A History of the Putnam Family in England and America. Recording the Ancestry and Descendants of John Putnam of Danvers, Mass., Jan Poutman of Albany, N. Y., Thomas Putnam of Hartford, Conn, Volume 1

Eben Putnam

ARMS OF
PUTTENHAM OF PUTTENHAM AND PENNE,
A.D. 1400.
AND OF
PUTNAM OF SALEM, MASS.

A HISTORY

OF THE

PUTNAM FAMILY

IN

ENGLAND AND AMERICA.

RECORDING THE ANCESTRY AND DESCENDANTS OF
JOHN PUTNAM OF DANVERS, MASS., JAN POUTMAN OF ALBANY, N. Y.,
THOMAS PUTNAM OF HARTFORD, CONN.

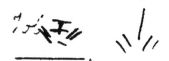

By EBEN PUTNAM

*Life member N. E. Historic-Genealogical Society; member Essex Institute; Danvers Historical
Society; American Association for the Advancement of Science; Massachusetts
Society Sons of American Revolution, etc.*

ILLUSTRATED.

SALEM, MASS., U. S. A.
THE SALEM PRESS PUBLISHING AND PRINTING CO.
The Salem Press.
1891.

8

COPYRIGHT 1891
BY EBEN PUTNAM.

PUBLISHER'S ANNOUNCEMENT.

This part, the first to be issued, is to become Part II in the final arrangement.

The history of the family in Europe will have a separate pagination and will be issued last in the series.

The next three parts will probably appear together, we hope before Christmas, and the balance of the work as soon as may be, completing the volume before the summer of 1892.

Subscribers are reminded of the terms of subscription, *i. e.*, payment in full for the work upon receipt of this part, unless directions have been previously given to deliver in bound volumes at a higher price.

The edition is limited to 300 copies of which nearly 200 are already taken.

Additions and corrections should be sent to Mr. Eben Putnam, Asylum Station, Essex Co., Mass., and subscriptions to the Salem Press Publishing & Printing Co., Salem, Mass.

(iii)

INTRODUCTORY NOTE.

At last! It is with a feeling of great relief that at last I offer to the subscribers the first part of the work upon which I have been engaged for so many years.

With the appearance of this part I feel that the Rubicon is passed; that I have burnt my bridges and that nothing further can now be added. For the past year I have been constantly upon the point of issuing this first part, but two important matters prevented: first, the conviction that more information pertaining to the early generations in America could and would be obtained; and, secondly, the fact that subscribers were few and far between.

As this goes to press, I lack over one hundred subscribers to make a number sufficient to reimburse myself for the actual cost of printing and publishing the work.

There are many, I feel assured, who would have contributed, had they been requested, to the fund for carrying the book through. To such, I state in brief that, as there remain nine parts to be issued, subscriptions are still welcome.

The first attempt to compile a genealogy of our family was made in 1733 by Deacon Edward Putnam, a grandson of John the first. He contented himself with the statement, given in full in the appendix, that John Putnam came over in 1634, and in giving a list of as many of the heads of families living in 1733, as he had knowledge of.

During the first part of this century, Gen. Rufus Putnam wrote a brief sketch of the family, particularly of his own line.

About 1820, the Rev. Eleazer Warburton Putnam collected materials looking towards the compilation of a family pedigree; but, some ten years later, learning that Col. Perley Putnam had commenced a genealogy of the family upon an extensive scale, he courteously provided him with such information as he then had.

To Col. Perley Putnam you owe this work; for, had he not collected, when he did, the records of so many families, it would have been almost impossible to present so complete a history as I hope this will be.

Colonel Putnam did not complete his work, but after his death the papers were deposited in the rooms of the Essex Institute and have been of service to many of our family who desired information concerning their ancestry.

During the period in which Colonel Putnam was working, others had taken an interest and several lines were worked out independently and some researches made in England, notably by the late George Palmer Putnam of New York.

Following Colonel Putnam, came Dr. Dana Boardman Putnam, who added much concerning the Maine families and later generations. Upon his decease the MSS. fell into the hands of Mr. Benjamin Putnam who in turn passed them to the Rev. Alfred Porter Putnam.

My own work commenced with the attempt to trace collateral lines in connection with some ancestral work. I was then but twelve years of age and entered into my work with great enthusiasm, having the libraries of Boston and Cambridge at my disposal. Soon I became interested in the family history in its broadest application and finally consulted with Rev. A. P. Putnam in regard to my work and offered to turn over to him all my notes, etc., if he would undertake the task of compiling a genealogy. His health forbade and so I found myself, figuratively speaking, the genealogical executor of my many worthy predecessors.

The labor of compiling this genealogy has been great; the letters that had to be written, the authorities to be consulted, the matter to be gleaned, — all have been a labor of love and one which has absorbed my entire time outside of business hours.

To the many who have encouraged me during this long period, and to those who have kindly furnished me with information concerning many lines apart from their own, I extend my cordial acknowledgments for the services rendered. The names of a few to whom I am most deeply indebted I mention below with great pleasure.

Dr. Henry Wheatland, Mr. Perley Derby, Hon. Deloss Putnam, Mr. Francis Barnes, Rev. Alfred P. Putnam, Mrs. Susanna Hartshorn, Hon. James O. Putnam, Mr. E. S. Jaqua, Mr. Henry Fitz-Gilbert Waters and Mr. Harrison Ellery. I am tempted to add many more but such a list would include most of my subscribers.

The reason for publishing the work in parts is to allow an opportunity for belated accounts to reach me, and further investigation to be made in England and Holland concerning both the ancestry of John Putnam of Danvers and Jan Poutman of Albany.

Our family is one of considerable antiquity and many surprises are in store for the great body of our name.

Should a reunion of the descendants of John Putnam ever be held, those present on that occasion will doubtless be struck with the resemblance existing between members of the family, even when separated by many degrees of kinship. Never have characteristics, mental and physical, remained so fixed as in our family. The Putnam type is somewhat as follows: good physique, Saxon features, of good height, inclined to stoutness but not fleshy, even temperament, honest intentions, fixedness of purpose, high principles, satisfied with a fair share of the good things of life, inclined to be too generous, patriotic and intensely military in spirit, more inclined to lead than to be led. There are many deviations from this standard as there are from all.

John Putnam has no reason to be ashamed of his descendants.

EBEN PUTNAM.

Beaver Brook, Danvers,
September 20, 1891.

THE PUTNAMS OF PUTTENHAM

PENN, AND WINGRAVE
CO. BUCKS, ENGLAND

AN ACCOUNT OF THE ANCESTRY OF
JOHN PUTNAM
1579–1662

ANCIENT CHURCH OF PUTTENHAM, HERTS.

ANCIENT CHURCH OF DRAYTON BEAUCHAMP, BUCKS.

VIEW FROM TRING HILL, LOOKING NORTHWEST, SHOWING WILSTONE RESERVOIRS WITH PUTTENHAM, WINGRAVE, MENTMORE, AND CHEDDINGTON.

are found in the Missendens, at Amersham, Chesham, Haw-ridge, Choulsbury, and other places between Penn and Puttenham, and to the north at Eddlesborough, Slapton, Stukeley, Woughton, and neighboring parishes, and at Hemel-Hempstead in Herts, as well as at one or two places in Essex.

Roughly speaking, the country for fifteen miles north and south of Tring, for a width of ten miles, was at the end of the sixteenth century nearly as thickly populated by people of our name as the country about Danvers is to-day, but at the present time I am only aware of one family in that whole territory, that of a respectable and well-to-do merchant of Aylesbury, who has a son in business in each of the towns of Tring and Thame. Even he spells his name Putman, which indeed is the usual form it is met with in the London directory, where a score of individuals are mentioned.

There are no memorials of the family in existence in all this territory, for, the elder line, the representatives of the family, were seated at Sherfield in Hampshire, and the younger branches were but small gentry or yeomen, entitled to and at times using coat-armor, but obliged to attend to their own affairs. Their position was similar to that of the "gentleman farmer" of to-day in England.

In early times the history of a family is that of the land with which it was identified. For this reason it is necessary, before beginning the genealogical account of the Putnam family in England, to describe in a brief manner the history of the territory of which their after possessions were a part.

The counties of Hertford and Buckingham are among the most fruitful, and the people have always been among the most progressive, in all England. In early times, before the Roman occupation, it is supposed to have been a part of the territory of the Catyeuchlani.* After the arrival of the Romans the province of Flavia Cæsariensis embraced this

---

* At the time of Cæsar's second invasion, this tribe, with the Cassi, under Cassibelaunus (Caswallon), proved a worthy match for the Romans.

district, and at St. Albans was an important Roman city
(Verulamium). The famous Watling Street and Icknield
Way intersect the counties, passing to the northward of
the "Putnam country," as we may call it.

The four centuries of Roman occupation affected principally the people in the southeastern part of Britain, and
after the Romans came the Saxons, who founded seven
kingdoms more or less independent, of which two founded
in the sixth century, Essex and Mercia, embraced the territory we are interested in. The Danes, too, at a later date,
permanently occupied a part of this same territory. Near
Hawridge may still be traced the lines of one of their fortified camps. During all these centuries, and to the coming
of the Normans, there is nothing to throw light upon so
small a section of the country as Puttenham and vicinity.
With the Norman occupation comes the first information
about the particular parish of Puttenham. Who then were
the inhabitants of the Vale of Aylesbury? Britons, Romans,
Saxons, or Danes? It is likely that the prevailing race were
most thickly distributed in those places the pleasantest, the
most easily defended, and the richest. In remoter spots the
former owners were less likely to be disturbed to as great an
extent. It is probable that while the greater part of the
population of Britain was Celtic, that is, a modified Celtic,
as would result from the admixture of the various conquer-
ing races, it being preposterous to suppose the original
inhabitants were either completely driven away or destroyed,
that in such spots as about Aylesbury, the prevailing race
would be either Saxon or Danish at the time of the Norman
invasion. Moreover, this part of the country was the scene
of stubborn resistance between the Britons and Saxons, and
later with the Danes.

When, in 1066, William the Norman conquered England,
there was an estimated population of two and one half
millions of people, and of these but three hundred thousand
are enumerated in Domesday Book. It is doubtful if the
total so called "Norman" contribution to the population of

Britain amounted to over 100,000 individuals, and of these a majority were drawn from the districts of France which were of the same race as the ancient Britons. It is, then, probable that our ancestors were of a mixed Danish-Saxon-Celtic race* and may have been identified with the land from the earliest times.

There is nothing to show to what extent the territory about there was "Normanized."

Puttenham is mentioned in the great survey ordered by William the Conqueror, and which took place in the years 1085 and 1086. The records of this survey are to be found in a volume called Domesday Book.

The inquisitors were to inquire into the name of every place, who held it in the time of King Edward, who was the present possessor, the extent of the manor, its capabilities, the number of inhabitants of certain classes, its present value and the value in King Edward's time. From this survey it appears that before the time of the Conquest the manor belonged to Earl Leuiun, the brother of Harold, and that it was given by William to Odo, Bishop of Baieux, his half-brother, on his mother's side, who held it at the time of the survey. "The manor answers for four hides, Roger holds it for the Bishop. There is land to four ploughs. There is one in the demesne and another may be made. Four villanes with two borders have there two ploughs. There are four cottagers and two bondmen, and two mills of ten shillings and eight pence. Meadow for four ploughs, and four shillings. Pasture for the cattle. It is worth sixty shillings, when the Bishop received it forty shillings. In King Edward's time four pounds."

The origin of the name seems to be from the Low Dutch or Flemish word "pütte," a well, plural pütten, and "ham," a house, or hamlet. The Danish word "putt" is

---

* I am inclined to think that the Danish rather than Saxon blood is predominant in our race, and was at the time of the Migration. Since then, in many branches of the family, the so-called Saxon must predominate. The late George D. Putnam used to say that the majority of the Putnams he had met would very well meet the supposed physical characteristics of the Danes of early times.

used to designate a well or spring.   Near Ghent, in Holland, is a village called Püttenheim, and there is a place called Puttenham* in Surrey, England.   It is probable that the Putmans † of Holland may have a similar origin for their name.

Mr. Cussans, in his *History of Hertfordshire*, states that Puttenham is singularly devoid of wells or springs; the sub-soil there is of stiff, blue clay, through which a boring of four hundred feet had then (1881) recently been made without reaching water.   A small stream rises at Astrope, a hamlet about one mile east of the village, where were proba-bly the two mills mentioned in Domesday, flows westward, close by the north side of the church, then north into the Thame.

The church of an ancient English parish is surrounded by even more interest than is the case in this country.   The church at Puttenham is a structure of the date of the thir-teenth century.   It is not a large building, but has ample accommodations for the needs of the parish, which is a small one.   Close by is an old straw-thatched cottage which has the appearance of extreme age and which is now used as a Sunday-school.   An ancient tree still survives near the porch, which looks as though it may have witnessed the going and coming of contemporaries of John Putnam.   The church itself can best be described by using the words of former historians.

"The church at Puttenham is dedicated to St. Mary, and consists of a chancel, nave, north and south aisles, and a modern south porch, and is one of the plainest and smallest in the county, being but 69 feet long inside measurement, and of which the chancel occupies 25 feet, and the tower 14 feet 6 inches.   The width is 31 feet 8 inches.

"Salmon writing of the church in 1728, says: 'The chancel

---

* Puttenham in Surrey is singularly devoid of running water.   It is not mentioned in Domesday.

† Mr. DeWitt C. Putman informs me he has investigated the history of the Putmans to some extent, and finds four distinct families in Europe, *i.e.*, the Continent, existing at the present date.

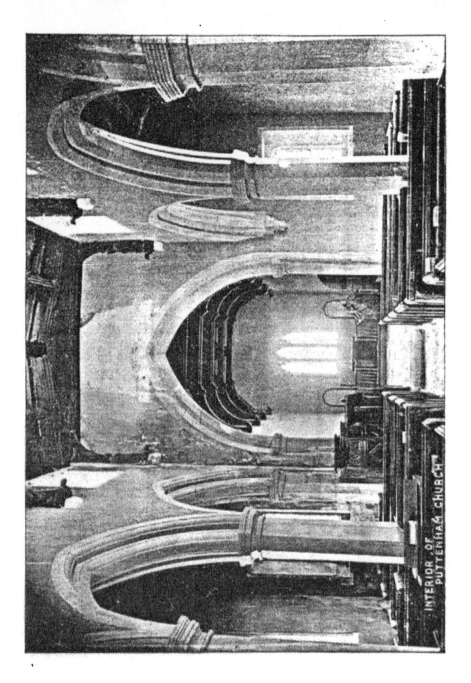

INTERIOR OF PUTTENHAM CHURCH

is dark and uninhabited, two round windows have been stopt up and it is shut out from the church. There are two old stones in it, the arms and inscriptions broke off.'"

The date of the structure is put by Cussans as about 1280 or 1290 or very early in 1300. The tower is large and beautiful. The original roof over the nave and south aisle are, however, decidedly decorated, while the windows are early Tudor. The chancel was rebuilt in 1851. The roof of the nave is supported by eight carved figures against the wall, apparently intended to represent saints, which serve as corbels. Between them and resting on the wall plates are smaller figures, each holding an uncharged shield on its breast. From the shape of the shields, at the intersection of the rafters and beams, it is safe to put the roof at the date of 1420. The easternmost shield is charged with the arms of Zouch, Gules, twelve bezants and a canton, indented at the base, ermine. The other, Argent, two chevronels sa. between three roses gu., for Wykeham.*

William Wykeham was Bishop of Lincoln (in which diocese Puttenham was situated) 1584-94, but Cussans thinks that too late a date to account for the arms.

Alan la Zouch of Ashley, Co. Northampton, died in 1314, and he and his father, Roger, and grandfather, Alan, were liberal benefactors of the priory there, and as this church belonged to the prior and canons of Ashley until the reign of Edward II. when it was granted to the Bishops of Lincoln, it is probable it was built by the Zouch and given to the priory. When the church was rerooved the arms were placed in a conspicuous position.

Clutterbucks adds that in one of the windows lighting the north aisle of the nave are these arms in stained glass: 1. Ar. a ship in full sail, in the dexter corner a bezant, in a chief gu. a lion passant gardant or. 2. A chief divided compartments; in the centre, Gu. a lion pass. gard. or; 3 and 4, Or. each charged with a rose gu.

---

* Chauncey describes but one coat as follows: A field arg., a cheveron sa., voided betw. chaplets gu.

The benches and pews are of solid oak and date back to the time of Henry VI. The construction of the tower is curious; it is built of long, squared blocks of Kelton stone, with spaces varying from eight inches to a foot between the ends of each block, filled in with flint.

There are three bells in the tower—one undated, one dated 1656, and the other 1714. In the last year of Edward VI. there were three bells in the steeple, a challisse of silver, etc.

The gravestones are modern and bear the names of Gregory, Gales, Chapman, Ives, Hancher, Hall, Collins, Clark, Nash, Tapping, etc. The rectory is in the diocese and archdeanery of St. Albans, and at the valuation at demolition of the religious houses in England was placed at £10. 1. 1½.

The prior and canons of Ashby presented the living till 1309; then the Bishop of Lincoln until 1852, but there was no resident minister from 1713 to 1849.

The registers begin in 1684 and are very carelessly kept; among the names which occur are Stonnell, Gurney, and Chapman.

The hamlets of Long Marston and Wilstone are included in the parish of Tring.

Urwick, in the *History of Nonconformity in Herts*, states that Long Marston was a stronghold of the Nonconformists, and that Hertfordshire was one of the first counties to embrace Nonconformity. The seat of Sir Nicholas Bacon and his lady was some few miles west of St. Albans, and was the rallying-place for many Puritan divines. In 1662, the widow Puttenham and many others of Tring and vicinity were either fined or imprisoned for not going to the parish church.

Odo, Bishop of Baieux, had at the time of the survey four hundred and thirty-nine lordships, of which thirty were in Buckinghamshire. Who Roger his undertenant was I know not; this same Roger seems to have held other of the Bishop's manors. The Bishop was also Earl of Kent, but before his death had lost his authority and influence in England. He left an illegitimate son.

The Beauchamps, afterward Earls of Warwick, were possessed of large estates in this section of the country soon after the conquest, as also were the Spigornells. The Putnams first appear during the latter part of the twelfth century, and soon after are undisputed lords of the manor of Puttenham.*

From this time to the middle of the sixteenth century Puttenham was a part of the possessions of the Putnams of Sherfield, after which time it passed by descent or purchase successively into the families of Skipwith, Saunders, Duncombe, Lucy, Meacher, Egerton, and was finally purchased by Baron Lionel Nathan de Rothschild.

Wingrave in Bucks, the home of the grandparents of John Putnam, was also a part of the possessions of the Beauchamps, and later that of the Nevilles. Early in the sixteenth century it became the property of the Hampdens and still later passed to the Dormers.

Wingrave includes Rowsham, which latter place is bounded on the west by Burstone, a part of the parish of Aston Abbotts. It is in Burstone that John Putnam probably lived, as his uncles, from whom his father inherited property, owned land in Wingrave, Rowsham, and in Burstone. Burstone bounds Aylesbury on the north. It will thus be seen that the direct ancestors of John Putnam continued to reside upon the same or nearly the same property which had been in the family for nearly four centuries.

* Chauncey errs in saying that the manor was early in possession of the family of Cheyne and from them passed to the Puttenhams ; he confesses ignorance concerning those Cheynes. In Browne Willis's MSS. will be found an account of the Cheyne family of Drayton Beauchamp, the adjoining parish, who are descended from Thomas ob. 1357, whose son Thomas was the grantee of Drayton Beauchamp in 1362 and who died in 1368. A Roger Cheyne, who died in 1415, of Drayton Beauchamp and grandson of the last-named Thomas, held land in Puttenham in 2 Henry V. (*Inq. p. m.*). Willis does not give Puttenham at all among the possessions of any of the Cheynes, and I have found no further evidence of their ownership there. Willis was descended from the Hampshire Putnams.

THE PUTNAMS OF PUTTENHAM.

Simon de Putteham* and **Ralph de Pudeham**, mentioned in the Rotuli Curiæ Regis, report of a court held in Hertfordshire, October, 1199.

Ralph de Putenham had property in Stivecle, Bucks, 1217-18. (*Fines, 2 Henry III.*) Ralph de Puteham held three carucates, *i.e.*, about 150 acres, of land in Puttenham by three parts of one knight's fee of the honor of Leicester (*Testa de Neville temp Henry III.*, prob. 1236). Simon de Mountford, the great Earl of Leicester, was the over-lord: his property was confiscated after his defeat and death in 1264. Ralph de Puttenham is also mentioned in the Rotuli Litterorum Clusæ, of 1st Henry III., 1217.

Richard de Putenham is mentioned under the Hundred of Bonestowe, Bucks. 2 Edw. I., 1273 (*Hundred Rolls*).

John de Puttenham and Agnes his wife, and Richard Payn and Agnes his wife, enter into an indenture concerning a messuage in Tykeford, near Newport Pagnell, 34 Edw. I., 1306 (*Fines No. 368*). John de Putham is assessed 70 shillings, Peter de Putham 5 shillings, and Walter de Putham 27 shillings 6 pence, 19 Edw. I., 1291 (*Lay Subsidies*), for property in Puttenham, John being the first person of the thirty-two named, with the largest assessment.

In 22 Edw. I., 1294, Johan de Putham also appears on the subsidy as of Totenhale.

Peter de Puttenham, mentioned above with John de Putham (*Lay Subsidy for Herts, 19 Edw. I.*), 1291, and in 34 Edw. I., 5 April, 1306, Peter de Puttenham, "manucaptor" of Ranulphus de Monte Caniso, knight of the shire returned for Herts. (*Parl. Writs.*)

---

* The name on old records is variously spelled Puttenham, Putenham, Potenham, Putham, Puteham, with the usual contractions; later, Putnham, Puttnam, Puttman, and Putnam.

Peter de Puthen held land in common socage as one thirtieth part of a knight's fee in Aston Clinton, Bucks (*Testa de Nevill*).

James de Puttenham was Bailiff of Southwerk, 1325 (*Rolls of Parl.*), and in 17 Edw. II., 1323, as " Janitor Dori Regis," brings certain persons into the Court of Kings Bench.*

Thomas Puttenham, temp. Edward I. (1272–1307), married Helen,† daughter and co-heir of John Spigornell, Lord of Buckingham (*Harl. MSS. 1553, fo. 41 b.*).

John Spigornell, was seized of the manors of Stondon in Essex, and Skegely in Notts, 1308–9 (*Inq. p. m. 2 Edw. II.*). He was brother and heir of Edmund who d. 24 Edw. I., 1295–6 (*Banks Baronia Anglica*), or, according to Morant (*History of Essex*), his son. They were descended from Godfrey Spigurnel, who had a grant of Skegeby, 9 John (1207–8). This was an important family during the succeeding two centuries, and possessed much property in Eastern Bucks. I fail to find that any Spigornell was ever the possessor of the lordship of Buckingham, which seems to have been at the time of Thomas Puttenham's marriage a part of the possessions of the Broas family.

Thomas left a son

Roger Puttenham (*Harl. MSS., 1553*), whom I identify with Roger de Puttenham, High Sheriff of Herts in 1322.

3 Edw. II., 1309–10, Roger de Puttenham and wife Aliva are parties to an indenture with Robert de Gravile and Alicia his wife, concerning lands in Penn, Bucks.

In consequence of his continuance with the king he was exonerated from the fine imposed on the knights and esquires of Essex and Herts. 15 Jan., 1321–2. (*Parl. Writs.*)

Roger left a son

---

* Beside the above there occur the names of Gilbert de Putesham of Melecombe in Cumberland, 1314–15 ; Phillip Puttesham, B.A., Oxford, 1454, supplicant as secular chaplain for B.C.L., March, 1462, instituted incumbent of Newton St. Loe, Somerset ; William Puttysham, supplicant for B.A. Oxford, 19 June, 1454.

† Somerby MSS. in the library of the Mass. Hist. Soc. calls her Catherine.

Henry Puttenham (*Harl. MSS., 1553*), about whom no further information has been discovered. He probably was living between 1300 and 1350. He probably had a brother or son

Sir Roger de Puttenham, Knt., who was knight of the shire for Bucks, 1354, 1357, 1362, 1364-5, 1366, 1368, 1370-1, 1378. He married Margery, and in 44 Edw. III., 1370-1, Robert Stratford, parson, granted by deed to Christian Bardolph the manor of Long Marston for life, with remainder to Sir Roger Puttenham, Knt., and Margery his wife, and the heirs of their body begotten, and for want of such issue the remainder to the heirs of said Roger.

Robert Puttenham * was a witness to a deed conveying the manor of Erle in Pittston in 1346, of which William Puttenham was later one of the enfeoffees.

William Puttenham of Puttenham and Penne, who married Margaret, the third daughter of John de Warbleton of Warbleton, Sussex, and Sherfield on Loudon, Southampton, by Katherine, daughter of Sir John de Foxle of Foxle, Bramshell, and Apuldrefield. This John de Warbleton died 21 Sept., 1375. He was son of John, who was great-grandson of Thomas de Warbleton of Warbleton and Sherfield about the middle of the 13th century. (*Vol. III. Topographer and Genealogist.*)

In 1422, William Puttenham, Esq., John Hampden, Esq., and others, were enfeoffed of the manor of Erle in Pittston, by John Southend of Eddlesboro, and others. In 1406 and 1427-8, Robert Puttenham was witness to similar grants of this same manor.

William Puttenham of Tring, Esq., in 1430 was one of the persons resident in Herts who "may despend X ls by yere and above."

---

* In the pedigree given by Berry in his *Hampshire Pedigrees* (taken from a *Visitation of Hampshire*, 1634?), the descent of Sir George is derived from a Robert Puttenham. At present the exact relationship of Sir Roger, Robert and William remains a matter of conjecture.

Margaret (Warbleton) Puttenham died prior to 8 Edward IV., 1468.   Children:

Henry, son and heir.

Robert (?), living 1406–28.

John (?), rector of Tewin, Herts, resigned 21 June, 1453.

Thomas (?), vicar of Ambrosden, Co. Oxford, 1458.

Henry Puttenham, son of William, was aged 60 and upwards in 8th Edward IV.; he died 6 July, 1473. (*Esch. 13 Edw. IV.*)

In 28 Henry VI., 1449–50, he, with Edmund Brudenall, Robert Foster, and Thomas Lombard, purchase of Thomas Hand and Johan his wife a messuage in Chalfhunt (*Fines 28 Hen. VI.*), and two years later, with Thomas Everdon and Thomas de la Hay, buys of Thomas More and Florence his wife, messuage and land in Wycombe and Huchenden (*Fines, 30 Hen. VI., No. 81*). In 1461–2 Barnard son and heir of Bernard Brocas of Horton, Bucks., Esq., gave to Richard Neville, Count Warwick,* John Neville, Lord Montague, Thomas Perkins, Henry Puttenham, Robert Rushford, Esqrs., John Bulman and John Malter, the manor of Haliborne, Estbroke et Westbroke, Trayle, Renstede, Slapton, Whaddon, Croston, Woketon, Dakenhale, Tisede, Betlow, Aldewyk, Marsworth, Ivingho, Aston Clinton, Picksliethorn, Wingrave, Wegeton and Roysden. (*Close Rolls 1st. Edw. IV.*)

Henry Puttenham married Elizabeth, the widow of Geoffrey Goodluck, whose will is recorded in Somerset House (*Prerog. Court of Canterbury, "Logge" 25*). It is dated 25 Dec., 1485 and proved 9 Oct., 1486. She desires to be buried in the Chapel of St. Mary the Virgin, in All Saints of Istelworth next to the burial-place of Geoffrey Goodeluck formerly her husband: to the high altar at Istel-

---

* Libscombe says the Nevilles, Lords Latimer, held Wingrave manor, which they had by marriage with an heiress of the Beauchamps, who were anciently possessed of it, and that John, Lord Latimer, died, seized of Wingrave in 1531. It was sold 1531 to William Hampden, Esq., whose heirs in 1617 sold to Sir Robert Dormer. Richard, Earl of Warwick, held the estates of his uncle George, Lord Latimer, during the later years of his uncle's life, who was non-compos. George, Lord Latimer, died in 1469.

worth church she gives her red girdle silver gilt, and to the lights of the Blessed Virgin, the Holy Cross, St. Nicholas, and All Saints at that church she gives 12 pence each. The minister and convent of Holy Trinity at Houneslowe, and the prior and convent of the House of Jesus at Bethlehem of Shene, the abbess and convent of Lyon, each receive 13 shillings and 4 pence. For repairs of parish church at Potenham in diocese of Lincoln, 20 shillings, at All Saints in Istelworth, 13 shillings and 4 pence, and at Twykenham, 6 shillings and 8 pence. She forbids Maude, the wife of John Chase and Thomasine the wife of Philip Payn, her daughters, to disturb John Anger or his heirs in the possession of a certain messuage in West Brayneford (Md.), called the "Belle" formerly the "Angel," which she had lately sold the said John. Residue of her estate to be devoted by her executors William Potenham, Philip Payn, and Richard Lovet, "to do other works of piety for my soul and for the souls of my parents, friends, and benefactors," etc. By a codicil of same date, she gives to her daughter Molte (Matilda) Chase her white bed with all apparel thereto belonging, in the great chamber, also a second pair "fuscians."

William Puttenham, of Puttenham, Penn, Sherfield, Warbleton, etc., eldest son of Henry, above, was probably born about 1430. He married Anne, daughter of John Hampden,* of Hampden, Co. Bucks. She was probably living in 1486.

William Puttenham was named executor in the will of Gilbert Stapleton, vicar of Aston Abbotts, in 1490. His will is dated 10 July, 1492, and was proved at Lambeth, 23 July, 1492. He directs that his body be buried before the image of the Blessed Virgin Mary in the Chapel within

---

* The Hampdens enjoyed the distinction of being one of the most ancient of English families, claiming descent from Baldwin de Hampden, who was of note before the Norman invasion. John, the father of Anne Puttenham, was Knight of the shire for Bucks in 1420 and 1430; of Beds, in 1450, in which year he died. He is said to have married Elizabeth, daughter of Sir John Whalesborough, Knt., of Whalesborough, Co. Cornwall. From John descended John Hampden, the "Patriot," noted for his resistance to the collection of ship-money, whose mother was Elizabeth Cromwell, aunt to Oliver Cromwell.

the church of the Hospital of the Blessed Mary, called the Elsingspytell, in London.   For his daughters he provides liberally, whenever they shall be married, except Agnes, to whom he gives £5 yearly, to be taken from his manor of Willeigh, in Co. Surrey.   The profits of his manors of Tannerigg and Willeigh, in Co. Surrey, and Merston, in Co. Hertford, are placed in trust until the marriages of his daughters, to provide their portions.   George, his son and heir, Sir William Bowlond, prior of the Hospital of the Blessed Mary of Elsingspytell, William Tysted, Esq., and William Oldacres, chaplain, are made executors.   (*P. C. C. Doggett 19.*)

Children :

Sir George, son and heir.

Edmund, of Puttenham.

Nicholas, of Penn., ancestor of the American family.

Frideswide.

Elizabeth.

Alionore, m. Richard Pigott, son of Richard Pigott, Esq., of Aston Rowant, Co. Oxon.   He held Milksoppe manor in Aston Rowant, etc.: Ch. Bartholomew, who m. Julianda, daughter of Thomas Lenthall, Esq., of Lachford, and was buried in 1558, at Aston Rowant ; Edmund ; Andrew ; Sybell ; Leonard.   Pigott quartered Puttenham, Sa., a stork arg., beaked and legged gu., between eight crosslets fitcheé of the second.   (*Harl., 1533: Lipscombe's Bucks.*)

Brigide.

Agnes.

Sir George Puttenham, of Puttenham, Sherfield, etc., son and heir of William, above, married, previous to 1479, Alice, daughter of Thomas de Wyndesor.   After her death he married Rose, daughter of Sir John Gainsford, of Crowhurst, Surrey.   She married, secondly, William Sackville, who died at Bletchingley, Surrey, 1538.   Myldred, daughter of William Sakevylle, gent., and Dame Rose Potingham, buried

1541 ; and on the last day of March, 1545, Dame Rose Potenham, wife of Mr. William Sakvylle, buried. (*Church Wardens' Accounts, Bletchingley.*)

Thomas Wyndesor, the father of Sir George's first wife, is the ancestor of the Earls of Plymouth and other noted English families. He was the son of Miles de Wyndesor, who died in 1452. Thomas Wyndesor, in his will of 13 Aug. 1479, provides for payment of what he owed to William Puttenham by his daughter's marriage. Sir George was knighted upon the occasion of the marriage of Prince Arthur, 17 November, 1501. His arms at that time are described as follows : Crest, a hind's head gu. Arms, quarterly, 1 and 4, Sable, crusily fitcheé and a stork arg.; 2 and 3, Lozengy, az. and or (for Warbleton). Motto, "Quære an sit caput vulpis vel clamæ." He was of considerable prominence in his county, and is named upon various occasions in the early part of the 16th century upon commissions of the peace, to collect subsidies, etc., etc. On the 2 May, 1512, a commission was issued to Thomas, Marquis of Dorset, Sir George Puttenham, and others, to review the captain, mariners, and soldiers under the said Marquis, about to depart for foreign parts and to arrest and punish rebels. In 1520 his name occurs among a list of noblemen and gentry to attend Henry the Eighth at the Field of the Cloth of Gold.

From a fine, 8th Henry VIII. (1516–17), passing lands and messuages in Long Merston, Gobilcote, and Tring, it appears that Alice, his wife, was still living.

From a fine levied 18 Henry VIII. (1526), it appears he had had possession of the manor of Stoke in Co. Northampton.

He owned land in Penn, Wycombe, Denham, Co. Bucks, as well as the manors of Puttenham, Long Marston, Sherfield, Warbleton, Willeigh, Tannerigge, Westfielde, Crighthing, Cateherst, Cuckstepe. He died in or prior to 1535, as upon Close Rolls, 27 Henry VIII., 2d part, is an indenture dated 15 May, 26 Henry VIII., between Robert Puttenham, Esq., son and heir of Sir George, deceased, and the

King, who agrees to grant, etc., all the lands, etc., which descended to the said Robert. By this document it appears that the manor of Sherfield was valued at £40, and Puttenham, Co. Herts., at £25; this manor was in the possession of Rose, widow of Sir George, while Tannerigge, Co. Surrey, was feoffeed to the use of Margaret, wife of Robert Puttenham. The other estates mentioned are Warbleton in Sussex, Wylkey in Surrey, Chyngham in Southampton, and Marston in Hertford. The total value was £145.

An inquisition post mortem was taken upon George Puttenham, Knt., 33-34 Henry VIII. (1542), by which it appears that Robert Puttenham was son and heir.

Children:

Robert, son and heir.

Bridget, m. Christopher Bullock, of Aberfield, Berks.

Dorothy, m. Thomas Dawbridgecourt, of Stratfield Say, son of Thomas of the same. He died 20 Jan., 1539–40. Their children were Thomas, Barnard, and Anne. (*Vis. Notts.*)

Anne, m. John Norton, of Tisted, whose son Robert married Mary, daughter of Richard Elyot, the Chief Justice. From this marriage Browne Willis derived his Putnam descent.

Audrey.

Dorothy, m. an Adams of Kent.

Elizabeth, m. Thomas Oxenbridge.

Robert Puttenham, son and heir of Sir George, married Margaret, daughter of Sir Richard Elliott. His name frequently occurs upon the State Papers concerning Hampshire. He was obliged to mortgage a part of his estate. Many of his indentures are recorded on the Close Rolls. One dated 13 July, 35 Henry VIII., mentions the manor of Long Marston, now in the tenure of John Duncombe, yeoman. John Duncombe died prior to 1558, when an inquisition found him possessed of lands in Stukeley, Puttenham, and Long Marston.

On the 6 June, 38 Henry VIII., Robert Puttenham, of
Sherfield, Esq., sells to Richard Puttenham, gentleman, his
son and heir-apparent, the manors of Puttenham, Sherfield,
and Marston, immediately after the death of Robert, upon
condition that Richard pays £5 semi-annually at the feast of
St. Michael the Archangel and the feast of the Annun-
ciation of our Lady; also, upon request, to pay a yearly
rent to Francis and George, younger sons of Robert, to be
taken out of the manor of Marston. Probably Robert
Puttenham died in 1546.

Children :

Richard, son and heir.

George, of Sherfield.

Rose, m. Thomas Blundeville, of Blundeville manor, New-
    ton, Co. Norfolk. In the church at Newton, re-built
    1385, over the vault where many of the family are buried,
    is a monument having Noah's Ark figured thereon, and
    on either side a square pillar, the whole supported by
    four marble pillars forming three partitions, on the first
    of which are three men in armor. The second contains the
    effigy of a man in armor, bareheaded, kneeling, and over
    him " Thomas Blundeville, filius Edwardi "; beneath are
    two shields, Blundeville impaling Johnson, and Blunde-
    ville impaling Puttenham, Sable, crusilly, a stork argent,
    quartering Warbleton, Lozengy, or and azure. The third
    part contains four effigies, viz., the two wives and two
    daughters, and above, " Rosa et Margareta Uxores
    Thome Blundeville cum Fil' suis Elizabetha et Patientia."
    This monument was erected in 1571.

Margaret, m. a Dockwray, who dying, she m., second, Sir
    John Throckmorton, the fifth son of Sir George, of
    Coughton, where Sir John and his wife Margaret are
    buried. Sir John Throckmorton was a well-known
    character in Elizabeth's reign. He was at one time,
    1558, Justice of Chester, and Master of Requests. He
    suffered the enmity of Lord Leicester. George Putten-
    ham found his brother-in-law his firm friend and adviser.

Lady Margaret survived her husband, who died 22 May, 1580, and lived to see her son Francis executed for treason, first having been terribly tortured on the "equuleus," an instrument shaped like a horse, to extort a confession. He was concerned in an attempt to liberate Mary Queen of Scots. He was conveyed from the Tower to Blackfriars Stairs, thence to the Old Bailey and delivered to the Sheriff of London. Then placed on a hurdle and drawn to Tyburn, to be hanged, disembowelled, and quartered. This was on the 10 July, 1584.

Anne, m. John Edwards, of Co. Denbigh.

Francis, living 1546.

William, prob. d. y.

Mary, m. Richard, son and heir of Robert Charnock, of Hulcote, Beds. Esq. Their children were: John, living in 1634, who m. Elizabeth, daughter of Sir John Arundell; and Florence, who m. Thomas Emery, of Arlesey, Beds.

Richard Puttenham, eldest son of Robert, married Mary daughter of Sir William Warham, of Malsanger (*Chancery Proc., Elizb.*) He leased to his brother George his manor of Sherfield upon conditions which would result in the end, of that property passing to George. As shown above, he had immediate possession of the paternal estate after his father's death, and that same year, as "of Warburton, Sussex," mortgaged that manor to William, Lord Windsor, for £400. He added to his estate at and near Sherfield (*Close Rolls, 1550*), but soon after fell into disgrace at Court and retired to the Continent, leaving his wife in the care of his brother. This was probably in 1561 (*vide Machyn's diary*). Later he returned, secretly, for which he was afterward pardoned,— those were troublesome times—and while visiting his son-in-law, Francis Morris, sold—22 Oct., 1567 to him and Anne, his wife, his estates, subject to the lease already mentioned. This transaction was the cause of a bitter lawsuit between George Puttenham and Morris.

By the terms of the indenture by which Morris got Sherfield, he was to pay £50 semi-annually at the tomb of Jeffery
Chaucer, within the Church of St. Peter, city of Westminster, also to deliver the carcass of a fallow deer, called a
buck, being in season, yearly. The property conveyed is
described as "his lordship of Sherfield on Loudon, within
the parish of Sherfield or Brameley Basing, Gowiche, Sel-
chester, Stratfield Saye, Stratfield Mortymer, Turgyes
Hartley, Odyam, or Rotherwick, or elsewhere within the said
county of Southampton."

Richard next appears as a prisoner in the Court of Kings
Bench. In 1574 Mary Puttenham asks Thomas Colby, who
has bought her husband's estate, "to pay her her pension
fixed on the estate, as her estate is very poor." (*Acts Privy
Council.*)

In 1578, during the troubles of George Puttenham with
his wife, Richard wrote him, which letter is on file (vol. 127,
fo. 32, *Dom. State Papers*). He accuses George of ungrate-
ful behavior to Sir John Throckmorton. It is a brotherly
letter.

In 1585, Richard Puttenham, "prisoner ye second time,"
petitions the Privy Council and makes complaint against Mr.
Sackford, Master of Requests. He had been in prison a
year and complains that he has had money taken from him;
that his income is diverted from him to his wife, who he
says Colby is maintaining against him; and that in consequence of all this, by reason of lack of funds, he will die of
cold and want of food, having been placed in the common
jail. Moreover, he says he was wrongfully condemned.
(*Dom. State Papers.*)

The will of Richard Puttenham, "the nowe prisoner in
Her Majesty's Bench," is dated 22 April, 1597, and was
proved by Catherine Puttenham 2 May, 1597. To his
"verily reported and reputed daughter Katherin Putting-
ham and her heirs forever," he gives all his goods and
chattels, etc., and makes her his sole executor. (*P. C. C.
Cobham 39.*) He was the last male representative of the
Puttenhams of Sherfield.

Children by Mary Warham :

Anne, m. Francis, son of Thomas Morris, of Copewell, Co. Berks. Sold Sherfield, in Hants, prior to 1574; Ch., Anne m. a Turner, of Clanfield, Oxon ; Martha m. Stephen Martin, of Sherfield, Berks.; Alice m. Edmond Hornejoy, of Lincoln ; Katherine m. Walter Louddon, of Cuiscott, Berks. ; Jane m. Bartholomew Weeks, of Ashbury, Berks. ; Mary; Warham, Thomas, of Copewell, son and heir, m. Dulsabell, daughter of Thomas Dennys, of the Isle of Wight, and had Thomas, Francis, Edward, Anne, Dulsabell. Morris quartered Johnes, Puttenham and Warham :

By an unknown :

Katherine, her father's executor.

George Puttenham, the younger of the two surviving sons of Robert of Sherfield, is best known as the author of the *Arte of English Poesie*. According to his own statement he was born in 1528. The early years of his life were spent abroad, probably in the train of some great noble or ambassador. In the *Arte of Poesie* Puttenham occasionally alludes to events in his life. He states that he was aged eighteen upon his addressing *Elpine* to Edward VI.—unfortunately this composition has not come down to us,—and that he was brought up in foreign countries and has less knowledge of English courtiers than those of other countries.

Whatever his education and associations, he leased Sherfield, with the intention of becoming its future owner, gave a bond of £1000 for the performance of the lease, and, according to the old documents on record, "farmed" it for his brother Richard's interest. I think this lease was made 15 Feb., 2 Elizb. (1560), about the time of his marriage with Elizabeth, Lady Windsor. That the marriage occurred about this time is probable, as Edward, Lord Windsor, granted Lady Windsor a settlement of £240 yearly 18 May, 2 Elizb. She was the daughter of Peter Cowdray and second wife of William, Lord Windsor, who died 1558. By a former marriage, with Richard Paulet, she was the mother of Thomas, Lord Paulet. Puttenham's married life was not happy. Whether the trouble was his own or of his wife's making it is hard to tell. The question of his control of her property had evidently something to do with it.

It was, however, ten years before the legal embarrassments of Puttenham reached a crisis. As we have seen, Richard secretly returned in 1567, and deeded the Sherfield estates to his son-in-law. In the meantime the Privy Council had ordered George to pay certain sums to Richard's wife, which he very properly reserved from the rent; but without legal right. This pretext was seized by Morris to regain possession of Sherfield, which he did in 1570. The matter was not finally settled till 1583. Puttenham resisted Morris, attempted to make a forcible entry upon one of his estates, and with his men was seized and thrown into prison, from which, however, he soon was released. His case going against him, he probably made use of some strong language against the court, and having denounced as a traitor one Hodges, retained by him as a go-between, Hodges lodged information against Puttenham, accusing him of a design to kill Secretary Cecil. The papers are in existence and are interesting reading. It seems he had armed his servants for the purpose of "terrifying" Morris, and so had rendered himself liable under the laws of the realm. This and his harboring a man accused of murder, together with a pretended offer to Hodges of 500 marks if he would kill Secretary Cecil, are in brief the chief accusations against him, of all of which he was acquitted.

Later Puttenham attempted to recover from the government a sum of money, £900, alleged to have been wrongfully taken from him by his obedience to the Queen's commands. In this he failed, but the following decision by the Privy Council seems to place him in a fair light: "I know no cause to move me to think otherwise but that George Puttenham ought to be relieved of the forfeature, whereof Morrise took advantage for I know that George Puttenham's relieving of his brother's wife, where by grew the cause of his forfeyture, was by order of the councill uppon the lamentable complaint made to her Ma⁺ⁱᵉ by Ri: Puttenham's wife." This forfeiture was that of his bargain of inheritance by the stopping of rent upon the ownership of Sherfield changing hands.

In the meantime Puttenham's troubles with Lady Windsor had reached a climax. In 1578 he was repeatedly summoned to appear before the Privy Council. On one occasion he excuses his refusal to appear on account of outrages feared from Lord Paulet, and says: " My danger is not small in respect to my wife and her children, who have long desired my death." Again, in a letter to Sir John Throckmorton, to whom he had transferred much if not all his property, and who was looking after his interests at court, he writes that he is now on the point of fifty years, and has been five or six times waylaid, twice by the Lord Thomas Paulet and his servants, and his goods taken away from him, and twice or thrice other times by Mrs. Paulet's servants, being assaulted with swords and daggers. He goes on to complain of the slanders against him by his wife and her favorites at Court. In another letter he writes of the great labor in his causes before the Privy Council which Sir John Throckmorton has been put to " for my cawse at the pursewt of the La. Wyndesore whereof ye write ye are assured we shall be eased."

Finally a safe conduct was issued and he proceeded to London, only to remain in hiding for three weeks, until Sir John Throckmorton, by means of a little French girl who was Puttenham's messenger, discovered his retreat, had him arrested and brought before the Council.

In his examination he testified that the first passing of writings between himself and Throckmorton was at the time of his final going beyond the seas, about the fifth year of Elizabeth (1563), which statement seems to contradict the statement of Haslewood, his biographer, that he was certainly at Spa about 1570.

A settlement of financial troubles was finally effected by Throckmorton between the mismated couple, and Puttenham continued to occupy Herriard, his wife's inheritance, which seems to have been his home after the loss of Sherfield.

Shortly after Throckmorton's death, Frederick, Lord Windsor, instituted a suit against Puttenham, claiming that certain lands chargeable with an annuity to Lady Windsor, granted by Edward, late Lord Windsor, had been transferred to Throckmorton, and that the payment of £20 yearly rent to Edward, Lord Windsor, due as long as Puttenham and Lady Windsor lived together, had been stopped some seven years since, when Edward, Lord Windsor, went beyond seas. Moreover, Puttenham had utterly wasted Lady Windsor's estate and he, Frederick, had been obliged to pay Lady Windsor £80 since Michaelmas, at which Puttenham was much displeased. Also that said Puttenham and Lady Windsor, the executor of William, Lord Windsor's will, had induced William, one of his sons, to claim a legacy they knew had already been paid, and confessed the demand.

As very little more appears on the court records it is probable that he was left in comparative peace the remainder of his life, and evidently he regained the favor of Elizabeth, the loss of which he so greatly bewailed in 1578, as he became one of her gentlemen pensioners, and toward the end of his life basked in the sunshine of the Court, in which life he so much delighted.

During his tours abroad he had used his powers of observation to good advantage, and he describes some of his experiences in his works. He visited the Courts of France, Spain, and Italy. Haslewood thinks it not unlikely he visited the Courts of Italy in the train of Henry, Earl Arundell, as he describes himself as witnessing a feast given by the Duchess of Parma to that nobleman at the Court of Brussels. This was probably in 1558, when the Lord Chamberlain, Lord Arundel, was joined on the commission for settling the terms of peace with France and Scotland. Of his numerous works only the *Arte of English Poesie* and *Partheniades*, published in 1579, are known to exist.   The first of these was entered upon the register of the Stationers' Company Nov. 9, 1588, and published anonymously in 1589, dedicated to Sir William Cecil, Knt., Lord of Burghley, the same Cecil whom he had been accused of a design to murder.   Until now no research has proved successful in determining the authorship of the *Arte of Poesie*.   In 1605, Edmund Bolton, in a manuscript entitled *Hypercritica*, notes that " Queen Elizabeth's verses, those of which I have seen and read to some extent in the elegant, witty, and critical Book of the Art of English Poetry (the work, as the fame is) of one of her gentlemen pensioners, Puttenham, are princely as her prose."

In 1615, Richard Carew, writing of the " Excellencie of the English Tongue," says : " You shall find that Sir Philip Sidney, Master Puttenham, Master Stainhurst and divers more have made use how far we are within compass of a fair imagined possibility in that behalf."

Puttenham thoroughly mastered the complex rules of expression then prevailing, but, while his verse has some merit, he was not a poet.   He advanced one or two original ideas, since accepted by modern writers, but his work should be judged from the standpoint he himself used, as he professes to have written for the Court, and not for the school.   He says : " Our chief purpose herein is for the learning of ladies and young gentlemen, or idle courtiers, desirous to become skilful in their mother tongue, and for their private recreation to make now and then ditties of pleasure."   It has been said of him that he was a candid but sententious critic.

His will is nuncupative and dated about the 1 Sept., 1590. He is styled George Putenham, of London, Esq.   To Mary Symes, widow, his servant, " as well for the good service she did him as alsoe for the money which she hath layed forth for him, all and singular his goods, chattels, etc.   It was proved by Mary Symes 14 Oct., 1594.   (*P. C. C. Dixy 69.*)

That Throckmorton's comment, perhaps made in a fit of petulance, that once his end was served he was careless of all men, was not deserved is shown by the following epitaph from the *Arte of Poesie* upon his "deere friende, Sir John Throgmorton, Knight, Justice of Chester, and a man of many commendable vertues,

> "Whom vertues rerde, envy hath overthrowen
> And lodged full low, under this marble stone :
> He never were his values so well knowen,
> Whilest he lived here, as now he is gone."

THE PUTNAMS OF PENN.

Nicholas Puttenham or Puttnam, as his name is most frequently spelled, lived at Putnam Place in Penn. He used the same coat armor as the Sheffield family. The probable date of his birth is about 1460. Nothing further is known about him than appears in the Visitations.
Children :
John of Penn.
Henry, who was living in 1526.

John Puttnam, of Penne, elder son of Nicholas above, died in 1527. His will, dated 25 Feb., 1526, was proved 6 May, 1527. His name in that document is spelled Puttenham. He directs that his body be buried in the " churche-yerd of the Holy Trynytye of Penn, nigh unto the aulter of the holy apostyll." To the mother church at Lincoln, to church at Penn, small legacies. To his daughter Margaret ; to his brother Henry, his " chamblett doblett at 20s " ; William Payn ; Robert Ffrend. To Margaret his wife his lands and tenements in Penn and Wicombe, co. Bucks, for life with remainder to his son and heir, John Puttenam (*sic*), in default of heirs to son George with remainder to son Robert, in default of his heirs to " Henry my broder, and in event of his death without heirs to Sir George Puttenham, Kt."

He makes his wife Margaret executrix, and Robert Dormar and Robert Cramfeld, supervisors. (*Arch. Bucks.*)

He married Margaret Pygott.
Children ; (with exception of Margaret, named in Visitation of 1566) ;

Margaret.

John, who d. *s.p.* He m. Mary, dau. of Richard Verney of Middle Claydon, Bucks., who m., second, Roger Snappe, of Stanlake, Co. Oxon., gent.

George, of Penn, his brother's heir.

Robert.

Hellen, died in infancy.

George Putnam, of Penne, second son of John of Penn, was heir to his elder brother John.

He married Isabel, daughter of John Shrympton* of Chipping Wicombe, Co. Bucks.

His will, dated 20 Sept., 1585, was proved 5 May, 1590. He directs that his body be buried in the church-yard at Penn, and divides his household stuff among his four daughters, after his wife Isabel's decease. He mentions son William, son Richard, and son-in-law Thomas Long, the last of whom with the relict Isabel were executors. (*Arch. Bucks.*)

Children; recorded in Visitation of 1566.

John, d., *s.p.*, subsequent to 1566.

William.

Richard, bapt. at Penn, 29 Nov., 1563.

Mary.

Susan, m. at Penn, 16 Nov., 1584, Christopher Childe.

Ellen,
Anne or Jane, } bapt. at Penn, 8 Oct., 1560.

Isabel, bapt. at Penn, 3 July, 1565.

Elizabeth, d. y.

One of the daughters married Thomas Long of Penn, gent., reference to whose will was kindly given me by Henry F. Waters, Esq. The will is dated 20 June, 1638, proved 6 May, 1639. He mentions brother William Puttenham, friend Richard Shrimpton the elder, of Penn, tallow-chandler, brother-in-law William Standley. Also kinswomen Anne

---

* John Shrympton et al. sells to Wm. Colkys et al. tent. in Danyngton, Bucks. (*Feet of Fines,* 24 *H. viii.*, 1532.)

William Schrympton of Chipping Wicombe left a will which was proved 1531. (*Arch. Bucks*).

Gosbell of Uxbridge, Ellen Woolfe and her sister Anne Woolfe, cousin Anne Clay of Colebrook. Sons Thomas Long, Francis Long and his children Thomas and Elizabeth, grandchildren Robert and Elizabeth children of son Richard Long, son Henry Long and his child Ellen, Thomas son of his elder son George Long, and Ephraim Long another son, also Anne and Ellen and other children of George. (*P. C. C. Harvey 66.*)

William Putnam or Puttenham, of Penn, gentleman, second son and heir of George of Penne, was buried there, 28 July, 1638. His wife Jane was buried 22 Sept., 1622.
Children, all bapt. at Penn:

Rhoda, bapt., 5 March, 1587; buried, 12 July, 1587.
Sarah, bapt., 3 May, 1590.
Joseph, bapt., 6 April, 1592.
William, bapt., 13 March, 1593. } ? d. y.
Barbary, bapt., 3 April, 1596; m. at Penn, 11 Oct., 1618, Thomas Evans.
Thomas, buried, 18 May, 1600.

Richard Putnam or Puttenham, of Penn, gentleman, brother of the above, was bapt., 29 Nov., 1563.
Administration on estate of Richard Puttenham of Amersham (Agmondesham) granted to his widow Mary Puttenham, 4 July, 1601. (*P. C. C.*)
Children, bapt. at Penn:

Isabel, bapt., 27 May, 1582, perhaps the Sybel, who m. at Penn, 13 Nov., 1613, John Harper.
Frances, bapt., 27 March, 1586; buried, 23 Sept., 1588.
Mary, bapt., 13 May, 1587; buried, 28 Jan., 1592.
Catherine, bapt., 13 May, 1587; buried, 15 Sept., 1631.
Martha, bapt., 28 Sept., 1589.
Ann, bapt., 26 May, 1591.
Grisette, bapt., 20 Nov., 1592.
Putnam Place in Penn is now a farm-house. Probably there are no male descendants of this Penn family, bearing the name, now living.

THE PUTNAMS OF WINGRAVE AND WOUGHTON.

Henry Putnam, younger son of Nicholas of Penn, was living in 1526.

His will has not been found.

Children:

Richard, of Eddlesborough and Woughton, born about 1500.

John, of Slapton and Hawridge.

Thomas, of Eddlesborough.

Richard Putnam, of Eddlesborough and Woughton, the probable eldest son of Henry Putnam, above, is mentioned in the Lay Subsidy of 16th Hen. VIII. (1524), as of " Edlesbury," while in those for the 14th and 15th Hen. VIII. he is styled Rychard Puttynhn. From this same roll it appears that John Pottman, of Slapton, was assessed 4s. The roll is badly mutilated. Eddlesborough is nearly surrounded by the county of Hertford. It was a town of considerable importance as early as 1332. Slapton joins on the west, and Woughton, whither Richard removed, perhaps on the death of his father, who may have been living there, is but a dozen miles to the north of Eddlesborough. Wingrave is about the same distance from Woughton. The early registers of Woughton, unfortunately, are so tattered and worn that it is impossible, except here and there, to glean any information from them. The register begins in 1556, but is illegible until 1558, and, until 1590, the outer half of each page has been destroyed. Thus in some instances the name and in some the dates suffer.

The church, a fine specimen of its style, has been recently restored, at his own expense, by the rector, Rev. Mr. Field, who is an enthusiastic antiquary.

Mr. Field located the farm occupied by the Putnams of the 17th century as lying nearly opposite the rectory and toward Stony Stratford, being on the farther or south side of the canal. The property is now owned by Mr. Bowles, while the name, remembered dimly by the aged parish clerk, has long since been lost in that vicinity. From the wills extant and from the churchwardens' accounts it is evident the younger branch of the family living at Woughton were substantial yeomen. Richard Putnam fortunately left a will, a copy of which is on record at Somerset House. The name of the testator in this instance is spelled Puthnam, and he is styled as of " Woughton on the Grene." He directs that his body be buried in the churchyard at Woughton. To Joan his wife, he leaves his house in Slapton, with remainder to his son John, and all the goods she brought with her at her marriage. To John he also gives £3. 6. 8 ; to son Harry, land in Woughton. To son John's wife, 6sh. 8d., and to every child that he hath one sheep. To his daughter Joan he gives £6. 13. 14, and to each of her children a sheep. The residue of his estate he gives to son Harry whom he makes his executor. To the high altar at Woughton he gave 4s. Overseers John, his son, and Rychard Brynkelowe. Witnessed by John Chadde, Laurence Wylson, with others. The will is dated 12 Dec., 1556, and was proved 26 Feb., 1556/7. (*Arch. Bucks.*)

The register for the year 1565 contains an entry of which but the name, Jone Putnam, is legible ; it may be the entry of burial of Richard's widow, who was likely a second wife, or the baptism of a daughter of Henry Putnam.

Children :
  John, of Wingrave, eldest son.
  Harry, of Woughton.
  Joan, married prior to 1556.

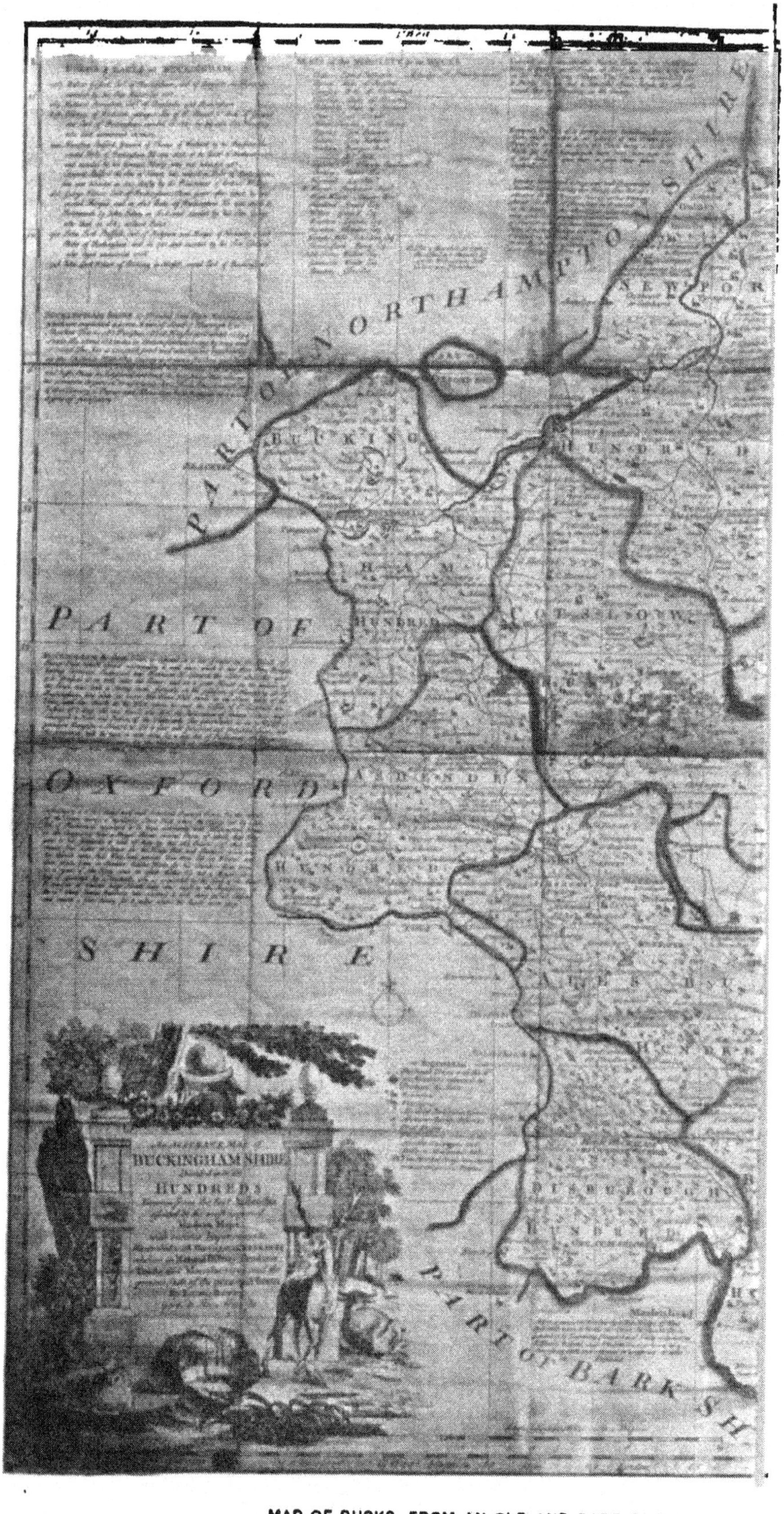

MAP OF BUCKS, FROM AN OLD AND RARE ENGRAVING OF

John Putnam, of Rowsham, in Wingrave, the eldest son of Richard of Woughton, was buried in Wingrave, 2 Oct., 1573. Margaret Putnam, who was buried 27 Jan., 1568, was probably his wife.

His will is dated 19 Sept., 1573, and proved 14 Nov., that year. He directs that he be buried in the church or church-yard of Wingrave. To son Nicholas he gives £30, as well as cattle, sheep, barley, etc., etc.; Richard receives the house and lands at Wingrave, and lands lying in the fields of Rowsham and Wingrave, also twenty nobles. He divides his flock of sheep thus: Nicholas, two of the best; Kateryne Mosse next best couple; Richard and Thomas five of next best; and bequeaths small legacies to the following persons: Ellyn Duncumbe, Katerin Mosse, William Brandon, godson; Robert Rowe, Mother Gillam, William Gillam, Harye Wakeman, Kempster, Skelton, widow Raffe. Overseers, Mr. Henshaw and John Duncumbe. Witnessed by Robert Nixon, clerk, John Rowe, Thomas Gryne, John Winchester. (*Arch. Bucks.*)

The registers at Wingrave are in excellent condition, beginning with 1550; but unfortunately from 1611 to 1640, there is a gap, and from 1645 to 1653, were poorly kept. The church has been considerably improved of late, the defacements of the church-wardens of the early part of the century having been removed, the old windows opened, and many interesting evidences of ancient church art, both painting and sculpture, revealed. The rector, Mr. Starbuck, has still to do much to the building, the tower needing a considerable expenditure of money. As here John Putnam, who came to Danvers, was baptized, this edifice is of more than ordinary interest.

A window or brass should be placed there to commemorate the events of his life. Wingrave includes Rowsham, and is between Aston Abbotts and Long Marston and Puttenham. Settled at Wingrave were the Goodspeeds, Duncombes, Hardings, Stonehills, and other families bearing the same names frequently mentioned in the wills of members of other branches of the family about this time. It is probable that intercourse between the people of the Vale of Aylesbury between Tring and Aylesbury was constant. As mentioned previously, non-conformity had a firm foothold at Long Marston and in other parts of Herts nearby. The farmers and yeomen of this part of Bucks were of good estate, the land being exceedingly fruitful.

Children:

Nicholas, probably born previous to 1550, and perhaps as early as 1540.

Richard, of Wingrave, d., *s. p.*, buried at Wingrave, 24 June, 1576. By his will, dated 21 June, and proved 17 Oct., 1576, he gives to his brother Nicholas his house at Wingrave, his free lands and leaseholds bequeathed him by his father, John Putnam. To brother John and his son Thomas, Ellyn Duncombe, Harry Wigge, William Brandon, Johan Duncombe. Brother Thomas executor. (*Arch. Bucks.*)

Thomas, of Rowsham, d., *s. p.*, buried at Wingrave, 2 July, 1576. He married, 16 Nov., 1574, Agnes Britnell. In his will, dated 26 June, proved 7 July, 1576, he mentions brothers John and Nicholas, and Thomas, John's son, also sister Johan Macham, and William Brandon, Ellyn Duncombe, Harye Wigge, brothers John and Richard Brickenell. Wife Annys, executor. Overseers, "my well beloved friend Maister Triamor Smithe of Edlesborough, and Maister John Blackenell of Wingrave."

Margaret, married at Wingrave, 14 June, 1573, Godfrey Johnson.

 ✳ **Nicholas Putnam**, eldest son of John of Rowsham, above, probably born about 1540; married at Wingrave, 30 Jan., 1577, Margaret, daughter of John and Elizabeth Goodspeed. She was baptized at Wingrave, 16 Aug., 1556, Nicholas Goodspeed ✳ being godfather and Margaret Theed and Margaret Milne godmothers.

✳ Nicholas Goodspyde, John Aged, and Nich. Grasse, were witnesses to the will of John Grace, the elder, of Rowsham in Wingrave, husbandman, 13 May, 1528. (*Arch. Bucks.*) The Grace family, toward the end of this century, was one of influence and wealth in

Nicholas Putnam lived in Wingrave until about 158 later when he removed to Stewkeley. He inherited prop from his father and from both his brothers, and undoubte for the times was exceedingly well to do. His will is da 1 Jan., 1597, and was proved 27 Sept., 1598. It is given ... full below :

In the name of God Amen the first daye of Januarie Anno D͞ 1597. I Nicholas Putnam of Stutely being sicke in bodie but of a whole mind Pfict memorrie thank be to god doe dedeyn and make this my last will and testament in maner and forme follow-inge, first I bequeath my Sowle to Almighti god my bodie to be buried in Christen menes buriall,

It. I geve unto John my Sonne all my howes and landes being in the fielde and towne of Abbots Aston when he cometh to age. It. I geve unto my wife all my goodes untill such time as my sonne John cometh to age and then he to have halfe (*with her?*). It. I will that yf my wife and my sonne cannot agree to dwell together that then my sonne John shall paye unto my wife V^{lb} a yeare as longe as she liveth yf she keepe her widdowe, yf she marrye then my sonne to paye her V^{lb} a year soe iij yeares after her marriage and no longer. It I geve unto my iiij children Thomas, Richard, Anne, and Elizabeth to everi one of them X^{lb} to be payd them by my wife and my sonne John when they come to the age of xxi yeares, It I make my wife and Sonne John my executors jointley together to Receive my debtes. Their hearing witness Wm. Meade, Bennet Conley and John Meade wth others Prov. xxvij. Sept. 1598. (*Arch. Bucks.*)

Margaret Putnam, married, second, at Aston Abbotts, 8 Dec., 1614, William Huxley, and, dying four years later, was buried there 8 Jan., 1618–19.

From the record of marriage licenses granted at St. Albans it appears that license to marry was had by William Huxley of Aston Abbots, widower, and Margaret Putnam of the same place, widow. John Putnam of Aston Abbotts, hus-bandman, was surety.

Wingrave. They appear, from their wills, to have been in about the same position as the Putnams there. John Goodspeed was buried at Wingrave, 20 Jan., 1602.

hildren, baptized at Wingrave;

Anne, bapt., 12 Oct., 1578; m. at Aston Abbotts, 26 Jan., 1604/5, William Argett.

John, bapt., 17 Jan., 1579; of Salem, Massachusetts.

Elizabeth, bapt., 11 Feb., 1581, m. at Aston Abbotts, 22 Oct., 1612, Edward Bottome. Ch.: Richard, bapt. 24 Nov., 1613. Marie, bapt. 5 Nov., 1615. Elizabeth, bapt. 16 Aug., 1618. John, bapt. 27 Dec., 1620. Robert, bapt. 5 Dec., 1624.* Edward Botham buried 31 March, 1642.

Thomas, bapt., 20 Sept., 1584.

Richard, baptism not found. Living in 1597.

John Putnam, of Slapton, a younger son of John of Wingrave, owned land in Eddlesborough. From his will, dated 5 March, 1594, and proved 28 Feb., 1595/6, it appears he was possessed of fair estate. He appoints his brother Nicholas Putnam and Richard Sawell, overseers, and his wife Margaret and son Thomas, executors.

It is likely Thomas, the elder son, was the issue by a former marriage.

The will of Margaret, widow of John, is dated 2 July, 1617, proved 1 Oct., 1617, by the executors. She mentions son Barnard to whom her freehold in Horton in Eddlesborough, he paying the four children of William Ames, £5 each; also her daughters Agnes and Margaret whom executors; also her son John's two children. Thomas and Joan, who may have been the wife of William Ames, are not mentioned. (*Arch. Bucks.*)

Children:

Thomas, b. prior to 1576.

John.

Margaret
Joan } under 16 in 1594.
Anne

Barnard, b. subsequent to 1585.

* There was a Robert Botham of Ipswich, Mass., in 1652.

Harry Putnam, of Woughton, husbandman, the younger son of Richard of Woughter, made his will 13 July, 1579, which was proved 3 Oct. the same year. He mentions his wife's daughter, Elizabeth Twytchill, his wife Jane, who is to live with his son Richard, three months after his decease, and the children given below. Supervisors to be Harry Goodman, the elder, and Arthur Mason. Witnesses were William Townlye, Harry Goodman, junior, Laurawnce Willson, James Robberds, Goylliam Kyswyck. (*Arch. Bucks.*)

Children:

Richard, executor of his father's will.

Harry.

Margaret Putnam who was m. November 157(6) to ——, at Woughton. She received for her unborn child, by her father's will, a ewe and a lamb.

Alice, under 22 in 1579.

Jhone, under 22 in 1579, perhaps the child (name effaced) of Henry who was bapt. Jan. 1569/70 at Woughton. She m. a Coleman, and had two children living in 1613.

Richard Putnam, of Woughton, yeoman, the eldest son of Harry of Woughton, had the house and lands. His will is dated 1 Dec., 1613 and was proved 12 Jan., 1613/14. To each of his children he gave generous bequests. He directs that his son John remain with his mother till her death, she providing for him. He also mentions sister Jane Coleman and her two children, and his brother Henry's children. Wife Ann to be sole executrix.

"Jonas Chapman and Agnes Puttenham married 14 Sept., 1615."—(*Woughton Register.*)

Children:

Henry.

John.

Anne, m. Pattison, and had two children living 1613.

Richard, bapt., 13 Mar., 1600.

William, bapt., 22 Jan., 1601/2. Adm. on estate of William Putnam of Stony Stratford, granted 29 March, 1678.

Edward, bapt., 19 Feb., 1601/2.
Margaret, bapt., 19 Feb., 1601/2.
Katherine, bapt., 19 Feb., 1601/2.

Henry Putnam, of Wolnerton, husbandman, brother of Richard, above. His will, dated 21 Sept., 1625, was proved 26 Oct,, 1625.
Children :
Thomas, of Wolnerton ; he had a dau., Elizabeth, mentioned in her father's will.
John, of Wolnerton, executor of his father's will.
Anna.

Henry Putnam, of Woughton, eldest son of Richard of Woughton, inherited his father's lands.
" Henry Puttenham and Ales Goodman, widow, married 15 Oct., 1615."—(*Woughton Register.*)
Children, baptized at Woughton :
Richard, bapt., 24 Mar., 1615/16.
Alicia,   "   23 Dec., 1618.

Richard Putnam, of Woughton, son of above. Administration upon the estate of Richard Putnam of Woughton, to relict Mary, 23 March, 1658.
Children :
" Mary, of Richard and Mary Putnam, born 25 Dec., 1650."—(*Woughton Register.*)
? Richard. " Alice, wife of Richard Putnam, buried 10 Dec., 1692."—(*Woughton Register.*) Richard buried at Woughton, 1717.

Edward Putnam, son of Richard of Woughton, bapt., there, 19 Feb., 1601/2. His will, dated 7 March, 1670/1, was proved 24 May, 1671. He makes Thomas White of Caldecot, Bucks, gent., and Roger Chapman of Newport Pugnell, gent., his kinsmen, trustees for his children, Charles, Thomas, Priscilla, Mary, Katherine, to whom he devises his lands in Great Woolston and Little Woolston, also the perpetual advowson of the parish church of Great Woolston.

Certain legacies to other children, viz., Richard, John, and Ann; wife Priscilla to be executrix. The seal is a coat-of-arms rather indistinct, probably, a bend, cottised, charged with three fleur de lys, between six fleur de lys. Crest, on an esquire's helmet, a griffin rampant. (*Original will, Somerset House.*)

Edward Putnam was matriculated at Oriel College, Oxford, 23 Nov., 1621, aet. 17; B.A., 7 Feb., 1623/4; M.A., 6 June, 1627. He was presented to the living of Great Woolston, May, 1634, on presentation by Agnes Chapman, widow, and John Harris, yeoman, and at the time of his death was rector there.

Woolston adjoins Woughton, and is a pleasant parish with, to-day, but a very small population. The old church has been pulled down and a small, plain affair erected. The living is an excellent one. The will of Priscilla Putnam, widow, of St. Bride's, London, dated 2 May, 1690, was proved 30 June, that year. She mentions son Charles, to whom land in Little Woolston; son Thomas, to whom money and plate; and daughter Priscilla Moody. Also her grandchild Priscilla Puttnam. (*P. C. C. Dyke 94.*)

John Putnam, of Wroughton of the Green, Co. Bucks, yeoman.

From his will, dated 8 Dec., 1761, proved 31 Dec., 1761 (*Arch. Bucks*), it appears that his grandfather was John Chadd. He makes Bernard Cheval and Hy. Ashby of Wroughton his executors. To his wife Dennis he left his cottage, where his sons George and Chadd then dwelt.

Children:

John.

Robert.

George.

Chadd.

Elizabeth, deceased prior to 1761. She had married ———— Fleet and left children, John, Elizabeth, and Edward.

Thomas Putnam, of Olney, Co. Bucks, senior, dealer. His will was made 1 May, 1729, and proved 22 Sept., 1729 (*Arch. Bucks*).

Children:

Thomas.
John.
Samuel.
Robert.
William.

Richard Putnam, of Olney, senior, chapman. Probably brother of the above. His will was dated 3 Dec., 1731, proved 10 May, 1732 (*Arch. Bucks*). He makes brother Hy. Butcher and Thomas Putnam of Olney, his nephew, executors, his wife having deceased.

Children:

Richard, under 21.
Hannah, under 21.

Thomas Puttenham, of Olney, Co. Bucks, dealer. Probably son of Thomas, above. His will was made 29 July, 1765, proved 7 Oct., 1765 (*Arch. Bucks*).

Children:

Thomas, of Olney.
Sarah, m. John Armstrong.
Hannah.

THE PUTNAMS OF HAWRIDGE AND CHOULSBURY.

John Putnam, of Hawridge, Bucks, the presumed younger son of Henry Putnam, and undoubtedly a brother of Richard of Woughton. Hawridge is within ten miles of Slapton and Eddlesborough, and is divided from Wingrave by the parishes of Drayton Beauchamp, where a branch of the family resided, and Puttenham. His will is dated 7 Oct., 1550, and was proved 20 April, 1551, by Agnes, the relict, his executrix. William Putnam of Choulsbury was one of the witnesses.

Children :

William, of Choulsbury.

Richard, of Hawridge.

Edward ; an Edward Putnam was married 6 Nov., 1564, at Chesham, Bucks, to Joan Cock.

Hugh, of Great Chesham, yeoman ; he left no issue ; his will is quite extensive. It is dated 26 Apr., 1590, and was proved 1 Sept., 1590. He wills that two tenements for the poor of the parish be erected on the plot of ground within the churchyard where the church house formerly stood ; to Christian his wife he leaves property she had when he married her and such as was Richard Boothe's, her son ; also £7 annually. His home and lands after death to go to Mark and John, sons of his brother, Richard Putnam. To his brother, John Putnam, his house and land bought of Richard Edmonds ; also a shop and barn, and his house and land at Bottey occupied by Thomas Gate and William Wier ; also his house in Hawridge, chargeable with a yearly payment

of 6/8 to the poor of Halberty and Chousbury. To
Mark, son of brother Richard, houses and lands in Great
Missenden, and in Churchfeild, also land on road from
Chesham to Hawridge; to John, brother of Mark, a
house in Hawridge and other property. To the three
daus., Agnes, Elizb., and Jane, of Richard Putnam, £5
each. To his sister Agnes Gate and her dau., Joan
Gate. Residue to brother John, whom executor. The
will of his widow is dated 1 July, 1603, and was proved
17 Aug., 1603. She bequeaths to her nephew Richard
Byrch and his children William, James, Jane, Mary,
Martha, and Richard; also to Jane, John, and James,
children of her cousin Stephen Byrche; to James, son
of her cousin John Byrche; to her cousin William Cul-
verhouse; to William Cartwright's children; and to the
poor of Chesham.

John, of Hawridge.

Agnes, perhaps married to (? Thomas) Gate, by whom she
had a dau. Joan, unmarried in 1590.

William Putnam, of Choulsbury, Bucks, the eldest son
of John of Hawridge. His will was made 14 Apr., 1575, and
proved 5 Aug., 1579. He made his son Thomas executor,
and gives to Henry lands in Wylteyne (Wilstone), " Parrats,"
in Drayton; Thomas had the house and lands in Choulsbury
and in New Grove, Drayton. He made his son John overseer. To all of his children he leaves legacies varying from
£2 to £13, 6. 8.

Among the Additional Charters in the British Museum is
one (# 5165) by which Frances Russell Lord Russell, Earl of
Bedford, grants to William Putman a messuage and land in
Choulsbury and Hawridge, Bucks, 8 Aug., 3 Eliz., 1561.

He is probably the William who married at Chesham, 18
Nov., 1547, Cicily Gaate. (*Chesham registers, Somerby's
MSS., Mass. Hist. Soc.*)

He left a wife Jane.

His children, except William, mentioned in his will were:

William, of Drayton Beauchamp, died in lifetime of his
   father.
Thomas, of Choulsbury.
John, of Tring.
Robert, of (see Chingford, Essex, family, below).
Henry, of Choulsbury.
Annis, m. —— Cocke.
Amye, m. 18 July, 1568, John Harding. (*Tring Reg.*)
Ellen, m. —— Duncombe. Tring register records the
   burial of Ellen, wife of Robert Duncombe, 26 Aug.,
   1600.
Jane, m. —— Byrche.
Jane, m. —— Feyld.

Robert Putnam, of Chingford, Essex. Administration on
his estate to widow Mercie, 4 July, 1614. (*Com. of London.*)

Reginald Putnam, of Waltham Holy Cross, Essex. Administration on his estate to widow Elizabeth, 21 Jan.,
1638/9.

Edward Putnam, of Chingford, Essex, yeoman. Will
dated 24 Oct., 1654; proved by his widow Elizabeth, 20
Dec., 1654. She may have been widow of Robert Sare, as
Edward leaves £5 each to Jane, Thomas, and Robert, left
them by their late father, etc.
Children :
Edward, joint executor of his father's will.
Robert.
Elizabeth.

William Putnam, of Drayton Beauchamp, Bucks, eldest
son of William of Choulsbury. His will is dated 20 Nov.,
1575, and was proved 30 April, 1576, by his widow the executrix. To his son William he gives £10 and the ground at
Wilstone in Tring which his father has promised him ; to
Henry, Robert, John, and Joyce each £10 when 21, and ten
sheep and a cow. To John and Anne Young a bullock each.
To Drayton Church, 20s. His brother Robert to be over-

seer. One of the witnesses is Henry Stonhill. He married, at Drayton, 23 July, 1564, Agnes Young, and was buried there, 20 Dec., 1575.

The register at Drayton Beauchamp, which begins with 1538, shows the baptisms of four of the children of William and Agnes Putnam.

Children :

William.
Henry, bapt., 27 Jan., 1565.
Joyce, " 30 Aug., 1568.
Robert, " 8 July, 1571.
Thomas, " 15 July, 1576.
John.

William Putnam, eldest son of William of Drayton, married Elizabeth, by whom he had two children, baptized at Drayton. He probably is the William who married, 18 May, 1590, Mary Cardell (*Tring Reg.*), and was buried there 8 April, 1592.

Children, by Elizabeth :

Mary, bapt. Drayton, 14 July, 1582.
William, bapt. Drayton, 19 May, 1588.

By Mary :

John, bapt. Tring, 27 Feb., 1590/1.

Thomas Putnam, of Choulsbury, second son of William of Choulsbury. His will was made 28 Sept., 1641, and proved 28 Sept., 1644, by his son Thomas. He mentions his wife, son-in-law Richard Ware and Mary his wife, and their son John ; to his son Thomas he gives his house and appurtenances in Choulsbury and Drayton, and after his death to his son James ; his son John £8, and to each of his grandchildren. Overseers, Kinsman Nicholas King and son John Putnam.

Children :

Thomas, of Choulsbury.
John, of Choulsbury.
Mary, m. Richard Ware, and had a son John living in 1641.

Thomas Putnam, of Choulsbury and Drayton, son of the above, had a son James under age in 1641, mentioned by his grandfather. Administration on the estate of James Putnam, of Choulsbury, was granted 3 June, 1679, to the relict Hannah. Inventory £104.

John Puttnam, of Wigginton, Herts., yeoman, the elder. Perhaps brother of Thomas, above. Will dated 16 Jan., 1690/1; proved 6 May, 1691. Inv. £240. 13. 6. To be buried at Choulsbury; to the poor of that parish and Hawridge; dau. Hester, "under a sad discomposure of mind," £80 in trust; grandchildren, Daniel, John, Thomas, and James Putnam when 21; granddau. Anne Putnam when 21; granddau. Elizabeth Bachelor; besides the children named below.
Children :
Hester.
Daniel ; executor of father's will.
Mary, wife of Francis Doggett.
John ; overseer, with Thomas Rutland of Wringsall, of
  father's will.

John Putnam, of Tring, yeoman, son of William of Choulsbury, and overseer of his father's will 1593. His will was made 30 July, 1611, and proved 3 April, 1613, by Richard his son, the executor. To Richard he gave Brians Grove, and to his other children, John, Robert, Joane Robinson, Alice Phillips, and Amy Stonhill, legacies.
Children :
John, bap. Tring, 25 Dec., 1566.
Annie, buried 12 Nov., 1568.
Annie, bap. Tring, 9 Oct., 1569.
Annie, "   "   24 Nov., 1570; m. 3 July, 1592, Henry
  Stonhill.
Richard, bap. Tring, 24 June, 1574.
Robert, "   "   14 Apr., 1577. Robert Putnam and
  Alice Wallis m. 15 Oct., 1601 ; Agnes, wife of Robert,
  buried 18 Dec., 1600 (*Tring Reg.*). Also Mary Putnam,
  m. 16 Sept., 1592, John Stonnell.

Joane, m. —— Robinson.

——, bap. Tring.

Alice, m. —— Phillips.

John Putnam, eldest son of the above, weaver, of Tring; married at Tring, 15 Oct., 1588,——; "Alice wife of John Putnam, buried 11 Apr., 1609"—(*Tring Reg.*). His will is dated 6 Sept., 1630, and was proved 17 June, 1631. He mentions wife Joan; Henry Bachellar, his daughter's son; son John Putnam.

The will of "Jone" Putnam, widow, is dated 3 June, 1635; proved 6 July, 1636, by Henry Bachelor, executor. She mentions Susan, dau. of her son John Putnam, and Henry, son of dau. Mary Bachelor.

Children:

Jane, bapt. Tring, 3 Aug., 1589, d. y.

John, of Tring, blacksmith.

Mary, bapt. Tring, 20 Jan., 1593/4; m. —— Bachellor, and had a son Henry in 1631.

John Putnam of Tring, blacksmith. His will, dated 30 June, 1632, proved 26 Feb., 1632/3, mentions his mother Joane Putnam of Willesthorne, wife Joane, and Henry Bachellor, his sister's son.

Child:

Susan, a minor at date of father's will.

Richard Putnam, of Tring and Drayton Beauchamp; yeoman. Probably the Richard son of John of Tring, bapt. 24 June, 1574. His will directs that he be buried in Drayton. He leaves to each of his children, viz., Richard, Alice, Marie, Susan, Elizabeth, and Judith, £20 when 22 years old. His son John and wife Susan to be executors. The witnesses are John Brown, of Tring, and John Putnam, of Willesthorne. Dated 10 Nov., 1625; proved 21 Apr., 1626.

Susan Putnham, widow, buried at Drayton, 6 Apr., 1642.

Susan Putnam, widow, appears on the Lay Subsidy of 4 Chas. I., 1628, as of Drayton.

Children :
  Elizabeth, bapt. Tring, 1612.
  John, bapt. Tring, 1615.
  Richard, bapt. Drayton, of "Richard and Susan," 23
     Aug., 1618.
  Alice, bur. at Drayton, 4 June, 1626.
  Marie, m. at Drayton, 26 Jan., 1631, John Harley.
  Susan.
  Judith, bapt. at Drayton, 29 April, 1621 ; m. 13 June, 1639,
     at Drayton, Edward Eames.

John Putnam, of Drayton Beauchamp, eldest son of
Richard, bapt. at Tring, 1615 ; buried at Drayton, 22 Jan.,
1682 ; married there 10 May, 1641, Alice Gurney.
Children, from Drayton register :
  Alice, bapt. 7 Feb., 1641/2.
  Susan,   "   19 May, 1648.
  John, born 2 Oct., 1653.
  Mary,   "   30 Dec., 1656, bur. 1 Jan., 1657.

Richard Putnam, brother to the above, of Drayton
Beauchamp, bapt. there 23 Aug., 1618 ; m. Susanna.
Children :
  Susanna, bapt. 25 Apr., 1653.
  Elizabeth, born 19 Oct., 1655.
  Maria, bapt. 27 Nov., 1672.

Henry Putnam, of Choulsbury, youngest son of William
of Choulsbury. His will was made 1 Apr., 1598, and proved
22 May, 1598. He makes his wife and son William executors. His brothers Robert Duncombe and Thomas Putnam
overseers. To son William his lands in Choulsbury ; to son
Robert, under 21, " Parratts " in Drayton, and to youngest
son Henry, " Marshell " in Hawridge ; to eldest dau. Jane
£20 on condition she do not marry Daumser ; other daus.,
Ellen and Agnes (youngest) ; sister Jane Byrche ; to Edmund Byrche.

Tring register records the marriage of Henry Putnam of
Choulsbury to Agnes Doncomb of Tring, 26 Nov., 1570.

Children:

William of Choulsbury.

Robert, of Hemel-Hempstead?

Harry, of Drayton and Hawridge.

Jane.

Ellen.

Agnes.

William Putnam, Hawridge, yeoman, eldest son of the above Henry. Will dated 11 May, 1647; proved by relict Jane, 4 July, 1648. Brother Henry Putnam, overseer.

Feet of Fines, 13 Chas. I., William Putnam sells John Penny, of Anynrvine Bryan, a messuage and 90 acres in Chesham, Bucks.

Children:

Henry, of Billendon, in Chesham.

Francis, of Barkhampstead, St. Mary, als. Northchurch, Co. Herts, yeo. His will is dated 5 Nov., 1673; and proved 17 Nov., 1673. His bro., Henry of Chesham, sole executor, to his bro. Henry's son Francis, £500; his bro.'s son Henry, £200; sister Jane Wright, of Chesham, £20. Residue to daus. of bro. Henry.

Thomas, *of Virginia?*

Mary.

Joyce.

Jane, m. John Wright.

Henry Putnam, of Billendon, in Chesham, yeoman, son of the above. In his will, dated 31 May, 1677, and proved 29 March, 1679, by Henry, son of the testator (William, the executor, being deceased), he mentions his father-in-law, Thomas Whitney, deceased, and brother Francis, deceased, and "all his daughters."

Adm. on estate of Henry Putnam, of "Billingden," 5 June, 1680.

Children:

William, executor of father's will but died before the presentation of the will.

Henry.

Francis, possibly the Francis of Hitchendon, called kinsman by his cousin Mark in 1690.

A daughter, m. ——— Buck.

Other daus.

Thomas Putnam, of Chesham, son of William, perhaps
the William above. He made his will on board the *Increase*,
bound for Virginia, 29 Dec., 1647.

To his son Thomas Putnam he gives £20 out of forty-
three pounds, nine shillings due him "in England by my
father Willliam Putnam's will dwelling ham shire in Chessum
parish." The remainder of the legacy he gives to his wife
Dorothy, provided she pay unto Sara Miller "at Holburne
Barre in Middle Rowe" the sum of £5; to John Salter he
gives £16, 16sh. due him from Henry Bottum of St.
Clement's Church.

Witnessed by Arthur Broniwell and John Bigge. Probate
on the above will was granted 22 May, 1659, to John Smyth,
husband of Dorothy Smyth alias Putnam, the late wife and
sole Extrix. named in will of Thomas Putnam the elder,
deceased, for the sole use and during the absence of the said
Dorothy and Thomas Putnam, the son of the said deceased,
now both in Virginia, beyond sea. (*P. C. C. Ruthen*, 197.)

Robert Putnam, of Hemel-Hempstead, Co. Herts. He
may have been a son of Harry of Choulsbury.

Children (*Somerby MSS.*):

Thomas, bapt., 28 Feb., 1613, N. S.

Stephen, bapt., 6 June, 1617.

Matthew, bapt., 3 Mar., 1621.

Thomas Putnam,* of Hemel-Hempstead, Herts, married
Sarah.

Children :

Sarah, bapt., 7 Oct., 1635.

John, bapt., 11 Nov., 1637.

Thomas, bapt., 11 Oct., 1639.

* Probably son of Robert Putnam, of Hemel-Hempstead. Found in the Somerby MSS.

John Putnam, * of Hemel-Hempstead, Herts, married Mary.

Children:

John, bapt., 27 Jan., 1637.

Mary, bapt., 10 Nov., 1637.

Anne, bapt., 3 Feb., 1640.

Henry Puttnam, of Woodcroft Hill, Barkhampstead, St. Mary, also Northchurch, Herts, yeoman. Probably son of Harry of Choulsbury. Will dated 10 Feb., 1664; proved 8 Oct., 1666. (*P. C. C. Mico, 147.*)

Left a wife, Anne.

Children:

Henry, died 1657/8.

Richard, executor of his father's will. Had land in Barkhampstead after death of his mother. The *Friends Records*, in London, contain the entry of baptisms of Richard Putnam, son of Richard and Ann Putnam of at Goshens End, Barkhampstead, 12–10–1664.

Mary.

Henry Putnam, of Dudswell, Barkhampstead, yeoman, son of above. Will dated 14 Aug., 1657; proved 5 Nov., 1658. (*P. C. C., Wotton, 599.*)

Married a daughter of Henry Norris.

Children:

Henry
John } under 21 in 1664.

Richard Puttnam, of Hawridge, husbandman, son of the first John of Hawridge. His will is dated 12 June, 1577, and proved 6 Oct., 1577, by the executrix, Joan, his widow. Overseers, Hugh Putnam and Richard Byrch, his brethren. Children, all of whom were under 10 years of age in 1577, all mentioned by their uncle Mark in 1590:

Agnes.

Elizabeth.

Jane.

* Probably son of Robert Putnam, of Hemel-Hempstead. Found in the Somerby MSS.

Mark, given land in Great Missenden by Hugh, his uncle.

John, born 1577/8; mentioned in will of uncle Hugh, 1590, and given a house in Hawridge.

Mark Putnam, of Missenden, Bucks, eldest son of Richard Puttnam, of Hawridge. Buried at Penn, 3 Dec., 1647. (*Penn Register.*) He was given property in Great Missenden by will of his uncle Hugh in 1590. Mr. Somerby (*Mass. Hist. Soc. MSS*) found the baptism given below:

Children :

Mary, bapt., Little Missenden, 8 Mar., 1618.

Mark, who by will dated 29 April, 1690, proved 17 Nov., 1694, leaves legacies to kinsman Francis Putnam, of Hitchingden, cousin Lewen, kinsman Joseph Putnam, of London, salter, Richard Edmonds, brother-in-law of kinsman (his nephew) Thomas Carter, whom executor, and kinsman Grimsdale, of Risborough, brickmaker.

Francis, of Hugenden.

Francis Puttnam, of Hitchenden, als. Hugenden, Bucks, the elder, yeoman. His will, dated 7 Apr., 1677, was proved 13 June, 1677.

Probably a son of Mark and brother of Mark, junior, who seems to call his nephews " kinsmen."

Children :

Richard.

Henry, lands in Hitchenden with remainder to Richard.

Francis.

Elizabeth, of Great Kingsell, Hugenden, m. 10th 1 mo., 1674 Robert Chearsley of Giles Chalfond. (*Friends Records.*)

Mary, m. —— Chapman.

Sarah, unmarried in 1677. The *Friends Records*, contain the entry of a marriage, 10th 1st mo., 1681, of Sarah Putnam of Dean Giles Chalfond, spinster, to John Newman of Stamwell.

Richard Puttnam of Stoke-Mandeville, Co. Bucks., yeoman. Will dated 17 Aug., 1682; proved 10 July, 1688. (*Peculiar of Banbury.*) To the poor of Lee. His godson Francis Puttnam. To John Harding of Wilsden and godson Thomas Jackson of Stoke-Mandeville. Perhaps son of Francis of Hitchendon.

Children:

A dau., m. to Richard Harding, executor of father-in-law's will. Ch., Sarah, Ruth, Richard, Easter.

Richard Putnam, of Hitchendon. Adm. on his estate to widow, Elizabeth Putnam, 14 Mar., 1694.

John Putnam, of Great Missenden, probably youngest son of Richard of Hawridge, and brother of Mark, senior.

He was given a house in Hawridge, and property in Great Missenden and elsewhere, by his uncle Hugh.

Administration on his estate was granted, 12 Nov., 1658, to Thomas Putnam, son of the deceased.

On the 16 May, 1640, was made a deed, put on record in the probate register of Arch. Bucks, 25 June, 1640, by which John Putnam, yeoman, of Ballinger in Great Missenden, gave, from natural love, etc., to his sons John and Thomas, all his estate.

A Lay Subsidy, of 4 Chas. I. (1628), names John Putnam and Zacheus Gould, of Great Missenden. (*Somerby MSS.*)

Children:

John.

Thomas.

John Putnam of Hawridge, Bucks, yeoman, youngest son of the first John of Hawridge. At the time of the making of his will 8 Dec., 1592, his children were all minors. To his wife Jane he leaves his lands in Hawridge, Chesham, Aberry, and elsewhere, until his sons are of age, when Thomas, the elder, is to have such as lie in Hawridge and Aberry, and John his lands in Botley in Chesham and houses in Great Chesham. He leaves many small legacies,

be, Bucks, paper worker, who
er Kezar of Wickomb, 5 sh.,
:o sh. (*P. C. C. Nabbs 190.*)
v of William, is dated 30 Apr.,
1671. Mentions her late hus-
la, wife of Bray Price; Robert,
Marlow, deceased; Ann, wife
of Robert Lockwood to pay
ɔod, daughter of said Robert
son of Ann White; widow
ım Lawrence, and her dau.,
ns; Elizabeth Murren. (*Arch.*

liam Murren, of High Wicombe, Bucks, paper worker, who is to pay Barbary, wife of Peter Kezar of Wickomb, 5 sh., and William Evins of Uborn 20 sh. (*P. C. C. Nabbs 190.*)

The will of Mary, the widow of William, is dated 30 Apr., 1668, and was proved 16 May, 1671. Mentions her late husband William, her sister Priscilla, wife of Bray Price; Robert, son of Lyonell Lockwood of Marlow, deceased; Ann, wife of William White; "the heir of Robert Lockwood to pay to his sister Elizabeth Lockwood, daughter of said Robert Lockwood, £5"; William, son of Ann White; widow Kezar; Joane, wife of William Lawrence, and her dau., Anne Lawrence; William Evans; Elizabeth Murren. (*Arch. Bucks.*)

VIEW FROM TRING HILL, LOOKING NORTHWEST.

THE PUTNAMS OF EDDLESBOROUGH.

Thomas Putnam of Eddlesborough, Co. Bucks, husbandman. Probably a son of Henry and brother of Richard and John. From his will, dated 31 Aug., 1575, proved 16 Sept., 1575, we learn he owned "Sewell" in Eddlesborough, and that his wife was to be supported by his son Anthony. From the context of the will, the following were probably his children.

Children :

Annis, m. to ——— Head.

Alice, m. to Thomas Crowshe and had children.

A dau. m. to John Crydgell.

"   "   Robert Sparke.

"   "   Richard Roberts.

Anthony, his father's executor.

Perhaps also the following :

Thomas Putnam who married at Leighton-Buzzard, 13 Feb., 1597/8, Ursula Jackeman. He had a son William who in will of Ralph Jackman, assistant steward on the ship *Royal Mary*, dated 17 July, 1633, is called kinsman and son of Thomas Putnam, living at Eddlesborough, Bucks. William Putnam, son of Thomas of Eddlesborough, matriculated at Magdalen Hall, Oxford, 12 Dec., 1628, æt. 20. He was B.A. 4 May, 1631 ; M.A. 30 Jan., 1633/4.

The Lay Subsidies for 1628, show Matthew and Thomas Puttenham as among the heaviest assessed inhabitants in Eddlesborough, and again in 1640 ; also in 1640, Gabriel Putnam of Eddlesborough, and Thomas Putnam of Marsworth, an adjoining parish.

The will of Matthew Puttenham of Hodenhall in Eddlesborough, yeoman, is dated 17 June, 1636, and proved 30
June, 1636; he gives to his brother-in-law, Thomas Cocke,
his house and freehold lands in Pitlesthorne, chargeable with
an annuity of £20 to the testator's wife Mary, whom he
makes sole executrix.

In 1638, 30 June, administration on estate of Thomas
or Gabriel Putnam, late of Eddlesborough, is granted to
Gabriel, his son. In his will dated 16 Dec., 1632, William
Newman of Milton Bryan, Beds. yeoman, mentions his
cousin Gabriel Putnam of Eddlesborough. (*P. C. C. Russell
13.*)

MISCELLANEOUS.

William Potenham, "girdeler," of London. Will dated 26 Sept., 1393, proved in the court of Hastings, 21 March, 1393/4. [*Roll 122(81)*.] Directs that his body be buried in church of St. Laurence in the Jewry before the image of St. Katherine, where lies his wife Christina. Devises to the said church and four orders of mendicant friars in London, viz., Minors, Augustinian, Preaching Friars, and Carmelites. To John Copelyn his brother, residing in Potenham, and John his brother in Wynchester. To Idonia, Matilda, Katherine, Johanna, junior, and William, children of John Potenham. Alice Dawe and others. To sons Thomas and William and to daughter Alice. Alice his wife to be guardian of said children until they reach age of sixteen years.

Poyntel Gilbert, "curreour," in his will dated at London, 26 Apr., 1372, proved 14 Feb., 1373/4, directs that his body be buried in St. Alphege Crupelgate. To wife Alice. To kinswoman Johanna Attewell. To Agnes, daughter of William de Potenham, whose wife Christina is testator's daughter. [*Court of Hastings, Roll 102 (10).*]

John Potman, fishmonger. Will dated at London, 24 Feb., 1373, proved 13 Oct., 1374. He directs that his body be buried in St. Magnus church near London bridge. Wife Juliana a tentement upon Fishwharf in parish St. Magnus, with remainder to sons Guydo and Henry. [*Court of Hastings, Roll 102 (147).*]

Robert Dymershe, alias **Putnam,** of St. Martyne Orgar, city of London, "stokefyshemunger." His nuncupative will, dated 9 March, was proved 15 March, 1550/1. Wife

Dorothy. Children Francis, Grace, and Thomas ; "the resi-due of his children should have nothing for they had their partes all redye." Wife to be executrix. (*Com. Court of London, Clyff 1a.*) He is probably the Robert Putnam alias Dymarshe of London, fishmonger, to whom protection was granted, June, 1528. He was travelling in the retinue of Sir Robert Wingfield.

Henry Poteman, of London, was one of several petition-ers regarding the selling of fish at retail. He was a whole-sale fishmonger of Fishwharfe 14 Edw. II., 1321.

Elizabeth Puttenham was bequeathed 6sh. 4d. by Nicho-las Talbot in his will dated 1501, proved at Bury Saint Edmunds 4 March, 1502. (*Camden Society Publications*, vol. 49.)

Indenture dated 17 Nov., 8 Hen. VIII., No. 46, between Richard Aldwyn of Puttenham and **Margaret Puttenham** concerning lands in Puttenham, Surrey. (*Palmer's Index to Close Rolls*, Hen. VIII.)

Francis Putnam, citizen and tallow chandler of London, gives bond to James Pyle, citizen and salter of London. (*Close Rolls*, 16 Elizb. Pt. 2.)

John Putnam, of Saint Bottolph without Bishopsgate, London. Adm. on his estate granted 8 March 1605/6, to his brother William Putnam. (*Com. of London, Act Book*, fo. 313.)

Jane Putnam, of London, widow. In her will dated 28 Jan, 1616/17, proved 16 March, 1617, she mentions son Richard Holmer and his daughters and the children of Daniel Andrew, "all of said daughter Holmer's children," cousin Proby, son Adrey's children, cousin William Hicks' wife, a diamond ring, cousin Kowman and his children, cousin Coe and her children, William Hicks executor. In codicil of 13 Nov., 1617, she mentions great-grandchild Martyn Rogers and cousin John Neeton. (*Com. London*, vol. 23, fo. 146.)

John Putnam sells Thomas Thorne et als., property in Gaddesdon parva, 1627. (*Feet of Fines for Herts., Mich. term* 3 Charles I.)

John Putnam was a deputy for the Admiralty commissioners at Hilbree, near Chester, in 1656. He wrote under date of 4 June, 1656, to the Commissioners that while Capt. Vessey of the frigate Nightingale was riding at anchor within his charge, he saw and heard of divers goods being sent on board for transportation to Ireland. His attempt to examine the same after going on board met with disaster, he being thrown overboard on the return trip, "being but a weakly man." He fears such actions will work great prejudice to the Commonwealth as regards customs, and of merchant vessels trading to Ireland. (*Dom. State Papers.*)

Edmund (or Edward Putnam?) **Putman**, of Greenwich, Kent, married, 10 Feb., 1623/4, Anne Compton.

Margery, daughter of Edmund Putman, bapt. 2 Feb., 1624/5.
Ellen,* bapt. 20 Apr., 1627.
Anne,* bapt. 4 Feb., 1629/30.
Edward,* bapt. 14 Dec., 1631.
Margery,* bapt. 6 Jan., 1633/4.
Elizabeth,* bapt. 24 Feb., 1635/36.
John,* bapt. 11 Nov., 1638.

(*Register Greenwich, Kent, Somerby MSS., Mass. Hist. Soc.*)

John Putnam bought Micklefield, Herts, of John Meyrick, 24 June, 1711, and sold the same to William Emmott, 30 Sept., 1717. (*Clutterbuck's Herts.*)

Henry Putnam was a dissenter in 1713. He lived in Northchurch, Herts. (*Nonconformity in Herts, Urwick.*)

Elizabeth Putnam, of Choulsbury, married, 12 June, 1660, John Judge of Great Missenden. (*Parish register, All Saints, Leighton Buzzard, Beds.*)

---

* These children are all entered as children of *Edward Putnam*. Did not the clerk or copyist make an error in recording the marriage and first baptism?

John Putnam, in 1670, lived in the parish of Saint Thomas, Island of Jamaica, where he owned 200 acres of land. (*State Papers Amer. and West Indies Series.*)

William Putnam, of Shipley, Yorkshire, was born about 1800. He was a maltster and was living in 1874.

George Putnam, of Wilstone, Tring, married Sarah, a daughter of John White, of the same place. John White died 2 June, 1892.

George Putnam, of Southampton, died in 1856.

Henry Puttenham, of Gravesend, died 4 July, 1886, leaving a widow Jane.

James Putnam, of High Wicombe, died 1886, leaving a son Fred Walter of that place.

Robert John Putman, of Hackney road, died 26 Oct., 1886, leaving a widow Emma Louisa.

James Puttnam, of Brompton road, died 1 March, 1888, leaving a daughter Ann, and an estate valued at £3200.

Henry Putnam, a music teacher in Hampstead road, had wife Lucy who died 1 Aug., 1888.

James Putnam, of Portsea, Southampton, died 19 March, 1888, leaving a widow Mary Ann.

John Putnam, of Willenhall, Stafford, died 15 July, 1888.

Undoubtedly many of the persons bearing the name of Putman or Putnam in London to-day, are descendants of emigrants from Holland. Prominent among these was Henry Putnam, who, born in Amsterdam in 1726, died in London 1 March, 1797, at his residence in Austin Friars. He was for forty years one of the ministers of the Dutch church. In 1793 he had intended to resign and return to Amsterdam, but the change in the government there prevented. He was a fellow of the Royal Society. (*Gentleman's Magazine*, vol. 67, page 256.)

William Putman, * of St. Giles in the Fields, Midd., cooper, bachelor, æt. about 30, and Unity Ward, of St. Clements Danes, Midd., spinster, æt. 20, with consent of the father, at St. Mary Savoy, 24 Sept., 1668.

Unity Puttenham, * of St. Mary Savoy, Midd., widow, æt. about 25, alleged by Laurence Vernier of the same, to Robert Goffe, of St. Giles in the Fields, Midd., citizen and vintner, widower, æt. about 40, 22 July, 1671.

Hannah Puttenham, * of St. Martin's in the Fields, widow, æt. about 27, to Richard Hull, of the same, chandler, bachelor, æt. 23, at Allhallows in the Wall, London, 24 Jan., 1661.

The wills of the following Putnams, probably of the Hawridge family, have not been examined. (*Arch. Bucks.*)

Henry of Bellingdon, adm. 1679.

John of Hawridge, 1716.

Daniel of Whitecraft, 1719.

Henry of Chesham, 1720.

Moses of Hitchenden, 1721.

"   "   Hugenden, 1723.

James of Hawridge, 1729.

Henry of Aston Clinton, 1735.

Francis of Chesham, 1736.

Richard "   "   1742.

Thomas of Hawridge, 1745.

John (Puttenham) of Ivingho, 1748.

Elizb. of Chesham, 1748.

William of Hawridge, 1755.

Elizabeth of Chesham, 1759.

Elizabeth of Hawridge, 1765.

John of Amersham, 1773.

William of Chesham, 1788.

Ann of Chesham, 1797.

George (Puttenham) of Aston Clinton, 1800.

Joseph of Aston Clinton, 1816.

* From *Marriage Allegations*, London, abstracted by H. F. Waters.

COAT–OF–ARMS.

The coat-of-arms of the Putnam family of Salem, Massachusetts, and its various offshoots, found in every State in the Union, in Canada, Australia, and in Old England, is a silver stork surrounded by eight crosses crosslet-fitchee, and placed upon a black field. The Crest is a red wolf's head.

Heraldically the above coat-of-arms would be described: Sable, between eight crosses crosslet-fitchee (or crusily-fitchee), argent, a stork of the last, beaked and legged gules. Crest, a wolf's head gules.

These arms have been borne by the Putnams from early times, prior to the Visitations, and are ascribed to Sir George Puttenham of Sherfield, and to Nicholas Putnam of Penn, the latter bearing a mullet for a difference. Such are the arms described in the Visitation of Bucks by Harvey in 1566 and 1634, and in the Visitation of Hampshire in the latter year.

The quarterings as given in the Visitations are: Lozengy, or and azure, which is for Warbleton.

The following coats-of-arms are found described by Burke in his *General Armory:*

PUTTENHAM of Sherfield, 1634, Argent, crusily fitchee sable, a stork of the last. Crest, as the last.

PUTTENHAM or PUTNAM, Bedfordshire and Penn, Co. Bucks, Sable, crusily fitchee argent, a stork of the last. Crest, a wolf's head gules.

PUTMAN or PUTNAM, Sussex, Sable, a martlet between six crosses crosslet argent.

PUTTENHAM or PUTNAM, Sable, a heron in an orle of crosslets argent, beaked and legged gules.

lxxii

PUTNAM, Sable, a bend between six crosses, crosslet, three, two, and one.

All of the above except the last are practically the same coat. I have been unable to locate any example of the one last described.

Several instances occur in the 16th century of families impaling or quartering Puttenham, and from the known rank of the ancestors of Nicholas Putnam it is probable that the stork and crosses have been borne from the beginning of our family history, certainly at the time of the intermarriage with Warbleton.

It seems that Nicholas Putnam could have added the following quarterings to his paternal coat beside that of Warbleton: Gules, two bars argent, for Foxle; Ermine, a bend vaire or and gules, for Apuldrefield; and Gules, a frette argent, on a chief or, a lion passant of the field, for Spigurnell.

John Putnam of Danvers, to our knowledge, never used coat armor, although entitled to by birth and position. He was the actual head of the family, as the two elder lines, those of Sherfield and Penn, had become extinct in the male line, and the Putnams of Woughton, Hawridge, and Eddlesborough were of younger lines than the Putnams of Wingrave.

The present head of the Putnam family must be looked for among the descendants of Thomas Putnam, the son of Thomas, and grandson of Thomas the eldest son of John Putnam the emigrant, and he is probably Thomas Burnside Putnam of Covington, Penn, or one of that family, he being descended from Samuel, the sixth and youngest son of Elijah Putnam, and the only one who lived to have children.

During the Revolution the Hon. James Putnam, the younger son of James Putnam, Esquire, of Danvers, and younger brother of Doctor Ebenezer Putnam of Salem, made enquiries, as may be seen from his letters printed in this history, about the origin of the American family, and his son, James Putnam, Esquire, obtained a confirmation of his claim to bear the same arms as the Putnams of Penn. This acknowledgment by the College of Arms was founded upon a presumption, since proved correct, as to the descent of John Putnam of Danvers from Nicholas of Penn.

While it is extremely probable that the various Putnam families in America whose ancestry is traced back to some other ancestor than John Putnam of Salem (Danvers), if of English descent, come from the same stock, presumably the Hawridge line, yet until that is proven they cannot consistently bear the stork and crosses.

The Putmans and Putnams descending from Jan Poutman of Albany are of Dutch descent. There is in existence an ancient tile, which may be as old as the migration, upon which is painted the arms described below, of undoubted Dutch origin. For many years this has been considered by them to represent their coat-of-arms, and I believe the right to bear those arms has never been questioned.

Arms of Poutman, Putman, Putnam : Gules on a fesse argent between three boars' heads erased close or, a lion passant sable. Crest, a boar's head or, snout and tusks argent.

THE PUTNAMS OF DANVERS

AND

THEIR DESCENDANTS.

JOHN PUTNAM. — Ancestor

1 John Putnam of Aston Abbotts, Co. Bucks., England, and of Salem, Massachusetts, born about 1580; died suddenly in Salem Village, now Danvers, 30 Dec., 1662, aged about eighty years; married, in England, Priscilla (perhaps Priscilla Gould), who was admitted to the church in Salem, 1641.

Children baptized at Aston Abbotts:

2 ELIZABETH, bapt. 20 Dec., 1612; "Eliza Putnam" admitted to the church at Salem, 1643.

3 THOMAS, bapt. 7 Mch., 1614-5; d. Salem Village, 5 May, 1686.

4 JOHN, bapt. 24 July, 1617; d. in infancy; buried at Aston Abbotts, 5 Nov., 1620.

5 NATHANIEL, bapt. 11 Oct., 1619; d. Salem Village, 23 July, 1700, æ. "about 79 or 80" (Danvers church records).

6 SARA, bapt. 7 Mch., 1622-3.

7 PHŒBE, bapt. 28 July, 1624.

8 JOHN, bapt. 27 May, 1627; d. Salem Village, 7 Apr., 1710.

JOHN PUTNAM, SEN., it is known, was resident in Aston Abbotts, England, as late as 1627, as the date of the baptism of his youngest son shows, but just when he came to New England I am unable to state. Family tradition is responsible for the date of 1634, and we know that the tradition has been in the family for over one hundred and fifty years. In 1641, new style, we find the following entry on the Town Records of Salem:

"At a meeting the 20th of the 11th moneth (1640 old style).

"Mr. Endecott.

"Mr. Hathorne.   ground (etc.).

"John Woodbury.   Graunted to Allyn Convers of planting

"Jeffry Massy.   .   .   .   .   .   .

"Graunted to John Putnam [ffiftie][1] one hundred acres of
"land at the head of Mr. Skeltons ffarme between it & Elias
"Stileman the elder his ffarme, if there be an hundred acres of
"it.   And it is in exchange of one hundred acres wch was
"graunted to the said John Putnam formerly & if it fall out
"that there be not so much there then to be made up neere
"Liuetennt Dauenports hill to be layd out by the towne.   And
"tenne acres of meadow in the meadow called the pine mead-
"ow if it be not there formerly graunted to others.

"Graunted ffiftie acres of land vnto Thomas [Putnam][1] and
"ffiue acres of meadow both to be layed [out by][2] the towne."

These are the earliest records we have of John unless the
following abstract from Lechford (12–27–1639, O. S.), refers
to him.   I am inclined to think, however, that in this case
Lechford refers to Thomas who was a resident of Lynn and
near neighbor of Gould and therefore likely to have engaged
Lechford (*see p. 238, Lechford's note book*).   "For drawing
Articles for Mr Cradocke & Gould and Putnam &c 12.27 (6s)."

Gov. Endicott arrived in Salem, 6 Sept., 1628, with a company of about one hundred; it is not likely that John Putnam
came with him.   If John Putnam came in 1634, he must have
witnessed the excitement over Mrs. Anne Hutchinson (1634–
8), the banishment of Roger Williams from Salem and the
colony (1635), perhaps taken part in the attempt to put the
colony in a state of defence against Charles I and Wentworth,
who were ruling England without the aid of a Parliament
(1635).   In 1636–7 occurred the terrible Pequot War, but
nowhere do we find mention of his name. Samuel P. Andrews, Esq., of Salem, a gentleman long interested in antiqua-

---

[1] Erased in original.
[2] Doubtful reading.   Essex Inst. Hist. Coll., p. 109, Vol. IX, 1869.

rian matters, especially in those relating to the Putnam family, is inclined to believe that John Putnam was here very early and at first owned land at the end of Broad street, extending to Essex where it joins the Boston turnpike. He bases his case upon an old deed which he found among the Peele papers, dated 1658 and now recorded, in which John Putnam (probably the younger) deeds a part of this land to Henry Kenny. Mr. Andrews thinks that here John Putnam built a house and brick-kiln and that this is the first grant spoken of above. At all events if John Putnam was in Salem in 1634 he lived quietly, and not until 1640–1 do we have any reliable information concerning him. [Here it is proper to state that the Book of Grants for Salem is a transcript from the Town Records of matters pertaining to land, and commences 1 Oct., 1634. The Town Records in existence to-day commence with Dec. 26, 1636, all previous records having been lost.]

John Putnam was a farmer and exceedingly well off for those times. He wrote a fair hand as deeds on record show. In these deeds he styles himself "Yeoman;" once, in 1655, "husbandman." The deeds on record run from "14th day 2d mo. 1652" to 31st Oct., 1662. The earliest deed is a grant of land from Ralph Fogg, conveying "a farme four score acres lying between old father Putnam's farm and Daniel Reies and more than eight acres near the house which John Hathorne built," recorded p. 481, L. VI, Essex Deeds. Under date of 2d, 1mo, 1653, he gives to Nathaniel Putnam one-half his lands or plains which he has in his possession and to this he affixes his mark; the next day he grants to Thomas one-half of all lands except what he has granted to son Nathaniel, p. 36, L. II.

It is probable that he may have experienced a shock of paralysis about this time and was expecting death. This method of disposing of their lands while living to their children, reserving enough for their own support however, was the rule among the earlier generations of the Putnam family.

The parents then had the pleasure of seeing that their children were comfortably settled before leaving them.

James and Jonathan Putnam owned his original estate in 1692, consisting of the town grant of one hundred acres in 1641; eighty acres granted to Ralph Fogg in 1636; forty acres (formerly Richard Waterman's) to Thomas Lothrop in 1642; and thirty acres to Ann Scarlet in 1636. The above estate was situated between Davenports Hill and Porters Hill and west of Daniel Rea's grant in Danvers (*Upham*). ✳The following account of the death of John Putnam was written in 1733 by his grandson Edward. "He ate his supper, went to prayer with his family and died before he went to sleep."

John Putnam was admitted to the church in 1647, six years later than his wife, and was also freeman the same year.

The town of Salem, in 1644, voted that a patrol of two men be appointed each Lord's day to walk forth during worship and take notice of such who did not attend service and who were idle, etc., and to present such cases to the magistrates; all of those appointed were men of standing in the community. For the 9th day, John Putnam and John Hathorne were appointed.

SECOND GENERATION.

My Ancestor

✱ II. 3 Lieutenant Thomas (*John*), eldest son of John and Priscilla Putnam, baptized at Aston Abbotts, Co. Bucks., England, 7 Mch., 1614–5; died at Salem Village, 5 May, 1686; married, first, at Lynn, Mass., 17th, 8 mo., 1643, Ann, daughter of Edward[a] and Prudence (Stockton) Holyoke. The Holyoke family were one of the most prominent and aristocratic families in the colony. Mrs. Ann (Holyoke) Putnam died 1 Sept., 1665 (1st, 7 mo., 1665).

Lt. Thomas married, second, at Salem, 14th, 9 mo., 1666, Mary Veren widow of Nathaniel Veren a rich merchant formerly of Salem. Mrs. Mary (Veren) Putnam died 16 (or 17th) Mch., 1694–5. In 1684, Mrs. Putnam in the apportionment of seats in the meeting house at the Village was seated in the first, or principal pew reserved for women.

Children of Thomas and Ann Putnam. With the exception of their daughter Sarah, the births of the children are recorded at Salem :

9 ANN, b. 25–6–1645; m. William Trask.

10 SARAH, bapt. 1st Ch. Salem, 23–5 mo.–1648; not mentioned in her father's will.

11 MARY, b. 17–8–1649; bapt. 1st Ch. Salem, 19–3–1650; not mentioned in her father's will.

12 THOMAS, b. 12–1–1652; bapt. 1st Ch. Salem, 16–2–1652.

⑬ EDWARD, b. 4–5–1654; bapt. 1st Ch. Salem, 9–5–1654.

14 DELIVERANCE, b. 5–7–1656; bapt. 1st Ch. Salem, 10–3–1657; m. Jonᵃ Walcott.

15 ELIZABETH, b. 30–6–1659; m. Joshua, son of John and Eleanor (Emery) Bayley, b. in Newbury, 17 Feb., 1653; will proved 6 Aug., 1722; a brother of Rev. James Bayley who m. Mary Carr, sister of Mrs. Ann Putnam (12). Joshua Bayley left no children and

---

[a] Great grandfather of Edward Holyoke, President Harvard College 1737–1769. For Holyoke Gen. see Vol. III, Essex Inst. Hist. Coll.

✱ President HARVARD College EDWARD Holyoke

after his wife's death his property fell to her nephews and nieces, viz., Susanna Putnam, Timothy Putnam, and Experience, widow of David Bayley.

16 PRUDENCE, b. 28-12-1661-2; bapt. 1st Ch. Salem, 29-4-1662; m. William Wyman.

Child of Thomas and Mary Putnam :

17 JOSEPH, b. 14 Sept., 1669; bapt. 4 Sept., 1670.

THOMAS PUTNAM, SEN., was an inhabitant of Lynn in 1640; freeman 1642; one of the seven men (selectmen) of Lynn in 1643; admitted to the church in Salem, 3 Apr., 1643.

The town of Salem granted to him, 20–11–1640, "fifty acres [of upland] and five acres of meddow." This was at the same time that his father received a grant of one hundred acres from the town ("in exchange of one-hundred acres formerly granted to him").

In 1645 the General Court passed the following order : "Mr Thomas Layghton, Edward Burcham, & Thomas Puttman are appointed by this Courte to end smale causes for ye towne of Lynne for ye yeere ensewing" 18 June, 1645. This commission was renewed the 20 May, 1648, "to end smale cawses, vnder twenty shillings."

11th, 9 mo., 1648, he was "Chosen for Gran-Juryman" in Salem and 10–10–1655 was chosen constable of Salem in place of Mr. William Browne. The office of constable at that date carried great authority and covered the entire local administration of affairs.

He was also the first parish clerk at Salem Village and was prominent in the local military and ecclesiastical, as well as town affairs.

Thomas Putnam wrote a very fine hand and had evidently received a good education, as had his brothers. In 1679 he gives to the Rev. James Bayley, upon his retirement from the ministry at Salem Village, three acres of meadow. During the long dispute over Bayley at the Village, Thomas and John seem to have supported Bayley, while Nathaniel was in opposition.

Thomas Putnam during a number of years held, besides the offices above mentioned, the various positions of "Layer out of highways," "Inspector of bridges," "to care for rates for the minister," etc. On the 29th day, 11 mo., 1658, "Jefferey Massey, Thomas Putname, Nath¹ Putname and Joseph Hutchensen are Impowered, or any three of them, to joyne with Topsfield about the Runninge & setlenge & full endinge of our sixe mile line in the extent of it in so many places as they shall see meet, for a full conclusion of the worke." Oct. 8, 1662, the General Court confirms his appointment as Lieutenant in the troop of horse.

When on the 8th Oct., 1672, the General Court permitted the inhabitants of Salem Farms to become a separate parish, Lt. Thomas Putnam was made chairman of the committee chosen to carry on the affairs of the parish (11 Nov., 1672), and on 25 Nov., 1680, it was voted "that Lt. Thomas Putnam and Jonathan Wolcott supply the place of deacons for year ensueing;" they were continued in office 27 Dec., 1681.

The above is the first mention of deacons in the Village records.[4]

In 1682 occurs the first list of tax-payers at the Village. There are ninety-four names on this list. The twelve largest amounts are here given set against the names of the persons paying them, also all of the family taxed in that year.

		£	s.	d.
— 1	Lt. Thomas Putman	18	6	3
2	Nathaniel Putnam	9	10	0
3	Thomas ffuller, sen.	8	6	0
4	Lt. John Putnam	8	0	0
5	Joshua Rea	7	7	0
6	Joseph Hutchinson	6	12	3
7	Joseph Porter	6	3	0
8	Daniel Andrew	5	19	3
9	Thomas Flint	5	2	0
10	William Sibley	4	16	0
11	Job Swinnerton, jr.	4	10	0

[4] In the Secretary's office at the State House are many documents relating to the religious disturbances at the Village. These show very plainly the attitude of the Putnams during that exciting period.

	£	s.	d.
12 John Buxton	3	15	0
22 Thomas Putnam, jr,	2	14	0
23 John Putnam, jr.	2	14	0
—— Edward Putnam	1	17	0
Jonathan Putnam	1	16	0

It will be seen from the above that the three Putnam brothers and their sons-in-law were by far the wealthiest in the "Village" or "Farms." Besides inheriting a double portion of his father's estate[5] Thomas Putnam by his marriage with widow Mary Veren came into possession of considerable property in Jamaica and Barbadoes. The homestead of Thomas although much enlarged is still standing and is now known as the "Gen. Israel Putnam house." This house is situated a little east of Hathorne's Hill in the northern part of Danvers, not far from the Asylum, and was occupied by his widow in 1692. Here also his son Joseph lived during his opposition to the witchcraft proceedings.

There was also a town residence in Salem situated on the north side of Essex street extending back to North River, its front on Essex street embraced the western part of the grounds now occupied by the North Church and extended to a point beyond the head of Cambridge street.

In his will dated, 8 Feb., 168⅚, and proved at Boston, 8 July, 1686, he gives the eastern half of the above estate to his son Thomas, the western half to his son Joseph; another estate on the western side of St. Peter's street, to the north of Federal, he gives to Edward.[6] To each of his children he gives a large estate in Salem Village and a valuable piece of meadow land. To a faithful servant Joseph Stacey, he gives eleven acres.

The children by his first wife attempted, unsuccessfully, to

---

[5] It was usual among many New England families for the eldest son to have a double portion; this became a law and continued in force until quite recent times.

[6] The Hon. Abner C. Goodell, jr., now owns and occupies a part of this estate. Near here was also the jail wherein were confined the condemned during the excitement of 1692.

break this will, claiming that undue influence was used to obtain for Joseph more than his share of the estate.

Mr. Upham in his Salem Witchcraft thus sums up the character and position of Thomas Putnam in contrast with his brothers "Possessing a large property by inheritance, he was not quite so active in increasing it, but enjoying the society and friendship of the leading men lived a more retired life. At the same time he was always ready to serve the community when called for as he often was, when occasion arose for the aid of his superior intelligence and personal influence," also in writing about the settlement of the "Farms" he says, "The Putnams followed up Beaver Brook to Beaver Dam, and spread out toward the north and west."

The will of Thomas Putnam is here given in full.

> Know all men by these p{r}sents, That I Thomas Putnam Sen{r} of Salem, being Ancient & sencible of the declining of old age, & weakness & sumptoms of mortality daily atending upon me, but being of sound mind & memory blessed be God, doe make this my last will & testament, this 8{th} day of february Ann{o} Dom. 168$\frac{2}{4}$ as followeth

> Imp.{r} I give my soule into the hands of Jesus Christ in whome I hope to live forever, & my body to the earth, In hope of a Glorious resurection with him when this vild body shalbe made like unto his Glorious body and for the estate God hath given me, in this world, (my debts being paid), I dispose of as followeth.

> It. I give & bequeath to my son Thomas putnam & to his hears & assignes the dwelling house he now lives in, with the Barne & oarchards, with all the land belonging there to containing by estimation, one hundred & fifty acres, be it more or lesse, according as it lyes bounded, as is heareafter exsprest, viz: from Hathorns medow as the water runs out of the medow, till it comes into Ipswich River, then from the bound by the river to the end of the Iland, to the great black oak betwixt my Cozen John Putnams land & mine, from thence to Cromwells, bound tree, & from thence to a walnut tree & a litle red oak where lyes a heape of

stones, the trees being falen down, which is alsoe the
bounds betwixt Joshua Reas land & this land, & from
thence to Reas bounds, that is a red oake where lyes stones :
& from thence to another heape of stones, & from thence
to the fence at Hathorns medow, where is a tree marked
by the fence, & from thence with or along by the fence,
all the upland & swamp, till it comes to the place where
the water comes out of the meddow, And from thence my
Spong of medow on the other side the brooke, & the upland on Jonathan Knites his side, till it comes to a marked
tree, neere the said Knights Corner of his feild next Beare
hill, & then Crosse the swamp, to the cart way that is at
the lower end, of the flaggy meddow, & to take in all the
meddow, & to run by the swamp, not over Andever waye,
till it comes at the tree where is three rocks & the tree
marked, & the tree is to the westward of the rockes : on the
north side, where Andever high way turnes, & from thence
to the bound where I Joyne to Topsfeild men, & soe to the
River ; till I meet mr. Balyes meddow at the Spring, that
runs into the River, a little above the bridg, & from the
bridg, Andever Road to be the bounds to the tree, where is
three stones, at the turne of the waye, & from thence to two
trees marked at the ridg or Top of the hill, that lyes on the
right hand of the path as wee come from the bridg to Thomas
Putnams house, and from the two trees to a great rock that
is neere Hathorns brooke where Thomas & Edward are to
make a bridg over the brook against the corner of Thomas
his feild by his Barne, within which bounds is included a
pcell of land, containing about fifty acres lying by the River,
which said fifty acres alsoe I give & bequeath to my said
son Thomas his heires & assignes together with the aforesaid
house Barne oarchards & about one hundred & fifty acres,
upland and meddow, all which my said son Thomas his
heires & assignes shall have & Injoy forever, after my decease

It.   I give and bequeath, to my sonn Edward Putnam & to
his heires & assignes a certaine tract of land, upland & meddow, containing about eighty Acres be it more or less, with
the house he now dwells in, & the barne & oarchard, upon

the said land, which said pcell of land, is bounde
land before Specifyed given to my son Thomas
easterly : & Ipswich River westerly : Alsoe I give
my son Edward one pcell more of land, lying upon
hill soe caled, containing about sixty acres more
being bounded as followeth, viz : from a forked waln
is alsoe Joshua Reas & nathaniell putnams bounds, from
thence to a stake & heape of stones neere the Cartwaye,
from thence to Cromwells bound tree soe caled, from thence
to a walnut & red oak blowed downe where lyes a heape of
stones, from thence to the forked walnut, Alsoe I give to
my said son Edward one pcell of land more, lying upon
Beare Hill, containing about sixty acres more or less : being
bounded, by the three Rocks & a tree standing by them
marked, from thence to the bound in the swamp, where my
land Joynes to Topsfeild land, from thence to william Hobs
his bounds, from thence to Phillip Knights his bounds behind Beare hill, & from thence along Knights his line till it
comes to a marked tree, & from the sd marked tree, Cross
the land to a red oak tree standing by a great Rock on the
north easterly side of Andev Road,—Alsoe I give my sd
son Edward, a pcell of pcell of meddow containing fower acres
more or less, lying on the west side of the River, neere his
house & the upland against his the sd meddow, from the
uper end of ye said meddow Cross my upland, to the top
of the high hill & soe Straite to my brother Nathaniells line,
& then to run along the line, to his bounds, at the lower end
of the meddow, which is a heap of stones upon the topp of
a hill about twenty pole from the meddow containing eight
acres more or less, of upland,—Alsoe I give him my sd son
Edward, all my meddow lying in Cromwells meddow soe caled,
contayning fower acres more or lesse, Alsoe I give my sd son
Edward, all that my part of meddow that lyes in Hathorns
soe caled, lying bounded by Joshua Reas medow on the
west, Ezekiell Cheevers meddow on the south, Jonathan
Knights upland on east & Thomas Putnams Spong of medow on the north, all which said pcells of land, boath upland
& meddow I give & bequeath to my said son Edward, & to
his heires & assignes forever, after my decease.

It. I Give & bequeath, to mary my beloved wife, & to my
son Joseph Putnam, borne by her, my said wife, all that my
farme I now live upon with all the buildings & houseing
theire upon with all the app^rtenances thereto belonging, both
upland & meddow oarchards fences & p^rvilidges thereto belonging, for them to have hold & Injoy the Same to them
& there assigne after my decease, for the terme of my Said
wives naturall life, (they making no Strip nor waste,) either
of them or theire assignes to Injoy the one halfe part thereof, whoe are to mainetaine & keep in good repaire either of
them theire said part the said terme, & after my said wives
decease, then my will is & I doe by these p^rsents bequeath
the whole of all the said farme buildings & app^rtenances to
my said sonn Joseph Putnam & to his heires & assignes,
from the time of my wives said decease & for ever after,
which said farme containes about one hundred & twenty
Acres, be it more or les, that is to say the upland & meddow or mowing ground that is adjoyning to the house which
is bounded as followeth, on the west with the land formerly
Richard Hutchensons, a red oak marked neere the house
where Bragg dwelt, from thence to a heape of stones & a
stake standing neere my oarchards, from thence to an other
heape of Stones, on the side of the hill, from thence to another heape of stones, which was the Said Hutchensons
Corner bounds toward the meddow, from thence to a heape
of stones, which is Reas bounds alsoe, & Hutchensons &
mine, from thence to another heape of stones, that is alsoe
the bounds of Joshua Reas & Thomas Putnams & mine, &
from thence Crosse the upland downe to the marked tree by
the meddow, which is my share of meddow in Hathorns
meddow, soe Caled (which meadow is to be und^rstood as
part of the said farme, as it now lyes fenced,) & from thence
the upland on the east, to a tree fallen where is a heape of
stones that is the bounds of Peeter Prescotts & m^r Cheev^rs
land, from thence to Hamer beame soe caled, where lyes a
heape of stones on the stump, from thence to a white oake
on the top of the hill, that is the bound, alsoe of Henry Kenny & m^r Cheevers, & from thence by the said Kenne to a
Rock in the waye, from thence along by the land of Robert

Princes to a great white oak at Beaver Dam, & from thence to the Red oack marked by Hutchensons land by Braggs house, alsoe as belonging to the said farme a pcell of upland & meddow, sixteen acres more or lesse, lying on the west side of he great River, from the logg Bridg downe the River, to the place, where the water runns, from Thomas Putnams and Edward Putnams meddow into the River, from thence to the top of the high hill, & soe Straite to my Brother Nathaniell Putnams bound or line, from thence to Princes bounds by ye pond, & soe to a great rock lying neere the high waye, where wee goe into the meddow, & soe along the waye to the bridg, Alsoe one pcell of meddow more containing two acres more or lesse lying in Hathorns litle meddow soe caled, with the fences as it now lyes, John Darling lying on the west, Joseph Hutchenson on the east, the brook on the south, Darlings upland on the north, alsoe five acres lying in Peeterses meddow soe caled be it more or lesse, alsoe my meddow at Bishops, soe caled, containing two acres more or lesse, alsoe my meddow lying by John nichols upland, about two acres Alsoe my old oarchard, with all the land fences & timber, with the share of Hathorns farme, as it now lyes bounded, by my brother nathaniell Putnams land, & my brother John Putnams land, & with the land, that was Robert Prince his all which said pcells of land & meddow, with all the prvilidges and apprtenances thereof, is a part & soe by me acconted as a part of my said farme as belonging there unto, & is to be understood intended by me as soe, & given to my said wife & son Joseph, the terme of her life & afterwards the whole to Joseph his heires & assignes forever after his mothers decease,

It. I give & bequeath, to my beloved wife mary & my son Joseph, all that my house & ground in the towne with all its aprtences & prvilidges according as is mentioned & bounded in my said wives bill of sale (which said house & ground my said wife bought of Phillip Veren before her marriage) to possess & Injoy the same the terme of my said wives naturall life,. after my decease: & after my wives decease, I give & bequeath all the said house & land as aforesaid to my son Thomas & my son Joseph, to have & to hold to them theire heires & assiges, forever after my said wives decease, and my will is, that when my said sons shall, them or either of them. devide the same betweene them in two distinct parts, they shall devid it equally: & at the front next the street to devide it there an equall breadth, each part,

It. I give & bequeath to my son Edward my halfe acre of land that I bought of Robert Temple & of John Simond deceased, & Job Swinerton Jun[r] as by theire deeds of Sale apeereth, to him & his heires forever after my decease

Item, I give to my daughter Ann, deceased late the wife of william Trask: to her fower children, viz: Ann, william, Sarah, & Susana ten pounds to each of them, to be paid as they com of age, the sons & daughters, as they com to the age of 21 yeares, in currant pay

It. I give to my daughter Deliverance one hundred pounds, to be paid her within one yeare next after my decease, in part in household goods in proportion as her sisters have had, & the rest in currant paye,

It. I give to my daughter Elizabeth, three & forty pounds, to be paid her in currant pay, within one yeare next after my decease

It. I give to my Daughter Prudence, fifty pounds, to be paid her within two yeares, next after my decease in currant pay.

It. I give to my three sonns, viz Thomas Edward & Joseph, ten acres of meddow more or lesse lying in the place caled blind hole, Joyning to Joseph Porters upland, to be equally devided between ym: to Injoy to them & there heires forever next after my wives decease

It. I give to mary my beloved wife, fifty pounds out of my estate after my decease, the plate to be a part, as Invintoryed: & the rest out of any of my other goods as shee pleases: (except any quined money which is to be excepted) & the sd fifty pounds with what shall remaine of it or other of the estate undisposed of, by this my will as she is executrix, at her decease to dispose of it, to & amongst my children as shee shall think fitt,

It. I give to my son Joseph, after my decease, all my plow geer & kart & tacking of all sorts, with all my tooles, implyments, of all sorts kind & quallyty what soe ever, my mill stone & grinston & Cider mill & app'tenances, & his mother to have halfe the use of them while shee lives: provided, she mainetaine the halfe of them, to keep them in repaire & make them good at her decease.

It. I give to my servant Joseph Stacy if he shall live to serve out his time, & be diligent, a pcell of land containing about eleven acres of upland & swamp, as it lyes bounded from the tree marked by Jonathan Knights feild, neere his corner next Beare hill, & soe by Thomas Canes land, to a tree marked, on the hill caled Beare hill, soe Cross, downe to a rock & red oak tree marked, on the north side of Andever Roade, & from thence along by the swamp, along by the flaggy meddow side, to the place where the carts have lately gon over, & soe Cross the swamp to the Said Knights marked tree

Item. I doe apoynt and ordaine my beloved wife Mary to be my executrix, & my son Joseph executor Joyntly together with his mother, of this my last will & testament, And it is to be understood & it is my will that in case I depart this life before my sonn Joseph comes of age, & my said wif see cause to marry an other man alsoe before he comes of age, that then before she marry the estate Shalbe devided betweene them, & either to pay theire proportion of what leagacies shall then be unpaid, & my said son Joseph, may then choose his guardian, to assist him & take care of his part, & my will is that my said son Joseph shall have the possession & improvem^t of his part at the age of eighteene yeares, & I doe desire my loveing freinds, & apoynt them, Viz! Ensigne Israell Porter and Searg! John Leach, to be overseers, to see this will pformed to whome I give twenty shillings each of them, In wittnes that this is my last will & testament, I have sett to my hand & seale, the day & yeare first above written: being the 8th of february Ann° Dom 168⅞

there was Interlyned in p: 1: betwene the 32 & 33 lynes the word (tree) & in the p: 3: betweene the 18 & 19 lynes the word (ground) & in p: 4: the words (about two acres) between the 15: & 16 lines in the same p: the words (ac-

3

counted as) between the 20 : & 21 lines & in the sam p : the word (them) betweene the 35 & 36 lines & in p : 6 : the words (before shee mary) betweene the 6 : & 7 lines & in the same page the word (eighteene) betweene the 12 & 13 lines & a word underneath blotted out & all these Interlinings, don by consent before signing & sealing.

Signed Sealed, & declared to be the last will & Testament of ye sd Thomas Putnam by him, after the severall enterlinings as above said, in the pʳsence of us : with this further addition Vizᵗ. That in case my son Joseph depart this life, before he come to have power to make his will, (which I conceive to be when he comes to the age of eighteene yeares, (when he is to possess his estate, as by my will), I say if he dy before then his estate, viz : the land to fall to his two brothers, viz : Thomas & Edward only out of ye land to his Brother nathaniell veren, the value of twenty pounds in pay : & the rest of his estate to be devided among his three sisters, my daughters. it is to be understood the housing is ment as the land, to ye brothers

Thomas Putnam sen. [Seal.]

witnes Hilliard Veren
Thomas feilld

This fourth of January one thousand six hundered Eigtie five

Where as my will being made some Considerable time past and therefore doe see cause to allter some perticulars in my said will and it being the plesuer of god to visit me with siknes and weaknes yet through his goodnes of sound mind and memory blessed be god for it

and whereas it is Exprest in my will that I have given to my three sons namely thomas Edward and Joseph : my meddowe it being ten Acers mor or Lese Lying in blinde hold soe called Adjoyning to the Land of Joseph Porter : I doe give & bequeth it to my twoe sons vide Thomas and Edward as allsoe part of the Land that I have purchesed and given to my sons : thomas and Edward Liying in topsfilld towneship at this time and thay thretening as if thay would deprive them of it the which if it should be : then my will is that my Land and orched belonging to my old house : as

allsoe my Land that was my brother John hathorns Share
of danforths farme all which Contains about Eighty Acars
more or Lese : I doe give to my three sons thomas Edward :
and Joseph Equily. to be divided between them After my
wifes deses.

and whereas I have given my wife fifty pound to be taken
out of my Esteate After prisell : I doe allsoe give and bequeth to my son Joseph out of my Estate after prisell his
Liberty of Choyse to take twoe oxen & twoe Cowes and sixe
sheep and A horse or A mare

and where as I have given to my daughter diliverance A
hundered pounds upon my will there Remains but fourty :
and three pounds to pay the Rest being all redy payd and
as allsoe my daughter Elizabeth haveing all Redy Receved
sixty and eight pounds : seven shillings & sixe pence there
Remains to make up to her an hundered pounds thirty &
one pounds : twelve shillings & sixe pence

my daughter Prudence allsoe haveing all Redy receved fifty
and nine pound five shilings there Remains : to make up to
her an hundered pounds : fourty pounds and fiften : shillings
Signed and Sealed as with som allterations : and with some
considerations in this my Last will and testament as witnes
my hand

Thomas Putnam sen. [seal.]

Witnes to the hole will
Israell Porter
John leach

Mr. Israel Porter and m^r. John Leach having renounced
their Legacyes of Twenty shillings P. man given in this will
and Thomas Feild all three sworne say that they were
present Feild on the Eighth of February 168⅔ and m^r Porter and Leach upon the fourth of Jan : 1685, and saw Leift.
Thomas Putnam signe seale and publish this will to which
this is annexed as his last will and Testament, and that
when he so did he was of sound memory and understanding
to their best Judgem^t and feild further adds that he saw M^r
Veren signe with him as a witnesse

Boston 8 July 1686

Jurat Coram J. Dudley presid^t
Attest^r Daniel Allin. Cler.

Boston this : 8ᵗʰ of July 1686.

To Thee Honorable Joseph Dudly Esqʳ President of His Majesties Council And Territory of New england In America. Thee Humble petition of thee several parsons under writen : son and sons in law of thee Late Lᵗ Thomas Putnam of Salem Deceased Humbly Sheweth.

That whare as there is an Instriment cald a will Left By our late Honord ffather Lᵗ Thomas Putnam Late of Salem In thee Hands of our Honored motherinlaw : which Instriment as wee Humbly conceive was occationd to be made as it is : by our Motherinlaw : by which Instriment as wee Humbly conceive wee shall all bee extreemly wronged if it must stand In fforce against us : And whereas our Brother Thomas putnam with good Advice as wee Humbly conceive hath entered caution against the said Instriment. our Humble petition to youʳ Honʳ is that he may have Liberty and time to make his plea By which meanes Yoʳ Honʳ May com to understand How much wee are all wronged : And so Hopeing Yoʳ Honʳ will bee pleased to heare the crie of thee ffatherles and Motherles : And not suffer such an injustice to stand in force against us to deprive us of that portion which by the Law of God and man belongs unto us : Butt that thee power (of) Administration of our Decceased ffathers estate may bee granted to our eldest Brother Thomas putnam : that he may bring in A true Inventory of thee same unto Yoʳ Honʳ, that soe each of us may Have that proportion of our Decceased ffathers estate which by the law of God and man belongs unto us : In which Requests If Yoʳ Honʳ shall Bee pleased to ffavour us : Yoʳ Humble petitioners shall evermore be bound to pray &ᶜ.

Edward Putnam,
William Traske,
Jonathan Walcott.

Boston June : 17, 1686

To the Honᵇˡᵉ Joseph Dudley Esqʳ President of his Majᵗⁱᵉˢ Council & Territory of New England in America—The humble Petition of Thomas Putnam Eldest son of Lieut. Thomas Putnam of Salem Village lately deceased. Humbly Sheweth

That whereas my late hon.^d ffather Lieu.^t Thomas Putnam deceased made an instrument in forme of a will for the disposall of his Estate which instrment or will is now in the hand of M.^s Mary Putnam relict & Executrix of my late Hon.^d ffather These are to Enter Caution against the said will Humbly intreating Yo.^r Hono.^r that there may not be any procedure in the probation of said will untill I be heard what I have to alledge concerning it and

Yo.^r Petitioner shall evermore be bound to pray &.^c

Thomas Putnam.

M^{rs}. Mary Putnam prayes ye allowance of Daniell Wicum for her atturney to answer ye plea of Thomas Putnam which is adjurned to July 22^d 1686.

J. D. PR.

NOTE.—Two of Massachusetts most honored citizens are direct descendants of Mrs. Mary (Veren) Putnam, viz., the Hon. Robert C. Winthrop and the Hon. William C. Endicott.

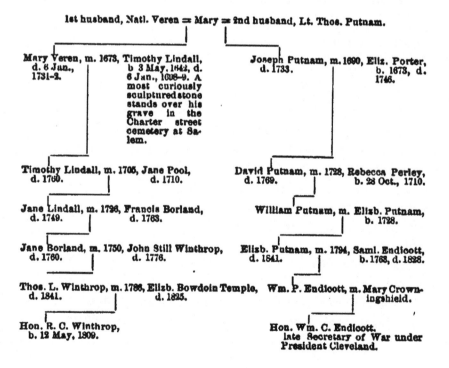

1st husband, Natl. Veren = Mary = 2nd husband, Lt. Thos. Putnam.

Mary Veren, m. 1673, Timothy Lindall, d. 6 Jan., 1731-2. b 3 May, 1642, d. 6 Jan., 1698-9. A most curiously sculptured stone stands over his grave in the Charter street cemetery at Salem.

Joseph Putnam, m. 1690, Eliz. Porter, d. 1733. b. 1673, d. 1746.

Timothy Lindall, m. 1705, Jane Pool, d. 1760. d. 1710.

David Putnam, m. 1728, Rebecca Perley, d. 1769. b. 28 Oct., 1710.

Jane Lindall, m. 1726, Francis Borland, d. 1749. d. 1763.

William Putnam, m. Elizb. Putnam, b. 1728.

Jane Borland, m. 1750, John Still Winthrop, d. 1760. d. 1776.

Elizb. Putnam, m. 1794, Saml. Endicott, d. 1841. b. 1763, d. 1828.

Thos. L. Winthrop, m. 1786, Elizb. Bowdoin Temple, d. 1841. d. 1825.

Wm. P. Endicott, m. Mary Crowningshield.

Hon. R. C. Winthrop, b. 12 May, 1809.

Hon. Wm. C. Endicott, late Secretary of War under President Cleveland.

The will of Mary, relict of Lt. Thomas Putnam, is dated 8 Jan., 1695; proved 20 May, 1695. She bequeaths to her husband's children, Thomas Putnam, Edward Putnam, Deliverance Wolcott, Elizabeth Bayley, Prudence Wayman, and to her own son, Joseph Putnam. In a deposition Mary Lindall, aged forty-five, wife of Timothy Lindall, calls Mrs. Mary Putnam, " Mother Putnam," and George Ingersoll, senior, calls her "sister Mary Putnam."

II. 5 Nathaniel (*John*), baptized at Aston Abbotts, 11 Oct., 1619; died at Salem Village, 23 July, 1700; married at Salem, Elizabeth, daughter of Richard and Alice (Bosworth) Hutchinson of Salem Village, born 20 Aug., and baptized at Arnold in England, 30 Aug., 1629; died 24 June, 1688.[7] In 1648, both Nathaniel and his wife Elizabeth were admitted to the church in Salem.

Children, born in Salem Village (births recorded at Salem) :

18 SAMUEL, b. 18–12–1652; bapt. 1st Ch., 17–2–1653.
19 NATHANIEL, b. 24–2–1655;   "   "   27–8–1655.
20 JOHN, b. 26–1–1657;   "   "   6–7–1657.
21 JOSEPH, b. 29–8–1659;   "   "
22 ELIZABETH, b. 11 Aug., 1662; "   "   11–2–1662; d. 6 Mar., 1697;
        m. Serg. George Flint.
·23 BENJAMIN, b. 24–10–1664.
24 MARY, b. 15–7–1668; bapt. 1st Ch., Dec., 1668; m. John Tufts.

Of these only John, Benjamin and Mary survived their father. In 1694, Nathaniel and John Putnam testified to having lived in the Village since 1641. Nathaniel Putnam was a man of considerable landed property; his wife brought him seventy-five acres additional and on this tract he built his house and established himself.

Part of this property has remained uninterruptedly in the family. It is now better known as the " old Judge Putnam place." He was constable in 1656, and afterward deputy to the General Court, 1690–1691, selectman, and always at the front on all local questions, whether pertaining to

---

[7] According to another account of ancient date, "1st June, æ. 60."

politics, religious affairs, or other town matters. "He had great business activity and ability and was a person of extraordinary powers of mind, of great energy and skill in the management of affairs and of singular sagacity, acumen and quickness of perception. He left a large estate."[8]

NATHANIEL PUTNAM was one of the principals in the great lawsuit concerning the ownership of the Bishop farm. His action in this matter was merely to prevent the attempts of Zerubabel Endicott to push the bounds of the Bishop grant over on his land. The real principals in the case were James Allen who had obtained the Bishop farm as part of his wife's dowry, and Zerubabel Endicott. The case was a long and complicated affair and was at last settled to the satisfaction of Allen and Putnam. Endicott was so chagrined that he was a different man and soon died from the effect of being cast by the courts. This Bishop grant which caused the trouble was sold by Allen to the Nurses and now belongs to Calvin Putnam. The above suit was settled in 1683.

During the unhappy trouble concerning the settlement of a minister over the parish at Salem Village, Nathaniel Putnam was a most determined opponent to the Rev. Mr. Bayley, but when Bayley was dismissed he joined with his brothers Thomas and John Putnam, Thomas Fuller, sr., and Joseph Hutchinson, sr., in a deed of gift to Mr. James Bayley of twenty-eight acres of upland and thirteen acres of meadow, which constituted a very valuable property. This was of date of 6 May, 1680. On 10 Dec., 1688, Lt. Nathaniel Putnam was one of four messengers sent to Rev. Samuel Parris to obtain his reply to the call of the parish. Parris put them off. His final engagement was settled by younger men, one of whom was Deacon Edward Putnam. Mr. Parris, however, was supported by Nathaniel Putnam, who four years later was completely deceived in regard to the witchcraft delusion. That he honestly believed in witchcraft and in the statements of the afflicted girls there seems to be no doubt;

---

[8] Upham's Witchcraft.

that he was not inclined to be severe is evident, and his goodness of character shows forth in marked contrast with the
almost bitter feeling shown by many of those concerned. Nathaniel lived to see the mistake all had made. That he should
have believed in the delusion is not strange for belief in witchcraft was then all but universal. The physicians and ministers
called upon to examine the girls, who pretended to be bewitched, agreed that such was the fact. Upham states that
ninety-nine out of every hundred in Salem believed that such
was the case. There can be no doubt that the expressed opinion of a man like Nathaniel Putnam must have influenced
scores of his neighbors. His eldest brother had been dead
seven years and he had succeeded to the position as head of
the great Putnam family with its connections. He was known
as "Landlord Putnam," a term given for many years to the
oldest living member of the family. He saw his brother
Thomas Putnam's family afflicted and, being an upright and
honest man himself, believed in the disordered imaginings of
his grandniece, Ann. These are powerful reasons to account
for his belief and actions. The following extract from Upham
brings out the better side of his character.—"Entire confidence was felt by all in his judgment, and deservedly. But
he was a strong religionist, a life-long member of the church
and extremely strenuous and zealous in his ecclesiastical relations. He was getting to be an old man and Mr. Parris had
wholly succeeded in obtaining, for the time, possession of his
feelings, sympathy, and zeal in the management of the church,
and secured his full coöperation in the witchcraft prosecutions. He had been led by Parris to take the very front in the
proceedings. But even Nathaniel Putnam could not stand
by in silence and see Rebecca Nurse sacrificed. A curious
paper, written by him, is among those which have been preserved :

"Nathaniel Putnam, Sr., being desired by Francis Nurse,
Sr., to give information of what I could say concerning his
wife's life and conversation, I, the above said, have known

this said aforesaid woman forty years, and what I have observed of her, human frailties excepted, her life and conversation have been according to her profession, and she hath brought up a great family of children and educated them well, so that there is in some of them apparent savor of godliness. I have known her differ with her neighbors, but I never knew or heard of any that did accuse her of what she is now charged with."

A similar paper was signed by thirty-nine other persons of the village and the immediate vicinity, all of the highest respectability. The men and women who dared to do this act of justice must not be forgotten :—

" We whose names are hereunto subscribed, being desired by Goodman Nurse to declare what we know concerning his wife's conversation for time past,—we can testify, to all whom it may concern, that we have known her for many years, and according to our observation, her life and conversation were according to her profession, and we never had any cause or grounds to suspect her of any such thing as she is now accused of.

Israel Porter	Samuel Abbey
Elizabeth Porter	Hepzibah Rea
Edward Bishop, Sr.	Daniel Andrew
Hannah Bishop	Sarah Andrew
Joshua Rea	Daniel Rea
Sarah Rea	Sarah Putnam
Sarah Leach	Jonathan Putnam
John Putnam	Lydia Putnam
Rebecca Putnam	Walter Phillips, Sr.
Joseph Hutchinson, Sr.	Nathaniel Felton, Sr.
Lydia Hutchinson	Margaret Phillips
William Osburn	Tabitha Phillips
Hannah Osburne	Joseph Holton, Jr.
Joseph Holton, Sr.	Samuel Endicott
Sarah Holton	Elizabeth Buxton
Benjamin Putnam	Samuel Aborn
Sarah Putnam	Isaac Cook
Job Swinnerton	Elizabeth Cook
Esther Swinnerton	Joseph Putnam "
Joseph Herrick, Sr.	

An examination of the foregoing names in connection with the history of the village will show conclusive proof, that, if the matter had been left to the people there, it would never have reached the point to which it was carried. It was the influence of the magistracy and the government of the colony, and the public sentiment prevalent elsewhere, overruling that of that immediate locality, that drove on the storm.

The above document shows the position taken by the heads of several of the Putnam families of the Village.

WILL OF NATHANIEL PUTNAM.

In the Name of God Amen, I Nathaniel Putnam of Salem, in y⁰ County of Essex in y⁰ province of y⁰ Massachusets Bay in New England being in perfect health & strength & sound in mind & memory, yet Considering that old age is come vpon me & y⁰ vncertainty of my life doe make This my last Will & Testament hereby revoaking all former & other wills by me heretofore at any time made.

Imp⁰ˢ   I resigne my soule to God whoe Gaue it & my body to decent burial hoping for a gloriours resurrecon in & through y⁰ merits of my blessed Redeemer Jesus Christ to whome bee Glory foreuer.

And   For my Outward Estate which God hath bestowed on me I Giue bequeath & bestow y⁰ same as hereafter in this my will is expressed.

Itm.   I Giue vnto my daughter Mary Tuft y⁰ wife of John Tuft one hundred and Twenty pounds in money to be paid by my Executor hereafter named within three yeares after my decease to which with y⁰ fifty pounds which I formerly gave her is in full & ouer & aboue what I promised her on marriage.

It.   I Giue vnto my said Daughter Mary y⁰ one half of my household goods that were in y⁰ house when my wife Deceased in y⁰ quality & condition that y⁰ said goods shall be at my departure.

Itm.   I Giue vnto my Grandchildren y⁰ sons & daughters of my daughter Elizabeth Flint Deceased, viz: to Mary who hath a lame hand twenty poundes in money & to y⁰ others Eight Ten pounds a peice if they shall ariue at Age, viz:

yᵉ sons at Twenty one yeares & yᵉ Daughters at Eighteen yeares or marriage to be paid by my Sonn John Putnam to each of my said Nine grand children as they come to age as aforesaid.

Itm.   I Giue vnto my Sonne John Putnam besides about an hundred acres of vpland & about sixteen acres of meadow which I haue already Giuen him by deed of Gift : viz : I giue & bequeath vnto him all my land & meadow which I haue lying on yᵉ Northwesterly side of yᵉ Riuer Caled Ipswich Riuer scituate in Salem bounds in seueral peices containing in yᵉ whole about Seuenty acres be yᵉ same more or less.

Itm.   I Giue vnto my said Sonne John Putnam about one hundred & sixty acres of land adjoyning to yᵉ hundred acres of land which I formerly gaue him by deed of Gift being his homestead he paying to my sᵈ nine grand children yᵉ legacies hereby giuen them.

Itm.   I Giue to my Said Sonne John all yᵉ remainder of that land (besides what I haue sold) That I formerly purchased of William Jeggles : all to be to him & his heirs foreuer.

Itm.   I Giue to my said sonne twenty pounds in money to be paid him by my Executor in three years after my decease.

Itm.   I Giue to my said Sonne halfe my wearing apparell.

Itm.   I Giue to my sᵈ son John Thirty pounds to be paid by my Executor within one yeare after my decease in graine & cattle at money price : which legacies with yᵉ hundred pound I Gaue him formerly for land sold which I had of Wm. Jeggles is in full of his portion.

Itm.   I Giue vnto my sonne Benjamin Putnam my homestead that is my farme that I now dwell on as alsoe all my other lands & meadows whether in possession or reuersion wheresoeuer scituate lying & being which are not perticularly in this will otherwise disposed off. to be to him & his hiers For Euer.

Itm.   I Giue to my said Sonne Benjamin all my personall Estate whether money Cattle corne Debts or other estate what ever.

Itm.   I make & Constitute my said sonn Benjamin Putnam to be yᵉ sole Executor of this my last will & Testament.

Lastly.   I Desire & apoint my Good friend Capt. Samuel Gardner & Sargᵗ John Leach to be ouerseers of this my will.

Itm: My Will further is that neither of my two sonns shall sell any of yᵉ lands hereby Giuen them nor any wayes dispose of yᵉ same vntill yᵉ Seuerall legacies & payments in this my will Giuen & apointed be respectively paid and fullfilled or Security Giuen for payment of yᵉ same: & yʳ lands respectiuely to stand bound for fullfilling of yᵉ same.

It. my will is that in Case either of my sonns should neglect & refuse to pay what I haue ordered them to pay or any differences arise either betwixt my two sonns or betwixt either of them & yᵉ Legatees. Then & in such case my will & desire is that my said ouerseers heare & determine yᵉ same & that Euery one acquiesce in what they shall doe.

In Testimoney that this is my last Will & Testament I haue herevnto set my hand & seale this 21 Day of February 1698–9, & in yᵉ Eleuenth yeare of yᵉ Reigne of William yᵉ 3ᵈ of England &c. King defenʳ of yᵉ faith.

Signed Sealed published   Nathaniel Putnam [SEAL.] & declared in ꝑsence of vs

Henry West
Henry West Juner
Stephen Sewall
Margaret Sewall

Essex ss. Before yᵉ Honᵇˡᵉ Jonathᵃ Corwin Esq. Judge of Probate of Wills &c. August 12ᵗʰ 1700 Majʳ Stephen Sewall, Henry West Senʳ & Henry West Junʳ all ꝑsonally Appeared and made Oath they were ꝑsent and did see Nathᵃ Putnam Signe Seal & heard him publish and Declare this Instrument to be his last Will and Testament and that he was then of A Disposing mind to there best undᵉstanding & that they then subscribed as Wittnesses in his ꝑsence.

Sworn Attest John Higginson Regʳ.

Vpon wᶜʰ this Will is proued Approued and allowed being ꝑEsented by yᵉ Executor therein named. Viz: Benjᵃ Putnam.

Attest John Higginson Regʳ.
Essex ss.   Probate Office.
Salem, Dec. 28, 1889.
A true copy of original will and of probate on file in this office.

Attest,

Ezra D. Hines, *Asst. Register.*

II. 8 Captain John (*John*), baptized at Aston Abbotts, England, 27 May, 1627; died at Salem Village, 7 April, 1710; married, at Salem, 3–7–1652, Rebecca Prince, "step-daughter of John Gedney," and perhaps sister of Robert Prince, a near neighbor.

Children, born at Salem Village:

25 REBECCA, b. 28 May, 1653; m. 22 Apr., 1672, John, son of Thomas Fuller (d. 26–6–1675). Ch. (Salem Rec.): Elizabeth; b. 22–6–1673. Bethiah, b. 22–1–1676.

26 SARAH, b. 4 Sept., 1654; m. July, 1672, John, son of Richard and Alice (Bosworth) Hutchinson of Danvers, b. there May, 1643; d. 2 Aug., 1676. Ch.: Sarah, m. Deacon Joseph Whipple.

27 PRISCILLA, b. 4 Mch., 1657; d. 16 Nov., 1704 (g. s. in Wadsworth cemetery); m. Joseph Bailey (*s. s.*), b. 4 Apr., 1648; killed by Indians at Kennebunk, Oct., 1728; son of John and Eleanor (Emery) Bayley. Ch.: Rebecca, b. 25 Oct., 1675. Priscilla, b. 31 Oct., 1676. John, b. 16 Sept., 1678. Joseph, b. 28 Jan., 1681. Hannah, b. 9 Sept., 1683. Daniel, b. 10 June, 1686. Judith, b. 11 Feb., 1690. Lydia, b. 25 Nov., 1695. Sarah, b. 14 Feb., 1698.

28 JONATHAN, b. 17 March, 1659.

29 JAMES, b. 4 Sept., 1661.

30 HANNAH, b. 2 Feb., 1663; m. 17 May, 1682, Henry, son of Henry and Abigail Brown, b. in Salisbury 8 Feb., 1658-9; rem. to Salem Village about 1695 and d. there 25 Apr., 1708; his widow made her will 9 May, 1730; proved 4 Jan., 1731. Ch.: John, b. 15 Apr., 1683; m. Mary Elsey. Rebecca, b. 1 Oct., 1684. Abraham, b. 4 July, 1686. Hannah, b. 20 Mar., 1689; d. y. Eleizer, b. 18 Feb., 1691; m. Sarah, dau. of Joseph Putnam, *q. v.* Henry, b. 17 June, 1693. Benjamin, b 25 June, 1695. Mehitable, b. 20 Sept., 1698. Nathaniel, b. 21 Dec., 1700. Joseph, bapt. 18 Sept., 1703. Hannah, b. 9 June, 1705; d. before 1734 (see Brown Gen. in preparation by Wilbur C. Brown, Esq.); m., 2d, 25 May, 1725, John, son of John and Ruth Rea, who, by a second wife, Ann Dodge, had a son Ebenezer, b. 20 Nov., 1745, and who m. Lydia Putnam of Danvers.

31 ELEAZER, b. 1665.

32 JOHN, b. 14 July, 1667.

33 SUSANNA, b. 4 Sept., 1670; m. prev. to 1695, Edward, son of Edw. Bishop of Danvers. (Upham.)

34 RUTH, b. Aug., 1673; bapt. 1st Ch., Salem, Aug., 1673.

On the 14–5–1667, the following children of John Putnam were baptized at the First Church in Salem: Rebecca, Hannah, John, Sarah, Priscilla, Jonathan and James.

JOHN PUTNAM was made freeman in 1665. He was constantly to the fore in all matters relating to town or church government. In 1668 and 1670, he with both his brothers signed a petition to be allowed a minister at the " Farms." His name occurs among the following Putnams on a petition of the Village to be set apart from Salem, dated 14 March, 1681–2.

Thomas Putnam senior*	Jonathan Putnam
John Putnam "	Thomas Putnam jr.
Nathaniel Putnam[10]	Edward Putnam.
John Putnam jr.	

1689, Nov. 10, the following members of the church at Salem were set off to form the church at Salem Village, now the North Parish in Danvers. They had had preaching for some years.

Bray Wilkins and wife	
Nathaniel Putnam	
John Putnam and wife	Peter Cloyce
Joshua Ray and wife	John Putnam jr. and wife
Nathaniel Ingersoll	Benjamin Putnam and wife
Thomas Putnam	Deliverance Wolcott
Ezekiel Cheever	Henry Wilkins
Edward Putnam	Jonathan Putnam and wife
Peter Prescott	Benjamin Wilkins and wife
	Sarah Putnam wife of James.

Summing up the connection of John Putnam with church affairs we have the following: He was not connected with the church in any official capacity except as occasion might arise when his influence was needed to collect rates, etc., for the minister; he himself was generous in providing for the wants of the minister and church. He was a man of decided opinions, naturally supported Bayley, who was the brother of his son-in-law, opposed Burroughs bitterly, accepted Par-

---

* 1679.—Thos. Putnam Sr. and Jr. and John Putname are among signers to a petition wishing the Gen. Court to refer the difficulty concerning Mr Bayley's settlement referred to the church in Salem. In this petition it is stated that " there are but 11 or 12 church members at the farmes & 50 freeholders on their own land, all English men & most of them town born children." (State Archives).

[10] John Putnam, jr., and Nathaniel Putnam are among the opposition, but desire a minister sent them.

ris. His house was occasionally the meeting place for the church meetings. He did not hesitate to invoke the law where the affairs of the church were concerned.

In his business career we find many interesting facts. Under date of 1678, John Putnam testifies to having heard a conversation in 1643 between Governor Endecott and one of his men, the deponent being then on the Endecott farm, and in 1705 he testifies that he had fifty years before been a retainer on Governor Endecott's farm and was intimately acquainted with the Governor. It is evident that his father had sent him to the Governor's farm to learn the science of agriculture, as this farm was known throughout the colony as a model place, where the latest and most approved theories were in practice. From this school of agriculture he seems to have gone forth well prepared to clear a farm for himself, for in 1658 he deeds some twenty acres of meadow land on north side of Ipswich river to Robert Prince, styling himself "Planter." As he was married in 1652 he probably remained with Endecott some time between his fifteenth and twenty-first years. From this time to his death he was constantly acquiring property, following the calling of a farmer of the highest and most intelligent class. He also entered more or less into the speculative enterprises of his time.

In 1674 at Rowley Village (now Boxford) Simon Bradstreet, Daniel Dennison and John Putnam established iron works. These were constructed and carried on upon a large scale, on contract, by Samuel and Nathan Leonard.

In this connection the following extract is interesting: "John Gould his book of accounts 1697 an account of the weaight of the iron plates that cozen Putnam had. Thomases waighed 260. Samuell weighed 330. Samuell Smiths waighed 170."

That John Putnam was successful in the management of his affairs is shown by his tax rate. He paid £8 in 1683 and until a few years before his death was among the heaviest tax payers in the Village. Some years previous to his death he gave his property to his children, always with reservations as to his maintenance, and the last year of his life his property was rated only for a few shillings.

It was in the military affairs and witchcraft delusion that his character is best shown. In 1672 he is styled corporal; on the 7 Oct., 1678, he was commissioned lieutenant of the troop of horse at the Village; after 1687 he is styled "Captain." As late as 1706 "Capt. John Putnam in company with Capt. Jonathan (his son) was empowered to settle town bounds." He served in the Narragansett fight and retained his military manners throughout his life. In 1679 and later he was frequently chosen to present Salem at the General Court to settle the various disputed town bounds. He was selectman in 1681.

He was deputy to the General Court in May, 1679, to succeed Mr. Bartholomew Gedney and again for the regular terms of 1680–1686–1691–1692, previous to the new charter. On the 12 May, 1686, he received the following order from the town of Salem: "In case Mr. Dudley &c. said to be nominated & authorized by his Majesty to Edict another Government here, do publish a Loyal Nullification of our charter and a commission from the King for their acceptance of the Government. Here then our instruction to you is— That you give no countenance to any resistance, but peasably withdraw yourself as representing us no longer." This was just previous to the Andros administration. It is seen above that he was returned to the General Court again in 1691, after the Revolution, but of the part that John Putnam played during the intervening time we know nothing.

That he was alive to the needs of education among the growing generation while absorbed in military and political affairs and his own business, the following entry shows: Jan. 24, 1677, "ordered and empowered to take care of the law relating to the catechissing of children and youth be duly attended to all the Village." He is desired to have "a diligent care that all the families do carefully and constantly attend the due education of children and youth according to law."

We come now to the part he took in the witchcraft delusion; the same causes alluded to under Nathaniel were active in his case. Family pride, the strong feeling of kinship, his stern education, quick temper and obstinate nature, all tended to influence his action ~~which was~~

Emery,	Rachel, b. 19	Judith. b. 3
~~n~~e, 1683	Oct., 1662; m. 16	Aug., 1665; d.
~~d.~~ 1 Apr.,	Feb., 1680, Sam-	20 Sept., 1668.
~~m.~~, 2nd,	uel Poor.	
~~a~~ Bart-		
~~le~~tt., 1700.		

~~r~~ence (46) = David	Isaac, m. Sa-	Joshua.	Judith.	Sarah, m.
Thomas | 3d son.	rah Titcomb,			Richard Carr.
(12).	who m., 2d,—			D
	Bartlett.			

| David. | Elizabeth. | Jonathan. | Nathan. |

~~1686~~ ~~Mr Burroughs and the inhabitants met at the~~ meeting house to make up the accounts in public, according to their

as to his maintenance, and the last year of his life his property was rated only for a few shillings.

It was in the military affairs and witchcraft delusion that

hi
or
tr
ta
w
b
hi
b
C
s

c
t
t
fi
n
G
c
o
l
j
t
t
c

f
f
5
l

attended to a

gent care that all the families do carefully and constantly attend the due education of children and youth according to law."

We come now to the part he took in the witchcraft delusion; the same causes alluded to under Nathaniel were active in his case. Family pride, the strong feeling of kinship, his stern education, quick temper and obstinate nature, all tended to influence his action which was excusable according to the ignorant and narrow superstitions of the times. One side of his character is known by the following extract from Upham :

In 1683, the Court order Rev. George Burroughs to settle with the parish at Salem Village. This settling was interrupted in a most arbitrary manner, as the following deposition shows :

["County Court, June, 1683 — Lieutenant John Putnam *versus* Mr George Burroughs. Action of debt for two gallons of Canary wine, and cloth, &c. bought of Mr Gedney on John Putnam's account, for the funeral of Mrs Burroughs."]

"DEPOSITION."

"We whose names are underwritten, testify and say, that at a public meeting of the people of Salem Farmes, April 24, 1683, we heard a letter read, which letter was sent from the Court. After the said letter was read, Mr Burroughs came in. After the said Burroughs had been a while in, he asked 'whether they took up with the advice of the Court, given in the letter or whether they rejected it.' The moderator made answer, 'Yes we take up with it;' and not a man contradicted it to any of our hearing. After this was passed, was a discourse of settling accounts between the said Burroughs and the inhabitants, and issueing things in peace, and parting in love, as they came together in love. Further we say that the second, third and fourth days of the following week were agreed upon by Mr Burroughs and the people to be the days for every man to come in and to reckon with the said Burroughs; and so they adjourned the meeting . . . . .

. . . We further testify and say, that, May the second, 1683 Mr Burroughs and the inhabitants met at the meeting house to make up the accounts in public, according to their

4

agreement the meeting before: and just as the said Burroughs began to give in his accounts, the marshall came in,
and after a while went up to John Putnam, Sʳ, and whispered
to him, and said Putnam said to him 'You know what you
have to do; do your office' Then the marshall came to Mr
Burroughs and said ' Sir, I have a writing to read to you.'
Then he read the attachment and demanded goods.   Mr Burroughs answered 'that he had no goods to show and that he
was now reckoning with the inhabitants, for we know not yet
who is in debt but there was his body.' As we were ready to
go out of the meeting house, Mr Burroughs said, ' Well, what
will you do with me?' then the marshall went to John Putnam Sr. and said to him ' What shall I do?' The said Putnam
replied, 'You know your business.' And then the said
Putnam went to his brother Thomas Putnam, and pulled him
by the coat; and they went out of the house together, and
presently came in again.   Then said John Putnam 'Marshall
take your prisoner, and have him up to the ordinary [that is
a public house] and secure him till the morning.' "

(Signed)   " Nathaniel Ingersoll, aged about fifty
          Samuel Sibley, aged about twenty four."

" To the first of these, I, John Putnam, Jr. testify, being
at the meeting."

Again—Thos. Haynes testified, " after the marshall had
read John Putnams attachment to Mr Burroughs, then Mr
Burroughs asked Putnam what money it was he attached
him for.   John Putnam answered 'For five pounds and
odd money at Shippen's at Boston, and for thirteen shillings
at his father Gedney's and for twenty four shillings at Mrs
Darby's;' then that Nathaniel Ingersoll stood up and said,
'Lieutenant, I wonder that you attach Mr Burroughs for the
money at Darby's and your father Gedney's when to my
knowledge, you and Mr Burroughs have reckoned and bal-
anced accounts two or three times since, as you say, it was
due, and you never made any mention of it when you reckoned with Mr Burroughs.' "

John Putnam answered "It is true and I own it." John Putnam as chairman of the Committee the previous year represented the inhabitants. "As there was really no case against Burroughs and as there was even while these proceedings were taking place, a balance due Burroughs, the case was withdrawn."

From the above we learn the obstinate character of John Putnam and those who sided with him.

Upham says, writing of the scene at the above described meeting, "We can see the grim bearing of the cavalry lieutenant, John Putnam, and of his elder brother and predecessor in commission . . . . . . But the chief figure in the group is the just man who rose and rebuked the harsh and reprehensible procedure of the powerful landholder, neighbor and friend though he was. The manner in which the arbitrary trooper bowed to the rebuke, if it does not mitigate the resentment of his conduct, illustrates the extraordinary influence of Nathaniel Ingersoll's character and demonstrates the deference in which all men held him." Burroughs lived with John Putnam nine months in 1680 after his first coming into the settlement.[11]

Another trouble in which John Putnam took a leading part was the matter of the bounds between Salem and Topsfield. There was a strip of territory claimed by both towns. This land had been granted to settlers by Salem who had taken up their farms in good faith. Topsfield claimed these lands, unimproved and improved, as part of its commons and refused to acknowledge the titles given by Salem. There were many fights in the disputed territory between the people of the two towns and much bad feeling existed.

John Putnam with two of his sons had land there and had two houses, orchards and meadows in the disputed territory. He maintained his ground throughout the dispute, resisting force with force. The records are full of this dispute; it was finally settled by a separate township being formed, called

[11] Burroughs was not a character easily gotten along with and reports of the troubles between his wife and himself have come down to us.

Middleton. The action taken by John Putnam in these matters shows him to have been a man without fear and tenacious of his rights.

His opponents in both of these cases were, however, among the accused during the witchcraft delusion, but I do not think that John Putnam used his influence against them. He does not seem to have appeared as a witness of any moment during the proceedings, although he was more or less prominent as shown above, in the quarrels immediately preceding the trials. That he did not believe in all of the statements of the afflicted children is evident, as his name, with that of his wife, occurs on the document testifying to the good character of Rebecca Nurse, and on testimony favorable to others of those accused, but he seems never to have spoken out in open opposition, as did his nephew, Joseph Putnam.

The will of John Putnam is not on record; he seems to have disposed of his property by deed to his children. As early as 1690 he deeds one hundred acres to Jonathan and to James, and in 1695, ninety acres to John.

His residence was on the farm originally occupied by his father, now better known as Oak Knoll, the home of the poet Whittier.

Rev. Joseph Green makes the following note in his diary:
"April 7 (1710). Captain Putnam buried by ye soldiers."

The graves of both Captain John and of his father are unmarked. The present Wadsworth Cemetery was originally the Putnam burial place and in some of the many unmarked graves probably their remains lie. Here are buried the families of his sons James and Jonathan and many others of his descendants in later generations. The oldest stone is dated 1682, and is that of Elizabeth the first wife of Jonathan Putnam. All of the graves seem to have had at some time head stones and foot stones but most are now broken off level with the ground. Many of those still standing are broken. Although the cemetery was presented to the parish by Rev. Mr. Wadsworth, no care is taken to preserve the ancient memorials of the dead. A shameful state of affairs, indeed!

III. 9 Ann (*Thomas, John*), born in Salem Village 25–6–1645; married there Jan. 18, 1666–7, William Trask of Salem, baptized Salem, 19–7–1640, son of Captain William and Sarah Trask. She died 14–9–1676.

William Trask married, second, Hannah———. His will is dated 5 Sept., 1690; proved 30 June, 1691. In this instrument he mentions his daughters, Hannah Brooks, Sara, Susanna, Elizabeth and Mary Trask; sons, William and John under age; wife Hannah and son William to be executors; brother John Trask, brother Thomas Putnam and Edward Flint to be overseers.

Children born at Salem :

85 ANN, b. 7 June, 1668.
86 ELIZABETH, b. March, 1669–70; d. young.
87 SARA, b. 14 June, 1672.
88 WILLIAM, b. 7–7 mo., 1674.
89 SUSANNAH, b. 8–9–1676.

Children by Hannah:

JOHN.
ELIZABETH.
MARY, b. March, 1683.
GEORGE, b. Jan., 1690.

Captain William Trask, one of the earliest settlers, had the following children, viz. :

1 SARAH.
2 MARY, bapt. 1–11–1636.
3 SUSANNA, bapt. 10–1638.
4 WILLIAM, bapt. 19–7–1640.
5 JOHN, bapt. 13–7–1642.
6 ELIZA, bapt. 21–7–1645.
7 MARY, bapt. 2 Oct., 1652.
8 ANN, bapt. 18 June, 1654.

Of these we have seen that William married Ann Putnam.

Sara married the second Elias Parkman and John married Abigail Parkman, probably his sister. For interesting facts concerning the writing of "Putnam" for "Parkman" on Connecticut Colonial Records, see appendix under "Elias Putnam."

III. 12 Sergt. Thomas (*Thomas, John*), born at Salem, 12–1–1652; baptized at First Church 16–2–1652; died in Salem, 24 May, 1699; married, 25–9–1678, Ann, youngest daughter of George and Elizabeth Carr of Salisbury, born there 15 June, 1661; died at Salem Village, 8 June, 1699.

Children born in Salem Village:

40 ANN, b. 18 Oct., 1679.

41 THOMAS, b. 9 Feb., 1681: bapt. 1st Ch., Salem, Aug., 1681; aged 14 and upwards, 4 Sept., 1699, when he chooses his cousin, John Putnam, jr., as guardian.

42 ELIZABETH, b. 29 May, 1683; bapt. 1st Ch., May, 1684; aged 14 and upwards, in 1702; guardianship to Jonathan Putnam.

43 EBENEZER, b. 25 July, 1685; bapt. Oct., 1685; 10 Oct., 1699, aged 14, appoints his uncle Edward, guardian.

44 DELIVERANCE, b. 11 Sept., 1687; bapt. 1st Ch., 1 July, 1688; not mentioned in her sister Ann's will, 1715, presumably dead; Rev. Jos. Green in his diary notes the funeral of "Dell Putnam" under date of Dec. 31, 1712.

44a Thomas Putnam's child; d. 17 Dec., 1689, not quite four mos.

45 TIMOTHY, bapt. in Salem Village, 26 April, 1691.

46 EXPERIENCE, bapt. at Salem Village, 20 Nov., 1693; m. David, son of Isaac and Sarah (Emery) Bailey, b. 12 Dec., 1687, and nephew to Rev. James Bailey, who m. Mary, sister of Ann (Carr) Putnam, died before 1722. Ch. David, who probably d. previous to 1722; Elizabeth, Jonathan, Nathan. Experience (Putnam) Bailey received a legacy from her uncle, Joshua Bayley, in 1722.

47 ABIGAIL, bapt. Salem Village, 30 Oct., 1692; aged 9, 23 April, 1702, guardianship to John Putnam, 3d.

48 SUSANNA, b. 1694; bapt. Salem Village, 20 Nov., 1698.

48a (Perhaps there was another daughter; "1694, Aug. 22, Sarah, daughter of Thomas Putnam died, 6 mos.; 'old record.'")

49 SETH, b. May, 1695; bapt. in Salem Village.

With the exception of Deliverance, all of the above named children, were alive in 1715. (See Ann Putnam's will.)

SERGT. THOMAS PUTNAM had received a liberal education for his times, but with others whom we should call more enlightened, he took a most prominent part in the witchcraft delusion of 1692, being in fact, second to none but Parris in the fury with which he seemed to ferret out the victims of his young daughter's insane desire for notoriety. His wife also took a prominent part in those proceedings. She was the sister of Mary Carr, wife of Mr. James Bayley, whose ministry at the village was the cause of so much dissension and which indirectly added to the bitterness of the witchcraft persecutions.

By nature, Mrs. Putnam was a woman of a highly sensitive temperament, apparently easily wrought upon and deceived. The Carrs seem all to have been rather weak in that respect, although of good social position.

Sergeant Putnam, on the contrary, was of a decisive and obstinate nature; he had great influence in the village and did not hesitate to use it; he had been in the Narragansett fight, belonged to the company of troopers and was parish clerk. Many of the records of the witchcraft proceedings are in his hand. He wrote a fine, clear and beautiful hand.

It was in the houses of Sergt. Thomas and of Rev. Mr. Parris that the "bewitched" children first met to accomplish their pranks. In the "circle" were the daughter Ann, and a maid-servant of Mrs. Ann Putnam, Mary Lewis by name.

Afterward, at the trials of the accused persons, Mrs. Putnam was often seized with strange attacks of imagination, evidently produced by the over-excitement and consequent strain on her brain. At these times she was a prominent witness, but after this was all over and Parris was attempting to retain his hold on the parish and to dicker with the inhabitants over terms of settlement, she seems to have refused to him her aid or encouragement.

That Sergeant Putnam and probably his wife were firm believers in the whole matter there seems to be but little doubt. He showed a lamentable lack of common sense, but so did many others. The strain was too much for him and he died shortly after the trials; his wife followed him to the grave a few weeks later.

III. 13 Deacon Edward (*Thomas, John*), born at Salem
Village; baptized in Salem, 4 July, 1654; died at Salem Village, 10 March, 1747; married 14 June, 1681, Mary Hale.
His will is dated 11 March, 1731, proved 11 April, 1748, "Edward Putnam of Middleton, yeoman." Mentions his wife Mary,
sons Edward, Joseph, Elisha, Ezra, Isaac, daughters Prudence
and Abigail, granddaughters Elizabeth and Anna Flint.

Children :

50 EDWARD, b. 29 April, 1682; bapt. at Salem church, Oct., 1682.
51 HOLYOKE, b. 28 Sept., 1683; killed by the Indians at Dunstable,
     3 July, 1706.
52 ELISHA, b. 3 Nov., 1685; d. at Sutton, 10 Jan., 1745.
53 JOSEPH, b. 1 Nov., 1687.
54 MARY, b. 14 Aug., 1689; bapt. at 1st Ch., Salem, Oct., 1689; d. before
     1726; m. 8 Jan., 1713, Thomas, son of Captain Thomas and Mary
     (Dunnton) Flint of Salem, b. 20 Aug., 1678. Ch.: Edward, b. 12
     June, 1714; d. 9 July, 1714. Elisha, b. 22 July, 1715; m. 28 Jan.,
     1744, Miriam Putnam. Elizabeth, m. 17 June, 1735, Thomas Dor-
     man. Anna, m. a Baker. Thomas Flint was a farmer in Danvers
     and had three wives; his first being Lydia Putnam (No. 137)
     whom he m. 6 Jan., 1704, and who d. 31 Aug., 1711. His third was
     Mrs. Abigail Ganson, whom he m. 1 Sept., 1726. There were
     four children by his first, none by his third wife. His will was
     proved 11 July, 1757. (Flint Genealogy.)
55 PRUDENCE, b. 25 Jan., 1692; m. 3 Dec., 1719, William, son of Wil-
     liam and Prudence (Putnam) Wyman of Woburn, b. 15 Jan.,
     1685; d. 1753. Five children: Elizabeth, b. 27 Dec., 1720. Nehe-
     miah, b. 25 June, 1722; m. Elizabeth Winne. This Nehemiah
     and Elizabeth had a son Abel, b. between 1745–1751, who. m.
     20 Oct., 1772, Ruth Putnam, who d. 20 Aug., 1812. Mary, b.
     13 July, 1724. Francis, b. 5 Aug., 1726. Stephen, b. 27 Aug.,
     1732. (See Wyman Genealogy in preparation by Jos. G. Wyman.)
56 NEHEMIAH, b. 20 Dec., 1693; bapt. at the village 1693–4.
57 EZRA, b. 29 Apr., 1696.
58 ISAAC, b. 14 March, 1698; d. in Sutton.
59 ABIGAIL, bapt. Salem Village, 26 May, 1700; d. in Lunenburg, Jan.,
     1764; m. in Middleton, 11 Nov., 1730, Joseph (b. 7 Aug., 1705;
     d. in Middleton while on a visit from Lunenburg, 5 Jan., 1769),
     son of Thomas and Elizabeth (Andrews or Buxton?) Fuller, of
     Middleton. Ch.: John, b. in Middleton, 15 Sept., 1731; d. Feb.,
     1801; prominent in Revolution, known as "Captain John Ful-
     ler." [12] Nehemiah, b. in Middleton, 26 Jan., 1733. Stephen, b. in
     Middleton, 11 Jan., 1735. Mary, b in Middleton, 15 Aug., 1736.
     Elizabeth, b. in Lunenburg, 13 May, 1739. On 8 April, 1739,

────────────

[12] Miss E. Abercrombie authority on Fuller, also Mrs. Averill.

Abigail, daughter of Deacon Edward Putnam, and wife of Joseph Fuller, received letters of dismissal to the church in Lunenburg; these were accepted there on 13 May, same year.

DEACON EDWARD PUTNAM was a man much respected and loved by his neighbors. He was made freeman in 1690, and on 3 Dec., 1690, was chosen deacon of the First Church in Danvers. His name stands second in the list of deacons, Nathaniel Ingersoll having been appointed on the 1 Dec., 1690. From 1690 to 1876, one hundred and eighty-six years, there have been in all twenty-five deacons in this church, of whom fourteen have borne the name of Putnam.[13] Like all of the family, he was a farmer, and in his will styled himself "yeoman." His farm was in what is now known as Middleton, but in the last years of his life he occupied a house not far from the church at the village. During the witchcraft troubles he was a member of the party which brought charges against so many innocent people. His whole course, however, shows that he acted only as he believed was right and good for the community. As soon as the girls were declared bewitched, he repaired to the house of his brother and there proceeded to examine them in order to ascertain whether or not they were truthful in their declarations. His own innocence of all wrong is shown by the ease with which he was deceived. After a thorough examination he was convinced that the girls were bewitched and then did what he considered his duty. His action, however, in the proceedings was never bitter or vehement; he merely testified as to what he had seen and to what appeared to him to be probable.

[13] The meeting-house of this society has recently (Feb., 1890) been destroyed by fire. This house was the sixth erected by the society. In 1889, several families placed stained memorial windows in the church, one of which was to Ebenezer Putnam, Esq., but on 23 July of that year, many of these were injured. The list of Putnams officiating as deacons is as follows, the first date being that of their election, the last that of their death: Edward, 1690-1747; Benjamin, 1709-1714; Eleazer, 1718-1732; Nathaniel, 1731-1754; Archelaus, 1756-1759; Samuel, jr., 1757, removed to Lunenburg; Asa, 1762-1795; Edmund, 1762-1810; Gideon, 1785-1810; Daniel, 1795-1801; Joseph, 1802-1818; James, 1807-1819; Eben, 18:0-1831; Ebenezer, 1845-1848; William R., 1861.

Since writing the above, the society has dedicated, in Sept., 1891, a fine new structure. There are several memorial windows, the family being well represented.

It was somewhat rare in those days to find men with any literary ability outside of the ministry, but Edward Putnam had had a good education and was evidently fond of his books and of writing. He expressed himself in a rather ornate style of language. The following is a fair example, from the records of the church, in his own handwriting. This tribute is to the memory of the Rev. Joseph Green who died 26 Nov., 1715.

"Then was the choicest flower and greenest olive tree in the garden of our God here cut down in its prime and flourishing estate at the age of forty years and two days, who had been a faithful ambassador from God to us eighteen years. Then did that bright star set, and never more to appear here among us; then did our sun go down, and now what darkness is come upon us! Put away and pardon our iniquities, O Lord! which have been the cause of our sore displeasure, and return to us again in mercy, and provide yet again for this thy flock a pastor after thy own heart, as thou hast promised to thy people in thy word: on which promise we have hope, for we are called by their name, and, oh, leave us not!"

Deacon Edward was also the first historian and genealogist of our family. His account written in 1733 is the basis upon which all of like nature have been founded. From this period is traced the tradition of the emigration in 1634, although the records would point to a later date (1640).

For many interesting facts concerning Deacon Edward Putnam and his generation, the reader is referred to "Upham's Witchcraft." In that work one will find much of value to the genealogist as well as to the historian, especially in regard to our own family.

WILL OF DEACON EDWARD PUTNAM.

In the name of God Amen   I Edward Putnam of the town of Middleton in the county of Essex Husbandman: I being oftentimes sick & weak in body But of perfect mind & memory: Blefsed be God for it And calling to mind the mortallity of my body. And that it is appointed for all men once to Die. Do make This my last Will & Testament (and do hereby revoke. And make Void & Null all former Wills & Testaments heretofore made by me) That is to say principally and first of all, I give and Recommend my Soul into the hand of God, through Jesus Christ my Redeemer with whome I hope to live with forever And my body I committ to the Earth. To be buried in a Christian like & Decent manner, at ye Difcretion of my Executors hereafter named: Nothing doubting But at the General Refurection to Receive ye same again by the mighty power of God And as touching my worldy estate wherewith it hath pleafed God to blefs me withall in this life. I Difpose of it in manner & form as followeth

Imp⁵ I give to my son Edward To him and his heirs Exuⁿ & assigns forever Aboute Ten Acres of land Joining his own land Which he had of me by a deed of Gift and being bounded with a stake and a heap of stones by the highway that goes from my house to his house, Which heap of stones is also this brother Ezra's bound Mark; and from his bound mark upon a Strait line over the Swamp & plain, till it comes where the water comes out of the Island into his Spong of meadow Then from that place upon a Strait line a crofs ye Island To a stone Lying in Ipswich River at the place called the Indian Bridge.

Item I give and bequeath to my son Joseph To him his heirs Exuⁿ & afsigns forever. A certain peice of land Lying on the West side of Ipswich River and containing by estimation Twenty Acres be it more or less. To begin at ye River at the Lower End of the Island belonging to the sons of John Putnam Decᵈ and from Thence to the top of the high hill and so upon the same line. till he meet with the land or line of the sons of John Putnam Then to turn North westward by Their line or land till it comes to the heap of Stones on the Top of ye hill near the river Then so down the hill to the two acres of meadow, which I bought of John Putnam Also I give to my son Joseph all that meadow that lyeth between this land and ye River I give him the whole of my land, upland & meadow Except that two acres of meadow that I bought of John Putnam which lyeth below this meadow that I have given to Joseph.

Item   I give and bequeath to my son Ezra Putnam To him his heirs Exec^{rs} & assigns forever a certain peice of land called ye Island on this side of the River To begin at the upper End of his brother Edward's Spong of meadow from thence he is to run upon a Strait line a crofs the Island To a great stone lying in the river, at the place called the Indian Bridge which stone is also his brother Edward's bound Mark. Then he is to turn Southwestward by the River Side Till he comes where the Island comes to the River; Then along by the River side to ye Spong of meadow, And then to turn Northwestward by the Spong of meadow. Till he meets with his brother Edward's Spong where he began; Also I give to my son Ezra my share of that land that I & Edward brought of Francis Ellyott lying near to the Iron works as it lyeth Divided between him & his brother Edward.

Also I give to my son Ezra my share in ye Iron works and that New house that I built for Coal I also give him my share of that house where ye Chimney is That I & Thos Cave & my son Edward built.

Item   I give and bequeath to my son Isaac Putnam To him his heirs Exec^{rs} & afsigns forever Aboute ten acres of land on the hill called by the name of Bear hill and lying on the south side of the hill. Being bounded at the south west corner, with a stake & a heap of Stones And from there to run up the hill, Eastward to a Walnut tree marked; Then to turn southeastward down ye hill to a White Oak Tree marked which Tree is his brother Edward's bound mark. Then to turn westward by ye land that my father gave to Joseph Stacie. Till he comes to a great rock; Then along untill he comes to and meets with the land of Deacon Ebenezer Putnam. Then up ye hill to ye bound mark first mentioned.

Item   I give to my four sons (Namely) Edward, Elisha, Ezra and Isaac Putnam That meadow that lyes behind The Island every one of them shall have an equal share of it as near as they can This meadow Lyes below that meadow, that I gave to my son Ezra in his Deed of gift (His two acres in his deed of gift Shall come down to the bounds there stated; which is a heap of stones by the Island side. And so strait to the River To another heap of stones) This meadow which I give to my four sons, Shall begin below these bounds and the bounds shall be the bounds of their meadow at the upper end. The first share of this meadow shall be for Isaac. To begin at the bounds first mentioned and so downward. And next share shall be for Elifha, and the third share shall be for Ezra, and the fourth share shall be for Edward being at ye lower end. Each of their shares shall come as strait as they can from the Island to the River.

And I do hereby oblige my son Ezra by virtue of my will, that he shall sell his share of this meadow. To his brother Edward if he sees caufe to buy it: and he shall lett him have it after the Rate of Ten pounds & acre of Pafsable money of New England —— or Good Province Bills: And if Edward will not give Him so then Ezra shall keep the meadow or sell it to any other whome he will. Only Edward shall have one years Liberty after my Decease to Buy This meadow before that Ezra shall sell it.

Item   I give and bequeath To my Daughter Prudence Ten pounds in or as money (besides what Shee hath already had) and to be paid to her by my son Elisha Putnam and that in one year after my decease.

Item   I give & bequeath my daughter Abigail Ten pounds in or as money (besides what shee hath already had) and to be paid to her by my son Isaac Putnam and that in one year after my decease.

Item   I give and bequeath to my two Grand Daughter's (namely) Elizabeth Flint & Anna Flynt each of them five Pounds a piece; in or as money (besides what I gave to their mother) and to be paid to them by my son Edward Putnam when they come to age of eighteen years old: And if either of them Die before That age the other shall receive ye whole of the ten Pounds.—

Also my will is that my son Joseph shall pay Four Pounds to his mother In or as money within one year after my decease end also twenty shillings to my grandson Elisha Flint within one year after my Decease

Also my will is that my wife Shall have the East end of my house to Dwell in and shee shall have the Inward Cellar and the whole of the House upward above it: And One half of the Garden;

And

Also my will is that my four sons (Namely) Edward, Elisha, Joseph & Isaac Shall pay to their mother fifty shillings a year in or as money That is: That each of them pay fifty shillings a piece; To their mother yearly if shee call for it, at their hand, for her need, or if others see shee need it & call for it for her relief, they shall surely bring it for her relief in due season And this no longer than shee remains my widow.

Item

My Will farther is that my son Ezra shall suitably Provide for his mother Things Comfortably for her and Convenient for her support while she Remains my widow: He shall provide & bring in those things for her In due season hereafter named and that yearly, He shall provide for her Suitable firewood & bring it into her house for her. He shall provide for her & bring her in Ten bushells of Indian Meal And two bushells of English Meal and four bushells of ground Malt and four barrills of good Cyder and find the barrills; and as many apples as she shall see cause; and he shall bring her in nine or ten score weight of good pork annually. and he shall Keep her two Cows Winter & Summer and no Longer than shee remains my widow

Item

I give to my son Ezra my part in the great Timber chain. I also give my Cross cutt Saw to my three sons Edward Joseph & Ezra. and the rest of my tools I leave to them to divide among themselves

I Also give my cane to my son Edward

I Also give to my son Elifha my great Bible

I Also give to my son Joseph a Book of Mr Jeremiah Burror's Works.

I Also give to my son Isaac a book of Mr Flavel's works.

And the rest of my books shall be at my wifes disposal

Also I give to my son Joseph my Girdle & Sword

Item

My will farther is That I give to Mary my Beloved wife Whome I make Exec^x Together with my son Ezra To this my last will and Testament:

I give to my beloved wife all my moveable estate Both

within Door & without Door. as to moveable estate without
Dor I mean as to Cattle Sheep or Swine : Yet not with standing I give to my son Ezra My Desk & that Box where in
there is so many Writings ; And what moveable estate shall
be left of mine within Door after my wifes Decease (undisposed of by her) Shall Equally be divided between my two
Daughters Prudence and Abigail

Item   My will also is that my wife's pew in the Village Meeting house shall be long to my son Joseph

Item   My will Alfo is That as to my funeral Charges My Son
Ezra shall bear the One halfe of it and my other four sons
Shall bear ye other halfe equally between them ; As to my
Wearing Apparrill I leave it to my wife to Dispose of yt
among my sons as she shall see fitt.

And now to Conclude ; This my last will and Testament ;
And I Now Nominate & Appoint Constitute & Ordain Mary
my beloved wife and Ezra my son. To be sole Executors
To this my last will & Testament ;

And In Witnefs whereof I Have Hereunto Sett my hand
& Seal this eleventh day of March One Thousand Seven
hundred and Thirty and One

Signed Sealed published   EDWARD PUTNAM Sen.
& Declared by me Testator
Edward Putnam Sen To be
My last Will & Testament
In presence of
Tho⁸ Fuller
Jon⁴ Fuller   Proved Approved and Al-
Tho Putnam   lowed at Ipswich April 11ᵗʰ
                 1748 Before Honⁱ Tho⁸ Ber-
                 ry Esq Judge of Probate

III. 14 Deliverance (*Thomas, John*), born in Salem
Village, 5–7–1656 ; married, 23 April, 1685, Jonathan Walcott of Salem Village, who died 16 Dec., 1699.

Jonathan Walcott was a man of the highest respectability,
and was exceedingly popular. He had held the positions of
captain of the troop of horse and deacon in the church. Although he had opposed the violent measures at the Village,
just previous to the witchcraft delusion, during the attempts

to settle a minister, he seems to have believed thoroughly the
stories of the girls, one of whom was his own daughter, Mary.
He seems to have investigated matters but being very much
under the authority of the church, was easily prejudiced and
afterward was prominent in the witchcraft trials.   He had
married, on the 26 Jan., 1665, Mary, daughter of John Sibley, who died 28 Dec., 1683, and by her he had the following
children :

Children of Jonathan and Mary Walcott :

    JOHN, b 7 Dec., 1666.
    HANNAH, b. 6–10–1667.
    JONATHAN, b. 1 Sept., 1670.
    JOSEPH, b. 25–7–1673; d. 30 June, 1674.
    MARY, b. 5–5–1675; one of the "afflicted girls" in 1692.   She was
        afterward married and settled in Woburn.
    SAMUEL, b. 12 Oct., 1678; H. C. 1698.

Children of Jonathan and Deliverance (Putnam) Walcott :

60 ANN, b. 27 Jan., 1685-6.
61 THOMAS, b. 25 March, 1688; d. 5 June, 1688.
62 THOMAS, b. 5 June, 1689.
63 WILLIAM, b. 27–1–1691.
64 EBENEZER, b. 19 Apr., 1693.
65 BENJAMIN, b. 23 Apr., 1695.
66 PRUDENCE, b. 10 July, 1699.

III. 16 Prudence (*Thomas, John*), born in Salem Village 28–12–1661-2, was living in Charlestown, 1745; married, first, William, son of Francis and Abigail (Read) Wyman
of Woburn who was born about 1656 and died in 1705.   He
was admitted Freeman in 1690.

Children :

67 WILLIAM, b. 18, d. 20 Jan., 1682-3.
68 PRUDENCE, b. 26 Dec. 1683; m. 28 June, 1704, Jacob Winn, Jr., of
      Woburn.   (See Sewall's Hist. of Woburn.)
69 WILLIAM, b. 15 Jan., 1685; m., for his second wife, Prudence dau.
      of Edward and Mary (Hale) Putnam (No. 55).   He was of Wo-
      burn and d. 1753.
70 THOMAS, b. 23 Aug., 1687; of Pelham, N. H.
71 ELIZABETH, b. 5 July, 1689; d. 25 June, 1690.
72 FRANCIS, b. 10 July, 1691; lived in Maine.

73 JOSHUA, b. 3 Jan., 1692-3; m., 1st, Mary Pollard; m., 2nd, Mary Green, 14 July, 1747.
74 A DAU., b. 1694 and d. young.
75 EDWARD, b. 10 Jan. 1695-6; of Pelham, N. H.
76 ELIZABETH, b. 16 Feb., 1697-8.
77 DELIVERANCE, b. 28 Feb., 1700; m. 1 Jan., 1732, Ezekiel Gowing, jr., of Lynn.
78 JAMES, b. 16 Mar., 1702; of Maine.

Mrs. Prudence (Putnam) Wyman married for a second husband Captain Peter Tufts of Charlestown. The articles of covenant to marry with him were dated 11 June, 1717. Peter Tufts was son of Peter and Mary (Pierce) Tufts of Charlestown and was born about 1648. He died 20 Sept., 1721, aged 73. His brother, John Tufts, had married Mary daughter of John Putnam, jr. Capt. Peter Tufts had been married twice previous to his marriage with Prudence Wyman: first, to Elizabeth Lynde; second, to Mercy Cotton.

III. 17 Joseph (*Thomas, John*), born in Salem Village 14 Sept., 1669; died there 1724-5. Will dated 15 Mar., 1722-3, wife Elizabeth to be executrix, mentions sons William, David and Israel minors, daughters Mary and Elizabeth Putnam, daughter Sarah Brown, daughters Rachel, Anna and Huldah Putnam, minors, and Mehitable. He married 21 April, 1690 (Salem town records), Elizabeth, daughter of Israel and Elizabeth (Hathorne) Porter, of Salem Village, born 7 Oct., 1673; died 1746.

The mother of Mrs. Elizabeth (Porter) Putnam was sister to Hon. John Hathorne, the witchcraft judge. Mrs. Elizabeth (Porter) Putnam married, second, 15 May, 1727, Captain Thomas Perley of Boxford. "20 July, 1730, Elizabeth Putnam, alias Perley, ex'trix, returns on will of Joseph Putnam, payment of legacies to John and Rachel Leach, Jonathan Putnam jr. in virtue of his wife Elizabeth, daughter of Joseph: Joseph, Jethro and Anna Putnam, Eleazer and Sarah Brown, Israel Andrews, grandson of said Mary Putnam, Eunice Putnam."—*Essex Probate.*

5

Children :

79   MARY, b. 2 Feb., 1690–1 (Salem town records) ; bapt. in Salem, Apr.,, 1692 (1st Ch. rec.) ; m. 1710, Bartholomew Putnam (No. 147).

80   ELIZABETH, b. 12 Apr., 1695 (Salem town records) ; bapt. Salem, 24 May,, 1694 ; m. 12 Feb., 1714-15, Jonathan Putnam (No. 141).

81   SARAH, b. 26 Sept., 1697 (Salem town records) ; bapt. Salem, 26 June, 1698 ; m. 7 Dec., 1716, Eleazer (*Henry,*[3] *Henry,*[2] *George*[1]), Brown of Salem (see No. 30) ; in 1739 was a party to a deed, "with her brother Israel Putnam both of Salem." Ch. : Mehitable, bapt. 21 June, 1719. Elizabeth, bapt. 30 July, 1721. Hannah, bapt. 5 Jan., 1723-4. Joseph, bapt. 9 Oct., 1726 ; m. a Towne. William, bapt. 16 Mar., 1728-9. Mary, bapt. 14 Nov., 1731. Eleazer, bapt. 24 Feb., 1733-4. Asa, bapt. 9 May, 1736. Sarah, bapt. 24 Sept., 1738. Rebecca, bapt. 16 Aug., 1741. All bapt. in Danvers.

82   WILLIAM, b. 8 Feb., 1700 ; bapt. (No. Parish, Danvers), 14 July, 1700 ; m. 1723, Elizabeth Putnam.

83   RACHEL, b. 7 Aug., 1702 ; bapt. (No. P., D.) 27 Sept., 1702 ; m., 1st, 1723, John Trask ; m., 2nd, before 1730, John Leach ; both living 1740.

84   ANNE, b. 26 Apr., 1705 ; bapt. (No. P., D.) 24 June, 1705 ; m. 1726, Jethro Putnam (No. 153) ; both living 1740.

85   DAVID, b. 25 Oct., 1707 ; bapt. (No. P., D.) 26 Oct., 1707 ; colonel.

86   EUNICE, b. 13 Apr., bapt. (No. P., D.) 18 Apr., 1710 ; m. 20 Sept., 1731, Thomas Perley, son of Capt. Thos. ;[14] d. 2 Feb., 1787. He d. 28 Sept., 1795. Ch. : Huldah, b. 13 Feb., 1731-2 ; m. Joshua Cleaves of Beverly. Rebecca, b. 12 Jan., 1733-4 ; d., unm., 22 Aug., 1813. Israel, b. 2 July, 1738 ; m. Elizabeth Moores, settled on St. John's River, N. B. Mary, b. 4 June, 1741 ; m. John Peabody of Boxford. Olive, b. 30 July, 1743. Thomas, b. 19 June, 1746 ; m. Sarah Wood. Enoch, b. 19 May, 1749 ; m. Anna Flint. Aaron, b. 18 Sept., 1755.

87   A SON, } twins ; b. and d. 4 Apr., 1713.
88   A DAU., }

89   HULDAH, b. 29 Nov. ; bapt. (No. P., D.) 30 June, 1717 ; m. 19 July, 1734, Francis Perley, son of Jacob and Lydia (Peabody) Perley, b. 28 Jan., 1705-6. Lydia (Peabody) Perley was a niece of Lydia, wife of Thos. Perley, being the dau. of Capt. John Peabody. Jacob Perley was a brother of Capt. Thos. Perley (see note below. Ch. : Capt. William, b. 11 Feb., 1735 ; d. 29 Mar., 1812 ;

[14] Capt. Thos. Perley was son of Thomas and Lydia (Peabody) Perley of Boxford ; b. 1668 ; m., 1st, 1695, Sarah, dau. of Capt. John Osgood of Andover, who d. 23 Sept., 1734 ; Capt. Perley d. 1745 ; he had ten children all by his first wife, viz., Lydia, b. 1696. Mary b. 1697. Hepzibah, b. 1699. Moses, b. 1701 ; d. 1702. Sarah, b. 1703. Thomas, b. 1704-5 ; m. Eunice Putnam (No. 86). Mehitable, b. 1708 ; d. 1723. Rebecca, b. 28 Oct., 1716 ; m. David Putnam (No. 85). Allen, b. 1714. Asa, b. 1716. Margaret, b. 1719.

m. Sarah. Clark. Wm. Perley commanded a company at Lexington and at Bunker Hill.

90 ISRAEL, b. 7 Jan., 1717-18, bapt. (No. P., D.) 2 Feb., 1717-18; general.

91 MEHITABLE, b. 12 March, 1720; d. 2 Sept., 1801; m. 24 Mar., 1741, Richard, son of John and Winifred (Sprague) Dexter of Malden,[15] a physician of Topsfield, b. 15 June, 1713; d. Topsfield, 25 Nov. 1783.

JOSEPH PUTNAM will always be remembered for his opposition to Mr. Parris and the witchcraft trials. The position which he took could only have been maintained by one who, like himself, was allied with the principal families of the county. He opposed from first to last the proceedings which disgraced Danvers and his immediate relatives and friends. This was a source of peril to even him, however, and for six months, one of his fleetest horses was kept saddled, ready at a moment's notice, should an attempt be made to seize his person. This fact was well known and it was also known that he would resist every attempt of that nature, even though it cost the lives of those who came to take him. It is a significant fact that his children were baptized in Salem, this being a very public manner of showing his disapprobation of the course followed by Mr. Parris. Joseph Putnam should be honored far above all others of his generation; for he showed that not only did he have the courage common to all of the family, but was above the ignorant superstition of the time by which such men as Judge Samuel Sewall and Cotton Mather were overcome.

It is proper to state at this juncture, that the romantic tale of a sister of Joseph Putnam being accused of witchcraft at a session of the Court to which she had been drawn by curiosity, and her flight and concealment in Middleton woods, is entirely without foundation. Mr. Tarbox in his History of Gen. Israel Putnam quotes from Mr. Rice, but however thrill-

---

[15] Their dau. Mehitable Dexter, who d. 25 Nov., 1783, m. the Rev. John Treadwell and their daughter Mehitable Treadwell, m. Charles Cleveland, whose brother William Cleveland m. Miss Falley and was father of Richard Falley Cleveland, and grandfather of Grover Cleveland, President of the United States.

ing and interesting a story this account may be, it has ababsolutely no foundation.

WILL OF JOSEPH PUTNAM.

In the name of God Amen I Joseph Putnam being Sick and Weeke in body but of Sound Mind and Memory, considering the uncertainity of life and the Duty of Setting my Estate in order to leave Peice in my Family Doe make this my last Will and Testament hereby revokeing and making Null and voide all former wills by me made

Imp[ed] I committ my sole to God my body to a Deacent Buriale hopeing for a glorious Resurrection in and through ye merritt of my Dear Redeemer the Lord Jesus Christ, and for my outward Estate I Dispose of as follows on

My will is that my Just Debts and funeral Expence be paid out of My Personall Estate or monies

Item I Give and bequeath to my beloved wife Eliz[a] in Lieu of her Dower that Peice of land in blind hole by John Curticies Containing about Twenty Eight acres yt was her Fathers, and that Jane Possest of by virtue of his will, to be wholey att her Dispose to sell or as shee shall see cause — and I further give to my wife towards her own Support and the Support and Maintenance of my children under age the Improvement of all the severall Tracts & parcells of lands and the Housein thereon, I have hereafter in this my will given my two sons David and Israell with the Improvement of so much of my Stock and Husbandry Utencells and so much of my Household Stuff bedding and Necefsaries as my Executors hereafter named shall Judge Necessary & Convenient for the Carring on the Farm and the Subsistance of ye Family until my sons David & Israell come Respectively to ye age of Twenty one years and then they are to be sear[d] and Posses[d] of their Parts hereafter given them and either of them first given their Mother Security to pay her yearly the sum of Ten Pounds each in Payable money in ye whole Twenty Pounds yearly and she is also to have a Room or two in my now Dwelling house and what wood Shee may have occasion to burn therein and part of ye Celler, and

Shee is to Keep Possition of sd Lands till shee hath Security to her Satisfaction, I also further give her towards her own Support and the Support and maintainance of my children under age the Leave and Liberty to Cutt and Sell what Wood Shee Shall See cause of from my Old Farm hereafter given my son William only I Desire itt may be cutt where itt may be with the Least Detriment My Wife Remaining unmarried

Item   I Give and bequeath unto my Son William Putnam his heirs and assigns forever Severall Tracts and peices of land viz all that my Farm called the Old Farm Containing about Eighty acres More or less with ye Houseing and fencing on itt (Excepting as above to his Mother) and also the one halfe of my land & Meadow Lying on the West side of Ipswich River and all my Interist In the Saw Mill and Damm att Bishops brook and also my two acres of Meadow Near said Damm and also two acres more of meadow Lying below the Saw Mill on Nichols & Porters land and all my land in Peters Meadow and the ten acres of land I bought of Joseph Allen In case he pay his sister Mahitable out of this last percell Eighty Pounds in Pafsible Bills of Publick Creditt or monies when Shee shall come to ye age of Eighteen years or If shee be married before shee is eighteen years old then to be paid her at Marriage —

Item   I Give and bequeath to my two Sons David and Israell these Severall Tracts & parcells of lands following they and each of them respectively performing what I have ordered to their Mother out of their parts, all that my Farm I now Dwell on Containing about one hundred and fifty acres more or less Including ye land I bought of Anthony Ashby and Capt Putnam and A Small bitt above the Toomb and also the other halfe of my Upland and Meadow on ye West Side of Ipswich River to be equally divided between them and to be to them their Heirs and Assigns forever and If either of my two sons David or Israell Dye before they come to ye age of Twenty and one years then ye one Moiety of his Part to be to my son William his heirs and Assigns forever and ye other Moiety of his Part to be to the Survivour and his heirs and assigns forever the bequest to my wife to be made good and complyed with out of Such part never the less.

I give and bequeath to my Daughter Mary Putnam five Pounds in Bills of Publick Creditt of this Provence.

I give to my Daughter Elizabeth Putnam, Ten Pounds in like money.

I give and bequeath to my daughter Sarah Brown fifteen Pounds in Like money all to be paid In six months after my Decease

I give and bequeath to my four Daughters Namely Rachell Anna Eunice & Huldah Eighty Pounds Each. to be paid them Respectively as they arrive att the age of Eighteen years or If they or any of them Marry before they are Eighteen years old then to be paid att their marrage, and in case of any of my Above named four Daughters Decease before they come to Eighteen years of age her or their parts then to be equally Divided amongst all the rest of my Daughters Married or unmarried or such as shall Legally represent them In like money also

I Give and bequeath to my Daughter Mehitabell the sum of Eighty Pounds as before expressed to be paid by my son William and in case of his not paying as before I then give to her my said Daughter Mehitable her heirs and assigns forever the Ten Acres of Land I bought of Joseph Allen

I Constitute Ordain and appoint my beloved Wife Elizabeth and my son William Putnam to be ye Executors to this my Will and I Desire a Just and Exact Inventory of my Parsonall Estate may be taken and in case there is not enough in mony and Stock yt may be Spaired and houshold Stuff yt may be spaired as before Exprest then my will is and I hereby Impower My Executors to Sell that peice of land of mine yt my Father formerly gave to Joseph Stacey and with ye money for yt Land and for what Stock and household stuff may be spaired and sold to ye best advantage to pay my Just Debts, funerall expence and all my Legaceys not otherwise Directed and In case my money and Stock and household stuff that may be spaired as my children come of age and att Present Is soficient to pay ye above then the said peice of land yt was last mentioned I give to my afore named two sons David & Israell to be Equally Divided and to be to them their heirs and assigns forever In testimony yt on mature consideration this is my Last Will and Teste-

ment I have hereunto Sett my hand and Seal this 15th Day
of March Anno Domini 1722–3

Joseph Putnam [Seal]

Signed Sealed & Declared to be the Last Will and Testament of the Testator in ye Presence of ye woords between ye 5th 16th Line from ye Topp being first Interlined

Benj^a Holton
John Dale jr
Zerobebell Endicott } Essex fs Ipswich May 25th 1723 Befoer the Honb^{le} John Appleton Esq Judge of the Probate of Wills &c In s^d County of Essex them Benj Holten John Dale jr & Zerobable Endicott all parsonally appeared and made oath yt they were Present and saw the within named Joseph Putnam Signe Seale and heard him Publish and Declare ye within written Instrument to be his Last will and Testament and when he so did he was of good understanding and of Disposeing Mind, to the best of their Descerning and they all att the same time Sett to there hands In his Presence as Wittnesses

Sworn Attest Danl Appleton Regt

Upon which this Will is Proved Approved and allowed ye Executors Appeared and accepted of said Trust and Promised to give In an Inven'ty by ye last of June next

Attest Daniel Appleton Regt

III. 18 Samuel (*Nathaniel, John*), of Salem Village, born there 18–12–1652, baptized First church, Salem, 17–2–1653; died, 1676; married Elizabeth ——.

Children :

92 ELIZABETH, b.——.
93 SAMUEL, b.——; bapt. at Salem 25 Dec., 1687.

Of SAMUEL PUTNAM we know nothing except that an inventory of his estate, which amounted to £191–07–03, was taken by Jacob Barney and Joshua Rea, 17th 9 mo., 1676, and was allowed 29th 9 mo., 1676. Administration was granted to Elizabeth Putnam, relict.

Probably the above Elizabeth is the "widow Elizabeth Putnam" who married Benjamin Collins of Lynn, 5 Sept., 1677.

They had : Priscilla, born 2 May, 1679 ; Elizabeth, born 3 Jan., 1682 ; Benjamin, born 5 Dec., 1684.

III. 20 **John** (*Nathaniel, John*), of Salem Village ; born there 26 Mar., 1657 ; baptized in Salem 6–7–1657 ; died in Salem Village, Sept., 1722 ; married in Salem, 2 Dec., 1678, Hannah, daughter of Samuel and Eliza Cutler of Salem, born Dec., 1655 ; living in 1722 ; baptized at First church in Salem the same date as her son Samuel.

Children :

94   HANNAH, b. 22 August, 1679 ; d. previous to 1721.
95   ELIZABETH, b. 26–9–1680 ; m. 12 Mch., 1701, John, son of John and (Abigail) Phelps of Reading, b. in Salem, 6–12–1670. Ch. : Elizabeth, b. 1702. Mary, b. 1706 (Eaton's Hist. of Reading). John, b. in Salem, 8 July, 1709. Nathaniel, b. 22 Oct., 1714.
96   ABIGAIL, b. 26 Feb., 1682 ; bapt. in Salem, 6 July, 1684.
97   SAMUEL, b. 5 Nov., 1684 ; bapt. in Salem, 8 Feb., 1684–5. "Hanna ye wife and Samuel the son of John Putnam jr., baptized."
98   JOSIAH, b. 29 Oct., 1686.
99   JOSEPH,[16] b. —— ; bapt. in Salem, 1 July, 1688.
100   MARY,[16] b. 29 Sept., 1688 ; bapt. in Salem, Oct., 1689.
101   SUSANNA,[16] b. 11 Apr., 1690 ; m. Nov., 1709, Isaac Buxton.
102   JOSHUA, b. ——. } These two sons are named by Perley
103   DAVID[16] or Daniel, b. ——. } Putnam ; there is no doubt concerning Joshua, but of David I find no further record. A son of John Putnam, jr. was bapt. in 1694 ; the margin of the page being worn away the date and name can not be supplied ; perhaps the same as "son to John Putnam died 25 Aug., 1695."
104   REBECCA, b. 16 Aug., 1691 ; unm. 1715 ; "John Rogers to niece Rebecca Putnam."
105   JOHN, b. 16 Aug., 1691 ; bapt. in Salem Village, 23 Aug., 1691.
106   SARAH, b. 5 Mar., 1693 ; bapt. in Salem Village, 12 Mar., 1692–3.
107   AMOS, b. 27 Jan., 1697 ; bapt. in Salem Village, 27 Nov., 1698.
108   PRISCILLA, b. 7 May, 1699 ; bapt. in Salem Village, 16 July, 1699.

On April 15, 1692, a daughter of John Putnam died, probably one of those referred to by note above.

JOHN PUTNAM'S farm was in that part of Danvers west of Hathorne's hill near the log bridge across Ipswich river.

---

[16] Presumably died previous to 1721 as no mention is made of them in the will of the father, who, however, mentions "son Isaac Buxton."

The farm, or part of it, is now owned by George H. Peabody, Esq. In this immediate vicinity his cousins Deacon Edward and Sergeant Thomas Putnam, lived. John Putnam was known as "Carolina John," and as "John Putnam, junior." During the witchcraft excitement, he was constable, and, of course, must have taken a more or less active part in the proceedings. At one time, Mercy Lewis, one of the "afflicted girls" had been living in his house as a servant and in May, 1692, he testifies, apparently in good faith, as to a fit she had when bewitched. It was at a church meeting at his house in 1698 that several of the wronged members of the church again met with the majority and all agreed to live in "love together." This occurred a week after the ordination of the Rev. Joseph Green.

Besides the office of constable, John Putnam was frequently tything man, surveyor of highways, especially towards Ipswich road, and was appointed to other minor positions.

In his will dated 30 Nov., 1721, he appoints Ebenezer and Thomas Putnam overseers; mentions his wife Hannah, sons Samuel, Josiah, John, Joshua, Amos, his son Isaac Buxton; daughters Priscilla, Abigail, Sarah and Rebecca Putnam, and Elisa Phelps. Proved 1 Oct., 1722.

III. 22 Elizabeth (*Nathaniel, John*), born in Salem Village, 11 Aug., 1662; died 6 Mar., 1697; married Sergeant George, second son of Thomas and Ann Flint of Danvers, born there, 6 Jan., 1652; died at North Reading, 23 June, 1720. He married, for a second wife, 2 Mar., 1699, Mrs. Susannah Gardner, who died Mar., 1729.

Children, all by Elizabeth Putnam :

109 ELIZABETH, born 19 Aug., 1685; m. Ebenezer Damon.

110 GEORGE, b. 1 Apr., 1686; m. 9 July, 1713, Jerusha, dau. of Joseph and Bethsua (Folger) Pope and sister of Joseph Pope (see No. 163); lived in North Reading.

111 ANN, b. 18 April, 1687; m. 21 Dec., 1706, Jonathan Parker.

112 EBENEZER, b. 16 Dec., 1689; m. 1714, Tabitha Burnap; lived in North Reading.

113　NATHANIEL, b. 21 Oct.; 1690; d. y.
114　MARY, b. 4 Nov., 1691; "unfortunate daughter Mary." She had
　　　been accidentally shot by her sister in the shoulder. Her grand-
　　　father Nathaniel Putnam bequeathed to her a double portion.
115　MERCY, b. 7 Oct., 1692; m. 9 Sept., 1714, Benjamin Damon.
116　NATHANIEL, b. 4 Jan., 1694; m. 1720, Mary —— of Lynnfield;
　　　lived in Tolland, Conn.
117　HANNAH, b. 12 Feb., 1695; m. 10 July, 1716, John Hunt.
118　JOHN, b. 4 Mar., 1696; d. y.

Sergeant George Flint removed to Reading and settled
before 1682 on land inherited from his father. His house was
used as a garrison house during the Indian troubles. He
was the first of his name in Reading and held the office of
selectman. (Flint Genealogy, pp. 10–11.)

III. 23 Captain Benjamin (*Nathaniel, John*), of Salem Village, born there, 24 Dec., 1664; died there about
1715; married, according to Col. Perley Putnam, 25 Aug.,
1686, Elizabeth, daughter of Thomas Putnam, but on the Salem records, the births of his children are recorded and it is
there stated that they were "by wife Hanna." His first wife
died 21 Dec., 1705; married, second, 1 July, 1706, Sarah
Holton.

Children :

119　JOSIAH, b. ——; bapt. 1st Ch., Salem, 2 Oct., 1687; prob. d. y.[17]
120　NATHANIEL, b. 25 Aug., 1686; bapt. in 1st Ch., Salem, 6 Nov., 1687.
121　TARRANT, b. 12 Apr., 1688; bapt. in 1st Ch., Salem, Aug., 1688.
122　ELIZABETH, b. 8 Jan., 1690; bapt. in No. Parish, Danvers, 22 Feb.,
　　　1690; m. 27 Dec., 1711, Robert, son of Joseph and Lydia (Bux-
　　　ton) Hutchinson of Danvers, b. there, 13 Nov., 1687; d. 1733.
　　　Ch.: Sarah, bapt. 12 Sept., 1712; d. Dec., 1800; m. William
　　　Shillaber. Robert, bapt. 16 May, 1716; d. before 1738. Robert
　　　Hutchinson, senior, m., 2d, Sarah Putnam, 6 June, 1717.
123　BENJAMIN, b. 8 Jan., 1692–3; bapt. 25 Jan., 1692–3.
124　STEPHEN, b. 27 Oct., 1694.
125　DANIEL, b. 12 Nov., 1696; bapt. at Salem, 17 Oct., 1697.
126　ISRAEL, b. 22 Aug., 1699; bapt. at No. Parish, 27 Aug., 1699.
127　CORNELIUS, b. 3 Sept., 1702; bapt. at No. Parish, 6 Sept., 1702.

[17] Author; Dr. Poore states that he d. 21 Oct., 1751.

BENJAMIN PUTNAM HOUSE,

BENJAMIN PUTNAM was a prominent man in Salem, and held many town offices. He had always the title of "Mr." unless other titles are given. He held the positions of Lieutenant and Captain (1706–1711). From the time he was chosen tything man at the Village in 1695-6, hardly a year passed but what he was honored by his fellow townsmen. He was constable and collector in 1700. He was constantly chosen tything man and surveyor of highways at the Village. He was one of the selectmen in 1707–1713 and that his judgment was considered of value is shown by the frequency with which he was returned to the Grand and Petit Juries. His last appearance on the Salem records was in 1712 when he was one of those chosen to perambulate the bounds between Salem and Topsfield. On 30 Dec., 1709, he was chosen deacon of the church at the Village. On 25 July, 1713, Rev. Joseph Green in his diary mentions the fact of his calling on "Landlord Putnam" and that he was very sick and out of his head. This was the beginning of the end, for he died in 1714 or 1715. In regard to his part in the witchcraft delusion it can be summed up thus : The Goods were dependents in his family and when the indemnities were paid by the General Court to the heirs of those accused and imprisoned and murdered, William Good through the instrumentality of Benjamin Putnam obtained a very large proportion,—Mr. Upham thinks more than his share. Among the signatures to the certificate of character of Rebecca Nurse both those of Benjamin and his wife Sarah are found. He never seems to have appeared as a witness of any account and probably steered clear as far as he was able, of the whole affair. The title "Landlord" was one often given to the eldest living Putnam.

The following entries are as yet unexplained, diligent search among the state archives failing to reveal the reason of Benjamin Putnam's imprisonment. These entries are also from Rev. Joseph Green's journal.

"1707, June 16. News of Captain Putnam having come to Marblehead.

June 17. Our country in great confusion. Some for the

army, others against it. I went to Boston to ye Governor
to release Benj. Putnam.

Sept. 21. Sab. 7 baptised. Discoursed Capt. Putnam
at night."

The Rev. Joseph Green often alludes to Benjamin Putnam
in his diary. "1708, July 29, I went with B. Putnam to
Reading to Deacon Fitches, to spend ye day in prayer for him,
he being almost blind, and old Mr. Weston quite blind, and
other disconsolate deaf, &c.   Mr. Pierpont began, I prayed,
Dea. Fitch, Landlord Putnam and Dea. Bancroft then sang
146 Psalm and I concluded with a short prayer and blessing."

During the following August there was more or less anxiety from attacks by the Indians at Haverhill.

"Oct. 23. I went with Major Sewall and Capt. Putnam
to Haverhill."

"Dec. 30 (1709). Benj. Putnam chosen deacon by every
vote except his own."

"March 1 (1711). Ye church kept a Fast at ye house of
Dea. Benj. Putnam's."

"May 4 (1711). Chh. meeting rec'vd to full communion
. . . ye wife of Dea. Ben. Putnam."

"May 10. I went to Capt. Putnam's house raising."

"Mar. 17 (1713). I visited Dea. Ben. Putnam who is ill
with a fall."

"July 25. Visited Landlord Putnam, very sick and out of
his head."

At the time covered by the above extracts, there were several "Capt. Putnams" viz. : John, Jonathan, Nathaniel and as
in the cases above Benjamin, it is possible that some of the
extracts may refer to Jonathan, who was extremely active
at this time.

The will of Benjamin Putnam is dated 28 Oct., 1706, proved
25 April, 1715. He gives to his son Daniel (minister at
Reading) "£150 for his learning." Overseers, "Uncle John
Putnam and Capt. Jon*. Putnam." All his children but Josiah are here mentioned.

30 June, 1715. The children of Benjamin who were of

age, viz. : Tarrant, Benjamin, Robert Hutchinson, Elizabeth Hutchinson entered into an agreement.

On April 1, 1717, Cornelius chose his brother Nathaniel his guardian.

WILL OF BENJAMIN PUTNAM.

In the Name of God Amen   I Benj^a Putnam of Salem in ye County of Essex in ye province of the Mass Bay in New England being in perfect health & of sound memory Blefsed be God for it.   yet Considering my own mortality Doe make This my Last Will & Testament In Forme and manner following

Imp^s   I Give up my Soul to God & my Body to Decent buriall hopeing for a glorious refurrection in & thro Jesus Christ my Redeem^r. and as for yt estate yt God hath bestowed upon me I give & Bequeath in Manner following

I Give to Sarah my beloved wife fifty pounds in or as Money to be payed within five years after my decease by my Exers hereafter named   Also ye use of ye lower room in ye west end of my house & halfe ye Cellar under it during her widowhood.

Item   I give this ffarme I now dweel upon to my Two eldest sons Nathaniel & Tarrant with all the buildings & fences thereon to be equally Divided between them only Nathaniel shall have twenty acres above halfe   They paying as is hereafter expressed

Item   I give to Benj^a & Stephen my two sons My part of Davenports farm ; also my part of the meadow that belongs to said farme, also ye land adjoining to ye meadow yt I bought of Mr. Israel Porter to be equally divided between them both land & Meadow they paying as hereafter is expressed.

Item   I Give to my son Israel That land which I bought of Mr Minziefs belongeing to Mr Humpherys farme alfo that six acres of meadow ground which I bought of my brother John Putnam belongeing to Grigeles his farme.

Item   I Give to my son Daniell one hundred and fifty pounds in or as money To be payed by my Two sons Nathaniel and Tarrant equalley betweene them as he shall neade it in his Larning or when he comes of age If he do not take to Larening.

Also my sons Nathaniell and Tarant shall pay fifty pounds Willed to my wife as above said and also fourty pounds to their sister Elizabeth and also twenty pounds to their brother Cornelius when they com of age each their part.

Item　My Will is that my son Cornelius be put out to larne som good Trade and that his brothers Benjamin and Stephen shall pay him Six Score pounds in or as mony within Three years after he comes of age That is forurty pounds a yeare To be Equally to be payed betweene them.

Item　I Give to my Daughter Elizabeth Sixty pounds to be payed out of my household goods at my decees proportunalle of every thing to be apprised to Her and the Remainder of my Household goods with my out dores Vseing Tooles I give to my Two sons Nathaniel and Tarrant.

Item　All my Stock of what Kinde soever I give to be equally devided amonges all my children except my son Daniel.

Item　I do appoint my two sons Nathaniel and Tarrant to be Joynte Executors of this my will　and my will is that if any of my children dye before they com of age that theire parte or portion shall be equalley devided between the servivors I Do desire and apointe my Well beloued frinds my brother John putnam and my Cozen Jonathan putnam to be the Ouerfeers of this my will and I do require all my children to sett down by the advice of my overfeers whare there may arise any mifsunderstanding of my will

In Testemony that this is my last Will and Testement I have hereunto set my hand and seele This Twenty eight day of October in the year of our Lord Seventene hundred and six Signed and Seeled published and declared in presence of us

Wittnesses

John Jeffards　　　　　　　　　　Beniamin putnam　[seal]

Hannah X Roberds
　　　her
　　　mark
Jonathan Putnam

Apprais and Allowed befr Hon Jnᵒ Appleton at Court at Ipswich April 25 1715

Endorsed Will of Leut Putnam

III. 24 Mary (*Nathaniel, John*), born in Salem Village, 15–7–1668 ; baptized at Salem, Dec., 1668 ; married, prior to 1688, John, son of Peter and Mary (Pierce) Tufts of Charlestown, that part now Malden, who was born about 1665 and who died 28 Mch., 1728, aged 63.

His will dated 9 May, with codicil 20 Nov., 1727, proved 12 Apr., 1728, devised to wife Mary the west end of house, to Nathaniel, Mary and grandson John, Peter, Benjamin, Thomas, son-in-law John Willis.

Freeman 1690 ; buys four lots of land in 1701 of John Putnam.

Children :

128 MARY, b. in Medford, 11 Apr., 1688; m. John Willis.

129 JOHN, b. in Medford, 28 May, 1690; m. 28 Mch., 1723, Elizabeth Sargent, who m., 2d, Nicholas George.

130 NATHANIEL, b. in Medford, 23 Feb., 1692; m., 1st, Mary Sprague; m., 2d, Mary Rand.

131 PETER, b. in Malden, 10 May, 1697; d. 5 Dec., 1776, in 80th year (gravestone) ; m. Lydia, dau. of Samuel and Deborah (Sprague) Bucknam, who was b. 1704; d. 31 Oct., 1776, in 72d year (g. s.). Deborah (Sprague) Bucknam was dau. of Capt. John and Lydia (Goffe) Sprague and granddau. of Ralph Sprague, one of the founders of Charlestown. Ch.: Nathan. Peter. Lydia. Timothy. Samuel, b. 1737; m. Martha Adams. Aaron. Susanna.

132 BENJAMIN, b. in Malden, 28 Nov., 1699; m., 1st, Mary Hutchinson; m., 2d, Hannah Johnson.

133 TIMOTHY, b. in Malden, 13 Oct., 1703; d. 2 May, 1727.

134 THOMAS, b. 4 Dec., 1704; non compos 1739.

135 STEPHEN, b.—— (in his 17th year 1728) ; d. in Malden, 5 Dec., 1785, in his 77th year.

136 MARY, b. 6 Sept., 1716.

(See Wyman's Estates of Charlestown.)

III. 28 Captain Jonathan (*John, John*), of Salem Village, born there 17 Mar., 1659; died there 2 Mar., 1739; buried in Wadsworth Cemetery; married, first, Elizabeth, daughter of Thomas and Elizabeth Whipple; " the oldest inscription in the Wadsworth Burying Ground reads : 'Here Lyes ye Body of Elizabeth, ye Wife of Jonathan Putnam, aged about 22 years. Deceased ye 8th of August, 1682." This gravestone was originally faced with lead. He married, second, Lydia, daughter of Anthony and Elizabeth (Whipple?) Potter of Ipswich. Her will is dated 14 Sept., 1742; proved 8 Apr., 1745, when administration of the estate was granted to John Porter of Wenham. She mentions her daughters, Elizabeth and Esther.

Children, born in Salem Village:

By first wife:

137 SAMUEL, "aged fifteen weeks, deceased about the last of November, 1682."

By second wife:

188 LYDIA. b. 4 Oct., 1684; bapt. at Salem May, 1685; d. 31 Aug., 1711; m. 6 Jan., 1794, Thomas Flint (See No. 54). Ch.: Thomas, b. 23 Nov., 1705; m. Priscilla Porter. Jonathan, b. 12 Oct., 1707. Lydia, b. 10 Sept., 1709. Mary, b. 19 Aug., 1711; m. Mr. Flint; he m., 2dnd, Mary, dau. of Deacon Edward Putnam (No. 54).

189 ELIZABETH, b. 2 Feb., 1686–7; bapt. at Salem 3 July, 1687; d. 8 Aug., 1728.

140 RUTH, b. 7 Apr., 1689; bapt. North Parish, Danvers, 27 Apr., 1690; d. 26 Mar., 1700.

141 SUSANNA, b. ——; bapt., No. Parish, Danvers, 25 May, 1690.

142 JONATHAN, b. 8 May, 1691; bapt. No. Parish, Danvers, 10 May, 1691.

148 ESTHER, b. 18 Nov., 1693; bapt. No. Parish, Danvers (1694?).

144 JERUSHA, b. 2 May, 1696; bapt. No. Parish, Danvers; d. 18 Nov., 1697; g. s. "aged 6 mos. 20 days."

145 JERUSHA, b. ——; bapt. North Parish, Danvers, 15 Sept., 1700; d. 16 Aug., 1716 (g. s.).

146 DAVID, b.; bapt. North Parish, Danvers, 8 Feb., 1706.

Perhaps still another Jerusha as there is a third stone bearing the name Jerusha Putnam, close to the grave of Samuel.

JONATHAN PUTNAM built himself a house, not far from his father's house, on the Topsfield road; part of this house is still standing. He was a farmer and in excellent circumstances. In 1680, Jonathan Putnam was one of several petitioners for a township on Casco Bay on a river called "Swegustagoe;" however, out of regard to the protests of the settlers in that neighborhood who objected to the petitions, the court granted them a township on the north of the Bay. Bartholomew Gedney was one of a committee to superintend this settlement. The committee was to build a fort and sell land there to the value of £100 for that purpose. It is not known whether Jonathan Putnam ever visited this plantation. The inhabitants who objected to the petitioners were Gorges men and seemed to have shown considerable opposition. The first time that Jonathan Putnam is mentioned on the Salem records is in 1683 when he was chosen to the grand jury. Mar. 17, 1684–5, he was chosen surveyor of highways. In 1689 he had the title of "captain" and was selectman. He was made freeman in 1690. On the 30th of Aug., 1691, he was chosen commissioner to join with the selectmen in taking a list of the male persons and estate of the town. Their report showed 402 heads of families. This commission was renewed in 1703. In 1691 he was constable. In 1704 he was one of a committee to look after the common lands, and in 1708 to value the estates of the town. He was constantly serving the town in one capacity or another until his death, being repeatedly surveyor of highways, or on committees to establish town bounds, tything-man, and selectman in the years 1689–1703–1705–1707–1709–1710–1718–1720–1721–1722.

He was representative to the General Court in 1710. In 1722, he, with Captain Bowditch, was desired to wait upon the justices of his Majesty's Court to request them to revive their order of 1688, establishing a House of Correction. In 1713 he was trustee for the commoners of Salem. In 1681, he was one of the petitioners to be freed from paying rates for the maintenance of a minister at Salem or to be erected into a separate township. This application was renewed in 1711 when he was again prominent.

During the witchcraft excitement, he appears in both an unfavorable and favorable light. He and Deacon Edward were the complainants for the warrant issued against Rebecca Nurse and Dorcas Good, the latter a child of but four or five years of age. Afterward, however, Jonathan Putnam saw his mistake and with characteristic manliness signed the paper declaring that in his belief Rebecca Nurse could not be guilty of the charge preferred against her. His wife Lydia also signed this document. In military affairs he kept up the reputation of the family, holding a captain's commission as early as 1689, and was always known as "Captain Putnam" there-

6

after except in 1699 and 1704 when he is styled on the records "Lieut."

III. 29 Lt. James (*John, John*), born in Salem Village, 4 Sept., 1661; baptized at First Church in Salem, 14–5–1667; died in Salem Village 7 April, 1727; married, first, Sarah, who was without doubt the mother of his children. On 10 Nov., 1689, she signed the petition presented to the Church in Salem, for dismissal and liberty to form a new church at the Village and in 1693 (4 Feb., 1692–3), she joins with her husband in a deed of that date, transferring land to Joseph and Caleb Boynton of Rowley; she died 25 Dec., 1717, aged fifty-three years, and is buried in the Wadsworth cemetery by the side of her son Archelaus. Lt. James married, second, 6 Mar., 1719–20 (Salem town records), Mary, widow of Daniel Rea. She died 14 Feb., 1726–27. Zerubabel Rea, son of Daniel and Hepzibah (Foster) Rea,[18] in his journal states under date of "16 Mar., 1720, then my mother-in-law was married again to Lt. James Putnam."

Children, by Sarah, born in Salem Village:

147   SARAH, b. 6 Jan., 1686; bapt. at Salem, June, 1686; m. 12 Sept., 1706, Israel, son of Israel and Elizabeth (Hathorne) Porter of the Village, b. there 4 Apr., 1686. Their children were: Ginger, bapt. 17 Aug., 1707. Sarah, bapt. 10 Feb., 1710; d. before 1729. John, bapt. 12 Mar., 1713; d., unm., in 1742. Israel, bapt. 24 June, 1716. Elizabeth, bapt. 26 Apr., 1719; d. about 1772. Amos, bapt. Sept., 1722; m. Oct. 22, 1741, Peter, son of Rev. Peter Clarke. Mary, bapt. 24 Apr., 1726; m. 31 Jan., 1745, Joseph, son of Joseph and Lydia (Flint) Putnam (No. 214).

148   BARTHOLOMEW, b. 1687; bapt. Salem, Oct., 1688.

149   JAMES, b. 1689; bapt. at Salem Village, 22 Feb., 1690.

150   NATHAN, b. 1692; d. 1723; a mariner, never m. Administration on his estate was granted to his elder brother, James, 11 Nov., 1723. The estate was divided between his brothers and sisters, viz.: James, Jethro, Sarah Porter, widow, Elizabeth Putnam, widow, and to the heirs of Bartholomew Putnam, deceased. (Essex Prob.) For some further facts relating to him see under Bartholomew, No. 148.

[18] See Vol. XVIII, Essex Institute Hist. Coll. and also Rev. A. P. Putnam's letters to the Danvers Mirror. Daniel Rea's first wife was Hepzibah, dau. of Lt. Francis and Mary (Foster) Peabody. No record of her death exists nor of Daniel Rea's second marriage, but the evidence of the diarist must be accepted as conclusive.

Salem Vital Records, IV, 231.

151 JONATHAN, bapt. in Salem Village, 1693; prob. d. y.

152 ARCHELAUS, bapt. in Salem Village, 4 July, 1697; d. at Cambridge, 14 May, 1718, while an under-graduate at Harvard.

153 ELIZABETH, b. 4 Aug., 1700; bapt. Salem Village, 4 Aug., 1700; m. William (No. 82, q. v.), son of Joseph Putnam. William is the only one of the Thomas branch known to be buried in Wadsworth cemetery, and his grave is close by that of Archelaus who d. at Cambridge. She m., 2d, 26-8-1730, John Gardner.

154 JETHRO, bapt. at the Village, 2 May, 1702.

JAMES PUTNAM was a farmer inheriting, from his father, the homestead at Oak Knoll. He in turn passed it to his youngest son Jethro. James Putnam was admitted to the church in Danvers on the 16 Feb., 1689–90; freeman 1690, and in the year 1710–11 was tything man at the Village. In 1720–21 he is styled on the records "Lieut." but with this exception he has only the title of "Mr.," which title was always scrupulously given him. Although never caring to hold office he was evidently esteemed by the townspeople.

The following from the Salem town records relative to the apportionment of the rights to the common land is interesting as showing that the original homestead remained in his hands.

	Cottage	House
"James Putnam for his house & Grandfather's "Cottage Right	1	1
"For his father's place sold and Mr. Freeman's "Cottage Right	2	1"

"These entitled to Rights in the Common Lands "whose Houses were Built after the year 1714

"Josiah Putnam House	1
"Joseph Putnam jr.	1
"Samuel Putnam house 1702.	1
"Mr. John Putnam Sen. his house. wooden lives in	1
"Dea Eleazer Putnam Dwelling house near "George Clays	1
"Tarrant Putnam house.	1
"James Putnam Jr. house.	1
"Jonathan Putnam Jr. house.	1
"Joseph Putnam house,	1
"Mr. Nathaniel Putnam house	1 "

Capt. Jonathan Putnam was the most active person in adjusting these common rights. He served the proprietors on the "Grand Committee" for twenty-two years, and it is doubtless due to him, who was frequently one of the selectmen during this period that we have the records of these latter meetings of the proprietors, so complete.

James Putnam had been taught a trade, and he in his turn taught his son the same trade, that of bricklayer. This was a custom among many of the early Puritan families. It is to the credit of all concerned, that far-sighted and wealthy men of that day brought up their sons to know a useful trade in case adversity should overtake them. "5th Dec., 1718, James Putnam, senior, bricklayer, deeds to his son James Putnam junior, bricklayer, land in Danvers." In 1721 and 1722 he deeds land to his sons Nathan, Bartholomew and James "from natural love and affection." In one of these deeds (1722) he mentions his daughter Elizabeth Putnam. (Essex Deeds, L. 39–40–35.)

His will is dated on the 2 Mar., 1723–4, and a codicil 1 April, 1727. Proved 8 May, 1727.

WILL OF JAMES PUTNAM, SR.

In the Name of God Amen I James Putnam Sen of Salem in the county of Essex in the Province of the Mafsach^{tts} Bay in New England, being sick & weak of body but of Perfect Mind and Memory Blessed be God for itt Do Make this my last will and Testament in form and manner following

Imp^s I Give up my Soul to God when he shall Please to Call for itt and my body to Deacent buriall att the Direction of My Exce^s. And as to my outward estate I despose of as followeth. (Item) I have Disposed of my lands already by Deeds of Gifts

Item I Give to My Daughter Sarah Porter One Hundred Pounds which I have already paid to her and also five Pounds which I formerly lent to her:

Item I Give to my Daughter; Elizabeth Putnam One Hundred Pounds of which I have paid fifty-three Pounds

Item   I give to my two Grandsons Joseph & William Putnam the Sons of my son Bartholomew Ten Pounds Apeace to be to them when they come to be Twenty one years of age

Item   I give to my two Grandchildren Bartholomew Putnam and Mary Putnam children of my son Bartholomew Five shillings Apeace when they come of age.

I also give to my aforsd grand Sons; Joseph & William Putnam, one of my Common Rights Equally between them.

Item   I give my son Jethro Putnam my great brass kittle and my biggest Iron pott and all the rest of my Estate, both within Doors and without Doors. I give in Equall haves between my two sons James and Jethro, they paying all my just debts, and the severall legaceys herein mentioned, in Equal parts between them.

My will is that the severall legaceys herein mentioned to be paid in Money, or other good pay equivelant to money

I constitute and Appoint my two Sons James & Jethro Joint Execrs of this My Will

In Testimony and Confirmation hereof I have here unto sett my hand and seal ye Second Day of March 1723-4

James Putnam & Seal

Wittnefs. Robert Hutchinson, Amos Putnam, Joseph Whipple, jr

Memorandum Aprill 1, 1727 As an Addition or Supplement to my within Written Will, in consideration of the great cost and pains My Son Jethro Puttnam hath been att for me, in my long sickness, I do give to my said son Jethro out of my stock before his Brother James and he divide the same, that is to say my two oxen and two Cows, and my two Horses and three Shots and six of my Sheep. in Confirmation that this is an addition to my Will I have here unto sett my hand and seal ye year and Day above written in presence of these Witnesses

Robert Hutchinson Amos Putnam Joseph Whipple jr

James X Putnam & C.
his
mark

Approved and allowed at Ipswich May 8, 1727, before John Appleton Judge of Probate

III. 31 Eleazer (*John, John*), born Salem Village, 1665; died there 25 Jany., 1732–3; married, first, Hannah, daugh-

ter of Daniel and Hannah (Hutchinson) Boardman, born in
Ipswich, 18 Feb., 1670–1; married, second, 14 Nov., 1711
(published 19 Oct., 1711), Elizabeth, daughter of Mr. Benj.
and Apphia (Hale) Rolfe of Newbury, born there 15 Dec.,
1679; died 2 Jan., 1752. She was a sister of Abigail, wife of
Nathaniel Boardman, a brother of Eleazer Putnam's first wife.

Children :

155   HANNAH, b. 8 Dec., 1693; bapt. Topsfield, 16 Sept., 1694. "16 Sept.,
         1694, Hannah Putnam, once Borman or Dorman[19] her daughter
         Hannah bapt.;" m. 29 Nov., 1711, Dea. Nathan, son of Capt.
         John and Hannah (Andrews) Peabody, b 20 July, 1682; d. 4
         Mar., 1733. Children: John, b. 2 Feb.; d. 23 Feb., 1713. Han-
         nah, b. 27 Apr., 1714. Nathan, b. 13 Mar., 1716. Elizabeth, b. 14
         Feb., 1718.   Nathan Peabody lived in Boxford; m., 2nd, 27
         Mar., 1723, Priscilla Thomas.

156   ELEAZER, b. 8 Sept., 1695; bapt. Topsfield, 9 Aug., 1696.

157   SARAH. b. 26 Sept., 1697.

158   JEPTHA, b. 24 Aug., 1699; bapt. Salem Village, 25 Aug., 1700.

158a   JOSEPH (not mentioned by Savage, and of whom we know nothing).

159   SAMUEL, b. 30 May, 1707; bapt. 15 June, 1707.

160   HENRY, b. 14 Aug., 1712; bapt. Salem Village, 17 Aug., 1712;
         killed 19 Apr., 1775.

161   APPHIAH, b. 8 July, 1716; pub. 27 Oct., 1733, to John, son of Ben-
         jamin and Hannah (Endicott) Porter, b. in Salem Village 1712
         or 1713, d. in 1759: Mrs. Apphiah (Putnam) Porter m., 2nd, 12
         Aug., 1762, Asa, son of Thomas and Sarah (Osgood) Perley of
         Boxford (see note p. 50). Children: Elizabeth, bapt. 12 Oct.,
         1735; m. Asa Leach of Beverly. John, bapt. 13 June, 1736; d.
         in 1774. Benjamin, bapt. 22 Oct., 1738. Abigail, bapt. 12 Mar ,
         1740. Ezra, bapt. 1 July, 1744. Nathan, m. 23 Mar., 1773,
         Lydia Goodridge. Anna, m. 12 Aug., 1762, Eliphalet son of
         Major Asa and Susanna Bailey. Apphia, bapt. 20 Oct., 1754.
         Mary, bapt. 30 May, 1756.

In the possession of the family in Cortland, N. Y., are
papers once the property of Henry (born 1712) and among
them is the following account of his immediate relatives.

"On Jan[y] the 25th 173$\frac{2}{3}$ Eleazer Putnam Departed this
Leife about 16 minutes after 3 O÷ the clock in the afternoon
in ye 65 year of his age.

[19] "Borman or Dorman." The town clerk of Topsfield at that time wrote the name
Dorman. The head of the family in question signed his name Bowman or Borman.
His descendants now spell their name Boardman.
     Nathaniel Boardman mentions in his will his cousins Putnam and among them
Henry Putnam of Charlestown.

Mother·Died Jany 2nd 1752 between 7 & 8 in ye morn"
Again
"The age of Hannah is 50[20] in 1749.
 The age of Eleazer is 54
 The age of Jeptha is 30[20]
 The age of Samuel is 42."

ELEAZER PUTNAM lived in Danvers and was more prominent
in town and church affairs than his brother James. He settled on a farm north of the Gen. Israel Putnam house and
near the Topsfield boundary on the present Preston place.
He was a farmer and probably well off.

Eleazer and Hannah Putnam were admitted to the church
in Salem Village, 7 May, 1699, and on 31 Jan., 1717–18, he
was made deacon of this church. In 1700 he was chosen tythingman for the Village and again in 1705. He was constable
during the year 1708 and surveyor of highways on Topsfield
road in 1711.

In 1690 Eleazer Putnam had been one of Captain William
Raymond's company enlisted for the "Canada Expedition."
The General Court thought so well of this command that in
1725 a grant of land was made to the officers and soldiers, or
their heirs, in Merrimack. Afterward this grant, being found
to be in New Hampshire, was located on the Saco river.
During the witchcraft delusion Eleazer Putnam "drew his
rapier" and punched at an imaginary devil or two which
seemed to be torturing one of the afflicted girls. According
to the ancient depositions his thrusts were as effective against
the witch as against the French and Indians a couple of years
before.

His will is dated 3 Oct., 1732, and probated 9 Apr., 1733;
in it he mentions his wife Elizabeth, his daughter Hannah
Peabody and her children, Nathan, Hannah, and Elizabeth;
his sons Eleazer and Jeptha and daughter Apphiah Putnam;
his sons Samuel and Henry to be executors. An inventory

[20] 50 and 30 are undoubtedly misreadings by my correspondent for 60 and 50.

of the estate was returned by Samuel Putnam, executor, 22 Jan., 1733–4.

——III. 32 John (*John, John*), born Salem Village, 14 July, 1637; baptized at Salem, 14–5–1667; will is dated 7 Jan., 1731–2; proved 21 March, 1737; married Hannah————. Children all born and baptized at Salem Village:

162   CALEB, b. 14 Feb., 1693–4; bapt. 169(6).

163   MEHETABLE, b. 20 July, 1695; bapt. same date as Caleb; m. 7 Feb., 1715–16, Joseph, son of Joseph and Bethesda (Folger) Pope, b. 16 June, 1687, d. 1755; in will of date of 25 Mar., proved 18 Oct., 1755, mentions wife Mehetable; Joseph Pope was own cousin of the famous Dr. Benjamin Franklin. Children, b. Salem Village: Joseph, bapt. 1 Sept., 1717; removed to Pomfret, Conn. Mehetable, bapt. 3 May, 1719; m. Jos. Gardner. Hannah, bapt. 3 Sept., 1721; m. Gen. Israel Putnam. Nathaniel, bapt. 17 May, 1724. Eunice, bapt. 30 Apr., 1727; m. Col. John Baker of Ipswich. Mary, bapt. 31 May, 1730; m. Sam'l Williams of Pomfret. Ebenezer, bapt. 9 June, 1734. Eleazer, bapt. 14 Nov., 1736. Elizabeth, bapt. 14 Oct., 1739. (See Vol. VIII, Essex Inst. Hist. Coll.).

164   MIRIAM, b. 9 Feb., 1698; bapt. 20 Nov., 1698; m. Stephen (*Benj., Nath'l, John*), Putnam (No. 124).

165   MOSES, b. 29 May, 1700; bapt. 9 June, 1700.

166   RUTH, b. 13 July,[21] 1703; bapt. 18 July, 1703; d. Sept., 1780; m. 6 March, 1722–3, Capt. Samuel, son of Capt. Thomas (*Thomas*) and Mary (Daunton) Flint of South Danvers, b. there 29 Sept., 1698, and d. 10 Mch.,1767. Children, b. there: Ruth, b. 14 Jan., 1723–4; m. Archelaus (*James, James, John, John*), Putnam (No. 375). John, 27 Aug., 1725. Mary, b. 10 Apr., 1730. Samuel, b. 9 Apr., 1733. Capt. Samuel Flint was a prominent and influential man.

167   HANNAH, b. 7 May, 1707; bapt. 11 May, 1707; d. 16 June, 1798; m. 2 Dec., 1730, James Prince, bapt. 12 Jan., 1700, and d. 1775, æ. 70 yrs. (g. s.). His w. d. 19 June, 1798, æ. 93 (g. s.). Buried in the Prince burial ground at Beaver Brook. Children: James, b. 15 Sept., 1731; d. 27 July, 1796, æ. 65 (g. s.). Huldah, b. 9 Feb., 1733–4; David, b. 27 Nov., 1738. John, b. 26 Jan., 1743–4. John, b. 20 Nov., 1745. Amos, bapt. 14 Feb., 1747–8.

JOHN PUTNAM is generally styled 3rd, on the records. He was made freeman in 1690, and held many minor town offices. In connection with his father he is supposed to have built the

——————————

[21] Or 13 February.

"old Clarke House," not far north of Oak Knoll.   In his
of 1732, he devises to wife Hannah, son Caleb, who is appointed
executor, daughter Mehetable Pope, daughter Ruth Flint,
daughter Miriam Putnam, daughter Hannah Prince, and
grandson Moses.

Under date of Apr. 1, 1709, Rev. Joseph Green notes the
burning of "John Putnam 3d's house."

PRESTON FAMILY OF DANVERS.

I   1. ROGER PRESTON, aged 21 years, came to America in the Elizabeth of London, 1635, and settled in Ipswich.   In 1657 he sold
his property there and in 1660 he was an innkeeper at Salem;
m. Martha ——. Children: (2) Thomas, b. 1643. (3) Samuel,
b. 1651. John. Jacob, b. 1658, lost on a fishing voyage, 1679.
Levi.

II   2. THOMAS PRESTON, m. 15 Apr., 1669, Rebecca, daughter of
Francis and Rebecca Nurse. He died 1697. Children: Re-
becca, b. 12 May, 1670; m. Ezekiel Upton of Reading. Mary,
b. 1671; m. Peter Cloyse, of Framingham. (4) John, b. 20
Nov, 1673. Martha, b. 21 Oct., 1676; m. 7 Dec., 1705, David
Judd. Thomas, m. Anna Leach. Elizabeth, b. 1680; d. 21
Nov., 1698. Jonathan. David.

II   3. SAMUEL PRESTON, m. in Andover, 27 May, 1672, Susanna Gut-
terson. Children: William, b. 11 Jan., 1674. Susanna, b.
30 March, 1677; m. 20 March, 1705, James Holt. Mary, b.
5 Jan., 1678; m. 26 March, 1702, Benj. Russell. Jacob, b. 24
Feb., 1681; m. Sarah Wilson. Elizabeth, b. 14 Feb., 1682; m.
John Holt. John, b. 1 May, 1685; m. Mary Harris. Mary,
b. 1 May, 1685. Joseph, b. 26 June, 1687; m. Rebecca Putnam (perhaps No. 104). Ruth, b. 7 Feb., 1689; m. Hugh
Tyler.

III 4. JOHN PRESTON, m., 1st, Elizabeth ——; m., 2d, 28 Dec., 1736,
Mrs. Mary Rea. Children: (5) Moses, b. 6 July, 1715. (6) John,
b. 4 Sept. 1717. Phillp, b. 6 Mar., 1719; m. Ruth Putnam
(No. 177).

IV 5. MOSES PRESTON, m. Mary Leach. Children b. in Beverly:
Elizabeth, b. 14 Dec., 1736; m. 18 Sept. 1755, James Prince of
Danvers.   Joseph, b. 14 June, 1733, drowned while bank
fishing, 1761.

IV 6. JOHN PRESTON, m. 12 July, 1744, Hannah Putnam (No. 264),
who d. 28 March, 1771. He d. 14 June, 1771.

FOURTH GENERATION.

IV. 40 Ann (*Thomas, Thomas, John*), born Salem Village, 18 Oct., 1679; died there, 1716; will dated 20 May, 1715, proved 29 June, 1716. In it she mentions her brothers Thomas, Ebenezer, Timothy, Seth; sisters, Elizabeth, Experience, Abigail and Susanna; her brother Thomas to be executor. Ann Putnam, so notorious in the year of 1692, never married. She made a public confession; her statement previously prepared by Rev. Mr. Green was read by him and received by the church, 25 Aug., 1706. Her health was broken by the excitements of 1692 and she sank into an early grave. As the story of Ann Putnam's life is the story of the Salem Witchcraft, the reader is referred, first, to the Rev. Mr. Upham's work on the subject, and secondly to the chapter of this work especially given up to the history of the part the Putnam family took in the delusion. There will also be found Ann Putnam's confession and each reader may decide for himself or herself whether or not Ann Putnam was demented, influenced by outside agencies, or entirely responsible for the fearful tragedy. Her interment was the last in the old Putnam tomb in the Thomas Putnam burial-ground.

IV. 41 Thomas (*Thomas, Thomas, John*), born Salem Village, 9 Feb., 1681; died there about 1757; married in Ipswich, 10 April, 1705, Elizabeth Whipple.

Aug. 3, 1712, Thomas Putnam and Elizabeth his wife admitted to Salem Village church.

Children, all baptized at Salem Village, now the North Parish, Danvers:

(74)

168 THOMAS, bapt. 25 Aug., 1706; d. y.

169 PHINEAS, bapt. 4 Apr., 1708.

170 MATTHEW, bapt. 10 Feb., 1709.

171 ELIZABETH, bapt. 6 July, 1712; m. (pub. 24 July, 1731), Daniel Farrington of Andover.

172 EBENEZER, bapt. 17 Jan., 1713-14.

173 ANNA, bapt. 6 May, 1716; m. (pub. 4 Oct., 1734), Daniel, son of Capt. John and Elizabeth (Weld) Gardner of Danvers, b. 25 Dec., 1709; will proved 1 Oct., 1759. Children: Samuel, b. 4 Mar., 1736-7. Daniel, bapt. 12 Nov., 1738: m. Emma Rea and removed to Lunenburg. Anna, bapt. 8 Oct., 1738; m. —— Brewer. Ruth, bapt. 31 Sept., 1740; m. —— Estes. George, bapt. 29 Aug., 1742. Benjamin. Ebenezer. Lydia, m. —— Clark. Elizabeth, Sarah, Esther, all bapt. 9 Oct., 1757. Mrs. Anna (Putnam) Gardner m., 2d, 19 July, 1764, Andrew, son of Lot Conant, of Concord. She was his third wife. (See Conant Genealogy).

174 THOMAS, bapt. 27 July, 1718.

175 SARAH, bapt. 13 Nov., 1720.

176 SAMUEL, bapt. 5 Jan., 1723.

177 RUTH, bapt. 22 Oct., 1727; m., 1st, 29 June, 1747, Phillip, son of John and Elizabeth Preston of Danvers, b. 6 Mar., 1719; d. s. p., 14 Apr., 1748 (see note p. 73); m., 2nd (pub. 26 Oct., 1751), Samuel Kimball, of Andover.

Perley Putnam also supplies him with a son Michael.

THOMAS PUTNAM was as he states in his will of date of 22 Mar., 1754, "of Danvers, husbandman." This will was proved 15 July, 1757. By it he bequeaths to his daughters, Elizabeth Farrington, Anna Gardner, Ruth Kimball, and appoints his son Samuel, executor. As no other children are mentioned it is probable they were deceased. Inventory was rendered 29 Mar., 1758.

IV. 43 Ebenezer (*Thomas, Thomas, John*), born Salem Village, 25 July, 1685; baptized First Church, Salem, Oct., 1685; died ——; married at Charlestown, 16 Oct., 1712, Margery, daughter of Joseph (*Lawrence*) and Mary (George) Dowse, born 22 Feb., 1685-6; baptized Roxbury, 13-4-1686. In 1728, Margery, daughter of Joseph Dowse was heir to her father's Narragansett rights. Joseph Dowse had been a trooper in Moseby's company, 1675.

EBENEZER PUTNAM was a mariner and probably resided in Charlestown. The following entries in Middlesex deeds relate to him: .

1716, recorded 1721. Stephen Butcher and wife (Mary, sister of Margery), E. Putnam and wife, Alice and Elizabeth Dowse (also sisters, Alice married Robert Wright, 1720; Elizabeth married —— Dyer) to William Rand. 1 Sept., 1719, E. Putnam buys of Dowse heirs one acre, and 5 Dec., 1720, sells the same to Eleazer Dowse. In this last deed he styles himself "of Charlestown, mariner." Not known to have had any children. (See Wyman's Estates of Charlestown and Dowse Genealogy, by A. M. Dows.)

IV. 45 Timothy (*Thomas, Thomas, John*), born Salem Village, baptized there, 26 April, 1691; died in Tewksbury after a long illness, 3 Nov., 1762; married in Newbury, 25 Sept., 1718, Eleanor Doare, died at Tewksbury of fever 5 May, 1765.

Children, born in Newbury:

178　THOMAS, b. 13 Jan., 1719–20.
179　ELIZABETH, b. 1 Aug., 1721; m. at Tewksbury, 28 Apr., 1744, Nathan son of Nathan and Experience (Putnam) Bailey (No. 46) of Tewksbury, b. in Newbury, 11 Dec., 1721. Children: Nathan bapt. 3 June, 1744. Betty, d. 31 Oct., 1744. Betty, bapt. 11 Aug., 1745. Experience, bapt. 22 Mar., 1747. Hannah, bapt. 2 Apr., 1749. Susannah, d. 9 July, 1750. Eleanor, bapt. 14 July, 1751. Molly, bapt. 3 June, 1753. Patience, bapt. 5 Apr., 1755.
180　ANNA, b. 2 Nov., 1723.
181　ELENOR, b. 6 Dec., 1725.
182　TIMOTHY, b. 24 June, 1728; d. at Tewksbury of a violent fever, 14 Feb., 1753.
183　SAMUEL, b. 10 Jan., 1730–1, d. at Lake George, of fever, 19 Sept., 1758.

TIMOTHY PUTNAM, in early manhood left Danvers, settling in West Newbury among his kinspeople the Baileys. In deeds of date from 1713 to 1743, he is styled weaver. He inherited property from Joshua Bailey the husband of his aunt Experience and about 1744 removed to Tewksbury; thither also many of the Baileys had removed. From the church records we learn that on the 1st of April, 1744, there were received into the church at Tewksbury, from the 3d church at Newbury, " widow Experience Putnam," David Bailey and wife and Jonathan Bailey. On the 17th Sept., 1748, Mrs. Anna and Elenor Putnam; on the 3 Sept., 1749, Mr. Nathan Bailey and Elizabeth his wife all from the 3d church at Newbury, and on the 13 Jan., 1760, Mr. Timothy Putnam and wife from the 1st church at Newbury. Doubtless all of these had been residents of Tewksbury for many years but had not obtained a dismissal from their old church. Timothy Putnam, jr., and his brother Samuel united with the Tewksbury church, the first on 29 July, 1750, the second on 29 Apr., 1753. Administration on the estate of Timothy Putnam of Tewksbury was granted 22 Nov., 1762. In 1769, Elenor Putnam his daughter complained of the administrator, Nathan Bailey.

IV. 49 Seth (*Thomas, Thomas, John*), born in Salem Village, May, 1695; died at Charlestown, N. H., 30 Nov., 1775; married 16 Sept., 1718, Ruth, daughter of —— Whipple, born ——, 1692; died in Charlestown, N. H., 1 Feb., 1785.

Children born at Billerica:

184 EBENEZER, b. 8 Aug., 1719.

185 RUTH, b. 11 Oct., 1720; d. ——; m. 3 Oct., 1746, Peter Larrabee of Salem afterwards of Charlestown, N. H. Children : Ruth, b. 1747. Elizabeth, b. 1749. Peter, b. 1750; m. Sarah Kennedy. Peter Larrabee, senior, was taken prisoner by the Indians in 1754, but escaped, and afterwards became one of the most prominent men in Charlestown.

186 SARAH, b. 16 Mar., 1721-2.

187 SETH, b. 14 Mar., 1723-4; killed by the Indians 2 May, 1746. Says Belknap in his history of N. H., Vol. II, p. 243: "The enemy was scattered in small parties on all the frontiers. At Number Four, some women went out to milk their cows, with Major Josiah Willard and several soldiers for their guard. Eight Indians who were concealed in a barn, fired on them and killed Seth Putnam; as they were scalping him, Willard and two more fired on them and mortally wounded two, whom their companions carried off."

188 ELIZABETH, b. 6 Sept., 1725.
189 THOMAS, b. 22 Oct., 1728.
190 SUSANNA, b. 8 Jan., 1730-1.
191 TIMOTHY, b. 25 Dec., 1732.

SETH PUTNAM was one of the earliest of the Danvers Putnams to go forth into the wilderness and make a home for himself and family. In 1719, March 21, he bought of Samuel Walker, for £200, a house lot and sixty acres of land in Billerica. His farm began at Shawshin bridge and was bounded by the river on the west. Here he lived until about 1750 when he removed to Number Four, now Charlestown, N. H. This frontier post had been fearfully exposed to Indian attacks, and but three of the original grantees had settled there. In 1746, Number Four had been abandoned by the inhabitants who took up their abode for the most part in Groton, Lunenburg and Leominster, Mass. In 1747, the place was again garrisoned and on 21 June, 1751, a company of the settlers was organized with Phineas Stevens as captain. On the rolls of this company are found the names of two sons of Seth, viz., Ebenezer and Thomas. The father was at Charlestown, but not on the company rolls. Ebenezer Putnam also served under New Hampshire in 1755. In 1755 upon a petition of the inhabitants of Charlestown, fourteen in number, among whom were Seth and Ebenezer Putnam, Massachusetts again garrisoned the town. There had been ten Indian attacks between 1753–1755, and New Hampshire had failed to afford the town any protection.

On the 18 Feb., 1754, a committee which had been appointed by New Hampshire to examine into the claims of persons to land at Charlestown, reported forty-three claims besides the heirs of Obadiah Sartwell. Among the forty-three were Mr. Seth Putnam, Ebenezer Putnam and Thomas Putnam, to each of whom was set apart $\frac{1}{64}$ of the whole.

After the close of hostilities, Charlestown was no longer a frontier town and by 1760 a tide of emigration set in which soon filled the country with desirable settlers and gave the inhabitants of old Number Four, among them the Putnam family, the opportunity long wished for, to cultivate their farms and establish a flourishing town.

Seth Putnam helped form the first church at Charlestown and was one of the first ten members. He seems to have been highly respected by his neighbors. On 14 Aug., 1753, the first town meeting at Charlestown was held and Seth Putnam was chosen tything man.

On his tombstone is the following inscription:

"The memory of the just is blest."

on his wife's,

"Sweet soul we leave thee to thy rest till we shall meet thee above with Christ."

IV. 50 Deacon Edward (*Edward, Thomas, John*), born in Salem Village 29 April, 1682; baptized at the church in Salem the following October; died in Middleton, 23 Oct., 1755; married, first, Sarah ——; married, second, 3 Sept., 1735, Mrs. Priscilla Jewett of Rowley, widow of Nehemiah Jewett who died 2 Feb., 1732–3. She was the daughter of Nathaniel and Priscilla (Carrell) Bradstreet and was born 22 Sept., 1689, and died in Rowley 6 Sept., 1736. By her first husband she had four children, viz.: Jeremiah. Jemima, who married Joseph Scott. Priscilla, who married, first, Zaccheus Perkins; second, Hon. Humphrey Hobson. Caleb.[22]

He married, third, 24 Feb., 1736–7, Martha Nurse widow of Francis Nurse of Reading. She was dismissed to the church in Middleton from Reading in 1738.

He married, fourth, 29 Nov., 1743, Mary Wilkins, perhaps widow of Daniel Wilkins[23] of Middleton.

Children baptized at Salem Village:

192 HOLYOKE, b. 29 Sept., 1706.
193 SARAH, b. 28 Nov., 1708; m. at Middleton, 2 Aug., 1731, Joseph Steele.
194 EDWARD, b. 30 June, 1711; d. 17 Feb., 1800.

[22] See p. 21. Vol. XXII, Essex Inst. Coll.
[23] If Mary Wilkins was widow of Daniel Wilkins, then she was the daughter of John and Mary (Gould) Hutchinson; Abigail, another daughter, married Benjamin Putnam.

195 SUSANNA, b. 17 Jan., 1713–4.

196 MARY, b. 10 Feb , 1717; m. previous to 1755, —— Flint; prob. the
      Mary who m., 26 Apr., 1737, Eben. son of Eben and Gertrude
      (Pope) Flint of Dracut. Children: Molly. Miles. Nehemiah.
      David. Elijah, b. 15 Nov., 1747. Samuel. Simeon, slain in
      battle of White Plains.

197 EUNICE, b. 18 Sept. 1719; m. 19 Sept., 1743, Thomas Lovell.

198 ABIGAIL, b. 11 Sept., 1720; m. 25 Apr., 1744, Israel Curtis.

199 LOIS, b. 19 April, 1724.

200 MILES, b. 5 Sept., 1725.

201 HANNAH, b. 23 April, 1727; m. 8 May, 1746, Amos Fuller.

EDWARD PUTNAM received from his father a gift of land in
Middleton and here he established himself although owning
property in Danvers, where he was taxed as late as 1755.
Jan., 1706, both he and his wife Sarah were admitted to the
church at Salem Village, and on 16 Nov., 1729, they, with
others, were dismissed to form the church in Middleton.[24] In
1738 Edward Putnam, jr., was chosen deacon of the church
there; he was also the first town clerk and one of the first
selectmen.

On 4 May, 1734, Edward Putnam, junior, of Middleton,
husbandman, sells, etc., to Thomas Cave of Middleton a parcel
of land and $\frac{1}{16}$ part of Iron works standing on Pout Brook
Pond, also $\frac{1}{8}$ part of stream, hammer, anvil, bellows, etc.
(Essex Deeds 78–5.)

Edward Putnam's farm was just within the limits of Middleton and here, according to Gen. Rufus Putnam, he died
at a good old age.

In his will Deacon Edward mentions his children[25] Martha
Nurse and Timothy Nurse, heirs of Jonathan Nurse and Samuel Swan, late of Reading.

IV. 52 Deacon Elisha (*Edward, Thomas, John*),
born in Salem Village, 3 Nov., 1685; died in Sutton,
10 June, 1745; married, first, at Salem, 10 Feb., 1710, Han-

---

[24] The vote of the church can be found p. 248, Vol. XII, N. E. H. G. Reg. The families
dismissed were those of Wilkins, Fuller, Kenny and Putnam.

[25] By her first husband, Martha Nurse had Jonathan, b. 1719; Martha, b. 1722; Timothy,
b. 1724; Samuel, b. 1726; Caleb, b. 1729.

nah Marble of Salem ; married, second, 15 Feb., 1713, Susanna, daughter of Jonathan and Susan (Trask) Fuller of Topsfield, born 1695.

Children (the first five born in Salem Village, the remainder in Sutton) :

202 ELISHA, b. 2 Dec.; bapt. 8 Jan., 1716; d. ——, 1758.

203 HANNAH, bapt. 8 Sept., 1717; d.——; m. in Sutton, 18 Aug., 1786, Jonathan, son of Samuel and Abigail (King?) Dudley; Ch. : Jonathan, b. 22 March, 1738. Hannah, b. 20 Jan., 1740. John, b. 20 Aug., 1743. Prudence, b. 4 May, 1747. Anne, b. 9 April, 1753. Samuel, b. 4 Jan., 1755. Peter, b. 10 Jan., 1758; d. 8 Sept., 1836.

204 NEHEMIAH, b. 22 March, and bapt. 29 March, 1719; d. 27 Nov., 1791.

205 JONATHAN, b. 19 July, bapt. 3 Sept., 1721.

206 SUSANNA. bapt. 8 Sept., 1723; d. ——; m., 1st, in Sutton, 24 Feb., 1742, Timothy, son of Timothy and Keziah Holton, b. 5 Sept., 1719. Ch. : Kezia, b. 16 Nov., 1743; m. 29 Nov., 1768, Solomon Cook. Timothy, b. 1 May, 1745. Elisha, b. 17 Feb., 1752. Susanna, b. Nov., 1755; m. 29 Aug., 1779, Benjamin Cogswell. Sarah, b. 20 May, 1758. Mrs. Susanna Holton m., 2d, John Whipple, and had perhaps John, b. 15 Mar., 1766. Perley, b. 6 June, 1769.

207 MARY, b. 12 June, 1725; d. 22 Apr., 1736.

208 STEPHEN, b. 4 Apr., 1728; d. 5 March, 1803, in N. H.

209 AMOS, b. 22 July, 1730; d. 19 Aug., 1804 (Perley Putnam MSS.), 17 Sept., 1811 (Hist. Sutton).

210 EUNICE, b. 6 July, 1732; d. at Windham, unm.

211 HULDAH, b. 25 May, 1734; m. Daniel Matthews, son of Daniel and Eunice (Morse) Matthews, b. 28 Oct., 1725. Ch : Sarah, b. 1764; d. 16 June, 1802; m. 8 Apr., 1782, Joseph Willson, who was grandfather of Rev. Edmund Burke Willson of Salem.

212 RUFUS, b. 9 Apr., 1738; d. at Marietta, Ohio, 4 May, 1824; General in Revolutionary army.

ELISHA PUTNAM of Topsfield, husbandman, Jonathan Kenny of Boxford, do., Joseph White of Salem, joyner, Josiah White of Salem, husbandman, Samuel White of Salem, do., Samuel Carril of Boxford, cooper, buy of William Wait of Sutton, husbandman, and Abiel his wife for £658, five hundred acres of land in the Nipmug country, being the northern half of the grant of 1000 acres to Col. Elisha Hutchinson and Isaac Addington by the General Court in 1713. One week afterward Elisha and Susannah Putnam, Jonathan and Rebecca Kenny, Joseph and Beatrix White, Josiah White, Samuel and Dinah White, Samuel and Rebecca Carril, mortgage the same tract to Thomas Hutchinson of Boston for £600. The mortgage to run until 10 Aug., 1723. This mortgage was witnessed by Jonathan, William and Anna Fuller. (Vol. 34, p. 239, Suffolk Deeds.)

Of the above, Elisha Putnam, Jonathan Kenney, Josiah White and Samuel Carriel, settled in Sutton. Exactly at what date Elisha Putnam took up his final abode in Sutton is not known; probably in 1725, perhaps in 1723. Isaac Putnam and Jeptha Putnam bought land in Sutton about 1723 and settled there. Nathaniel and Stephen Putnam bought land there in 1726.

In the year 1726, the name of Putnam first appears on Sutton Records, and the particular mention is that of Elisha Putnam being appointed one of a committee to treat with their minister, an important matter to our ancestors. From this time to his death Elisha Putnam was prominent in church and town affairs. He had the executive ability which his father had shown in Danvers; and the people of Sutton, realizing this, honored him in many ways. He was representative to the General Court, town clerk and treasurer, besides holding many minor offices.

In 1730 he was admitted to the church and chosen deacon in 1731. Gen. Rufus Putnam in his memoirs of the Putnam family says, "In justice to the character of my father I ought to mention that he was much respected as a citizen and a christian."

The Rev. Dr. Hall in his diary says that "Deacon Elisha Putnam was a very useful man in the civil and ecclesiastical concerns of the place. He was for several years deacon of the church, town clerk, town treasurer and representative in the General Court, or Colonial Assembly of Massachusetts. He died in June, 1745, in the joyful hope of the glory of God."

The farm upon which Elisha Putnam settled in Sutton is the place now known as the Freeland estate. The remains of the old cellar were still to be seen a few years ago. The house, which succeeded the first house, was a fine specimen of a colonial mansion and was built to resemble the house of an English nobleman.

IV. 53 Joseph (*Edward, Thomas, John*), born in Salem Village 1 Nov., 1687; died there. Will dated 8 June, 1772, proved 26 Nov., 1773. Mentions sons Joseph and Oliver, Lydia, daughter of his son Joseph, and grandson Joseph. He married Lydia Flint.

Children :

213 OLIVER, bapt. Salem Village, 21 Oct., 1722.
214 JOSEPH, bapt. Salem Village, 26 Apr., 1724.

JOSEPH PUTNAM was known as Joseph "Junior" until the death of his uncle. He was one of the first selectmen of Danvers, 4 March, 1752.

IV. 57 Ensign Ezra (*Edward, Thomas, John*), born in Salem Village, 29 Apr., 1696; died Middleton, 22 Oct., 1747. Will dated 5 Sept., 1747, proved 30 Dec., 1747. Mentions widow Elizabeth, daughter Mary, son Nehemiah to be sole executor, son Ezra a minor; married 6 March, 1719 (another authority 16 March, 1719), Elizabeth, daughter of Thomas and Elizabeth Fuller bapt. Salem Village, 21 Sept., 1707; died in Middleton, 21 Oct., 1747.

Children :

215 ELIZABETH, bapt. Salem Village, 7 May, 1721; d. in Middleton 17 Sept., 1747.
216 MARY, bapt. Salem Village, 3 March, 1722; d. 14 Dec., 1786. Mrs. Averill, with apparent reason, thinks she m. 17 Feb., 1749, Ephraim Fuller, a brother of Amos (see No. 201). Ephraim Fuller d. 20 Feb., 1792. Their sister, Rachel Fuller, m. Rev. Wm. Phipps, 13 Nov., 1751, and removed to Douglas.
217 NEHEMIAH, bapt. at Salem Village, 5 Sept., 1725; d. in Middleton, 23 Oct., 1747.
218 EZRA, bapt. Salem Village, 8 June, 1729.
219 RUTH, bapt. 17 Mar., 1734; d. in Middleton, 16 Dec., 1747.

'TNAM, SENIOR, was of Middleton and was styled
He bought land in Topsfield from his brothers and
psfield then included part of Middleton. The farms
dward and his sons are all in that part of what is
now Middleton near Danvers, and in some instances crossing
the Danvers line. Deacon Edward gave each of his sons a
farm. To Isaac, within a week of his removal to Sutton, he
gave the homestead. Isaac sold to Ezra.

IV. 58 Isaac (*Edward, Thomas, John*), born in Salem
Village 14 March, 1698; died in Sutton, 1757; married 20
Dec., 1720, Anna Fuller.

Children :

220   PHINEAS, b. Salem Village, 1 Oct. and bapt. 7 Oct., 1722.

221   ASAPH, b. Salem Village, 11 Sept. and bapt. 20 Sept., 1724.

222   ANNA, b. Salem Village, 27 July and bapt. 31 July, 1726; probably
     m., 31 Oct., 1745, Josiah Trask of Sutton. Ch.: Peter, b. 23
     May, 1746; d. 7 Oct., 1803. John, b. 2 Dec., 1747; d. 19 Mar.,
     1748. Isaac, b. 22 May, 1749.

223   SUSANNA, b. in Sutton, 20 Aug., 1728; m. 15 Jan., 1746, John Sadler
     of Upton.

224   NATHAN, b. in Sutton, 24 Oct., 1730.

225   EDWARD, b. 5 Feb., 1733; d. young. (Gen. Rufus Putnam's ac-
     count.)

226   ISAAC, b. 4 Nov., 1734.

227   LYDIA, b. 20 Oct., 1736.

228   DANIEL, b. 28 March, 1739.

ISAAC PUTNAM of Topsfield, yeoman, buys 23 May, 1726,
of John Hutchinson of Salem, yeoman, 125 acres in Sutton
for £310. This land bounded on Jeptha Putnam's purchase.
He also in Dec., 1726, bought 33 acres of the Davenport
farm, which adjoined his former purchase. He was "of Topsfield" when this last deed was drawn, but probably soon afterward settled on his purchase in Sutton. He was dismissed
from the church in Salem Village to the church in Sutton, and
was admitted there 1 Feb., 1730. His name does not appear
on Sutton records later than 1740, and it is not known that
any of his posterity now live there. His son, Phineas, had
the homestead in Sutton.

IV. 82 William (*Joseph, Thomas, John*), born in Salem Village, 8 Feb., ——; baptized 14 July, 1700; died 19 May, 1729 (gravestone Wadsworth cemetery); married in Salem, 30 Jan., 1723, Elizabeth, daughter of Lt. James (*John, John*) Putnam (No. 133), born 4 Aug., 1700; married, second, 26–3– 1730, Capt. John, baptized 16 Feb., 1706–7, son of John and Elizabeth (Weld) Gardner of Salem. Mrs. Gardner died of apoplexy, 4 Feb., 1764. Capt. Gardner died 15 Jan., 1784; married, second, Elizabeth Herbert; third, Mary Peale.

Children:

229 ELIZABETH, bapt. 15 May, 1726; d. 30 March, 1759; m. 28 June, 1748. Jonathan, son of Josiah and Sarah (Ingersoll) Orne of Salem, b. 1722–3; d. 1 Jan., 1774, æ. 51, merchant of Salem. Children: Joseph, b. 4 June, 1749; m., 1st, Mary Leavitt; m., 2nd, Therese Emery. William, b. 4 Feb., 1752; d. 18 or 14 Oct., 1815, an eminent merchant in Salem; m. Abigail, dau. of Hon. Nathaniel Ropes. Elizabeth, bapt. 29 Sept., 1754. Samuel, bapt. 10 Oct., 1756, probably d. y. Mehitable, bapt. 20 April, 1759, prob. d. y. Jonathan Orne, m., 2d, 21 Aug., 1760, Elizabeth Bowditch.

230 SARAH, bapt. 22 Dec., 1728; d. ——; m., 2 Jan., 1753, Capt. Jonathan, son of Jonathan and Elizabeth (Gardner) Gardner Salem, mariner, b. in Salem 25 May, 1728; d. 2 March, 1791. Ch.: Jonathan, b. 16 Mar., 1755; d. 26 Sept., 1821; m., 1st, Sarah Fairfield; m., 2d, 27 Oct., 1799, Lucia, dau. of Israel and Lucia (Pickering) Dodge, b. 16 June, 1768; d. 24 Mar., 1812, *s. p.* (See Pickering Genealogy.)

Child of Capt. John and Elizabeth (Putnam) Gardner:

230a JOHN, b. 23 June, 1731; d. 27 Oct., 1805; m. 11 July, 1757; Elizabeth, dau. of Timothy and Mary (Wingate) Pickering, b. 11 Jan., 1737; d. 12 Oct., 1823. (For descendants see Pickering Genealogy).

IV. 85 Colonel David (*Joseph, Thomas, John*), born in Salem Village, 25 Oct., 1707; died 1768; married 24 Nov., 1728, Rebecca, daughter of Thomas and Sarah (Osgood) Perley of Boxford, born 28 Oct., 1710. (See note on page 50.)

Children, born and baptized in Salem Village:

231 WILLIAM, bapt. 8 March, 1729–30.

232 LUCY, bapt. 23 Apr., 1732; m. Major Ezra Putnam.

233 ALLEN, b. 1732; bapt. 4 Apr. 1734; d. ——, 1759.

234 MEHITABLE,[26] b. 1734; bapt. 18 Mar., 1736–37; m. previous to 1767; Rev. Edward Perkins, son of Rev. Nathaniel and Elizabeth (Perkins) Sparhawk, of Lynnfield, b. 10 July, 1728. He m., 2nd, a Mrs. Adams. (See Sparhawk genealogy.)

235 JOSEPH, bapt. 14 Oct., 1739; d. 9 Mar., 1818.

236 ISRAEL, b. 29 June, 1742.

237 EUNICE, bapt. 28 Apr., 1745; d. y.

238 DAVID, b. ——, 1747; d. ——, 1766.

239 EUNICE, b. ——, 1751; d. 26 Nov. 1846; m. Nathaniel, son of Joshua and Eunice (Jennison) Richardson, tanner, formerly of Woburn but afterwards of Salem, in which latter place he was killed 25 Jan., 1796, while superintending the moving of a building. He was born in Woburn, 20 Mch., 1742. Ch.: Jesse, b. ——, 1774, of Salem. Joshua, of Portland. Nathaniel, a merchant of Malaga, Spain. William P. of Salem. Israel of Portland.

240 JESSE, b. 8 Jan., bapt. 13 Jan., 1754.

COLONEL DAVID PUTNAM was one of the most prominent men in Danvers for over fifty years. He was not only influential in town and parish affairs but was known throughout the colony as a dashing cavalry officer. Col. Timothy Pickering was accustomed to mention among the recollections of his boyhood that "David Putnam rode the best horse in the Province."

For many years the inhabitants of Salem Village had been petitioning the General Court to set them off as a separate town and in these attempts David Putnam sided with the popular party. In 1752, they partially gained their point and David and James Putnam are among the subscribers to a petition to Daniel Eppes, Esq., for calling the first town meeting in the District of Danvers, 18 Feb., 1752. This meeting was held on the 4th of March, and Lt. David was chosen one of the highway surveyors, an important office in a new town. Previous to the separation he had held various offices in the old town.

---

[26] Mehitabel, in History of Sanbornton, N. H., is said to have m. Laban Harriman, a Quaker and to have had a child, Mehitabel, b. 20 Sept., 1762; m., 1789, John Abrams of Sanbornton. He was b. in Amesbury, 3 March, 1766. This must refer to some other Mehitable, though whom, I know not. (See No. 289.)

In 1751, he was selectman of Salem from the Village and doubtless did much to influence the town to consent to the separation.

In 1753, he was chosen selectman of Danvers and in 1757 was one of a committee of five to regulate the grammar school. Hardly a year passed but that he held some one or another town office, being at various times selectman, surveyor of highways, tythingman, overseer of the poor, warden, and on special committees. He was last taxed in 1767, his estate was taxed in 1768, and his will proved in 1769.

This will is an interesting document; by it he provided for his son William, his daughters Lucy, Mehetable Sparhawk, and Eunice, then gives the remainder to his sons, Joseph and Israel leaving it to them to divide, they to furnish their youngest brother, Jesse, with the means to carry him through college.

The terms of the will were fulfilled in every particular and tradition states that when Joseph and Israel came to divide the property each had chosen that which the other did not want. This property comprised the estate now known as the Gen. Israel Putnam place, the Col. Jesse place, about fifty acres, now owned by the state, included in the Insane Hospital grounds, and the houses of Eben S. Flint, Eben Jackson, Mrs. Daniel Verry, Mrs. Julia A. Philbrick, and the schoolhouse grounds.

The section known as the Col. Jesse estate fell to Joseph and the part known as the Gen. Israel place fell to Israel.

The sword carried by Col. David long remained in the hands of his descendants and never left the homestead until presented on the 19 May, 1890, by Granville B. Putnam, Esq., to the Danvers Historical Society.

IV. 90 Major-General Israel (*Joseph, Thomas, John*), born in Salem Village, now Danvers, 7 Jan., 1717–18; baptized 2 Feb., 1718; died Brooklyn, Conn., after an illness of two days, 29 May, 1790; married, first, at Danvers, 19 July, 1739, Hannah, daughter of Joseph and Mehitable (Putnam,

No. 163) Pope of Danvers, born there; baptized 3 Sept., 1721; died Brooklyn, Conn., 6 Sept., 1765, in the 44th year of her age; married, second, 3 June, 1767, the widow Deborah (Lothrop) Gardiner. Madame Gardiner was daughter of Samuel and Deborah (Crow) Lothrop of Norwich, Conn., and widow of John Gardiner, fifth proprietor of Gardiner's Island, who died 19 May, 1764. She died at Putnam's Headquarters at Fishkill on the Hudson, 14 Oct., 1777, and was interred in Beverly Robinson's family vault. Mr. Gardiner she had married as his second wife, 21 Nov., 1755, being then the widow of Rev. Ephraim Avery of Pomfret. The children of Mr. Gardiner by Deborah (Lothrop) Avery were *Hannah*, born 31 Dec., 1757; married Samuel Williams of Brooklyn; died *s. p. Septimus*, b. 28 Dec., 1759; died unmarried 1 June, 1777. He was with General Putnam during many of his campaigns.[27]

Children, all by his first wife:

241 ISRAEL, b. Danvers, 28 Jan.; bapt. there 8 June, 1740.
242 DAVID, b. Pomfret, Conn., 10 Mar., 1742; d. y.
243 HANNAH, b.   "   "   25 Aug., 1744.
244 ELIZABETH, b. "   "   20 Mar., 1747; d. y.
245 MEHITABLE, b. "   "   21 Oct., 1749.
246 MARY, b.   "   "   10 May, 1753.
247 EUNICE,   "   "   10 Jan., 1756.
248 DANIEL, b. "   "   18 Nov., 1759.
249 DAVID,   "   "   14 Oct., 1761.
250 PETER SCHUYLER, b. Pomfret, Conn., 31 Dec., 1764.

GEN. ISRAEL PUTNAM was born, Jan. 7, 1718, in a house which is still standing on its original site, near the eastern base of Hathorne or Asylum hill, in Danvers. It has several times been enlarged and is still in an excellent state of preservation. Its first proprietor was his grandfather Thomas, who left it to his youngest son Joseph. Joseph wedded Elizabeth Porter, daughter of Israel and Elizabeth (Hathorne) Porter, and granddaughter of John and Mary Porter, the emigrant progenitors of the Porters of Essex county. From this marriage sprang

---

[27] See "Lionel Gardiner and his Descendants."

MAJOR-GENERAL ISRAEL PUTNAM.

the soldier whose history we are to trace. Elizabeth Hathorne was a daughter of Major William and Ann Hathorne, whose country seat was where the Danvers Asylum now stands, on the hill above mentioned. Nathaniel Hawthorne, the celebrated novelist, was also a lineal descendant. John Porter, likewise, was of "Salem Village," now Danvers. For many years he was deputy in the General Court, first from Hingham and then from Salem; and, as the Colonial Records testify, he was a man "of good repute for piety, integrity and estate."

The ancestry of the future soldier-patriot, in various lines, is thus seen to have been of Essex County stock. His later boyhood was probably spent in Boxford at the home of his step-father, Capt. Thomas Perley, while yet he would be a frequent visitor at the Putnam homes in Danvers. His early education was defective, partly because school advantages were then very meagre in the rural district in which he passed his youth, and partly, no doubt, because his strong natural inclinations were for farming and active out-of-door life, rather than for books and sedentary occupations. Robust and full of energy, he was as a boy given to sports, and to feats of strength and daring; and numerous trustworthy traditions of his courageous exploits in those days have been handed down in the old home from then until now, somewhat prophetic of his more extraordinary prowess and achievements in maturer years. Having attained an age when he would care for a share of his father's farm, he returned to Danvers and settled upon the portion set off to him, and here built a small house, the cellar of which yet remains. On the 19th of July, 1739, he married Hannah, daughter of Joseph and Mehitable (Putnam) Pope. The spot is still pointed out, not far from that of his nativity, where stood the humble habitation in which for a brief period the young couple dwelt, and in which their first child, Israel, was born. Shortly afterward, they removed to Pomfret, Conn., borne on by the continued tide of emigration that had already carried a large number of settlers into the eastern part of that state from towns about Massachusetts bay.

There at length he was the head of a numerous family of children, some of whom removed to other parts of New England or to the west, their descendants being now widely scattered abroad through the country. The ancient homestead in Danvers has been occupied by successive generations of his brother David, "the lion-hearted Lieutenant of the King's troops," as he has well been called.

In 1739, Israel, and his brother-in-law, John Pope, bought of Gov. Jonathan Belcher, a tract of land of about five hundred acres, of which he became sole owner in 1741. It was part of a large district known as the "Mortlake Manor," which, while it had special privileges of its own, was included in the territory that in 1786 was detached from Pomfret and erected into a separate and distinct township under the name of Brooklyn. Certain foundation stones, and a well and pear tree, have long marked the place where our brave pioneer built for himself his first house in Connecticut. Here was the family home, until larger accommodations were required, when he built the plain, but more commodious and comfortable house to which the domestic scene was transferred and in which many years afterward the old hero died. This, with its narrow chamber in which he breathed his last, is still standing and is an object of great interest with patriot-pilgrims who year after year visit it from afar. From the outset, his fondness for agriculture and horticultural pursuits was conspicuously shown in the vigorous way in which he subdued and cultivated his land, and introduced into Pomfret and its neighborhood all its best varieties of fruit trees, while it is chiefly due to his taste, sagacity, and enterprising spirit that were planted the long lines of ornamental trees which have graced the streets and added so much to the beauty of Brooklyn. Although at first the exemptions which the owner of Mortlake Manor enjoyed created a jealousy among the inhabitants of Pomfret and rather estranged him from participation in their affairs, yet his sterling worth was early recognized and his public spirit became more and more manifest. He was among the foremost in establishing good schools in the town and did not fail to ensure to his sons and daughters a higher education than he had received himself. Before he entered upon his military career, he joined other leading settlers in a library association which had a marked effect in developing a love of reading among the people and in elevating their general character. He was not only a thrifty and highly prosperous farmer, but, from first to last, he was also an earnest and helpful friend of all the best interests of the little, but growing colony.

The familiar story of his entering the wolf-den, together with the accounts of his many other bold adventures in his earlier manhood, needs not to be repeated in this brief sketch of his life. The late Hon. Samuel Putnam, a native of Danvers and judge of the Supreme Court of Massachusetts, wrote, in a letter to Col. Perley Putnam of Salem, July 16, 1834 :—
" I was once in his house in Brooklyn where he treated me with great hospitality. He showed me the place where he followed a wolf into a cave and shot it, and he gave me a great many anecdotes of the war in which he had been engaged before the Revolution, tracing the remarkable events upon a map."

In 1755, there was a call upon the New England colonies and New York for a large military force for the relief of Crown Point and the regions about Lake George, where the French had gained a strong foothold. The quota from Connecticut was to consist of a thousand soldiers. Though it would require him to leave behind a large property and a numerous family, Putnam was prompt and quick to respond to the summons. Brave, energetic and popular, he was at once appointed to the command of a company, which he soon succeeded in recruiting for Lyman's regiment, under the supreme command of Gen. William Johnson of New York. He received his "first baptism of fire and blood" in the unsuccessful encounter of Col. Ephraim Williams and his twelve hundred men with the enemy under Baron Dieskau, in the forests between Fort Edward and Lake George. This defeat of the

provincials was soon followed by a brilliant victory, in honor
of which Johnson built a fort, named Fort William Henry,
on the spot where it was won. The autumn of 1755 was spent
in constructing defences and in opening means of communication between different parts of the immediate country. As
winter approached, most of the men returned to their homes,
but enough remained to garrison the fortresses. Putnam's
regiment was disbanded with the rest, and he himself returned
to Pomfret to spend the season with his family. The next
year witnessed a renewal of the campaign, the entire forces
being under the command of General Abercrombie. Putnam
was reappointed as captain, to serve as before in Lyman's
regiment. During the service which he rendered in all this
war against the French and their Canadian and Indian allies,
he acquired a great reputation as a soldier and hero, by his
dauntless spirit and marvellous deeds. These, taken in connection with his many perilous exposures, severe hardships,
and hairbreadth escapes, gained for him swift and repeated
honors from the Legislature of his adopted state, and made
him immensely popular with all classes of his countrymen.
The accounts of them, as given more or less fully by his
biographers, Humphreys, Peabody, Cutter, Hill and various
others, are no doubt exaggerated in some particulars.[26] But
enough is true to warrant the fame and distinction that were
then and subsequently accorded to him in abundant measure.
In 1757, he was promoted to be major. He had previously
connected himself with the famous band of rangers, whose
chief was the notorious Major Robert Rogers. Near the
time of the outbreak of the revolution, this remarkable hunter, scouter and roving adventurer, notwithstanding all his
ardent promises and professions of loyalty and devotion to
the cause of the colonies, went over to the British and received from them an appointment as colonel. His volume of
"Journals" makes but very few and slight allusions to Putnam,

---

[26]Gen. Rufus Putnam, who was a soldier in the Massachusetts contingent, kept a diary
which has been printed and which corroborates Humphreys' narrative.

who on one occasion had saved his life and who had borne so conspicuous a part with him in their hard and hazardous campaigning; and this circumstance, together with the fact that some of his friends and apologists grew to be virulent defamers of his gallant comrade, makes it quite evident that no very strong tie of trust or affection united the two. Putnam could hardly have had much confidence in such a strange and lawless man as Rogers, and Rogers must have found little that was congenial to him in such a true-hearted and straightforward man as Putnam, whatever they may have had in common as free and fearless rangers. Here, in this capacity, they were still, as Colonel Humphreys says, "associated in traversing the wilderness, reconnoitering the enemy's lines, gaining intelligence and taking straggling prisoners, as well as in beating up the quarters and surprising the advanced pickets of their army."

On the 3d of August, 1757, Montcalm, the French commander, arriving with a large force from Ticonderoga, laid siege to Fort William Henry, whose surrender after six days was followed by a dreadful massacre of the garrison. Putnam had vainly endeavored to procure reinforcements from Fort Edward. His saving the powder magazine of Fort Edward, amidst the terrible conflagration that visited it, was one of the numerous daring deeds which he accomplished. His descent of the falls of the Hudson, at Fort Miller, and his happy escape from a strong party of Indians who fired at him incessantly as he skilfully steered his bateau down the dangerous rapids, was another of his characteristic achievements, which made his savage foes think that he was under the special protection and smile of the Great Spirit. Yet he was not so successful in escaping their barbarities, when once he was in their power. For it was about the same time, in 1758, that, in one of the forest expeditions in which he and Rogers and five hundred men were engaged, they took him prisoner and subjected him to the most brutal treatment. Judge Putnam's letter, which we have already quoted, states that they

tied him to a tree to be put to death according to their custom
under such circumstances, and then goes on to say: "They
threw their tomahawks into the tree by the side of his head,
and after amusing themselves in this way for some time, they
lighted up the fire, and danced and yelled around him. When
they were thus engaged, one of the tribe, a chief, who had
been once a prisoner of Putnam and treated kindly by him, arrived on the spot, and, recognizing his friend in their intended
victim, immediately released him from impending slaughter.
Gen. Putnam said that their gestures in the dance were so
inexpressibly ridiculous that he could not forbear laughing.
I expressed some surprise that he could laugh under such circumstances, at which he mildly replied that his composure
had no merit, that it was constitutional; and said that he had
never felt bodily fear. I can as easily credit that assertion as
the one Gouverneur Morris made of himself, viz.: that *he never
felt embarrassed by the presence of any one whomsoever, in his
life;* and I am inclined to think that both of them spoke the
truth concerning their own sensations." The wounds which
these cowardly savages inflicted upon the fearless but helpless
sufferer left scars which he long afterward carried with him
to the grave. The almost incredible outrages and tortures
which they perpetrated upon him were not brought to an end
by the cutting of the cord that bound him to the tree, but
were still continued, in other forms, all the while they marched
him through a rugged country to Ticonderoga and thence to
Montreal. There Col. Peter Schuyler, who had been held
a prisoner in that city, hearing of his miserable condition,
hastened to his rescue, supplied him with clothing and other
necessities, and managed to procure his release. Putnam's
tenth and last child was born afterward and he named it
in grateful honor of this noble friend and benefactor. Nor
was this the only kindness which the generous man rendered
at this juncture. Among those whom the Indians had made
captives was a Mrs. Howe, whose first and second husbands
the redmen had murdered and the story of whose wretched

lot under her inhuman masters is familiar to American read-
ers. Schuyler paid the price of her ransom and entrusted
her to the care of Putnam, who, on his return, safely conducted her beyond the reach of her persecutors.

In pursuance of a plan of 1759, to expel the French from
their American possessions, General Wolfe was to lead an expedition against Quebec, General Prideaux one against Fort
Niagara, and General Amherst another against Ticonderoga
and Crown Point. Putnam, who had now been raised to the
rank of lieutenant colonel, was with Amherst and assisted
him in the reduction of both the objects or places of his meditated attack, being subsequently employed at Crown Point
in strengthening its defences. In 1760, the British having captured Quebec, Amherst projected another expedition
against Montreal, in which Putnam again accompanied him
and rendered important service. The city, without resistance, capitulated at the formidable approach, and Canada was
soon lost forever to the French. In 1762, the conquerors turned
their attention to the French and Spanish possessions in the
West Indies, France and Spain having entered into a coalition
with each other. Martinique and the Caribbees were taken,
and a naval force of ten thousand men landed on the island of
Cuba. Presently a reinforcement of two thousand men arrived,
half of the number being a regiment from Connecticut under
the command of General Lyman. Putnam was with him as
on previous occasions, and was ere long placed at the head of
the regiment from his own state, Lyman being appointed to
take charge of the whole body of these provincial troops. The
former had been cool and courageous during a fearful gale
which had been encountered at sea, and on reaching shore he
was busy and efficient in constructing accommodations for the
soldiers. In due time the British Commander, Albemarle,
besieged one of the strong fortresses of Havana and stormed
the city, which finally surrendered, and with it a large part
of Cuba temporarily became a possession of the power that had
now well-nigh gained the mastery of the continent. In 1763 a

Treaty of Peace was concluded between France and England. On the northern frontier there was still some trouble from the Indians under Pontiac, the great chief of the Ottawas. The next year, Amherst sent forces to occupy several of the more important posts and avert the threatened danger. Under Colonel Bradstreet, Putnam, who had himself now been promoted to the rank of colonel, marched to Detroit with a Connecticut regiment of four hundred men. The savages soon dispersed, and all sounds or signs of war were finally at an end.

The year 1764 found the veteran again at home. Nearly a whole decade he had spent in fighting the enemies of his country. Forest, mountain, valley, river, lake and sea had witnessed his arduous service. It had given him a very wide, varied and valuable experience. It had been full of heroic deeds and romantic adventures and incidents; full of duties and responsibilities faithfully discharged, and of dangers and trials nobly met and overcome. After his original appointment as captain, he had been three times promoted. He had been under the command of some of the ablest and most celebrated generals of his time, and had been intimately associated with officers and patriots of high distinction. He had seen many parts of the land, and much of Indian as well as colonial life, and his activities had extended from Montreal to Havana. At every stage of his service, from first to last, he enjoyed the absolute confidence of his superiors and of his state, and was always in demand. How, under all these circumstances, his quick eye, his sagacious mind, his superabundant energies and his natural soldierly qualities and aptitudes, were trained for other and greater military trusts and performances, coming events were destined to show. What has thus far been written of him may well be remembered, as he appears before us in more momentous scenes.

More than another decade was to follow, however, before his advent there. Shortly after he exchanged the sword for the ploughshare and once more began to engage in his peace-

ful agricultural pursuits, the beloved wife of his youth and
the devoted mother of his large family of children, died; and
it was in the same year, 1765, that the husband and father,
who had always, like his ancestors, been a sincere and faithful attendant upon public worship, united with the church at
Brooklyn which was then under the pastoral care of Rev.
Josiah Whitney, and made a formal profession of his Christian
faith. It was during this year, also, that the news of the passage of the infamous *Stamp Act* reached the colonies and
aroused them to stern protest and resistance. Putnam was
foremost in making its execution impossible in Connecticut,
and from that hour he stood forth as a ready and resolute
defender of the imperilled liberties of the people. In 1767,
two years after the death of his first wife, he married Mrs.
Deborah Gardiner, who was the widow of John Gardiner, Esq.,
the fifth proprietor of Gardiner's Island, and who accompanied
him in most of his campaigns of the Revolution, until her
death in 1777 at his head-quarters in the Highlands. For a
time he threw open his house for the accommodation of the
public, and one of his biographers says; "The old sign, which
swung before his door, as a token of good cheer for the weary
traveller, is now to be seen in the Museum of the Historical
Society of Connecticut, at Hartford." During the interval
of time from the close of the French and Indian war to the
outbreak of hostilities between England and her American
colonies, he received many marks of confidence from his
fellow citizens, attesting what they thought of his capacity,
judgment and good sense, for municipal or civil functions also.
He was placed on important committees; was elected moderator of the town meeting; was thrice chosen a member of the
board of selectmen, the last time in 1771; and was deputy to
the General Assembly. In the winter of 1772–73, he went
with General Lyman and others to examine a tract of land
on the Mississippi, near Natchez, which the British government had given to the men of Connecticut who had suffered greatly from exposures and hardships during the West

8

India campaign, of which a brief account appears above. They also visited the Island of Jamaica and the harbor of Pensacola. There is still extant, in the possession of one of his descendants, a curious diary, "probably the longest piece of writing that he ever executed," which Putnam kept in his absence, and in which he jotted down, hastily and imperfectly, many of his own and the party's experiences by the way.

Immediately prior to the Revolution, Putnam held various conversations in Boston with General Gage, the British commander-in-chief, Lord Percy and other officers of the royal troops, quartered in that city, and told them plainly his opinion, that, in the event of war between England and her American colonies, the former could not subjugate the latter, while he gave them to understand, clearly, that he himself should side with the cause of the patriots. In 1774, the enemy were strengthening their forces there and were thus subjecting the inhabitants to manifold privations and embarrassments. Bancroft relates how Putnam rode to Boston with one hundred and thirty sheep as a gift from the Parish of Brooklyn, and "became Warren's guest and every one's favorite." Soon after his return to Connecticut, an exaggerated rumor reached him of depredations of the British in the neighborhood he had just quitted, whereupon he aroused the citizens of his state to a fiery determination to avenge the attack. Thousands were quickly on their way to Massachusetts for this purpose, but the extraordinary excitement subsided when it was ascertained that only a powder magazine between Cambridge and Medford had been captured.

The news of the battle of Lexington, April 19, 1775, arrived at Pomfret by express on the morning of the twentieth. The intelligence reached Putnam as he was ploughing in the field, with his son Daniel, who was then but sixteen years of age, and who afterward wrote; "He loitered not, but left me, the driver of his team, to unyoke it in the furrow, and not many days after to follow him to camp." Having doubtless made haste to consult with the authorities, the old soldier received in the afternoon the tidings of the fight at Concord and at once set out on horseback for the scene of hostilities, riding a distance of well nigh a hundred miles. He was in Cambridge on the following morning, and also in Concord, writing from the last-named place under date of April 21, the second day after the battle, to Col. Ebenezer Williams of Pomfret :—

"Sir, I have waited on the Committee of the Provincial Congress, and it is their determination to have a standing army of 22,000 men from the New England Colonies, of which, it is supposed, the Colony of Connecticut must raise 6000." And he urges that these troops shall be "at Cambridge as speedily as possible, with Conveniences ; together with Provisions, and a Sufficiency of Ammunition for their own use." From Cambridge he wrote again, on the 22nd, for troops and supplies to be forwarded without delay. On the next day the Provincial Congress took definite action for raising a New England army, having already sent delegates to Rhode Island, New Hampshire and Connecticut to request their coöperation, and having now already established a Camp at Cambridge, with Gen. Artemas Ward as commander-in-chief. On the 26th, the Committee of Safety issued a circular letter appealing to the colonies to aid in the common defence ; and on the 3rd of May, the immortal Warren, as President of the Provincial Congress, wrote to the Continental Congress, earnestly pleading the great peril and need of Massachusetts, saying that she had resolved to raise a force of her own of 13,600 men and was now to propose corresponding action by the other New England colonies, and suggesting an *American Army* "for supporting the common cause of the American colonies." No effort was wanting to give to what some writers have called an "army of allies," a truly patriotic spirit and a most effective and consolidated union. Any suggestion or indication, that, under such circumstances, Massachusetts, who appealed so piteously for help, was to arrogate to herself privileges and honors that might not be shared as well by the colonies which she called to her assistance, would have made the mustering army but "a rope of sand."

The appeal was of a nobler character and it was not in vain. New England responded to it with alacrity. Stark and Reed came with their New Hampshire regiments and fixed their head-quarters at Medford, the whole forming substantially the left wing. Troops arrived from Rhode Island under the command of General Greene and were stationed at Jamaica Plain, while General Spencer with his First Connecticut regiment and with two thousand Massachusetts men was posted at Roxbury and Dorchester, the whole constituting the right wing, under Gen. John Thomas. Putnam, with his Second Regiment from Connecticut and with Sargeant's Regiment from New Hampshire and Patterson's from Massachusetts, was assigned to Cambridgeport, where he and his men formed a part of the centre, whose main body, composed of numerous Massachusetts regiments, was under the immediate command of General Ward at old Cambridge. Our Pomfret hero, soon after his prompt arrival on the 21st of April, had been called back to Connecticut to assist in raising and organizing the quota from that state, whose legislature now appointed him to be Brigadier General. He was absent only one week, and, as he set forth again to join the new army, he gave instructions that the troops should follow him as quickly as possible. His post at the centre, where he occupied the Inman House as his head-quarters, was an exposed one, and was deemed to be of special importance from the apprehension that the British might there make their first or chief attack. While he was here, he served at one time as commander-in-chief, during a temporary absence of General Ward in Roxbury. On another occasion he led a large body of the troops which had then gathered in Cambridge, numbering about 2,200 men from Massachusetts and New Hampshire, to Charlestown, marching them over Bunker Hill and Breed's Hill, and into the main street of the town, and then back again to the encampment, so as to inspire them with more confidence and courage. He himself thus came to know still better the ground where he was soon to be a conspicuous actor.

On the 27th of May, he commanded a party of Provincials sent to Chelsea to drive off the live stock on Hog Island and Noddle's Island in the harbor, so as to prevent it from falling into the hands of the enemy. They were attacked by a force of the British marine appearing with a schooner and sloop, but were completely successful in the hot engagement that ensued, only one of the Americans being killed and four wounded, while the loss on the other side, it is said, was twenty killed and fifty wounded. The victors seized the abandoned schooner, and, having taken possession of her guns, rigging and other valuables, set her on fire. In this expedition, General Putnam was accompanied by Dr. Warren, who went as a volunteer. On the sixth of June, these two patriot friends, under the escort of Captain Chester's Connecticut company, proceeded to Charlestown to effect an exchange of prisoners taken in one or more encounters. Having accomplished their object in a manner highly creditable to all concerned, they returned to Cambridge. Putnam was now more popular than ever. The Continental Congress caught the enthusiasm of the people and soon raised him to the rank of Major General. It conferred the honor upon Artemas Ward and Charles Lee on the 17th of June, the day of the battle of Bunker Hill, and upon Israel Putnam and Philip Schuyler, on the 19th, two days after it, not knowing at the time about the great conflict at Charlestown, even as such of these officers as were engaged in the strife were not aware of their promotion until the eventful day was quite of the past.

On the 15th of June, the Massachusetts Committee of Safety recommended to the Council of War, that "Bunker Hill be maintained by sufficient force being posted there," as it was supposed that the enemy were about to make a movement in that direction. The Council of War met on the following day and approved the plan, though Ward and Warren op-

posed it as a rash and perilous measure. Among those of
the council who strongly favored it, Putnam was foremost
and Gen. Seth Pomeroy was also prominent, the former believing it to be necessary as a means of drawing the enemy
out from Boston and bringing on an engagement, the people
being impatient for action. On the evening of that day, the
16th, a detachment of about 1000 men, comprising three regiments under Colonels Prescott, Frye and Bridge respectively,
and nearly 200 Connecticut troops taken principally from
General Putnam's regiment at Cambridgeport, together with
Capt. Samuel Gridley's artillery company of forty-nine men
and two field-pieces, was sent forth to occupy Bunker Hill
and there intrench. Col. Samuel Swett's History of the Battle, which was first published in 1818, and which, as the
fullest and best of all the earlier accounts of it, came to be
regarded as of "classical authority" and to serve as the
"basis" of all reputable subsequent sketches, says: "General
Putnam, having the general superintendence of the expedition, and the chief engineer, Colonel Gridley,[29] accompanied
the detachment." After they had passed the Neck and reached
the peninsula, a halt was made at Bunker Hill, when a con-
sultation of the officers was held, and it was decided to push
on to Breed's Hill and intrench there instead. Arriving at
the summit of that eminence, the ground having been laid out
by Putnam, Gridley and Prescott, the men began at midnight
to throw up a redoubt, eight rods square and six feet high,
with a breastwork extending from its northeast angle a hundred yards or more over the brow and down to a point near
the base of the hill, in the direction towards the Mystic
river. As soon as the British discovered at sunrise what the
Provincials had done during the night, they at once opened
fire on the small fort from their ships in the harbor and from
Copp's Hill in Boston. Putnam, who had readily divined

---

[29]Colonel Richard Gridley, who was a veteran of the French wars, was Chief Engineer
of the army and planned the works on Breed's Hill. He afterward rendered distinguished service and received the rank of Major-General from the Continental Congress.

the need, had proceeded at earliest dawn to Cambridge for
reinforcements and provisions, but, hearing the first firing of
the guns, he immediately started back for Charlestown. Perhaps it was about this time during the day, that he wrote to
the Committee of Safety the following message, of which the
original copy is in the possession of Hon. Mellen Chamberlain : "By the bearer I send you eighteen barrells of powder
which I have received from the Gov. and Council of Connecticut for the use of the army ;"—a much needed and most
timely gift which his energy had procured for the emergency.
The men at the redoubt had toiled long and hard, and wanted
rest as well as refreshments, while yet the breastwork was
not completed. The authorities at headquarters had promised,
on the previous evening, that the detachment should be *relieved* in the morning, and, in fact, early on that next morning
General Ward had accordingly ordered another detachment
of regiments to take its place, with three new colonels, Nixon,
Little and Mansfield, to command them, instead of Prescott,
Frye and Bridge ; but, what with the well-known dilatoriness
that then marked the conduct of affairs at Cambridge, these
fresh troops were not required to parade and march until late
in the afternoon. Meantime there was growing discontent at
Breed's Hill. The soldiers applied to some of their officers,
who in turn appealed to Prescott. The Colonel refused to
send for the promised *relief*, but on a second appeal he con-
sented to send for *reinforcements*, and dispatched Major, afterward Governor, John Brooks, to Cambridge to procure
them, Putnam himself hastening thither again about the same
time, or earlier, to effect the result. Ward hesitated, from
fear that the principal attack would yet be made nearer at
hand, in which case all available forces would be needed there.
Finally, though reluctantly, he ordered a third part of Stark's
regiment, or about 200 men under Colonel Lyman, to march
to Charlestown. Afterward, through the strong influence of
Richard Devens, in the Committee of Safety which was then
in session, he was prevailed upon to order the remainder of

the New Hampshire troops to the scene of action. Putnam's post was at Bunker Hill. He had seen from the start, as others did not then, but as all see now, how imperatively necessary it was to fortify that eminence as well as Breed's Hill, as the former was situated nearer the Mystic and the Neck than the latter, and so might be made instrumental in preventing the enemy from flanking the redoubt, or might serve as a safe retreat in case the fort itself should have to be abandoned. He saw the chief point of danger and the one key of the situation. There he could best survey the whole scene and superintend its general operations. Under his command, various parties which he took from Prescott's detachment, and from the New Hampshire forces as they arrived, were soon employed in throwing up on Bunker Hill the intrenchments he was so anxious to construct. In anticipation of an aggressive movement on the part of the enemy, whose barges had landed several thousand troops at Moulton's Point, at the eastern end of the peninsula, the Americans were set to work in constructing the famous rail-fence which forms so important a feature in any satisfactory account of the battle. It extended about 600 feet, in a northwesterly direction, from near the northern end of the breastwork, at the base of Breed's Hill, towards the eastern slopes of Bunker Hill, thence for about 900 feet northward to the Mystic river. It was especially the latter section of it that was now sought to be made a barricade against the foe, as it came to be evident to Putnam that there was not time to complete his intrenchments on the hill in the rear. It was formed by placing portions of fence-work near each other in parallel lines and by stuffing between them and capping them with new-mown hay from the immediate vicinity, the work being chiefly wrought by the men from New Hampshire and Connecticut, who with others were to line it in the hour of action. Stark and his men were at the extreme left of the lines, by the Mystic; Reed was at his right; and next to him, at the right again, were Captain Knowlton and his Connecticut braves, while still further towards Breed's Hill were parts of Massachusetts regiments and companies, Prescott being in immediate command of the redoubt, at the extreme right. With the more extended field as just indicated, he had nothing to do. As Mr. Richard Frothingham, the historian, candidly admits: "Colonel Prescott was left in uncontrolled possession of his post. Nor is there any proof that he gave an order at the rail fence or on Bunker Hill." Of the *supreme* command, the late Mr. W. W. Wheildon, who was exceptionally familiar with all these local history matters, writes: "Of course, this could only be assumed by a superior officer, and this officer, beyond all question, would be General Putnam," who "necessarily became commander of the Battle and very sensibly and satisfactorily left Colonel Prescott in full command of the redoubt."

Soon after three o'clock, General Howe, the British commander, led on his formidable double column of grenadiers and light infantry solidly against the rail-fence and the yeomanry who were there, while the fire of his left wing under Pigot was kept up on the fort as a feint to divert the attention of the Provincials from the more serious point of attack. Putnam, who had charged his men "not to fire until they saw the white of the enemy's eyes," and to take good care to pick off the officers by aiming at their waistbands, was now, as in all the action, at the front, assigning fresh troops their places as they arrived, riding back and forth along the lines, encouraging his soldiers to be valiant and faithful, and exposing himself to the greatest peril. Tremendous as was the onset, it was in vain. The proud foe was hurled back with fearful confusion and destruction. Again the British General rallied his forces and made another and most vigorous and determined assault. Putnam, during the lull, had ridden over Bunker Hill to urge on the expected, but tardy re-inforcements, yet with little effect. He returned to be once more conspicuous in the fight, and again there was a gallant and effective repulse, "as murderous as the first." Here, along these more exposed, unsheltered lines, was the most protracted and terrible fighting of the day. Said Stark, "The dead lay as thick as sheep in a fold." Then it was that the enraged enemy, who had thus twice been foiled in their efforts to flank the redoubt, directed their main force against the redoubt itself, enfilading the breastwork, storming the height, rushing into the little enclosure and furiously assailing the greatly reduced garrison. It became a hand-to-hand and bloody, but unequal contest. Prescott soon ordered a retreat, and the escape of his surviving heroes was followed by the flight of the cowardly "reinforcements" who had kept aloof from the strife and had rendered no service during the day. The colonel pursued his sad way to Cambridge to report to Ward that the battle was lost. Seeing that the redoubt had been taken, Putnam and what was left of the main body of the army, who had been so brave and stubborn, were also obliged to retreat from the rail-fence. In vain he passionately besought and sternly commanded his men to make one stand more on Bunker Hill. Finding this impossible, he led them forth to Prospect Hill, where he intrenched that same day in full sight of the enemy. There he was still recognized by the central authority as the leader of the host. Immediately and repeatedly, General Ward sent him reinforcements from Massachusetts regiments, until he had in a short time not less than four or five thousand men under him, at that important point.[30]

Though compelled to surrender his post, Prescott was an admirable soldier. His only military distinction, previous to the Revolution, had been that he had served as lieutenant under General Winslow in the conquest of Nova Scotia and had been urged by British officers to accept a commission in the royal army. But this latter he had declined to do. His experience in war had been quite limited. As General Heath, who praised him highly, said, he was "unknown to fame." However meritorious his conduct as the immediate local commander at the *redoubt*, comparatively little contemporaneous or subsequent mention was made of him in connection with

[30] Stark and his brave New Hampshire men had withdrawn to Winter Hill.

the battle of Bunker Hill. He was never promoted, but continued for two years to serve in the army, for a part of the time at least under Putnam himself. He then retired to his home in Pepperell, where among old friends and neighbors he was still honored and useful to the end of his days. That such an unknown and inexperienced man should have been singled out for the supreme command of so hazardous an enterprise, when there were on the ground a half dozen or more generals who ranked him, and who were equally brave and competent and far more trained and distinguished, and that he should have been charged with the responsible trust instead of Putnam, who was not only his superior in office and service both, but who was first to suggest and the most strenuous to urge the movement, is to the last degree improbable.[31]

Owing to the secrecy with which the original detachment and expedition were partially veiled, and to the fact that Warren had been recently appointed Major General and was actually in the battle, it was for some time supposed by many that he, the illustrious patriot-martyr, must have led the American forces. As he came on the ground, Putnam offered him the command, which he refused, not having yet received his commission and having come only as a volunteer. He repaired to the redoubt where Prescott tendered him his own command, but this also he declined. The erroneous impression, as to his supremacy, gradually wore away as the facts be-

[31]Col. Samuel Adams Drake, the eminent historian, in his admirable pamphlet, entitled, *General Israel Putnam, the Commander at Bunker Hill*, says: "He (Putnam) was a veteran of the army campaigns. Beyond question he was the foremost man of that army in embryo which assembled at Cambridge after the Battle of Lexington. Not Ward, or Thomas, or Pomeroy, or even the lamented Warren, possessed its confidence to the degree that Putnam did. Mr. Frothingham truly says he 'had the confidence of the whole army.' Nature formed him for a leader; and men instinctively felt it." And with reference to the Battle of Charlestown Heights, he adds: "He alone, showed the genius and grasp of a commander there, in posting his troops, in his orders during the action, and in his fruitless endeavor to create a new position on Bunker Hill;" and "in estimating the services of General Putnam and Colonel Prescott, from a military view, the former must receive the award as the commanding officer of the field." In connection with this matter of the Bunker Hill controversy, the very able and keen discussion of the subject by Rev. Increase N. Tarbox. D.D., embraced in his Life of General Putnam, also deserves special mention. His argument, like Drake's, seems to us unanswerable.

came more and more known. Not Prescott, but Putnam, was
hailed far and near as the hero of the hour. At home and
abroad, toasts were drunk to his honor, and engravings and
other pictures of him appeared in American and European
cities, representing him as chief; and as such he passed into
history, as numberless newspapers, poems, orations, school-
books and chroniclers have borne witness. As never before,
he was now the idol of the people. Yet it was this "unbounded
popularity" and the high promotion that accompanied it,
which he never meanly sought for himself or begrudged to
others, that inspired with a feeling of envy and jealousy certain military officers whose unfriendly spirit was never wholly
repressed or concealed while yet he lived, but broke forth
with peculiar violence long after his death and when most
of those who knew him best and loved him most were in their
graves. We shall have occasion to refer to this matter again,
at the conclusion of our story.

What Washington thought of General Putnam and what he
probably thought of his action and preëminence in the battle
of Bunker Hill, he that runs may read, in the events which it
remains to outline. On the 2d of July, the "Father of his
Country" arrived at Cambridge, as the commander-in-chief
of the American Army. He brought with him the commissions for the four distinguished officers who have been mentioned as having been promoted by the Continental Congress to
be Major Generals. They occasioned much "dissatisfaction"
and "disgust" among those who thought that their own claims
to honor had been overlooked. The commissions of Ward,
Lee and Schuyler were withheld for a time in consequence.
But Putnam's, which alone had received the unanimous vote
of Congress, was presented at once by Washington's own
hand. Some of the offended officers threw up their commissions in the army by reason of the fancied slight, but were
ere long persuaded to return to the service.

In the reorganization of the army, which was to carry on
the siege of Boston, Washington gave to Putnam the com-

mand of the centre, near himself at Cambridge; to General Ward the command of the right wing at Roxbury and Dorchester; and to General Lee that of the left wing, toward the Mystic river. In the autumn Putnam fortified Cobble Hill and Lechmere's Point. In March, 1776, Washington appointed him to head a formidable force of 4,000 men in an attack on the British lines, but the plan was frustrated by a most violent storm, which prevented the boats from landing the troops. During the night of the 16th of the same month, Nook's Hill, a Dorchester height nearest Boston and commanding it, was fortified, and such was the advantage which was thus gained by the beleaguering host, that the next morning the enemy evacuated the city, and, boarding their vessels, put to sea. Putnam, with a strong force, immediately entered the town and took possession of all its important posts amidst the exultant shouts and cheers of its long-suffering people.

Washington, having previously learned that the British meditated an attack on New York, had already sent General Lee thither to construct a system of defences for the protection of that city. These works, after the departure of General Lee for the south, were pushed forward by Lord Stirling, a brigadier in the American army. Under the apprehension that the British fleet, which had sailed from Boston, would soon appear in New York harbor, Washington forwarded his troops with all possible despatch to that point, ordering Putnam to go on and temporarily take the command while he himself was to follow shortly after. Putnam, on the 7th of April, sent Colonel Prescott's Bunker Hill regiment and other parties to take possession of Governor's Island and erect on it a breastwork, and also a regiment to fortify Red Hook on the Long Island shore, directly across the narrow channel, so as to hinder more effectually any operations of the enemy's ships in that quarter. The battle of Long Island took place a few months later. In the latter part of June, the British landed in great numbers on Staten Island, and in August crossed over to Long Island and advanced towards the American lines that extended across the Brooklyn peninsula from Wallabout Bay to Gowanus Creek. General Sullivan had been in command on that side of the East river, but was now superseded by Putnam, to whom Washington thus again gave proof of his trust and confidence. Putnam retained Sullivan at the centre to guard the passes and fight the Hessians. Both of them accompanied Washington as, having come over from New York for a brief visit, he rode towards evening on the 26th of August down to the outposts and examined the situation of affairs. The fierce engagement came on during the next morning, and it was while the two armies were in deadly conflict, that General Clinton, who during the night had led a column of 10,000 British soldiers by a long, circuitous and lonely road at the distant left, where he was guided by a few tories, suddenly appeared at the rear of the Americans and overwhelmed them with disaster, Stirling who was fighting Grant far at the right sharing in the common misfortune. The wonderful retreat to New York of Washington and his shattered army amidst the darkness and fog of the succeeding night, is too well known to call for details in this connection. Certain writers, without just warrant, have blamed Putnam for the defeat because he did not anticipate and prevent Clinton's movement. The most exact, thorough and impartial, and altogether the best account of the battle, is that of Mr. Henry P. Johnston, as contained in his "Campaign of 1776," published in 1878, as Vol. III of the "Memoirs of the Long Island Historical Society." That careful and conscientious writer says that such an accusation against Putnam is "both unjust and unhistorical." . . . "No facts or inferences justify the charge. No one hinted it at the time; nor did Washington in the least withdraw confidence from Putnam during the remainder of the campaign." He adds that the responsibility cannot be fastened upon Putnam, who had just taken the command, "any more than upon Washington, who, when he left the Brooklyn lines on the evening of the 26th, must have known precisely what dispositions had been made for the night at the hills and passes." He then proceeds to show how the responsibility, if it falls on any one, falls on Sullivan, and on Colonel Miles and his regiment, whose duty it was to guard the left.

In occupying New York after the retreat, Washington assigned to Putnam the command of the city as far up as Fifteenth street, while Spencer and Heath were to guard the island from that point to Harlem and King's Bridge. On the 15th of September, five British frigates appeared and took position in Kip's Bay, on the east side, opening a tremendous fire upon the breast-work and lines of Colonel Douglas with his 300 Connecticut militia and his battalion of levies. The Colonel's panic-stricken forces fled in all directions, nor could the desperate and almost superhuman exertions of Washington and Putnam, who were soon on the ground, avail to stay their flight. Other New England troops quickly joined in the stampede, and from all points the Americans were soon flying in wild disorder towards Harlem Heights, except that General Putnam "was making his way towards New York when all were going from it," his object being to rescue Sullivan's Brigade and some artillery corps that were still in the city and conduct them to the place of safety. This was successfully accomplished, and Col. David Humphreys, who was the earliest biographer of Putnam and who was in the army and saw him frequently during that day, says: "Without his extraordinary exertions, the guards must have been inevitably lost and it is probable the entire corps would have been cut in pieces."

The battle of Harlem Heights took place on the next day, the fugitives having been vigorously pursued by the British. The advantage was with the Americans, and General Greene, referring to the engagement, said that Putnam was "in the action and behaved nobly." In the battle of White Plains, Washington sent Putnam with a detachment to the support of McDougall, but not in season to succor him before his safe retreat. Subsequently he sent him to command 5,000 troops

on the west side of the Hudson river, for the protection of
Gen. Greene who was there at Fort Lee, and who it was feared
might be attacked by the enemy. The speedy capture of
Fort Washington on the east side by the British, was the di-
rest calamity to the American cause in all the Revolutionary
War. As the commander-in-chief led his wasted army across
the Jerseys, hotly pursued by the foe, he sent Putnam forward to take command of Philadelphia which was supposed to
be in danger, and construct fortifications for its defence. Colonel Humphreys, who was still with Putnam, gives a glowing
account of his herculean labors and great success in this work,
attended as it was with manifold obstacles and discourage-
ments. While he was thus engaged, Washington crossed
the Delaware and soon won his brilliant victories at Trenton
and Princeton, which electrified the country and raised the
spirits of the tired and dejected army. As the loss of Philadelphia was now no longer feared, Putnam was stationed for the
winter at Princeton, whence he made various expeditions
against foraging parties of the enemy, taking nearly a thousand prisoners, more than 120 baggage wagons and large
quantities of provisions and other booty.

It was now of prime importance to seize and hold the Highlands on the Hudson. In May, 1777, a commission, consisting
of Generals Greene, Knox, McDougall, Wayne and George
Clinton, Governor of New York, were directed to proceed
thither, examine the defences, see what was needed, and report accordingly. This they did, and among the various works
which they recommended was an enormous boom or chain
across the river at Fort Montgomery, with other obstructions
at that point, to bar the ascent of the enemy's ships. Washington gave the command of the region to General Putnam,
who fixed his headquarters at Peekskill, on the east side of
the Hudson, and whose troops were from New York and New
England. But on the 12th of June, just as he began to exe-
cute the plan of the commission, he was ordered to forward
most of his men to Philadelphia which was now again threat-

ened by General Howe. At the same time he was obliged
to hold various regiments in readiness to march against Burgoyne, who was expected at any moment to come down from
the north. Again and again Washington called upon him for
detachments for the Delaware, directing him to reinforce
himself by militia recruits from the neighborhood or from
Connecticut. What with these many changes, the presence
around him of watchful foes, incessant marches and counter-
marches, and the miserable condition of his soldiers, so many
of whom were new and raw, Putnam's situation was pain-
fully perplexing. Some of his men deserted and others he
deemed it advisable to dismiss from the service which they
wished to abandon and for which they were unfit. He wrote
to Washington, representing to him the danger he appre-
hended from his weakened condition and saying to him that
he could not be held responsible for whatever serious conse-
quences might ensue.

Sir Henry Clinton saw his opportunity. Sailing up the
river from New York with three or four thousand troops, he
appeared in Tarrytown Bay on the 5th of October, and after
much manœuvering landed his forces at Verplanck's Point,
just below Peekskill, transferred a large body of his men to
the west side, and filed them off amidst a dense fog behind
the high banks until they reached the rear of Forts Montgomery and Clinton, whence they stormed these strongholds
which soon fell into their possession, though the commission
of generals in their report had declared them to be inaccessible from that quarter, owing to the very mountainous character of the region. The river was now open to the enemy,
who at once proceeded to ravage the country. Putnam, with
the advice of a council of officers, removed his headquarters
to Fishkill, a few miles north of Peekskill, for the safety of
his little army. The immediate commander of Fort Montgomery was Governor Clinton, who, as danger was imminent,
had been summoned from the legislature at Kingsbury by
Putnam and was urged to bring a body of militia with him.

9

Here, also, Putnam was subsequently blamed for the defeat, but Clinton nobly demanded that the censure should fall on himself and not on others, and a later court of inquiry decided that the disaster was due to a lack of men and not to the neglect or incompetency of those who were in command. Says Washington Irving : "The defences of the Highlands on which the security of the Hudson depended, were at this time weakly garrisoned, some of the troops having been sent off to reinforce the armies on the Delaware and in the north."

Sir Henry returned to New York and Putnam reoccupied Peekskill and the neighboring passes. The latter shortly wrote to Washington, announcing to him the sad intelligence of his wife's death, but with it, also, the glorious news of the surrender of Burgoyne. Five thousand men now came to Putnam from the northern army. Washington had previously suggested to him a descent upon New York and he now recommended it again, but afterward, hearing that Sir Henry was in New York and fearing he might join General Howe, he despatched Alexander Hamilton to Putnam at Peekskill and to General Gates at Albany, with orders to them to forward large bodies of troops to the vicinity of Philadelphia, the British being in possession of that city.. Putnam delayed compliance with Hamilton's instructions, being perhaps too intent on the long-meditated attack upon New York. The youthful martinet, scarcely out of his teens, wrote a bitter letter to Washington in consequence and also an insolent one to the old scarred veteran himself, who very properly sent the missive he had received to the commander-in-chief, alleging that it contained "unjust and ungenerous reflections," mentioning some of the reasons for the delay, and saying, "I am conscious of having done everything in my power to succor you as soon as possible." But the order had been a peremptory one, and Washington for the first and only time in his life reprimanded his old, trusted companion-in-arms, even as he once reprimanded Hamilton himself for an act of tardiness by saying to him, "You must change your watch, or I must change my aid." Putnam was now unpopular in New York. The people of the state were strongly prejudiced against New Englanders, and the feeling had notably manifested itself at the time of the "cowardly" and "disgraceful" flight of Connecticut and Massachusetts soldiers at Kip's Bay, while it was but natural that this dislike should be warmly reciprocated. "Yorkers" and "Yankees" were epithets which were freely bandied between the two parties. Hamilton and other leading men of his state wanted their Governor to be placed in command. Many of them held Putnam responsible for all the misfortunes on the Hudson, accused him of being too lenient with the tories in the neighborhood, and were unwilling to support the cause of their country so long as he retained his position. Colonel Humphreys, whose testimony here is very significant, avers that the chief cause of the animosity in question is to be referred to Putnam's determined opposition to the dishonesty and selfish greed of influential men who were charged with the care of the sequestrated property of tory families. But it seemed to Washington all-important to hold the state of New York to the support of the army and the government, and this was the only reason he presented for the change, when, some months after Hamilton's mission to Albany and Peekskill, he gave the command to General McDougall. As we shall see, Washington still regarded Putnam with unabated friendship and affection, and still honored him with high trusts.

Meanwhile, in the latter part of the year 1777, Putnam had set on foot several expeditions which were more or less successful. During the winter he was at the Highlands, whence he wrote to Washington, who was with his suffering army at Valley Forge :—"Dubois' regiment is unfit to be ordered on duty, there being not one blanket in the regiment; very few have either a shoe or a shirt, and most of them have neither stockings, breeches nor overalls." In company with Governor Clinton and others, he selected West Point as the site of the chief fortress, and began vigorously to put the

defences of the Hudson on a respectable footing.   About this
time he made a visit to Pomfret to attend to his private affairs.   After his return and his removal from the command
of the Highlands, he again went to Connecticut, in obedience
to orders, to hasten on the new levies of militia from that
state for the coming campaign.   Subsequent to the battle of
Monmouth, we find him in charge of the right wing of the
army, in place of General Lee who was under arrest.   In the
early autumn of 1778, he was again in the neighborhood of
West Point for the defence of the North river.   In the winter he was posted at Danbury with three brigades, to protect
the country lying along the Sound, to cover the magazines
on the Connecticut river, and to reinforce the Highlands in
case of need.   It was while he was here, that he very successfully quelled a serious mutiny that arose among some
of the troops who had endured much hardship and received
no pay, and who were preparing to march in a body to Hartford and demand redress from the General Assembly at the
point of the bayonet.   It was in this region, also, that he
posted himself with 150 men on the brow of a high, steep
eminence at Greenwich, or Horse Neck, and, as General Tryon
advanced towards him with ten times the force, dashed on his
steed down the precipice to the amazement of his pursuers
and escaped unharmed, bidding his little company to secure
their own safety by retiring to a neighboring swamp which
was inaccessible to cavalry.   He immediately collected a
party of militia, joined with them his original handful, and
hung on the rear of Tryon in his retreat, taking forty or fifty
of his men as prisoners.   These he treated with so much
kindness that Tryon, as the biographers tell us, addressed to
him a handsome note in acknowledgment, accompanied with
a present of a complete suit of clothes, though it does not
appear that there was any attempt again to supersede the
General for such manifest and highly appreciated "aid and
comfort" to the enemy !

General Putnam's military career was now hastening to its

close.   In the spring of 1779, Sir Henry Clinton was preparing for a campaign up the North river.   Late in May, Washington moved his army towards the Highlands from Middlebrook.   Putnam crossed the river and joined the main body in the Clove, one of the deep defiles, where in the latter part of June he was left in immediate command, while Washington took up his headquarters at New Windsor, and then, about a month later or a few days after the brilliant capture of Stony Point by Wayne, at West Point.   Putnam's post was at Buttermilk Falls, two miles below.   As if it was determined by his great chief, that he should not be sacrificed to the enmity of his foes, he was here given the command of the right wing of the army, having under him troops from Pennsylvania, Maryland and Virginia.   It was from July to December, of this year, that the most important works at West Point and in its vicinity were chiefly constructed.   One of his biographers says ; "Experienced in this department, he took an active and efficient part in completing the fortifications which had been laid out under his own eye and the site for which had been selected through his agency.   He had the honor of giving his own name to the principal fort."   Sir Henry contented himself with depredations in other quarters.

While the army was in winter quarters, Putnam again visited his family in Pomfret.   On returning to the camp, he was attacked with paralysis, which seriously affected the use of his limbs on one side and which obliged him to retrace his steps and pass the remainder of his days at home.   He had strong hopes that he might yet be well enough to join once more his comrades and engage in active service, but this was not to be. Yet he lived for ten years more, was able to take a moderate amount of exercise in walking and riding, retained full possession of his mental faculties, was an object of great interest and veneration on the part of his neighbors and the people generally, was fond of relating stories of the wars in which he had been engaged to groups of young and old who were wont to gather around him, and was quick and eager to learn all he could about the campaigns in which he could not now participate and the affairs of the country he could no longer serve. When in 1783 the Treaty of Peace had been concluded between England and America and the cause he loved had gloriously triumphed, he sent his congratulations to Washington, from whom he received in reply a beautiful and touching letter, full of grateful recollections and of the old undying friendship.

"In 1786," says the letter of Hon. Samuel Putnam from which we have already twice quoted, "he rode on horseback from Brooklyn to Danvers and paid his last visit to his friends there. On his way home, he stopped at Cambridge at the college, where the governor of the college paid him much attention. It was in my junior year; he came into my room. His speech was much affected by palsy."

In the month of May, 1790, he was violently attacked with an inflammatory disease, which from the first he was satisfied would prove mortal. It was of short duration, continuing but a few days. On the 29th[32] he passed to his rest, "calm, resigned, and full of cheerful hope." And the narrator adds: "The grenadiers of the 11th Regiment, the Independent Corps of Artillerists and the militia companies in the neighborhood, assembled each at their appointed rendezvous early on the morning of June 1st, and having repaired to the late dwelling house of the deceased, a suitable escort was formed, attended by a procession of Masonic brethren present and a large concourse of respectable citizens, which moved to the Congregational meeting-house in Brooklyn; and, after divine service performed by the Rev. Dr. Whitney, all that was earthly of a patriot and hero was laid in the silent tomb, under the discharge of volleys from the infantry, and minute guns from the artillery." Mr. Whitney's funeral sermon, afterward published, dwelt touchingly upon the exalted virtues and merit of his departed parishioner whom he had

---

[32] We correct here a long perpetuated error as to the dates of General Putnam's death and burial. See account in *Salem Press Record*, of May and June, 1892.

known intimately for many years, rendering the highest testimony to his character as a Christian man, as an ardent lover and noble defender of his country, and as a most faithful, excellent and beloved citizen, husband, father and friend. In due time a monument was erected over his grave, bearing an epitaph which was written by the celebrated Rev. Timothy Dwight, D.D., President of Yale College, who also knew him well, and whose marble inscription states that "he dared to lead where any dared to follow," that his "generosity was singular and his honesty was proverbial," and that "he raised himself to universal esteem, and offices of eminent distinction, by personal worth and a useful life."

In 1818, long years after the old warrior had sunk to his rest and a grateful country had recorded his name high on the roll of her noblest defenders, the malignant feeling which has been adverted to on a previous page and which had all the while lain smothered and rankling in the breasts of a few surviving officers of the Revolution, at length found vent in a published "Account of the Battle of Bunker Hill," by General Henry Dearborn. It denied to Putnam, not only the command, but also any active participation in that engagement; represented him as cowardly, unfaithful, and base in his conduct on the occasion; and otherwise sought to blacken his memory. The public was stung to indignation and rage. The press denounced the calumny and its author. Notable men came forward to voice the righteous anger of the people, and confute the statements and allegations of the accuser. Col. Daniel Putnam, the able and highly esteemed son of the departed veteran, whom we have seen with his father at the plow in Pomfret, on the arrival of the news from Lexington, April 20. 1775, wrote and published an eloquent and triumphant answer, of which, with another letter from the same source, John Adams said; "Neither myself nor my family have been able to read either with dry eyes ;" they "would do honor to the pen of Pliny." Other distinguished sons of Connecticut, like Thomas Grosvenor and John Trumbull, confirmed the manly and telling reply with their weighty words. Hon. John Lowell, of Boston, gave to the press a series of trenchant articles in which he exposed the envious and vindictive spirit of the attack and effectually riddled the attempted falsification of history. Daniel Webster appeared on the scene and in his own masterful way vindicated the character of the slandered dead. Col. Samuel Swett issued his fresh and full account of the battle already mentioned, in which he set forth, in detail, the patriotic and heroic part which Putnam had taken in it, as the chief of the contending provincial forces. Aged soldiers, who were perhaps supposed to have also passed away, but who were still lingerers on the stage in many a section of New England, rose on every side as from their graves, to testify anew their love and loyalty to their lamented leader, and to stamp as false his traducer's charges and declarations. And the state of Massachusetts had not long to wait for an opportunity to set its formal and final seal to the just and general verdict.

Yet Dearborn was not alone in his bitterness at what he repeatedly and ruefully refers to as the "extraordinary popularity," the "universal popularity," or the "ephemeral and unaccountable popularity" of Putnam; nor was he alone responsible for the groundless and wicked aspersions which he made. The substance of these first appeared, as early as the year 810, in a sketch of General Stark, published in a New ampshire paper which was not less hostile to Putnam than was favorable to the "hero of Bennington," the editor's personal friend. Stark, who was an able officer and a very brave in battle, was the reputed author or source of the actions. He was a person of strong passions and prejudices, sensitive to slights and had on several occasions during his ry career thrown up his command when he had thought s own claims to preferment had been overlooked, or when had been promoted and he had not. He was one of ho had been made unhappy by Putnam's high honors and pularity; and the annoyance was not a little intensihe circumstance that he had been worsted in a court

AN INTERIOR. JOSEPH PUTNAM HOUSE, DANVERS.
CHAMBER WHERE GEN. ISRAEL PUTNAM WAS BORN.

trial, at which a case of Putnam's interference with certain irregularities among the New Hampshire troops was brought forward for examination and decision. The enmity seems never to have died out. It was shared not only by Dearborn, who was a captain in Stark's regiment at Bunker Hill, but also by Major Caleb Stark, the colonel's or general's son. One of these, at least, was at length busy in seeking supports for their strange story of the battle and in privately disseminating it abroad as he found opportunity. During the year following the great event, Stark, the father, appears to have given his version of it to the infamous General James Wilkinson. When, in 1815, the latter was preparing for publication what McMaster, in his new *History of the people of the United States*, justly describes as his "three ponderous volumes of memoirs, as false as any yet written by man,"—he wrote to Major Stark for fuller information about the occurrences of June 17, 1775, asking him for aid in procuring subscriptions for his work, and informing him of his desire or purpose to correct certain prevalent misconceptions concerning matters of Revolutionary history ! He had already heard from Dearborn.

The bait took. The major was pleased, sent him some things that he wanted, referred him to *Dearborn for more*, and wished him abundant success in his literary enter, ise. And then it was, that Wilkinson embraced in his "false" and "ponderous" volumes an account of the battle as written by himself, and as based upon the testimony of this little coterie o. Putnam's enemies. It is with reference to these memoirs, published in 1816, that Richard Frothingham himself says, in his *Siege of Boston;* "This work contains the earliest reflections on General Putnam's conduct on this occasion, either printed or in manuscript, that I have met." The historian had not seen the New Hampshire paper of 1810. Its detraction had died an early death. Wilkinson's renewal of it, six years later, also produced no particular effect on the public mind. It was left to Dearborn to stir it into life again, and it was only when one who had creditably filled so many prominent positions as he had held, dragged it forth once more, two years later yet, for wider notice, charged with a still more venomous spirit, that it received any general attention, or that it was deemed worth the while to brand it as it deserved. And now it remains to be added, that it is just these perversions and falsifications of the truth, which were prompted by such unworthy motives and had such ignoble beginnings, and which were then brought forward in their more amplified and offensive form forty-three years after the battle of Bunker Hill and more than a quarter of a century after General Putnam and the vast majority of his contemporaries had passed from earth, but *only a few months after the death of Colonel Humphreys*, his old personal friend, his intimate companion in war, and up to the time of this juncture his sole biographer—a circumstance, of which Mr. Webster makes mention—that, in lack of better material, were seized upon by partisans of Prescott as props for their new theory of his supreme command on the ever memorable day. Whoever will read attentively what these friends and eulogists of the Pepperell soldier have written about the battle cannot fail to see what eager and extensive use they have made of the discredited testimony, and with what pains-taking and disingenuous skill they have woven it into their narratives for the end in view. Certain Stark men, of New Hampshire, in their antipathy to Putnam, feel that they can safely enough extol Prescott, his supposititious rival, while yet they labor to lift to proud preëminence their own hero and essay to remove the one fatal obstacle by alleging that the army in the field, as a whole, was without an actual and responsible head. The Prescott men regard the latter con-tention with complacency, so long as their own favorite is exalted, and common cause is made against Putnam. Whatever jealousy exists between the two parties is held in abeyance, as both alike are made to realize that there is another com-mander whose claims are paramount to those of either Stark or Prescott, and whom it is for the interest of both parties to disparage, to ignore and to get rid of. Hence their constant and studied endeavor, while they may not still venture the more brutal defamations that were found to be so unprofitable in earlier years of the century, to minimize as much as possible Putnam's best action or service; to magnify and give credence to idle things that have been said to his prejudice; to conceal or weaken the force of the evidence that goes to establish his supremacy; and, as in some recent instances, to leave him out of sight altogether, not even his name being mentioned, as if he had no part or lot in the matter. And this is the way that some men write history. A late cycloramic representation of the battle, following such authorities, made Prescott and the redoubt at the extreme right of the lines the only real object of attention or interest, had nothing to show of the tremendous conflict at the rail-fence, and Dearborn-like placed Putnam far in the safe background, quietly sitting on his horse, and apparently engaged in conversation with a bystander and unconcerned about what was going on in full view before him.

But General Putnam, however he has himself been maligned or wronged, never by word or act betrayed any such feeling of jealousy, hatred, or revenge towards others. He was swift and severe to upbraid and chastise those who were cravens or skulkers in the hour of imminent peril. But the records furnish no proof that he ever regarded with even the slightest envy or rancor any of his comrades. He never sought to undermine the good reputation or the fair fame of those who deserved well of their country. He was not troubled at their popularity or promotions, and as little did he seek by unworthy means or with a selfish spirit his own advantage or distinction. The honors and the praise that came to him were the free, unbought and spontaneous gifts of the state, the government and the people, whom he so gallantly served, and to whom he so gladly devoted the strength of his earlier and later years. He was as kind as he was generous, and he was as brave as he was magnanimous. Foremost in the strife, he was also last at the post of danger when others fled the scene. He knew how to spare a fallen foe, and he knew as well how to be loyal and true to his friends. He wore no masks, but was frank, open and honest, and as transparent as the day. His was no dark, sinister, tricky or deceitful nature; and President Dwight most truthfully said of him;—"His word was regarded as an ample security for anything for which it was pledged, and his uprightness commanded absolute confidence."

He was not without his faults, defects, or mistakes. Neither were any of his contemporaries, however great or good. If, like others, he was bluff and unlettered, it may be remembered that he had but few early school or social advantages, and that very much of his maturer life was spent on the frontiers or in the camp. If his words lacked polish or refinement, they were, at least, clear and vigorous and to the point.[33]

If he was not one of the great commanders or strategists, yet was he a bold and fiery leader and inspirer of men, whose rare natural genius and aptitudes for military service were everywhere recognized and always called into requisition, and whose more daring, and dashing kind of warfare was often quite as necessary and useful as the faculty which he may not have so fully possessed for arranging complicated plans and combining numerous forces for a more extensive scene of operations. Washington said of him, that he was "a most valuable man and a fine executive officer," and it has been seen how frequently and how continuously he assigned to him the most important trusts he had at his disposal, until the growing infirmities of age unfitted him for the burden. Against all attempts of smaller men, who did not know him, or have

[33] We copy, by way of illustration, the characteristic letter which General Putnam wrote to Sir Henry Clinton in reply to an insolent and threatening message sent him by that British commander under a flag of truce, demanding the release and return of a tory spy who had been caught in the American camp. It runs as follows:

" HEADQUARTERS, 7 AUGUST, 1777.

" Sir: Edmund Palmer, an officer in the Enemy's service, was taken as a spy, lurking within our lines. He has been tried as a spy, condemned as a spy, and shall be executed as a spy and the flag is ordered to depart immediately.
                                                        "ISRAEL PUTNAM.

P. S.—He has been accordingly hanged."

not learned who or what he was, to write him down by be-
littling his capacity or his patriotism, we place that simple and
sufficing testimony of one who knew him long and well,
who was "first in war, first in peace, and first in the hearts
of his countrymen," and whose judgment may perhaps be
not unreasonably preferred to that of the critics and censors
of a later time.   Like so many of the military officers of his
day, Putnam, it is said, often indulged in profane language.
If he did, he had the manliness and grace openly to confess
and renounce his sin and express his sorrow for it, thereby
giving to all who villify, as well as all who blaspheme, a good
example which they may well follow.   Whatever forbidden
word he may have made use of under the sway of vehement
passion, and amidst the heat and stress of battle, few men
were at heart more reverent of God and sacred things than
was he.

A distinguished grandson of the General, Judge Judah
Dana, who was formerly United States Senator from Maine,
wrote the following description of the subject of our sketch:

"In his person, for height about the middle size, very erect, thick-set,
muscular and firm in every part. His countenance was open, strong, and
animated; the features of his face large, well proportioned to each
other and to his whole frame; his teeth fair and sound till death.   His
organs and senses were all exactly fitted for a warrior; he heard quickly,
saw to an immense distance, and though he sometimes stammered in
conversation, his voice was remarkably heavy, strong and commanding.
Though facetious and dispassionate in private, when animated in the heat
of battle his countenance was fierce and terrible, and his voice like thunder.
His whole manner was admirably adapted to inspire his soldiers with
courage and confidence, and his enemies with terror. The faculties of
his mind were not inferior to those of his body; his penetration was acute;
decision rapid, yet remarkably correct; and the more desperate the situation, the more collected and undaunted. With the courage of a lion, he had
a heart that melted at the sight of distress; he could never witness suffering in any human being without becoming a sufferer himself. Martial
music roused him to the highest pitch, while solemn sacred music sent him
into tears.   In his disposition he was open and generous almost to a fault,
and in his social relations he was never excelled."

Of the many other just and eloquent tributes which eminent Americans have paid to General Putnam's memory, the

following from Washington Irving may fitly conclude our story :

"A yeoman warrior, fresh from the plough, in the garb of rural labor; a patriot brave and generous, but rough and ready, who thought not of himself in time of danger, but was ready to serve in any way, and to sacrifice official rank and self-glorification to the good of the cause. He was eminently a soldier for the occasion. His name has long been a favorite one with young and old. one of the talismanic names of the Revolution, the very mention of which is like the sound of a trumpet. Such names are the precious jewels of our history, to be garnered up among the treasures of the nation, and kept immaculate from the tarnishing breath of the cynic and the doubter."[34]

IV. 97 Samuel (*John, Nathaniel, John*), born in Salem Village, 5 Nov., 1684; baptized 8 Feb., 1684–85, at Salem; died at Sudbury, 20 Dec., 1753; married at Salem, 19 Oct., 1709, Mary, daughter of John and Elizabeth (Flint) Leach, born 3 Mar., 1684–5.

Children, born at Salem Village :

251　SAMUEL, b. 24 Feb., 1711–12; probably m. 1748, Mary Pratt.[35] Perhaps the Samuel who was taxed in Framingham, 1737.

252　JOHN, b. 8 Oct., 1715; bapt. 6 May, 1716; d. Apr., 1762.

253　DANIEL, b. 27 Nov., 1717; bapt. 11 Oct., 1719; d. Sudbury.

254　ELIZABETH, b. 2 Dec., 1719; bapt. 10 Sept., 1721; m. —— Robbins of Bolton where they settled.

255　HANNAH, b. 7 July, 1722; bapt. 16 Dec., 1722.

256　NATHAN, b. 7 June, 1725; bapt. 5 Sept., 1725.

257　MARY, b. 13 Feb., 1729; bapt. 23 Feb., 1728; m. —— Whitcomb, of Bolton, where they settled and had a small family.

SAMUEL PUTNAM was at one time a large land owner and prosperous farmer in Danvers, but having become surety for a friend was obliged to surrender his property, except a small farm in Sudbury, in order to meet this endorsement. On this Sudbury farm he spent the remainder of his days. His grandson, John Putnam, stated, in 1833, that Samuel was a short thick-set man. He remembered him well.

"Dec. 20, 1753. This day between ten and eleven at night

---

[34] My thanks are due to the Rev. Alfred P. Putnam of Concord for this valuable and interesting account of the life of Gen. Israel Putnam.—E. P.

[35] Framingham Records say "Samuel Putnam, m. 27 July, 1748, Mary Pratt of Framingham. There was also a Samuel Putnam who went from Sudbury to Crown Point in 1756.

Died Mr. Samuel Putnam of a fever taken on Monday night, æ. 66." [36]

IV. 98 Josiah (*John, Nathaniel, John*), born at Salem Village, 29 Oct., 1686; died at Danvers, 5 July, 1766; will proved 2 Sept., 1766, dated 8 June, 1762, wife Ruth, sons Josiah, Enos, Asa, daughters Ruth and Elizabeth; married at Salem Village, 19 Feb., 1712–13, Ruth, daughter of Joseph and Elizabeth (Swinnerton) Hutchinson of the Village, born there 26 Feb., 1690–1.

Children, baptized at Salem Village :

258   Asa, b. 31 July, bapt. 15 Aug., 1714.
259   Enos, b. 6 Oct., 1716; bapt. 10 Feb. 1717; d. 1780.
260   Josiah, b. 8 Mar., 1718–19; bapt. 8 May, 1719.
261   Peter, bapt. 5 Apr., 1724.
262   Elizabeth, bapt. 4 July, 1725; m. William Putnam[37] of Sterling.
263   Elisha. bapt. 24 Mar., 1727–28.
264   Ruth, bapt. 4 June, 1732; m. —— Russell.

Josiah Putnam and his wife were received into the church 10 Dec., 1727. He is styled "Yeoman" and seems not to have taken much part in town affairs. He lived in a house built after 1714.

IV. 103 Joshua (*John, Nathaniel, John*), born in Salem Village, between 1690 and 1694; died in 1739; married in Salem, 2 Feb., 1721, Rachel Goodale. Administration on estate of Joshua Putnam was granted to his widow Rachel, 8 Mar., 1730–1, and 1 Aug., 1744, administration on estate of Rachel Putnam and also of Joshua Putnam to their son-in-law, John Preston.

Children, baptized in Salem Village :

265   Hannah, b. 16 June, 1722; bapt. 15 Jan., 1726; d. 28 Mar.,[38] 1771; m. 12 July, 1744, John, son of John and Elizabeth Preston, b. in Salem Village, 4 Sept., 1717; d. 14 June, 1771. Ch. : Elizabeth, b. 9 May, 1745; m. Abel Nichols, Dec. 30, 1766; m. 2nd, Bartholomew Trask, 1785. John, b. 3 Sept., 1746; m. Mehitable White.

[36] Ancient diary kept by a Sudbury gentleman.
[37] Authority of Rufus Putnam.
[38] See account of Preston family on page 73.

Philip, b. 30 Oct., 1748; d. 29 May, 1749. Joshua, b. 27 March, 1751; d. 11 May, 1751. David, b. 20 March, 1752; d. 16 Jan. 1774. Hannah, b. 3 Aug., 1754; m. Amos Tapley, 19 May, 1772; d. 20 Oct., 1825. Capt. Levi, b. 21 Oct., 1756; m. Mehitable Nichols. Moses, b. 20 Apr., 1758; m. Sarah Berry. Aaron, b. 24 Mar., 1760; d 9 Apr., 1760. Daniel, b. 11 June, 1761; d. 1 July, 1762.

266 MARY, b. 26 June, 1727; bapt. 15 Oct., 1727; m., 1744, Timothy, son of Joseph and Elizabeth C. (Robinson) Prince. Ch.: Samuel, bapt. 31 May, 1747. Phebe, bapt. 18 Dec., 1748. Betty, bapt. 22 Dec., 1751. Timothy, bapt. 7 Nov., 1756. Hannah, bapt. 19 Oct., 1760.

267 RACHEL, b. 2 Dec., 1728; unm. in 1744.

IV. 105 John (*John, Nathaniel, John*), born in Salem Village, 16 Aug., 1691; baptized there, 23 Aug., 1691; died 10 Feb., 1764. Will dated 8 Oct., 1763; proved 9 Apr., 1764. He married, first, 16 Mar., 1717, Rachel Buxton; married, second, Lydia, daughter of Samuel and Love (Howe) Porter, born, 1692; died, 22 Apr., 1777, mentioned in her husband's will. In his will he gives his son Amos 10s.; son Edmund, £40; son John all his lands and buildings.

Children, born in Salem Village, all mentioned in their father's will :

268 LYDIA, b. 1718; d. 22 Nov., 1789 (pub. 14 Jan., 1737-8); m. 2 Mar., 1737-8, David Goodale, of Salem. Ch.: David, b. 16 Dec., 1738. Lydia, b. 20 Nov., 1740. Emma, b. 21 Jan., 1743. Phebe, b. 4 Feb., 1745. Ede, b. 16 Sept., 1747; d. 12 Apr., 1770. Huldah, b. 5 Apr., 1750. Sarah, b. 5 July, 1754. Hannah, b. 5 June, 1758. Judith, b. 20 Apr., 1761; d. in Cambridge, 4 May, 1837; m. 15 June, 1780, Daniel Harris.[39] Andrew, b. 11 Nov., 1765.

269 ISRAEL, mentioned in his grandmother Love's will dated 12 July, 1759; proved 13 Sept., 1762.

270 JOHN, b. 1720; bapt. 11 Oct., 1724.

271 AMOS, b. 1722; bapt. 11 Oct., 1724.

272 EDMUND, b. 1724; bapt. 27 June, 1725.

273 EMMA, b. 1727; bapt. 9 July, 1727; m. 20 July, 1748 (pub. 30 Apr.,

[39] Daniel Harris was b. in Dorchester, July, 1752; d. in Fitchburg, 16 Dec., 1820. His parents were Thomas and Lucy (Pierce) Harris. He was at Bunker Hill and served throughout the Revolution. There were twelve children born to Daniel and Judith Harris, the third child and oldest son being Daniel, b. in Fitchburg, 21 June, 1784; d. 18 June, 1858, who was captured in the war of 1812 and confined in Dartmouth Prison. He was grandfather of A. Scott Harris, of Chelsea, who is also descended from William Towne, the father of Rebecca Nurse and Mary Estey.

1748), James Swinnerton. of Danvers. Ch.: Emma, bapt. 16 Mar., 1755. Phebe, bapt. 15 Feb., 1761. James, bapt. 11 Jan., 1767.

274 PHEBE, b. 1723; bapt. 22 Sept., 1723; m. (pub. 11 Mar., 1746-7) Gilbert Tapley, of Danvers. Ch.: Daniel, bapt. 23 Dec., 1750. Joseph, 11 Apr., 1756. Aaron, bapt. 4 Feb., 1759. Asa, bapt. 20 Sept., 1761. Elijah, bapt. 6 July, 1766. Seelah, bapt. 24 May, 1772.

275 EDE. b. 1733; bapt. 29 July, 1733; m. John Swinnerton. Ch.: Ede. Hannah. Both bapt. 16 Nov., 1760.

IV. 107 Amos (*John, Nathaniel, John*), born in Salem Village, 27 Jan., 1697; baptized there, 27 Nov., 1698; died, 1774. Will dated 15 June, 1773, proved 8 Nov., 1774, son Daniel, executor. He married Hannah, mentioned in her husband's will.

Children :

276 HANNAH, bapt. Salem Village, 1 Oct., 1727; d. before 1773.
277 AMOS, b. 1723; bapt. 31 Oct., 1729.
278 JOSHUA, b. 1732-3; bapt. 25 Feb., 1732-3.
279 UZZIEL, b. 1735; bapt. 12 Oct., 1735.
280 DANIEL, b. 1738; bapt. 26 Nov., 1738.
281 LYDIA, bapt. 14 June, 1741; m., 1st, Samuel Putnam (No. 397); m., 2d, Capt. Timothy Page.

In a will, dated 29 Mar., 1769, Amos calls himself "Yeoman, of Danvers." He gives to his three eldest sons his lands in New Salem, to his son Daniel, his farm and property in Danvers and Middleton.

IV. 120 Deacon Nathaniel (*Benjamin, Nathaniel, John*), born in Salem Village, 25 Aug., 1686; died 21 Oct., 1754; married in Salem, 4 June, 1709, Hannah Roberts, who died about 1763.

Children, born in Salem Village :

282 NATHANIEL, b. ———; bapt. 1 Oct., 1710; d. 4 Mar., 1711.
283 JACOB, b. 9 Mar., 1711-12; bapt. 20 Apr., 1712.
284 NATHANIEL, b. 4 Apr., 1714; bapt. 2 May, 1714; d. 11 Feb., 1720.
285 SARAH, b. 1 June, 1716; bapt. 2 Sept., 1716; unm. in 1763.
286 ARCHELAUS, b. 29 May, 1718.
287 EPHRAIM, b. 10 Feb., 1719-20; bapt. 3 Apr., 1720.
288 HANNAH, b. 4 Mar., 1721-2; d. in Amherst, N. H., 1802; m. (pub. 22 Oct., 1746), Solomon, son of Ebenezer and Hannah (Gould) Hutchinson, of Souhegan West (Amherst, N. H.), b. in Salem Village, 1721; d. Fayette, Me., about 1815. Ch.: Sol-

10

omon, b. in Salem Village, 10 Nov., 1750; d. in Fayette, Me.,
1821. Ebenezer, b. in Danvers, 22 Mar., 1753; d. in Ohio, 1828.
Asa, b. in Amherst, N. H., 17 Nov., 1759; d. in Fayette, Me.,
27 June, 1848. Hittie, b. 1760; d. Hillsboro, N. H., 1799; m.
———— Crain. Hannah, b. 1778; d. Sept., 1821.

289 NATHANIEL, b. 28 May, 1724; bapt. 21 June, 1724.
290 MEHITABLE, b. 26 Feb., 1726–7; bapt. 19 Mar., 1726–7; m. Reuben
Harriman, of Haverhill, N. H. (see note, p. 86). (Salem Records
state that on 4 June, 1747, Reuben Harrington of Haverhill,
N. H., and Mehitable Putnam of Salem were married.)
291 KEZIA, m. ———— Marble.

NATHANIEL PUTNAM was a yeoman and lived in Danvers,
perhaps part of the time in North Reading. Elected deacon
of the First Church at Danvers, Nov. 15, 1731.

The following children and grandchildren were living in
1763 and signed receipts for their share of the estate of widow
Hannah Putnam.

Son, Jacob Putnam.
Daughter, Sarah Putnam.
    "   Hannah Hutchinson.
Son, Reuben Harriman, for his wife Mehitable.
Daughter, Kezia Marble.
Grandson, Archelaus Putnam, jr.
Asa Putnam, for his daughter Hannah, a daughter-in-law of above
    Hannah Putnam deceased.
Grandson, Elisha Putnam.
Grandchildren, Jeremiah and Sarah Hutchinson.

IV. 121 Tarrant (*Benjamin, Nathaniel, John*), born in
Salem Village, 12 Apr., 1688; died, 1732 or 1733; married
8 June, 1715, Elizabeth, daughter of Jonathan and Elizabeth
(Giles) Bacon, born 26 Nov., 1695; died 23 Aug., 1761.

Administration was granted on his estate to his widow
Elizabeth who was then with child, 10 Mar., 1732. Elizabeth Putnam gave bonds with Nathaniel and Jonathan Putnam. The will was probated 9 April, 1733.

Children, all born and baptized at Salem Village:

292 TARRANT, b. 3 Apr., bapt. 6 May, 1716.
293 ELIZABETH, b. 20 May; bapt. 8 June, 1718; m. Samuel (*Eleazer,
John, John*) Putnam (No. 159).
294 SOLOMON, b. 5 June, bapt. 19 June, 1720; adm. on estate granted

to his brother Gideon, 26 Apr., 1752. Of Salem in 1747. Blacksmith.

293 MARY, b. 26 April, bapt. 3 May, 1724; m. 27 Feb. 1752, Samuel[40] Endicott.

296 GIDEON, b. 29 May, 1726; bapt. 12 June, 1726.

297 ISRAEL, b. 24 Sept., 1730; bapt. 27 Sept. 1730.

298 SARAH, b. 29 Apr. 1733; bapt. 6 May, 1733, "of Elizabeth widow of Tarrant Putnam." On 14 May, 1752, guardianship was granted to Samuel Putnam.

TARRANT PUTNAM inherited the homestead from his father under the latter's will of date of 28 Oct., 1706.

IV. 123 Benjamin (*Benjamin, Nathaniel, John*), born in Salem Village, 8 Jan., 1692-3; died at Danvers, 1744. His will is dated 28 May, and was proved, 15 Oct., 1744. He married, first, 9 June, 1715, at the Village, Bethiah, daughter of Joseph and Elizabeth Hutchinson of Danvers, born 24 Dec., 1693, died 9 Dec., 1726; married, second, 5 Mar., 1727-8, Abigail, daughter of John and Mary (Gould) Hutchinson of Danvers, an own cousin of his first wife, born at Salem Village, 17 Mar., 1702; survived her husband. John Hutchinson, father of Abigail (Hutchinson) Putnam, was a farmer in Danvers, but owned land in Sutton, out of which he sold a farm to Cornelius Putnam.

Children, by Bethiah, all born and baptized at the Village:

299 A dau., b. 2 Sept.; d. 10 Oct., 1716.

300 A dau., b. and d. 8 Oct., 1717.

301 BENJAMIN, b. 12 Oct.; bapt. 18 Oct., 1718; d. 26 Apr., 1796.

302 A son, b. and d. 31 May, 1721.

303 EUNICE, b. 21 May, bapt. 10 June, 1722; m. 19 Mar., 1739-40, Francis, son of Samuel and Dorothy (Faulkner) Nurse,[41] b. in Danvers, 6 June, 1717; d. there 7 Apr., 1780. They lived on the old Nurse homestead. Francis Nurse m., 2d, 1769, Hannah Endicott. Ch.: by Eunice (Putnam) were, Samuel, b. 25 Mar., 1742; d., unm. 1766. Peter, b. 25 Mar., 1744; m. Lydia Law, removed to Rockingham, Vt. Philip, b. 10 July, 1748. Eunice, b. 2 May, 1752; m. William Fiske, of Amherst, N. H. Benjamin, b. 5 Apr., 1755;

---

[40] According to the Endicott Genealogy printed in the N. E. H. & G. Reg., Vol. 1, she married Samuel, son of Samuel and Anna (Endicott) Endicott. b. in Danvers, 12 Mar., 1717; d. 10 Dec., 1773. Ch.: Sarah, b. 1733. Samuel, b. 1734. Solomon, b. 1757; Mary, b., 1758. Anna, b. 1762; d. unm. Deborah, b. 1767.

[41] See Putnam's Monthly Historical Magazine, Vol. I, for genealogy of Nurse family.

d. 5 Feb., 1818; m. 20 Nov., 1781, Ruth Tarbell, and had twelve children. Among his descendants is Benjamin Nurse Goodale, of Saco, Me. Phebe, b. 21 or 25 of Sept., 1757; d. unm. Jacob, b. 11 May, 1760. Abigail, b. Jan. or June, 13, 1762; m. O. Spaulding, of Merrimac, N. H. Edie or Edith, b. 17 May, 1765; m. John Odell, of Amherst. By the second marriage, there was one child: Allen, b. 30 July, 1771; m. Ruth Putnam and had the following children: Polly, Pamella, Ruth, Samuel, Endicott, Hannah, Eliza.

304   A son, b. and d. 10 Mar., 1725.
305   A dau., b 26 Nov.; d. 11 Dec., 1726.

By Abigail:

306   ABIGAIL, b. 27 June, 1727, d. y.
307   ABIGAIL, b. 1 Jan., 1729; bapt. 4 Jan., 1729–30.

BENJAMIN PUTNAM was of Danvers, was a yeoman, and of good estate. He joined with the church, 4 Mar., 1715. Bethia, his wife, joined 30 Nov., 1715.

In his will dated 28 May, 1744, he appoints his son Benjamin executor, and his brothers Stephen and Nathaniel to be overseers. His widow and children, Benjamin, Eunice and Abigail, are mentioned in that instrument.

IV. 124 Lieutenant Stephen (*Benjamin, Nathaniel, John*), born in Salem Village, 27 Oct., 1694; died 1772; married, at Salem, 30 May, 1718, Miriam, daughter of John and Hannah Putnam (No. 164) of Salem Village, born 9 Feb., 1698.

Children, born and baptized at Salem Village:

308   STEPHEN, b. 19 Mar., 1718–19; bapt. 17 May, 1719; d. young.
309   MIRIAM, b. 11, bapt. 18 Apr., 1721; m. 28 Jan., 1743–4, Elisha, son of Thomas and Mary (Putnam) Flint, a farmer of South Danvers, b. 22 July, 1715. Children: Mary, b. 12 Mar., 1744–5; m. 4 Jan., 1765, Dea. Eleazer Spofford; lived in Jaffrey, N. H., and Bradford, Mass. Moses, b. 17 July, 1746; d 25 Nov., 1754. Rebecca, b. 25 Jan., 1749; m. 22 Apr., 1774, David Kimball of Boxford. Mehitable, b. 9 Jan., 1758; m. 17 June, 1779, Bartholomew Brown of Danvers. Miriam, b. 4 Nov., 1759; d. 20 Oct., 1830; m. 5 Mar , 1777, Benjamin Putnam, jr. (*Benj.,*[5] *Benj.,*[4] *Benj.,*[3] *Nathl.,*[2] *John*[1]), Hannah, b. 1 Nov., 1763; m. Parker Tyler of Townsend, Mass.
310   RUFUS, b. 10 Sept., 1723; bapt. 15 Sept., 1723.

311 TIMOTHY, b. 9 Jan.; bapt. 27 Mar., 1725–6.

312 PHINEAS, b. 10, bapt. 16 June, 1728.

313 AARON, b. 30 Aug., bapt. 11 Oct., 1730.

314 SARAH, b. 21, bapt. 25 Feb., 1732; m. ——— Ingalls.

315 HANNAH, b. 13, bapt. 18 May, 1735; unm. in 1769.

316 MOSES, b. 23, bapt. 30 Sept., 1739. H. C. 1759.

317 STEPHEN, b. 14 Feb., 1741.

STEPHEN PUTNAM, senior, was occasionally honored with an election to some minor town office, but does not seem to have sought such preferment. In 1739, he was made lieutenant of the third company of foot in town of Salem. Lieut. Stephen's will is dated 1 Feb., 1769; proved 5 May, 1772. In it he mentions his wife Miriam and all his children except Rufus and Timothy.

Mr. Gyles Merrill supplied the dates and names of the above-mentioned children from an old paper, evidently over a century old, given to his mother by a daughter of Miriam and Elisha Flint.

IV. 125 Rev. Daniel (*Benjamin, Nathaniel, John*), born in Salem Village, 12 Nov., 1696, died in Reading, 20 June, 1759, married 25 Feb., 1718, Rebecca Putnam, born 16 Aug., 1691 (family record of Mrs. Howard has it 16 Aug., 1695), who survived her husband.

Children, born at North Reading (the majority of the dates, etc., given below are from a record in Rev. Daniel Putnam's own hand, made in one of the church books) :

318 REBECCA, b. 7 May, 1720; m. 21 Nov., 1751, Ebenezer Emerson of Lynnfield, son of Ebenezer and Mary (Boutwell) Emerson of Reading, b. 1716–17. His first wife was Anna Nichols whom he m. 1746 and who d 1749. They had one son, Ebenezer, b. 1747. By Rebecca he had Daniel, b. 1760, who inherited the homestead and m. 1781, Lucy, daughter of Isaac Pratt.

319 DANIEL, b. 8 Nov., 1721; d. 5 Nov., 1774.

320 AARON, b. 3 Oct., 1723; d. in infancy.

321 SARAH, b. 5 Sept., 1724; d. 8 Apr., 1756; m. 18 Aug., 1742, Henry Ingalls of Andover.

322 HANNAH, b. 31 July, 1726; m. 7 May, 1747, James, son of Deacon William and Abigail (Nichols) Flint of North Reading, b 25 July, 1724; d. 8 Oct., 1802. Children: James, b. 30 Mar., 1754; d. unm. Kendall, b. 6 Mar., 1756; d. y. Hannah, b. 5 Feb.,

1759; m. 7 Sept., 1786, Benjamin Buxton. Samuel, b. 1 Sept.
1761. James Flint, senior, m., 2nd, 10 July, 1765, Mary Hart
and had: Mary, Adam, Jacob, Elizabeth, Mary, James, Charlotte,
bapt., 1784. (See Eaton's Hist. of Reading.)

823   ELIZABETH, b. 28 May, 1728; m. 28 May, 1772, John Payson of
      Pomfret, Conn.
324   MARY, b. 13 May, 1730.
325   JOSHUA, b. 23 Feb., 1732; d. 22 Nov., 1745.
326   AARON, b. 15 Dec., 1733.
327   BETHIAH, b. 29 Nov., 1735.
328   SUSANNAH, b. 17 April, 1737; d. 28 May, 1737.

REV. DANIEL PUTNAM was graduated from Harvard College with the class of 1717.   His father had in his will, probated in April, 1715, given to him £150 for his learning.   In
1717, the North Precinct of Reading, which had been set off
in 1713, voted "to settle a minister amongst them as fast as
they can and in the best method they can."   The next year
it was voted "to give Mr. Daniel Putnam twenty acres of land,
exchanged with Sergt. Flint and Sergt. Eaton, if Mr. Putnam
be our minister."   Also "to build Mr. Putnam an house of
28 feet long, 19 feet wide, and fifteen feet stud, a 'Leuter'
on the back side 10 feet stud, three chimneys, from the ground,
and chamber chimney, and convenient parlor, and convenient
well, in lieu of the 100 pounds, if Mr. Putnam find nails and
glass for the house."

Mr. Putnam had been preaching in the North Parish some
while, until they could settle a minister.   He was married in
the same year as the above offer was made and probably the
two events were closely connected.   It was not until 29 June,
1720, that he was ordained.   The church then consisted of but
thirty-nine members, hence his support from a financial point
of view, must have been slight.   In 1722, the older parish of
the town "took up a contribution in aid of Rev. Daniel Putnam, of North Precinct, who is represented to be in great
straits."   The amount collected was £5–17s.   In 1724, the
North Precinct voted "to apply to the Governor and Council
in relation to Mr. Putnam's troubles."   In spite of the slight
financial support he received, his ministry was a success.   The

parish was pleased with him and did what they could for him. We imagine that times became easier for him after the last entry. In 1759 his death occurred; he was much lamented. During his ministry of thirty-nine years he had added 194 persons to his church, baptized 491, and married 111 couples. He was succeeded by Rev. Eliab Stone in 1760.[42]

The house and farm of the Rev. Daniel Putnam are now, in 1800, occupied by his descendant Henry Putnam, Esq., of North Reading.

IV. 126 Deacon Israel Putnam (*Benjamin, Nathaniel, John*), born in Salem Village, 22 Aug., 1699; died in Bedford, 12 Nov., 1760; married probably about 1720–21, Sarah, daughter of Jonathan and Elizabeth (Giles) Bacon, of Billerica (that part now Bedford), born 25 Dec., 1696.

Children, born in Bedford:

329 ISRAEL, b. 20 Mar., 1723; d. at Chelmsford, 23 Feb., 1800, aged 77 years (g. s.).

330 BENJAMIN, b. 2 Aug., 1725.

331 JONATHAN, b. 16 July, 1727.

332 SARAH, b. 29 June, 1729; m. (pub. 6 Jan., 1750–1), Matthew Whipple of Salem.

333 ELIZABETH, b. 18 July, 1731.

334 TARRANT, b. 2 Sept., 1733.

335 MARY, b. 8 Nov., 1735.

336 BRIDGET, b. 11 Feb., 1737.

ISRAEL PUTNAM left the homestead as soon as he was of age and bought, June 1, 1721, of John Lamon, fifty acres of land in Billerica. Here he settled and made a home for himself. This part of Billerica was set off as Bedford in 1729, and Israel Putnam became the first constable of the town. He also was the first to hold the position of deacon in the first church established there. From time to time he added to his estate by buying adjoining lands; and in 1763 an inventory of his estate made by his widow Sarah, and her son Israel amounted to £444. The old burying ground at Bedford was once part of his estate but he had given the land to the town for that purpose before his death.

[42] For an interesting account of the early ministers at Reading see Putnam's Monthly Historical Magazine for July, 1892.

IV. 127 Cornelius (*Benjamin, Nathaniel, John*), born Salem Village, 3 Sept., 1702; died in Sutton, 1761, will dated 20 Apr., proved 29 May, 1761; married, first, 17 Nov., 1725, Sarah, daughter of Benjamin and Jane (Phillips) Hutchinson of the Village, born 26 Dec., 1701; died in Sutton, 9 June, 1741; married, second, 12 Nov., 1741, Elizabeth widow of William Perkins of Sutton and daughter of ——— Nelson of Newbury, born 18 April, 1734.

Children :

337 SARAH, b. 3 Jan., 1726; d. 30 May, 1738.
338 BETHIA, b. 18 Dec., 1728; not mentioned in her father's will.
339 CORNELIUS, b. 23 May, 1730; m. 2 Aug., 1753, Elizabeth or Deborah Perkins.
340 BENJAMIN, b. 13 May, 1732; d. y.
341 NATHANIEL, b. 3 May, 1734.
342 TARRANT, b. 28 Mar., 1736.
343 BARTHOLOMEW, b. 19 Apr., 1739; d. y.
344 DAVID, } twins, b. 31 May, 1741; d. y.
345 SARAH, }

By second wife :

346 SARAH, b. 18 Mar., 1743; m. 16 Oct., 1765, Capt. Archelaus Putnam (No. 432).
347 BARTHOLOMEW, b. 21 Apr., 1745.
348 DAVID, b. 14 May, 1747.
349 ELIZABETH, b. 28 Sept., 1749.
350 ANNA, b. 21 Nov., 1754; d. y.

CORNELIUS PUTNAM was probably settled in Sutton as early as 1726. He and his wife Sarah joined the church there in 1729, and in 1733-4 he was one of the selectmen. During his lifetime he was much respected and held many offices.

IV. 139 Elizabeth (*Jonathan, John, John*), born Salem Village, 2 Feb., 1686–7; died 8 Aug., 1728; married (pub. 9 Dec., 1708) John son of John and Lydia (Herrick) Porter of Wenham, born 21 July, 1683. He died about 1775. John Porter removed to Ellington, Conn., about 1740.

Children, all born in Wenham :

351 JOHN, b. 16 Apr., 1710; d. 27 Jan., 1722.
352 JONATHAN, b. 1 Apr., 1712; d. 5 July, 1783.

353   ELIZABETH, b. 14 Aug., 1714; d. Jan., 1715.
354   DAVID, b. 10 Mar., 1716, d. 22 Apr., 1716.
355   LYDIA, b. Sept., 1717; m. prob. Samuel Burroughs of Windsor 30
        Oct., 1745.
356   RUTH, b. 28 Oct., 1719; prob. m. 1 Jan., 1743, Samuel Bowles.
357   DANIEL, b. 19 Sept., 1721; d. 5 Jan., 1760.
358   JOHN, b. 17 Jan., 1723
358a JERUSHA, b. 8 Nov., 1724.
358b ELIZABETH, b. 23 May, 1726.

IV. 142 Jonathan (*Jonathan, John, John*), born Salem
Village, 8 May, 1691; died 17 Jan., 1732 (gravestone, Wadsworth cemetery); married 12 Feb., 1714–15, Elizabeth,
daughter of Joseph and Elizabeth Putnam (No. 80)[43], who
married, second, 25 Nov., 1736, Capt. Benjamin, son of Benjamin and Sarah Houlton, of Salem,[44] born 14 Jan., 1689;
died 1744. She was his second wife. She married, again,
7 Nov., 1745, Edward Carlton of Haverhill.[45] Jonathan
Putnam, jr., was a farmer in Salem.

Children, all baptized at the church in Salem Village:

359   JONATHAN, b. 13 July, bapt. 24 July, 1715; d. 1762–3.
360   DAVID, b. 7, bapt. 17 Nov., 1717; guardianship to Israel Andrews,
        granted 3 June, 1732.
361   ELIZABETH, b. 28 Nov., 1719; bapt. 19 June, 1720; d. 8 Aug., 1728.
362   AARON, b. 23, bapt. 31 Dec., 1721; d. 4 Aug., 1728.
363   NATHANIEL, b. 6, bapt. 8 Dec., 1723; in 1744, of Boston, chair-
        maker (Suffolk D. 208-74). Will dated 16 Jan., 1747; proved
        1 Aug., 1748; mariner; mentions sister Mary Cleaves, Elizabeth
        Cleaves, brother David Putnam.
364   MARY, b. 19, bapt. 20 Feb., 1725–6; guardianship to Nathaniel
        Brown, 5 Dec., 1742; m. (pub. 9 June, 1744) William Cleaves,
        jr., of Beverly.
365   ELIZABETH, b. 19, bapt. 24 Nov., 1728; guardianship to Nathaniel
        Brown, 13 Dec., 1742; m. ——— Cleaves.

IV. 143 Esther (*Jonathan, John, John*), born in Salem
Village 18 Nov., 1693; died ———; married 22 June, 1721,

---

[43] Rev. Jos. Green in his diary makes the following entry "Feb. 25, 1714-15, I went
to Mrs. Joseph Putnam's and married Jonathan Putnam."
[44] Mrs. Sarah Houlton married for her second husband Capt. Benjamin Putnam (No.
23).
[45] See Houlton Genealogy by Eben Putnam.

Daniel, son of Samuel and Rebecca (Andrews) Marble, born 5 Feb., 1693, died April, 1755.

Children :

365*a* ESTHER, b. Feb., 1723; d. 19 Jan., 1799; m., 1st, 18 Sept., 1746, Jonathan, son of William and Margaret (Derby) Osborn, b. 1722; d. 1754; m., 2nd, John, son of Benjamin Proctor, b. 1705; d. 8 Sept., 1773.

365*b* DANIEL, b. 1726; d. 30 Oct., 1775; m. Ann ———, b. 1728, d. 19 Jan., 1779.

365*c* JONATHAN, b. 1730; d. Jan., 1730.

365*d* JONATHAN, b. 1732; d. 27 Mar., 1815.

365*e* JOHN, b. 1734.

365*f* SAMUEL, b. 1735; d. 7 Jan., 1799; m. Abigail who was b. 1738 and d. 3 May, 1773.

IV. 146 David (*Jonathan, John, John*), born Salem Village, baptized there, 8 Sept., 1706; died 3 Feb., 1760; married (published at Salem, 27 Apr., 1745) Anna, daughter of Samuel and Anna (Edwards) Houlton (of Danvers) born 4 Sept., 1729, died 25 Sept., 1763.

Children, born Salem Village, baptized at North Parish :

366   EUNICE, bapt. 31 Mar., 1750-1.

367   DAVID, b. 15 July, 1755, bapt. 17 Aug., 1755.

368   HOULTON, bapt. 28 Aug., 1757, d. y.

The will of David Putnam, jr., of Danvers, yeoman, is dated 8 Jan., 1760, and was proved 31 Mar., 1760. Mentions his wife Anna and son David, under age.

David (*Joseph, Thomas, John*) is usually styled senior on the records.

IV. 148 Bartholomew (*James, John, John*), born Salem Village, 1687; baptized at Salem, Oct., 1688; died at sea 23 May, 1723; married 6 July, 1710, Mary, daughter of Joseph Putnam (No. 79) born 2 Feb., 1690-1.

Children :

369   BARTHOLOMEW, b. 3 Mar., bapt. 9 Mar., 1711-12.

370   JOSEPH, b. 1, bapt. 15 Aug., 1714.

371   WILLIAM, b. 1, bapt. 4 Aug., 1717.

372   MARY, b. 19, bapt. 20 Sept., 1719.

BARTHOLOMEW PUTNAM was of Salem. He was a mariner

as the following marine protest shows. It also throws light
upon the dangers to which our early mercantile marine were
exposed.

Province of the Maſsachusetts ⎱ Anno Regni Regis Georgii Nunc
Bay in New England Eſsexſ co ⎰ Magnæ Brittaniæ &c Nono.

[SEAL]

By this Publique Instrument of—Protest be
it knowne & Manifest to all Christian People
that on the Sixth day of July Anno Dom 1723.
personally appeared before me Stephen Sewall
Esqʳ. Notary Publique at my office in Salem
within the County & province aforeſ⁴ Mʳ Nathan Putnam of Salem
aforeſ⁴ Marriner Lately mate of Capᵗ Bartholᵒ Putnam in the
Skooner Eſsex who Departed this Life at Sea on their paſsage from
Jamaica to New England Since which the sᵈ Nathan Putnam as is
Customary in Such Cases was master and Commander in Cheife who
for & in the nature of a protest Did on the Day aforeſᵈ in Salem
aforeſᵈ Solemnly Declare make knowne & Averr in Manner following viz That on the 10ᵗʰ day of March 1722/3 they Set Sayle from
the Island of Saltateodos Laden with Salt their veſsell being very
Leaky bound for New England that on the 12ᵗʰ day of March
aforeſᵈ at Night they Sprang thier foremast by reason of which &
thier veſsells remaining very Leaky on the 14ᵗʰ they bore up to
Jamaica where they arived the 24ᵗʰ of the Same month & after they
had Stopt thier Leaks & Strengthned their mast refitted thier veſsell what was necefsary which they were forc't to doe at a Great
Disadvantage by Selling a Considerable parcell of Salt—being at a
Low rate there; on the 24ᵗʰ of Aprill 1723 they Set Sayle from
Port Royal in Jamaica bound for Salem in New England & on the
8ᵗʰ of may following in the Lattiᵈᵉ of 21 Degrees North Latt: they
unhappily met with Loe the famous pyrate who had 2 Sloops or
veſsells under his Command and the Pyrats Carried the Master
Bartholᵒ Putnam & 2 of our men on board the veſsell he himselfe
was aboard & the rest of us on board the Lefser pyratical veſsell
Called the ranger & then the Pyrates went on board our veſsell
broke open the Chests Trunks & Ransackt & tooke away what
Silver & Gold was aboard that they could find & the Cloths &
Every thing Else they See cause beat the master with the Cuttlash
& on the 9ᵗʰ of May Dismist us when we made the best of our way
to New England on the 23ᵈ day of May our Master Capᵗ Bartholᵒ

Putnam Dyed haveing been Sick from the time they Came out of
Jamaica & that on the 5ᵗʰ day of July 1723. they arived at Salem
in New England with about Twenty Tunn of Salt.

Wherefore I the Notary aforesᵈ at the motion & request of the sᵈ
Nathan Putnam doe Solemnly protest against the Leakinefs of the
vefsell the Springing of the fore mast & their being taken & plundered by the Pyrates to be the Causes & the onely Causes of all the
Lofses Damages Delays hindrances Demurrages Mischeives Incon-
veniencies already Suffered & Sustained or hereafter to be Suffered
& Sustained. this Done an protested the day & year abovesᵈ.   In

Testimonium—veritatis Signo meo manuali Solito Signavi &
S·gillum apposui Rogatus.

Stephen Sewall Notʸ Pubᶜᵘˢ

John Gray & Timothy Mackmazza Two of the Crew—
    made oath to the Truth of the matter of fact Contained
    in the foregoeing protest.
Sworne by both July 8ᵗʰ 1723. Curiam

Steph Sewall Just peace

On 20 July, 1723, administration on his estate was granted
to his father James Putnam and to his brother-in-law, Israel
Porter.   The father died shortly afterward and the duties of
settling the estate devolved upon James Putnam, jr., who on
29 Dec., 1729, rendered an inventory of the estate.   On 18
June, 1733, Sarah, widow of Israel Porter, is appointed administratrix on this estate and on 29 June, 1733, a division
was effected in which Bartholomew, Joseph, William, and
Mary, participated.

During 1736–38, the three sons disposed of lands which
had come to them from estate of their uncle Nathan.

This seems to have been one of the most thrifty of the
Putnam families, a trait which has shown itself in many of
James Putnam senior's, descendants.

IV. 149 James (*James, John, John*), born Salem
Village, 1689; died probably late in the winter of 1763; will
dated 6 July 1751, proved 14 Jan., 1764, inventory 1 Apr.,
1765; married (published 15 Jan., 1714–15), Ruth, daughter

WADSWORTH CEMETERY, SUMMER STREET, DANVERS.

JAMES PUTNAM HOUSE
BUILT ABOUT 1718.

ABOUT AND BEYOND THE TREE AND IN
ITS SHADOW ARE THE EARLIEST
PUTNAM GRAVESTONES.

OAK KNOLL.

PHOTO. BY FRANK COUSINS.

of Col. John and Ruth (Gardner) Hathorne, of Salem, baptized Sept., 1694; living in 1751.

Children, born in Salem Village:

373 SARAH, bapt. No. Parish, 4 Dec., 1715; m. (pub. 28 Nov., 1733) Jonathan Browne of Newbury.

374 EBENEZER, b.——, 1717; bapt. No. Parish 20 Oct., 1717; d. 12 Aug., 1788.

375 ARCHELAUS, b.——, 1721; bapt. No. Parish, 14 May, 1721.

376 ABIDE, not on town or church records; d. y.

377 NATHAN, not on town or church records; d. s. p.

378 JAMES, b.——, 1726; bapt. No. Parish, 31 July, 1736.

JAMES PUTNAM lived in the house just to the southeast of Oak Knoll on the same road. The house is still standing in a fine state of preservation. The following entry is of interest in this connection; 4 Feb., 1714, Israel Porter, Junior, conveys to James Putnam Sr., mason, three and one-half acres of land, "on which his son James hath lately built him a house." He had joined the church on 4 Sept., 1713, and was probably married about the time of the above deed. His wife belonged to one of the most influential families in Salem.

During his long life James Putnam took considerable interest in town affairs. He was one of those who succeeded in obtaining the establishment of the District of Danvers and was elected tythingman at the March meeting in 1758. Previous to this he had been surveyor of highways in 1729, and in 1747 was selectman from the "Farms." In 1730, he paid the ninth largest tax in the Village. His will is given below.

WILL OF JAMES PUTNAM.

In the Name of God Amen I James Putnam of Salem in the county of Essex yeoman being att this time in a good measure of health, and of Perfect mind and memory. Thanks be given Unto God, but Calling unto mind the mortallity of my body. And not knowing how soon it may Please God to Take me out of this world Do make and ordain this my last Will and Testament viz: Principally and first of all I give and recommend my Soul into the hands of God that gave it. And my body I Recommend to the earth to be Buried in Decent Christian Buriel. And Touching Such Worldly estate wherewith it hath Pleased God to Bless me in this Life. I give & dispose of the same in the following manner & Forme.

Imp[r] I give and Bequeath to my well Beloved wife Ruth the use and improvement of one-third part of all my real Estate during her natural life I also give to my said Wife all my household goods within door Forever.

Item I give to my daughter Sarah Brown one pound six shillings Lawfull money which is her full Portion out of Estate with what I have given her att her marriage.

Item I give to my son Ebenezer Putnam Twenty-eight Pounds Thirteen shillings and four pence Lawfull money which is his full Portion out of my Estate with what I have given him before viz a Liberall Education and other things.

Item I give to my son James Putnam one pound Eight shillings Lawfull money which is his full Portion out of my estate with what I have given him before viz: a Liberall Education and other things.

Item I give to my son Archelous Putnam and to his heirs and assigns forever all my lands and all the buildings standing thereon situated in said Salem and Middleton with all the Priviledges and Appurtinances thereunto belonging. I also give to my said son Archelous all my live stock of creatures. And all my Personal Estate that I have not Disposed of and further my will is that my said son Archelous Shall pay all and every of the aforesaid Legacies within the space of two years after my Decease and he shall pay all my just Debts, and the charges of a Decient funeral for my self and my said wife out of what Estate I have given him in and by this will. And I hereby constitute and appoint my said son Archelous Putnam to be my sole Executor of this my last will and Testament and I do hereby Revoke and Disanull all and every other Former Testament Wills Legacies and Bequeaths Ratifying this and no other to be my last will and Testament in witness whereof I have hereto sett my hand and seal this sixth Day of July A. D. 1751.

JAMES PUTNAM [Seal]

Signed Sealed Published and Declared by the said James
Putnam as his last will and Testament in the Presence of us
Elijah Porter
Israel Clark jr } Essex fs Ipswich January the 14 1764 Before the
Dorothy Porter } Honble John Choate Esq Judge of Probate this
will was Proved Approved and allowed.

IV. 154 Jethro (*James, John, John*), baptized Salem
Village, 2 May, 1702; died —— 1751; married 14 Apr.,
1726 Anne (No. 84), daughter of Joseph and Elizabeth
(Porter) Putnam, who survived her husband.

Children, born in Salem Village:

379 HULDAH, bapt. 16 Apr., 1727; d. 1 May, 1802; m. 8 Jan., 1746,
Deacon John, son of Capt. Samuel and Ruth (Putnam) Flint,
of Middleton. Ch.: Jeremiah, b. 23 June, 1749. Ruth. Anna, b.
26 July, 1753; m. Enoch Perley. John, b. 1 Mar., 1756.

380 ENOCH, b. 18 Feb., bapt. 26 Feb., 1731-2.

381 REBECCA, bapt. 5 Sept., 1736; m. Peter (*Caleb, John, John, John*),
Putnam.

382 NANNY, bapt. 18 Feb., 1738-9; prob. d. y.

JETHRO PUTNAM lived on the old Putnam place, now Oak
Knoll. In 1730, his name stood tenth on the tax list for the
Village. Although holding a good position and good property
he seems not to have taken much part in public affairs.

His will is dated 24 Jan. and was proved 18 Feb., 1750-1.
In it he mentions his wife, his daughter Huldah Flint, his
daughter Rebecca, under eighteen years of age, and son
Enoch.

IV. 156 Eleazer (*Eleazer, John, John*) born Salem
Village, 8 Sept., 1695; died Preston, Conn., 13 Jan., 1741;
married at Preston, 7 Jan., 1730, Mrs. Hannah (Williams)
Billings of Groton, Conn., who died Aug., 1780, aged
seventy-two.

ELEAZER PUTNAM settled in Preston, Conn., previous to
1730. He was a farmer there and much respected.

Children, born at Preston:

383 APPHIA, b. 9 Oct., 1731; d. 1800; m. Samuel Andrews of Groton,
Conn. Ch.: Eleazer, of Preston. Elisha. Lucy. Eunice. Sally.

384 JOHN, b. 13 May, 1734; d. 10 Aug., 1786.
385 CHARLES, b. 13 Oct., 1737.
386 EUNICE, b. 2 Nov., 1740; d. y.

VI. 158 Jeptha (*Eleazer, John, John*), born Salem Village, 24 Aug., 1699; died in Sutton, 23 Apr., 1772; married, first, 11 Mar., 1728, Ruth Fuller, who died 1742–3, or, according to the History of Sutton, Ruth Ray; married, second, at Beverly, 8. Jan., 1746, Mrs. Ruth Hayward of Beverly, born, 1727; died Jan., 1779.

Children, probably all born in Sutton:

387 BENAJAH, b. 27 Aug., 1725; d. y.
388 SAMUEL, b. 19 May, 1727[46].
389 HANNAH, b. 13 Aug., 1728[46]; m. 28 May, 1748, Benjamin son of Benjamin and Ruth (Conant) Woodbury of Sutton (formerly of Beverly), b. 5 Feb., 1726; d. Royalston, 17 Oct., 1793, whence he had removed from Sutton in 1760. Ch. all but last b. in Sutton: Benajah, b. 21 Feb., 1748. Ruth, b. 12 Feb., 1749. Apphia, b. 31 July, 1751. Elizabeth, b. 21 Mch., 1753. Lot, b. 10 July, 1755. Jesse, b. about 1758. Hannah, b. about 1760. A child, b. Royalston.
390 EBENEZER, b. 22 Feb., d. 5 Mar., 1730.
391 FULLER, b. 13 Jan., 1731[46].
392 RUTH, b. 18 Oct., 1732 or 33[46]; m. 5 Nov., 1751, Stephen Holman of Sutton, who d. 15 Nov., 1800. Ch.: Ruth, b. 13 Sept., 1754. Stephen, b. 7 Dec., 1756. Judith, b. 21 Feb., 1759. Called "Ruth Bartlett" in her father's will dated 18 Oct., 1763.
393 JOHN, b. 27 July, 1738[46].
394 MARY, b. 23 Oct., 1741[46].
395 BENAJAH, b. 7 Sept., 1747[46].
396 GIDEON,[46] b. ———.

JEPTHA PUTNAM probably moved to Sutton as early or earlier, than 1725. 26 Dec., 1723, John Hutchinson of Salem, husbandman, sold for £150, to Jeptha Putnam of Salem, carpenter, a farm of 129 acres, more or less of said farm being in town of Sutton. This grant bounded on the west on Cornelius Putnam's land. This deed was done at Salem; but on 14 Dec., 1726, Jeptha Putnam "of Sutton or living on the farm formerly Mr. Davenport's of Boston that adjoins to the town of Sutton" for £80, sells to Isaac

[46] Mentioned in will of Jeptha Putnam "housewright" dated 18 Oct., 1763, proved 4 May, 1772.

Putnam of Topsfield, yeoman, thirty-three acres of Davenport's farm which bounded on said Isaac's land. This was done at Sutton and Elisha Putnam and Jonathan Fuller were witnesses. Both Jeptha and his wife Ruth were admitted to the church at Sutton, 6 Oct., 1728. His son Fuller inherited the farm and lived there.

IV. 159 Samuel (*Eleazer, John, John*), born in Salem Village, 30 May, 1707; died there, 14 or 15 Dec., 1781; married there, 29 Dec., 1736, Elizabeth (No. 293), daughter of Tarrant and Elizabeth (Bacon) Putnam, born 10 or 20 May, 1718; died 21 May, 1784.[47]

Children, born and baptized in Salem Village:

896a ELIZABETH, b. ——, 1738; d. 14 Apr., 1791; m. Daniel Putnam.
397 SAMUEL, b. 13 June, bapt. 14 June, 1741; d. 1786.
398 MARTHA, b. 9 Sept., 1742; bapt. 27 Mar., 1742–3; d. 3 Sept., 1821;
    m. ——, John, son of John and Elizabeth (Jacobs) Endicott
    of Salem, b. 1739, bapt. 7 June, 1741, d. 4 Mar., 1816. Ch.:
    Samuel, b. June, 1763; m. Elizabeth (No. 632), dau. of William
    Putnam of Sterling.[48] John, b. 13 Jan., 1765; m., 1st, Mary
    Putnam. Moses, b. 19 Mar., 1767. Ann, b. Jan., 1769; m. Sol-
    omon Giddings of Beverly. Elizabeth, b. Aug., 1771; m. James
    Gray of Salem. Jacob, b. 9 July, 1773; d. 1816. Martha, b. Sept.,
    1775; m. Jeremiah Page of Danvers. Nathan, twin with Martha,
    d. y. Sarah, b. Sept., 1778; d. y., unm. Rebecca, b. 20 May, 1780;
    m. Daniel Hardy. William, b. 1782; d. unm., 1806. Timothy,
    b. 27 July, 1785; d. *s. p.;* m. Harriett Martin of Sterling. John,
    Endicott, the father of the above children, was a great, great
    grandson of Doctor Zerubbabel Endicott who had the law suit
    with Nathaniel Putnam and Allen. Zerubbabel was son of Gov-
    ernor John Endicott.
399 TARRANT, b. 8, bapt. 26 Feb., 1743–4; d. 14 Apr., 1776.
400 RUFUS, b. 31 Mar., bapt. 6 Apr., 1746; d. 21 Nov., 1749.
401 SOLOMON, b. 13, bapt. 20 Nov., 1748; d. 12 Nov., 1749.
402 RUFUS, b. 18 Oct., bapt. 11 Nov., 1750; d. 1 Sept., 1757.
403 RUTH, b. 28 bapt. 31 Mar., 1751.
404 HANNAH, b. 19 bapt., 25 Mar., 1753; d. 20 Aug., 1757.
405 MARY, b. 24 Oct., bapt. 16 Nov., 1755; d. 26 Aug., 1757.

[47] Another authority Nov. 5 or 21st and another 19 May.
[48] Their son, William Putnam Endicott (b. 5 Mar., 1803: m. Feb. 1826, Mary, dau. of Hon. Jacob Crowninshield), was father of the Hon. William C. Endicott (b. 19 Nov., 1826), late Secretary of War under President Cleveland. His dau., Mary C., m. 15 Nov., 1888, Hon. Joseph Chamberlain of Birmingham, England.

406   ELEAZER, b. 4, bapt. 6 May, 1759; d 30 May, 1836.

407   HANNAH, b. 1, bapt. 28 Feb., 1762; d. 23 Aug., 1796; m. 11 Dec., 1783, Major Elijah Flint.

SAMUEL PUTNAM was a man of considerable influence in Danvers. He was much respected by his townspeople, this fact being shown by the frequency with which he was called to occupy the various town offices. At one time he lived in Topsfield, but the most of his life was spent in Danvers.

His will is dated 1 Mar., 1781; was proved 7 Jan., 1782. In it he styles himself "of Danvers, Yeoman;" he mentions his wife Elizabeth, son Eleazer to be executor; his daughter Elizabeth wife of Daniel Putnam, his daughter Hannah, his granddaughters Lydia, Mary, and Sarah, daughters of his son Samuel, deceased, also Sally, Betsey, Samuel, Perley, children of his son Tarrant.

IV. 160 Henry (*Eleazer, John, John*), born in Salem Village, 14 Aug., 1712; killed at Lexington, 19 Apr., 1775; married Hannah ——.

Children:

408   HENRY, b. 1737 (by a curious error the record dates his birth as 1747), bapt. at the church in Salem Village, 2 Dec., 1753.

409   ELEAZER, b. 5 June, bapt. 13 Aug., 1738.

410   ELIJAH, b. 23, bapt. 26 July, 1741. Probably the Elijah who was graduated from Harvard College, 1766.

411   ROGER, b. 10, bapt. 16 Oct., 1743.

412   JOHN, b. 11 Oct., bapt. 13 Oct., 1745; administration on his estate granted to his father, with Caleb Brooks and Thomas Reed as bondsmen, 9 May, 1763. (According to the Perley Putnam MSS. this John had removed to St. John.)

413   BILLINGS, b. 11 May, 1749.

414   BENJAMIN, b. 26 Aug., bapt. in Salem Village, 15 Sept., 1751; d. Savannah, Ga., 1801.

There is considerable difficulty in tracing the history of this family as the father left Danvers and his son Henry seems to have remained there, causing some confusion in regard to localities; added to this are various contradictory statements received from descendants now scattered throughout the United States and who are limited somewhat in their knowledge by the tradition which variously states that Henry, senior, and Henry, junior, were killed at Lexington.

The whole life-history of both father and son would undoubtedly prove interesting as they seem to have had the same love of adventure, the reckless bravery and patriotism of Gen. Israel Putnam, with whom they were allied by marriage as well as blood.

There is a romantic story concerning the courtship of Henry Putnam. It is related that on one of his journeys from Medford to Connecticut, he stopped over night at Bolton, fell in love with his host's daughter, proposed in the morning, was immediately married and with his bride drove back her dowry consisting of two cows and twelve sheep.

He is said to have been at the capture of Louisburg; being in command of a company there; his son Henry was also there from Danvers.

In 1738, he united with his brother, Samuel Putnam of Topsfield and their mother Elizabeth, in a deed of sale of land in Danvers to Benjamin and Joseph Knight. In or about the year 1745, he sold his father's homestead to Phineas Putnam, but had not disposed of all his property in Danvers as he was on the tax list there in 1752, and on the 4th of March of that year was one of the three tellers at the first town meeting in Danvers to collect and count the votes for selectman. At this meeting he was chosen surveyor of lumber. Probably about this time he removed to Charlestown as the name of Henry Putnam does not occur on the Danvers tax list until 1757, when we may suppose it is the son and not the father who is mentioned.

Henry Putnam[49] was taxed in Charlestown from 1756–1765 (he had purchased of J. Hartwell, forty-five acres in 1753), kept school without the neck. He was then styled "Gentleman" and, according to Wyman, from Danvers.

On 9 May, 1763, Henry Putnam, of Charlestown, "Gentle-

[49]Since writing the above all doubt as to the identity of Henry of Charlestown has vanished; see will of Nathaniel Boardman in Essex Probate.

man," was appointed administrator on estate of his son John late of Charlestown. It appears from the above extracts that he was more or less of a soldier, a scholar, and a man of some consequence, else he would not have had the title of gentleman. Some time, soon after 1763, he probably removed to Medford and was perhaps there when the Alarm of the 19th of April was sent out and may have joined his old friends among the Danvers minute men. It is worthy of notice that the Danvers militia marched from Danvers to West Cambridge, a distance of over sixteen miles, in four hours. It was at West Cambridge that the greatest loss was met with by the Americans; it was at that point that the Danvers companies, hoping to intercept the retreating British, took possession of a small, walled enclosure and with shingles attempted to form a breastwork. There were nearly two hundred men from Danvers and Beverly. Henry Putnam, senior, of Medford, was killed, his son Henry badly wounded, Perley Putnam was killed and his brother Nathan wounded; all but the first being members of the Danvers company. Another son of Henry, Eleazer, who went out with his company from Medford, was near or among the Danvers men.

There Henry Putnam gave up his life for his country at the age of sixty-three years; he had volunteered his services as he was exempt from military duty. I have seen it stated that five of his sons were there. His son Henry remained in Medford wounded, probably at the home of his brother Eleazer; but was at the battle of Bunker Hill.

IV. 162 Caleb (*John, John, John*), born in Salem Village, 14 Feb., 1693–4; died 1757; married, Salem Village, 7 Dec., 1720, Silence Phillips, daughter of Jacob[30] and Sarah (Rea) Phillips, born 8 Dec., 1689. The Salem Records state that her name was Duncklee. He married, second, Elizabeth——.

---

[30] Jacob Phillips died of small pox 19 Sept., 1689, aged 27 (record of Rev. Saml. Parris). Mr. Moses Prince thinks the stone, from which the inscription is chipped off, bore date 24 Aug., 1689. It was erected in the Wadsworth Cemetery. The widow m., 2d, James Prince.

Children,. born in Salem Village, and baptized there:

415 MOSES, b. 18 Nov., bapt. 3 Dec., 1721; d. 5 Oct., 1735.
416 MEHITABLE, b. 6, bapt. 10 Nov., 1723; m. Archelaus Putnam.
417 CALEB, b. 10, bapt. 13 Feb , 1725; d. 17 Apr., 1751.
418 JOHN, b. 25, bapt. 31 Dec., 1727; d. 25 (or 21) Aug., 1728.
419 MARY, b. and bapt. 8 Nov., 1729; d. 12 Mar., 1734.
420 JOHN, b. 23, bapt. 28 Apr., 1733.
421 PETER, b. 3, bapt. 6 July, 1735.
422 MOSES, b. 31 Aug., bapt. 4 Sept., 1737.
423 MARY, b. 16, bapt. 29 July, 1739.

CALEB PUTNAM was a farmer in Danvers. His name does not occur on the tax lists of that town, later than 1756. Both he and his wife Silence owned the covenant at the church at Salem Village, 1 Oct., 1721, admitted to full communion 5 Apr., 1728. No descendant in the male line now lives in Danvers.

IV. 165 Moses (*John, John, John*), born in Salem Village, 29 May, 1700; baptized 9 June, 1700.

Children:

424 MOSES.
425 CALEB.
426 PETER.
427 JOHN.

Of Moses I have no record. His name is not on the tax list or town or church records of Danvers.

FIFTH GENERATION.

V. 176 Samuel (*Thomas, Thomas, Thomas, John*), born in Salem Village, baptized there 5 Jan., 1723–4; died in Lunenburg, 2 Jan., 1775, aged fifty-two; married 4 April, 1742, Sarah Nurse, living 1777.[51]

Children,[52] born and baptized in Salem Village:

428   ELIZABETH, b. 24 Nov., 1744.
429   THOMAS, b. 10 Nov., 1747; d. 26 Dec., 1747.
430   SARAH, b. 10 Nov., 1748; d. July, 1787.
431   ANNA, b. 8 May, 1753; d. 8 June, 1753.
432   MITCHELL, b. 18 June, d. 25 June, 1754.
433   MARY, b. 4 July, 1755; d. 20 Sept., 1789.
434   SAMUEL, b. 4 May, 1757; d. 26 May, 1758.
435   SAMUEL, } twins, b. 30 July, 1758; { d. 12 Aug., 1758.
436   ANNA,   }   { d. in New Hampshire.
437   ELIJAH, b. 1 June, 1761; d. 11 Aug., 1825; bapt. in Lunenburg.
438   LUCY, b. 15 Nov., 1764; d. 11 Aug., 1825.
439   CLARISSA, b. 9 Jan., 1768; d. 11 May, 1794.

SAMUEL PUTNAM, in 1752, was elected one of the first tythingmen chosen by the new town of Danvers. On 4 Sept., 1757, he was chosen deacon of the church, but soon afterward removed to Lunenburg and was chosen deacon of the church there. He was selectman of Lunenburg, 1767–70.

V. 184 Ebenezer (*Seth, Thomas, Thomas, John*), born in Billerica, 8 Aug., 1719; died in Charlestown, N. H., 2 Feb., 1782; married Mary Parker, who married, second (published 27 Feb.), 1791, Capt. Sylvanus, son of Dr. John and Hannah (White) Hastings, of Charlestown, born 22 Mar., 1721, died 12 Jan., 1807; she was his second wife.

[51] Probably daughter of Ebenezer and Elizabeth (Mitchell) Nurse; if so, b. 14 Nov., 1722.
[52] Did he also have a daughter Martha, b. 9 Sept., 1742?

Children, born in Charlestown, N. H. :

440 SETH, b. 24 Aug.; d. 26 Sept., 1746.

441 MARY, b. 4 Jan., 1747–8; d. 12 Aug., 1762.

442 RUTH. b. 13 Jan., 1749–50; d. Canada, 1823; m. Solomon Grout, b. 27 June, 1751; Ch.: Ebenezer, b. 12 April, 1772; d. 4 July, 1773. Solomon, b. 20–21 Jan., 1774, m. Sebra Allen of Middlesex, Vt. Jesse, b. 15 May, 1775; d. 16 Sept., 1776. Charlotte, b. 29 Nov., 1777; d. 7 or 12 Mar., 1829; m. William McClintock of Elmore, Vt. Ebenezer, b. 9 April, 1779; d. 12 Mar., 1853; m. Abigail Clarke, of Rockingham, Vt. Ruth, b. 24 Nov., 1780; m., 1st, 1812, Josiah Hart of Charlestown, N. H.; 2d, Judah Center of Chatham, Canada. Polly, b. 1 Sept., 1782; m. Philip Wheeler of Morrisville, Vt. Levi, b. 7 or 14 July, 1784; d. 28 Oct., 1820, m. Polly Nichols. Don,[44] b. 6 or 12 Mar., 1786; d. 22 Jan., 1841, m. 4 April, 1811, Beulah Elmore, b. Sharon, Ct., 28 Feb., 1787; d. 22 April, 1864. Phila, b. 20 Aug., 1788; d. unm. 8 Oct., 1811.

443 EBENEZER, b. 25 Jan., 1751–52.

444 SETH, b. 9 Aug., 1754.

445 LEVI, b. 11 Feb., 1757.

446 REBECCA, b. 15 May, 1759; d. Charlestown, 1819; m. Julius Silsbee. Ch.: Polly ——; Uriah ——; Isaac, b. 23 Jan. 1787; Betsey ——; Samuel ——; Theodosia ——; Caroline ——; Seth ——; Phineas.

447 PAMELIA, b. 25 May, 1761; d. Charlestown, 1831; m. Moses, son of Ensign Moses and Elizabeth (Holden) Wheeler. b. 29 Aug., 1752. Ch.: George ——. Laura, b. 31 Oct., 1784. Horace, b. 12 May, 1792. William, b. 15 Jan., 1796. Lucia, b. 13 Sept., 1800, d. 1814. Marcia, b. 7 Feb., 1803.

448 MARY, b. 22 April, 1763; d 8 Oct., 1781.

448a ISAAC, b. 6 May, 1765; d. 24 Jan., 1766.

449 ISAAC, b. 27 May, 1766.

450 TERZA, b. 4 Aug., 1768; m. Nathan Benton. Ch. :Fanny ——; Laura ——; Polly ——; Hyram ——; Permelia ——; Charlotte ——; Clarissa ——; Phila ——.

451 JACOB, b. 18 Mar., 1771.

452 BENJAMIN, b. 27 Dec., 1775.

[44] The ch. of Don and Beulah Grout were: Jesse C., b. 16 Jan. 1812; d. unm. 14 Feb., 1842. Phila. b 18 July, 1813; m. Edwin Richmond. Ralph, b. 4 Mar., 1815; d. 10 Nov., 1825. Horace, b 9 April. 1816; m. Melinda Bullock. Silvia, b. Feb., 1818; m. George Hill, who was b. Montpelier, Vt., 13 May, 1806; d. Medway, Mass., 15 Jan., 1875; their ch. are the Rev. Calvin Grout Hill, Don Gleason Hill, the Dedham antiquary. Rev. George Edwin Hill, and William Francis Hill. Levi, b. 4 Mar., 1821; d. 22 Sept., 1821. (Major) Luman M., b. 9 Mar., 1823; m., 1st, Philura French; m., 2d, ——, Sarah, b. 1 Jan., 1825; m. Nathan Camp. Calvin, b. 4 Aug., 1828; d. 23 Feb., 1842.

EBENEZER PUTNAM was early in Number Four or what is now Charlestown, being one of the grantees. He was there in 1745, and in 1746 was on Col. Josiah Willard's roll of the company stationed at Fort Dummer; also in 1748 and several of the following years. He also served under Capt. Phineas Stevens. The early settlers of Number Four had to contend with the French and Indians, who were constantly hovering about these frontier posts on the Connecticut.

Fort Dummer was a post established by Massachusetts to protect her frontier and when, in 1745, New Hampshire, having previously obtained a grant of this country from the King, refused to garrison the posts on the Connecticut, Massachusetts sent troops to Fort Dummer, under Capt. Willard, and later a troop of Rangers under Capt. Stevens to Number Four. Shortly after Capt. Stevens' arrival, that place repulsed a fierce Indian attack. Many of the troopers under both of these captains were former settlers from Massachusetts, in that section of the country, among them the Putnams.

Ebenezer Putnam helped to form the first church at Number Four, and was one of the first ten male members. He was also their first deacon. He was selectman in 1755, '56, '61, '65, and moderator 1765, '66, '69.

V. 189 Thomas (*Seth, Thomas, Thomas, John*), born in Billerica, 22 Oct., 1728; died in Charlestown, N. H. 20 Aug., 1814; married in Lunenburg, Mass., 24 Jan., 1754, Rachel, daughter of Capt. Ephraim and Joanna (Bellows) Wetherbee of Charlestown, born 3 April, 1733, died 12 June, 1812.

Children, born in Lunenburg:

452a HEPSIBETH, b. 2 Feb., 1755.
452b SUSANNAH, } twins, b. 16 Sept., 1756.
452c SETH.
452d THOMAS, b. 27 Feb., 1758.

Children, born in Charlestown:

453 EPHRAIM, b. 16 Oct., 1759; d. 16 Oct., 1769.

454 RACHEL, b. 9 April, 1761; published 1 Nov., 1792, to James Thurber of St. Johnsbury.

455 JOANNA, b. 30 Dec., 1763; m. Samuel, son of Joseph and Huldah Willard, of Charlestown. She was his second wife; they had twelve children.

456 ABIJAH, b. 31 Jan., 1765.

457 ABEL, b. 29 June, 1766.

458 ELISHA, b. ——, 1768; m. 1791.

459 HEPSY, b. ——, 1767; d. unm.

460 EPHRAIM, b. 9 June, 1770, never married.

461 MARTHA, b. Acworth ——; m. Charlestown 24 Nov., 1802, John Hackett. Ch.: Betsy; Harvey, b. 1810, a soldier in the Mexican and Civil wars; d. at New York, 17 June, 1864, from wounds received before Richmond, of 11th Vt. Battery M; m. 27 April, 1854, Charlotte dau. of Nathan and Nancy (Grinnell) Putnam, q. v. b. 28 Mar., 1818. Ch.: Henry Clark, b. 11 Feb., 1855, at Charlestown, N. H.

462 DOROTHY, b. Acworth.

463 ASA, b. Acworth.

464 ABIGAIL, ——; m. (pub. 6 Dec.) 1812, John Temple, son of Timothy and Hannah (Glidden) Holden, b. 17 Jan., 1793. Ch: John Temple, b. 9 Feb., 1818; see History Charlestown.

THOMAS PUTNAM took part in the French and Indian wars as soon as he was able to bear arms, for in 1750 we find his name on the roll of Capt. Stevens' company at Number Four. Shortly after this we find him settled in Lunenburg, but in 1759 he is again at Charlestown. He marched from Acworth to Bennington in August, 1777, in Capt. Abel Walker's company and may have taken part in the battle of Bennington, where, according to Stark, "had every man been an Alexander, or a Charles of Sweden, they could not have behaved better."

In civil and religious affairs Thomas Putnam was more prominent; he was one of the first members of the church at Charlestown and afterward their deacon. After his return to Charlestown from Acworth, where he had gone in 1771 to live in the southern part of the town, he was standing moderator of the church meetings from 1793. During his residence in both towns he was constantly in office. In Acworth he was the first justice of the peace, likewise the first miller for he built the first grist mill erected there.

Moderator of Acworth town meetings in 1775, 1779. Selectman 1772, '73, '75, '76, '78, the most important years of the Revolution. He was also deacon in the Acworth church.

V. 191 Timothy (*Seth, Thomas, Thomas, John*), born in Billerica, 25 Dec., 1732; died in Charlestown, N. H.; married Susanna Badger, who perhaps married, second (published 19 Dec.), 1790, Josiah Hart of Charlestown, N. H. His first wife was Mehitable. Children by Susanna were thirteen in number. See Hist. Charlestown, where a curious error is made.

Children :

465 TIMOTHY, b. 4 Oct., 1760.
466 SAMUEL, b. 14 June, 1762.
467 JOHN, b. 4 June, 1764.
468 EXPERIENCE, b. 8 Feb., 1766; d. 27 May, 1844.
469 SARAH, b. 14 June, 1768; m. (pub. 5 Mar.), 1789, Luther, son of Joseph and Lucy Spencer.
470 BAILEY, b. 8 Mar., 1770 (8 May, Hist. Charlestown).
471 DAVID, b. 7 June, 1772.

TIMOTHY PUTNAM[54] was a member of Col. Bellows' Regiment which marched in May, 1777, to reinforce Ticonderoga, and again in June of the same year, but found the fort had been evacuated.

V. 192 Holyoke (*Edward, Edward, Thomas, John*), born 27 Sept., 1706;[55] baptized in Salem Village, 29 Sept., 1706; married, first, in Middleton, Sept., 1731, Eunice, daughter of John and Hannah (Howard) Hutchinson of Salem, born 9 April, 1712; married, second, 4 May, 1742, Esther, daughter of Thomas and Martha (Herrick) Lovell of Ipswich and Sutton, born 27 Mar., 1717.

Children :

472 EUNICE, b. Middleton, 4 Sept., 1732.

---

[54] A certain Ensign Timothy Putnam reported the details of his scout about Lake Champlain to Capt. Rogers in 1755.
[55] On page 79 the error is made of giving the dates of baptism instead of dates of birth of the first five children of Edward 50.

473 SARAH, b. (*Sutton ?*) 6 Oct., 1785; m. 8 Nov., 1757, Eleazer Bateman.
474 EBENEZER, b. 7 Sept., 1738.
475 HANNAH, b. 26 April, 1741.

By Esther:

476 MARTHA, b. 27 April, 1743.
477 EUNICE, b. 10 Feb., 1745.
478 SUSANNA, b. 16 Aug., 1747.
479 JOSEPH, b. 19 April, 1749.
480 EZRA, b. 2 Nov., 1751.
481 THOMAS, b. 1 July, 1754.
482 MARY, b. 5 April, 1758.

HOLYOKE PUTNAM was dismissed from the church at Middleton, where he had formerly lived, to the church in Sutton in Mar., 1744. This is probably about the time of his settlement in Sutton. He chose to settle in that part of the town now forming a part of Millbury having been set off from Sutton in 1813.

V. 194 Edward (*Edward, Edward, Thomas, John*), born 25 June, 1711; baptized in Salem Village, 30 June, 1711; died in Sutton, 17 Feb., 1800; married, first, 3 Dec., 1734, Ruth Fuller of Middleton, daughter of John and Phebe (Symonds) Fuller.

Children:

483 JOHN, b. Middleton, 25 Aug., 1735.
484 ANDREW, bapt. Middleton, 1738.
485 STEPHEN, b. 20 Apr., 1739; killed in French and Indian war.
486 RUTH, b. 6 June, 1741; d. 28 Dec., 1811; m. 18 Mar., 1761, Samuel, son of Samuel and Elizabeth Rich, b. 30 July, 1735. Ch.: Stephen, b. 3 Jan., 1762. Elijah, b. 4 Apr., 1764. Ruth, b. 31 July, 1766. Samuel, b. 26 Feb., 1769. Elizabeth, b. 23 Jan., 1772.
487 ARCHELAUS, b. 16 Feb., 1743; d. 14 Jan., 1809.
488 PHŒBE, b. 2 Nov., 1745; m. 25 Sept., 1766, Nathaniel son of Elisha and Mary (Davis) Rich, b. 20 Mar., 1742.
489 SARAH, b. 12 Mar., 1747; m. 2 Dec., 1766, Paul, son of Jonathan and Hannah (Burnap) Sibley, b. 26 Apr., 1748. They removed to Spencer. Ch.: James, b. 10 Mar., 1767. Paul, b. 14 Aug., 1769. Caleb, b. 16 Aug., 1771. Sarah, b. 18 Jan., 1774. Jonathan, b. 17 Apr., 1776. Molly, b. 17 Sept., 1778. Betty, b. 1. Jan., 1781. Ruth, b. 19 Feb., 1783. Rufus, b. 2 Mar., 1785. Simeon, b. 12 Apr., 1787.

490 MOLLY, bapt. 22 Apr., 1750; m. Bartholomew Putnam (No. 347).
491 DAVID, b. 19 July, 1752.
492 CALEB, b. 27 Oct., 1754.
493 PETER, b. 29 May, 1757.
494 LUCY, b. 2 June, 1760; d. Sutton, 1841; m. 19 Aug., 1777, Henry,
son of Henry Phelps of Sutton. Ch.: James, Simeon, Stephen,[54]
b. Sutton, 1792; d. Rochester, N. Y., 1827.
495 ASA, b. 30 Apr., 1768.

EDWARD PUTNAM and his wife were dismissed from the
church in Middleton to the church in Sutton in 1744. It is
presumed that either in 1742 or 1743, he had established his
home there; there are evidences of his having been in Sutton
as early as 1737, although he was taxed in Middleton as late
as 1739.

The original farm where Edward first settled is now owned
by a descendant, Mrs. Harriet Augusta Putnam, wife of
Peter Holland Putnam, a great granddaughter of Edward's
youngest son, Asa, having inherited the farm from her father
Bradford Putnam. On page 225 of the History of Sutton,
there is a wood-cut of the house now standing on the place.

V. 197 Eunice (*Edward, Edward, Thomas, John*),
born in Middleton, 13 Sept., 1719; married 19 Sept., 1743,
Thomas, son of Thomas and Martha (Herrick) Lovell. They
removed to Sutton about 1742.

[54] Stephen Phelps was a merchant in Maine, and m. at Paris, Me., 1808, Elizabeth, dau.
of William and Catherine (Nixon) Stowell, who was b. there, 5 Oct., 1785; d. there,
Nov. 1830. Catherine Nixon was the dau. of Col. Thomas Nixon of the 6th Mass. Reg.
during the Revolution. The son of Stephen and Elizb. Phelps is Rear Admiral
Thomas Stowell Phelps, U. S. N., who was b. Bucksfield, Me., 2 Nov., 1822, m. 25 Jan.,
1848, Margaret R. Sevy. Their ch. are Lt. Thomas Stowell Phelps, U. S. N., b. Portsmouth, Va., 7 Nov., 1848; Edmonia Taylor, b. Portsmouth, Va., 1 Feb., 1856; m. 30
Sept., 1875, Lieut. T. B. M. Mason, U. S. N.; Margaret Jane, b. Portsmouth, Va., 25 Jan.,
1864, m. 6 May, 1873, Lieut. James Dexter Adams, U. S. N.

Admiral Phelps graduated at Annapolis, 11 July, 1846, and performed service in the
Mexican War. He also took part in the Paraguayan Expedition in 1858-59. When
the Civil War broke out Lieut. Phelps was selected by ballot to perform a survey of
the Potomac River in 1861, an appointment not only exceedingly dangerous, but re-
quiring great skill and care in engineering. This duty was accomplished successfully and he received the compliments of the Secretary of the Navy. Constantly being
detached for special service, he performed many gallant deeds and at the close of
the war was commissioned Commander, 5 Aug., 1865. Since that date Admiral
Phelps has had charge of Mare Island Navy Yard and other service on the Pacific
coast. He now resides in Washington.

Children, born in Sutton :

496 SARAH, b. 22 Aug , 1744; m. 15 Mar., 1775, Josiah, son of William and Ruth (Lovell) Waite, of Sutton, b. 7 May, 1746. Ruth (Lovell) Waite was aunt of Josiah Waite.

497 JOHN, b. 8 Aug., 1746.

498 EZRA, b. 29 Mar., 1749; m. Mary, dau. of Elias and Hannah (Twist) Jennison of Sutton, b. there, 18 Nov., 1754. Ch.: Elias, b. 12 Jan., 1778. Polly, b. 17 Feb., 1779. Lydia, b. 5 June, 1782. Ezra, b. 8 July, 1787.

499 EUNICE, b. 2 Oct., 1751.

V. 198 Abigail (*Edward, Edward, Thomas, John*), born in Middleton, 11 Sept., 1720 ; married there 25 April, 1744, Israel, son of Thomas and Phebe (Gould) Curtis, born in Middleton, 14 June, 1719. Will of Israel Curtis proved 2 April, 1776. Lived in Middleton.

Children, born in Middleton :

500 RUTH, b. 17 Feb., 1744–5; d. 27 Jan., 1810; m. 13 Dec., 1769, Andrew Peabody, son of Zerubbabel and Jerusha (White) Peabody of Middleton, b. there, 21 July, 1745; d. 14 Oct., 1813. Ch.: Lucy Peabody, b. 28 Sept., 1770, m. 25 June,1795, Abraham Gage of Middleton, and d., 1801; Andrew Peabody, b. 29 Feb., 1772.[57] Hannah, b. 22 Aug., 1773; m. 2 June, 1808, Benjamin Averill of Middleton whose son, Edward Putnam Averill is living there.

501 ELI, b. 27 Oct., 1745; m. 12 April, 1772, Susanna, dau. of Ichabod and Mary (Clark) Wilkins of Middleton. Lived in Lyndeborough, N. H.

502 ANDREW, b. 27 Feb., 1749. Killed by lightning in Andover, when a young man.

503 DUDLEY, b. 12 Feb., 1751; m. 16 July, 1777, Sarah Marble. Removed from Middleton.

504 ISRAEL, b. 20 Oct., 1754; m. 2 Sept., 1779, Elizabeth Wilkins, sister of Mrs. Eli Curtis. Lived in Middleton.

505 LEVI, b. 12 Nov., 1756; prob. d. y.

506 SARAH, b. 25 Feb., 1759.

507 BETTY, b. 22 June, 1764; m. 2 July, 1786, Daniel Barnard. Lived in Bridgton, Me.

V. 200 Miles (*Edward, Edward, Thomas, John*), born in Middleton, 1725 ; baptized at the church in Salem Village, 5 Sept., 1725 ; died in Grafton, Vt., 19 April, 1800 ;

[57] Andrew Peabody b. 29 Feb., 1772; d. Dec., 1813; m. 30 May, 1808, Mary dau. of Robert and Mary (Preston) Rantoul of Beverly, b. 22 July, 1783. Ch.: Andrew Preston Peabody, D. D., of Cambridge, and Mary, who m. John P. Lyman of Portsmouth, N. H.

married in Middleton 23 Sept., 1747, Rachel Wilkins of Middleton.

Children, born in Middleton :

508 RUTH, b. 16 Jan., 1747.
509 AARON, b. 5 May, 1751; d. 22 Mar., 1813.
510 SUSANNA, b. 22 June, 1753.
511 EDWARD, b. 20 Aug.. 1755; d. Grafton, Vt., 2 Dec., 1843.
512 RACHEL, b. 6 Sept., 1757; living in Rindge, N. H., in 1848.

Born, away from Middleton :

513 DANIEL, b. —— ; d. Grafton, Vt., 30 Sept., 1802.
514 JOHN, b. 10 Dec., 1768; d. (Harvard, 12 Aug., 1867, family records), Grafton, Vt., 27 Sept., 1810.
515 MARY, b. 9 Jan., 1760.
516 SALLY, b. 20 Apr., 1765.
517 MILES, b. 6 July, 1774; d. Plainfield, N. J., 25 Dec., 1827.

MILES PUTNAM lived in Middleton until 1757, when he moved with his family to Harvard ; from there he went to Winchendon where he was in 1772, for on 23 Aug., 1772, the church at Middleton dismissed him, and his wife Rachel, to the church at Winchendon.

From Winchendon, they removed to Tomlinson and, finally, about 1783, to Grafton, Vt.

V. 201 Hannah (*Edward, Edward, Thomas, John*), born in Middleton, 23 April, 1727; married 8 May, 1746, Amos (probably), son of Joseph and Susanna (Dowman) Fuller of Middleton, if so, born 5 April, 1720. Removed to Wilton, N. H., before the incorporation of that town.

Children, born in Middleton :

518 SUSANNA, b. 11 Mar., 1747.
519 SARAH, b. 15 Nov., 1749. In 1775 said to be "daughter of Amos Fuller of Wilton, N. H." She m. 26 Mar., 1776, Dea. John Nichols of Middleton.
520 ENOCH, b. 13 Feb., 1754.
521 EUNICE, b. 24 Feb., 1756.
522 JOSEPH, b. 21 July, 1760.
523 AMOS.[58]
524 AARON.[58]

[58] In the History of Wilton, N. H., Amos Fuller is said to have had three sons, Amos, Enoch and Aaron.

V. 202 Elisha (*Elisha, Edward, Thomas, John*), born in Topsfield,[50] 2 Dec., 1715; died, in 1758, at, or near, Crown Point; married 3 Mar., 1742, Lydia, daughter of Philip and Mary (Follansbee) Chase, born 12 Aug., 1722. She married, second, 26 May, 1762, John Daniels.

Children, born in Grafton, Mass.:

525 ANDREW, b. 2 May, 1742; m. 10 Jan., 1764, Lucy Park.
526 ELISHA, b. 4 Dec., 1745; d. 25 May, 1784.
527 ANTIPAS, b. 24 July, 1747; d. at Havana in 1764.
528 JOKTON, b. 1 May, 1750.
529 LUKE, b. 5 Oct., 1755; served as private in Revolution.
530 WILLIAM, b. 7 Jan , 1758.

ELISHA PUTNAM lived in Sutton, or in that part of the town now called Oxford. During the French and Indian War he served in the Provincial army and during the campaign of 1758 against Ticonderoga, he lost his life. Great numbers of the Provincial troops were killed or lost during this campaign, as the commander of the expedition, Gen. Abercrombie, was not only a coward in battle but an incompetent leader. The assault on Ticonderoga was continued all day by the Provincials and Regulars and over 1,900 were slain.

V. 204 Nehemiah (*Elisha, Edward, Thomas, John*), born in Salem Village, 22 Mar., 1719; died Sutton, 27 Nov., 1791; married in Sutton, 5 Oct., 1742, Sarah Manning. They lived in Sutton.

Children:

531 AARON, b. 23 Mar., 1744.
532 SARAH, b. 10 Mar , 1746.
533 HANNAH, b. 26 July, 1748; m. 25 Nov., 1773, Jonathan Willard.
534 RACHEL, b. 17 Apr., 1750.
535 SUSANNA, b. 19 Jan., 1752; m. 26 Mar., 1771, John Fuller.
536 EUNICE, b. 4 Dec., 1753; m. 4 Apr., 1773, Benjamin Shumway.
537 REUBEN, b. 9 Apr., 1757. " Deacon "
538 JOSEPH, b. 20 Sept., 1760.
539 BENJAMIN, twin with Joseph. "Reverend "

V. 205 Jonathan (*Elisha, Edward, Thomas, John*),

---

[50] That part now Middleton.

born in Salem Village, 19 July, 1721; died in Sutton;
married 3 Nov., 1743, Mrs. Anne (Chase) Stockwell,
daughter of Philip and Mary (Follansbee) Chase, and widow
of Nathaniel Stockwell, born 28 Sept., 1719. By her first
husband she had a son Nathaniel, born 1 April, 1741.
Nathaniel Stockwell, senior, died 2 April, 1741.

Children:

540   ADONIJAH, b. 6 or 9 Oct., 1744; m. 27 Nov., 1766, Mary Wilkins.
541   MARY, b. 25 Dec., 1755; m. Luke Putnam (No. 529).
542   FRANCIS, b. 24 Sept., 1758. "Captain."
543   JOHN.
544   JONATHAN FOLLANSBEE, b. 9 May, 1763; d. 30 Oct., 1858.

JONATHAN PUTNAM was carried to Sutton by his father,
and lived there always. He built a grist mill which the Sutton Cranberry Company now own. This property with the
water privilege descended through his son, Captain Francis,
to the latter's son Silas who sold it.

V. 208 Stephen (*Elisha, Edward, Thomas, John*),
born in Sutton, 4 April, 1728; died, according to Gen. Rufus
Putnam's account, at Northampton, 5 Mar., 1803; another
account states the death as occurring in May, 1802. He married 14 Mar., 1755, Mary, daughter of John and Abigail
(Chase) Gibbs of Sutton, born 10 Mar., 1737.

Children, nearly all born in Sutton:

545   SOLOMON, b. 17 July, 1755.
546   MARY JANE, b. 10 June, 1757.
547   RHODA, b. 3 July, 1759; m. John Evans and had several ch. This
         family removed to western New York.
548   JOHN, b. Winchester, N. H, 10 May, 1761, of Chesterfield, Vt.
549   GIDEON, b. 17 Apr., 1763.
550   ELISHA, b. 13 May, 1765.
551   LEWIS, b. ———. In 1854 was of Lansingburg and without children.
552   CHARLOTTE, b. 11 Jan., 1767; m. James Ross and had several
         children. This family removed to the western part of New York.
553   DAVID, b. 21 Mar., 1771; d. 9 Aug., 1832.
554   RUFUS, b. 22 Mar., 1773.
555   ABIGAIL, b. 10 Feb., 1776; m. Mr. Robertson. Lived in western
         New York.
556   LAVINA, b. 5 May, 1780.

JTNAM.

STEPHEN PUTNAM removed from Sutton to Hampshire county, but finally settled in Winchester, N. H.

V. 209 Amos (*Elisha, Edward, Thomas, John*), born in Sutton 22 July, 1730; died there, 17 Sept., 1811; married 26 June, 1760, Sarah, daughter of Samuel and Eliphal (Tilley) Swift, of Boston.

Children, born in Sutton:

557 ELIPHAL, b. 8 July, 1762; d. 25 Sept., 1845, m., 1st, Ebenezer Larned of Oxford; m., 2nd, Thomas Rice, jr., of Worcester.
558 LUCRETIA, b. 6 Sept. 1764; d. Jan., 1852; m. John Nichols, 3d, of Charlton.
559 REBECCA, b. 18 Feb., 1767; d. 29 Dec., 1854; m. Andrew Adams.
560 PAUL, b. 4 Mar., 1769; d. 1779.
561 SUSANNA, b.———; d. y.
562 ELIZABETH, b. 22 Oct., 1772; m. Ebenezer Newton.
563 POLLY, b. 1775; d. 1851, m. Benjamin Edwards.
564 SARAH T., b. 1779; m. Ebenezer Bryant. Both died about 1 Nov., 1855.
565 MARTHA, b. 25 Oct., 1781; d. 8 Oct., 1852; m. Silas Livermore.

V. 212 General Rufus (*Elisha, Edward, Thomas, John*), born in Sutton, 9 April, 1738; died in Marietta, Ohio, 4 May, 1824; married April, 1761, Elizabeth, daughter of William Ayers, Esquire, of Brookfield, who died 1762; married, second, 10 Jan., 1765, Persis, daughter of Zebulon Rice of Westborough, born 19 Nov., 1737; died at Marietta, Ohio, 6 Sept., 1820.

Children, by first marriage:

566 AYRES, b. and d. in 1762.

By second marriage:

567 ELIZABETH, b. 19 Nov., 1765; d. unm., 8 Nov., 1830.
568 PERSIS, b. 6 June, 1767; d. Sept., 1822.
569 SUSANNA, b. 5 Aug., 1768.
570 ABIGAIL, b. 7 Aug., 1770.
571 WILLIAM RUFUS, b. 12 Dec., 1771.
572 FRANKLIN, b. 27 May, 1774; d. April, 1776.
573 EDWIN, b. 19 Jan., 1776.
574 PATTY, b. 25 Nov., 1777.
575 CATHARINE, b. 17 Oct., 1780; d. Mar., 1808.

12

RUFUS PUTNAM was left fatherless at the age of seven. At no time during his youth would one have predicted that of the two great soldiers which the Putnam family has given to this country, he was to be one; yet such has proven to be the fact, and by some he is considered to far excel his cousin and fellow patriot in military qualities, even as he excelled in education. Yet he obtained this education only by the most persistent perseverance, for, with the exception of two years spent in Danvers immediately following his father's death, during which time he was an inmate in the family of his grandfather, Jonathan Fuller, he had no schooling. Upon his mother's marriage to John Sadler he returned to Sutton where Sadler kept an inn. Sadler was not inclined to encourage the fondness of his stepson for "book learning," so young Putnam was obliged to do his studying at odd moments, and at night by candle light; moreover, such text books as he had were obtained by his own efforts, he, occasionally earning a few pennies, by attention to the guests at the inn. With what he earned in this wise, he bought ammunition and by means of an old gun shot small game, which abounded in the neighborhood, from the sales of which he obtained the money necessary for elementary text-books. At the age of fourteen he chose his brother-in-law, Jonathan Dudley, of Sutton, guardian, and two years later we find him apprenticed to Daniel Matthews of Brookfield to learn the trade of millwright. This trade required some knowledge of geometry, and although Matthews did not send the boy to school, yet he did not discourage him in his studies as his stepfather had done. "During this time his physical frame grew fully as rapidly as his mind, so that when he was 18 years old he possessed the brawny limbs, the muscular power, and the full stature of a man six feet high." Early in his nineteenth year he enlisted as a private soldier in the company of Capt. Ebenezer Learned. The detachment left Brookfield on the 30th of April, 1757, reaching Fort Edward on the 15th of June. Determined to see service, he joined a company of rangers as a volunteer, and, on the 8th of July, marched under Lt. Collins,

on a scout around the lower end of Lake Champlain. Being
detailed with two comrades to reconnoitre South Bay, Putnam, being some time absent, the detachment supposing
them captured returned to camp, leaving the three scouts to
their fate. After forty-eight hours, without food, they reached
camp. This was his first taste of the work which lay before
him. Shortly afterward he did scout duty under the command
of Israel Putnam, then a captain in provincial service.

The expiration of his term of enlistment drawing near, and
it becoming evident that the provincial troops were to be kept
beyond the agreed time of their discharge, the company to the
number of seventy, under the leadership of their captain, having made snowshoes, silently left the camp and started through
the forest for home. They carried with them provisions for
fourteen days, but the hardships of the road, the difficulty of
proceeding in a proper course, and so many froze their feet and
hands, that from the lack of transportation facilities much of
their provision was abandoned. Their suffering, indeed, was
terrible; death from starvation or freezing stared them in the
face, but on the 15th of February, he arrived at his home
and in the following April reënlisted under Captain Whitcomb
for another campaign in the provincial service. In his journal
he records that from Northampton to Greenbush, at which
place he arrived June 8th, there was, with the exception of a
small fort on the Housatonic River, but one house. On account of his mechanical ability he was engaged with the
"regiment of carpenters" in such work as they could do.
Rufus Putnam kept a journal during this and his subsequent
terms of service, from which we learn of the feeling existing
in the camp at the cowardly manner in which General Webb
left the garrison at Fort William Henry to their fate. At
the end of the campaign of 1759 he was offered a lieutenant's
commission in the army but declined. Upon the close of
the campaign and war, having seen nearly four years service,
he resumed the business of building mills and cultivating his
farm, at every opportunity however, adding to his knowledge
of surveying.

It was in 1761 that he married Miss Elizabeth Ayers, but inside of a year was left alone with an infant son who, however, soon followed his mother. In his journal he touchingly alludes to his forlorn condition after this double bereavement, but in 1765 again married, this time Miss Persis Rice, and settled in North Brookfield.

Always an active man, and much interested in the schemes of the times, it was but natural that the project of the colonial officers to secure a grant of land from the Crown and to settle thereon should have had his support. They styled themselves the Military Adventurers, and engaged General Lyman to prosecute their claims; Lyman obtained a promise of lands in West Florida. The company appointed a committee, of which Col. Israel Putnam and Rufus Putnam were members, to prospect the proposed location. Having chartered a sloop they sailed from New York, 10 Jan., 1773, and arrived at Pensacola, 1 March, and although Governor Chester had received no instructions from the home government they pushed on and explored the Mississippi as far as the mouth of the Yazoo, thence some thirty miles up that river. Upon their return to Pensacola, although the Governor as yet had received no instructions he took it upon himself to promise them, upon very satisfactory terms, the location they had chosen and where they had laid out nineteen townships. Encouraged by the committee's report, quite a number of New Englanders seized the opportunity to emigrate to new lands; but, unfortunately, Governor Chester had in the meantime received positive orders not to grant or sell any more lands for the present. Thus the colonists, thrown upon their own resources in an unhealthy country, and being allowed to take only what unoccupied land they could find, soon became discouraged, and as many died the colony was abandoned. Rufus Putnam found awaiting him on his return more stirring matters than new schemes for colonization, for the relations between the colonies and the home government were daily becoming more strained.

As soon as the news of bloodshed on April 19th, 1775, reached Worcester County, Rufus Putnam was up and ready

to do his part with his neighbors and friends. As lieuten-
ant-colonel of a regiment commanded by David Brewer, he
marched to Roxbury, and after the battle of June 17th, he was
called upon to direct the raising of fortifications. He immediately constructed a line of fortifications on Roxbury Neck
and Sewall's Point, which attracted Washington's favorable
notice on his arrival. In December, he accompanied General
Lee to Providence and Newport and laid out works there,
particularly a battery to defend the harbor.

Upon returning to Boston, he found the American army still
shutting the British up in Boston, and Washington trying
to devise some method to force the issue favorably. During
a call on General Heath, Putnam's eye fell on a work of "Mul-
ler's Field Engineer," which after some entreaty he obtained.
From this work he procured the idea for effecting a lodg-
ment on Dorchester Heights, and which he accomplished on
the night of the 4th of March, thus forcing the evacuation of
Boston. These signal successes of Putnam proved to Washington what a valuable engineer he had with him and when
subsequent occasion offered he showed his appreciation of Putnam's ability in this capacity.

During 1776, he was charged with the supervision of the
works in and about New York. On the 11th Aug., 1776,
he was informed by Washington of his appointment by Congress as engineer with the rank of colonel. He rendered
signal service on the retreat from, and after the battle of
Long Island. On Dec. 17, 1776, he accepted the command of a regiment in the Massachusetts line. Upon being
notified of this, Washington wrote to Congress as follows :
"I have also to mention that for want of some establishment
in the department of engineers agreeable to the plan laid before Congress in October last, Colonel Putnam, who was at
the head of it, has quitted and takes a regiment in the state
of Massachusetts. I know of no other man even tolerably well
qualified for the conducting of that business. None of the
French gentlemen whom I have seen with appointments in that
way appear to know anything of the matter. There is one in

Philadelphia who, I am told, is clever; but him I have not seen."

Putnam's regiment was engaged in the campaign which culminated at Saratoga with the surrender of Burgoyne, and behaved themselves very creditably throughout. They went into winter quarters at Albany. In the following March he was called upon to fortify West Point, and was obliged to tear down much of what the French engineer in charge had accomplished. The Fort at West Point, built by his own regiment, is named for him. Gen. Israel Putnam was in command there at this time. During the early part of 1780, he was in Boston on leave of absence, and availed himself of this opportunity to obtain relief for the Massachusetts troops, then suffering greatly from lack of money and supplies. It was through his prompt action and forethought that a mutiny amongst the Massachusetts troops was prevented. During the autumn of 1782, he decided to withdraw from the army,[1] and on the 17th of December he wrote Washington, expressing his final determination to retire from active service and return to the care of his private affairs. During the absence of Colonel Putnam from home, Mrs. Putnam, with a family of small children was endeavoring to make an unproductive farm of fifty acres yield a sufficient income, helped out by the meagre allowance which her husband's pay permitted him to spare for her use. The distaff and needle helped to fill the breach; rigid economy and industry did the rest. The women of the revolution did their share in the struggle, and none were more noble hearted and self denying than was Mrs. Putnam. In 1780, Putnam bought on easy terms the confiscated property of Colonel Murray, a tory. This property was situated in Rutland and consisted of a large farm and spacious mansion. Although the war was over and Colonel Putnam had intended to devote himself to his own affairs, yet he was not permitted to retire completely to private life, for soon he was called upon to survey the eastern lands of the state of Massachusetts, and at once proceeded to the Passamaquoddy. In the year 1786,

---

[1] Congress voted him a Brigadier General's commission 7 Jan., 1783.

he was appointed commissioner to treat with the Penobscot Indians, together with General Lincoln and Judge Rice of Wiscasset. In January of the following year, he joined General Lincoln as a volunteer aid against the insurgents under Shays, and remained with him until their dispersion at Petersham. This year he was also appointed a justice of the peace and was elected to the legislature representing Rutland. During the year 1783–4, Putnam had urged upon Washington plans for the settlement of the western country, and as agent for the retired officers of the continental army had endeavored to bring this about; but, circumstances not being wholly ripe for the successful culmination of these plans, it was reserved for Dr. Manasseh Cutler, the prominent patriot and botanist of Essex County, Massachusetts, to obtain, three years later, the concessions asked for. Dr. Cutler not only obtained the grant of 1,500,000 acres of land to the Ohio Company upon easy terms, but was also instrumental in procuring the passage of the ordinance of 1787, which prohibited slavery north of the Ohio River. The one it is said was dependent on the other. Cutler and Putnam, working together, were the chief spirits in the enterprise. Therefore when on the 23d Nov., 1787, the directors of the Ohio Company appointed Putnam, superintendent of all the business relating to the commencement of their lands in the territory northwest of the Ohio River, he gladly undertook the difficult position. "The people to go forward in companies employed under my direction, were to consist of four surveyors, one blacksmith, and nine common hands, with two wagons, etc., etc. Major Hatfield White conducted the first party, which started from Danvers the first of December. The other party was appointed to rendezvous at Hartford, where I met them the first day of January, 1788." The two parties joined 14th Feb., 1788, at the Youghiogheny River, thence they proceeded by boat to the mouth of the Muskingum where they arrived on April 7, 1788, and commenced the settlement of Marietta.[60]

_____

[60] The first of the party to jump ashore is said to have been Allen Putnam of Danvers.

The four surveyors who accompanied Putnam were Colonel Sproat, Colonel Meiggs, Major Tupper, and Mr. John Mathers. The family of Rufus Putnam arrived at the settlement in 1790. The early years of the settlement were years of watch and ward against the Indians, and many suffered at their hands. If it had not been for the careful management of the affairs of the company by Putnam and his associates, disaster must surely have come. Financial trouble threatened the company in their early years, but Congress was disposed to treat the adventurers with generosity, appreciating the great difficulties of their position. General Putnam, himself, lost quite heavily in advances to the settlers. The expense of the Indian wars to the Ohio Company was $11,350, a very heavy burden for them to bear. On May 5, 1792, Putnam received the news of his appointment as brigadier-general in the army of the United States and immediately proceeded to carry out the orders of the Secretary of War, which were to procure the signing of a treaty with the Wabash Indians and in which he was successful. It is impossible in the limited space at hand to give but an inadequate idea of the services of General Putnam to the northwest. He was active in all schemes for the advancement of the settlements in educational, social and more material projects.

In 1798 he, with others, founded Muskingum Academy, and, in 1811, was appointed by the territorial legislature, one of the trustees of the Ohio University, in the welfare of which he had the deepest interest, and was instrumental in obtaining endowments and placing the college on a firm foundation.

His last public office was that of a member of the convention which met in 1802 to form a state constitution, and to his firm and determined opposition was due the failure to incorporate in the constitution the right to hold slaves. The slavery party was defeated by but one vote.

The latter years of his life were spent among the scenes of his success, and during these years the church had many occasions to bless him for his kindly and substantial interest. Cared for by his maiden daughter, Elizabeth, he calmly waited for the end which came on the 4th of May, 1824, and was laid to rest in the Mound Cemetery, so called from the ancient mound, the preservation of which is due him who rests so near it. Even in that early day, when American archæology was as yet unheard of, he manifested a keen appreciation of the relics of the people who had once inhabited that fruitful region. He was nearly the first to realize the importance of preserving the memorials of a bygone race if we would know aught concerning them, and to another of the name, Prof. Frederic W. Putnam, more than any other, we owe what knowledge we have of the wonderful works and customs of those people.

Throughout the Ohio valley to-day, a deep and sincere veneration is felt for the pioneer of that vast territory, and to none can the title be more truly given than to Gen. Rufus Putnam, the "Father of the Northwest."

The following inscription is upon his gravestone:

GEN. RUFUS PUTNAM

A revolutionary officer, and the leader of the colony which made the first settlement in the Territory of the Northwest at Marietta, April 7, 1788.

BORN APRIL 9, 1738

DIED MAY 4, 1824

PERSIS RICE, WIFE OF

RUFUS PUTNAM

BORN NOVEMBER 19, 1737.

DIED SEPTEMBER 6, 1820

"THE MEMORY OF THE JUST IS BLESSED."

NOTE. As it is not in the power of the author to do full justice in these pages to Gen. Putnam's career, the reader is referred to Hildreth's Lives of the Early Settlers of Ohio; Walker's History of Athens Co., Ohio; Life of Rufus Putnam, with extracts from his journal, by Mary Cone; History of Sutton, Mass.; The Marietta Centennial Number of the Ohio Archæological & Historical Quarterly (June, 1888); Journal of Gen. Rufus Putnam, 1757-1760, by E. C. Dawes; Essex Institute Historical Collections, XXV; New England Historical Genealogical Register, Vol. 42.

V. 213 Oliver (*Joseph, Edward, Thomas, John*), baptized at Salem Village, 21 Oct., 1722; died between 1789 and 1794; married 22 Dec., 1743, Hannah Brown who was living in 1794. Lived in Danvers, just beyond Hathorne's Hill. The house is still standing.

Children, baptized North Parish, Danvers:

576 WILLIAM, bapt. 27 May, 1744.

577 MEHITABLE, bapt. 16 Aug., 1747; m., 1794, Joseph Knight of Middleton.

578 OLIVER, bapt. 4 Feb., 1753.

579 LYDIA, bapt. 29 Dec., 1754; m. Benjamin Ray, tailor, living in Penobscot, Hancock Co., Me., 1794.

580 LUCY, bapt. 80 Jan., 1763; m. Richard Luscomb, junior, of Salem, joiner. Ch.: Samuel and Richard. Both parents and children died previous to 1794.

V. 214 Joseph (*Joseph, Edward, Thomas, John*), baptized Salem Village, 26 April, 1724. Will dated 3 Mar., 1781; proved 17 April, 1781; married 31 Jan., 1745, Mary, daughter of Israel and Sarah (Putnam) Porter (No. 147), baptized 24 April, 1726; died 1811.

Children, born in Danvers:

581 LYDIA, bapt. 27 July, 1746.

582 SARAH, bapt. 29 Jan., 1748-9; d. y.

583 JOSEPH, bapt. 21 Apr., 1751.

584 ISRAEL, bapt. 24 June, 1753.

585 MARY, bapt. 14 Sept., 1755; d. y.

586 LYDIA, bapt. 26 Feb., 1758; not mentioned in father's will.

587 JOHN, bapt. 18 Jan., 1761; not mentioned in father's will.

588 BETTY, bapt. 30 Oct., 1763.

589 MARY, bapt. 26 Jan., 1767.

590 PORTER, bapt. 25 Mar., 1770.

JOSEPH PUTNAM was more or less prominent in the local affairs of Danvers. He was tythingman, 1754 and 1758; surveyor of highways, 1756; constable 1764.

V. 218 Major Ezra (*Ezra, Edward, Thomas, John*), born at Salem Village; baptized there 8 June, 1729; died Marietta, Ohio, 19 Mar., 1811 (gravestone); married 21

June, 1750, Lucy (No. 232) Putnam, probably daughter of Col. David Putnam, who died at Marietta, 20 July, 1818, aged eighty-seven (gravestone.)

Children, born in Middleton:

591 BETTY, b. 18 Mar., 1751; m. 11 Nov., 1767, Archelaus Batchelder.

592 NEHEMIAH, b. 14 Oct., 1753.

593 LUCY, b. 4 Jan., 1757; d. 19 May, 1802; m. 9 Mar., 1780, Samuel Small, of Danvers, who m., 2nd, 25 Nov., 1802, Mrs. Jerusha (Upton) Fuller, widow of Jacob Fuller. The following obituary was found among some old papers: "May 19, 1802, Mrs. Lucy Small died in the 74th (?) year of her age. She was wife of Mr. Samuel Small, and 2nd daughter of Major Ezra Putnam, now at the Ohio. She lived much beloved, and died greatly lamented. Her sickness was short, but attended with the most excruciating pains, which she bore with an uncommon share of Christian patience, and met death with a calm composure of mind in the animating hope of a blessed immortality, through the merits of the great Redeemer."

594 EZRA, b. 5 July, 1759; killed by the Indians during the winter of 1791–92. Ezra had gone to Marietta about 1788, and some of his letters are extant. In one under date of 29th May, 1788, to his mother, he speaks well of the settlement at Marietta and mentions his brother Small of Middleton.

595 DEBORAH, b. 19 Jan., 1761; m. Feb., 1785, David, son of Andrew and Elizabeth (Clark) Fuller of Middleton. Ch.: Andrew, b. 6 Feb., 1786; d. 5 Aug., 1810. Jedediah, b. 7 Oct., 1788, settled in Ohio, but d. while a young man. Betsey, b. 17 Jan., 1791; m. Jabez Farley of Salem. Eunice, b. 19 Mar., 1793; d. 5 Aug., 1795. Lucy, b. 31 July, 1795; m. 10 Apr., 1817, John Ross. Nehemiah Putnam, b. 15 Sept., 1797; m. 25 Dec., 1823, Mary Ann Perkins. Ezra, b. 23 June, 1800; d. in Ohio while a young man.

596 DAVID, b. 10 July, 1767; d. of some sickness at Marietta previous to 1792. He was graduated from Phillips Andover Academy.

597 JOHN, b. ——— (not on town records); killed by the Indians at the same time that his brother Ezra was.

EZRA PUTNAM lived in Middleton, but on the Lexington Alarm Lists at the State House he is named as lieutenant in Capt. Asa Prince's company, and as of Danvers. His time of service there is given as two days.

From a "General Return of the Army of the United Colonies at Cambridge, Jan. 8th, 1776," we learn that he then held the commission of Major in Col. Israel Hutchinson's Regiment, the 27th Foot. Among the other officers of this

regiment were Captain Enoch Putnam, Adjutant Tarrant Putnam, Lieutenant (second) Tarrant Putnam, Ensign Jeremiah
Putnam.

On the Coat Rolls, *i. e.* rolls of men who served eight
months from May to December, 1775, at the siege of Boston,
occurs the name of Ezra Putnam, drummer, of Middleton;
probably, this was the young son of Major Ezra.

After the Revolutionary War, Major Ezra settled on the
old farm but in 1789[61] he and his wife joined his sons Ezra,
David, and John in Ohio. Many letters still remain in the
possession of Miss Susan Putnam of Danvers which throw
much light on the incidents of the early settlements on the
Ohio. From these letters and other sources we find that
the sons went up the Muskingum River to their and their
father's "donation land" in the fall of 1790. Soon after came
the Big Bottom Massacre and the sons lost their lives. The
old people were obliged to take refuge in Campus Martius
and there for many years Mrs. Putnam kept a "domestic
boarding house." They had many trials; the death of their
son Nehemiah whom they had endeavored to persuade and
settle in Ohio, the gradually failing memory of the Major,
the severe times and high price of labor, all these are mentioned.

During the long evenings in Campus Martius it was a
common occurrence to get the Major to sing a seventy verse
ballad on the taking of Capestown, and to recount the many
stories of the French and Indian War in which he had taken
part, having held an officer's commission at the taking of
Cape Breton.

Both the Major and Mrs. Putnam are buried in the northern end of Gen. Rufus Putnam's lot at the Mound cemetery.

Upon their gravestones are the following inscriptions:

"Sacred to the Memory of Major Ezra Putnam: a native
of Massachusetts, who died March 19th, 1811, aged 83 years."

[61] Dismissed from the church at Middleton at his own request, with his wife, 27
Sept., 1789.

"Sacred to the Memory of Lucy Putnam, who died July 20th, 1818, aged 87 years."

Major Ezra Putnam was short but not of heavy build, his wife was stout, and both were of lively and cheerful disposition.

Among the old letters mentioned above is one of date of 29th June, 1790, in which description is given of the excitement and unbelief in Ohio of "a scheme to bring vessels to Marretta by *fire works.*" Gen. Rufus Putnam, however, the writer goes on to say, endorses the scheme.

Gen. Rufus Putnam in his Memoirs states that all three of Major Ezra's sons left male issue; this is probably a mistake.

V. 220 Phineas (*Isaac, Edward, Thomas, John*), born in Salem Village, 1 Oct., 1722; of Sutton.

Children, probably born in or near Sutton:

598	LEVI,	; removed to Washington, Vt.
599	ENOCH, b.	
600	DANIEL,	
601	BETTY,	; d. 5 Apr., 1784 or 5.
602	HULDAH,	
603	EUNICE,	

V. 221 Asaph (*Isaac, Edward, Thomas, John*), born in Salem Village, 11 Sept., 1724; married 7 Sept., 1743, Sarah, daughter of Jonathan Park. Asaph Putnam was carried to Sutton when a boy but left there about 1760. The baptisms of his children are from Sutton church records.

Children:

604 ABIJAH, bapt. 21 Oct., 1744.
605 ASAPH, bapt. 18 June, 1749.
606 JONAS, bapt. 16 Aug., 1752.
607 EPHRON, } bapt. 7 July, 1756.
608 PARK, }

V. 224 Nathan (*Isaac, Edward, Thomas, John*), born in Salem Village, 24 Oct., 1730; died Sutton, 6 Aug., 1813; married 2 Aug., 1752, Betsey, daughter of James Buffington of Salem, born there, 28 Feb. (another authority Sept.,) 1734; died 26 Aug., 1810.

Children, born in Sutton :

609 ZADOCK, b. 29 Dec., 1752.

610 MICAH, b. 8 April, 1754.

611 JAMES, b. 26 Nov., 1755.

612 BETTY, b. 12 Jan., 1758; d. 21 Dec., 1812; m. 14 Nov., 1776, Lt. Stephen, son of Samuel and Lucretia (Richardson) Marble, of Sutton, a sadler by trade. Ch.:[68] Nathan, b. 29 June, 1778. Betsey, b. 10 Jan., 1780. Polly, b. 10 Sept., 1781. Palmer, b. 20 Sept., 1784. Charlotte, b. 7 Dec., 1786. Samuel, b. 3 Dec., 1788. Nancy, d. y. (of lockjaw).

613 LYDIA, b. 31 Dec , 1759; m. 7 Nov., 1777, Stephen Fuller of Vermont, and had twelve children.

614 NATHAN, b. 16 May, 1761.

615 HANNAH, b. 13 Mar., 1763; d. 28 Sept., 1818; m. 15 Dec.. 1796, John (but according to John Putnam of Grafton in 1836,'Waters'), son of Stephen and Huldah (Flagg) Fuller, as his second wife. Ch.: Stephen, b. 6 Aug., 1797; d. 22 Sept., 1850. Nathan, b. 24 May, 1799. Richard, b. 1 Nov., 1802; d. 29 Mar., 1876. Betsey, b. 17 Jan., 1804, m. Tyler Carpenter.

616 ABNER, b. 17 Mar., 1765; m. Abigail Waters. Abner Putnam followed the business of scythe-making; in 1835 he was a resident of Ludlow, Me.

617 SALLY, b. 27 Feb., 1765; m. 26 Feb., 1790, Jesse, son of Samuel and Patience (Gale) Marble, of Rutland. Ch.: Lewis, b. 7 Sept., 1790. Esther, b. 12 Jan., 1792. Sally, b. 22 Aug., 1793. Sukey, b. 25 Sept., 1796. Betsey, b. 22 May, 1798.

618 TAMAR, b. 23 Oct., 1768; d. 6 Dec., 1819; m. 17 Mar., 1785, John, son of John and Elizabeth (Town) King, of Ward. Ch: Tamar, b. 7 July, 1785. John, b. 7 Feb., 1787. James.

619 POLLY, b. 1 Apr., 1770; d. prev. to 1802; m. 4 July, 1791, Amos, son of Amos and Abigail (Cobb) Waters, a blacksmith, b. 18 Feb., 1764; d. 18 Mar., 1856. They had one child.

620 JOHN, b. 3 Sept., 1771; m. Anna Hodgskins of New Ipswich, N.H. Scythe-maker.

621 OLIVER, b. 19 July, 1773; d. *s. p.*; m. Elizabeth Newton. A farmer of Dixfield, Me., in 1836.

622 GEORGE W., b. 17 May, 1778; d. *s. p.* Farmer.

623 ABIGAIL, b. 20 Mar., 1775; m. Simon Rawson, a farmer of Uxbridge, Mass.

NATHAN PUTNAM was an energetic and popular man. He was known as "Esquire" Putnam and was noted for the great number of marriages he performed. He bought the

---

[68] There were several more children born previous to 1835, but their names are unknown to me.

original homestead of Isaac Putnam from Phineas Putnam, but his son Capt. Abner Putnam sold the place. Nathan Putnam operated a trip-hammer run by horse-power and carried on the manufacture of scythes, enjoying the credit of being the father of scythe-making in Massachusetts. Many of his descendants have been in the same line of business.

V. 226 Isaac (*Isaac, Edward, Thomas, John*), born 4 Nov., 1734; published to Rachel Pratt, 22 Mar., 1760. Mrs. Putnam died at the home of his son David, at Becket, aged one hundred and four years.

Children :

624 DAVID.
625 ISAAC, bapt. 1763. (This is doubtful date.)

V. 228 Capt. Daniel (*Isaac, Edward, Thomas, John*), born in Sutton, 28 Mar., 1739; died Cornish, N. H., 1809; married 25 June, 1761, Anna, daughter of Hon. Samuel Chase of Sutton.

They removed to Cornish in 1764, and spent the winter in a camp built for the use of men who had been cutting masts for the Royal Navy.

Children, born in Cornish :

626 SAMUEL.
627 DANIEL, drowned in the Conn. River, while quite young.
628 ISAAC.

Town clerk of Cornish 1775. Served in Continental Army under Col. Jona. Chase in 1777 for three years. In 1781 member of Capt. Moody Dustin's Co., 1st N. H. Continental. Selectman in 1784.

V. 231 William (*David, Joseph, Thomas, John*), born in Salem Village; baptized there 8 Mar., 1729–30; will dated at Watertown 4 June, probated at Worcester, 7 July, 1807; married in Danvers, 5 Nov., 1751, Elizabeth daughter of Josiah and Ruth (Hutchinson) Putnam who died previous to 1807.

Children :

629 REBECCA, b. 26 April, 1753; d. Danvers, Sept., 1814; m. Capt.
Samuel, son of Col. Jeremiah and Sarah (Andrews) dau. Daniel
and Ginger (Porter) Hutchinson. Ginger Porter was dau. of
Israel and Sarah (dau. Lt. James Putnam) Porter Page of
Danvers; b. there 1 Aug., 1753 (or 1 July); d. 2 Sept., 1814.
Capt. Page was at the storming of Stony Point. For their dau.
Rebecca's descendants see Pickering Gen., 38 vii-182. For their
son Jeremiah's dau., Laura Deland, descendants see ditto, 26
ix-417.

630 ANDREW, b. 2 April, 1755.

631 WILLIAM. b. 15 Mar., 1757.

632 ELIZABETH, b. 25 Mar., 1764; d. 9 Nov. 1841; m. May, 1794, Capt.
Samuel Endicott of Salem, son of John and Martha (Putnam)
Endicott, b. June, 1763; d. 1 May, 1828. Ch.: Sam'l, b. Mar.,
1795; d. unm., May, 1828. Eliza, m. 7 Jan., 1838, Augustus
Perry. Martha, m. July, 1823, Francis Peabody. William Put-
nam, b. 5 Mar., 1803.[63] Clara, m. Sept. 1827, George Peabody.

WILLIAM PUTNAM settled in Sterling, Mass., and in 1780
was a member of the Convention which framed the State
Constitution.

V. 235 Joseph (*David, Joseph, Thomas, John*), born
in Salem Village, 23 Sept., 1739; died in Danvers, 9 Mar.,
1818; married there 26 Mar., 1770, Ruth Flint.

Children, born in Danvers :

633 RUTH, b. 29[64] June, 1773; d. 22 Jan., 1849, m. 5 Nov., 1799, Allen
Nourse, of Danvers. Ch.: Polly, b. 29 Aug., 1800; d. unm. 3 Jan.,
1825. Pamelia, b. 6 June, 1802; d. 9 Oct., 1872, unm. Ruthy, b.
6 Dec., 1803; d. 5 Sept., 1883; m. 6 Dec., 1832, Elijah Hutchinson.
Samuel Putnam, b. 14 Feb., 1806; d. 8 May, 1872; m. 24 May, 1836,
Mary E. Proctor; m., 2d, 21 Jan., 1846, Phebe W. Proctor. Daniel E., b. 5 Apr., 1808; d. unm. 16 Oct., 1887. Hannah Endicott, b.
25 Dec., 1810; d. 31 Dec., 1832; m. 5 Dec., 1831, Thomas E.
Dodge. Sally, b. 3 Oct., 1813; m. Orrin Putnam. Eliza Flint, b.
26 Dec., 1816; d. 27 Feb., 1887; m. 14 June, 1843, Stephen
Franklin Reed.

634 DAVID, b. 10 Oct., 1774; d. 1775.

635 DAVID, b. 4 May, 1776; d. 1776.

636 JESSE, b. 3 April, 1778; d. 10 Feb., 1861.

[63] See page 145, number 398, and footnote.
[64] Family Bible record.

637 PARMELIA or MELLY, b. 13 Nov., 1780; d. 24 Dec., 1797.
638 POLLY, b. 19 April, 1784; d. 8 Oct., 1831; m. 16 Jan., 1806,
 Ebenezer, son of Benj. and Rebecca (Putnam) Upton of Reading,
 b. 14 Jan., 1788; d. 18 Aug., 1822. Ch.: Daniel Putnam, b. 18
 Dec., 1806.
639 CATHARINE, b. 16 May, 1791; d. æt. 4 weeks.

DEACON JOSEPH PUTNAM was a smaller man than his
brother Israel, was of a light complexion, his countenance was
open and pleasant. In his old age he retained the agility of
youth. Throughout his long life he was prominent in town
and parish affairs and held the office of deacon in the church,
having been chosen 2 Sept., 1802.

V. 236 Israel (*David, Joseph, Thomas, John*), born
in Salem Village, 29 June, 1742; died in Danvers, 23 Feb.,
1825; married there, 7 Feb., 1771,[65] Sarah Eppes who died
8 Oct., 1784; married, second, 22 Feb., 1785, Mrs. Emme
Prince, widow of Ezra Prince of Danvers, who died 10 July,
1831. She was born 21 Jan., 1743.

Children, born in Danvers:

640 ALLEN, b. 11 April, 1772; d. at sea 10 Nov., 1793, unm.
641 DANIEL, b. 8 Mar., 1774; d. 10 Feb., 1854.
642 ISRAEL, b. 29 Sept., 1776; d. 15 July, 1795, unm.
643 SALLY, b. 6 Mar., 1779; d. 20 Aug., 1811.
644 BETSEY, b. 9 Oct., 1782; d. 23 Oct., 1864.

ISRAEL PUTNAM inherited that part of the David Putnam
estate upon which stands the Gen. Israel Putnam house. His
brother Deacon Joseph had the other half of the farm.

Israel Putnam lived all his life in Danvers on his ancestral
acres. He was a man of great breadth and warmth of character, generous, of pure tastes and of a deep religious nature.
It is said by his granddaughter, Mrs. Harriet (Putnam)
Fowler that he resembled the portrait of his uncle, Gen. Israel
Putnam, having a round pleasant face, blue eyes, but display-
ing his firmness and decision of character although frank and
good natured.

[65] Town Records.—They were married by "Benj. Prescott, Esq."

13

These traits in his character led to the seeking of his advice on town matters as an opinion given by him was rarely at fault.

For his time he was a close observer of affairs and reader of books, especially those pertaining to scripture.

V. 240 Jesse (*David, Joseph, Thomas, John*), born in Danvers, 8 January, 1754; died in Boston, 14 April, 1837; married 11 Feb., 1776, Susanna Thatcher, daughter of Col. Samuel and Mary (Brown) Thatcher, of Cambridge, born 1755, died 8 April, 1839. A son of Col. Ebenezer Thatcher, who was a prominent citizen during the Revolution, married Lucy, daughter of Gen. Knox.

Child :

645   CATHARINE, b. in Boston, 9 Jan., 1777; d. in Peterborough, N. H., 27 Mar., 1862. Miss Putnam was a most cultivated and worthy woman. Throughout her life she was constantly doing good and by her example urging others to be charitable and patriotic. When the Civil War broke out she presented the Putnam Guards of Danvers with a stand of colors and in other ways encouraged them. Peterborough owes much to her benevolence, among other things a fine public park.

JESSE PUTNAM was one of the foremost of Boston merchants, universally respected by all who knew him. He was graduated from Harvard College in 1775.

In a letter of date 1834, he states he had become separated from his family in early life and never had returned to the homestead except on visits.

He was more or less prominent in public affairs in Boston.

The inscription upon the opposite page was placed upon his monument at Mount Auburn.

JESSE PUTNAM
LONG KNOWN
AS THE FATHER OF THE
MERCHANTS OF BOSTON
A DISTINCTION
NOT CLAIMED BY HIMSELF
BUT ACCORDED BY OTHERS,
IN CONSIDERATION OF THE
INTELLIGENCE, ENERGY AND INTEGRITY
WITH WHICH
FOR MORE THAN HALF A CENTURY,
AT HOME AND ABROAD
HE FOLLOWED AND ADORNED
HIS PROFESSION.

On the same monument:

HERE REPOSE
WITH THOSE OF HER HUSBAND
THE REMAINS OF
SUSANNAH
FOR MORE THAN SIXTY YEARS THE WIFE OF
JESSE PUTNAM
SHE DIED APRIL 8, 1839
AGED 84.

V. 241 Col. Israel (*Gen. Israel, Joseph, Thomas, John*), born in Salem Village, 28 Jan., 1739–40; died in Belpre, Ohio, 7 March, 1812; married ——, 1764, Sarah Waldo of Pomfret, Conn.

Children, born in Pomfret:

646 SARAH, b. 25 Oct., 1764; d. 1818; m. Samuel Thornily.
647 ISRAEL, b. 20 Jan., 1766; d. 9 Mar., 1824.
648 AARON WALDO, b. 18 April, 1767; d. 21 Aug., 1822.
649 DAVID, b. 24 Feb., 1769; d. Marietta, Ohio, 31 Mar., 1856.
650 WILLIAM PITT, b. 11 Dec., 1770; d. Marietta, 8 Oct., 1800.
651 MARY, b. 5 Aug., 1773; m. Daniel Mayo.
652 GEORGE WASHINGTON, b. 27 July, 1777; d. ——, 1800; of Verney, Ind.
653 ELIZABETH, b. 19 Jan., 1780; m. Joel Craig.

Of the above children only David was living in 1852. Mary and Elizabeth settled in Newport, Ky.

COL. PUTNAM spent his boyhood, as most boys of his time, on the farm, only receiving such education as the country schools afforded, but of which he made good use.

When his father hastened to Cambridge in 1775, Israel raised a company of volunteers and joined the army shortly after, where he remained under his father's orders until the arrival of Washington.

Upon the appointment of Col. Israel Putnam as Major-General, Capt. Israel Putnam was appointed an aide (22 July). In this capacity he served on the Hudson, but after three years' service he retired to his farm. During the time he was in the army he acquitted himself with distinction.

When the Ohio company was formed, Col. Israel Putnam joined the company, and, with two of his sons, crossed the mountains with a wagon load of farming utensils. Mrs. Putnam remained on the farm at Pomfret. At the formation of the settlement at Belpre, Colonel Putnam settled there, devoted himself to clearing a farm, and in 1790 he returned to Connecticut to bring out his family. During his absence from Ohio the Indian War broke out, which delayed his return for five years.

At Belpre, he took a leading part in the affairs of the community, and his wealth which, though not great, was greatly in excess of that of most of his neighbors, enabled him to introduce many improvements. In church affairs he was prominent, being an earnest Episcopalian, and often read the services for the church.

As a farmer he was constantly on the lookout for means to improve his stock and was the means of introducing in Ohio a fine breed of cattle, which he had gotten by improving the native Connecticut cattle by crossing with imported stock, obtained during the Revolution.

"Col. Putnam was a man of sound, vigorous mind, and remarkable for his plain common sense; abrupt and homely in his manner and address, but perfectly honest and upright in his intercourse with mankind."

V. 243 Hannah (*Gen. Israel, Joseph, Thomas, John*), born in Pomfret, 25 Aug., 1744; died 3 April, 1821; married 26 Oct., 1764, John Winchester, son of Isaac[66] and Sarah (Winchester) Dana of Pomfret, Conn., born in Pomfret, 6 Jan., 1739–40, died Feb., 1813.

Children :

654 ISAAC, b. 28 Nov., 1765; d. 2 Mar., 1831; m., 1st, Sally Dean; m., 2d, Laura Miner. One of his children was Rev. Judah Dana, b. 29 Sept., 1817; Dartmouth College, 1845; he m. 5 July, 1847, Marcia Holmes Weld of Hartland, Vt.

655 BETSEY, b. ——, 1768; d. 81 Mar., 1841; m. 1790, Jonathan, son of Jonathan and Melatiah (Metcalf) Ware, b., Wrentham, 27 April, 1767; d. 1 Feb., 1838, H. C. 1790. Ch.: Jonathan, b. 1796. Camilla, b. 28 Nov., 1804; d., Cabot, Vt., 10 Aug., 1871. Mary Betsey, b. 13 Sept., 1800; d. 3 Jan., 1849; m. Sam'l Butterworth of Andover, N. H. John, b. 1798. Elinor, b. 1807; d. y.

656 BENJAMIN, b. ——, 1770; d. 21 July, 1838; m. Sarah Shaw; res. at Waterford, Ohio. Ch.: a dau. m. to A. M. Dawes.

657 JUDAH, b. 25 April, 1772; d. 27 Dec., 1845.

658 ISRAEL PUTNAM, b. 3 April, 1774; of Danville, Vt.; State Counselor, etc.; m. Sarah Smith.

659 HANNAH PUTNAM, b. ——, 1775; d., Pomfret, Conn., 14 April, 1850; m. Zebulon Lyon, who d., Woodstock, Vt.

[66] Isaac Dana was son of Benjamin, whose father, Richard Dana, settled in that part of Cambridge, now Brighton, about 1640.

660 JOHN WINCHESTER, b. 16 Jan., 1777.
661 DANIEL, b. 28 Mar., 1778.
662 SARAH WINCHESTER, b. ——, 1779; m. Major Elisha Smith of
      Pomfret, Vt.
663 DAVID, b. 24 Mar., 1781; d. 12 Mar., 1839.
664 EUNICE, b. ——, 1783; m. Harvey Chase of Cornish, N. H.; Yale,
      1800. Attorney.
665 SCHUYLER, b. ——, 1785; d. inf.
666 MARY, b. ——, 1787; d. ——, 1816; m. —— Greet.

John Winchester Dana removed, in 1773, to the grant which Governor Wentworth had made to his father in the New Hampshire Grants in 1761. The new town was called Pomfret. Here he became prominent in the affairs of town and state. Representative in the legislature in 1878, '80, '81, '92, and a member of constitutional convention of 1777.

V. 245 Mehitable (*Gen. Israel, Joseph, Thomas, John*), born in Pomfret, Conn., 21 Oct., 1749; died 28 Nov., 1789; married, 1771, Capt. Daniel Tyler,[67] of Brooklyn, Conn., an aide-de-camp of Gen. Israel Putnam at Bunker Hill. Captain Tyler was born 1750; died 29 April, 1832; married, second, Sarah,[68] widow of Deacon Benjamin Chaplin. She was a granddaughter of President Jonathan Edwards and a sister of Aaron Burr's wife.

Three of the sons of Captain Tyler graduated at West Point, Septimus, Edwin and Daniel.

Children :

667 MARY, b. ——; d. 12 June, 1832.
668 PASCAL PAOLA, b. 15 May, 1774; m. Betsey Baker. Ch. : Caroline
      E., m. Hulings Cowperthwait of Philadelphia. Daniel Putnam,
      lawyer in Brooklyn, formerly Secretary of State for Conn.; m.

[67] Captain Tyler was son of Daniel Tyler who was born at Groton, 22 Feb., 1701; died 20 Feb.. 1802, aged 100 years 11 mos. 26 days. He married thrice and had 21 children; at the time of his death there were living 6 children, 50 grandchildren and 120 great-grandchildren.
[68] The children of Captain Tyler by his 2d wife were Sally, b. 29 May, 1791; d. Nov. 1857; m. Rev. Sam'l P. Williams of Newburyport, Mass.; Frederic, b. 5 July, 1795; d. at Hartford, Conn., æt. 85; m. Sarah Sharp of Abington, Conn., and was father of Gen. Robert O. Tyler, U.S.A. Edwin, b. 5 Jan., 1794; d. 4 Aug., 1838; m. Alla Mary Edwards who d. 22 Sept., 1833, æt. 31. He m. again. Gen. Daniel P., was of the late war.

his cousin Emily C. Tyler. Mary B., m. James Holbrook of Brooklyn, Conn.

669 DANIEL P., b. ———; d. 18 Jan., 1798, æt. 21 years.

669a SEPTIMUS, b. ———; d. 26 May, 1782, æt. 2 yrs. 8 mos.

670 WILLIAM P., b. 7 Oct., 1781; d. 2 Dec., 1859; m. 1 Jan., 1809, Waty, dau. of Nathan and Hannah (Putnam),[69] Williams of Canterbury, Conn. They lived a few years at Warner, Vt., but returned to Brooklyn. Ch.: Hannah Putnam, b. 15 Mar. ——; d. 30 Jan., 1892; m. 14 July, 1840, David Gilmur of Elizabeth, N. J. Elizabeth, b. 19 Oct., 1809; d. unm. 29 Apr., 1839. Maria Cordelia, b. 3 Sept., 1811; d. 1 Mar., 1882; m. 11 Sept., 1832, John Gallup, 3d, of Brooklyn, at one time general manager of Lake Shore R. R. Emily Cecilia (twin with Maria), d. 13 Feb., 1869; m. Daniel P. Tyler above. Waty Williams, b. 27 Aug., 1814; m. 30 May, 1842, Rev. Benjamin Howe, b. Ipswich, 3 Nov., 1807; d. Hudson, N. H. (Ch.: Homer, b. Wells, Me., 16 Aug., 1848, of Hudson, N. H. Cecil Putnam, b. Meredith, N. Y., 8 Nov., 1857; d. 13 Feb., 1866.) William P., b. 7 July, 1815; d. 10 Sept., 1816. William Williams, b. 30 July ——; d. 27 Jan., 1865; m. 22 Jan., 1855, Joanna Farrington.

671 BETSY, b. 18 June, 1784; m. ———, Eldredge of Warren, Vt. Ch.: Betsy. Frederick. Daniel. Lucretia. Edward. Lucy.

672 SEPTIMUS, d. on passage home from St. Domingo, on board the frigate Congress, 17 Sept., 1817, æt. 27 years. He was commercial agent of U. S. at the Island of St. Domingo.

V. 246 Mary (*Gen. Israel, Joseph, Thomas, John*), born in Pomfret, Conn., 10 May, 1753; married 2 Nov., 1773, Samuel, son of Zachariah Waldo of Pomfret, Conn., a brother of Dr. Albigence Waldo and a descendant of deacon Cornelius Waldo of Chelmsford, Mass., born 28 Aug., 1747, died 14 Feb., 1810.

Children :

673 BETSEY, b. 22 Sept., 1774; m. 12 May, 1799, John Augustus Gleason.

674 ISRAEL, b. 12 Dec., 1776; d. 2 Jan., 1786.

675 SAMUEL, b. 12 Mar., 1779; d. Hartford, Mar., 1826, author of many biographical works.

676 FRANCIS, b. 22 April, 1783; m. 12 May, 1805, Lucinda Clement Cheney. Ch.: Catharine, b. 14 May, 1806. Samuel, b. 1 June, 1810. Mary Putnam, b. 12 Sept., 1812. Frances Lucinda, b. 12 April, 1815.

677 LEWIS, b. 25 June, 1787; d. 1 May, 1788.

[69] Hannah Putnam was dau. of John (*Eleazer, Eleazer, John, John*) Putnam and was born 1 Jan., 1763.

678   POLLY, b. 18 April, 1789.
679   LEWIS PUTNAM, b. 22 Mar., 1796; d. 28 Mar., 1796.

V. 247 Eunice (*Gen. Israel, Joseph, Thomas, John*), born in Pomfret, 10 Jan., 1756; died 27 June, 1799; married, first, Elisha son of Rev. Ephraim and Deborah (Lothrop) Avery of Brooklyn, Conn., born 3 December, 1744. A sister Elizabeth married Rev. Aaron Putnam (No. 326);[70] married, second, 7 Sept., 1783, Brig. Gen. Lemuel Grosvenor, son of Ebenezer, jr., and Lucy (Cheney) Grosvenor, born 18 April, 1752; died in Pomfret, 19 Jan., 1833; he married, second, 9 Mar., 1801, Sarah Perkins, born 27 Oct., 1771, died 16 Oct., 1831. Six children, viz., Perkins, born 25, died 28 April, 1802. Eunice Putnam, born 24 April, 1803; died 5 July, 1883. Sarah Perkins, born 5 Feb., 1806, living 1892; married Charles Coit of Norwich, Conn. Ellen Douglas, born 27 Feb., 1814; died 16 Nov., 1831. Two died in infancy.

Child by first marriage:

680   ELISHA.

Children by second marriage:

681   LEMUEL, b. 26 Oct., 1784; d. 19 Jan., 1858; m. Clarissa Downs of Boston. Ch.: Charlotte Otis, b. 30 Jan., 1810; d. 22 Oct., 1847; m. James Shepard Pike[71]. Louisa, b. 23 Feb., 1814; d. Providence, 10 Aug., 1869. Rev. Lemuel, b. 27 April, 1815; d. *s. p.*, 8 Aug., 1870, of London, Eng.; m., 1st, 20 Oct., 1845, Miss Pearce, dau. of Daly Pearce of Newport, R. I.; m., 1866, Grace Duganne of Boston, who d. London, 17 Dec., 1891. Clarissa, b. 6 July, 1817; d. 10 June, 1890; m., 1845, Charles Stockbridge son of Ebenezer and Ruth (Otis) Thompson and had (Rev.) Ebenezer of Biloxi, Miss., b. 21 Nov., 1846,[72] and Charles Otis, b. 19 June, 1849, of Pomfret. Caroline Downs, m. Dr. Thomas Perry of Providence.

[70] Avery Genealogy, by W. W. Avery.

[71] J. Shepard Pike, minister to the Hague 1861-5. Associated with Greeley on the Tribune.

[72] Rev. Ebenezer Grosvenor, m. 17 May, 1882, Julia E. Curran. Ch. are John Ebenezer Grosvenor, b. 8 Mar., 1883; d. 17 Oct., 1887. Charles Curran, b. 17 Feb., 1886. Paul Stockbridge, b. 3 Aug., 1890, Episcopal minister at Biloxi, Miss. Charles Otis Grosvenor, b. 19 June, 1849; m. 14 Feb., 1889, Caroline Wadsworth. Ch. Dorothy Otis, b. 29 Aug., 1890.

682 GUY, b. 5 Sept., 1786; d. 10 Sept., 1788.
683 (MAJOR) EBENEZER, b. Pomfret, Conn., 26 Feb., 1788; d. there 10
     Nov., 1817; Yale 1807, lawyer; m. Brooklyn, Conn., 3 May, 1815,
     his cousin, Harriet Wadsworth, dau. of Daniel and Catherine
     (Hutchinson) Putnam. No living issue (1890).
684 CLARK GUY, b. 28 June, 1790; d. 21 Oct., 1809.
685 LEWIS, b. 12 April, 1794; d. 12 Aug., 1833; m. Harriet Winchester
     of Boston. One dau. d. y., three more died in infancy.

V. 248 Daniel (*Gen. Israel, Joseph, Thomas, John*),
born in Pomfret, Conn., now Brooklyn, 18 Nov., 1759; died
there 30 April, 1831; married in Boston, 2 Sept., 1782,
Catherine, daughter of Shrimpton and Elizabeth (Malbone)
Hutchinson, born in Boston, 11 April, 1757; died in Hartford,
31 Oct., 1844.

Children, born in Brooklyn, Conn. :

686 WILLIAM, b. 1 Jan., 1783; d. 5 Dec., 1846; m. Mary Spalding.
687 CATHERINE, b. 17 Nov., 1785; d. 2 Oct., 1842; m. Geo. Brinley.
688 ELIZABETH, b. 18 Feb., 1789; d. 10 May, 1794.
689 HARRIET WADSWORTH, b. 22 Sept., 1792; d. 20 Sept., 1869; m. her
     cousin Ebenezer Grosvenor, *q. v.*
690 ELIZABETH, b. 24 Sept., 1794; d. ; m. George Sumner, *q. v.*
691 ISRAEL, b. May, 1796; d. 2 June, 1796, æt. 10 days.
692 ANNE COFFIN, b. 17 April, 1798; d. 2 July, 1840.
693 EMILY, b. 17 Jan., 1800; d. 14 Mar., 1873; m. James Brown.

DANIEL PUTNAM was a farmer on a very large scale in
Brooklyn, Conn., and a man of much worth. He was an
earnest supporter of the Protestant Episcopal church.

V. 250 Peter Schuyler (*Gen. Israel, Joseph, Thomas, John*), born in Pomfret, Conn., 31 Dec., 1764; died
Sept., 1827; married July, 1785, Lucy, daughter of Nathan
Frink of Pomfret, counsellor at law, born ———— ; died Oct.,
1829.

Children :

694 JOHN POPE, b. Brooklyn, Conn., 9 May, 1786.
695 NATHAN, b. Brooklyn, 22 Aug., 1787.
696 PETER SCHUYLER, d. 1858, æt. 69.
697 OLIVER, b. ———— ; d. æt. 6 yrs.

PETER SCHUYLER was landlord of the Mansion House at Williamstown. It was at his home in Pomfret that Gen. Israel Putnam lived during the last years of his life and died.

V. 252 John (*Samuel, John, Nathaniel, John*), born Salem Village, ——, 1715; died at Oswego, April, 1762; married at Sudbury, 25 April, 1737, Sarah, eldest daughter of James and Mary Maverick of Sudbury.[73] At the time of his marriage John Putnam lived in Framingham.

Children:

698　ELIZABETH, b. Sudbury, 18 Jan., 1738; d. unm. "at middle age."
699　SAMUEL,
700　JAMES, } twins, { d. in infancy.
701　JESSE, b. Framingham, 25 Mar., 1743. In 1759 he was on the roll of a militia company in Sudbury. In 1835 his brother John gave the following account of him. "He went out in the French and Indian War, became entirely blind but was cared for and cured by the British surgeons, after which he remained in the British service. During the Revolution he held the commission of Ensign. At the close of the war he was in New York and died there. He was buried with the honors of war." It is worth noting that this Jesse, with the exception of Hon. James Putnam, and his son James, is the only one of the name who has held commissions in the British service since 1775.
702　JOHN, b. Sudbury, 8 June, 1746.
703　NATHAN, b. Sudbury, 15 July, 1749.
704　ENOS, b. Sudbury, 8 June, 1752. His brother John relates that Enos was bound out when a boy, but being ill-treated left his master and travelled almost naked, to his brother's in Marlboro, who clothed him, afterward went to Templeton, but left there and never heard from.
705　DANIEL, b. Sudbury, 27 Sept., 1755. Was at Concord, 19 April, 1775.
706　ASA, b. Sudbury, 5 Sept., 1758. Served in the Revolution.
707　SARAH, b. Sudbury, 25 Sept., 1761.

[73] James Maverick was married twice, first to Mary, the mother of his children, secondly to Lydia Sanderson, 28 April, 1742. His children were Sarah, m. as above. Mary, b. 4 Mar., 1720. Abigail, b. 4 June, 1725; m. 10 Aug., 1743, Moses Hill. James, b. 4 Aug., 1729. Esther, b. 30 April. 1732. Silence, b. 16 April, 1735. Bathsheba. d. unm. Of these ch. those whose dates of birth are given are known to have been born in Sudbury. All but the last married and had children.

JOHN PUTNAM was presented with a farm in Framingham by his father and had settled there. When his father was forced to surrender his property to his creditors, this farm of John's was also taken, he being unable to show title deeds. His home was on the south side of Green Hill about three quarters of a mile from that spot where Wadsworth and his men were slain in 1676.

It is said that the loss of his farm in this manner so disheartened him that he enlisted in the army during the last French and Indian war. He died in the service at Oswego in 1762.

V. 253 Daniel (*Samuel, John, Nathaniel, John*), bapt. in Salem Village, 11 Oct., 1719; died in Sudbury, 15 Dec., 1753; married ——, Thankful ——.

Children, born in Sudbury:

708 LUCY, b. 18 May, 1748; d. y.
709 RELIEF, b. 6 Nov., 1751; m. in Sudbury, 23 May, 1770, Ephraim Curtis.

DANIEL PUTNAM received as a gift from his father a farm in Sudbury, and there he lived and died. He followed the trade of a shoemaker.

Abstract from an ancient diary: " Dec. 15, 1753 died Mr. Daniel Putnam, of a voilant fever of which he lay sick a week. Has left behind one child and a widow who has been in a sorrowfull condition for a considerable time. The Lord support her under this heavy bereavement and also do her soul good by it and bring her out of the distressed condition take care of her and the child its father has forsaken. Taken away in the prime of life about 36 years old & being one of my nearest neighbors the call is louder both to me & mine to get ready."

This same diarist notes the death of the father, Samuel Putnam, under date of Dec. 20.

V. 258 Deacon Asa (*Josiah, John, Nathaniel, John*), born in Danvers, 31 July, baptized 15 Aug., 1714; died in Danvers, 1795; married, first, in Salem, 30 Nov., 1738, Sarah Putnam, who died in Danvers, 25 Sept., 1762; married, second, at Danvers, 23 Aug., 1764, Mary Walcott.

Children, born in Danvers, baptized at the North Parish :

710 SARAH, b. 22 Oct., bapt. 28 Oct., 1739; d. Oct., 1781; m. 11 April,
1760, Jeremy, son of Ebenezer and Hannah (Shaw, née Southwick)
Hutchinson, b. Salem Village, 29 June, 1738; d. 7 April, 1805.
They lived in Danvers. Ch. b. there: Sarah, b. 12 Feb., 1762;
d. 14 July, 1815; m. 13 Oct., 1788, Jethro Russell, jr.; lived in
Danville, Vt. Ebenezer, b. 10 July, 1764; d. Danville, Vt., 25
Aug., 1849; m. 4 June, 1792, Anna Caves of Danvers. Bethiah,
b. 8 Mar., 1766; d. 2 July, 1801.   Mehitable, b. 10 Jan., 1768; d. 2
Mar., 1835. Joseph, b. 9 April, 1770; d. 1 Jan., 1832; m. 9 Feb.,
1806, Phebe Upton of No. Reading; lived in Danvers. Hannah,
b. 23 Mar., 1772; d. 9 April, 1813.

711 ELISHA, b. 16 Mar., 1741; bapt. 21 Mar., 1741-2.

712 JOSIAH, bapt. 11 Mar., 1743-4; d. 6 Oct., 1754.

713 ASA, bapt. 27 May, 1750; d. 8 Oct., 1754.

714 PETER, bapt. 18 Feb., 1753; d. 8 Oct., 1754.

715 HANNAH, b. 9 Jan., 1755, bapt. 18 Jan., 1756; m. Benjamin
Russell. Ch.: Asa. Hannah. Betsey, b. 21 Jan., 1780; m. 5 May,
1811, Levi, son of Joseph and Hannah (Fuller) Hutchinson of
Middleton.

By second wife :

716 MARY, b. 4 Aug., bapt. 11 Aug., 1765; m. Rufus Putnam.

717 ELIZABETH, b. 2 Feb., bapt. 8 Feb., 1767; m. Major Elijah Flint.

ASA PUTNAM was a farmer in Danvers. He was a man of
an inventive turn of mind and was much respected for his
Christian character and generous, kindly disposition.   Mr.
Putnam was always thoroughly acquainted with the results
of investigations of the great minds of his day. He was a
man to be guided by and any one could follow the dictates
of his conscience.   His life is aptly described by Dr. Wadsworth in the text delivered at his funeral " Mark the perfect
man, and behold the upright for the end of that man is
peace."

Deacon Asa was a man of small stature but athletic and
vigorous power, both in mind and body, dark eyes which
retained their lustre to the last, an expression conveying a
mixture of firmness and gentleness to those who met him.

Corporal in Capt. John Putnam's Co., two days' service at
Lexington Alarm.

V. 259 Enos (*Josiah, John, Nathaniel, John*), born in Salem Village, 6 Oct., 1716; died there ——, 1780, will proved 2 Oct., 1780; married 5 May, 1774, Sarah Goldthwaite. Not known to have had any children.

Elected constable 19 Mar., 1767, which seems to have been his only public office. His name is on the Danvers tax lists from 1752 to 1773, after which date the lists are missing. There was an Enos Putnam in Capt. John Putnam's Co., which marched to Lexington, April 19, 1775.

V. 260 Josiah (*Josiah, John, Nathaniel, John*), born in Salem Village, 3 Mar., 1718-19; died in Warren, Mass., 4 Feb., 1795; married 13 Jan., 1740, Lydia Wheeler of Brookfield, born 14 Aug., 1721; died (numb palsy) 25 Mar., 1805, after a sickness of five years.

Children :

718   Asa, b. 10 Aug., 1743; d. 7 Sept., 1795.
719   Lydia, b. ——; d. May, 1810.
720   Thankful, b. 6 May, 1747; drowned 7 Aug., 1814.
721   Josiah, b. 8 June, 1749-50; d. 1 May, 1835.
722   Ruth, b. 24 July, 1752; m. ——, Juda Daman.
723   Mary, b., Western, 15 April, 1759; d.; m. 23 Sept., 1777, Jeremiah Gould. Lived in Pomfret, N. Y. Ch.: Polly, b. 6 June, 1778. Jeremiah, b. 31 July, 1780. James, b. 2 Aug., 1782. Phares, b. 20 Dec., 1787; m. Melina Osgood, only sister of Mrs. Harvey Putnam. Abram Putnam, b. 14 Aug., 1794. Lydia, b. 4 Mar., 1797. Laura, b. 2 Mar., 1800.

Josiah Putnam was a captain in Col. Jedediah Foote's regiment. He was at Lexington on the 19th April, 1775, and among his men was his son Josiah.

V. 270 John[74] (*John, John, Nathaniel, John*), born in Salem Village, 1720; died in Danvers; will made 29 June 1786, proved 6 Nov., 1786; married, Salem, 4 Feb., 1741, Ruth Swinnerton.

Children, all born and baptized in Salem Village :

724   Nathan, b. 8 Nov., 1742, prob. d. before 1786.

[74] Mentioned in father's will, also "granddau. Lydia," and wife Ruth.

725   JOHN,[75] b. 10 Dec., 1748; bapt. 1 May, 1744.
726   DANIEL, b. 19 April, 1748; bapt. 24 April, 1748.
727   JAMES, b. 16 July, 1750; bapt. 5 Aug., 1750.
728   PETER, b. 8 Oct., 1751; bapt. 5 Oct., 1755.
729   AMOS, b. 25 May, 1752; bapt. 7 June, 1752.

V. 271 Doctor Amos (*John, John, Nathaniel, John*),
born in Salem Village, Sept., 1722; died 26 July, 1807;
married 18 Mar., 1743, Hannah Phillips perhaps daughter of
James Phillips of Danvers, who died 2 Oct., 1758, aged
thirty-three; married, second, 13 Aug., 1759, Mary Gott of
Wenham who died 15 Feb., 1803.

Children, born and baptized in Salem Village:

730   JAMES PHILLIPS, b. 21 April, 1745; bapt. 28 April, 1745.
731   HANNAH, b. 18 Sept., 1749; bapt. 24 Sept., 1749; m. Nathan
      Putnam.
732   ELIZABETH, b. 8 Mar., bapt. 18 Mar., 1753; d. *s. p.*; m. Nathaniel
      Oliver of Marblehead.

DR. AMOS PUTNAM studied medicine under Dr. Jonathan
Prince of Danvers, and practised in Danvers until the opening of the French and Indian War, when he entered the
colonial service as surgeon.   At the close of the war he
returned to Danvers and practised until over eighty years of
age.

During the Revolution he was a member of the committee
of safety, was often moderator at town meeting and held
other positions of public concern.   He was a firm and out-
spoken patriot and one of the most influential citizens of the
town.

His grave, in a small enclosure near the Collins house, is
marked by a plain stone with the following inscription:
" Sacred to the memory of Doct. Amos Putnam and Hannah
Phillips the wife of A. P."

During his life Dr. Putnam lived near Felton's corner, in
the house afterward occupied by Daniel Tapley.   A portrait
painted, in 1762 or thereabouts, is in the possession of the

---

[75] Probably the Capt. John Putnam who commanded a company at Lexington. He
was constable in 1774 and held many offices before and after the Revolution.

Danvers Historical Society having been presented by Charles Putnam, Esq., of Cambridge, a descendant. This portrait represents a man with large chin, small mouth, blue eyes and a good intellect.

The following obituary appeared in the Essex Register, printed at Salem, Mass., 3 Aug., 1807.

We have received the following notice of the character of Dr. AMOS PUTNAM, whose death, in Danvers, was mentioned in our last :—

"He was born in Danvers, 11th Oct. O. S. 1722. After having enjoyed the benefits then derivable from a common school, he commenced the study of Physic and Surgery with the late Dr. Prince, to the attachment of whose family he particularly recommended himself by the propriety of his conduct, and the uniform serenity of his disposition. In 1744, he applied to practice the rich acquisitions of his retentive mind, with that success which never attaches itself to superficial knowledge, and gained that extensive reputation which invited his advice and assistance, in the most dangerous diseases, with undiminished confidence, for 56 years; at which period an asthmatical disorder, which he had previously experienced, began to corrode his strength with more superior force, though not sufficiently to counteract the energy of medicinal application, or prevent him from the duties of his profession, until 1805; when his age, united with his debilitating disorder, more obstinately prohibited his future usefulness in society. He was emulous in the principles, and unremitting in the practice of the religion he professed, and a retrospective view of his life, sanctioned by the approbation of his conscience, produced that resignation to the will of his MAKER, which mantled his mind in serenity. As a husband he never infringed the sacred state by an unfeeling word or angry frown; as a father, the object of his fond exertion was to infuse into the minds of his children those virtues which shone with eminent lustre in his own; and as a friend he was social, sincere, and innocently cheerful, was never known to slander the character even of an inveterate enemy, but with benevolence involved every injury in oblivion."

V. 272 Deacon Edmund (*John, John, Nathaniel, John*), born in Salem Village, 1724; bapt. 27 June, 1725; died there 1810; married Oct., 1745, Anna, daughter of Israel and Anna (Porter) Andrews, born in Danvers, 26 Dec., 1726.

Children :

733 HULDAH, b. 18 May, 1746; bapt. 3 May, 1747; m., Danvers, 6 May, 1766, Joseph, son of Peter and Hannah (Batchelder), Woodbury of Beverly, b. there 21 Sept., 1741; d. 5 Feb., 1816. He m., 2d, 7 Mar., 1775, Abigail, dau. of John and Mary (Kimball) Porter. Ch.: Nancy, b. 6 Dec., 1767; d. 23 July, 1823; m. 8 Oct., 1786, Nathaniel Pierce of Lexington. Huldah, b. 8 Jan., 1771; m. 23 Jan., 1791 (John or William), Fiske.

734 ANDREW, b. 15 Jan., 1750; bapt. 27 Jan., 1750-1.

735 ISRAEL, b. 20[76] Nov., 1754; d. ——, 1820; m. his cousin Anna, dau. of Elias and Eunice (Andrews) Endicott.

736 SARAH, b. 19 Dec., 1756; d. Newport, N. H., ——; m. as his 1st wife, Samuel, son of Sam'l and Mary (Putnam) Endicott, bapt. 14 Dec., 1754; d Newport, N. H., April, 1810. He was a surgeon's mate in the Revolutionary army. Ch.: Sally, b. ——; m. Andrew Bryant of Newport, N. H.

737 EDMUND, b. 15 Jan., 1772; bapt. North Parish, Danvers, 12 Feb., 1772.

EDMUND PUTNAM, in 1753, bought land of John Baker and removed to Topsfield; but in 1758 he sold it to Rev. John Emerson and returned to Danvers, buying there of Daniel Rea a farm of sixty acres. Here he occupied, until his death, what is known as the old Rea Putnam House, now the property and residence of Mr. Augustus Fowler. For a portion of his life, Edmund was a tailor as well as a farmer, and an old manuscript account book, still extant, shows how extensively he provided outfits for his neighbors or customers, in that line of business. In 1762, he was chosen deacon of the First Church, serving twenty-three years. After the death of Rev. Peter Clarke, the third minister, which occurred June 10, 1768, the parish was without a pastor for the space of four years or more. During this interval, its affairs were

---

[76] According to Church Records, bapt. at Topsfield, 17 Nov., 1754.

entrusted to a committee of seven, consisting of John Nichols, Capt. Elisha Flint, Dr. Amos Putnam, Lieut. Archelaus Putnam, Dea. Asa Putnam, Dea. Edmund Putnam, and Dr. Samuel Holton. It was at a time of serious troubles in the society about the settlement of a successor to Mr. Clarke, but the committee wisely and usefully discharged the duties which had been assigned to them.

"Deacon Edmund," as he has usually been called, shared largely the patriotic spirit of the hour, as the outbreak of the Revolutionary war was drawing near. We copy the following from Force's *American Archives*, Vol II: "At a meeting of the people of the Alarm List of the Third Company in Danvers, held in said Danvers the 6th of March, 1775, for the purpose of electing officers for said Alarm List Company, Rev. Benj. Balch, chairman; said people unanimously made choice of Dea. Edmund Putnam for Captain, Rev. Benjamin Balch for Lieutenant, and Mr. Tarrant Putnam for Ensign. The said gentlemen, being present, declared their acceptance. Attest, Arch. Dale, clerk of said meeting." Orators and authors, like Hon. Daniel P. King, Hon. Charles Hudson, and Mr. J. Wingate Thornton, have referred to this record as illustrative of the fact that ministers and deacons, as well as others, were ready for military service, at that momentous crisis.

Deacon Edmund was now captain, and under that title he also commanded one of the eight Danvers companies which flew to encounter the British on the day of the Battle of Lexington, April 19, 1775. The company was a small one, gathered from the more sparsely settled district of the town to which its captain himself belonged. Like others of the number, it may have intercepted and harassed the enemy in his hurried retreat on the way from West Cambridge to Charlestown. All were alike paid for their two days' service, as the records at the State House attest.

On the 11th of March, 1776, Captain Putnam was chosen, by a unanimous vote, as selectman, and also as assessor of

14

the town. At a meeting of the citizens of Danvers, held April 13, 1778. he was appointed one of a committee of thirteen to consider and report upon a form of government for the State of Massachusetts which had been adopted by the General Court on the 28th of February of the same year, and was subject to the approval of the people by a two-thirds vote. The other members of the committee were Col. Israel Hutchinson, Mr. Archelaus Dale, Maj. Samuel Epes, Mr. Gideon Putnam, Capt. Jonathan Procter, Maj. Caleb Lowe, Mr. Ezra Upton, Mr. Stephen Needham, Capt. John Putnam, Capt. William Shillaber, Mr. Benjamin Procter and Mr. David Prince. They reported, at an adjourned meeting, adversely to the proposed Constitution, and their action was ratified by the unanimous vote of those who were present. The objectionable draft was defeated by an overwhelming majority of the people of the commonwealth. The better form of Constitutional Government was adopted in 1780.

Deacon, or Captain Putnam, was a man of large frame and great physical strength. He was of strong mind; was possessed of much intelligence; and was one who thought for himself and who was honest and free to form and express his opinions. Not the least interesting event in his life was his conversion to Universalism. He has been claimed as the original adherent to that faith among the inhabitants of the town. His official and personal relations with the First Church ceased in 1785, and it was probably about that time that he became unalterably confirmed in his belief of the new doctrine. Moreover, that was the year, when, at Oxford, Mass., the Universalists held their first convention and adopted their denominational title. In previous years, the celebrated Rev. John Murray, the founder of Universalism in America, had been settled in Gloucester, and had earnestly and diligently proclaimed his views in the neighboring towns. "Deacon Edmund" could hardly have failed to become acquainted with his teachings, if, indeed, he was not on one or more occasions a hearer. At all events, he imbibed his tenets and was henceforth a stout advocate of them. His prominence and zeal in this matter are set forth in a few of the lines of the quaint Ode written by Dr. Andrew Nichols for the Danvers Centennial Celebration, of June 16, 1852 :

> " Still people would think, read their Bibles, embrace
> Other doctrines than those we have named ;
> Deacon Edmund, with new-fangled views of God's grace,
> Universal Salvation proclaimed.
>
> It found little favor, his converts were few,
> When he with his forefathers slept ;
> Still the seed he had sown died not, the plant grew,
> Reproduced till it thousands accept."

The officiating minister at his funeral was Rev. Edward Turner, who was then the pastor of the Universalist church in Salem. One who was present recalled to us, a half century later, the scripture words which Mr. Turner quoted on the occasion : "Thou shalt come to thy grave in a full age, like as a shock of corn cometh in his season." The interment took place in the old burial ground at Danvers Plains.

V. 277 Amos (*Amos, John, Nathaniel, John*), born in Salem Village, 1723 ; died in New Salem previous to 1797 ; married Lydia Trask of New Salem, born in Salem Village, 1733 ; died in Houlton, Me., 8 April, 1820, aged 87, probably daughter of John and Elizabeth Trask of the Middle Precinct now Peabody, baptized there 27 Nov., 1737. Mrs. Putnam's father died while serving under Wolfe at Quebec.

Children :

738 HANNAH, b. 15 June, 1754; d. at New Salem; m. Varney Pearce of New Salem, one of the proprietors and early settlers of Houlton. Ch.: Lydia, m. Amos, son of Uzziel Putnam. Varney, m. a sister of Simeon Holden. Amos, b. New Salem; d. at Houlton. Polly, m. Simeon Holden of New Salem. Sally, b. New Salem, June, 1791. Hannah, b. New Salem, 29 Nov., 1793; d. in Houlton, 18 April, 1878; m. 21 April, 1829, John Tenney.[77] Melissa, b. ———. Abraham, b. New Salem, 1799; d. in Houlton, 5 Oct., 1850; m., 1st, 18 Feb., 1828, Polly Cook who d. 14 Dec., 1828; 2d, 1 April, 1841, his sister-in-law Fanny Cook, who d. May, 1870.

[77] Their son is Charles Pearce Tenney, Esq., a prominent and influential citizen of Houlton and an enterprising merchant.

739   AMOS, b. 9 Sept., 1755; d. from exposure, while on the road to
        Lexington in April, 1775. He had started immediately upon the
        alarm being given.
740   JACOB, b. New Salem, 2 Nov., 1758; d. there.
741   SARAH, b. 16 July, 1762; d. in Houlton, 3 Aug., 1843; m. prob. in
        1782, Joseph Houlton[78] of New Salem, and the founder of
        Houlton, Me.
742   AARON, b. 10 April, 1767; d. y.
743   LYDIA, b. New Salem, 24 Nov., 1770; d. in Houlton, Me., 7 Aug.,
        1751; m., as his second wife, Jonas Wheeler, of Petersham,
        Mass. Ch.: Varney Pearce, b. 25 Oct., 1802; d. 12 May, 1812.
        Amos Putnam, b. 25 Feb., 1805; d. 28 April, 1812. James, b. 7
        May, d. 2 Aug., 1807. Cordelia, b. 21 Sept., 1809; d. New Salem;
        taught school at the South. Hannah Putnam, b. 12 Mar., 1813;
        d. 17 Jan., 1814.
744   SAMUEL.[79]
745   AARON, b. 19 July, 1773; d. in Houlton, 13 Feb., 1849.

AMOS PUTNAM probably removed from Danvers to New
Salem about the time of his father's death, as he inherited
with his two eldest brothers, their father's lands in New
Salem. After his death his widow removed to Houlton, Me.,
where her sons and nephews had already gone to hold the
Academy Grant.

The history of this grant shows the character of these brave
New England people.

In the year 1724, many inhabitants of Salem being "much
straitened for land" prayed for a grant in the western part
of the Province. This petition was allowed with the conditions that one lot should be reserved for the first settled
minister, one for the ministry, and one for a school. Each
grantee was required to give a bond for twenty-five pounds to
be on the spot, have a house seven feet stud and eighteen feet
square at least, seven acres of English hay ready to be mowed,
help to build a meeting house and settle a minister within
five years.

One of the Danvers Holtons led the party who settled
New Salem, which was incorporated in 1753. The New

---

[78] See Houlton Genealogy by Eben Putnam.
[79] Not mentioned by Francis Barnes, Esq., of Houlton, Me., to whom I am deeply indebted for the larger part of the Houlton family records.— E. P.

Salem Academy was incorporated in 1795, and two years later, in response to a petition, a township was granted to the Academy, in the Maine District. In consequence of the depreciation of land at this time the Academy was not benefited by this grant as had been anticipated, and much disappointment ensued. At this juncture, rather than that the Academy should be given up, members of the Putnam and Holton families came forward, mortgaged their farms in New Salem, which had by that time attained a good value, and bought the Maine lands with the money so received, thus supplying the Academy with funds, they themselves going into the wilderness to make new homes.

The pioneers of Houlton started in wagons to Boston, thence in a coasting vessel to St. John, N. B., thence up the river by sloops to Fredericton, thence by barges and canoes to Woodstock and then struck through the forest and reached their location. Even horses, at a much later date, could not penetrate the woods for the whole distance. This settlement is now the most prosperous town in northern Maine, and is the shire town of Aroostook. In and about Houlton are settled many families of Putnams all of whom have been much respected and honored by their townspeople. Francis Barnes, Esq., of that town, himself connected with the family, and a painstaking antiquarian, has written and collected much pertaining to Houlton and its early settlers.

He writes that Mrs. Putnam, the widow of Amos, was of an extremely generous nature, very courageous and most highly esteemed; in the "cold years" of 1816–17 she was the means of sustaining many a starving family. She would ride forth with her saddle bags filled with food and medicine and visit the less fortunate families during the most inclement weather, notwithstanding the fact she was of slight frame. Her death was widely lamented, for her great charity had reached the entire community.

Amos Putnam is probably the one of that name from New Salem, who was in the American army during the siege of Boston.

V. 278 Joshua (*Amos, John, Nathaniel, John*), born in Salem Village, 1733 (according to family tradition, baptized 1732); died in New Salem, ——; married ——, Eunice Trask, the sister of Mrs. Lydia Putnam, (No. 227).

Children, born in New Salem:

746 JOHN.

747 EUNICE, b. 15 May, 1766; d. in Houlton, Me., 11 Aug., 1837; m. in New Salem, 19 Dec., 1785, Dea. Samuel, son of Samuel and Ann Kendall of New Salem, b. there 29 Dec., 1748, d. in Houlton, 18 April, 1835. Ch. b. in New Salem: Samuel, b. 16 Mar., 1787; d. in New Salem, 9 Nov., 1795. Joshua Green, b. 15 April, 1789; d. in Houlton, 16 Oct., 1841. Catherine, b. 24 Aug., 1791; d. in New Salem, 2 Sept., 1791. Eunice, b. 30 Dec., 1792; d. in New Salem, 10 Mar., 1793. Samuel, b. 3 April, 1794; d. in Fredericton, N. B., 3 April, 1828. Joseph, b. 6 May, 1796; d. in Houlton, 28 Oct., 1872; m. 1 Sept., 1835, Hannah H. North, of Bangor, Me. Lucy, b. 26 Jan., 1799; d. in New Salem, 18 May, 1800. John, b. 20 Jan., 1801; d. in New Salem, 20 Jan., 1801. Sally, b. 27 Jan., 1802; d. in Houlton, 23 April, 1843; m. 22 Jan., 1820, Samuel Houlton, of Houlton. Elizabeth, b. 28 May, 1805; d. in Houlton, 13 June, 1875; m. there, 22 Mar., 1847, Leonard Pierce[50] of Houlton. Nancy, b. 24 July, 1808; m. in Houlton, 15 July, 1844, Samuel W. Bennett.

748 JOSHUA, b. 8 Feb., 1772; d. 14 June, 1835.

749 ELIZABETH, b. ——; d. Dennysville, Me.; m. in New Salem, Dr. Samuel Rice, as his second wife. The first wife of Dr. Rice was a Woodman of New Salem, by whom he had two ch., a son Woodman, and a dau. Delia, still (1891) living near Woodstock. Dr. Rice bought out one of the proprietors of Houlton and moved there from New Salem in 1811, in company with Joshua Putnam. At first he built himself a log-hut. For nine years he was the only physician in town and was highly respected. Later he removed to Woodstock. The last years of his life were spent with Mr. and Mrs. Lincoln. Ch. of Samuel and Elizabeth (Putnam) Rice were, Elizabeth, for many years governess in the family of Judge Theodore Lincoln of Dennysville, m. his son Bellah Lincoln, a grandson of Gen. Benjamin Lincoln of Revolutionary fame. They had six children: Charles Darwin, m. Jane Cronkhite of Eel River Settlement, and d. at Eastport, Me., in 1853. He was a physician of much ability. Mrs. Rice died 14

---

[50] Leonard Pierce was b. in Dorchester, Mass., 2 June, 1795; d. in Houlton, Me., 1 Dec., 1773. His first wife was Mary Prince, who was b. in Newburyport, Mass. After her death he m. her sister Ann Laura. By his third wife, Elizabeth Kendall, he had one son, Clarence, b. 17 Feb., 1848, who m., 25 Aug., 1881, Francis E. Madigan of Houlton. Mr. Pierce is of the firm of A. H. Fogg & Co., Houlton, Me.

Dec., 1890, at Woodstock. Samuel Dwight, entered the Methodist church at an early age, became a bishop and lived and died at Hamilton, Ontario, leaving quite a large family. Mary, removed to Massachusetts where her cousin Franklin Putnam followed and married her. They removed to Minneapolis, Minn.

V. 279 Deacon Uzziel (*Amos, John, Nathaniel, John*), born in Salem Village, 1735; died in New Salem; married —— Ganson.

UZZIEL PUTNAM was a deacon in the Congregationalist church in New Salem.

Children, born in New Salem:

750 DANIEL.
751 SAMUEL.
752 JOSEPH.
753 UZZIEL.
754 MARY, b. ——; m. Deacon Shaw of New Salem. Ch.: Hannah, m. James Lander in Houlton. Putnam, m. Julia Stacy of New Salem, and d. in Hodgdon, Me. Putnam Shaw was brought up in the family of John Putnam, son of Joshua Putnam, and was a man of considerable importance.

V. 280 Deacon Daniel (*Amos, John, Nathaniel, John*), born in Salem Village, ——; died in Danvers, 13 Nov., 1801; married in Danvers, 27 Mar., 1760, Elizabeth, daughter of Samuel Putnam.

Children, born in Danvers:

755 ELIZABETH, b. 26 Feb., 1761.
756 DANIEL, b. 3 Oct., 1762.
757 HANNAH, b. 16 Mar., 1765.
758 PHEBE, b. 26 Jan., 1767.
759 SAMUEL, b. 23 May, 1769.
760 AMOS, b. 11 Oct., 1778.

DANIEL PUTNAM inherited his father's Danvers and Middleton property. He was a deacon in the North Church at Danvers, and marched to Lexington upon the Alarm, as lieutenant in the company of Capt. Samuel Flint. In 1777, he was on the Committee of Correspondence.

V. 283 Jacob (*Nathaniel, Benjamin, Nathaniel, John*), born in Salem Village, 9 Mar., 1711; died in Wilton, N. H.,

10 Feb., 1781; married at Salem, July, 1735, Susanna Harriman (styled Henman on Salem Records) of Danvers; married, second, Susanna Styles, who died 27 Jan., 1776; married, third, Patience, mentioned in his will proved 28 Feb., 1791.

Children :[31]

761 SARAH, b. in Salem Village, 28 June, 1736; died in Wilton; m. John. Cram of Wilton. Ch.: Sarah, b. 21 Feb., 1760. Jonathan, b. Nov., 1764. Philip, b. 24 Feb., 1766; d. unm. 7 Jan., 1832. Susanna, b. 27 Jan., 1769; m. Abiel Bridges. Mary, b. 27 Jan., 1769; m. 12 June. 1794, Joseph Gage. Mehitable, b. 14 July, 1772; d. unm. 7 Oct., 1842. Zerviah, b. 20 Sept., 1775; d. 10 Feb., 1859; m. 21 Feb., 1799, David Carlton.

762 NATHANIEL, b. in Salem Village, 24 April, 1738.

763 PHILIP, b. in Salem Village, 4, bapt. 9 Mar., 1739–40; d. y.

764 STEPHEN, b. in Salem Village, 24 Sept., bapt. 18 Oct., 1741. Removed to Rumford, Me., and became the founder of the Rumford family of Putnam.

765 PHILIP, b. in Wilton, N. H., Mar., 1742; d. there 10 Oct., 1810.

766 JOSEPH, b. in Wilton, N. H., 28 Feb., 1744.

767 MEHITABLE, b. in Wilton, N. H., 25 Dec., 1745; d. in Wilton, 20 Jan., 1800; m. Daniel Holt.

768 JACOB, b. in Wilton, N. H., 15 Nov., 1747; d. 2 June, 1821.

769 ARCHELAUS, b. 15 Oct., 1749; d. 22 Oct., 1816.

770 CALEB, b. 20 Mar., 1751; d. in the army, one account says 1776; another " before Ticonderoga."

771 ELIZABETH, b. 15 April, 1753; m. 26 Nov., 1778, Jacob Hardy of Alexandria, removed to Hyde Park, Vt., and brought up a large family.

772 PETER, b. 8 Jan., 1756; d. 3 July, 1776, while serving in the army during the Ticonderoga campaign.

JACOB PUTNAM was a pioneer of Salem, Canada, now Wilton, N. H. It is stated that he was there in 1738. It is known that in June, 1739, Ephraim and Jacob Putnam and John Dale, all of Danvers, made the first permanent settlement in Wilton, and (1889), the remains of a cellar nearly opposite Michael McCarthy's barn, mark his house site. This house was two stories in front and one in the back. For three years the wife of Jacob Putnam was the only woman who resided permanently in town. During one winter, such

[31] The History of Wilton varies a few days on some of the dates of birth of children.

were the depth of snow and distance from neighbors that she saw no one outside her immediate family, for six months. In 1829, a part of Jacob's farm was in the possession of Caleb Putnam, his grandson. Ephraim Putnam, mentioned above, removed to Lyndeborough shortly after the settlement of Wilton. Both of these towns were cut out from what was originally Salem, Canada. It is said that the brothers Jacob, Ephraim and Nathaniel were all early at Wilton, and finding the Indians troublesome, returned to Danvers, then a second time settled at Wilton and Lyndeborough.

Salem, Canada, was a grant of land to soldiers under Sir William Phips in the Canada Expedition of 1690, and was made in 1735.

Jacob Putnam was a man of great industry and at one time operated a saw mill, besides his farm. In his old age he employed himself in making cans.

The reader is referred to History of Wilton, N. H., History of Lyndeborough, N. H. (in preparation), and Peabody's Centennial Address at Wilton, 1839, for many interesting anecdotes concerning the Putnams and allied families.

V. 286 Archelaus (*Nathaniel, Benjamin, Nathaniel, John*), born in Salem Village, 29 May, 1718; died in Danvers. Administration on estate granted to widow Mehetable, 25 Oct., 1756 (elsewhere it is stated that he died in 1759); married 12 April, 1739, Mehetable, daughter of Caleb and Silence (Phillips) Putnam, born in Danvers, 6 Nov., 1723. The widow married, secondly, Col. Israel, son of Elisha and Genger (Porter) Hutchinson, of Danvers, baptized 12 Nov., 1727; died 15 Mar., 1811. Col. Hutchinson was a veteran of the French and Indian Wars, and of the Revolution. For twenty-one years he represented Danvers in the General Court. Col. Hutchinson was the father of several children by his first wife, Anna Cue; by Mehetable he had one son, Israel, born in Danvers, 27 Sept., 1760; married, first, Susan Trask, 15 Dec., 1785; married, second, 18 July, 1795, Eunice Putnam, born in Danvers, 3 Jan., 1766.

Children, born in Danvers:

773 A DAUGHTER, b. 25 Oct., 1739 (family bible).
774 ARCHELAUS, b. 6 Nov., 1740; bapt. 23 Nov.
775 MEHITABLE, b. 11 Nov., 1742; bapt. 14 Nov.
776 EPHRAIM, b. 14 Sept., bapt. 30 Sept., 1744.
777 NATHANIEL, b. 17 May, 1746; bapt. 18 May.
778 MARY, b. 13 Mar., 1747-8.
779 JACOB, b. 21 Nov., 1749; bapt. 26 Nov., guardianship to Edmond
       Putnam, 2 Jan., 1769.
780 SALAI (son), b. 21 Nov., 1749.
781 PHEBE, b. 27 Nov., bapt. 1 Dec., 1751.
782 CALEB, b. ———; bapt. 22 July, 1753.
783 SARAH, b. 14 Sept., 1755; bapt. 21 Sept., 1755; d. 19 Nov., 1847;
       m. 4 Mar., 1773. Samuel, son of Joseph and Mary (Prince)
       Fowler, b. Ipswich, 9 Jan., 1748-9; d. Danvers, 20 April, 1813.
       Samuel Fowler settled at New Mills, Danvers. He was a
       member of Capt. Jeremiah Page's company, which marched to
       Lexington, 19 April, 1775. Sarah (Putnam) Fowler, was the
       first white child born at Danversport. She was considered a
       very handsome woman, having a snowy complexion and bright
       dark eyes. Ch. John, b. 13 Aug., 1774; d. 21 Aug., 1774. Samuel
       b. 15 Sept., 1776; m. Clarissa Page. John, b. 15 Sept., 1778; m.
       Martha Page. Jacob, b. 13 Sept., 1781; d. 1 Dec., 1782. Sarah,
       b. 14 Oct., 1783; m. Robert H. Stimpson. Mary, b. 9 Jan., 1787;
       m. John Page.

In the spring of 1754, Deacon Archelaus Putnam moved
a building which had been used as a shop, from his father's
farm, now known as the "Judge Putnam farm" on Meeting
House Lane, down Crane river, by floating it from the
upper mill pond near his father's house, to the bank of the
river, at what is now Danversport. The building was landed
near where the depot now stands and taken to a spot south
of what is now Warren's store. This was converted into a
dwelling and here his daughter Sarah was born. (Fowler
Gen.)

This settlement at New Mills was, in 1772, incorporated
into a separate Highway District, there having been much
feeling, provoked by the action of the settlers at the Port in
building roads and bridges. The thickets were so dense
formerly at the Port that once Mrs. Putnam became lost in
making her way from the mill to the house.

Here were established grist and chocolate mills by

Archelaus Putnam, and by Archelaus Putnam and others, a saw mill.

Archelaus Putnam was chosen Deacon of the First church 26 Jan., 1756.

V. 287 Deacon Ephraim (*Nathaniel, Benjamin, Nathaniel, John*), born in Salem Village, 10 Feb., 1719-20; died in Lyndeborough, N. H., 13 Nov., 1777; married Sarah Cram of Reading (perhaps Wilmington), Mass., daughter of Jacob Cram, who is said to have been the first settler in Lyndeborough; died 15 Oct., 1777, aged fifty-nine years (gravestone).

Children:

784 HANNAH, b. Lyndeborough, 26 Feb., 1743, said to be the first white child born in Lyndeborough; m. Eleazer Woodward. She had five sons and five daughters; one of the latter m. Aaron Woodward, Esq.

785 EPHRAIM, b. (in Salem Village ?), 15 June, 1744.

786 SARAH, b. 8 June, 1746; m. John Bradford. They had four sons and three daughters.

787 HULDAH, b. 15 May, 1748; d. 1778; m. Jonas Kidder; three sons and one daughter.

788 JESSE, b. in Lyndeborough, 21 Sept., 1750.

789 DAVID, b. in Lyndeborough, 6 Mar., 1753; d. 1820.

790 KETURAH or KATHARINE, b. 29 June, 1756; m. John Smith. They had five sons and four daughters.

791 AARON, b. in Lyndeborough.

792 JOHN, b. in Lyndeborough.

793 REBECCA, b. ———; m. Ward Woodward. They had four sons and three daughters.

The home of Deacon Ephraim was destroyed by fire a short time after his death (it was then occupied by one of his sons) and at that time the family records were destroyed. The children were all baptized by Rev. Mr. Wilkins, of Amherst, and births recorded by Jacob Wellman, society clerk.

EPHRAIM PUTNAM was an early settler in Salem, Canada. He settled first in what is now Wilton near the intersection of roads near the North Cemetery, but later removed to Lyndeborough. The garrison house was near his home and he had charge of it. It is said that the three early settlers of Lyndeborough, each living on a hill, would each morning signal the others if all was well. We can imagine the anxiety with which each watched for the return signal of the others. Mrs. Hartshorne, of Lyndeborough, a descendant, writes "The family of Ephraim Putnam had dark eyes and black hair; they were an honest, conscientious and God-fearing family, and these characteristics are noticeable in the families immediately descended from him. The older families were rather above medium height and thickset. Their descendants now living are about medium size."

In 1834, Daniel Putnam of Lyndeborough, who supplied Col. Perley Putnam with much information concerning his branch of the family, wrote "There are living in the town of Lyndeborough twenty-six male descendants of Ephraim Putnam including his son Aaron. Up to the present date there have been three 'Deacon' Putnams and six 'Captain' Putnams in Lyndeborough."

While the early settlers of Wilton and Lyndeborough seem to have feared the Indians greatly, and even in 1744 petitioned Gov. Wentworth for soldiers to protect them, they seem never to have been molested. The petition of 1744 is signed by Ephraim Putnam and several of the Crams; in it they state they are but recently come into the province.

None of the Wilton or Lyndeborough Putnam families are known to have supplied men for the French and Indian Wars.

V. 289 Nathaniel (*Nathaniel, Benjamin, Nathaniel, John*), born in Salem Village, 28 May, 1724; died July, 1763, in the vicinity of Dunstable, while on his way home from a trip East. His sudden death was caused by drinking cold water; married in Middleton, 6 Feb., 1744, Abigail Wilkins.

Children :

794 .MARY, b. in Salem Village, 24 July, 1744; d. unm.

795 SARAH, b. in Salem Village, 24 April, 1747; d. y.

796 FRANCIS, b. in Salem Village, 24 Oct., 1748, bapt. there 6 Nov., 1748. Enrolled 23 April, 1775, from Wilton, as second sergeant of Capt. Walker's company, and was present at the battle of Bunker Hill. About 1779, or 1780, he removed from Wilton to Cherry Valley, N. Y.

797 ABIGAIL, b. in Salem Village, 24 Sept., 1746; m. —— Scripture; settled in Cherry Valley.

798 MEHETABLE, b. in Wilton, 1750; m. Thomas Lewis of Wilton, b. 21 Mar., 1758.

799 RACHEL, b. in Wilton, 12 April, 1751; m. Timothy Carlton, who was killed, 7 Sept., 1773, by the falling of the meeting-house at Wilton; m., 2nd, her cousin Jesse (*Ephraim*) Putnam of Lynde borough, and settled first in Guildford, Vt., then in Buffalo, N. Y.

800 MIRIAM, b. in Wilton, 16 May, 1753; m. Isaac Peabody, jr., of Wilton.

801 SUSANNA, b. in Wilton, ——; m. Israel Jones, settled in Halifax, N. Y.

802 SARAH, b. in Wilton, 20 April, 1755; m. Enoch, probably son of Amos and Hannah (Putnam) Fuller, of Wilton, who died before 1835. Ch.: Amos, b. 27 April, 1780. Sally, b. 5 Nov., 1781; m. Peter Putnam of Andover, Vt. Benjamin, b. 1 Sept., 1783; m. 11 Oct., 1804, Naomi Burton; lived in Andover, Vt. Daniel, b. 20 Sept., 1785; d. in Wilton, 3 Oct., 1858; m. 1810, Betsey Burnham. James, b. 26 June, 1787. Frederic, b. 15 Mar., 1790. Mary Putnam, b. 5 July, 1794. Enoch, b. 5 Aug., 1796. Mrs. Fuller d. in Andover, Vt., subsequent to 1835.

803 DANIEL, b. in Wilton, 27 Feb., 1760; d. unm.

804 BENJAMIN, b. in Wilton, 9 Mar., 1762; d. unm. Mariner.

NATHANIEL PUTNAM was in Wilton early; but, on the breaking out of the Indian troubles, returned to Danvers. About 1750, he returned to Wilton and settled upon what is now known as the Batchelder place.

V. 292 Deacon Tarrant (*Tarrant, Benjamin, Nathaniel, John*), born in Salem Village, 3 April, 1716; died in Sutton, 27 Aug., 1794; married 9 Dec., 1742, Priscilla Baker of Topsfield who died in Sutton, 16 Mar., 1812, aged eighty-nine.

Children, born in Sutton:

805 TARRANT, b. 24 April, 1744; d. 17 Dec., 1770.

806 MOLLY, b. 18 July, 1745; d. 24 Mar., 1768.

807 ELIJAH, b. 23 Jan., 1746; d. *s. p.*, 14 April, 1787. H. C. 1766.
808 ELIZABETH, b. 30 May, 1749; m. 2 Mar., 1773, Abraham Brown of Sutton. No issue.
809 PRISCILLA, b. 22 Aug., 1751; m. 3 Dec., 1772, Adam Brown.
810 SARAH, b. 4 Aug., 1753; m. 21 June, 1775, Timothy Merriam.
811 MARTHA, b. 15 July, 1755; m. —— Merriam, dec. prev. 1794, leaving ch.: John, Tarrant Putnam, Samuel, Martha, of Concord.
812 REBECCA, b. 5 May, 1759; d. unm. 13 Mar., 1796.
813 LYDIA, b. 27 July, 1761; d. unm. 8 Sept. 1787.
814 MOLLY, b. 15 Nov., 1763; m. —— Williams.
815 ISRAEL, b. 22 May, 1767.

DEACON TARRANT PUTNAM went from Danvers to Sutton, and was admitted to the church at Sutton by letter from the Danvers church, 1747.

He owned a large tract of land in Sutton, embracing what are now the poor farms, and the John Rich, and Brigham farms. He left all his real estate to his son Israel.

When in 1775, Gen. Israel Putnam rode through Sutton on his way to Bunker Hill, he stopped at the Deacon's and had dinner there. The flag stone from which he mounted his horse is still shown.

V. 296 Gideon (*Tarrant, Benjamin, Nathaniel, John*), born in Salem Village, 29 May, 1726; died 17 May, 1811; married 4 June, 1752, Hannah, daughter of Abraham and Jerusha (Raymond) Browne of Beverly, who died 6 Nov., 1813, aged eighty-one.

Children, born in Danvers:

816 HANNAH, b. 1 May, 1753; d. 24 Nov., 1773.
817 GIDEON, b. 19 Sept., 1756; d. 19 Dec., 1773.
818 SOLOMON, b. 24 May. 1759; d. 19 July, 1759.
819 ANNA, b. 12 April, 1761; d. 2 May, 1761.
820 ABRAHAM, b. 16 Dec., 1762; d. 25 July, 1782.
821 JONATHAN, b. 12 Feb., 1765; d. 24 April, 1765.
822 ELIZABETH, b. 24 Oct., 1766; d. 25 Feb., 1767.
823 SAMUEL, b. 13 May, 1768.
824 ELIJAH, b. 26 Feb., 1771; d. 25 Mar., 1771.
825 HANNAH, b. 29 Jan., 1774; d. 29 Aug., 1795.

GIDEON PUTNAM was a store keeper[32] at Danvers, and was more or less influential in town affairs previous to the Revolution, but he became still more so after the struggle commenced. In 1772, he was one of a committee of three to see about taking some action concerning the civil rights of the town. In 1780, however, he was proved to have sold cheese at a higher price than that fixed by law, as the following abstract from the Town Records shows: "The town taking into consideration the conduct of Gideon Putnam — Voted, Mr. Gideon Putnam has violated the Resolves of the convention at Concord by selling cheese for nine shillings pr. pound as by evidence fully appeared, Voted, Mr. Gideon Putnam be reported in one of the Public Papers of this State for Breaking one of the Resolves." The above action was taken at a town meeting, held Sept. 13, 1779, over which Dea. Edmund Putnam was moderator.

However, this backsliding on his part seems not to have affected his popularity as he was constantly moderator of the town meetings and held many other important offices in the gift of the town.

On the 28th of April, 1785, he was chosen deacon by the First church.

He was a man of good ability and impartial judgment.

V. 297 Israel (*Tarrant, Benjamin, Nathaniel, John*), born in Salem Village, 24 Sept., 1730; died (drowned near Baker's Island) 5 Nov., 1756; married 20 June, 1754, Betty Dale, who married, second, Archelaus[33] Fuller, of Middleton. She returned an inventory of Israel Putnam's estate as Betty Fuller, 28 May, 1770.

Children :

826 ISRAEL, b. 15 April, 1755; d. in Salem, 1774; at first he was called "Solomon" but afterward christened, Israel; m. Polly Shays.

---

[32] He is styled joyner in partition of his father's estate, 1747.
[33] Ch. of Archelaus and Betty (Dale) Fuller: Betty, b. Feb., 1760. Sarah, b. 17 Feb., 1762; m. Eleazer Putnam (No. 406). Mary, b. 6 Jan., 1764. Benjamin, b. 13 Sept., 1767; Daniel, b. 14 Nov., 1770-1. Archelaus Fuller d. 25 Aug., 1776.

V. 301 Benjamin (*Benjamin, Benjamin, Nathaniel, John*), born in Salem Village, 12 Oct., 1718; died in Danvers, 26 April, 1796; married 28 July, 1741, Sarah Putnam, who died in Danvers, about 1793, aged about seventy years.

Children, born in Danvers:

827 BENJAMIN, b. 29 Aug , 1742; d. 26 May, 1747.

828 SARAH, b. 17 May, 1745; d. 10 Sept., 1766.

829 BETHIAH, b. 10 Sept., 1748; d. 10 Mar., 1815; m. 6 Aug., 1766, William Putnam, junior.

830 EUNICE, b. 31 July, 1751; d. 26 Jan., 1755.

831 RUTH, b. 26 June, 1752; d. 26 Oct., 1773; m. 28 Nov., 1771, Francis Perley of Beverly.

832 BENJAMIN, b. 28 April, 1756; d. 9 July, 1812. Inherited his father's real estate.

BENJAMIN PUTNAM was elected to a minor office upon the organization of the town of Danvers in 1752, *i. e.*, that of fence viewer. He was afterward, hayward, surveyor of highway, warden, etc., but between 1755 and 1768, he held no office. In 1771 he was tithingman.

He was a sergeant in Capt. Edmund Putnam's company. His son Benjamin was a private in Capt. Jeremiah Page's company. Both marched to Lexington 19 April, 1775.

In 1782, a return was required for purposes of taxation, of coaches, chariots, phaetons, chaises, and riding chairs. There were returned for Danvers, eighteen fall-back chaises, and twenty-two standing-top chaises; of these Benjamin Putnam owned one, Aaron Putnam one, Col. Enoch Putnam, Esquire, one, Nathaniel Putnam one, Archelaus Putnam one, Phineas Putnam one.

In 1787 in company with Nathan Putnam he was on the committee to regulate schools for the winter.

Benjamin and Sarah Putnam joined the Congregationalist church at Danvers, 29 Nov., 1741. From an old diary quoted by Rev. A. P. Putnam in his letters to the Danvers Mirror occurs the following "The mourners followed the corpse in the following order, Capt. Benjamin Putnam and mother; Mr. William Putnam and wife; Capt. Porter and

.wife; Mr. Eben Putnam and Capt. Putnam's wife; Mr. Joseph Porter junr. and wife, Stephen Putnam junr., Ruthy and Miriam Putnam, Seth and Benjamin, and Sarah Thomas.

The pall bearers were Dea. G. Putnam, Dea. Edward Putnam, Col. Page, Col. Hutchinson, Mr. Archelaus Rea and Benjamin Porter."

V. 311 Timothy (*Stephen, Benjamin, Nathaniel, John*), born in Salem Village, 10 Jan., 1725; died 1756, will dated 4 Aug., 1756; proved 4 July, 1757; married 1755, Elizabeth (Nurse) Putnam, widow of Caleb Putnam; she married, third, previous to 1759, Richard Upham, of Reading, and moved to Nova Scotia.

Children:

833   TIMOTHY, b. ——, 1756, after his father's death; bapt. 14 Nov., 1756.

TIMOTHY PUTNAM[84] joined the church 27 April, 1755; this was probably about the time he married. He had held a few minor town offices previous to 1755. On 8 March, 1756, he was elected tythingman.

Various Danvers historians have stated that Timothy was a Tory, probably because his descendants are now resident in Nova Scotia. Such could not be the case as he died in 1756; his father's will made in 1769 does not mention him. His widow had formerly been wife of Caleb Putnam and by him had three sons. After the death of Timothy Putnam she married, and previous to 1759, Richard, son of Richard and Abigail (Hovey) Upham of Topsfield and Reading, bapt. 9 Dec., 1716. Richard Upham's first wife was also Elizabeth and she died 7 June, 1756. In 1759, Richard Upham, with wife Elizabeth, deeded land. In 1773, Elizabeth wife of Richard Upham, of Onslow, Nova Scotia, was heir, with William and Caleb Putnam (her children by her first husband Caleb Putnam) to a Putnam estate in Essex Co.,

---

84 In 1755 an Ensign Timothy Putnam reported the details of his scout near Lake Champlain to Capt. Rogers.

(see Essex Deeds).   By her third husband, Richard Upham,
she had Richard, bapt. 28 May, 1758. Mary, bapt. 5 April,
1761. In 1758, Richard Upham was of Boston (see Vol. 23,
N. E. H. Gen. Reg.).   It is probable that Richard Upham
and family removed to Nova Scotia and settled in Onslow
township in 1761.   Haliburton says, in his history of Nova
Scotia, "The first British settlers came from the Province of
Massachusetts and were of various origin.   They landed in
Onslow in the summer of 1761, to the number of thirty
families, ... they were compelled to undergo the most
severe privations . . . . During the second year the government supplied them with Indian corn. . . . . On their arrival
they found the country laid waste to prevent the return of
the Acadians, but 570 acres of marsh land were still under
dyke, and about 40 acres of upland round the ruins of the
houses were cleared. . . . Remains of the French roads. . . .
are still visible, as also parts of their bridges, ... the settlers
encountered great difficulty in procuring their grant and it was
different from what they had been led to expect." This grant
was registered on 23 Feb., 1769.   The Acadians, or French
neutrals, had been forcibly and cruelly removed from these
lands by the British government in the fall of 1755.

   The present family of Putnam in Nova Scotia, settled principally in Truro, are descended from the three half-brothers,
sons of Elizabeth Putnam Upham.   They also have had the
impression that they were descended from American Loyalists,
which only shows how superficial evidence can distort genealogy and history.

   V. 312 Phineas (*Stephen, Benjamin, Nathaniel, John*),
born in Salem Village, 10 June, 1728; died in Danvers, 1817;
married in Danvers, 10 Aug., 1752, Mary Whipple of Andover.
   Children :
   834   PHINEAS, b. 23 Feb., 1753.
   835   MATTHEW, b. 2 Aug., 1756.

836 JOSEPH, b. 12 April, 1761; m. his cousin, Fanny Putnam.
837 TIMOTHY, b. 17 Feb., 1763.
838 EZRA, b. 6 Mar., 1771.

PHINEAS[85] PUTNAM bought in 1784, the Nurse homestead in Danvers, from Benjamin Nurse, great grandson of Rebecca Nurse.

V. 313 Aaron (*Stephen, Benjamin, Nathaniel, John*), born in Salem Village, 30 Aug., 1730; died in Danvers, 20 (30 Jan.) Feb., 1810; married 4 Jan., 1759, Lydia daughter of John Waters, born May, 1737; died 23 Jan., 1831, aged ninety-four.

Children, born in Danvers :

839 LYDIA, b. 27 Oct., 1759; d. ——, 1776.
840 AARON, b. 17 April, 1762; adm. on estate of Aaron, junr., granted to his father, Aaron, 20 April, 1791.
841 RUFUS, b. 7 May, 1764; d. Beverly 14 Mar., 1836.
842 ISRAEL, b. 2 July, 1766; adm. on estate of Israel Putnam, granted to his father, Aaron, 20 April, 1791.
843 ELIZABETH, bapt. 28 April, 1771; d. y.
844 MARY, b. 23 May, 1774; m. Capt. Johnson Proctor.
845 SIMEON, b. 22 Nov., 1776; d. Danvers, 29 July, 1834.

AARON PUTNAM was a farmer and carpenter in Danvers. He was a private in Capt. Edmund Putnam's company, Lexington alarm.

V. 316 Moses (*Stephen, Benjamin, Nathaniel, John*), born in Salem Village, 30 Sept., 1739; died in Wilton, N. H., 25 July, 1801; married 3 April, 1768, Rebecca, daughter of Aaron and Sarah (Wood) Kimball of Boxford, born 29 March, 1740; died in Wilton, N. H., 15 Oct., 1797.

Children, born in Danvers :

846 STEPHEN, b. 20 May, 1772; d. 18 Sept., 1821.
847 SARAH, b. 5 Nov., 1773; d. 10 Sept., 1809; m. 28 Sept., 1806, Ebenezer Stiles. Ch.: Willard, b. 5 July, 1807. Sarah, b. 18 June, 1809.

[85] Two by the name of Phineas, probably father and son, went from Danvers on the Lexington Alarm, one in Capt. John Putnam's and the other in Capt. Asa Prince's Co.

Born at Wilton, N. H. :

848　Moses, b. 24 July, 1777; d. 20 Sept., 1807.
849　Aaron Kimball, b. 11 Jan., 1784.

Moses Putnam was graduated from Harvard College in 1759. He taught school a while in Boxford and in 1776 or thereabouts, removed to Wilton, N. H. There he obtained the respect and trust of the people and on 9 March, 1778, was elected one of the committee of safety, served as selectman for several years, and was often on important committees. In 1778, he was chosen to represent the town in convention to be holden at Concord for " establishing some regulations by which our sinking currency may be raised and set upon some more stable basis."

V. 317 Stephen (*Stephen, Benjamin, Nathaniel, John*), born in Salem Village, 22 Feb., 1742; married, first, Ruth, daughter of Nathaniel Putnam ; second, Susanna, daughter of Samuel and Elizabeth (Jones) Herrick, born 25 July, 1750, died 25 Feb., 1825.

Children, born in Danvers :

850　Stephen, b. 22 Oct., 1773; d. unm. 1848; by first wife.
851　Moses, b. 4 Nov., 1775.
852　Susanna, b. 22 April, 1777; m. Daniel Putnam and lived in the "Gen. Putnam " house.
853　Ruth, b. 1 Jan., 1779; m. Andrew Batchelder, a clock maker. They lived on the Lindall place. Mr. Batchelder m. a second time.
854　Jacob, b. 17 Nov., 1780.
855　Samuel, b. 30 Oct., 1782.
856　Eben, b. 5 Feb., 1785.
857　Hannah, b. 17 Jan., 1787; d. unm.
858　Sally, b. 10 Mar., 1795; d. unm.

Stephen Putnam was a carpenter and lived in the house (taken down, 1839), built by his father not far from where Israel H. Putnam, Esq., now lives. He is credited with two days' service on the Lexington Alarm under Capt. Jeremiah Page.

V. 319 Deacon Daniel (*Daniel, Benjamin, Nathaniel,*

John), born in Reading, 8 Nov., 1721; died 5 Nov., 1773; married Hannah, daughter of Henry[86] and Hannah (Martin) Ingalls of North Andover, born there 12 Sept., 1723, died 11 May, 1761.

Children, born in Reading:

859 HANNAH, b. 23 Jan., 1745 (unm. in 1774); fam. rec. says she m. Thos. Brown and d. 26 Jan., 1799.

860 DANIEL, b. 10 Oct., 1747, in Reading; a physician; d. 3 Nov., 1773; adm. on both his and his father's estate granted at same time.

861 JOSHUA, b. 27 Jan., 1751 (fam. rec. has it 1750); a man of note in North Reading; d. 25 Oct., 1773; m. Eunice ———.

862 REBECCA, b. 18 Jan., 1752; d. 17 Sept., 1785; m. 20 Dec., 1770, Benjamin, son of Amos and Sarah (Bickford) Upton of Reading, b. 7 May, 1745, d. 12 Aug., 1827. Ch.: Benjamin, b. 12 May, 1773. Ebenezer, b. 14 Jan., 1783; d. 13 Aug., 1822; m. 16 Jan., 1806, Polly, dau. of Joseph Putnam (No. 638). Elijah, b. Aug., 1785; d. 25 Mar., 1860; m. 2 July, 1809, Phebe Wood, a dau. of Israel, b. 23 Mar., 1787, d. 12 July, 1821. Rebecca, b. 1778; d. y. Rebecca, b. 22 Sept., 1780.

863 HENRY, b. 7 May, 1755; d. 27 Nov., 1806.

864 AARON, b. 11 April, 1757; d. May, 1812.

865 SARAH, b. 25 June, 1760; d. in Boston, 16 Mar., 1798, of consumption (aged 38 ?); m. Dr. Nahum Fay of Boston; Wyman states they were m. 17 June, 1794; see under Dea. Henry, son of above. A daughter, Maria Augusta, m. Nahum Fay (Harvard, 1790); d. 1804.

DANIEL PUTNAM was elected deacon of the church in North Reading in 1754; in 1763, 1768 and 1771 he was selectman of Reading, and in 1773 represented Reading in the General Court. On 4th Jan., 1774, Hannah Putnam, spinster, was appointed administratrix on his estate.

V. 326 Rev. Aaron (*Rev. Daniel, Benjamin, Nathaniel, John*), born in Reading, 15 Dec., 1733; died in Pomfret, Conn., 28 Oct., 1813 (15 Oct., gravestone); married 23 or 30 Oct., 1760, Rebecca, daughter of Rev. David and Elizabeth (Prescott) Hall of Sutton, born 1 Sept., 1736, died 17 July, 1773, from the effects of a fall, having been thrown from the carriage while driving with her husband. She

---

[86] Son of Henry and Abigail (Emery) Ingalls and grandson of Henry and Mary (Osgood) Ingalls. See Osgood Gen. edited by Eben Putnam, also Emery Gen., both published by the Salem Press.

died within three days of the accident. Mrs. Putnam was a lady of distinguished endowments. Her brother was Dr. D. Hall of Pomfret, and her sister married Col. John Putnam of Sutton. He married, second, May, 1777, Elizabeth, daughter of Rev. Ephraim Avery of Brooklyn, Conn., born 5 Dec., 1746, and died in Cherry Valley, N. Y., 7 Dec., 1835.

Children :

866 AARON, b. 30 July, 176.; d. 1 April, 1765.
867 REBECCA, b. 5 May, 1763; d. 25 Jan., 1767.
868 ELIZABETH, b. 24 Jan., 1765; d. Oct., 1808; m. Elijah Belcher of Cherry Valley; they removed to Bushue, Tioga Co., N. Y. She left two sons.
869 MARY, b. 25 Jan., 1766; d. 9 Oct., 1848; m. 20 Feb., 1790, Nathan Allen, a farmer of Pomfret, and had nine ch. See p. 243, Hall Genealogy.
870 REBECCA HALL, b. ———; d. 28 Jan., 1819; m., 1810, Nathaniel Frye, son of Moody and Hannah (Carlton) Morse, of Sutton, b. 6 Dec., 1750; d. 1828. Dr. Morse's first wife was Hannah Gibbs, who was mother of his eleven children.

By his second wife :

871 DEBORAH, b. in Pomfret, 13 Feb., 1778; m. Matthew Campbell.
872 HANNAH, b. 14 Feb., 1780; d. in Cherry Valley, 1 Sept., 1857; unm.
873 RUTH, b. 31 Oct., 1782; d., unm., at Cherry Valley, 14 Mar., 1864.
874 SALLY, b. 13 Oct., 1784; d. Cherry Valley, Mar., 1821; m. Samuel P. Storrs.
875 AARON, b. 26 Oct., 1786; d. 20 Dec., 1831; graduated at Brown Univ. A Presbyterian minister settled at Cherry Valley.

REV. AARON PUTNAM was graduated from Harvard, in 1752. On 17 Nov., 1755, he was called to Pomfret, Conn., and accepted 8 Feb., 1756. Ordained 10 March, 1756. He was pastor of this church until 1802, and was universally respected and beloved by his people. He was a member of the Library Association of Pomfret, having been elected upon his arrival. This society was noted for the character of its members.

Rev. Aaron Putnam was very thorough and severe in his discipline and entertained high notions of the sanctity of the Sabbath. He lost his health and finally his voice, rendering it necessary for his deacons to read the sermons he wrote.

From his tombstone the following tribute to his memory is taken: "a kind father, an affectionate husband, a good man, and a minister of truth, whose virtues will be remembered long after the marble shall have crumbled to dust."

V. 329 Israel (*Israel, Benjamin, Nathaniel, John*), born in Bedford, 20 March, 1722; died in Chelmsford, 23 Feb., 1800, aged seventy-seven years (gravestone); married ————.

Children :

876   JOHN, b. about 1755; "removed to the Eastward."[97]
877   ISRAEL, b. about 1757; "I think had no sons;"[97] served 10 days in Capt. John Moore's Co. from Bedford during the Lexington Alarm.
878   DANIEL, b. ——, 1761; had two sons.

V. 330 Benjamin (*Israel, Benjamin, Nathaniel, John*), born in Bedford, 2 Aug., 1725; will dated 3 Sept., 1763, brother Israel to be executor; son Benjamin married Rebecca, who probably married again, in 1764, Eleazer son of Eleazer and Rebecca (Chandler) Davis, born 30 May, 1734. Mr. Davis' first wife was Mary Davis who died 28 Jan., 1763. See History of Bedford.

Child :

879   BENJAMIN.

V. 331 Jonathan (*Israel, Benjamin, Nathaniel, John*), born in Bedford, 16 July, 1728; died in Chelmsford, 1784, aged fifty-eight (gravestone); married, first, at Concord, 21 Aug., 1750, Hannah, daughter of David and Mary (Farrar) Melvin of Concord, born there 9 Oct., 1730; married, second, 1760, Hannah Worcester, died 15 May, 1826, aged ninety-five years (gravestone).

Children :

880   MARY,[88] b. in Bedford, 18 Nov., 1750; m. Peter Proctor. Ch.: Leafy, b. 1770. Zaccheus, b. 1771. Hannah, b. 1773. Polly, b. 1774.[88]
881   SARAH, b. in Chelmsford, 1758; m. Daniel Blood. Ch.: Daniel, b.

[97] Letter of Daniel Putnam to Perley Putnam 1883.
[88] Living 1784.

1775. Michael, b. 1776. Joseph, b. 1778. Sarah, b. 1780. Jonas, b. 1781. Martha, b. 1783. Putnam, b. 1785. Jonathan, b. 1787.

882 HANNAH, b. in Chelmsford, 1754; m. 1771, Daniel Spaulding. Ch.: Daniel, b. 1772. Jonathan, b. 1774. Willard, b. 1776.

883 LUCY, b. in Chelmsford, 1756; m. 1775, Samuel Adams; Ch.: Samuel, b. 1776; not ment. in settlement of her father's estate 1784.

884 DAVID, b. in Chelmsford, 1758 (living March, 1784).

885 BETSEY, b. in Chelmsford, 1759; m. Amos Curtis. No issue.

886 EUNICE, b. in Chelmsford, 1761; d. y.

887 JONATHAN, b. in Chelmsford, 1763; d. 4 June, 1790, aged 21 yrs. (*sic*) aged 2 days (g. s.).

888 REBECCA, b. in Chelmsford, 1764; prob. d. prev. 1784.

889 DANIEL, b. in Chelmsford, 1766; prob. d. prev. 1784.

890 EUNICE, b. in Chelmsford, 1768; d. prev. 1784.

891 POLLY, b. in Chelmsford, 1769; d. 29 June, 1785 (g. s.).

892 JOSEPH, b. in Chelmsford, 4 Mar., 1771; living 1784.

893 ISRAEL, b. in Chelmsford, 1773; d. 1862; no male issue; m. Patty Trask; m., 2d, in 1817, Mary Lindsey.

894 STEPHEN, b. in Chelmsford, 1776; living 1784.

JONATHAN PUTNAM lived at first in Bedford, but afterward removed to Chelmsford. On 9 May, 1766, he bought a farm in Chelmsford, still in possession of the family. The house had formely been a garrison house and was one of the first erected in that town, and had double walls of brick. This house was torn down in 1817 and the present building erected on the same spot. When Jonathan Putnam first lived in Chelmsford, he found the Indians still there.

The following epitaph is on the gravestone of either Jonathan or Hannah Putnam,

"Affliction sore long time I bore
Physicians were in vain, till God did
please and death did seize, to ease
me of my pain."

V. 334 Tarrant (*Israel, Benjamin, Nathaniel, John*), born in Bedford, 2 Sept., 1733; died in Newbury, Vt., 1804; married, first, at Danvers, 1 July, 1756,[89] Mary, daughter of Eleazer Porter, of Danvers, baptized 22 Aug.,

[89] According to Porter Gen., married 19 Jan., 1758.

1736; married, second, Eunice, daughter of Daniel and
Eunice (Cue) Porter of Wenham, born there 3 March, 1750.

Children by Mary :

895 ELEAZER PORTER, b. in Danvers, 8 Dec., 1758.
896 ISRAEL, b. in Danvers, 22 Nov., 1760, of Topsham, Vt.
897 ASA, b. in Danvers, 28 Dec., 1765, of Essex, N. Y.
898 ABIGAIL, b. in Danvers, 13 July, 1768; m. 1794, Joseph Putnam.
899 MARY, b. 5 April, 1771; m. Wyman Wyman, of Newbury, Vt.
     10 ch.

Children, by second wife :

900 BETSEY, b. 16 Feb., 1786; m. John Buskett, of Newbury.
901 SARAH, b. ———; m. and lived in Newbury, Vt.
902 DANIEL (DAVID), b. ———; d. ———, aged about 2 years.
903 TARRANT.
904 EUNICE, b. ———; d. unm.
905 RUTH.
906 ELISHA, b. ———; lived near Brookfield, N. Y.

TARRANT PUTNAM lived in Danvers, near the Topsfield
line until 1789, then in Bakerstown, Me., and finally settled
in Newbury, Vt., where most of his children also settled.

A brother of Mrs. Mary (Porter) Putnam, was Samuel
Porter the Tory, a graduate of Harvard, whose estate was
confiscated. He died in London.

Tarrant Putnam was at Lexington, in Capt. Edmund
Putnam's company. He held the rank of ensign.

V. 341 Nathaniel (*Cornelius, Benjamin, Nathaniel,
John*), born in Sutton, 3 May, 1734; died in Sutton 1812;
will dated 27 June, probated 4 Aug., 1812; married ———,
Deborah ———, who died 24 June, 1810, in her seventy-
fifth year. "Gentleman."

Children :

907 MOSES, b. 23 Jan., 1758, perhaps the private in B. Woodbury's Co.,
     from Sutton, who served 8 mos. at siege of Boston.
908 MOLLY, b. 25 Feb., 1759; m. ——— Jenison. Ch.: Nathaniel,
     Maverick, Joseph, Gardner.
909 HANNAH, b. 11 May, 1761; m. ——— Sibley. Ch.: Stephen,
     Tarrant (jr.), Francis, Lot, Nathaniel, Tyler, Nahum.
910 STEPHEN, b. 17 Jan., 1764; d. July, 1779.

16

V. 347 Bartholomew (*Cornelius, Benjamin, Na-thaniel, John*), born in Sutton, 21 April, 1745; will dated 16 May, 1822; probated 6 Sept., 1825; married, first, ———, Mary (No. 490), daughter of Edward Putnam, who was born 1750, died 1796; married, second, Hannah Axtell, who was executrix of her husband's will.

Children, born in Sutton:

911 BARTHOLOMEW, b. 19 July, 1774; d. prev. 1822.
912 LUCY, b. 8 July, 1779; m. Simeon Howard.
913 EDWARD, b. 26 Jan., 1782.
914 PRUDENCE, b. 13 Nov., 1784; m. Daniel, son of Simeon Hathaway, of Sutton. Ch.: Prudence, b. 12 Nov., 1805; d. 18 Oct., 1807. Phebe, b. 24 Oct., 1807. Daniel, b. 18 Aug.. 1808. Prudence, b. 10 Mar., 1810. Joseph Hall, b. 19 Nov., 1812. Mary, b. 17 Aug., 1815.
915 PHEBE, b. 11 Oct., 1787; d. prev. 1822; m. Capt. Elijah Bigelow. Ch.: Phœbe.
916 LEWIS, b. 15 July, 1796.
917 CYNTHIA, b. 27 Aug., 1804, not mentioned in father's will.

V. 348 Ensign David (*Cornelius, Benjamin, Na-thaniel, John*), born in Sutton, 14 May, 1747; died there, 1814; married there, 12 April, 1770, Elizabeth, daughter of Joseph and Elizabeth (Fuller) Woodbury, born 3 March, 1745; died 27 Dec., 1831. "One of the best of Christian women" (History of Sutton).

Children, born in Sutton:

918 DAVID, b. 30 April, 1771; d. y.
919 BETTY, b. 14 April, 1773; d. 2 Feb., 1815; m. 30 Mar., 1791, Aaron, son of Aaron and Lydia (Taylor) Elliot, b. 1 Dec., 1768. Ch.: John, b. 20 April, 1791. Lucy, b. 14 Mar., 1794. Betsey, b. 2 Oct., 1796. Jerusha, b. 1 Jan., 1799. Aaron, b. 5 Mar., 1801. Lydia, b. 25 May, 1803. Betsey, b. 22 Sept., 1805; m. 1826, Sylvanus Putnam. Jerusha, b. 9 Jan., 1808. May, b. 29 July, 1810. Lucy Ann and Julia Ann, twins, b. 17 Jan., 1815.
920 ABNER, b. 14 May, 1775; d. 25 June, 1859.
921 CYRUS, b. 21 Aug., 1777.
922 JERUSHA, b. 13 Dec., 1779; m. 28 Aug., 1803, Thomas Bigelow.
923 CORNELIUS, b. 28 Jan , 1782.
924 SALLY, b. 28 July, 1784; m. 27 Dec , 1806, Samuel Bigelow.
925 LUCY, b. 8 Sept., 1787; m. 1 June, 1805, Simeon son of Aaron and Lydia (Taylor) Elliot, b. 6 May, 1779. Ch.: Nancy Gibbs, b. 5

Dec., 1805. Lucy Putnam, b. 2 Mar., 1808. Lula Maria, b. 14 June, 1810. Madison, b. 3 Aug., 1812. Laury Ann, b. 12 Nov., 1814.

926   Joseph, b. 23 Feb., 1790.

DAVID PUTNAM marched to Lexington upon the alarm of 19 April, 1775, in Capt. John Sibley's company.

V. 359 Jonathan (*Jonathan, Jonathan, John, John*), born in Salem Village, 13, baptized 24 July, 1715; died there Dec., 1762; married 2 Nov., 1736, Sarah, daughter of Lieutenant Thomas and Hannah (Goodhue) Perley of Boxford, born 12 May, 1716.

Children, born and baptized in Salem Village:

927   Jeremiah, b. 31 Oct., 1737.
928   Sarah, b. 2 March. 1738; m. Henry, son of Henry Putnam.
929   Jonathan, b. 30 Dec., 1740; prob. d. Nov., 1762.
930   Hannah, b. 10 Dec., 1742; m. —— Foster.
931   Elizabeth, b. 11 Jan., 1744-5; prob. d. prev. to 1762.
932   Lydia, b. 15 July, 1747; d. 22 Nov., 1825; m. about 1769, Ebenezer Rea, b. 7 Dec., 1745. Ch.: Lydia, b. 8 June, 1770; d. 26 Aug., 1834. William, b. 6 Oct., 1771. John, b. Nov., 1773. Ebenezer, b. 23 July. 1775; d. 28 Feb., 1822. Perley P., b. 24 Jan., 1778. Jeremiah, b. May, 1781. Aaron, b. March, 1784. Lucy, b. June, 1786; d. 1824. Benjamin, b. Oct., 1789; d. 1812.
933   Nathan, b. 8 Sept., 1749; d. 13 Dec., 1813.
934   Levi, b. 1 Aug., 1751.
935   Perley, b. 17 March, 1754; killed at the battle of Lexington, 19 April, 1775.
936   Aaron, b. 6 Sept., 1756.

JONATHAN PUTNAM lived in Danvers; after the town of Danvers was established he held various offices, such as tythingman, hayward, constable, etc. On the 3 Feb.; 1767, the guardianship of Nathan and Levi Putnam, minor children of Jonathan, was granted to Gideon Putnam.

V. 367 David (*David, Jonathan, John, John*), born in Salem, 15 July, 1755; died 12 Aug., 1825; married ——, Elenor Haskell.

Children :

936a ELENOR, b. 29 May, 1784.

937 DAVID, b. 18 March, 1786; d. 27 April, 1812.

938 JOSHUA, b. 3 Sept., 1789.

939 ANNA, b. 27 Aug., 1792; d. — June, 1871; m., says Dr. A. P. Put-
        nam, 27 Oct., 1792, Nathl. Boardman whose 1st w. was Nancy,
        dau. of Israel (*Edmund*) Putnam, *q. v.* Ch. by Anna : Nancy Ellen.
        Caroline Haskell and Nathl. Holton, twins. Alonzo Bishop.
        Horace Webster.

940 HOLTON, b. 14 July, 1795; d. 27 May, 1813.

V. 369 Bartholomew (*Bartholomew, James, John,
John*), born in Salem, 3 March, 1711–12; died there about
1753; married 2 Nov., 1734–5, Ruth daughter of John and
Elizabeth (Weld) Gardner of Salem, born 12 May, 1716,
died 19 March, 1808; married, second, 24 Feb., 1771,
Captain Benjamin Goodhue, born in Ipswich, 11 July, 1707,
died 20 Jan., 1783.

Children :

941 MARY, bapt. So. Parish, Danvers, 22 Aug., 1736, born Aug., 1736.

Born in Salem :

942 BARTHOLOMEW, b. 2 Feb., 1737; bapt. 5 Feb., 1737–8.

948 NATHANIEL, b. 19 Oct., 1739; prob. d. y.

944 RUTH, b. 15 April, 1740; bapt. 19 April, 1741; d. 7 Dec., 1786; m.
        17 May, 1761, William, son of Ebenezer and Rachel (Pickman)
        Ward of Salem, b. 9 Aug., 1736; d. 9 Oct., 1767. For their desc.
        see Essex Institute Hist. Collections; also Pickering Gen. chart
        17, VII–105.

945 SARAH, b. 17 Jan,, 1743; d. in Sanbornton, N. H., 4 Oct., 1824; m.
        in Salem, 8 May, 1763, John, son of John and Abigail (Archer)
        Elkins of Salem, b. 1739, d. there, May, 1781. Ch. : Sarah, b.
        28 April, 1766; d. 22 Aug., 1801; m. —— Webb. Abigail, b. 16
        July, 1768; d. 15 April, 1851; m., 1st, George Curwen Ward of
        Salem; 2d, Hon. Nathan Taylor; 8d, Eliphalet Ordway, 4 April,
        1842; d. 4 Oct., 1844. John, b. 4 March, 1770; d. in the army.
        William, b. 7 March, 1772, drowned at sea. Ruthey, b. 30 April,
        1779. Jonathan, b. Oct., 1781; d. in West Indies. Mrs. Elkins
        m., 2d, Major Chase Taylor of Sanbornton, N. H., b. 1728, d.
        13 Aug., 1805.

946 WILLIAM, b. 25 Feb., 1745.

947 JOHN, b. 2 Dec., 1748.

948 WILLIAM, b. 7 April, 1751.

BARTHOLOMEW PUTNAM lived in Salem, on Essex street,
nearly opposite the Essex Institute. This estate he sold

about 1750. He was a tailor and of good estate. His will is dated 19 June, 1753. He appoints his beloved wife Ruth sole executrix, his brothers-in-law Jonathan and Samuel Gardner trustees. His six children, Bartholomew, John, William, Mary, Ruth and Sarah Putnam are to have the benefit of his property after the death of their mother.

V. 370 Joseph (*Bartholomew, James, John, John*), born in Salem, 1 Aug., 1714; died in Boston. Will dated 23 Feb., 1786, proved 19 July, 1788; married, first (published 30 Jan., 1735), 19 Feb., 1735, Sarah daughter of Joseph and Sarah (Stacey) Urann, born 16 Dec., 1716; married, second (published 7 Oct., 1765), Elizabeth Comeston.

Children, born in Boston:

949 SARAH. b. ———; d. aged 8 yrs. (g. s.).
950 MARY, b. 5 May, 1737; m. (pub. in Boston, 21 Feb., 1760) to James Kenny.
951 MEHITABLE, b. 1 Feb., 1739; m. (pub. in Boston, 14 March, 1765) Robert Earl. Mrs. Bradford of Rutland, Vt., is a granddau.
952 JOSEPH, b. 1 —, 1740; d. 19 Feb., 1741, aged 3 mos. (g. s.).
953 ELIZABETH, b. 14 Oct., 1742; m. (pub. 17 June, 1771), at King's Chapel 14 July, 1771, Jonathan Carey.
954 REBECCA, b. ———; m. (pub. 16 July, 1778) Nathaniel Carey; m., 2d, John Wise.
955 HANNAH, b. ———, 1758; d. 4 May, 1793; m. 7 Aug., 1777, Josiah Bradley, son of Samuel and Mary (Andrews) Bradley of Boston, b. 24 March, 1754, d. 2 Oct., 1793; m., 2d, 1 Dec., 1793, Lydia Callender.

JOSEPH PUTNAM lived in Sudbury street, Boston, and like his brother William, was a chair maker. In 1736 (28 May), he sold his share in his uncle Nathan's estate to David Putnam of Salem.

The executor of his will was Mr. Jesse Putnam, of Boston. In the will of Nathan Putnam, mariner, of Salem, the brother of Jonathan (No. 359), Joseph and his brother William are called "his good friends of Boston."

At the time of the making of his will, viz., 1783, his son-in-law, Josiah Bradley, occupied the other half of his house in Sudbury street.

V 371 William (*Bartholomew, James, John, John*),
born at Salem, 1 Aug., 1717, baptized 4 Aug., 1717; died
at Boston, 1749; administration on his estate to widow Ruth,
30 May, 1749; inventory, 25 July, 1749, £2511.12; married
(published 18 Sept., 1740) 16 Oct., 1740, at Boston, Ruth
Leach.

Children, born in Boston :

956 RUTH, b. 13 Dec., 1741.
957 HANNAH, b. 4 Aug., 1743.
958 WILLIAM, b. 5 July, 1747.

V. 374 Doctor Ebenezer (*James, James, John, John*),
born in Salem Village, ——, 1717; baptized North Parish,
20 Oct., 1717; died in Salem, 12 Aug., 1788; married 28
Oct., 1764, Margaret, daughter of John and Elizabeth (Pratt)
Scollay of Salem, baptized in Marblehead, 6 Dec., 1724;
died in Salem, April, 1808.

Children, born in Salem :

959 SARAH, b. 30 Aug., 1765; d. 20 Dec., 1801; m. Nath'l Ropes.
960 EBENEZER, b. ——, 1768.

EBENEZER PUTNAM was graduated from Harvard College
in the class of 1739. Of his youth and early manhood very
little is known; but that he studied medicine and practised in
Danvers, Salem, and very generally throughout the county,
and that he obtained the entire confidence of his patients, is
well known. From family letters of his younger brother,
Judge James, we learn that he had a decided adversion to
the state of matrimony, yet in the fall of 1764, when he
had arrived at the mature age of forty-seven years, he surrendered to the charms of Miss Margaret Scollay, who it is
said was a most beautiful woman. John Scollay, the father
of Mrs. Putnam, had originally been settled in Marblehead
and belonged to the Charlestown family of that name, to
one of whom General Warren was betrothed at the time of
his death. John Scollay had married as his second wife,
Elizabeth Pratt of Salem, whose mother was a Maverick of
Boston, and had moved to Salem about 1736. Soon after
his marriage, Dr. Putnam bought the large house formerly

standing on the corner of Washington (then Court street) and Church street, and built in 1768. Nearly opposite was the fine mansion of Col. Benjamin Pickman, now known as the Brookhouse estate. But eight years had passed since the very court house, in which the persons accused of witchcraft in 1692 were tried, had been torn down. This had stood between Dr. Putnam's and Colonel Pickman's. Colonel Pickman's house was afterward sold to Elias Haskett Derby, Esquire.

In this house Doctor and Mrs. Putnam lived during the exciting years preceding and during the revolution and entertained liberally. Among those whom they numbered as friends were many who upon the outbreak of the revolution remained loyal to the Crown and these associations probably led to the charge that the doctor, too, was a tory. This charge as we shall soon see was utterly false. On the 9th Nov., 1774, Doctor Putnam was chosen ruling elder of the church at Salem, in place of Nathaniel Ropes deceased. During the Revolution he entertained Judge Trowbridge, and seems to have been much invited out.

The period from 1760 to 1775, mentioned above, was one of constant agitation, on the one hand for a more liberal government of the colonies, and on the other a determined effort by the merchants and government of England to force the American trade into such channels as they willed. The gentry of the colony were uniformly loyal to the crown as well as patriotic.

That men of wealth and position did not join in the popular hue and cry is not to be wondered at, whether their sympathies were with or against the popular party. Nearly all true-spirited colonists desired to be treated fairly but men of education perceived the great power of Great Britain and did not believe that violent measures would be successful, and therefore held aloof from the popular demonstrations.

Governor Hutchinson upon his departure for England was presented with addresses from the principal people of the

colony, for although accused of subserviency to the home
government and of attempting to overthrow the liberty of his
countrymen, yet those who enjoyed his confidence knew how
false such statements were. As a token of esteem and as an
act of courtesy, these addresses were signed by the principal
merchants and gentlemen of Boston, Salem and elsewhere.
Among the signers were the brothers Ebenezer, Archelaus
and James Putnam. The signers were later stigmatized as
Hutchinson " Addressers " and all manner of vile calumnies
thrown at them by the people and press of that period. Indeed, so hot became the popular feeling that in many places
it became necessary for those who had innocently signed, to
withdraw their signatures publicly. This was done by the
following Salem gentlemen on 30th May, 1775, John Nut-
ting. N. Goodale, Ebenezer Putnam, Francis Cabot, N.
Sparhawk, Andrew Dalglish, E. A. Holyoke, William Pynchon, Thomas Barnard,[90] Nathaniel Dabney, William Pickman, C. Gayton Pickman.[91] These gentlemen declared that
in affixing their signatures to the address given below, they
did so with the best intentions, and they state "that we were
so far from designing by that action, to show our acquies-
cence in those acts of Parliament so universally and justly
odious to all America, that on the contrary, we hoped we
might in that way contribute to their repeal . . . and
our serious determination is to promote to the utmost of our
power, the liberty, the welfare, and happiness of our country."

That this statement was made on the 30th May, 1775, almost one year later than the date of the address, June 11, 1774,
is in itself significant. In 1774, the feeling of a personal
loyalty to the Crown was nearly universal and this deep
respect for King George did not disappear till after blood had
been shed. In 1775, the feelings of a very great many of the
signers had changed, for the effect of the battle of Lexington

<hr/>

[90] The patriotic minister who so wisely advised Leslie at the North bridge, that bloodshed was averted.

[91] Lived opposite Dr. Putnam.

was like that caused by the fall of Sumpter. The addresses which were presented to the departing Governor were very like in their phraseology, merely expressing regret at the difficulties under which he left the country, wishes for his future welfare, and prayer that he would attempt, in some measure, to relieve the colonies of the troubles then prevalent. These moderate expressions of courtesy so inflamed the passions of the people that mills were burnt, property of all kinds destroyed, if belonging to the hated "Tories," themselves tarred and feathered, "smoked" out of house and home and finally in many cases driven to Boston for protection. Thus the colony in its need lost its best brain and blood, for probably not one in ten of the refugees was so from choice. Some few remained at home and after the first outburst of mob fury were left alone. The friends of Dr. Putnam were mostly numbered in this class and he himself was often troubled by the lawless element; but the people of Salem knew that his patriotism was unsullied and that very year, 1775, saw him elected as one of the committee of safety. No better proof of his integrity and the belief of his fellow citizens in his loyalty to his country is needed. In 1776, under date of Jan. 29, William Pynchon entered in his diary, "News from Doctor Putnam at Providence where he and the Salem companies have arrived well." Doctor Putnam was then fifty-nine years old.

Some years later, certain persons in Salem presented to the selectmen a list of those whose property they desired confiscated, for, as they claimed, adhering to Great Britain. On this list occurs the name of Ebenezer Putnam but the authorities promptly erased his name, again clearing him of the charge. Doubtless much of this enmity to Doctor Putnam was due to the fact that his brother, James Putnam, was widely known as having remained loyal to the Crown and that his nephew held an officer's commission in the British army.

As will be seen from the letters of the Hon. James Putnam printed hereafter, that the brothers were in instant com-

17

munication and that James was distressed beyond measure at
the lamentable war, and though he refused to return yet was
deeply grateful to the brother who, more patriotic than he, had
the power to obtain the restitution of his Worcester estates if
he would return.

Doctor Putnam, by his extensive practice accumulated a
very handsome property, and thus was enabled to leave to
his children ample means. It is said that he was a man of
great physical strength and courage. His death occurred at
his home 12th Aug., 1788. He lived to witness the recog-
nition of the independence of his beloved country and to
perceive the beneficial results which followed. He was buried in the Charter street cemetery, the pall bearers being,
Elias Haskett Derby, Esq., Mr. Ward[92] and Doctor Holyoke.

V. 375 Archelaus (*James, James, John, John*),
born in Salem Village, baptized 14 May, 1721; died previ-

[92] Probably Joshua Ward whose grand-daughter Elizabeth Appleton married Eben
Putnam, grandson of Dr. Putnam.

ous to 1786; married 4 Dec., 1740, Ruth, daughter of Capt. Samuel and Ruth (Putnam) Flint.

Children, born in Salem Village:

961 EBENEZER, bapt. 2 May, 1742.
962 ARCHELAUS, bapt. 9 Dec., 1744.
963 MARY, bapt. 20 Mar., 1747-8.
964 JAMES, bapt. 9 Aug., 1747.
965 EBENEZER, bapt. 8 Apr., 1750.
966 RUTH, bapt. 12 Jan., 1751-2; m. 18 Dec., 1771, Francis Perley of Boxford. Children: Fanny, Nancy, Francis, Ebenezer Putnam. Mrs. Perley was probably the daughter who died 1783-4, spoken of by James Putnam as an only daughter.

ARCHELAUS PUTNAM was ensign in 1760 and lieutenant in 1770. He was one of the selectmen of Danvers at the outbreak of the Revolution and was often chosen to fill such minor offices as surveyor of highways, etc.; he was frequently chosen moderator of the town meetings and presided with great dignity and impartiality. He signed the address to Governor Hutchinson upon his departure in 1774, for a further account of which, see the biographical notice of his elder brother, Dr. Ebenezer Putnam. Will made 18 June, 1784, proved 2 Aug., 1785, son Archelaus executor; to grandchildren, Fanny Perley, Nancy Perley, Francis Perley and Ebenezer Putnam Perley.

V. 378 Hon. James (*James, James, John, John*), born in Salem Village, baptized 31 July, 1726; died at St. John, New Brunswick; married, first, 14 Aug., 1750, Eleanor Sprague; married, second, 20 Sept., 1754, Elizabeth, daughter of Col. John and Hannah (Gardiner) Chandler, born 15 Jan., 1733, died 2 May, 1798.

Child, by first wife:

967 ELEANOR, b. Worcester, 15 July, 1751; m. 18 Nov., 1770, Rufus son of Col. John and Mary (Church) Chandler, b. 18 May, 1747; d. 11 Oct., 1823. Child: Elizabeth Putnam, b. 1 June, 1771; m. Solomon Vose, Esq., of Portland, Me.

Children, by second wife:

968 JAMES, b. 16 Nov., 1756; d. 2 Mar., 1838.

969 JOHN, b. 27 Sept., 1758; d. in infancy.
970 EBENEZER, b. 26 Jan., 1763; d. 8 Apr., 1798.
971 ELIZABETH. b. 7 May, 1769; d. 14 Aug., 1787; m. —— Knox. Their
        only child was Elizabeth Putnam.

HON. JAMES PUTNAM was graduated from Harvard College
in 1746; there were eleven others in his class among whom
was Dr. Edw. A. Holyoke, whose father Edward Holyoke was
then president of the College.   He studied law, under Judge
Trowbridge, who, according to John Adams, controlled the
whole practice of Worcester and Middlesex counties, and
settled in Worcester, 1749, taking up the practice of the law.
   In 1750, Aug. 14, he married Eleanor Sprague by whom
he had one daughter, Eleanor, who married Rufus Chandler.
In a letter to his brother Dr. Ebenezer Putnam, of Salem,
dated July 8, 1754, he writes, after speaking of his better
health.   "That which you think or care but little about,
[Dr. Putnam did not marry until 1764] as to your own part
is not wholly out of my thoughts.   I mean (tho' you could
tell without further explanation what you care least about) a
Female Companion.   If I pursue this design which I am
sometimes almost tempted to do with one of my neighbors,
it will not be very speedyly.   But it is an affair of consequence,
and tho' such a one as you yourself don't incline to meddle
with, yet may perhaps with less partiality than others, prejudiced in favor of it give your friendly and brotherly sentiments upon, tho' not as to the person yet as to the *thing* itself which I shall expect in some future epistle unless you
will be so kind as to make me a visit this summer, and if you
will Doct. Tufts[23] will be your company and then you may
see and not be at the trouble of writing on that *Head* or giving your judgement but in part. . . . Postscript—My
little daughter Nelly is very healthy and well, tho' she has
not the pleasure of knowing any of her relations."

* Doct. Tufts—probably Cotton Tufts, H. C. 1749, son of Doct. Simon Cotton Tufts,
m. a Quincy and aunt of Mrs. John Adams. He was an ardent patriot. Simon Tufts
of Boston, merchant, was banished in 1778.

He seems to have changed his mind in regard to "not very speedyly" pursuing this design, for the 20th Sept., 1754, he was united in marriage to Elizabeth, daughter of Col. John Chandler, of Worcester, Judge of Probate, and who was afterward known in England as the "honest refugee." Judge Chandler was driven from his home, his house spoiled and even the clothing of the females plundered when the Whig Committee made their inventory. Judge Chandler died in London in 1800. His portrait is preserved at the rooms of the Antiquarian Society in Worcester. His son Rufus Chandler, by his second wife, Mary Church, born May 18, 1747; (Harvard College, 1766); married Eleanor Putnam, daughter of Hon. James and Eleanor (Sprague) Putnam, Nov. 18, 1770. Rufus Chandler studied law with his father-in-law and practised in Worcester until 1774, when he left the country and went to Boston and afterwards to London, where he died Oct. 11, 1823.

James Putnam, says Sabine, in 1757, held the commission of Major under General Loudon and saw service. Between the years of 1755 and 1758, John Adams (Harvard College 1755) afterward president of the United States, taught school in Worcester and studied law with Mr. Putnam. He also boarded in his family. Mr. Adams remarks that Mr. Putnam possessed great acuteness of mind, had a very extensive and successful practice, and was eminent in his profession.

In 1774, Jan. 14, Mr. Putnam in writing to Dr. Putnam, speaks of an illness which prevented his attending at the class arranged for inoculation[94] and desires to know about the future arrangement of classes as he may come down and bring his son Ebenezer.

James Putnam was one of the twenty signers to the address from the barristers and attorneys of Massachusetts to Governor Hutchinson, May 30, 1774. His brothers, Dr. Ebenezer and Archelaus, both addressed Governor Gage on his arrival on June 11, 1774. In Feb., 1775, he, with others,

[94] For small-pox.

was forced by the threatening attitude of the popular party
to leave Worcester and seek refuge in Boston.

On the 14 Oct., 1775, eighteen "of those gentlemen who
were driven from their habitations in the country to the town
of Boston," addressed Governor Gage on his departure. The
signers were:

John Chandler	Jonathan Stearns
James Putnam	Ward Chipman
Peter Oliver, sr.	William Chandler
Seth Williams, jr.	Thomas Foster
Charles Curtis	Pelham Winslow
Samuel Price	Daniel Oliver
David Phips	Edward Winslow, jr.
Richard Saltonstall	Nathaniel Chandler
Peter Oliver, jr.	James Putnam, jr.

In 1778 the Massachusetts Legislature passed an act confiscating the estates of 308 Loyalists and banishing them;
if they returned a second time, to suffer death without the
benefit of clergy. Among these was the Hon. James Putnam, who had in 1777 succeeded Jonathan Sewall as attor-
ney-general of Massachusetts, the last under the Crown.

From the battle of Lexington until the evacuation of Boston the British were shut up in Boston [95] On the 17 Nov.,
1775, the following order was issued by the British commander. "Many of his Majesty's Loyal American subjects, having offered their services for defence of the place" are to be
formed into three companies under command of Hon. Briga-
dier-General Ruggles to be called the Loyal American Associates, to be designated by a white sash around the left arm.

James Putnam was commissioned captain of the second
company, and James Putnam, jr., was commissioned second
lieutenant of the second company.

Sabine says of this command: "Gen. Timothy Ruggles
tried to raise a corps of loyalists during his residence in Boston but did not succeed. At evacuation he went to Halifax

[95] 19 Apr., 1775 to 16 Mar., 1776.

with the army thence to Long and Staten Islands, where the attempt to embody a force for the King's service was renewed. He organized a body of some three hundred and fifty local militia but does not appear to have done much active duty.

Both James Putnam and his sons, James and Ebenezer, accompanied the army to Halifax and New York, where his sons engaged in business. He sailed for Plymouth, Eng., Dec., 1779, with Mrs. Putnam and his daughter Elizabeth.

COPIES OF LETTERS FROM JAMES PUTNAM TO EBENEZER PUTNAM.

LONDON, JUNE ye 1st 1780.

DEAR BROTHER,

It is so long since you have heard from me, especially by letter that you have perhaps, almost forgot me. I had many reasons for not writing to you while I was in America. But as I am in England it can do you no harm to be informed that I am alive and well. I arrived at Plymouth in England the 22 of Jany. last, and rode from thence up to London where we arrived the 29 of the same month. My wife and daughter came over with me. My two sons I left at N. York in business. Our passage from N. York here was 30 days very blowing, boisterous weather, and we were the first ship that arrived of a fleet of between 90 and 100 sail yt. came out of N. York together.

This is a fine country and the husbandry, seems to be carried to the greatest degree of perfection; and by this means the land produces the greatest crops, of grass, & corn &t. Nature has furnished this Island with great abundance of the best manure, and by the industry & labor & skill of the husbandman these are so mixed with the different soils, as to yield the greatest abundance. The soil in its natural state so far as I am able to judge is not in general equal to ye soil in America. And what surprised me most of anything was to find so much land wast and uncultivated still, on this Island; a considerable part of which appears to be as fit for improvement as the adjoining which are loaded with the finest crops. In our journey from Plymouth up to London we must have rode over many thousands of acres of such lands. And I am informed a very considerable proportion of the Island is yet unimproved. That being the case it is hard setting bounds to the additional increase of the produce of the ground, and of cattle and of course to the still greater abundance of inhabitants that might be supported here.

The air of this country is not so cold in winter or hot in summer as in N. Eng. But in winter there is a dampness and chilliness in the air much more disagreeable than the clear cold of N. Eng. yet the people of the Island in general seem to be remarkably healthy.

In this city you see but little of natural simplicity. Everything is art or artifice and there is so much of the latter interwoven with the Government of the Country, that it needs simplifying. If you should have an opportunity to write to me here, let the letter be directed to be left with Mr. Samuel Rogers Mercht., Queens Square, Bloomsbury, London. I hope you are all well. Present my love particularly to your wife and children and to my Brother and his famerly and all friends. Mrs. Putnam & Betsey join in this request. _ .

I am and ever shall be your loving and affectionate brother

JAMES PUTNAM.

P. S. If you should ever write as I hope you will I want you to enquire & send me an account what were the Christian names of our ancestors who first went from this country to N. Eng; at what time they came over; where they first settled and what part of England they went from; And by old writings, or otherwise, if they always spelt their names as we do now Putnam, or whether they have not spelt it some times Putman For of the latter name there are people here; and I suppose we have altered it. If you can make this matter certain I shall endeavor to find out something more about it. J. P.

LONDON Novᵣ· 13ᵗʰ 1783.

DEAR BROTHER

On the 10ᵗʰ of Octʳ I had the very great pleasure of receeiving your kind & affectionate letter of the 13ᵗʰ· of July last. It was very agreeable to me to hear that your wife children, & Brother Archelaus were well, but the mention of your ill health gives me much concern. I sincerely wish you better, and that you may enjoy every blessing the times will permit. .

My countrymen have got their independence (as they call it) and with it in my opinion, have lost the true Substantial civil liberty. They doubtless exult as much at the acquisition they have gained, as they do at the loss the Tories, as they call them, have sustained.

I have long ago made up my mind about the matter. I know the peace was shameful, disshonorable, & scandalous on the part of Great Britain. But it was such as the Ministers of the day chose to have it, not as they were under the necessity of makeing. Indeed, America had, during the whole war, all the aid & assistance a powerful party in this Kingdom could afford, as well as having the command of the British forces in weak or withered hands during the most important periods of the War. It is true that such was the faction, & such the temper & prejudice of a principal person in administration here during the most critical season of the war, that the properest person, if not the only person fit for the chief command in America, was prevented out of Malice, while it was entrusted in hands that every body knew was not competent to

America, the thirteen states, at last seperated from this country, never more to be connected. For you may believe me when I say, I firmly believe and on good grounds that even the present Adm—r would not now accept of the connection, if America would offer it on the old footing. The reasons & arguments for this are to long & too many to be handled in the compass of a short letter. I therefore dismiss the subject.

You may be assured there is nothing I wish for more than to see my dear Brother, and other dear friends in America again. At the same time I can tell you with truth unpleasing as you may think the situation of the Loyalist to be, I would not change with my independent countrymen, with all imaginary liberty, but real heavy taxes & burdens, destitute in a great measure, as I know they are, of order & good government &c.

Having this view of things you cant expect to see me in Massachusetts soon even if I was permitted or invited to return with, perhaps, the offer [of] the restoration of my estate. For what would it be worth, but to pay all away in taxes in a short time.

I am not yet determined whether to remain in this country or go abroad to Nova Scotia or elsewhere. When my affairs are settled here which I hope may be in the course of the ensuing summer I shall conclude on something & I will inform you what.

If you have opportunity & inclination as I hope you will, to write to me again, unless you send by somebody who will deliver it, and even in that case, least I should be out of the way let your letters be directed to the care of Mr. Sam'l Rogers, Queens Square, Bloomsbury, London. My wife and daughter wish to be remembered in the most affectionate manner to your wife & children & all our connections, in which I sincerely join.

Ever yours

JAMES PUTNAM.

LONDON, JULY 20ᵗʰ 1784.

MY DEAR BROTHER,

I acknowledge with pleasure the receit of your two affectionate letters of the 10ᵗʰ of March & 18ᵗʰ of April. I was glad to hear in the latter that you was better in health—I was sorry to hear my Brother Archel' had lost his only Daughᵗ and glad to hear he was getting well of a dangerous fever.

Let me be remembered to him. I don't like to hear my son James has been so inattentive to his uncle as never to have wrote. I hope he will reform in that particular, in other respects, I have the pleasure to think he is a pretty good boy. As to poor Ebenʳ he has been confined almost all Winter at New York with the Rhumatism. and this Summer has got the Augue & fever. He is there yet and if *that as one of the thirteen flourishing independant united American States* should prove favorable for trade, perhaps he may try it.—You say you wish to see me once more, I say I wish to see you often, but it seems fate has determined otherwise.

Your country is so changed since I left it and in my opinion for the worse, that the great pleasure I should have in seeing my dear friends would be lost in a great measure, in the unhappy change of governᵗ. I mean for them who have accomplished it.

You may perhaps hear of me quickly in Nova Scotia, or rather New Brunswick, a New Province to the Wˢᵗ· ward of N. Scotia. Where if I go out you will hear from me

Your loving & affectionate Brother

JAMES PUTNAM.

PARR,⁹⁶ ON THE RIVER ST. JOHNS NEW BRUNSWICK, NOVEMB. 18ᵗʰ, 1784.

DEAR BROTHER :

I have been at this place about ten days, and am surprised to find a large flourishing Town regurly laid out, well built consist-

96 Parr town in New Brunswick was settled by refugees from Boston before the hostilities fairly begun.

In 1783 about 13000 refugees arrived in Nova Scotia assisted by Gov. Parr who did

ing of about two thousand houses, many of them handsome & well finished—And at the opposite side the river at Carlton about 500 more houses on a pleasant situation. A good harbour lies between the two towns which never freeses, and where there are large ships & many vessels of all sizes. I left Mrs. Putnam & Betsey in England & find that Eben.ʳ sail'd from New York for London about a fortnight before I left it, and where I hope he arrived safe soon after my departure. I write to you now only to let you know where I am, hoping to hear from you soon and I hope I shall be able to give you more particular accounts of our settlement in due time. The Country appears to me to be very good, and am satisfied will make a most flourishing Province.

Give my love to your wife & children, Brother Archelaus & all friends.

I am most affectionately yours

JAMES PUTNAM.[97]

PARR RIVER, ST. JOHN, NEW BRUNSWICK, JAN.ʸ 20, 1785.

DEAR BROTHER

I have wrote you once before since my arrival in this province. I write again now least the former may have failed, to

everything in his power to help them. Soon however the loyalists about the St. John river became dissatisfied with the delay in surveying their grants, and with their representation in the assembly. Having influence at court they succeeded in having New Brunswick set off and a governor, Colonel Carlton, appointed. This news arrived in Nova Scotia in August, and in October. Colonel Carlton and family arrive i in the St. Lawrence, Captain Wyats, at Halifax from London being out eight weeks. On Sunday, Nov. 21, Gov. Thos. Carleton (brother of Baron Dorchester who was governor general of Canada during the Revolution, until General Burgoyne superseded him. Gov. Thomas Carleton had commanded a regiment in the Revolution) arrived at St. John from Digby and was enthusiastically welcomed by the Loyalists. He was escorted to the house of Mr. Leonard at York Point (close to the estate purchased by Mr. James Putnam, in 1785, where he resided for a time. In 1822 it was the residence of Governor Smith.

On the next day Governor Carleton was sworn in and also George Duncan Ludlow, chief justice, and James Putnam second justice. These with ten others constituted the council and were appointed by the crown. Ward Chipman received appointment of attorney general.

[97] J. W. Lawrence, president of New Brunswick Hist. Soc., in a paper read before the society in 1874, "First Courts and Early Judges of N. B.," says: James Putnam "was not one of the original grantees of Land. The lot where he built his house and resided he purchased Dec. 13, 1785, from John Sayre, Jr. (son of Rev. John Sayre) for £35: it was No. 84. east side of Dock Street and the 3d from Union. At this time and for many years this was the fashionable section of St. John. The price paid by Judge Putnam at that time seems high."

Both James and James J. were grantees of Carleton, across the river from St. John, in 1783. *Daniel* Putnam was a grantee of Parr in 1783.

inform you where I am, where I hope and expect to spend the remainder of my life and that I am now in good health.

I left my wife and daughter in London, last Aug.ᵗ My son Eben arrived there about a fortnight after my leaving it, and will I hope, be here with me in the spring all of them. James is yet at Halifax but I hope he will be able to settle to advantage in this Province that my family may be all together, at least in the same Province again.

You may wonder perhaps at my saying I hope I am settled in this Province for life. That I can be contented or happy in the place formerly called Nova Scotia. It is true I have not yet seen much of the Province. But I am now well acquainted with many gentlemen of the best credit and veracity, who have seen and well know the most of it. And from what I myself know and from their information, I believe there is not better land in America.

But then the climate! You say that is dreadful—I feared it was a thousand times worse than I find it. It is what I will now describe, during my residence here which is since about the 10ᵗʰ of Nov. Till sometime in Decemᵇ· in general, warmer than the autumn used to be in N. England. Nor have I seen a foggy day since I have been here.

About Christmas the weather grew very cold and to this time has been generally clear and cold, one or two (snow?) intervening. I have known colder days in N. England & even in N York than any I have seen here yet and not more snow than enough for good sleding The greetest difference between this & N England, I believe, is that here the cold last longer in general; but is seldom or never colder, or more snow, on the sea coast, than there.

Everybody will allow there is no better way of judging of the quality of the soil, than from what it produces. And I declare I never saw so good roots of all Kinds commonly raised in gardens and fields as I have seen, and have in daily use, here,

Such as I have seen in the gardens in this new place, after I arrived in Novᵇʳ raised without manure, exceeded everything I ever saw of the kind Turnips beets, potatoes parsnips & cabbages, larger & better than any I ever saw before And there were rhadishes growing in Col Tyng's garden, without manure, for there the frost had not hurt them, as big as my leg and as tender as any used to be commonly in the spring, I have seen a man by the name of Van Jcoik who lives about 60 or 70 miles up this river, who has been but about two years in this country, who tells me he raised last year, a thousand bushels of grain including wheat, rye, barley, oats, Indian corn, & pease; above half of the whole wheat fit for the market at New York. He lives at a place called Maysville

I hope the more reason to believe this man as sundry of his neighbors have told me they think he has raised as much. I myself have bought of him a quarter of beef, out of a drove he brought down the river with him as fat as any beef I have been used to see in New or old England. He brought twenty with him and says he has sixty more fat cattle to bring.

The price paid is dear for America but meat of all kinds here, is about the same price it was in the London market.

I want to see you and my friends, if I have any I dont wish to live in your country, or under your government I think I have found a better No thanks to the Devils who have robbed me of my property, I do not wish to live with, or see such infernals

God bless you! you — wife, your son, your daughter, my brother &c, who I should be glad to see again, but not in the American States.

Forever yours

JAMES PUTNAM.

ST JOHN NEW BRUNSWICK, MAY 13, '85.

MY DEAR BROTHER:

I wrote you last winter by M^r. Simion Jones from this place, and I hoped before this to have had a letter from you with the agreeable news of your and your family's health &c and of my brother Archelaus also. I shall always be glad to hear of the health and happiness of you both As to seeing you any more you have no reason to expect (in) your State. And I fear your inclination to see me hear, tho' I doubt not of your esteem and love will not be strong enough to overcome a voyage to this place.

You may be assured I should be exceeding happy in seeing you both here. I can give you a comfortable lodging, and wholesome, good fresh provisions, excellent fish and good spruce beer, the growth and manufacture of our own Province.

Mrs. Putnam, my daughter Betsey & Son Eben arrived at Halifax about the 27th of last month on their way to this Province. After remaining a few days with my son James at Halifax they will come forward.   I suppose they are now on their way and I expect their arrival every moment and then our rambling beyond the limits of this Province I hope is over.   Tho' we should be to glad see the few friends we have remaining there among you we don't wish to give them the pain of seeing us in your state, which is evidently overflowing with *Freedom:* and *Liberty*[98] without restraint.

The people of the States must needs now be very happy, when they can all & every one do just what they like best.   No taxes to pay No *Stamp Act. more money* than they know what to do with *Trade* and *navigation free as air.*

Have they advanced to any promising degree in the art of baloon making and the navigation of the air.   They may be the first to have the honor of making a voyage to the moon.   It is not altogether improbable if the navigation could be made safe, & easy, that the balance of the trade in favor of the States, could become immediately profitable.   And really if they kept it all to themselves only for six or seven years, it seems to me it might go a great way toward discharging your national debt.   I hope you will not communicate this sheet to the Congress without a premium. Let (me) be remembered to all your family in the kindest manner & to my brother Archelaus to.

And am ever yours

JAMES PUTNAM.

CITY OF SAINT JOHN JANRY 22d 1786.

DEAR BROTHER:

It is not because I have any thing very particular to write about, that I send you this But because I know you will be glad to hear from me sometimes as I am alike gratified of hearing of your health and prosperity.

My family, except my eldest son who is at Halifax are now together here.   My wife & son Eben: were very sick when they arrived here, and had long been so, but are now both in good health. The climate is undoubtedly one of the healthiest in the world, ow-

---

[98] During 1785 Shay's Rebellion occurred in Massachusetts and was put down by General Lincoln.

ing to that with the particular, attention, care, and skill of Doctor Paine, they are well

Since I wrote you last, I have been up this river about one hundred miles. It was in August before they had done reaping. I made particular observations on many fields of wheat, rye, and Indian corn &c and I am fully satisfied that I never saw apparently better crops growing on the ground in any country. I went through a field of wheat in a foot path which gave an opportunity of observing it the better. And I thought then and do really believe, I never saw larger or better growing in the highest cultivated field in England. This had been under cultivation ten or twelve years, and never had manure put on it. It is however lyable to be sometimes over run in a high spring freshet.

It is my opinion that and am very sure I never saw so much good land together in any part of the world that I have been, It wants nothing but the common cultivation to be one of the most productive countries in the world. I mean particularly for corn & cattle you will be surprised perhaps, to hear me say corn But in a few years you will see it fully verified. A gentleman who is one of the most distant sett'ers up this river. told me himself, and has been confirmed by many others of veracity. who have seen it, that he had about seventy acres of wheat on the ground last summer, which on an average, was supposed from the appearance would yield twenty bushels (paise?). He a few days since told me he had threshed out about five hundred bushels before he left home, and from what that yielded he had reason to suppose it would hold out in that proportion. This crop was partly of winter and partly of summer wheat, and never a tree out on the place but about two years ago.

The wheather has been very cold for a week or more the prepart of this month, but no one day colder, since I have been in the Province, than I have known in Worcester & New York. The summer at Saint Johns are not so hot up the river are much hotter than here. The southerly winds in summer are cool here but these north fogs which frequently come in here go but a few miles up the country.

I have not time now to write you more particu'arly

We hope you and your family are all well

We all join in hearty wishes for the health and happiness of you & family Remember me to my brother if living.

Your ever loving brother

JAMES PUTNAM

SAINT JOHN Novr 4th 1786

DEAR BROTHER

By Mr. N. V. Call I had your letter of the 11th of Sept. I had not heard till I rec^d yours that Brother Archelaus was dead————.

The people of your State seem to be stiring up another revolution What do they want now? Do they find at last, to be freed from the British Government, and becoming an independant state does not free them from the debts they owe one another, or exempt them from the charge of taxation. I wish they would pay me what they justly owe, they may then have what government they please, or none, if they like that best. As to their connection with European, or any other foreign power or state, if the affairs of this world are corrupt as they always have been, it will depend entirely on the principle of advantage. It appears as likely to me that Great Britian will resign their sovereignty & independence and give up to the American state the advantages resulting from the British *Navigation Act.* It is an object that a wise administration will never depart from. To encourage ship building in England, even in preferance. to their own British colonies is now be come an object of great importance with them. And it is expected there will be a duty laid on ships built in the British colonies And the government seems determined to admit no foreign. on any pretence whatever into a participation of their own carrying trade. Since other European trading nations, and they are almost all of them so, or aiming to be such now; see the great *advantage* derived from being their own carriers, they will of course entertain the same jelousy of encroachments on their own trade and navagation. I don't think there is the least probability that the American State will be admitted to participate of the advantages of the trade of any European trading nation, particularly. England, France, Spain, Portugal, or Holland, farther than the interest of each will draw it. Your Southern States having exports that will answer in some foreign markets may do something. But I cant conceive how the Northern can expect ever to become a trading people.

As to my own affairs, you know what I receive as a salary from govermt. Private chamber business as a Judge may be from £50 to a £100 a year more. As to compensation I have just been informed that I stand reported for the next dividend. I am not certain how much this first payment is to be but I hope not less then £1500 or

£2000. There are three equal payments as I am informed, and what I now mention is only the first, and it is for real estate only. Loss of business & personal estate is not included in this. I am not certain what my first proportion is but think it cant possibly be short of £1200.— This I say to you only. Benj^a Massten is at a place called Mirimichion the Gulf of the river S^t. Lawrence & County of Northumberland in this Province. I dont think he is able to pay any debts at present. Perhaps he may be quickly as he is making a settlement & going into the fishery there. Nathl. Hayward I can hear nothing of yet. I have a grant of some good lands here & may have as much more as I want. Mrs Putnam & Betsy join in their best wishes for you and your familys health & happiness.

Yours most affectionately

JAMES PUTNAM

SAINT JOHNS SEPT^r 19th 1787

DEAR BROTHER,

As I have so good an opportunity of writing by Doctor Paine, I could not excuse myself from writing. It is not because I had anything particular pleasing to write about. On the contrary we are pretty gloomy in our family, and have great reason for it. My dear & only daughter died on the 14 of Aug. last. Tho' she had been ill many weeks we had not the least apprehension of danger till about a week before her death. Her husband Mr. Knox was then & now is in Canada. He went away in June last on business of his office. We were all well pleased with her marriage, and She had a pleasing expectation of living well and happy. But that is all over and if there is a future State of happiness we have all good reason to hope & believe she will have a good portion in it. We hope you and yours are well and so to continue for a long time to come.

Your affectionate & loving brother

JAMES PUTNAM

S^t. JOHN JUNE 28th, 1788.

DEAR BROTHER,

The last letter I had from you which is not long since gave me the pleasing information of your better health. I

18

hope it will long continue, and that you may enjoy the blessing of health & comforts of your children & family as long as you can reasonably expect or desire.

I and all my family are in pretty good health I hope yours are to.

My son James has been lately here on a visit from Halifax, for the first time since I arrived in this country. He left us very well last week.

I am dear brother ever most affectionately yours

JAMES PUTNAM

Judge Putnam was the first of the council and bench of New Brunswick who died from failing health; he had not attended council meetings for over a year. He died 23 Oct., 1789, in his sixty-fifth year. Mrs. Putnam survived her husband nine years.

In character he was upright and generous; his health was never robust; and loss of country, friends and wealth must have been a severe blow.

Of his life in London I can find nothing beyond what his letters tell us. Chief Justice Parsons said of him, "He was, I am inclined to think, the best lawyer in North America."

Sabine says, "While the majority of the bar took the side of the people, the Giants of the Law sided with the Crown."

In the Cemetery at St. John is the Putnam tomb containing the remains of Judge Putnam and many of his family. The inscription is upon the opposite page.

SACRED
To the memory of
The Honorable James Putnam Esquire
Who was Appointed
A Member of His Majesty's Council
And
A Justice of the Supreme Court
In the Organization of the Government
of this Province
At its Original Formation
A. D. 1784.
He had been for many years before the war
Which terminated in the independence
of the United States of America
an eminent Barrister at Law
and was the last Attorney General
Under his Majesty
In the Late Province of Massachusetts Bay
He Died on the 23d Day of October A. D. 1789 aged 64 years.
In this Vault are also Deposited the Remains
Of his Wife
Elizabeth Putnam
Who Died on the 2d Day of May A. D. 1798, aged 66 years.
And of His Daughter
Elizabeth Knox
Who Died on the 14th Day of August A. D. 1787, Aged 18 years
And of His Grand Daughter
Elizabeth Knox Putnam
Who Died on the 19th Day of November A. D. 1789 aged 5 months
And of His Son
Ebenezer Putnam Esquire
A Merchant of this City
Who Died on the 3d Day of April A. D. 1798 aged 36 years.
And of His Great Grand Son
James Putnam
Who Died on the 13 Day of Jan. A. D. 1825 aged 11 months
Vivit Post Funera Virtus
VIRTUE SURVIVES THE GRAVE

The term "tory" as applied to New England loyalists has long since ceased to be a term of reproach. Fortunately the terrible guerilla warfare which engaged the residents of states to the south of New England was spared us, so that there are no memories of rapes and burnings to renew a hatred which was chiefly caused by the passions of the hour. The loyalists of Massachusetts were her best blood. They should be divided into three classes: those that took service in the British army and served against their country (which is truly the class we may condemn), those that became refugees and settled in foreign lands, and absentees who returned, during and after the war, to their homes. This latter class is much larger than is generally known. · Many of the refugees left relatives here who for a while suffered from their connection, but in many cases regained the confidence of the people and served in high office. The loyalist and patriot families were largely connected by marriage.[99] But no family connection availed in preventing confiscation of property and banishment. The feeling between both parties was intense. The whig or popular party committed acts of violence having no excuse, and which in 90 per cent of the cases was the cause of the recipients of abuse seeking the protection of the British army. We lost the representatives of many of our first families and the condition of affairs for many years showed this, for the respect due to magistrates and officers, civil and military, for many years during and after the revolution, was often very meagre and much begrudged. However, the remnant of the cultivated class soon resumed their former position and with the education of the masses, the true American spirit overcame the at first evident tendency to the revolutionary principles afterward rampant in France. Stability came from necessity and we of Massachusetts can still make the proud claim that the best of England's blood is represented on our soil.

That the heated passions soon cooled after the first years

[99] An instance is that of Gen. Knox who married Secretary Thos. Flucker's daughter.

of the war is shown by the position returning refugees took, and the frequent marriages between patriot and refugee families. One of the prime causes of the flight of many persons of wealth and standing was doubtless the fear that republicanism would degenerate into a sort of communism; for the establishment of a republican form of government then, was to the minds of persons educated under monarchical principles, as great a mishap as we to-day would view the establishment of the socialistic party in power at Washington.

Had men of different calibre than Washington and his intimates assumed control, the fears of these worthies might have been well founded. The fears of Americans to-day, with a vast minority of our people of alien birth and education, superstitious and lawless, are a thousand times better grounded than the fears of the loyalists of 1775.

NOTE.—In June, 1783, the British Parliament appointed a committee to examine into the conditions and claims of the American refugees. In 1790 the twelfth and last report of this committee was presented. 3225 claims had been examined of which 343 had been disallowed, 38 withdrawn, 553 not prosecuted, leaving 2291 claims favorably considered. The whole amount of claims preferred was £10,358,413, or about $50,000,000 in our money and of this £3,033,910 was allowed.

The annual pension list was £25,785 besides generous annual payments to 588 persons chiefly widows, orphans and merchants.

Sir William Pepperell was the agent of the Massachusetts Loyalists.

About 30,000 loyalists were driven to Nova Scotia, New Brunswick, and other parts of Canada. 13,000 were from New England in one year, 1783. Many others settled in the Barbadoes, Florida and the West Indies.

TREATY OF PEACE, 1783.

One of the most difficult questions was in regard to the settlement to be made with the tory who had suffered confiscation and banishment for the cause of the Crown. The British Government was quite firm in its demand that the U. S. recognize the tory and make good their losses. This was declared impossible by Franklin who said the commission had no power, nor did Congress itself do more than recommend the tories to the clemency of the different state governments.

"Franklin demonstrated that Great Britain had forfeited every right to intercede for them by its conduct and example, to which end he read to Oswald the orders of the British in Carolina for confiscating and selling the lands and property of all patriots, under the direction of the military". Bancroft's Hist. Vol. X, Chap. 29.

"The Am. Comm. agreed that there should be no further confiscation nor prosecutions of loyalists, that all pending prosecutions should be discontinued, and the Congress should recommend to the several states and their legislature, on behalf of the refugees, amnesty and restitution of their confiscated property." Bancroft's Hist. Vol. X, Chap. 29.

Dr. Ramsay says "From the necessity of the case, the loyalists were sacrificed, nothing further than a simple recommendation for restitution being stipulated in their favor."

Ramsay further says to many worthy tories, restitution was made, according to recommendation of Congress. Vol. II, Chap. 27.

The return of the tories to their homes was not at all relished by their former neighbors and often outrages were committed on the persons and property of returning loyalists.

V. 380 Col. Enoch (*Jethro, James, John, John*), born in Salem Village, 18 Feb., 1731–32; died in Danvers about 1796; married, first, in Danvers, 12 April, 1754, Hannah Putnam who was born 13 May, 1736, died 18 Dec., 1776; married, second, 25 Mar., 1778, Elizabeth Stratton, of Lincoln.

Children, by first wife, born in Danvers:

972 JETHRO, b. 22 Dec., 1758; d. May, 1815.

973 ANNA, b. 22 April, 1759.

974 FANNY, b. 7 Aug., 1764; d. 28 June, 1858; m. Joseph Putnam (No. 836).

975 HANNAH, b. 24 May, 1771; d. 29 June, 1830; m. Timothy Putnam (No. 837).

ENOCH PUTNAM lived in Danvers on the old homestead. In 1757, he was first elected to a town office, and continued for nearly forty years serving the town in one capacity or another. He held previous to the Revolution, the offices of highway surveyor, warden, constable, tythingman, and during and after the Revolution he held still more important positions, serving on committees to see about raising the necessary men for the army, taxes, supplies of beef for the army, schools, highways, etc. He was often moderator at the town meetings.

In 1775, he went to Lexington, upon the alarm, as lieutenant of Capt. Israel Hutchinson's company. This company suffered as much if not more, than any other single company in that fight. Those of its members who were killed were Perley Putnam and Jotham Webb; Nathan Putnam was wounded.

Jethro Putnam the son of Enoch was also at Lexington being in Capt. Jeremiah Page's company, of which company Henry Putnam was lieutenant.

By 1776, Enoch Putnam was captain and shortly after was commissioned colonel.

V. 384 John (*Eleazer, Eleazer, John, John*), born in Preston, Conn., 13 May, 1734; died there 10 Aug., 1786;

married there 25 Feb., 1762, Martha Woodward of Preston[100] who died 25 Dec., 1798.

Children, born in Preston:

976 HANNAH, b. 1 Jan., 1763; m. Nathan Williams of Preston. Ch.: Fanny, b. 8 July, 1784; m. 24 Oct., 1802, Eleazer Mather. Betsey, b. 1 Apr., 1786; m. 17 Feb., 1805, Dr. Eleazer Baker. Waty, b. 30 Mar., 1788; m. 1 Jan., 1809, William Tyler.[101] The parents lived at Brooklyn, Conn., as late as 1838.

977 JOHN, b. 7 Mar., 1765; living at Preston in 1786.

978 EUNICE, b. 6 or 7 Apr., 1767; m., 1st, Davis Dunnell. Ch.: Davis and John. Mrs. Dunnell m., 2nd, John Reament and was mother by him of several children. They lived in Mantua, N. Y.

979 JEDIDIAH, b. 6 Feb., 1769; d. Volney, N. Y., 1826.

980 MARTHA, b. 23 Mar., 1771; m. Jesse Cheeseboro of New London (another account, Stonington), Conn., and had five sons and three daughters. This family settled in New York State.

981 CHARLOTE, b. 22 or 23 May, 1775; m., 1st, Ebenezer Curtis and had Charlotte, Sophia and Ebenezer; m., 2nd, William Gray, and had one son in 1839. This family lived at Mantua, N. Y.

JOHN PUTNAM's name is on the Connecticut "Lexington Alarm Lists" as "sergeant" and he is credited with three days' service. He also served in the army for a short period.

V. 385 Charles (*Eleazer, Eleazer, John, John*), born at Preston, Conn., 13 Oct., 1737; died in Paris, N. Y., previous to 1838; married 27 May, 1762, Martha Rose of Norwich. They removed from Preston to Paris, N. Y. about 1765.

Children:

982 FREDERICK, b. in Preston, 20 Aug., 1763.
983 ELEAZER, b. in Preston, 4 Dec., 1764.
984 SARAH.
985 APPHIA.
986 CATHERINE.

V. 388 Samuel (*Jeptha, Eleazer, John, John*), born in Salem Village, 19 May, 1727; married 22 Sept., 1757, Kezia Hayward. Lived in Sutton.

---

[100] Family Records state that her name was Thomson; the Town Records, Woodward.
[101] Emily Cecelia, a dau. of Wm. and Waty (Williams) Tyler, b. 3 Sept., 1811; m. 9 June, 1837, Daniel Putnam Tyler, a descendant of Gen. Israel Putnam. See No. 670.

Child :

987　HOWARD, b. ——, 1758; killed in battle during the Revolution.

V. 391 Fuller (*Jeptha, Eleazer, John, John*), born in Salem Village, 13 Jan., 1731; died at Sutton; married, first, 4 Dec., 1752, Mary, daughter of Stebbins and Ruth Cummings, of Sutton, born 22 Oct., 1733; married, second, 23 Nov., 1756, Eunice Hayward.

Children :

988　DAVID, b. 26 Jan., 1753.

989　ELI, b. 27 Sept., 1754; d. *s. p.* prev. to 1835; m. Elizabeth, dau. of John and Hannah (Greenwood) Harback. Removed to Ludlow, Me. He owned land and a mill in Ballston, now Jefferson, Me. which he sold prior to 1806. A bridge over the Sheepscot River was long known as " Putnam's Bridge."

990　RUTH, b. 4 Dec., 1757.

991　JOHN, b. 8 July, 1760.

992　JEPTHA, b. 24 Sept., 1762.

993　SARAH, b. 20 July, 1765; m. ——, 1785, Nathan Putnam.

994　LUCY, b. 16 Feb., 1768; m 9 Mar., 1791, Tyler, son of Caleb and Ruth (Dodge) Marsh, of Sutton. Ch. : Betsey, b. 28 Dec., 1793. Seraph, b. 7 Apr., 1796. Harriet, b. 28 May, 1798. Lewis, b. 22 Oct., 1800. Willard, b. 17 June, 1802.

995　RUBY, b. 20 Sept., 1770.

996　PRUDY, b. 20 July, 1774; m. 1 Jan., 1794, Caleb, son of Paul and Sarah (Putnam) Sibley, of Sutton, b. 16 Aug., 1771.

996a　Perhaps a son Rufus.

FULLER PUTNAM lived in Sutton. He served in the Worcester Regiment, at Fort Dummer, N. H., from 13 July, to 12 Oct., 1749, during the Indian war.

V. 393 John (*Jeptha, Eleazer, John, John*), born 27 July, 1738; married 9 April, 1761, Mary, daughter of Jacob and Mary (Marble) Cummings, of Sutton, born 5 May, 1741. The widow Mary was appointed administratrix of the estate of her husband, late of Sutton, 29 April, 1771.

Children, born in Sutton :

997　REBECCA, b. 13 Sept., 1763.

998　JACOB, b. 21 Nov., 1764.

999　JOHN, b. 18 Mar., 1766.

1000 OLIVE, b. 28 Aug., 1767; m. ——Marble.[102] Ch.: John Putnam,
      who lived in Worcester.
1001 SIMEON, b. 10 Aug., 1769.

V. 395 Benajah (*Jeptha, Eleazer, John, John*), born
7 Sept., 1747; died some years previous to 1835; married
13 Dec., 1770, Sarah Fitts, daughter of Jonathan and Mary
(Hutchinson) Fitts, born 12 Sept., 1747 (History of Sutton,
page 641). Removed from Sutton to Montpelier, Vt.

Children :

1002 SARAH, b. 5 July, 1771; married 30 Sept., 1803, Peter Stockwell.
1003 PHEBE, b. 26 Nov., 1773; m. 15 Feb., 1795, Samuel Dudley.
1004 MEHITABLE, b. 25 Apr., 1775; m. Capt. Samuel, son of Alpheus
      and Anna (Dudley) Marble of Sutton, b. 27 Mar., 1776. Ch.:
      Samuel. Alpheus. Leonard.
1005 ANN,[103] b. 11 May, 1777.
1006 ABIJAH, b. 30 July, 1779.
1007 EUNICE,[103] b. 17 June, 1782.
1008 MOLLY, b. 2 May, 1784; m. Andrew Sibley.
1009 JAMES, b. 2 Nov., 1786; d. at Montpelier, Vt., in 1813.
1010 SYLVESTER, b. 11 May, 1791.

V. 396 Gideon (*Jeptha, Eleazer, John, John*), born
——; married 28 Nov., 1775, Abigail Holten, perhaps
daughter of John and Ann Holten, of Sutton, born Nov.,
1757.

Children :

1011 GIDEON, b. 7 June, 1776.
1012 NABBY, b. 23 Apr., 1778.
1013 ARTEMAS, b. 31 May, 1780.

He is probably the Gideon Putnam who marched to Lexington and served two weeks in Capt. John Putnam's company from Sutton. Gideon Putnam removed from Sutton
to Calais, Me.

V. 397 Samuel (*Samuel, Eleazer, John, John*), born in
Salem Village, 13 June, 1741; died prior to 1781; married

[102] Since page 248 was printed I have learned that No. 997 married 16 Nov., 1784, Aaron
Marble of Charlton. Ch.: Jacob. Aaron. Ruth. Luther. Mason. Sarah. Hiram.
Russell.
[103] One m. a Knight and the other a Hammett; both lived in Montpelier, Vt.

19

5 May, 1763, Lydia Putnam (born in Danvers 1742), who married, second, Capt. Timothy Page of New Salem, and had, besides three daughters, William, one of the first settlers of Springfield, Oneida Co., N. Y., and Asahel of New Salem.

Children, born in Danvers:

1014 LYDIA, b. 9 April, 1764; m. ——— Shaw. Several children.
1015 MARY, b. 9 Aug., 1765; married Daniel Putnam. Five ch.
1016 SARAH, b. 24 Jan., 1767; m. Col. Jacob Putnam who d. 1850, aged 91.

V. 399 Tarrant (*Samuel, Eleazer, John, John*), born in Salem Village, 8 Feb., 1743; administration on his estate to widow, 6 May, 1776; married 16 Nov., 1768, Sarah Page, who married, second, Capt. Robert Foster of revolutionary fame and well known to Salem by his action at the North Bridge affair, called "Leslie's Retreat." Children by him were, Abigail married Benjamin Cheever. Hannah married Samuel West. Nancy[104] married Capt. Samuel Flint. Lydia died young. Robert died in war. Daniel.

Children:

1017 SARAH, b. 5 Oct., 1769; d. 28 Feb., 1858; m. Capt. Hezekiah Flint.
1018 ELIZABETH, b. 9 Aug., 1771; m. John Derby.
1019 SAMUEL, b. 30 July, 1773; d. 9 Mar., 1826.
1020 PERLEY, b. 16 Dec., 1776.

TARRANT PUTNAM was graduated from Harvard College in 1763. In June, 1772, he was one of the committee appointed by the town "to take into consideration the condition of our civil liberties." He was a private in Captain Israel Hutchinson's company and marched to Lexington on the alarm of 19th April, 1775.

He was a bright, progressive man, popular and fearless.

---

1 + Their dau., Mary, m. Dr. Elisha Quimby and had Ann Mary a music teacher in Salem. Elisha Hervey d. y. Dr. Elisha Hervey. George Augustus. Samuel Foster, a physician in Salem. Ferdinand Page.

V. 406 Eleazer (*Samuel, Eleazer, John, John*), born in Danvers, 4 May. 1759; died there 30 May, 1836; married in Middleton, 29 Jan., 1784, Sarah, daughter of Archelaus and Betty (Dale, widow of Israel Putnam) Fuller, of Middleton, who died at Danvers 20 Dec., 1802. She was born 17 Feb., 1762. He married, second, 18 Sept., 1803, Mrs. Sally Webster of Danvers, who died 19 Feb.,1808. She was the widow of Lake Webster and daughter of Judge Samuel Holten. Married, third (published 10 Nov., 1815), Dorcas Foster, of Middleton; born in Boxford, and who died 2 Oct., 1835, aged 63 years.

Children, born in Danvers :

1021 SALLY, b. 14 Dec., 1784; d. 14 Aug., 1811.

1022 ISRAEL WARBURTON, b. 24 Nov., 1786; d. 3 May, 1868. He assumed the middle name of Warburton in after life, by act of Legislature.

1023 BETSEY, b. 22 Dec., 1788; d. in Middleborough, 1 Jan., 1868; m. —— Pope, of Danvers.

1024 ARCHELAUS FULLER, b. 3 Oct., 1792; d. in Beverly, 11 Aug., 1859.

1025 SAMUEL, b. 14 July, 1794; d. in Brooklyn, 20 Mar., 1859.

1026 MARY, b. 13 Nov., 1801; d. 19 Dec., 1802.

By second wife :

1027 MARY ANN, b. 5 Aug., 1805; d. 15 Nov., 1844; m. John Taylor, of Boxford, who d. 30 Nov., 1827; m., 2d, —— 1836, Sylvanus B. Swan, who d. 25 Jan., 1880. Mr. Swan was b. in Bristol, N. H., in 1806; m., 2d, 1846, Lydia Adams, of Londonderry, who survived him. By his 1st wife he had three daus., one d. in inf.; the others in 1857.

ELEAZER PUTNAM was a farmer and surveyor in Danvers. For many years he was constable and tax collector, tythingman, and held various other offices. He was universally liked and respected and was known as "Squire Ely."

He and his sons Archelaus and Samuel, were very tall. Israel was of medium height. All of the children had blue eyes and brown hair, excepting Israel whose hair was very dark. The gravestones of Samuel, father of Eleazer, and of his children are in the burying ground on Nichols street.

V. 407 Hannah (*Samuel, Eleazer, John, John*), born in Danvers, 1 Feb., 1762; died 23 Aug., 1796; married, 11 Dec., 1783, Major Elijah, son of Samuel and Ede (Upton) Flint; born in Danvers, 16 July, 1762; died 26 Nov., 1841. He married, secondly, 7 March, 1797, Elizabeth, daughter of Asa and Sarah Putnam, who was born 2 Feb., 1767; died 27 March, 1853. Elizabeth (Putnam) Flint was of slight build and like most of her family had black eyes and dark hair.

Children, born in Peabody, then South Danvers:

1028 BETSY, b. 21 Oct., 1784; d. 20 Mar., 1840.
1029 SAMUEL, b. 8 Jan., 1787; m. Sarah Carter.
1030 ELIJAH, b. 23 April, 1789; m. Mrs. Mary (Tewksbury) Bruce; m., 2d, Esther Newton Clay.
1031 PERLEY, b. 4 Aug., 1791; d. 6 July, 1833, unm.
1032 TARRANT PUTNAM, b. 21 Mar., 1795; d. in Belmont, Ohio, 8 Oct., 1822; m. Eunice Healey, of Lynnfield.

Children of Major Elijah and Elizabeth (Putnam) Flint:

1033 HANNAH, b. 13 Jan., 1798.
1034 CHARLOTTE, b. 12 May, 1801; m. 9 Mar., 1848, Nathaniel Pope. Lives in Roxbury.
1035 THOMAS, b. 11 Oct., 1802; m. Jan., 1831, Mrs. Sophia Fellows (Clark), wid. of David Needham; she was b. 1806.
1036 MARY P., b. 29 Mar., 1805; m. Benjamin Needham.
1037 KENDALL, b. 4 Feb., 1807; m. Mary C., dau. of Phineas Carlton; physician in Haverhill; graduated Amherst 1831.

V. 408 Henry (*Henry, Eleazer, John, John*), born in Danvers, 1737; died in Danvers, ——; married 8 Mar., 1762, Sarah, (No. 928), daughter of Jonathan and Sarah (Perley) Putnam, born 2 March, 1738.

Children, born in Danvers:

1038 ALLEN, b. 25 Oct. 1762.
1039 ALICE.
1040 OLIVE, b. 25 Sept., 1764.
1041 JONATHAN, b. 13 Sept., 1766.
} bapt. by Mr. Diman at North Parish Church, 31 July, 1768.
1042 RHODA, bapt. 30 Oct., 1768.
1043 FREDERICK.
1044 LUCRETIA, bapt. 25 Nov., 1770; m. John Wells.
1045 MARY CHEEVER.

V. 409 Eleazer (*Henry, Eleazer, John, John*), born in Danvers, 5 June, 1738; died probably in 1806; administration on his estate granted 14 March, 1806, "Eleazer Putnam of Medford, yeoman." His children are described in a document at the Middlesex Probate Court, as "Samuel, victualler; Elijah, now out of this government."

He married Mary Crosby of Billerica, published in Charlestown, 20 Mar., 1761 (Wyman).

Eleazer Putnam was in Capt. Isaac Hull's company and received credit for five days' service on the Lexington alarm.

Children :

1046 SAMUEL, b. ——— ; d. unm. According to family tradition (Putnams of Cortland, N. Y.) Samuel went South; but in 1806 we find him quit-claiming land in Topsham, Me., to William Putnam and styling himself " of Medford, victualler, gent." This William Putnam "yeoman" of Topsham, sells this same land or part of it, the same year. In 1809, William was of Turner, Me. (Reg. of Deeds, Wiscasset, Me). This William had previously in 1803, joined with the heirs of Samuel Thompson, in deeding land in Topsham. to Samuel Putnam of Medford. "The land where William Putnam now lives."

1047 JOHN.

1048 HENRY.

1049 ELIJAH, b. 1769.

1050 HANNAH, m. Eben Thompson.

1051 RHODA, m. ——— Locke.

V. 411 Roger (*Henry, Eleazer, John, John,*) born in Danvers, 10 Oct., 1743; "Eleazer Putnam, yeoman, appointed administrator on estate of Roger Putnam of Medford, yeoman, 4 Oct., 1797"; taxed at Charlestown, 1764.

Children :

1052 SALLY, b. ——— 1774; d. 1858; m. in Cambridge, 14 Jan., 1798, Adam, son of Lieut. Samuel and Susanna (Francis) Cutter of Charlestown, b. 12 Apr., 1774; d. 1855. Ch.: Harriet, m. 1826, Charles Whittemore. Sarah, m. 1819, Philip Whittemore. Charles. of Arlington; and five others. See p. 164 Cutter Gen.

1053 JOHN, b. Apr., 1777.

1054 HENRY.

1055 GILBERT, b. ——— 1785.

1056　DAVID, b. in Medford, 20 April, 1791.
1057　BENJAMIN, living in Waltham, 1836.
1058　CHARLES, of Charlestown.
1059　EBENEZER, of Charlestown.

V. 413 Billings (*Henry, Eleazer, John, John*), born in Danvers, 11 May, 1749; died in Newburyport, 28 Jan., 1814; married 19 April, 1775, Hannah Wier Allen, of Newburyport, born in Newbury, 9 Nov., 1756; died 14 Oct., 1798; married, second, 12 Nov., 1810, Mary Harris.

Children :

1060　JOHN ALLEN, b. 27 Nov., 1775; d. 19 Jan,, 1823.
1061　HENRY, b. 30 Mar., 1777; d., unm., 16 Feb., 1794.
1062　JOANNA, b. 3 Feb., 1779; d., unm., 9 April, 1807.
1063　HANNAH, b. 14 June, 1781; d. 24 July, 1831; m. John Hardy, of Deer Isle, Me.
1064　APPHIA, b. 12 June. 1783; d. 20 Oct., 1783.
1065　APPHIA, b. 15 Nov., 1784; d., unm., 15 Feb., 1800.
1066　JANE, b. 22 Apr., 1786; d. 20 Nov., 1818; m., but no ch.
1067　REBECCA, b. in Danvers, 7 Apr., 1791; d. 20 Nov., 1818; m. 19 Feb., 1809, Thomas, son of Thomas and Rachel (Moore) Chipman, a mariner; b. in New London, Ct., 14 Aug., 1778; d. in New Orleans, 20 May, 1813. They lived in Newburyport. The father of Thomas Chipman was a second cousin of Hon. Ward Chipman, the loyalist (see p. 301, Vol. xi, Essex Inst. Hist. Col.). Ch.: Hannah Wier, b. 7 May, 1809; m., 1st., Joseph Carlton, of West Newbury; m , 2d, Joel B. Parker, of West Newbury, who d. 5 Apr., 1854. Thomas Joseph, b. 8 Apr., 1811, a ship carpenter at West Newbury. Benjamin Putnam, b. Jan., d. 20 Sept., 1813.
1068　BILLINGS, b. 6 Sept., 1793; d. 12 Nov., 1800.
1069　JOSEPH, b. 15 Apr., 1794; d. 16 June, 1873.

V. 414 Dr. Benjamin (*Henry, Eleazer, John, John*), born in Danvers; died in Savannah, Ga., 1801; m. Ann Sophia, daughter of Alexander and —— (Bruce) Malcolm, of Washington. Alexander Malcolm was a Scotchman and had been an officer in the British Army.

Children :

1070　JOHN, d. before 1801, at a very tender age.
1071　HELEN, d. before 1801, at a very tender age.
1072　AUGUSTUS
1073　JOHN GUSTAVUS, b. in Savannah, Ga., 1796.

1074 CHARLES, b. 1797; d., unm.; minister at Darien, Ga., 1847.

1075 CAROLINE, d. in New Jersey, Oct., 1839; m., 1816, Peter Mitchel, who died on his way to Florida, in Nov., 1839. No issue.

1076 BENJAMIN ALEXANDER, b. 1804.

DOCTOR PUTNAM served as surgeon in the army during a portion of the Revolution and was married shortly after that war, when he removed to the South, and settled near Savannah.

V. 417 Caleb (*Caleb, John, John, John*), born in Danvers, 10 Feb., 1725; died there 17 April, 1751; married Elizabeth Nurse, who married, second, Timothy Putnam, and third, Richard Upham, and settled about 1761 in Maitland, N. S. (See under Timothy Putnam No. 311).

Caleb Putnam and wife Elizabeth joined the church 3 Aug., 1746. He was styled "yeoman." Elizabeth Upham and her sons William and Moses Putnam, were, in 1773, heirs to an estate in Danvers.

Children :

1077 WILLIAM, bapt. North Parish, Danvers, 10 Aug., 1746.

1077a MOSES, bapt. North Parish, Danvers, 15 May, 1748; drowned previous to 1773 while crossing one of the bays of Nova Scotia; d. *s. p.*

1078 CALEB, bapt. North Parish, Danvers, 15 June, 1750.

V. 421 Peter (*Caleb, John, John, John*), born in Danvers, 2 July, 1735; will dated 21 Nov., proved 7 Dec., 1773; married in Danvers, 27 July, 1756, Lydia, daughter of Samuel and Margaret (Pratt) Endicott, born 1734; married, second, Rebecca, daughter of Jethro Putnam (No. 365) born 5 Sept., 1736, who is mentioned in his will.

In this will he names "brother-in-law Enoch Putnam" to be executor. In 1774, 4 Jan., Jeremiah Page is appointed guardian of Peter, Hannah, John, Mary, and Caleb.

Children, born in Danvers :

1079 ANNA, b. 4 July, 1756.

1080 PETER, b. 15 Jan., 1758. There are two Peter Putnams of Danvers, on the Lexington alarm lists.

1081   CALEB, b. 20 Jan., 1759; d. 7 May, 1764.
1082   HANNAH, b, 13 Mar., 1761; d. in Danvers, Jan., 1854.
1083   JOHN, b. 20 Sept , 1762.
1084   MARY, b. 7 Sept., 1764.
1085   CALEB, b. 3 July, 1766.
1086   LOIS, bapt. 6 March, 1768.
1087   LYDIA, bapt. 2 July, 1769.
1088   REBECCA, bapt. 26 April, 1772.

SIXTH GENERATION.

VI. 437 Elijah (*Samuel, Thomas, Thomas, Thomas, John*), born 1 June, 1761; died 11 Aug., 1825; married Betsey Fayton, who died soon after the birth of her daughter; married, second, Lucy Redington.

Child, by Betsey:

1089 BETSEY TAYLOR, b. 29 Nov , 1784; m. in Langdon. 15 Nov., 1805, John Dunkin, of Bornet, Vt. Ch.: John D., b. Nov., 1806. Caroline, b. May, 1808. Jane, b. June, 1810. Chapman, b. 1 July, 1812. Homer, b. 10 Jan., 1815. Betsey, b. Sept., 1818. Christiana, b. 10 Oct., 1820. Emily, b. 6 Nov., 1822. Dummer, b. 1824. Ellen, b. 23 Dec., 1826. Mrs. Dunkin in 1837 kept a boarding house in Lowell; at that date two of the daughters were working in the cotton mills there, and two of the sons were brick-makers in Missouri.

Children, by Lucy:

1090 LUCY, b. 11 Aug., 1788.
1091 THOMAS, b. in Langdon, N. H., 19 June, 1790.
1092 CHRISTIANA, b. 16 July, 1792.
1093 SALLY, b. 19 July, 1794.

ELIJAH PUTNAM lived in Luningburg, Mass., Langdon, N. H., and afterwards removed to Covington, Penn., with his family. Farmer. In 1796, Captain Elijah Putnam was licensed to keep tavern in Langdon, N. H. Mrs. Lucy Putnam received license to keep tavern there from 11 March, 1809, until 1 Oct., 1809. Capt. Elijah Putnam was often chosen to town offices in Langdon, and town meeting was held at his house from 1796 to 1805. He is always mentioned as "Captain."[105] One of a committee to build a meeting house in 1800.

---

[105] There is an Elijah Putnam on the Mass. Revolutionary Rolls.

VI. **443 Ebenezer** (*Ebenezer, Seth, Thomas, Thomas, John*), born in Charlestown, N. H., 25 Jan., 1751-2; died in Middlesex, Vt., 1824; married Hannah Russell.

Children:

1094　ALATHEAH, m. David Church.
1095　EBEN.[106]
1096　ABIGAIL.[106]
1097　LEWIS,[106] d. before 1839.
1098　RUSSELL, d. in Middlesex, Vt., 1825; m. Miss Blaisdell.
1099　POLLY, m. Levi Lewis.
1100　SUSANNAH, m. Jeremiah Stone.
1101　SALLY, d. in Middlesex, Vt., 1828; m. Caleb Bailey.
1102　CALVIN, m. Miss Walcott.
1103　BETSEY, m. ——— Sawyer.
1104　PAMELIA, d. in Waitsfield, Vt., 1828; m. Mr. Knight.

There was an EBENEZER PUTNAM enrolled in Capt. Samuel Wetherbee's company from Charlestown, at Fort Independance, Nov., 1776. This company had marched to join the northern army. Perhaps the same Eben[r] who served one month in Capt. William Carey's company from Sept. 21, 1777. Capt. Carey was of Lempster, and his company marched to reenforce Gates.

New Hampshire State Documents R. 2–134. Deposition of Ebenezer Putnam. "Charlestown, Jan. 23d, 1778, does testify and say that some time in July, 1776, Capt. Weatherbee ask[d] me what I would give him to Discharge me : I told him Nothing where uppon he told me he would discharge me for Twenty Dollars or five week's work. I told him I would give it, then he turned about and went and got a man to go in my Rhoom and I set off to go home, but Before I got home I got sick of my Bargain and went and told him I would go myself and pay him for his trouble for gitting the man . . . after I was Inlisted I ast the Capt. if he was willing that I should take the Small Pox, he said No by No means, for perhaps we may be call[d] for before you will be Ready to march, then I was advis[d] by Capt. Geer and Mr. Olcott to ask Col.

---

[106] This account is taken from a MSS. written in 1839. It may be that this should read : " Eben, m. Abigail Lewis and d. before 1839."

Hunt's advise about the matter where upon he said he would advise any man that was a going to Enocolate as he thought it was not safe to go without."   EBENEZER PUTNAM.

VI. 444 Seth (*Ebenezer, Seth, Thomas, Thomas, John*), born in Charlestown, N. H., 9 Aug., 1754; married,[107] first, Dolly Holden; married, second, Waity Wetseot.

Children:

1105 HOLDEN. There was a Holden Putnam of Middlesex, Vt., in 1835.
1106 PHILA, d. at Middlesex, Vt., Nov., 1824.
1107 SOPHRONA. d. at Middlesex, Vt., Oct., 1838; m. Mr. Arbuckle.
1108 SETH, m. Miss Rockwell.
1109 CATHERINE, d. at Middlesex, Vt., Sept. 1830; m. Mr. Cushman.
1110 LEWIS, d. at Middlesex, Vt., Oct., 1814.
1111 ROSWELL, d. at Peacham, Vt., Feb., 1839; m. Miss Fletcher.
1112 FLETCHER (doubtful).
1113 GEORGE, m. Miss Watson.

SETH PUTNAM was a farmer in Charlestown, N. H. In June, 1776, he was a member of Capt. Sam'l Wetherbee's company in the regiment raised for Canadian campaign.

In June, 1777, he marched in Bellows' regiment to reenforce Ticonderoga. In Sept., 1777, this same regiment marched to reenforce Gates. In Capt. Carey's company were Ebenezer and Seth Putnam. There was another Seth Putnam in Capt. Flood's company from Alstead.

VI. 445 Levi (*Ebenezer, Seth, Thomas, Thomas, John*), born in Charlestown, N. H., 11 Feb., 1757; died there, 1835; married there, 29 March, 1784, Rebecca, daughter of Richard and Dolly Holden; born in Charlestown, N. H., 20 Oct., 1765.

· Marched in Capt. Abel Walker's company, Col. Bellows' regiment in June, 1777, to reenforce Ticonderoga. This regiment saw but 12 days' service.

Children:

107 A Seth Putnam was published at Charlestown, N. H., to Jane Kai Hall, 15 Feb., 1807.

1114 IRA, b. 1786; m., Feb., 1823, Susan Kimball.
1115 PARKER, b. Apr., 1789; d. in Charlestown, May, 1814.
1116 BETSEY, b. Dec., 1791; m. Abner Doty.
1117 HIRAM, b. 1798; m. Emily Griswold.
1118 SOPHIA WILLARD, b. June, 1800; m. (pub. 10 Nov., 1822) William
    Farwell.
1119 LEVI, b. Mar., 1805; m. Miss Wentworth.

VI. 449 Isaac (*Ebenezer, Seth, Thomas, Thomas, John*), born in Charlestown, N. H., 27 or 28 May, 1766; married Oct., 1795, Sarah Wing, who died 29 April, 1823; married, second, Oct., 1824, Sally Daggett, who died at Montpelier, Vt., 19 Aug., 1837. Known as "Captain" Isaac Putnam, of Montpelier, in 1835.

Children, by first wife:

1120 HARRIET, b. 29 July, 1796.
1121 DAVID WING, b. Nov., 1799.
1122 ISAAC, b. 9 May, 1804; d. in Montpelier, Vt., 11 Apr., 1827.

VI. 451 Jacob (*Ebenezer, Seth, Thomas, Thomas, John*), born in Charlestown, N. H., 18 March, 1771; married Polly Worth.

Children:

1123 LORENA, m. Mr. Cummings.
1124 LEANDER, m. Cynthia Stone.
1125 CHRISTOPHER COLUMBUS, of Montpelier, Vt.; m. Eliza Stone.
1126 EDWARD, unm., in 1839.
1127 NANCY, unm., in 1839.
1128 JACOB, unm., in 1839.

VI. 452 Benjamin (*Ebenezer, Seth, Thomas, Thomas, John*), born in Charlestown, N. H., 27 Dec., 1775; married Sally, daughter of Aaron and Mary (Smead) Willard, born 12 May, 1782.

Mr. Putnam served in the war of 1812.

Children:

1129 WEALTHY, m. Lemuel Gibson, of Hartland. Ch.: Laura M., m.
    Wm. H. Larabee, of Charlestown, N. H. Lemuel P. Leonard.
    Harriet P.
1130 SALLY, m. George Dorr, of Honeoye Falls, N. Y. Ch.: Putnam.
    Marcia.

1131 SCIENA,[100] m. Luke Allen. Ch.: Caroline. Sarah. Mrs. Allen after the death of Mr. Allen, continued to reside at Decatur, - Ill.

1132 DANIEL, m. Elizabeth Jones.

1133 JEMMEROON.

1134 ZYLPHA, m. Henry Kimball, of Charlestown, afterwards of Springfield, Ill. Ch.: Marcia. Nettie, m. Samuel West.

1135 MARIA.

1136 LUCRETIA, m. July, 1836 (she was then of Unity, N. H.) 1st, Samuel Hunt Stevens, b. 17 Aug., 1812; son of Enos and Martha (Hunt), of Rochester, Ill. Ch.: Samuel Phineas, b. 1838. Mrs. Stevens m., 2d, Samuel, son of Dea. Benj. West, of Charlestown. Ch.: Martha. Samuel. Charles. Lucy.

1137 LOUISA M., m. James B. Dinsmoor, b. 1825, son of John and Polly Dinsmorr. Ch., b. at born at Boston: Louise Maria, b. 1852. Carrie Ellen, b. 1855; both of whom married.

1138 BENJAMIN WILLARD, b. 17 Sept., 1821.

1139 MARIA WHEELER, unm., in 1839.

VI. 452c Seth (*Thomas, Seth, Thomas, Thomas, John*), born in Lunenburg, Mass., 16 Sept., 1756; died in Putnam, Ontario, 3 Sept., 1827. His gravestone erected in 1847, states that he was born at Charlestown N. H., in 1758. Married 14 Feb., 1790, Sarah Harden, born in Nova Scotia, 14 May, 1763; died probably in 1827.

Children :

1140 LEWIS, b. 11 Nov., 1791; d. 13 Feb., 1793.

1141 WILLIAM, b. 6 Nov., 1793; killed at Windsor, Canada, 4 Dec., 1838.

1142 JOSHUA, b. 5 Jan., 1798; d. 19 Sept., 1859.

1143 FANNY, b. 16 May, 1802; m. 21 June, 1820, Warner S. Dygert; m., 2d, Joseph Nicholas, a farmer, near Ontario. They had one son and one daughter.

1144 THOMAS, b. 28 Oct., 1804; d. 26 Mar., 1880.

SETH PUTNAM was a private in Capt. Samuel Wetherbee's company, Col. Isaac Wyman's regiment, which marched to reenforce the Northern army in June, 1776. According to his gravestone he was an officer in the Revolutionary army. His son Thomas is authority for the statement that he was a member of the "Boston Tea Party."

[100] Another account has this child's name Sylva.

VI. 456 Abijah (*Thomas, Seth, Thomas, Thomas, John*), born in Charlestown, N. H., 31 Jan., 1765; died 22 May, 1842; married 13 March, 1794, Susannah Durant, who died in 1843, aged 75 years.

Child :

1145 EPHRAIM, b. in Charlestown, 10 Aug. 1794.

ABIJAH PUTNAM is reported to have been a man of great goodness of character, a worthy citizen. For many years he was deacon. Resided in Charlestown, N. H.

VI. 457 Abel (*Thomas, Seth, Thomas, Thomas, John*), born in Charlestown, N. H., 29 June, 1766; married Polly Whipple. Lived in Charlestown, N. H.

Child :

1146 JOHN WHIPPLE, b. 25 Jan., 1804.

VI. 458 Elisha (*Thomas, Seth, Thomas, Thomas, John*), born in Charlestown, N. H., 1768; died in the U. S. army, during the war of 1812–15; m. (published 27 Aug.,) 1791, Mrs. Lydia (Durant) Parker, who married, 2 Dec., 1816, for her third husband, Samuel S. West, of Ohio. Both Mr. and Mrs. West died in Columbus, Ohio.

Children, born in Charlestown, N. H. :

1147 HENRY, b. 28 Feb., 1792; of Quincy, Mass.; m. Mary Adams, of Quincy.

1148 NATHAN P., b. 23 Aug., 1793.

1149 LYDIA, b. 10 Dec., 1794; d. Mar., 1876, *s. p.*; m., as his third wife, 16 Jan., 1833, Major Jonathan, son of Elijah and Mary (Willard) Grout, b. 24 Apr., 1760; d. 1854. The following notice was sent to the paper by the groom : "Married in Charlestown, Major Jonathan Grout, aged 73, and Miss Lydia Putnam, somewhat younger."

1150 ELISHA D., b. 26 Feb., 1797.

1151 SUSANNA, b. 3 Mar., 1799; m. John L. Bowman, of Royalton, Vt.

1152 RACHEL, b. 14 Mar., 1801; m. 29 Feb., 1824, Samuel Hurlburt, of Dalton, N. H.

1153 ASAHEL, b. 18 Dec., 1803; d. young.

1154 PATTY, d. in inf.

1155 LAVINA, b. ———; m., 1st, 28 Sept., 1824, Joseph Dill, of Lafayette, Ind., and had four children, all of whom died; m., 2d, Gen. James Burns, of Stoyestown, Penn., and died there.

VI. 465 Timothy (*Timothy, Seth, Thomas, Thomas, John*), born in Charlestown, N. H., 4 Oct., 1760; died there probably about 1835; published to Sarah Hewitt, 4 Oct., 1778.

Children :

1156 SARAH, b. in Langdon, 4 Nov., 1779; d. 18 Apr., 1814; m. (pub. 30 June, 1799), to Joseph Currier.

1157 TIMOTHY, b. 13 July, 1781; d. 1834.

1158 ABRAHAM, b. 27 July, 1783.

1159 SAMUEL, b. 18 July, 1785.

1160 BETSEY, b. 3 May, 1788; m. 17 Nov., 1808, Levi, son of Taylor and Mary (Davis) Spencer, b. 18 Dec., 1785. Ch., all b. in Charlestown: Benjamin P., b. 15 Sept., 1809; d. 31 Oct., 1834. Sally, b. 25 Aug., 1812; d. 1848. Eliza, b. 22 Mar., 1815; d., 1827. Belinda, b. 22 Mar., 1818; d. 1874. Susan, b. 21 April, 1823; m. and lives in Springfield, Vt. Mary, b. 24 Mar., 1825; d. 1827. Moses and Aaron, twins, b. 26 Nov., 1827; Moses d. in 1872; Aaron d. in 1874. Eliza Ann, b. 25 Nov., 1830; d. 6 Aug., 1837.

1161 OLIVE, b. 5 Feb., d. 5 Apr., 1791.

1162 POLLY, b. 27 May, 1792; m. 3 Jan., 1813, William Stoddard, of Springfield, Vt., and removed to Cleveland, Ohio.

1163 OLIVE, b. 7 Feb., 1794; m. 7 Dec., 1817, Nathan White, of Springfield, Vt.; eight children.

1164 MOSES, b. 12 Oct., 1796.

1165 JOHN, b. 24 June, 1799.

1166 OLIVER, b. 5 June, 1802.

1167 JOSEPH, b. 16 Nov., 1804.

1168 BENJAMIN, twin with Joseph, d. 6 Aug., 1808.

1169 SUSANNAH, b. 30 June, 1809; living in 1875; m. 20 Dec., 1826, Deacon Joseph Smart, of Concord, N. H., who d. in Charlestown, N. H., 31 Mar., 1864. Ch., b. in Charlestown: Susan, b. 24 Apr., 1828; d. May, 1847. Joseph Henry, b. 23 June, 1831; m. Mary Boutwell, settled in Ascutneyville, Vt. Moses Putnam, b. 20 Nov., 1833; m. Delia Garland; lives in Springfield, Vt. Sarah Abigail, b. 11 June, 1843; m. George Henry Griggs, of Roxbury

VI. 466 Samuel (*Timothy, Seth, Thomas, Thomas, John*), born in Charlestown, N. H., 14 June, 1762; died there 20 Dec., 1848: married (published 15) Nov., 1789, Ruth Spencer, born 9 Feb., 1771; died at Charlestown, 21 March, 1855.

Lived in Charlestown, N. H., and Weathersfield, Vt.
Samuel Putnam served in the war of 1812.

Children :

1170 ROSWELL, b. in Charlestown, 13 Nov., 1790; died somewhere in the West, leaving descendants.

1171 HORACE, b. 7 July, 1793; d. 4 May, 1822.

1172 ALPHEUS, b. 29 Aug., 1795; d. in Missouri, 1875.

1173 ORIN, b. in Weathersfield, Vt., 6 Sept., 1797; d. Apr., 1842.

1174 JEREMY, b. in Weathersfield, Vt., 2 Sept., 1799; d in the West, and has descendants.

1175 LUKE, b. in Weathersfield, Vt. 2 May, 1802; d. in Danvers, Mass., 5 Feb., 1890.

1176 CLARISSA, b. 25 June, 1808; d. previous to 1870; m. 2 Apr., 1834, George H. Phillips, b. in Westmoreland, N. H., 10 Jan., 1813; d. in Charlestown, Mass., Nov., 1888. Ch.; George Edwin, is coal dealer in Melrose or Malden. Abby Jane, m. 19 May, 1861, George W. Currier. Mr. and Mrs. Phillips lived in Claremont, N. H., for many years.

1177 LEWIS, b. 14 May, 1811; d. in Cambridge, Mass., 1888.

1178 ASAHEL, b. 24 Aug., 1814; of Melrose, Mass.

VI. 467 John (*Timothy, Seth, Thomas, Thomas, (John,* born in Charlestown, N. H., 4 June, 1764; died in Montpelier, Vt., 9 June, 1848; married, first, Catherine Case; married, second, at Charlestown, N. H., (published 1 April 1810), Mrs. Peggy Glidden, widow of Moses Willard, of Charlestown, born 25 Oct., 1781; died in Montpelier, 19 Feb., 1852.

John Putnam was a farmer in Montpelier, Vt., and was a Revolutionary pensioner.

Children :

1179 MARY, b. 29 Oct., 1786.

1170 CATHERINE, b. 12 Jan., 1789; m (pub. 1 Mar., she of Springfield, Vt.), Mar., 1807, Jabez Beckwith.

1181 MATILDA.

1182 GEORGE.

1183 CHARLES.

1184 CAROLINE.

By second wife :

1185 JOHN GLIDDEN, b. in Montpelier, 3 Feb., 1811.

1186 JAMES MADISON, b. in Springfield, 6 July, 1813.

1187   MARK RICHARDSON, b. in Springfield, 6 Nov., 1817; d. 1873.
1188   LUKE S., b. in Montpelier, 24 Jan., 1820; d. 1879.
1189   SARAH WILLARD, b. in Montpelier, 10 Apr., 1826; m. 3 May, 1843,
       Samuel Dudley, a teacher of vocal music at New England Con-
       servatory in Boston. Ch.: George.

VI. 470 Bailey (*Timothy, Seth, Thomas, Thomas, John*), born in Charlestown, N. H., 13 May, 1770; died Sept., 1827; married, first, 5 Mar., 1795, Anna Bailey; married, second, Jerusha, daughter of Joseph and Lucy Spencer, of Charlestown, N. H.

Children :

1190   ROSELANA,[109] b. 4 Mar., 1797.
1191   HIRAM, b. 27 Mar.. 1798.
1192   GUY, b. 11 June, 1800.
1193   BENJAMIN.[109]

VI. 471 David (*Timothy, Seth, Thomas, Thomas, John*), born in Charlestown, N. H., 7 June, 1772; married Feb., 1798, (8 March, 1802, Charlestown Records), Hannah Bailey. Lived in Malden, Mass.

VI. 474 Ebenezer (*Holyoke, Edward, Edward, Thomas, John*), born probably in Sutton, 7 Sept., 1738; died in Bethel, Vt., 4 May, 1808; married 16 Jan., 1766, Hannah, daughter of Daniel and Mary (Witt) Dike, who died in Barre, Vt., about 1832.

Children :

1194   AZUBAH, b. in Sutton; m. John Lothrop.
1195   JOSHUA, b. in Sutton, 2 Nov., 1769; d. 13 Sept., 1856.
1196   ANTHONY, b. 4 Mar., 1772; left descendants.
1197   POLLY, b. 5 Apr., 1774; m. Leonard Woodward.
1198   HANNAH, b. 7 Jan., 1776; m. Leonard Gibbs.
1199   SALLY, b. 20 Feb., 1778; m. John Willard.
1200   REUBEN, b. 5 June, 1780.
1201   RHODA, b. 8 Jan., 1783; m. Leonard Randall.

EBENEZER PUTNAM settled in Bethel, Vt., where he was a prosperous farmer. Mr. Ahiah Putnam, a grandson, states

---

[109] Joseph b. 1803 is given by one account and Benjamin omitted. This same authority gives the date of marriage as January. Roselana is called Roxia.

that "there was an old deed in town a few years since given by Holyoke Putnam. My grandfather and wife started from Sutton to Bethel; when they got as far as Westminster, Vt., they heard of the burning of Royalton, and stayed there five years, then came to Bethel." The dates of birth of the above children are taken from an old bible once the property of Mrs. Hannah (Dike) Putnam, now in the possession of her grandson, Abel Putnam.

VI. 480 Ezra (*Holyoke, Edward, Edward, Thomas, John*), born 2 Nov., 1751; died in Bethel, Vt., 1 July, 1841; married 14 Dec., 1780, Rebecca, daughter of Daniel and Mary (Witt) Dike, of Sutton, born 1 Aug., 1755; died 28 May, 1823.

Ezra Putnam removed to Bethel from Sutton in 1787.

Children :

1202   DANIEL, b. 18 April, 1782.
1203   CHARLOTTE, b. 12 June, 1783; d. 1 Sept., 1853; m. ——
1204   LUCINDA, b. 11 June, 1787; d. 1866.
1205   EZRA, b. 29 June, 1792.
1206   WILLARD, } b. 30 Aug., 1796.
1207   SIMEON,

VI. 483 John (*Edward, Edward, Edward, Thomas, John*), born in Middleton, 25 Aug., 1735; died in Sutton, 13 January, 1809; married 13 April, 1758, Mary, daughter of Rev. David and Elizabeth (Prescott) Hall, a sister of Mrs. Aaron Putnam, of Pomfret, Ct., born 14 Dec., 1738; died 1826.

Children, born in Sutton :

1208   JOSEPH, b. 25 Dec., 1758; d. in 1776, in the army.
1209   STEPHEN, b. 5 Apr., 1761; m. and removed to Whitingham, Vt.
1210   ELIZABETH, b. 31 July, 1763; m. 25 May, 1784, Thomas Eddy.
1211   JOHN, b. 27 June, 1766; physician; settled in Upton.
1212   CHARLES, b. 10 Nov., 1768.
1213   MARY, b. 3 Feb., 1781; m. 18 May, 1790, Aaron Putnam.
1214   DEBORAH, b. 3 May, 1773; d. abt. 1790.
1215   REBECCA HALL, bapt. 4 July, 1776; d. young.
1216   SARAH, bapt. 17 May, 1778; m. 14 Apr., 1798, Rufus Marble.
1217   JOSEPH HALL, b. 5 Apr., 1780.
1218   REBECCA PRESCOTT, b. 16 Apr., 1783; m. 20 Sept., 1805, Solomon Putnam (No. 1228.)

JOHN PUTNAM was a prosperous farmer in Sutton. He served in the French and Indian war, and upon the formation of bands of minute men in 1775 was chosen Captain of one in Sutton. There was another company of minute men there, and both marched upon the receipt of the alarm on the 19th of April. In Captain John Putnam's company were: Elisha, Gideon, James and Peter Putnam. In Capt. Andrew Elliott's company were: Adonijah, Archelaus, David, Ebenezer, Ezra, Luke and Moses Putnam, in all, twelve Putnams from Sutton.

After the Revolution Capt. Putnam received a commission as Colonel in the militia.

He was at various times, subsequent to the Revolution, assessor and selectman. His farm is now owned by his grandson, Joseph Hall Putnam.

VI. 487 Captain Archelaus (*Edward, Edward, Edward, Thomas, John*), born in Sutton, 16 Feb., 1743; died in Rutland, 14 Jan., 1809; married 10 Oct., 1765, Sarah Putnam; living in 1809.

Minute man in Capt. Andrew Elliott's company from Sutton.

Children, born in Sutton:

1219 AARON, b. 13 July, 1766; of Sutton, 1809.

1220 ARCHELAUS, b. 17 Aug., 1768; d. 9 Feb., 1854; of Sutton, 1809.

1221 SARAH, b. 26 Dec., 1770; d. 30 April, 1823; m. 27 Nov., 1788, Isaac, son of William and Silence (Dwight) King, of Sutton, born there 17 Sept., 1762; d. 8 Nov., 1859; Ch.: Tamar, b. 15 Nov., 1789. William, b. Oct. 5, 1791. Sally, b. 19 Feb., 1793. Prudence, b. 11 Feb., 1795. Luther, b. 14 Feb., 1797. Rufus, b. 28 Mar., 1799. Eliza, b. 21 Feb., 1801. Charles, b. 11 Mar., 1803. Maria, b. 25 July, 1805. Nancy, b. 14 Nov., 1808. Putnam, b. 10 Apr., 1810. Samuel, b. 26 Mar., 1814.

1222 ANDREW, b. 24 Sept., 1773.

1223 ABNER, m. previous to 1809, Anne ———.

1224 RUTH, b. 22 Mar., 1776; m. Adonijah Bartlett, of Rutland.

1225 AMY, b. 7 Oct., 1779; m. 13 Mar., 1799, Abner Putnam.

1226 BETSEY, b. 14 Sept., 1781; m. after 1808, Capt. Cyrus Carpenter.

VI. 491 Deacon David (*Edward, Edward, Edward, Thomas John*), born in Sutton, 1 July, 1752; died in Croyden, N. H., 21 March, 1840; married in Sutton, 3 July, 1776, Phebe, daughter, of Dea. Benj. and Ruth (Conant) Woodbury, of Beverly and Sutton, born in Sutton, 9 Sept., 1752; died in Croyden, 4 Jan., 1839.

Children :

1227   PHEBE, b. in Sutton, 23 Apr., 1777; d. 13 July, 1819; m. in Croyden, 13 Apr., 1806, Noah Lanswell, of Croyden.

1228   SOLOMON, b. in Sutton, 30 Sept., 1779.

1229   BETTY, b. in Croyden. N. H., 10 Jan., 1782; d. autumn of 1845; m. 6 May, 1802, Benjamin Whipple, of Croyden.

1230   POLLY, b. in Croyden, 22 Feb., 1784; d. 21 June, 1804, unm.

1231   LUCY, b. in Croyden, 26 Sept., 1786; d. 18 Oct., 1821; m. in spring of 1810, Simeon Wheeler.

1232   CHILD unnamed, b. 24 Mar., 1789.

1233   DAVID, b. in Croyden, 2 Oct., 1790.

1234   RUTH, b. in Croyden, 16 Aug., 1793; d. 31 May, 1826; m. in Croyden, 5 Nov., 1817, James Wheeler, of Newport.

1235   JOHN, b. in Croyden, 11 Nov., 1797; d. 18 Feb., 1884; the last of the family to die.

DAVID PUTNAM, in company with Caleb Putnam, left Sutton and settled in Croyden, which place was settled in 1766 by families from Grafton and Sutton, Mass. David Putnam was selectman seven years between 1781 and 1796; tythingman, 1787–9; moderator, 1793 and 1796; surveyor of highways, etc., auditor, 1794 and 1804. He was a man of great industry, and of a rugged constitution. His health was as usual on the day of his death.

He served in the Revolutionary army previous to his settling in Croyden.

VI. 492 Caleb (*Edward, Edward, Edward, Thomas, John*), born in Sutton, 27 Oct., 1754; died in Croyden, N. H.; married in Sutton, 21 Aug., 1776, Judith, daughter of Samuel and Abigail (Park) Libby, of Sutton, born there 6 June, 1757; died suddenly at Croyden, æ. 54.

Children :

1236 MEHALETH, m. 1812, Reuben Winter, of Grantham, N. H.
1237 SARAH, m. 17 Nov., 1808, Nathaniel Cole, of Croyden and of Claremont, N. H.
1238 CALEB, b. 24 Feb., 1779.
1239 JUDITH, b. 22 Dec., 1780; m. in Croyden, 18 Jan., 1800, William Whipple, of Grantham, N. H.
1240 RUTH, b. 18 Oct., 1782; m. Ethan Powers, of Vermont.
1241 LU, m. —— Phelps.
1242 SAMUEL, b. 28 Mar., 1785.
1243 EDWARD, b. 12 Dec., 1786; m. in Croyden, 21 June, 1810, Lydia Melandy, of Croyden. Selectman 1819. Afterward migrated to Illinois and died at an advanced age, leaving children.
1244 HIRAM, m., 1st, Rachel Chapman; m., 2d, Mrs. Carroll.
1245 PETER, b. 1795.

About 1781, CALEB and his brother Daniel removed from Sutton to Croyden. Caleb Putnam bought 100 acres of land for £100 of the town in 1784. In 1785, he held the office of constable, a position of much more importance then than now.

He was often chosen to office, particularly to such as had control of the highways.

VI. 493 Peter (*Edward, Edward, Edward, Thomas, John*), born in Sutton, 29 May, 1757; died 22 Nov., 1827, suddenly, while at dinner; married 16 Oct., 1782, Sarah Marble, born in Sutton, 31 Jan., 1760; died there, at the residence of her son Peter, 14 Oct., 1842.

Children, born in Sutton :

1246 SARAH, b. 2 Apr., 1784; m. 16 Dec., 1801, Moses, son of Moses and Elizabeth (Rich) Sibley, of Sutton. Ch.: Moses.
1247 PETER, b. 22 Mar., 1788.
1248 FANNY, b. 2 June, 1800; m. 12 May, 1822, Perley, son of Reuben and Tamar (Sibley) Waters, b. 9 Dec., 1795. Ch.: Henry M., b. 5 Nov., d. same month, 1824. Sarah M., b. 26 Jan., 1826; d. 15 Aug., 1828. George P., b. 28 Apr., 1833; d. 3 Nov., 1860.
1249 PERSIS, b. 21 Aug., 1802; m. 11 Dec., 1823, Rufus Bacon. One daughter m. Mr. Fairbanks, of Worcester.

VI. 495 Asa (*Edward, Edward, Edward, Thomas, John*), in Sutton, 30 April, 1763; living in 1816; married,

first, Rachel Harwood, of Barre; married, secondly, Mrs.
Taft, of Douglas.

Children:

1250   POLLY, b. 13 Aug., 1787.
1251   PERLEY, b. 28 Oct., 1789; d. 20 Dec., 1808.
1252   DAVID, b. 7 Feb., 1793.
1253   ASA, b. 13 June, 1795.
1254   DELIA, b. 12 May, 1798; m. Capt. Perley Howard; no ch.
1255   DARIUS, b. 2 Feb., 1801; d. 2 Aug., 1838.
1256   RACHEL, b. b. 15 Apr., 1803; m. 24 May, 1825, John, son of John
           and Rhoda (Hunt) Rich. Ch.: Mary, b. 12 Aug., 1825. · Ruth,
           b. 30 Jan., 1828.
1257   REBECCA, d. soon after the birth of a son; m. Maynard Dodge.
1258   JULIA, b. 13 Nov., 1808; m. 15 Dec., 1831, Leonard, son of Josiah
           and Huldah (Carriel) Dodge. Ch.: Julia Putnam, b. 14 Oct.,
           1832; d. 25 Jan., 1854; m. Andrew J. Morse. Richard Leon-
           ard, b. 22 Oct., 1834; m. Sarah Ann Fairbanks; lives in Ox-
           ford. Asa Putnam, b. 13 Sept., 1836; m. Frances A. Putnam.
           Sarah Cornelia, b. 4 June, 1839.

ASA PUTNAM was a farmer and carpenter in Sutton.   His
son David inherited the homestead, which was the the farm
of his grandfather Edward, and passed it to his son Bradford.
Asa Putnam accumulated considerable property by his industry; he was often selectman and assessor.

VI. 509 Aaron (*Miles, Edward, Edward, Thomas,
John*), born in Middleton, 5 May, 1751; was early in Grafton, Vt.; thence to Stillwater, N. Y.

Children:

1259   PATTY, b. 9 Dec., 1782; m. and went to England.
1260   AARON, b. 26 Feb., 1784; lived in Glen Falls,[110] N. Y.; left a large
           family.

VI. 511 Edward (*Miles, Edward, Edward, Thomas,
John*), born in Middleton, 20 Aug., 1755; died in Grafton,
Vt., 2 Dec., 1843; married, Aug., 1779, Mary Mastick;
married, secondly, 30 June, 1805, Hannah Mitchell.

Children, born in Sutton, Mass.:

[110] There are people of this name in Glen Falls to-day, but no communications could
be obtained from them.

1261 LEVI, b. 15 Apr., 1781; d. in Natchetaches, La., 6 Oct., 1808.

1262 EDWARD, b. 18 Aug., 1782; m. and had four sons and four daughters. In early life a merchant, but later ran a farm in Warsaw, New York.

1263 HANNAH, b. 29 July, 1784; m., 1812, Capt. Henry Blood, of Grafton, Vt; later (1836) of Lewis, N. Y. In 1835 they had had five or six children.

1264 LUKE, b. 15 Sept., 1788; unm. in 1848; at which date he was farming at Warsaw, N. Y.

EDWARD PUTNAM served in the American army at Cambridge, 1775. During 1776, he was a member of Captain Gates' company, Holman's regiment, and was present at the battle of White Plains. Later he was stationed at Albany. He enlisted from Winchendon.

VI. 513 Daniel (*Miles, Edward, Edward, Thomas, John*), born in Sutton; died in Grafton, Vt., 30 Sept., 1802; married 3 Dec., 1790, Dorcas Bone. Farmer, of Grafton, Vt.

Children :

1265 ELIJAH V., b. 29 Aug., 1791; in 1848 had had two sons and was living in Galway, N. Y.

1266 FLETCHER, b. 12 Aug., 1793; in 1848, lived in Florence, N. Y. Four sons.

1267 MARY, b. 7 Mar., 1796.

1268 NABBY, b. 12 Mar., 1798.

1269 DANIEL, b. 22 Mar., 1800; in 1848, lived in Delaware County, New York.

VI. 514 Captain John (*Miles, Edward, Edward, Thomas, John*), born in Harvard, 12 Aug., 1767; died in Grafton, Vt., 27 Sept., 1810; married 4 Sept., 1796, Susannah, daughter of Ebenezer Page, of Salem, N. H.

Children :

1270 JOHN, b. 2 Jan., 1798; d. 15 Oct., 1853.

1271 ASHER, b. 5 Oct., 1799; of Grafton, Vt., 1835.

CAPTAIN JOHN PUTNAM obtained his commission while in the infantry branch of the service. He was a firm and earnest member of the Congregationalist church. In 1848 his two sons occupied the farm originally owned by their grandfather Miles Putnam in Grafton.

VI. 517 Miles (*Miles, Edward, Edward, Thomas, John*), born in Winchendon, 6 July, 1774; died in Plainfield, N. J., 25 Dec., 1827; married 30 Oct., 1800, Martha, daughter of John and Sarah Davis, born in Barnard, N. J., 12 Feb., 1786. Previous to her marriage Mrs. Putnam was a school-teacher. Miles Putnam settled in Plainfield, N. J., where he taught school.

Children :

1272 JOHN W. DAVIS, b. 21 Sept., 1801.
1273 ANDREW WILKINS, b. in Barnard, N. J., 9 June, 1803.
 1274 SALLY, b. in Barnard, 31 July, 1805; m. 12 Jan., 1825, Azell Noe.
 1275 CLARINDA, b. in Piscataway, 9 Sept., 1807.
1276 WILLIAM, b. in Warren (formerly Barnard), 15 June, 1809.
 1277 ABRAHAM DAVIS, b. 23 Apr., 1811; d. 8 June, 1811; buried at Scotch Plains, N. J.
1278 ELLIS, b. in Warren, 19 Dec., 1813.
 1279 PAMELIA DAVIS, b. in Warren, 6 April, 1815.
 1280 OLIVE DAVIS, b. in Warren, 19 June, 1817.
 1281 ZEMIAH STED, b. in Warren, 13 Jan., 1821.
 1282 MARTHA MARIA, b. in Warren, 9 July, 1823; d. 24 March, 1826; buried at Scotch Plains.
 1283 RACHEL ANN, b. in Warren, 7 May, 1828.

VI. 525 Andrew (*Elisha, Elisha, Edward, Thomas, John*), born in Sutton, 6 (or 4) May, 1742; died in Townsend, Mass., aged above 70 years; married 10 Jan., 1764, Lucy Parks, of Sutton, who died in Townsend, aged above 70 years.

Children :

1284 ANDREW, b. in Winchester, 11 Mar., 1769.
1285 MALICHI, b. in Winchester.
1286 PETER, b. in Winchester.
 1287 STEPHEN, b. in Greenfield.
1288 DAVID, b. in Greenfield, 11 Jan., 1783.
 1289 ELIZABETH, m. Eliphaz Allen, of Rindge, N. H.
 1290 SALLY, m. Isaac Colburn, of Rindge, N. H.
 1291 LUCY, d. in child-birth; m. David Ball, of Townsend.
 1292 MARY, m. in Townsend, John Humphrey, of Boston.

ANDREW PUTNAM owned and cultivated a farm in Greenfield, besides fitting young men for college. He accepted farm work as an equivalent for board. About 1794, the farm in Greenfield was sold and a smaller one in Townsend bought,

whither the family, now consisting of but Mr. and Mrs. Putnam and the three youngest children, the elder boys having
sought their fortunes in the West, removed.

Mr. Putnam was fond of dress and had a fine carriage, being six feet two inches in height. The boys were all tall,
being over six feet in height. It is said that Mrs. Putnam
was the handsomest girl that ever entered Sutton meeting
house; she was rather short in stature. Her daughter, Mrs.
Ball, was quite ready with the brush and many of her re-pro-
ductions of domestic animals and scenes, were greatly admired, although she had no instruction. Some of the
present generation of this family, with modern facilities for
study, are doing good work as artists.

VI. 526 Elisha (*Elisha, Elisha, Edward, Thomas,
John*), born in Sutton, 4 Dec., 1745; died 25 May, 1784;
married 2 April, 1765, Abigail, daughter of Joseph and Hannah Chamberlain, of Sutton, born 26 Dec., 1746.

Children, all born in either Winchester or Greenfield:

1293 MOLLY, b. 23 Feb., 1766; m. Moses Sibley.
1294 VASHTI, b. 28 Jan,, 1768; m. ——— Wheelock.
1295 HANNAH, } b. 20 Jan., 1770; d. Feb., 1779.
1296 DEBORAH, } d. 6 Feb., 1770.
1297 ELISHA, b. 8 Aug., 1772; m. Levina Ellis.
1298 ABRAHAM, b. 19 Jan., 1775; d. 14 Apr., 1777.
1299 LUCY.
1300 ABNER, b. 28 Mar., 1777; m. ——— Stearns.
1301 LUCY, b. 16 Nov., 1779; m. Oliver Sibley.

VI. 528 Jokton (*Elisha, Elisha, Edward, Thomas,
John*), born in Sutton, 1 May, 1750; died probably at
Gloucester, R. I.; married in Gloucester, R. I., 7 April,
1770, Anne, daughter of John Harris, of Gloucester.

Children, born in Gloucester:

1302 LUCINDA, b. 24 May, 1771; m. there 12 April, 1789, Daniel Curtis.
1303 JOSEPH, b. 6 July, 1773.
1304 ISRAEL, b. 23 Dec, 1775; d. 7 Apr., 1776.
1305 SARAH, b. 13 Feb., 1777.
1306 MOLLY, b. 28 Apr., 1779.
1307 LYDIA b. 4 July, 1781.
1308 WILLIAM, b. 26 Feb., 1784.

21

JOKTON PUTNTM, during his minority, was ward of John Taft (1766), but soon removed from Sutton to Uxbridge, (while there, in Sept., 1772, he was appointed guardian of his brother William), thence to Gloucester, R. I. On the 3d Feb., 1778, he was drafted into the Continental army from Uxbridge to serve in Massachusetts, till 5th Nov., 1778. They were, however, ordered to the Hudson, and he, with three others, failed to appear.

In May, 1783, he petitioned the General Court of Rhode Island for his discharge from prison. From this petition it appears that he with others had been convicted of high crimes and misdemeanors and sentenced to pay £100 lawful money and costs and remain in goal till paid. He states that his property is under attachment for debt; that his family is large and suffering for want of his services. His petition was granted upon payment of costs.

In May, 1786, he again petitions, stating that in March, 1783, he and others were convicted of riotous proceedings at at Gloucester and sentenced, etc.; that by the indulgence of f the court he was liberated, having given security for his share of the costs, viz., £70, lawful money; that his property being small and family large, he prays that he may do as others have done, pay the costs in state notes. This was also granted.

Probably the disturbances above alluded to, were caused by the immense depreciation of paper money which followed the large issues by the state and federal governments, and which caused great suffering.

VI. 529 Luke (*Elisha, Elisha, Edward, Thomas, John*), born in Sutton, 5 Oct., 1755; m. 23 Nov., 1786, Mary, daughter of Jonathan and Anne (Chase) Putnam, born 25 Dec., 1755,

Luke Putnam marched from Sutton upon the Lexington Alarm, 19 April, 1775, and served during the seige of Boston.

Child:

1309 TYLER, b. in Sutton, 11 Sept., 1791.

VI. 530 Lieut. William (*Elisha, Elisha, Edward, Thomas, John*), born in Sutton, 7 Jan., 1758; died in Buckland, 22 July, 1818; married 25 June, 1778, Submit Fisk, born 27 Oct., 1759; died 19 Sept., 1818.

Children:

1310 LYDIA, b. 7 Mar., 1779; d. 6 July, 1822.

1311 POLLY, b. 8 April, 1780; d. 20 May, 1780.

1812 HANNAH, b. 14 June, 1781; d. 9 May, 1800.

1813 ZILPHA, b. 15 Apr., 1784; d. 1862; m. Nehemiah Sabine, and removed to Halifax, Vt. Ch.: Duncea, b. 1807; m., 1826, Jacob, son of Jonathan Whiting, born 1762; d. 1835; whose son Danforth, b. 1830; d. 1867, m. Laura Ballou, dau. of Hosea Ballou, b. 1833, and had a dau. Florence Danforth, b. 1861; who m. Charles E.. son of John Brown, of Concord, b. 1850.

1314 ELISHA, b. 18 May, 1786; living in 1836. He had been a member of the Vermont Assembly, and was formerly a joiner and carpenter and afterward farmer.

1315 WILLIAM, b. 15 Mar., 1788; farmer.

1316 DANIEL, b. 28 Feb., 1790; d. 6 Dec., 1828. Deacon of the Baptist church at Ashfield.

1317 SARAH, b. 6 Feb., 1792. .

1318 ABNER, b. in Buckland, 28 July, 1794; farmer.

1319 SUBMIT, b. 11 July, 1797; outlived all the family.

LIEUT. WILLIAM PUTNAM removed from Upton to Buckland, Mass. He was a successful farmer. Upon the Lexington Alarm he marched, as a private in Capt. Robert Taft's company, from Upton, and served through the siege.

VI. 531 Aaron (*Nehemiah, Elisha, Edward, Thomas, John*), born in Sutton, 23 March, 1744; died in Brookfield, 3 Oct., 1777; married 6 June, 1770, Patience, daughter of Daniel Potter, who married, secondly, previous to 1780, Michael Smith, an Englishman, and died 8 May, 1811.

Children, born in Brookfield:

1320 SARAH, b 26 June. 1771; m. John Cameron, of Oakham. She was living in 1798.

1321 CALVIN, b. 5 Feb., 1773: m Nabby Davidson.

1322 LUTHER, b. 23 Nov.. 1775; d. young.

1323 FRANKLIN, b. 17 Nov., 1776; d. young.

VI. 537 Deacon Reuben (*Nehemiah, Elisha, Edward, Thomas, John*), born in Sutton, 9 April, 1757; died

in Sutton, June, 1797; married 7 Nov., 1780, Elizabeth
Mason, who survived her husband.

Deacon Reuben Putnam was a cabinet-maker in Sutton.

Children, born in Sutton:

1324 AARON, b. 29 Aug., 1781; d. 27 Feb., 1854.
1325 JONAS, b. 5 Mar., 1783; d. prior to 1834.
1326 MASON, b. 20 Dec., 1784.
1327 MANNING, b. 12 April, 1787. At first a saddler; but afterward
    became a Methodist preacher and removed to Ohio, where he
    had two or three sons who d. in infancy.
1328 RUFUS, b. 1 Aug., 1789; d. young.
1329 RUFUS AUSTIN, b. 18 Nov., 1791; of Cornish, N. H.
1330 JOHN MILTON (christened Polycarp), b. 24 Feb., 1794.
1331 JONATHAN, b. 16 July, 1796; d. prev. to 1834.

VI. 538 Joseph (*Nehemiah, Elisha, Edward, Thomas,
John*), born in Sutton, 20 Sept., 1760; died in Sutton; married Tamar Towne, who was appointed administrator on her
husband's estate, 3 Jan., 1797.

Appointed administrator of his brother Aaron's estate upon
decease of their father, Nehemiah Putnam, 7 Aug., 1792.

Children:

1332 TAMAR, b. 8 July, 1786.
1333 JOHN TOWNE, b. 24 Sept , 1787; adm. on his estate to wid. Sarah,
    5 Mar., 1816; shoemaker of Sutton.
1334 DANIEL, b. 80 Aug., 1789; Baptist clergyman in California.
1335 BENJAMIN, Baptist minister in California.

VI. 539 Rev. Benjamin (*Nehemiah, Elisha, Edward, Thomas, John*), born in Sutton, 20 Sept., 1760; died
previous to 1834; married Patty Mason.

Joiner and carriage-maker; afterward a Baptist clergyman.

Children:

1336 SIMEON, b. in Rutland, 1785.
1337 RUFUS, d. in childhood.
1338 JOHN, of Hardwick, N. H.; farmer.
1339 JOSEPH, d. in childhood.
1340 JOSEPH,[111] d. in childhood.

VI. 540 Adonijah (*Jonathan, Elisha, Edward, Thomas, John*), born in Sutton, 6 or 9 Oct., 1744; died in Guil-

---

[111] Perley Putnam names another son, Rufus of "Hardwick."

ford Centre, Vt., 1791–2; married 27 Nov., 1766, Mary Wilkins.

Children, born in Guilford, Vt. :

1841 JOHN, } m. and had children. They removed to the Holland
1842 ELIHUE, } Purchase, N. Y.
1843 ASA, }
1844 LEMUEL, m. and had children.
1845 LUCY, unm.
1846 JANNA, } m. and had children.
1847 ISRAEL, }
1348 JARED, b. May, 1788; d. 6 May, 1844.

Guilford was the scene of many conflicts between the "Yorkers" and "Green Mountain Boys." Each party alternately held control and committed depredations upon the property of the opposing faction. This state of things lasted until Vermont was finally admitted to the union as a state. In 1788, a grant of land was made by New York to those inhabitants of the grants, who had suffered from their attempt to uphold New York authority. Among these was Adonijah Putnam, who received 212 acres in Clinton, now Bainbridge, Chenango Co., N. Y.

About this time (1792) it is stated by a gentleman writing from the settlements in Western New York, that $265 above the cost of land was the least that a family should attempt a settlement. This was the cost of a log hut $100—a yoke of oxen, a cow, farming utensils, etc.

The children of this son Adonijah are mentioned in will of their grandfather Jonathan, made 10 May, 1791; probated 6 March, 1798.

VI. 542 Captain Francis (*Jonathan, Elisha, Edward, Thomas, John*), born in Sutton, 24 Sept., 1758; died there; will dated 6 May, 1831, probated Dec., 1840; married there, 11 Dec., 1783, Joanna, daughter of Abner and —— (Fairweather) Leland, born 1760.

Children :

1349 NANCY, b. 8 Feb., 1784: m., 1st, Isaac Torrey, of Dixfield, Me. Ch., all b. in Dixfield: Susan, b. 1800; m. Rufus Joffan, of Dixffield. Adeline, b. 1802; m. Wm. Walker, of Wayne, Me. Grace G. H., b. 1804. Hall, b. 1806. Francis P., b. 1808. Joanna L., b. 1808. Mr. Torrey died and his widow m., 2d, 9 April, 1809, Charles Rich.

1350 PHEBE, b. 7 Feb., 1786; m., 1st, Daniel Sheffield. Ch.: Daniel C., b. prev. 1831. William, b. 1837. Francis, b. 1839. Mrs. Sheffield m., 2d, Levi Ludden.

1351 SILAS, b. 15 Oct., 1788.

1352 ROYAL, b. 16 Apr., 1791; d. in Westboro, Mass.

1353 OLIVE, b. 27 May, 1794; unm., in 1831.

1354 MARIA, b. 28 June, 1796; m. Aaron Elliott. Ch.: Francis J., b. in Worcester, 1824. Maria A., b. 1826. Mirias M., b. 1826. Stephen D., b. 1828. Sophia B., b. 1831. Aaron, b. 1833.

1355 PRUDENCE, b. 28 Feb., 1799; m. 16 June, 1822, Simeon L., son of Andrew and Sarah (Harback) Marble, of Sutton, b. 5 Oct., 1792. Ch.: Andrew A., b. 12 Apr., 1823 Mary H., b. 14 May, 1825. Joanna L., b. 25 Dec., 1828. Hannah G., b. 14 Jan., 1830. Albert Augustus, b. 15 June. 1840. Martha, b. 29 June, 1842; d. 1845. Franklin H., b. 12 July, 1833. Ann Louisa, b. 29 June, 1836.

1356 PLINEY, b. 15 Feb., 1801.

1357 FANNY, b. 28 May, 1804; m. —— Leland. Ch.: James. Francis E.

CAPTAIN FRANCIS PUTNAM served in the Revolution, volunteering as a private upon the call for troops after the Lexington alarm. During the siege of Boston he was in Col. Gridley's regiment. He also saw service in other parts.

A man of great agility and strength, he could out-jump every man in the regiment except Jacob Severy. It is re corded of him that he could jump a bar six inches higher than his head.

The grist mill owned by Jonathan Putnam, was operated by Francis, who afterward gave it to his son Silas, who in turn sold it to his brother Pliney. The property was afterward included in the property of the Sutton Cranberry Company.

VI. 544 Jonathan Follansbee (*Jonathan, Elisha, Edward, Thomas, John*), born in Sutton, 9 May, 1763; died there, 30 Oct., 1858; married 6 July, 1786, Philana Leland.

Mr. Putnam was a miller in Sutton.

Children, born in Sutton:

1358 JONATHAN FOLLANSBEE, b. 6 May, 1787.
1359 PHILANA, b. 1 Nov., 1789; m. 7 Apr., 1813, Major Rufus, son of Jonathan and Lilote (Bartlett) Burdon, of Sutton, b. 7 Mar., 1786. Ch.: Mary Ann, b. 11 Aug., 1813.
1360 JIM, b. 11 July, 1795; d. 13 June, 1855.

VI. 545 Solomon (*Stephen, Elisha, Edward, Thomas, John*), born 17 July, 1755; died in Claremont, N. H., previous to 1830; married 20 Oct., 1779, Miriam Elmer, who was born 23 July, 1755.

Mr. Putnam was a farmer in Claremont, N. H.

Children, (two of the daughters died by suffocation):

1361 ELECTA, b. 24 Feb., 1781; m. John Smith. Ch.: Lucia. Chester. Charles.
1362 PHILINA b. 31 June, 1782; m. Thadeus Rogers. Ch.: Elisha. Mary Ann. Fanny. Louis. Melinda. Adaline. Charles.
1363 ZELOTUS, b. 2 Mar., 1784.
1364 SALLY, b. 3 Feb., 1786; m. Jesse Cooper. Ch.: Mary. Hiram. Willard. Jane.
1365 CHESTER, b. 11 Aug., 1787; d., *s. p*, prev. to 1834.
1366 JOHN, b. 30 Mar., 1789; m. Lucia Cody.
1367 SOPHIA, b. 17 Dec., 1790; m. Oliver Hubbard. Ch.: Mary. John. George. Milena.
1368 MARY, b. 17 Aug., 1792; m. Charles Perry. Ch.: Charles. Westly. Hannah. Samuel.
1369 ELISHA, b. 15 July, 1794; d. prev. to 1834.
1370 FANNY, b. 28 May, 1796; m. Samuel Rogers. Ch.: James. Samuel. William. Fanny. Samuel. George.
1371 SAMUEL, b. 28 May, 1798; of Claremont, N. H.
1372 HIRAM, b. 6 Mar., 1800; of Claremont, N. H.

VI. 548 John (*Stephen, Elisha, Edward, Thomas, John*), born in Winchester, N. H., 10 May, 1761; died in Chesterfield, N. H., 17 Nov., 1849; married, 1801, Mary, daughter of Joseph and Elizabeth (Davis) Converse, born 13 July, 1777; died 14 Sept., 1853.

Children:

1373 MARY ADALINE, b. 13 Oct., 1802; m., 1824, Austin Richards, of Newfane, Vt. Ch.: Charles. Mary. Chester.

1374 ELIZABETH, b. 3 May, 1804; d. 2 July, 1877; m., 1822, Dr. Timothy S. Gleason, of Claremont, N. H. Ch.: John. Wiston. Henry. Mary.

1375 CHARLOTTE, b. 1 Mar., 1807; d. 22 Sept., 1858; m. Dr. Robert S. Gleason, brother of Dr. Timothy Gleason, of Claremont, N. H. Ch.: Elijah. Francis. $6-23$

1376 CHARLES LEWIS, b. 10 Sept., 1810; d. 17 July, 1877; m. 1835, Dorothy Flagg, of Keene, N. H. Graduated at Dartmouth College and studied law in the office of Hon. Joel Parker. From Keene he removed to Worcester. Mass., and became Secretary of a Fire Insurance Co., and held various other offices of trust.

1377 FRANCES MARIA, b. 18 July, 1816; d. 29 June, 1817.

1378 JULIA, b. 17 Aug., 1819; m. Orrin Rawson, a native of Richmond, N. H. Mr. Rawson was a prosperous merchant and lived in Worcester Boston. Cleveland and Louisville. He d. 1 Aug., 1873. Mrs. Rawson was in 1822, living at Louisville.

1379 JOHN JAY, b. 21 May, 1823.

JOHN PUTNAM in his boyhood lived in the family of Ebenezer Harvey, Jr., at Chesterfield. In 1779, he enlisted in Col. Hercules Mooney's regiment, which regiment was ordered to Rhode Island. After his marriage he lived in Centre Village. Although Mr. Putnam commenced life in humble circumstances, he acquired a considerable fortune.

He was trustee of the academy and selectman several years between 1808 and 1826. He was representative between 1816 and 1826.

VI. 549 Gideon (*Stephen, Elisha, Edward, Thomas, John*), born in Sutton, 17 April, 1763; died at Saratoga Springs, 1 Dec., 1812, of inflammation of the lungs; married 1784, Doanda Risley, of Hartford, Conn., who died 10 Feb., 1835, æ. 67 years.

Children:

1380 BETSEY, b. 30 June, 1786; m. 6 Oct., 1805, Isaac Taylor. Ch.: Israel P. Washington. Eliza D. Aurelia Putnam. John B. Asher, d. 30 May, 1821, æ. 5 yrs., 9 mos., 21 dys.

1381 BENJAMIN RISLEY, b. 23 July, 1788; d. 10 Oct., 1846.

1382 LEWIS, b. 17 Aug., 1790; d. 5 July, 1873.

1383 ROCKWELL, b. 3 Nov., 1792.

1384 AURELIA, b. 14 Mar., 1794; m. Joel C. Clement. Ch.: William H.,

who became a great railway magnate, (his son is H. S. Clement, of Congress Hall, Saratoga).   John.   Mary.   Caroline.
Francis.

1385 NANCY, m. 29 Sept., 1814, Ferdinand Andrews.   Ch.: Mary A.
Caroline.   Matilda.   Ferdinand.

1386 WASHINGTON, b. 29 Sept., 1798; of Saratoga.

1387 PHILA, b. 25 July, 1801; d. 22 Aug., 1805.

1388 LORIN, b. 20 Sept., 1803; d. 11 Sept., 1841.

1389 PHILA, b. 23 Jan., 1806; d. 15 Mar., 1808.

1390 PHILA b. 12 May, 1808; m. 22 Sept., 1824, Abel A. Kellogg, lawyer.   Ch.   Laura.   Sarah Rebecca.

GIDEON PUTNAM started in life without other means than a good wife and ample courage.   Their first settlement was at Middlebury, Vermont, where a log cabin was built by the young husband, and here they kept house.   An inventory of their household goods would have shown but three cups and saucers, three plates, knives and forks, an earthen tea-pot, and spider.   The site of the log cabin is now covered by Middlebury College.

Not being satisfied with Middlebury, a removal was made to Rutland, Vt., where their eldest son was born.   Thence to "Five Nations" or "Bemis Flats," where they were joined by Dr. Clement Blakesley and wife, who was a sister of Mrs. Putnam.   In consequence of a severe freshet which caused him considerable loss, Mr. Putnam left the locality and following the Indian trail went, in 1789, to Saratoga Springs, then comparatively unknown.   There he leased three hundred acres, and building a cabin commenced anew. Within two years he had paid for his farm in full, the lumbering business in which he engaged proving profitable.

In 1802 he erected seventy feet of Union Hall upon land bought for that purpose.   Union Hall was sold in 1864, to Leland Bros., and the hotel is now called the Grand Union.

In 1805, having bought 150 acres of land, he laid out the Village, reserving a burial place and church site, upon which the Baptists built in 1821, theirs being the first church to organize.   The next year Washington or Clarendon spring was excavated and tubed, and also the Columbian; besides all this he erected a bath house just north of Congress Spring, and excavated a spring about fifteen feet distant from the present Congress Fountain.

He next tubed Hamilton Spring, and in 1811 commenced the erection of Congress Hall, during the building of which he fell from a staging and broke several ribs. The following November he was seized with inflamation of the lungs which proved fatal. He was buried in the cemetery he had presented to the town.

The sign, a rude representation of Gen. Putnam and the wolf, used by Gideon Putnam at old Union Hall, is in the possession of Dr. Loren B. Putnam, a grandson.

VI. 550 Elisha (*Stephen, Elisha, Edward, Thomas, John*), born 13 May, 1765; died in Albany, N. Y., 11 Feb., 1854; married in Lansingburgh, N. Y., 25 Dec., 1792, Hester, daughter of Stephen Johnson, born 2 Mar., 1776; died in Albany, 3 Nov., 1855.

Stephen Johnson was a shipmaster and used to say that he was in Boston Harbor and took part in the Tea-party, disguised as an Indian.

Children :

1391 RUFUS, b. in Lansingburg, N. Y., 8 Oct., 1793; d. 18 May, 1845.

1392 ELIZA, b. in Albany, 5 Nov., 1795; d., *s. p.*; m. in Albany, 2 Jan., 1815, John D. Hewson.

1393 LAURA, b. in Albany, 4 Jan., 1798; d. there, 18 Jan., 1801.

1394 STEPHEN, b. in Albany, 14 Jan., 1800; d. 20 July, 1851.

1395 LAURA, b. in Albany, 27 Jan., 1803; d. there, 11 Sept., 1880; m. there, 1 Dec., 1825, William, son of Matthew and Elizabeth (Given) White, b. in Omagh, co. Tyron, Ireland, 9 Dec., 1798; d. in Albany, 26 Jan., 1882. He was a successful business man, one of the proprietors of the Albany Evening Journal for many years; and in later life, a merchant, bank director and president. Ch.: Ann Elizabeth,[113] b. 17 Sept., 1826. William W., b. 7 July, 1829; d. 12 Aug., 1830. Harriet, b. 6 Oct., 1830. James, b. 18 April, 1832. Eliza, b. 15 July, 1834.

1396 HANNAH JOHNSON, b. in Albany, 5 April, 1805; d. there, 5 Sept., 1888; m. there, 25 Mar., 1825, John Given White, brother of

[113] Rev. Wm. Durant, of Baltimore, is a grandson. To him I am much indebted for information regarding this branch of the family. E. P.

William White above; b. at sea, just out of New York, 21 July, 1801; d. in Albany, 16 Apr., 1889. He was a printer, publisher and bank president. Ch.: Elizabeth, b. 6 Jan., 1826. Rufus, b. 28 Dec., 1827. John, b. 28 Feb., 1880; d. 12 May, 1831. John, b. 9 July, 1832; d. 26 July, 1834. Matthew, b. 18 Feb., 1834.

1397　JOHN SMITH, b. in Troy, 9 Aug., 1808; d. 14 May, 1812.

1398　HARRIET, b. 21 June, 1811; d. in Moreau, N. Y., 20 Oct., 1843; m. in Albany, 7 Apr., 1880, Sperry Douglas Brower. Ch., all b. in Albany: Walter Scott, b. 6 Jan., 1831; m. 28 Oct., 1852, Harriet A. Moore; both living at Albany in 1891. Mr. W. S. Brower is the head of the Brower Electric Manfg. Co.; their ch. were: Hattie M. and Mary S. Harriet Douglas, b. 18 Nov., 1833; m. Thomas M. Newson, and lives in St. Paul, Minn. George, d., unm. Henry Douglas, d. unm.

1399　JOHN SMITH, b. in Albany, 4 Mar., 1814; living in 1891, at 220 W. 185th street, New York. He m. at Buffalo, 1 Nov., 1838, Catherine Dubois, who d. 1840; m., 2d, 1843, Pauline E. C. Chalet, and has one daughter.

1400　MARTHA, b. 4 Nov., 1816; m., 1st, 31 Aug., 1837, Silah Belden; m. 2d, about 1870, Mr. Smith.

1401　MARY, b. in Albany, 31 Mar., 1820; d. there, 10 Feb., 1885; m. there, 15 Aug., 1838, Samuel, son of John S. Pruyn. In early life Mrs. Pruyn became active in religious and charitable work. Through her energy, prudence and influence, two industrial schools and the House of Shelter were established in Albany, nor were her efforts abandoned even then. In May, 1871, she went to Japan as a missionary under the auspices of the Woman's Union Missionary Society. She established at Yokohama the first institution for the education of girls in that country. After five years she returned to Albany, but in Jan., 1888, she went to Shanghai, China, and established an institution similar to that in Yokohama.

In 1884 her health gave way from nervous exhaustion, and she returned home to die after a long and painful illness. Mrs. Pruyn was the author of "Grandmother's Letters from Japan." Mr. Pruyn m., 1st, Helen Vandervort. Ch.: Agnes, b. 6 July, 1839; m. 12 Apr., 1860, Robert, son of Joseph and Elizabeth (White) Strain, b. in Albany, 30 Nov., 1832. Mr. Strain's mother was a sister of Wm. and John White above. Five children. Mr. and Mrs. Strain live in Albany. Charles Elisha, b. 11 Nov., 1840; d. 15 June, 1864, unm.; killed at the head of his regiment, the 118th N. Y. Vols. Samuel Stephen, b. 17 Nov., 1842; d. 14 Aug., 1844. Edward Putnam, b. 24 Dec., 1844; drowned 21 June, 1856. Samuel S., b. 7 Dec., 1846; m. 12 Jan., 1869, Jane Agnes Lasher. He is asst. librarian of the N. Y. Geneal. and Biog. Soc., N. Y. City. (Ch.: Chas. E., b. 1 Jan., 1870. Samuel, b. 10 Oct., 1871.) Mary Esther, b. 28 Jan.,

1849; m. 27 Apr., 1871, Worthington, son of Stephen M. La-
Grange, who d. abt. 1884; Mrs. LaGrange lives in Albany with
her daughter. Francis Warranaer, b. 30 April, 1851; d. 23
June, 1852. Annie Warranaer, b. 7 Apr., 1854; d. 21 Jan.,
1857.

ELISHA PUTNAM was tall and spare, of quick intelligence,
inventive genius, independent and positive opinions even to
the extent of voting for his own candidates for presidential
electors. By occupation he was a carpenter, builder, civil
engineer, architect and contractor; he built the first nail
mills near Troy, N. Y., two or three churches in Albany,
one or more sections of the Erie canal, part of the Chesa-
peake and Ohio canal, laid the first pipes of hollowed wood
to supply Albany with water, and was for many years superintendent of the water works there. Before completing the
first nail works at Troy for the Brinckerhoffs, he got admission
into the only other establishment in the country where a certain secret process was carried on, disguised as an ignorant
countryman seeking work. In one day he mastered the special machinery, and was able from memory to set up similar
and improved machinery in the mills he was building.

A member of the Presbyterian church in Albany, in his
late years he gave especial attention to theological matters.
At the age of eighty, he wrote and published " The Crisis,
or Last Trumpet," which is an able presentation of the pre-
millenial views of the second advent.

A portrait is in the possession of his granddaughter, Mrs.
John D. Capron, Albany, N. Y.

VI. 553 David (*Stephen, Elisha, Edward, Thomas,
John*), born in Massachusetts, 21 March, 1771; died in Albany, N. Y., 9 Aug., 1832; married in Albany, 29 May,
1798, Jeannette Angus, born there, 19 Sept., 1779; died
there, 17 June, 1862. She was the daughter of James Angus, who had come from Aberdeen, Scotland, and Jeannette
(Ham) Angus, a native of Holland.

Children, born in Albany:

1402 MARIA, b. 18 Mar., 1799; d. in Albany, 4 July, 1854; m. Matthew
Gillispie. They lived in Albany. Ch.: Thomas, b. and d. in
Albany. Theodore. James. Charles.

1403 JAMES ANGUS, b. 2 Nov., 1801; d. 2 Dec., 1874.

1404 MARY MAGDALENE, b. 28 July, 1803; m., as his second wife, James
Lansing, who d. in Corning, N. Y. Ch.: Edward, b. abt. 1837,
in Albany; d. in San Francisco, abt. 1881.

1405 ADELINE, b. 22 June, 1805; d. 8 Mar., 1884; m. 6 Nov., 1836, as
his second wife, John A., son of Joseph Wilson, who d. 8 Oct.,
1848. They lived in Albany Ch.: William Putnam, b. 27 Aug.,
1837; living in 1891, in Baltimore, Md.; m. in Albany, 5 Aug.,
1858, Asenath Dorida, dau. of Levi and Sophia Phebe (Balcom)
Harvey, who is a granddaughter of Aaron Burr. John Annan,
b. 19 Mch., 1839; living at Albany in 1891; m. abt. 1869, Mary
Coulter. Edward, b. 11 July, 1840; d. in Albany, 24 Oct., 1844.
Lavina, b. 3 Sept., 1842; d. 7 Mar.. 1845. Helena, b. 2 Dec.,
1846; living in New York City in 1891; m. in Albany, 16 April,
1884, John Wilmot, from whom she obtained a divorce in
1885.

1406 CHARLES, b. 10 Dec., 1806.

1407 ELISHA, b. 10 July, 1808.

1408 CHARLOTTE, b. 1 May, 1810; d. 9 Oct., 1863; m. 15 Sept., 1834,
David H. Woodruff, who d. 23 May, 1888. They lived in Albany.
Ch.: Harriet E., b. 7 Apr., 1838; d. 10 July, 1843. Frances Mary,
b. 23 Feb., 1840; living at Albany, 1891, unm. Charlotte, b. 30
Dec., 1841; d. 14 Jan., 1845. William H. DeWitt, ·b. 7 March,
1849; m. in Emporia, Kas., 19 Sept., 1888, Pontia Waite, b. in
Hartford, Ct. They live in Albany.

1409 HARRIET, b. 5 Dec., 1811; d abt. 1865; m. 5 May, 1835, William
H. Ross, who d. abt. 1871. They lived in Albany. Ch.: Howard, b. 9 Sept., 1836; living, unm., at Hartford, Ct., in 1890.
Charlotte, b. 7 Apr., 1838; living, unm., 1891, at Miles City,
Montana. Harriet, 22 July, 1840; d. 25 Oct., 1783; m., Dec.,
1865, Rev. Alfred S. Collins, who m. again and was living in
1891.

1410 STEPHEN, b. 25 Nov., 1813.

1411 JANE ANN, b. 25 Nov., 1813; d. abt. 1879; m. William Parks, who
d. abt. 1867. They lived at Greenbush, N. Y. Ch.: Jennett, d.
abt. 1881; m. Charles Rawson; living in 1891. Stephen, living,
unm., 1891. Charlotte, m. John Ford; both living in 1891.

1412 ALMIRA, b. 10 Feb., 1817; d. 2 July, 1855; m. 17 Sept., 1839, Robert H Weir, who was living in 1891 at Albany. Ch.: Magdalene, b. 10 July, 1840; living at Albany in 1891, unm. Mary E.,
b. 3 July, 1843; m. 25 May, 1871, John A. Goffe; they live in
Albany. Robert H., b. 16 Sept., 1845; d. 9 July, 1847. Robert
b., b. 17 Jan., 1848; d. 28 Apr., 1881, unm. Franklin, b. 27
Feb., 1851; d. 25 Nov., 1851. Almira, b. 23 June, 1853; d. 7
June, 1857.

1413   WILLIAM HENRY, b. 5 July, 1819.
1414   HIRAM, b. 3 Aug., 1821.

VI. 554 Rufus (*Stephen, Elisha, Edward, Thomas, John*), born in Sutton (probably), 22 March, 1773; of Winchester, N. H.

Children :

1415   A SON, living in 1817.
1416   A DAUGHTER, living in 1817.
      Twelve children deceased previous to 1817.

VI. 568 Persis (*Gen. Rufus, Elisha, Edward, Thomas, John*), born in Brookfield, 16 Sept., 1767; died 22 Sept., 1822, at Belpre, Ohio; married 20 May, 1798, Perley, son of Capt. Perley and Tamar (Davis) Howe, b. 14 May, 1768; died in Belpre, Ohio, 17 May, 1855.

Children :

1417   JOSEPH. b. 14 July, 1800; d. 23 Aug., 1823, unm.
1418   PERLEY, b. 28 May, 1802; d. 5 Oct., 1823, unm.
1419   ABIGAIL, b. 31 Dec., 1804; d. Dec., 1835; m. Nov., 1825, W. R. Walker; 5 ch. Lived at Amesville, Ohio.
1420   RUFUS WILLIAM, b. 17 June, 1807; d. 24 July, 1866; m. 24 Jan., 1835, Polly Proctor, of Watertown. They lived in Belpre, O. One of their four children was George A. Howe, of Belpre.
1421   PERSIS, b. 7 Sept., 1810; d., Jan., 1832, unm.

Perley Howe was of Killingly, Conn., but became one of the early settlers in Marietta, where he taught school within the stockade. Soon after his marriage he settled in Belpre. He was a captain of militia, and on account of his proximity to Blennerhassett's residence, a witness at the Burr trial. An active Presbyterian, he was chosen deacon in that church.

VI. 569 Susanna (*Gen. Rufus, Elisha, Edward, Thomas, John*), born in Brookfield, 5 Aug., 1768; married 13 Dec., 1787, Ensign Christopher Burlingame.

Children :

1422   PERSIS.

1423 MARIA, m. Mr. H. Mills. Ch.: Christopher. Hannah. Isabella. Arthur. Joseph.

1424 SUSANNA, m. George Cunan. Ch.: Henry. Rebecca. Maria. Persis. Sarah. George. John. Susan. Mary.

1425 PATTY, m. Rev. S. P. Robbins, Ch.: Samuel. Persis. Hannah. Gilman. Jane. Chandler. Martha. Rufus.

1426 LUCY, m. Zephaniah Bosworth. Ch.: Lucy. Jerusha. William.

1427 EDWIN.

1428 WILLIAM.

1429 CHRISTOPHER, m. Miss Bartlett; 4 ch.

1430 RUFUS, m. Jane Morrow; 2 ch.

1431 JOHN, m. Eveline Morrow; 1 ch.

1432 BETSEY, m. ——— Porter; 4 ch.

1433 SARAH, m. Rev. Mr. Callahan; no descendants.

VI. 570 Abigail (*Gen. Rufus, Elisha, Edward, Thomas, John*), born in Brookfield, 7 Aug., 1770; died Feb., 1805; married, March, 1790, William, son of William Browning.

Children:

1434 WILLIAM RUFUS, m. ——— Barker. Ch.: Joseph. Abba. Synthia. William. Alexander Hamilton. Rufus Putnam.

1435 GEORGE, merchant; m. ——— Bryant; 2 ch.

1436 SAMUEL McFARLAND, unm.; a lawyer in Newark, Ohio.

VI. 571 William Rufus (*Gen. Rufus, Elisha, Edward, Thomas, John*), born in Brookfield, 12 Dec., 1771; married, Dec., 1802, Jerusha Gitteau.

Children:

1437 WILLIAM, d. a few days after birth.

1438 WILLIAM RUFUS, b. 13 June, 1812.
Three ch. d. in inf.

WILLIAM RUFUS was educated for the ministry, but on account of failing health devoted himself to farming and surveying. He held many important offices.

He was trustee of Ohio University from 1823–43. Lived in Marietta, Ohio.

VI. 573 Hon. Edwin (*Gen. Rufus, Elisha, Edward, Thomas, John*), born in Sutton, 9 Jan., 1776; died in Putnam, Ohio, 1844; married 12 June, 1800, Eliza Davis.

Children :

1439 FRANKLIN.
1440 JANE. m. Dr. R. Safford. Ch.: Jonas Putnam. Jane. Edward.
1441 RUFUS.
1442 WILLIAM RICE.
1443 CATHARINE, m. Mr. Bristar.

JUDGE PUTNAM served during the Indian war of 1791–5; in 1795 he was private secretary to Gov. St. Clair, enjoying the rank of Lieutenant Colonel.

He was graduated from Carlisle College in 1779, and began the study of law with Gov. Meigs, and was admitted to the bar in 1802. During the war of 1812 he served as Adjutant under Gov. Meigs. After settling in Putnam he established there the first printing office, bookstore and bindery.

In 1827 he was elected Judge of the Court of Common Pleas and held that office fourteen years; and was also Trustee of the Ohio University at Athens from 1820 to 1840. He was universally respected and beloved. For thirty years he was elder of the Presbyterian church in Putnam.

VI. 574 Patty (*Gen. Rufus, Elisha, Edward, Thomas, John*), born in Brookfield, 25 Nov., 1777; married 1802, Col. Benjamin, son of Gen. Benjamin and Huldah (White) Tupper, of Putnam, Ohio.

Children :

1444 CATHERINE, m. Cyrus Merriam. Ch.: Phebe; 2 others.
1445 ABIGAIL, m. Milton B. Cushing. Ch.: Benjamin. Edward. Roena; one other.
1446 SOPHIA, m. A. S. Culbertson; no ch.
1447 ELIZABETH, d. a few weeks after m. with Dr. C. Brown.
1448 EDWARD WHITE, of Putnam; m. Rachel Cushing. Ch.: Edward.

VI. 575 Catherine (*Gen. Rufus, Elisha, Edward, Thomas, John*), born in Brookfield, 17 Oct., 1780; died, March, 1808; married, 1805, Ebenezer Buckingham, of Ohio.

Children :

1449 CATHARINUS PUTNAM, b. Mar., 1808; m. Mary Gird. Was graduated at West Point; Prof. of mathematics at Kenyon College, Ohio; afterward connected with the steel works in Chicago. Ch.: Mary, b. in Cedar Lake, N. Y., 27 Aug , 1831; m. in Mt. Vernon, O., 29 Jan., 1856, Dean Kimball,[113] son of Samuel and and Thankful (Kimball) Fenner, of Palatine Bridge, N. Y., b. 17 Sept., 1813; d. in Irvington on Hudson, N. Y., 10 Feb., 1870. (Ch.: Ira Buckingham, b. 21 Aug., 1858. Alice, b. 3 Aug., 1864; d. 26 Apr., 1870. Frederick Cooper, b. 2 Aug., 1866. Charles Putnam, b. 28 Mar., 1868. Gertrude, b. 26 June, 1870.) Helen Buckingham, b. in Mt. Vernon, O., 6 July, 1846; m. 20 Oct., 1874, at Chicago, Frank Cotton, son of Franklin and Sarah Ann (Gilbert) Hatheway, of Chicago. Ch.: Maria Buckingham, b. 1883.

VI. 576 William (*Oliver, Joseph, Edward, Thomas, John*), born in Danvers, 1744; bapt. 27 May, 1744; will dated 11 Aug., probated 1 Sept., 1800; married 6 Aug., 1766, Bethiah Putnam.[114]

He inherited the homestead, and lived in the house, yet standing, on the western slope of Hathorne Hill.

Children :

1450 SALLY, b. 29 Oct., 1769; m. Amos Felton and removed to Tunbridge.
1451 EBENEZER, bap. 19 July, 1767; d. 29 Oct., 1831.
1452 ABIGAIL, b. 12 Feb., 1772.
1453 WILLIAM, not mentioned in his father's will.
1454 MEHITABLE.

VI. 577 Oliver (*Oliver, Joseph, Edward, Thomas, John*), born in Danvers, 4 Feb., 1753; died in Newburyport, 1794; married in Topsfield (published 12 Nov., 1775), Sarah, daughter of Eleazer and Sarah (Perkins) Lake, born in Topsfield, 1 Oct., 1754; died 12 Sept., 1811.

Children :

1455 OLIVER, b. 17 Nov., 1777; d. 11 July, 1826.
1456 SARAH, b. 9 Aug., 1779.
1457 BETSEY, b. 6 Mar., 1785; m. Dr. Hackett.

---

[113] Mr. Fenner, by his first wife, Julia A. Almy, had five children. He was a man of much energy and executive ability. His children are said to resemble him in these characteristics as well as in his fine personal appearance.
[114] Called Brown on Danvers Records.

22

1458 THORNDIKE, b. 1787; d. 21 May, 1858.   There was a Thorndike
      Putnam of Allantown, N. H., in 1825.
1459 THOMAS, b. 17 Jan., 1789.
1460 SARAH, b. 12 Nov., 1790.
1461 CHARLES, b. 28 Jan., 1793; d. 25 Oct., 1834.
1462 LUCY, b. 16 July, 1795; d. 6 July, 1839.
1463 JOSHUA, b. 23 July, 1798; d. at sea.

VI. 583 Joseph (*Joseph, Joseph, Edward, Thomas, John*), born in Salem Village; bapt. there, 21 April, 1751; died in Salem, 25 Sept., 1834; married 2 Dec., 1773, Anna Putnam, who died 21 Sept., 1815.

Children, born in Danvers :

1464 ANNA, b. 10 May, 1774; m. Joseph Putnam, of Chelmsford.
1465 JOSEPH, b. 15 Feb., 1777.
1466 LYDIA, b. 14 Aug., 1780; m. William Gifford, of Danversport.
      Ch. : Samuel.
1467 JOHN, b. 17 June, 1782; of Newburyport.
1468 PETER, b. 15 Jan., 1785.

1469 MEHITABLE, b. 14 Oct., 1788; ⎫ One m. —— Smith, and has de-
                                     ⎟ scendants in Lynn; the other m.
1470 POLLY, b. 7 Dec., 1789;   ⎬ —— Knight; a grandson is Wm.
                                     ⎟ Knight of Great Falls, N. H.
                                     ⎭

JOSEPH PUTNAM was a man of great physical strength and quick wit. He was a farmer and carpenter. When the alarm of 19 April, 1775, reached Danvers, he was in Marblehead, but, meeting his father, who had ridden over on the alarm, with his equipments, he donned them, and unhitching his horse from the team started for Lexington. It was past noon when he received the news but he reached Lexington in time to help attend the wounded and collect the dead. He drove the Danvers dead home. In after years he received a pension from the U. S. government.

VI. 584 Israel (*Joseph, Joseph, Edward, Thomas, John*), born in Salem Village; bapt. 24 June, 1753; married Mrs. Polly (Ramsdoie) Shays, widow of John Shays, of Middletown, who died 1 Dec., 1786.

Children, born in Danvers :

1471 ISRAEL, b. 9 Aug., 1792.
1472 RACHEL, b. 9 Apr., 1795.
1473 ALLEN, b. 18 July, 1797.
1474 LUCY (LEVI?) b. 6 Mar., 1801.

VI. 590 Porter[115] (*Joseph, Joseph, Edward, Thomas, John*), born in Danvers; bapt. there, 25 March, 1770; died in Hudson, N. H., Jan., 1836; m. in Danvers, 10 June, 1798, Sarah Tapley, born in Danvers, 19 Oct., 1771; died there, 25 Aug., 1849.

Children, born in Danvers:

1475 MARY, b. 28 Apr., 1799; d. 1837.
1476 SALLY, b. 30 Aug., 1801; d. in Danvers, 7 Feb., 1874; m. Jacob Demsey. Adop. ch: Mary Jane, dau. of William Tullock, who d. in Danvers, 21 Apr.. 1881, aged 22 yrs., 4 mos., 2 dys.
1477 CLARISSA, b. 29 June, 1808; d. 4 July, 1851; m. Daniel W. Fuller, b. in Wheelock, Vt., Sept., 1805; d. in Danvers, 9 June, 1879. Ch.: Sarah Putnam, b. in Danvers; d. there, 22 Nov., 1874; m. 21 Aug., 1861, Malcolm[116] Sillars, who was b. in Ryegate, Vt., 17 Sept., 1837. Mary, b. and d. in Danvers; m. William Tullock, and had one child, Mary Jane, who was adopted by her aunt, Sally (Putnam) Demsey. Clarissa E., b. and d. in Danvers; m., 1st, Wm. H. Ogden; m., 2d, George Wylie; 2 ch. by each husband.
1478 JOHN PORTER, b. 8 Aug., 1811.
1479 BETSEY, b. 17 June, 1815; m. 16 Dec., 1835, Daniel M. Very, of Danvers, b. there there 6 Nov., 1812; d. 4 May, 1884. Ch.: Nellie, b. 31 May, 1841. Elizabeth, P., b. 31 Mar., 1844; d. Oct., 1846. Eugene, d. aged 3 mos.

VI. 592 Nehemiah (*Ezra, Ezra, Edward, Thomas, John*), born in Middleton, 14 Oct., 1753; died 1792–3, while in Ohio, locating a settlement; married Betsey Fuller. Farmer in Middleton.

Children:

1480 BETSEY, b. 22 Aug., 1784; m. Israel Fuller, of Danvers.
1481 LUCY, b. 22 May, 1790; m. —— Fuller.

[115] There was a Porter Putnam at Pownalborough, Me., in 1785–6.
[116] Ch. of Malcolm and Sarah R. (Fuller) Sillars, were: William, b. 22 Apr., 1862; d. 25 Aug., 1864. Henry M., b. in Danvers, 16 May, 1864. Walter A., b. in Danvers, 15 June, 1866. Alice Putnam, b. 24 July, 1870. Capt. Sillars married again and has several ch. by his second wife. He is a prominent republican and has held many offices.

VI. 600 Daniel (*Phineas, Isaac, Edward, Thomas, John*), born probably in Sutton; married Phebe Walker, of Upton.

Child:

1482 AUSTIN, b. 16 Mar., 1796.

VI. 609 Zadock (*Nathan, Isaac, Edward, Thomas, John*), born in Sutton, 29 Dec., 1752; died in Grafton, 2 Oct., 1819; married, 1774, Abigail, daughter of Major Elliot, of Sutton, who died 29 May, 1822.

Children:

1483 ABIGAIL, b. Sept., 1776; m., 1795, Samuel, son of Samuel and Anna (Brigham) Harrington, of Grafton, b. 3 Aug., 1769; d. 3 Oct., 1802. Ch.: Charles. Martin. Nancy. Lucy. Mrs. Harrington m., 2d, Capt. David Trask, of Leicester. Ch.: James. Abigail. David. Adaline. Jane. Francis.

1484 JOHN, b. 7 Feb., 1778. "To John one-half of ye mills with privilges, etc."

1485 GEORGE WASHINGTON, b. 5 June, 1780; "to have blacksmith shop and tools."

1486 LEWIS, b. 16 May, 1782; lived in Eastport, Me.; has descendants.

ZADOCK PUTNAM marched as "fifer" in Capt. Luke Drury's company of minute men, on the alarm of 19 April, 1775, and continued in service until August of that year.

On August 21st, 1777, the state militia were ordered to march to Bennington and we find him serving as sergeant in Capt. Joseph Warren's company. He was a blacksmith and lived at Grafton. He owned land in Millsbury, Shewsbury and Rutland.

VI. 610 Micah (*Nathan, Isaac, Edward, Thomas, John*), born in Sutton, 8 April, 1754; married in Sutton or Grafton, 26 May, 1774, Anna Carriel, who died in Paris, now Marshall, N. Y., 24 Aug., 1794.

Children:

1487 REBECCA, b. in Sutton, 3 Oct., 1775; d. 7 Oct., 1858; m. 22 Dec., 1794, James Cowing. Lived in Marshall, N. Y. A grandson, Sylvester Gridley, lives in Waterville, N. Y.

1488 TIMOTHY, b. in Sutton, 7 Apr., 1776.

1489 NATHANIEL, b. in Grafton, 7 May, 1786.

1490 POLLY, d. 24 Aug., 1804.

1491 ANNA, d. 24 Aug., 1833; m. —— King, a carpenter and builder, who lived between Winfield and Litchfield, Herkimer Co., N. Y. Ch. Azina. Amanda. Zera, and another son.

1492 JAMES, said to have been a scythe manufacturer at Whitingham, Vt.

1493 RUFUS, b. 1792; d. 1844.

MICAH PUTNAM is said by an ancient authority to have had 11 children and 17 grandchildren living in 1835.

VI. 611 James (*Nathan, Isaac, Edward, Thomas, John*), born in Sutton, 26 Nov., 1755; killed by the breaking of a grindstone; administration on his estate to widow, 6 Sept., 1785; married Betsey Willard.

James Putnam is said to have had five grandchildren in 1835.

Children:

1494 JAMES, not mentioned in his grandfather's will, 1813.

1495 BETSEY, b. in Grafton, 12 Mar., 1782; living in 1813.

1496 HANNAH, b. in Grafton, 6 Apr., 1784; living in 1813.

VI. 614 Nathan (*Nathan, Isaac, Edward, Thomas, John*), born in Sutton, 16 May, 1761; married 25 March, 1785, Sarah Putnam.

Children, born in Sutton:

1497 RUTH, b. 2 Sept., 1785; d. young.

1498 RUTH, b. 23 Sept., 1787; m. 23 Mar., 1806, Judah, son of Judah and Olive (Fuller) Waters, b. 23 July, 1783. Ch. Sarah. Nathan P., b. 12 Feb., 1810. This family removed to central New York.

OTHERS.

VI. 616 Capt. Abner (*Nathan, Isaac, Edward, Thomas. John*), born in Sutton, 17 March, 1765; married Abigail, daughter of Amos Waters. They were settled in Ludlow. Me., in 1835, and at that time had three children.

VI. 620 John (*Nathan, Isaac, Edward, Thomas, John,*), born in Sutton, 3 Sept., 1771; married Anne Hodgkins, of New Ipswich, N. H; scythe-maker.

Children:

1499 STEPHEN, b. 25 Apr., 1799; d. 5 Nov., 1822.
1500 HARVEY, b. 27 Mar., 1800.
1501 GARDNER, b. 26 Oct., 1801; d. 26 Oct., 1802. Said to have had three other ch., all b. prev. to 1835.

VI. 625 Isaac (*Isaac, Isaac, Edward, Thomas, John*), born in Sutton, 1762, (g.s. 1763); died in Worcester, 23 April, 1808; married 18 Jan., 1784, Martha, daughter of Charles and Abigail Adams, a grandaughter of Aaron Adams, one of the first town officers of Worcester in 1722. Mrs. Putnam died 24 Aug., 1816, aged 52 years.

Mr. Putnam removed from Auburn (formerly part of Sutton) to Worcester in 1784.

Children, born in Worcester:

1502 SALLY, b. 1785; d. 1850; m. —— Baird.
1503 EBENEZER, b. 1787; d. 1848.
1504 JOEL, b. 1789 (g.s. 1788); d. 1858.
1505 WILLIAM, b. 1790; d. 30 Sept., 1796.
1506 CHARLES, b. 1792; d. 1840.
1507 SAMUEL, b. 1794; d., 1861.
1508 AARON, b. 21 Nov., 1797; d. 20 Sept., 1800.
1509 WILLIAM, b. 1799; d. 16 Sept., 1822.
1510 MARTHA, b. 1801; d. 1865.
1511 MARY, b. 1801; d., 1860; m. —— Blackman.

VI. 526 Samuel (*Daniel, Isaac, Edward, Thomas, John*), born in Cornish, N. H.; married Lois Liscomb.

Children:

1512 JOHN LISCOMB, b. 16 Mar., 1792.
1513 SARAH MARIA, b. 12 Jan., 1803; living in 1880.
1514 ANNIE ELIZABETH, b. 29 Mar., 1808; d. 26 Feb., 1847.

VI. 628 Isaac (*Daniel, Isaac, Edward, Thomas, John*), born in Cornish, N. H.

Children:

1515 ALEXANDER C.
1516 NORMAN W.
1517 SOLON, (Rev.).

VI. 630 Andrew (*William, Col. David, Joseph, Thomas, John*), born in Danvers, 2 April, 1755; died in Sterling, 13 Mar., 1809; will dated 12 Feb., 1809, probated 2 May, 1809; wife Jerusha, executrix; married 5 Oct., 1790, Jerusha, daughter of Joseph Clapp, born 29 May, 1767; died 1 Nov., 1834. In her will, probated 1834, she gives $1000 to George in trust for Andrew; rest to youngest son George.

Children :

1518　ANDREW, b. 9 Aug., 1791; d. 8 Mar., 1845.
1519　SAMUEL PAGE, b. 22 Sept., 1793; d. 8 Feb., 1815.
1520　CHARLES, b. 8 Oct., 1795; d. 12 Aug., 1812.
1521　WILLIAM, b. 14 Aug., 1797; d. 30 Oct., 1814.
1522　ELIZA, b. 4 July, 1805; d. 14 July, 1825.
1523　GEORGE, b. in Sterling, 16 Aug., 1807; d. 11 Apr., 1878.

VI. 636 Col. Jesse (*Joseph, David, Joseph, Thomas, John*), born in Danvers, 3 April, 1788; died there, 10 Feb., 1861; married in Middleton, 2 June, 1804, Elizabeth, daughter of Dr. Silas Merriam, of Middleton, born there, 14 Nov., 1784; died in Danvers, 20 Sept., 1887.

Children, born in Danvers :

1524　CATHERINE, b. 4 Apr., 1805; d. 1874; m. 22 Nov., 1834, Israel F. Ober. Ch.: Maria F., b. 8 Sept., 1835; m. 17 June, 1858, Chas. H. Killam. Israeletta, b. 28 Jan., 1839; d. 11 Dec., 1842. Mrs. Ober m., 2dly, Abram Doyle.
1525　ANDREW MERRIAM, b. 13 Feb., 1807; d. 6 May, 1881.
1526　ELIZABETH, b. 16 Jan., 1809; d. 21 June, 1843; m. 8 Nov., 1838, George A. Putnam (*Samuel, Stephen, Stephen, Benj., Nath¹., John.*)
1527　FRANCIS PERLEY, b. 6 Apr., 1811; d. 18 Oct., 1883.
1528　HENRY FLINT, b. 2 June, 1813; d. 10 Oct., 1884.
1529　CALVIN, b. 30 May, 1815.
1530　MARY JANE, b. 1 July, 1817; d. 29 Sept., 1883; m. 18 Aug., 1836, William A. Burnham. Ch.: Inf. dau., b. and d. 15 Nov., 1837. Samuel E., b. 31 March, 1840. Joseph W., b. 25 Nov., 1842. Mary A. b. 25 Aug., 1844; d., unm., 29 May, 1885. Elizabeth P., b. 21 April, 1846; m 3 Oct., 1866, Alex. M. Mervin. William A., b. 1 Aug., 1848. Anna W., b. 30 Aug., 1850; d., unm., 4 Feb., 1871. Sarah L., b. 22 Feb., 1853. James A., b. 13 Sept., 1855. Martha C., b. 30 July, 1859.

Mr. Burnham came to Danvers from Derry, N. H., and taught in both private and public schools. He was finally called to take charge of the Burr Seminary at Manchester, Vt.

1531   MARTHA ANN, b. 19 Apr., 1819; d. 25 July, 1887; m. 6 May, 1849, Judge Mellin Chamberlain, of Chelsea. He was at one time Librarian of Boston Public Library.

1532   SALLY WEBSTER, b. 17 Sept., 1821; m. 29 Nov., 1855, George W. Fuller. Ch.: Jessie P., b. 12 April, 1860.

1533   CHARLES AUGUSTUS, b. 20 Sept., 1823; d. in St. Louis, 2 Jan., 1854; m. 17 Aug., 1853, Lydia A. P. Tapley.

1534   EMILY ALMIRA, b. 3 Dec., 1825; m. 22 Dec., 1847, Rev. Richard F. Searle, b. in Georgetown, 2 Apr., 1814; d. in Danvers, 30 June, 1880. Ch : Walter J., b. 18 Feb., 1851; d. 20 May, 1861. Charles Putnam,[117] b. 21 July, 1854. Alonzo T., b. 13 Sept., 1856.

1535   JOHN MILTON,[118] b. 1 Mar., 1858.

COL. JESSE PUTNAM lived and died on his ancestral farm in Danvers, and with many of his family is buried in the Putnam cemetery near Asylum station in Danvers. This cemetery is known as the "Daniel and Jesse Putnam Burial Ground." In it are the remains of most of the descendants of Thomas Putnam who have lived on or near his original farm. Here in the old tomb, now overgrown, was laid the body of Ann Putnam of witchcraft memory.

Jesse Putnam was constanly improving the farm inherited from his ancestors, and early obtained the premium offered by the Essex County Agricultural Society for the best managed farm in the county.

He was an active temperance man in principle and practice, never supplying his men with the liquor customary in those days. His independent character was shown in many ways, especially in his active anti-slavery work and other moral and political reforms. His title of colonel was obtained during the war of 1812, he having commanded an artillery

117 Charles P. Searle is a councillor at law in Boston. He m 8 Jan., 1885, Cora A. W. Hogg. Ch.: John Endecott, b. 1 Oct., 1885. Charles P., b. 4 Nov., 1889. Richard Whiting, b. 7 July, 1891. Alonzo Thurston Searle, m. 17 Sept., 1882, Margaret B. Irwen. Ch.: Richard Jewett, b. 23 Nov., 1883. Charles P., b. 15 April, 1885.

118 In 1889 the descendants of Jesse had numbered 86, viz.: 12 children. 43 grandchildren, 31 great grandchildren.

JESSE PUTNAM HOUSE, MAPLE STREET, DANVERS.

company stationed at Beverly, although he was never in actual service.

In church affairs he was ever to the front in contributing financial and moral aid to every good cause. He had united with the First Church in 1832 and was a constant attendant.

In town affairs he was frequently called upon to take a prominent part and held many official positions. His character was strongly marked. Generous, brave, hearty in his friendships, fond of children and of fun, thoroughly in earnest in whatever he undertook, hospitable and kind to the poor, he was a typical American country gentleman.

Mrs. Putnam was as remarkable a woman as her husband was a man. She was of inestimable service to him and their long married life was unmarred. Living to a great age she retained her faculties to the last. On her 102d birthday, surrounded by her descendants, she received her many friends, and enjoyed the occasion as much as any, being keenly alive to all the affairs of the day. At the time of her death she was the oldest woman in Essex County.

VI. 641 Daniel (*Israel, David, Joseph, Thomas, John*), born in Danvers, 8 March, 1774; died there, 10 Feb., 1854; married at Putnamville, Danvers, 30 Nov., 1797, Susanna, daughter of Stephen and Susannah (Herrick) Putnam, (No. 852), born in Danvers, 22 April, 1777; died 15 March, 1869.

Children, born in Danvers:

1536 ELIZA, b. 10 Nov., 1798; d. 31 July, 1826; m. 6 Dec., 1821, Porter Kettelle. Ch.: Lydia W., b. 23 Aug., 1822; d. 19 Aug., 1834. Eliza P., b. 26 Feb., 1824; d. Mar., 1828. John Porter, b. 28 Dec., 1825; d. 3 Oct., 1826.

1537 EMMA, b. 6 Nov., 1800; d. 24 July, 1867; m. 18 Oct., 1826, John Kettelle.

1538 ALLEN, b. 31 Oct., 1802; d. 21 Oct., 1887.

1539 DANIEL FRANKLIN. b. 20 Oct., 1804; d. 7 Oct., 1839.

1540 AHIRA HERRICK, b. 21 May, 1807; d. 30 Nov., 1839.

1541 ANCEL, b. 23 Jan., 1809; d. 5 Mar., 1809.

1542 WILLIAM RICHARDSON, b. 28 May, 1811; d. 8 Sept., 1886.

1543 SUSAN, b. 27 Mar., 1813. Resides at the Putnam homestead. Miss
      Putnam has probably met more of the descendants of John Put-
      nam than any person living. She is always glad to receive
      visitors and show them the room in which Gen. Putnam was
      born. Many of these notes have been supplied by Miss Putnam
      and her sister, Mrs. Philbrick, who have always taken a deep
      interest in family affairs.
1543a MARIA, b. 22 Feb., 1816; d. 12 June, 1841, unm.
1544 JULIA ANN, b 4 Aug., 1818; m. 24 Aug., 1843, John Dudley Phil-
      brick; b. Deerfield, N. H., 27 May, 1818; d. in Danvers, 2 Feb.,
      1886; grad. Dart. Col., 1842, and was appointed assistant in the
      Latin School in Roxbury. His success was immediate and
      marked.   To him is due the present system of grammar schools
      in Boston; he was called to Conn., and organized the State
      Normal School at New Britian. He soon returned to Boston
      and was Supt. of Public Schools there from 1857 to 1874 and
      from 1876 to 1878. When he resigned his office he left these
      Schools the best organized and conducted public institutions in
      this or any other county. In 1878 he was sent to Paris to rep-
      resent our educational affairs and was successful in overcom-
      ing the many difficulties encountered and was decorated with
      the cross of the Legion of Honor. The Univ. of St. Andrews
      conferred on him the degree of Doctor of Laws. His entire
      life was devoted to the development of our educational institu-
      tions; his work and writings are known throughout the world.
      John G Whittier. his near neighbor in Danvers, wrote of him
      " He was deeply depressed with the imperative necessity of the
      education of all the people of the United States, as the only
      safeguard of liberty and progress, regarding the ballott in the
      hands of ignorance a cause for serious apprehension of national
      danger. A good and true man, who served his generation
      faithfully and successfully, he deserves to be held in grateful
      remembrance."
1545 ANCEL WALLACE, b. 11 Mar., 1821; d. 30 Jan ,1892.
1546 BENJAMIN WADSWORTH, b. 2 Oct., 1825.

DANIEL PUTNAM inherited from his father the farm now
known as the Gen. Israel Putnam place. There the general was born and the room to-day is in many respects un-
changed, although the outside of the house is much altered.
The old road passed by what is now the back of the house and
by the huge willow was a running book.

The estate is now owned by Miss Susan Putnam. The
state took a large part of the original farm, when the asylum

was erected, yet to-day the farm is one of the best cultivated in Danvers.

Daniel Putnam was a shoe manufacturer and farmer. He was representative to General Court in 1811–17–19, and often selectman.

VI. 647 Israel (*Israel, Gen. Israel, Joseph, Thomas, John*), born in Pomfret, Conn., 20 Jan., 1766; died in Marrietta, Ohio, 9 March, 1824; married 26 Feb., 1792, Clarina, daughter of Peter and Mary (Hodges) Chandler, of Pomfret, Ct., born 8 April, 1767; died 29 Nov., 1801. It is a tradition that Mrs. Putnam on the journey to Marrietta rode a horse 28 years old and gave birth to a child in a wagon. He married, secondly, 24 Aug., 1802, Elizabeth Wiser, of Marrietta, who died 16 Jan., 1842, æ. 60 yrs.

Removed to Ohio with his father Hon. Ephraim Cutler and Col. Israel, 1795, being 31 days upon the river.

Children, by first wife :

1547   FRANCES MAY, b. in Pomfret, 12 Apr., 1793; d. 5 Apr., 1809.
1548   AN INFANT, b. on journey to Ohio; d. soon.
1549   WILLIAM, d. 26 May, 1799.
1550   EMELINE E., d. 18 May, 1799, aged 2 yrs.
1551   CLARINDA CHANDLER, d. 25 Dec., 1838, aged 40 yrs., in Marietta.
1552   HARRIET, b. 16 Aug., 1800; d. 26 Aug., 1800.

By second wife :

1553   PASCAL PAOLI, b. 10 Nov., 1802; d. 23 Aug., 1831.
1554   HELENA PENELOPE, b. 9 Apr., 1804; d. 8 Jan., 1892; m. 9 Dec., 1829, William Devol.
1555   LOUIS JOHN POPE, b. 2 Mar., 1808; d. 1 Dec., 1888.
1556   LAURA ANN, b. 22 Dec., 1810; d. 27 Nov., 1835; m. 14 Dec., 1832, M. A. Chappell.
1557   FRANCES MARY, b. 22 Sept., 1817; d. 23 Aug., 1831.
1558   ELIZABETH AUGUSTA, b. 14 Oct., 1821; d. Jan., 1852; m. 10 Sept., 1840, W. B. Clarke.
1559   SUSAN CATHARINE, b. 14 July, 1824; d. 19 Mar., 1852; m. 20 Sept., 1843, John Newton.

VI. 648 Aaron Waldo (*Israel, Gen. Israel, Joseph, Thomas, John*), born in Pomfret, Conn., 18 April, 1767; died in Belpre, Ohio, 21 Aug., 1822; married 24 June,

1791, Charlotte, daughter of Col. Daniel Loring, of Ohio, born 12 June, 1773; died 21 Sept., 1822, æ. 50.

Children:

1560 WILLIAM PITT, b. in Farmer's Castle, Ohio, 2 Apr., 1792; d. 31 May, 1871.

1561 CHARLOTTE LORING, b. 11 Mar., 1794; d. 21 Aug., 1890; m. A. Stone, of Belpre.

1562 ALBIGENCE WALDO, b. in Belpre, Ohio, 11 Mar., 1799, d. 20 Jan., 1869.

1563 JULIA HOWK, b. 1 July, 1796, d. 26 Apr., 1824; m. 25 Mar., 1823, —— Rathbone.

1564 ISRAEL LORING, b. 31 Mar., 1801; d. s. p., of yellow fever at Natchez, 29 Sept., 1829.

1565 LUCY EATON, b. 1 Jan., 1804; m. G. N. Gilbert.

1566 CATHERINE, b. 6 May, 1806; m. —— Rathbone.

1567 BATSHEBA, b. 13 Sept., 1808; m. —— Henderson.

1568 ELIZABETH, b. 5 Sept., 1817; m. —— Henderson.

AARON WALDO PUTNAM accompanied his father to Ohio in 1788, and arrived at Marietta after a long and tedious journey full of peril and adventure. While crossing the North River at Fish Kill a severe accident befell the party, but, by the presence of mind of Aaron, his father's oxen, upon which so much depended, were saved.

Upon obtaining his land, which fell to him in the middle settlement at Belpre, he immediately commenced clearing. During 1791 the settlers went into garrison and young Putnam shared the perils of the Indian war during the succeeding four years.

As his clearing was over a mile and a half from the fort, visits to it were of great danger, and twice he narrowly escaped capture by the Indians.

As soon as circumstances permitted Mr. Putnam took up his residence on his farm and his chief delight centered in his home. Here he entertained the hosts of friends, among whom were the Blannerhassetts, and when their beautiful home was destroyed by the mob, and Madame Blannerhassett, after her husband's flight, left the island, Mr. Putnam supplied her with money and everything necessary. Indeed he was the last person to visit her.

Mr. Putnam had little taste for public office although constanly tendered him.

In height he was of medium size, with dark hair and expressive eyes, and an expression beaming with intelligence and good will.

Both he and his wife died during the epidemic of 1822. For further account of his life see Hildreth's Early Settlers of Ohio.

VI. 649 David (*Col. Israel, Gen. Israel, Joseph, Thomas, John*), born in Pomfret, Conn., 24 Feb., 1769; died in Harmar, Ohio, 31 March, 1856; married, 16 Sept., 1798, Elizabeth, daughter of Dr. Elisha Perkins and Sarah (Douglas) Perkins, of Plainfield, Conn., born 6 Nov.. 1778; died in Marietta, 18 May, 1866.

Children :

1569   BENJAMIN PERKINS, b. in Marietta, 26 Feb., 1800; d. in Marietta, 2 Jan., 1825; m., 1st., 14 Aug., 1821, Mary Dana, of Waterford. O., who d. 14 Dec., 1822; m., 2d, 3 Oct., 1824, Sarah Henshaw, dau. of Thomas and Elizabeth (Denny) Ward, b. 3 Nov., 1800; was living at Shewsbury, Mass., 1892.

1570   CHARLES MARSH, b. 24 Feb., 1802; d. 17 Apr., 1870.

1571   PETER RADCLIFFE, b. 8 Feb., 1804; d. 20 Mar., 1824.

1572   DOUGLAS, b. 7 Apr., 1806.

1573   DAVID, b. 17 May, 1808; d. 7 Jan., 1892.

1574   MURRAY, b. 10 June, 1810; d. 16 Apr., 1812.

1575   CATHERINE HUTCHINSON, b. 6 July, 1812; d. 17 Aug., 1829.

1576   MURRAY, b. 1 Aug., 1815; d. 27 Sept., 1823.

1577   GEORGE, b. 1 June, 1817; d. 12 Jan., 1876.

1578   ELIZABETH PERKINS, b. 18 Aug., 1819; d. 20 Apr., 1846; m. D. E. Gardiner. 15 ch.

1579   SON, (still born).

1580   MARY, b. 7 Dec., 1822; d. 11 Apr., 1825.

DAVID PUTNAM was graduated from Yale in 1793, settled in Marietta, Ohio, and practiced law. He was the first teacher in Muskingum Academy, founded by Gen. Rufus Putnam and his friends in 1797, at Marietta.

VI. 650 William Pitt (*Col. Israel, Gen. Israel, Joseph, Thomas, John*), born 11 Dec., 1770; died 8 Oct.,

1800; married, 1794, Bethia, daughter of Dr. Glyssam, of Woodstock, Conn.

Child:

1581 ISRAEL WALDO, b., 1824.

WILLIAM PITT PUTNAM began the study of medicine when eighteen years of age, with Dr. Albigence Waldo, of Pomfret, Conn., and also attended the lectures of Warren and Waterhouse, celebrated teachers at Harvard.

In May, 1792, he removed to Marietta, Ohio, and commenced the practice of medicine, spending a portion of his time at Belpre, where his brother was located. In 1794 he visited Connecticut, and returned to Ohio with his father and family and his young wife. Five years later he abandoned his profession and bought 200 acres of land on the Ohio eight miles above Marietta. The labor of clearing the land and developing a farm brought on a fever from which he died, leaving but one child. His widow married Gen. Edward Tupper and was living in 1852.

VI. 652 George Washington (*Col. Israel, Gen. Israel, Joseph, Thomas, John*), born in Pomfret, Conn., 1771; lived in Verney, Ind.

Child:

1582 GEORGE WASHINGTON.

VI. 657 Hon. Judah Dana (*Hannah, Gen. Israel, Joseph, Thomas, John*), born in Pomfret, Conn., 25 April, 1772; died 27 Dec., 1845; married in 1800, Elizabeth, daughter of Prof. Sylvanus and Abigail (Wheelock) Ripley, of Hanover, N. H. She died 15 Nov., 1819, æ. 35, and Mr. Dana married Mrs. Mehitable McMillan, who died 18 Nov., 1858.

Children:

1583 CAROLINE ELIZABETH, b. 20 Mar., 1801; d. 18 Oct., 1822.
1584 MARIA ANNETTE, b. 29 Apr., 1805; m., 1826, Joseph Howard, b. in Brownfield, Me., 14 Mar., 1800; d. there, 12 Dec., 1877. He

was graduated at Bowdoin College, 1821; read law with Judge Dana, and became U. S. District Attorney in 1837, when he removed to Portland, of which city he was mayor in 1860, Judge of Supreme Court 1848–55; he was a member of the Episcopal church and a great friend of young men. Ch.: Elizabeth Dana, b. 1827; d. 1831. Rebecca, b. 1829; d. 1831. Caroline Elizabeth, b. 10 Sept., 1831; d. 8 Feb., 1875; m. 1864, Nathan Cleaves, b. in Bridgton, Me., Jan., 1835; d. Sept., 1892; Bowdoin College 1859, Judge of Probate and member of legislature, of Bowdoinham and Portland. Joseph Dana, b. 15 July, 1833; d. 15 July, 1872. Maria Annette, b. 20 Aug., 1835; m. 1 June, 1858, Bishop Alexander Burgess, (Ch.: Caroline, b. 24 Jan., 1861. George, b. 11 July, 1864; d. 20 July, 1865. Christiana Maria, b. 8 May, 1866; m. 31 Oct., 1888, Homer Charles Royce. Katherine A., b. 1 Aug., 1871; d. 4 Aug., 1872). Henry Ripley, b. 5 May, 1838; m. 1864, Eleanor L., dau. of Franklin Glazier, of Hallowell, Me.: ordained to the Episcopal ministry in 1860; now settled in Potsdam, N. Y.; archdeacon.

1585 JOHN WINCHESTER, b. 21 Jan., 1808; d. near Rosario, Buenos Ayres, 22 Dec., 1867; m. 28 June, 1834, Eliza Ann, dau. of Jas. and Eliza L. Osgood, of Fryeburg, Me., where she d. 14 Dec., 1863, aged 50. He was Gov. of Maine, 1847–50; U. S. minister to Bolivia, 1854–5; he was a great political power in the state for many years. Ch.: Mary Sherburne, b. 6 May, 1835; m. 24 Dec., 1861, Henry Hyde Smith, b. in Cornish, Me., Feb., 1832, a lawyer of Boston, (Ch.: Winchester D., b. 18 Dec., 1863). John Winchester, b. 1 July, 1838; d. 12 Mar., 1839. Francis Judah, b. 11 Oct., 1839; of Buenos Ayres. Annie Winchester, b. 18 Aug., 1843; m. 31 Oct., 1867, James McMillan, son of Dr. Royal and Abigail (McMillan) Ayer, of Danville, Vt., where he d. 22 Aug., 1892; he was a surgeon at Buenos Ayres, (Ch.: Annie W., b. 18 Aug., 1870. Howard D., b. Aug., 1873; d. Oct., 1874. Harold Osgood, b. 9 July, 1877).

1586 FRANCIS PUTNAM, b. 1 Mar., 1810; d. 13 Mar., 1810.

1587 ABIGAIL RIPLEY, b. 12 Sept., 1811; m. 6 May, 1835, Edward L. Osgood. who d. in Fryeburg. Me., 9 Apr., 1864. Ch.: James Ripley, b. 22 Apr., 1836; d. in London, Eng., 18 May, 1892; Bowdoin College, 1854; member of the publishing house of Ticknor & Fields, and later of James R. Osgood & Co., and of James R. Osgood, McIlwaine & Co., of London. Elizabeth Dana, b. 21 Aug., 1838; d. 25 Jan., 1852. Catherine Putnam, b. 25 May, 1841; of Boston; favorably known as an author. Edward Louis, b. 6 Aug., 1843; m. Hannah Draper. Frances Caroline b. 21 Sept., 1845. George Phillips, b. 13 May, 1849; d. in Australia.

1588 CATHERINE PUTNAM, b. 7 Aug., 1814; d. 21 May, 1887; m. Henry B. Osgood, b. in Fryeburg, 5 Oct., 1811; Bowdoin College, 1832.

He was a lawyer in Portland, and d. 1843, leaving one son, Henry B., captain U. S. A. Mrs. Osgood m., 2d, Judge Daniel Goodenow, of Alfred, Me. They have a dau. m. to James H. Smith, of Portland.

1589 EMILY WHEELOCK, b. 7 June, 1816; d. 8 Dec., 1842.

1590 SARAH MALLEVILLE, b. 31 Oct., 1818; d. 18 May, 1821.

HON. JUDAH DANA was graduated from Dartmouth College in 1795, and began the study of law with Benjamin A. Gilbert, of Hanover, N. H. Three years later he began to practice at Fryeburg, Me., and was county attorney 1805–11; judge of probate, 1805–22; common pleas, 1811–23; member of the constitutional convention in 1819, and of the state executive council in 1833; U. S. senator 1836–7.

VI. 658 Israel Putnam Dana (*Hannah, Gen. Israel, Joseph, Thomas, John*), born in Pomfret, Vt., 13 April, 1774; died 22 June, 1848; married 29 April, 1798, Sarah Sophia, daughter of Elisha and Frances (Sessions) Smith, of Pomfret, who died 7 May, 1853.

Children :

1591 FRANCES MARY, b. 13 June, 1800; m. 1 June, 1819, Rev. Austin Hazen, of Dartmouth College, 1807; pastor successively of the First and Dothan churches in his native town of Hartford, and for 17 years in Berlin, Vt., where he died 25 Dec., 1854; his wife d. 11 June, 1831. Ch.: Alphia Dana, b. 23 July, 1820; d. in Northampton, 11 Mar., 1891. She was a student in Ipswich Female Seminary, and graduated at Mt. Holyoke Seminary 1841; associated with Miss Lyon as a teacher there until her marriage 14 Feb., 1851, to Rev. Daniel L. Stoddard, missionary to the Nestorians, her home being in Oroomiah, Persia, until his death 22 June, 1857. Returning to America she was again connected with Mt. Holyoke, and acting principal 1865–7; m. 4 Sept., 1867, Dea. William H. Stoddard, of Northampton, brother of her first husband, and remained there after his death, 14 June, 1884. She was a woman of rare qualities of mind and heart, beloved as a teacher by the multitudes of her pupils. Allen, b. 30 Nov., 1822; Dart. Col. 1842, and Andover Theological Seminary 1845, and for many years of the Marathe Mission of the A. B. C. F. M. in Western India. His alma mater conferred the honorary degree of D. D. in 1873. He was in America 1859–62 and from 1874–91, when he returned to India, after attending as a dele-

gate, the International Congregational Council in London. He m. 18 Sept., 1846, Martha Ramsay Chapin, of Somers, Ct., a graduate and teacher at Mt. Holyoke Seminary, who d. in Greenfield, 20 Jan , 1884; (Ch. : Henry Allen, b. 1 Jan., 1849; of Dart. Col. 1871; connected since 1880 with the Signal Service and Weather Bureau in Washington, where his services have gained marked distinction. William Oliver, b. 21 Aug., 1850; d. in the Mediterranean, while returning to India, 28 July, 1871; classmate of his brother in Dart. Col. Frances Anna, b. 9 July, 1852; grad. Mt. Holyoke Seminary, 1875; m. 20 Oct., 1875, Lorin Samuel Gates, of N. C., 1871; Yale Theo. Seminary, 1875; a missionary in Sholapur, India. Mary Sophia, b. 4 Nov., 1854; grad. Mt. Holyoke Seminary, 1877, and is with her father in India. Harriet Stoddard, b. 10 Oct., 1857; d. 11 Oct. Martha Chapin. b. 18 May, 1859; d. 8 Sept. Charles Chapin, b. 17 Aug., 1862; d. 31 Aug.).

1592 SARAH SOPHIA, b. 6 Feb., 1802; d. 31 Oct., 1820.

1593 HANNAH PUTNAM, b. 6 Mar., 1804; m. 15 Feb., 1832, Allen, son of Asa and Susannah (Tracy) Hazen, of Hartford, and brother of Austin (above). He was for two years a member of the Dart. Col. class of 1817; some time in Wheeling, Va., and in the custom house at New Orleans, but returned and spent his life on the farm of which his grandfather, Thomas Hazen, was the first owner; selectman 1829–33, and representative in the legislature 1845-6 and 9. He was often called to positions of trust for which his sterling integrity and intelligence specially fitted him, and was a man of literary tastes and high Christian character. He d. while on a visit at St. Johnsbury, 2 June, 1871; his wife d. 11 Dec., 1879. Ch.: Henry Allen, b. 27 Dec., 1832; Kimball Union Academy, 1850; Dart. Col. 1854, and Andover Theo. Seminary, 1857; ordained at St. Johnsbury, Vt., 17 Feb., 1857, and acting pastor at Barnard and Bridgewater, 1857-8; Hardwick, 1858-9; Barton, 1859-60; West Randolph, 1861-2; pastor Plymouth, N. H., installed 21 Jan., 1863, dismissed 15 July, 1868; Lyme, installed 2 Sept., 1868, dis. 30 Sept., 1870; Pittsfield, installed 22 Dec., 1870, dis. 30 Nov., 1872; Billerica, Mass. installed 21 May, 1874, dis. 4 May, 1879; secretary National Council and Congregational churches of the United States, and editor of their Year Book since 1883; Marietta College gave him the honorary D. D. 1891; trustee of Kimball Union Academy, 1869-86; Home school, Billerica, 1875-86; of the N. H. missionary society, 1872-4; besides being connected in various responsible capacities with many other societies and institutions. In July, 1891, he was appointed assistant secretary of the International Congregational Council in London; an historian of well known ability he is a member of the Vt. and N. H. Hist. Soc., and the N. E. Historic Geneal. Soc. Among his pub-

lished works is the History of Billerica, Mass , with genealogies.
He m. 9 July 1863, Charlotte Eloise, dau. of Dr. George Barrett
and Mary Hatch (Jones) Green, of Windsor, Vt., who d. in
Auburndale, 8 Feb., 1881, æ. 37 yrs. and 9 dys.; m., 2d, 31 Aug.,
1889, Martha Bethia, dau. of George W. and Sarah (Norris)
Heathe, of Boston. (Ch.: Mary, b. 23 Nov., 1864; d. 30 Sept.,
1865. Emily, b. 5 Aug., 1866; grad. Smith College, 1889; teacher
of Latin and Greek, Pueblo, Col. Charlotte, b. 6 Nov., 1868).
Israel Putnam, b. 28 Apr., 1837; d. 4 Jan., 1838. Charles Dana, b.
11 Feb., 1842; lives on the ancestral farm at Hartford; m. 28
May, 1868, Abby M., dau. of Horace P., and Martha L. (Dewey)
Coleman, of Norwich. (Ch.: Allen, b. 28 Aug., 1869; chemist
in charge of State Experimental Station, Lawrence, Mass., 1887.
Anna Putnam, b. 22 Sept., 1872; grad. from Smith College.
Louise Coleman, b. 1 Jan., 1877. Charles Dana, b. 3 Feb., 1881.
Richard, b. 12 July, 1887.) Emily Hannah, b. 2 Aug , 1844.

1594 EMILY EUNICE, b. 22 June, 1807; m. 25 Nov., 1828, Andrew Mc-
Millan, of Fryeburg, Me.; a merchant for a short time there
and afterward in Danville, Vt. He was in the legislatures of both
Maine and Vermont, and d. 11 Mar., 1875; his wife d. 17 May,
1844. Ch.: Putnam Dana, b. in Fryeburg, 25 Aug., 1832; m.
6 May, 1858, Helen E., dau. of Hon. Bliss N. Davis, of Danville,
who d. near Rosario, Buenos Ayres, of cholera, in 1867; m. 29
Nov., 1870, Catherine K., dau. of Hon. Moses Kittredge, of St.
Johnsbury, Vt. (Ch.: Emily Dana, b. 14 July, 1860. Helen
Margaret, b. 25 Jan., 1876; d. 18 Apr., 1879. Margaret, b. 27
Nov., 1878. Putnam Dana, b. 15 Nov., 1881.) Since 1870 Mr.
McMillian has been in the real estate and insurance business in
Minneapolis. Sarah Dana, b. in Danville, 12 May, 1836; grad.
from Kimball Union Academy, 1856; teacher in Putnam, O.,
Plattsburg, N. Y., and Pinkenton Academy, Derry, N. H.; m.
there, 11 July, 1865, Rev. Ebenezer G. Parsons, who was after-
ward principal; settled at Freeport, Me., and Derry, N. H.;
principal of Dummer Academy, Byfield, 1872-82. John, b. 27
Sept., 1838; a farmer, residing in Chester, La.; m. 28 Oct.,
1878, Mrs. Carrie A. Wagner. (Ch.: Putnam Dana, b. 18 Aug.,
1882). Julia Dana, b. 10 Nov., 1841; d. Jan., 1844.

1595 ISRAEL PUTNAM, b. 27 May, 1809; blind; m. 24 June, 1835, Charlotte O. Stanley, of Rochester, N. Y., who d. Aug., 1836; m.,
2d, 29 July, 1839, Almira L., dau. of Elijah and Susan (Hoar)
Dutton, of Hartford, Vt., who d. 23 June, 1890. Mr. Dana was
widely known as a teacher of music. After 1860 his home was
in St. Johnsbury, where he d. 27 May, 1875.

1596 JULIA ANN, b. 21 May, 1812; d. 28 May, 1838.

1597 CHARLES SMITH, b. 18 Nov., 1815; of Dart. Col., 1838; read law
at Waterbury with Gov. Dillingham, and Woodstock, Vt.; a

few years merchant in Danville, in firm of Dana, Weeks & Stanton; judge of probate for Caledonia county, 1846–54; removed to St. Johnsbury, and clerk of the county court, 1856–64; collector of internal revenue for the state, 1877–81; in Kansas City afterward; several years representative; and senator, 1854. At the outbreak of the civil war he was very active in raising troops and funds; he was talented and faithful in public office, the embodiment of honor and integrity; pure, gentle and affectionate in his home life, and a man of wide influence, from his strong convictions and sterling character; he was an active member of the Episcopal church. He m. 14 Feb , 1848, Arvilla H., dau. of Simeon P. and Sally (Bugbee) Sinclair, of Hardwick, Vt., where she was born 23 Aug., 1826. Mr. Dana d. 19 April, 1888. Ch.: Israel Putnam, b. 12 Aug., 1849; H. C., 1871; he engaged in the practice of law in Kansas City, in 1880. Sarah Sophia, b. 23 June, 1851; of Vassar College, and some years a teacher in Syracuse, N. Y.; m. 23 Aug., 1883, Chester, son of Chauncy C. and Lucy E. (Hicks) Loomis, of Syracuse. Their home is in Englewood, N. Y. Mr. Loomis is an artist. (Ch.: Charles Dana, b. 11 Dec., 1884. John Putnam. b. 9 May., 1889.) Abby Helen, b. 1 Dec., 1856; of Vassar College and a teacher for some years; m. 14 Feb., 1888, John A. Loomis, brother of Chester. Their home is on a large ranch, Point Rock, Concho County, Texas. (Ch.: Sarah Dana, b. 9 Feb., 1889. Chauncy Chester, b. 18 Aug., 1892).

ISRAEL PUTNAM DANA removed to Danville, in 1805, where he was one of the pioneers in the settlement of the town and of northern Vermont. He was a successful merchant for many years; also inn-keeper 1805–8, and an extensive farmer, devoting much attention to sheep raising. His sterling qualities gained and held the public confidence. He was high sheriff 1808–13, and took the first prisoners to the new state prison in Windsor.

In the war of 1812 he was an active supporter of the administration, raising volunteers for the service and furnishing the commissariat for numbers of soldiers quartered at Danville. In 1814 he raised a company and was on his way to Burlington when the news of the battle at Plattsburg was received. After the war was collector of the direct tax for a large district in northern Vermont; 1822–7, a member of the Governor's council; for several years the first president of the Vermont Mutual Fire Insurance Company. For 30 years he was an efficient and consistent member of the Congregational church, and earnest in support of its work at home and abroad.

VI. 660 John Winchester Dana (*Hannah, Gen. Israel, Joseph, Thomas, John*), born 16 Jan., 1777; married Susan, daughter of Rev. George Damon.

Children :

1598   GEORGE DURTON, b. 18 Feb., 1803; d. 1851.
1599   MARY ANN, b. 14 Nov., 1804.
1600   SUSAN ELIZA, b. 22 Dec., 1807.
1601   JOHN W., b. 8 Sept., 1811; d. 8 Nov., 1811.
1602   CATHERINE PUTNAM, b. 10 June, 1813.
1603   OSCAR FINGALL, b. 31 Mar., 1815.
1604   MARTHA ELIZA, b. 23 Mch., 1818.
1605   ANDREW JACKSON, b. 16 May, 1820.
1606   JOHN W., b. 4 Nov., 1822.

VI. 661 Daniel Dana (*Hannah, Gen. Israel, Joseph, Thomas, John,*) born 23 March, 1778; married Persis Brown; married, second, Mrs. Abigail Dudley, of Woodstock.

He held a colonel's commission in the war of 1812. By his first wife he had several children. They lived in Woodstock.

Children :

1607   GEORGE W.
1608   DANIEL P.
1609   GILES COLLINS, m. 19 May, 1836, Ruth Thomas; lived in Peoria, Il. Ch.: Martha Porter, b. 4 Jan., 1840; m. 10 Sept., 1863, Rev. Peter McVicar, b. in N. B., 15 June, 1829; pres. Washburn College. Alice R., m. James D. Gilchrist; lives in Pasadena, Cal. Mary Adams, m. 17 May, 1876, Hon. Henry H. Markham, of Pasadena, Cal.

VI. 663 David Dana (*Hannah, Gen. Israel, Joseph, Thomas, John*), born 24 March, 1781; married 25 Nov., 1805, Alice Hewitt; married, second, 3 Feb., 1814, Rebecca H., daughter of Jonathan Chase, of Cornish, N. H. He was a farmer in Pomfret, where he died 12 March, 1839.

Children :

1610 ELISHA, b. 1807.

1611 LUCY, b. 18 June, 1809; d. in Unionville, Ct., 14 Apr , 1890; m.
24 May, 1830, Rev. Joseph Marsh, b. in Sharon, Vt., 24 Aug.,
1799; d. 5 Feb., 1885; of Dart. Col., 1824; pastor at Pomfret,
1828–31; Hinsdale, N. H., 1835–8; and other churches. Ch.:
Joseph Putnam, b. 18 Sept., 1839; m. L. S. Balch; he was a
farmer in Minnesota. (Ch.: Lucy N. Charles B.) Daniel
Dana, b. in Oxford, N. C., 11 Apr., 1842; of Dart. Col., 1865:
ordained in Georgetown, Mass., 16 Sept., 1868; pastor there,
1868–88; Unionville, Ct., since; m. Abbie W. Cass. (Ch.: Carrie Tapley. Lucy D. Susie Preston).

1612 DANIEL PUTNAM, b. 1811.

1613 ALICE HEWITT, b. 17 Feb., 1815; m. 10 May, 1836, Dr. Stephen
Tracy, missionary in Siam, but practiced his profession afterward in Hudson, O., Windsor, Vt., Worcester and Andover,
Mass.; professor of Theory in practice of medicine in the New
England Female Medical College, many years. He died 13 Jan.,
1873. Mrs. Tracy lives with her son in Detroit, Mich. Ch.:
Martha Evarts, b. in Singapore, 8 Nov., 1837; of Abbot Academy; m. 17 May, 1860, Rev. William W. Livingston, b. in Pot-
ton, P.Q., 15 Dec., 1832; missionary in Siam, Turkey, 1860–72;
pastor, North Carner, Mass., 1873–8; Jaffrey, N. H., since. His
wife d. 19 Sept., 1874. (Ch.: Alice, b. 1 Mar., 1861. William
Farrand, b. 5 July, 1862; rector of Epis. ch., Augusta, Me.; m.
27 Dec., 1890, Margaret V. Farrington, of Augusta, Me. Steph-
en Tracy, b. 29 Dec., 1864; ordained 8 July, 1891, So. Egre-
mont, Miss.; m. 21 Oct., 1891, Lucia Towle, of Fryeburg, Me.
Rebecca, b. 10 Sept., 1867; of Mt. Holyoke Sem., 1887; d. in
Chattanooga, Tenn., 21 Apr., 1889. Edward M., b. 14 Aug.,
1869. Judith L., b. 12 June, 1872; d. 13 Oct., 1872.) Rebecca
Dana, b. in Pomfret, Vt., 19 July, 1840; of Abbot Acad.; missionary of A. B. C. F. M., Sivas, Western Turkey, 1868–70; m
1870, Mr. McCalloun, and now resides in Lansing, Mich. William W., resides in Detroit. Edward. Stephen Prince.

1614 DANIEL CHASE, b. Jan. 21, 1817; d. 12 Sept, 1843; m. Almira
King. Ch.: Hugh Ware, b. 18 Nov., 1841; d. 1842. Daniel C.,
b. 31 Mar., 1843; d. 23 Aug., 1862, in the U. S. Army.

1615 REBECCA HART, b. 17 Jan., 1819; m. 9 Aug., 1814, Rev. Edward
Elias Atwater, b. in New Haven, Ct., 28 May, 1816; of Yale
College, 1836; ordained 24 Nov., 1841, at Ravenna, O.; has
published Atwater Genealogy; History of the Colony of New
Haven; History of the City of New Haven, etc. Died in
Hawthorne, Fla., 2 Dec., 1887.

1616 PERSIS CHASE, b. 22 Sept., 1820; m. 15 June, 1842, Elisha Hewitt,
of Pomfret, who d. 12 Dec., 1882. Ch.: Stephen, b. 11 June,

1843. Lucy Maria, b. 1 Jan., 1845. David Dana, b. 14 Aug.; 1846. Mary B. Ware, b. 16 Sept., 1848; m. John J. Myers, of Cincinnati, and is now living a widow in Washington. Rebecca Atwater, b. 28 June, 1850. Persis Dana, b. 8 May, 1852; teacher in St. Johnsbury Academy, Vt. Alice Dana, b. 13 Mar., 1855. Elisha, b. 13 Mar., 1857; of New Haven, Conn. Emily Hamilton, b. 16 Feb., 1859. Jason D., b. 16 Dec., 1860. Ella Chase, b. 6 Oct., 1863; d. 1 Apr., 1880.

1617 BENJAMIN, b. 25 Jan., 1823, and d. a few days after.

1618 ISABELLA, b. Sept. 12, 1826; m. 30 Aug.,.1848, Oliver C. Woodward, and lived in Northfield. Ch.: Isabella D., b. 28 April, 1852; m. 25 May, 1874, Charles A. Smith. (Ch.: Eunice D. Albert O.) Jessie H., b. 10 Dec., 1856.

VI. 667 Mary Tyler (*Mehituble, Gen. Israel, Joseph, Thomas, John*), died 12 June, 1832; married, 23 Jan., 1793, Samuel, son of Samuel and Dorothy (Williams) Sumner, of Pomfret, Conn., born there, 1 Nov., 1766; died 31 Dec., 1821.

Children, all born at Pomfret:

1619 GEORGE, b. 13 Dec., 1793; m. Elizabeth, dau. of Daniel Putnam. His family will be found under No. 690.

1620 SARAH MAY, b. 25 July, 1796; d. Oct., 1873; m. John C. Howard.

1621 MARY, b. 3 June, 1799.

1622 ELIZABETH TYLER, b. 15 Aug., 1801; d. 30 Mar., 1841.

1623 SAMUEL PUTNAM, b. 8 Feb., 1807; d. 21 Oct., 1880; m. 19 April, 1830, J. Ann Goffe, of Pomfret, who d. 7 Feb., 1875. Ch., b. at Pomfret: Samuel, b. 24 Apr., 1831; d. 19 June, 1852. George, b. 1 Mar., 1833. Joseph, b. 12 July, 1836. Edward Tyler, b. 11 Mar., 1839; d. in Pomfret, 13 Aug., 1884; sergeant 11th Conn. Vol. Inf. Israel Putnam, b. 20 Jan., 1842; d. a pris. at Belle Isle, Va., 13 Feb., 1864; sergeant 7th Conn. Vol. Inf. Charles, b. 19 Feb., 1845; d. 23 May, 1852. Mary Elizabeth, b. 27 Mar., 1847; m. 17 Mar., 1869, Albert E. Potter, of Woodstock.

VI. 673 Betsey (*Mary, Gen. Israel, Joseph, Thomas, John*), born in Pomfret, Conn., 22 Sept., 1774; died 14 July, 1846; married 12 May, 1799, John Augustus, son of Elisha Gleason, of Pomfret, Conn., born there, 24 June, 1770; died 11 July, 1842.

Children:

1624 LEWIS PUTNAM, b. in Pomfret, 28 Feb., 1800; d. 22 Jan., 1885; m. 3 Mar., 1826, Sophronia Butler, who d. 6 Jan., 1827; m., 2d, 2

Oct., 1827, Lucy Butler, who d. 30 Oct., 1846; m., 3d, 20 Oct., 1847, Susan Davis. (Ch.: Caroline, b. and d. 1827. Henry Augustus, b. 6 Jan., 1829. Charles Edwin, b. 18 Apr., 1830. Caroline Maria, b. 10 June, 1832; d. 27 Jan., 1833. Elizabeth Frances (m. Marcus B. Webber), and John Francis (Rev.) b. 28 May, 1835. Lewis P., d. young. Alfred Waldo, d. young. Lewis Putnam, b. 1 June, 1839; d. 27 July, 1872. Lucy Caroline, d. young.

Lewis P., Sr., was a shoemaker, and stopped in Bedford while on a trip to his grandmother Waldo in Maine. From him the Bedford family descends.

1625 CAROLINE, b. 5 Feb., 1804; m. Daniel Clark, of Arlington.

1626 MARY WALDO, b. 15 Aug., 1807; m. 11 Oct., 1835, William Webber, who d. Feb., 1848. Ch.: Charles W., b. 1836. William A., b. 1840. Edwin F., b. 1843.

1627 ELIZABETH, b. 22 Aug., 1810; m. David Clark, of Arlington.

VI. 686 William (*Daniel, Gen. Israel, Joseph, Thomas, John*), born in Brooklyn (then Pomfret), Conn., 1 Jan., 1783; died there, 5 Dec., 1846; married there, 17 April, 1805, Mary, daughter of Ebenezer and Mary (Payne) Spalding, of Brooklyn, born there, 17 April, 1786; died there, 29 Dec., 1880.

Children:

1628 CAROLINE MARY, b. in Pomfret, 17 Feb., 1806; d. 10 Apr., 1882; m. 6 Jan., 1834, Edward Fogg.

1629 DANIEL, b. in Brooklyn, 23 Feb., 1808; d. 5 Oct., 1814.

1630 HARRIET WADSWORTH, b. in Holland, Mass., 5 Feb., 1810.

1631 WILLIAM HUTCHINSON, b. in Holland, Mass., 2 Feb., 1812; d. 17 July, 1880.

1632 ELIZABETH, b. in Brooklyn, 15 Dec., 1813; m. 1836, Benjamin Bacon Spalding.

1633 DANIEL, b. in Brooklyn, 9 Jan., 1816; d. 11 Aug., 1818.

1634 ISRAEL, b. in Brooklyn, 31 Aug., 1818; d. 3 Apr., 1819.

1635 ASA SPALDING, b. in Brooklyn, 16 July, 1820; d. 30 July, 1868.

1636 JANE, b. in Brooklyn, 25 Apr., 1823; m., as his 2d wife, Rev. Riverius Camp, D. D.; no ch.

1637 ANNE, b. in Brooklyn, 20 Mar., 1825; m. Charles Bacon. Mrs. Bacon lives at 304 Sibley street, Cleveland, Ohio.

WILLIAM PUTNAM was a farmer in Brooklyn, Conn., and held various town offices. He was highly respected and held a prominent position in the community

VI. **687 Catherine** (*Daniel, Gen. Israel, Joseph, Thomas, John*), born in Brooklyn, Conn., 17 Nov., 1785; died in Hartford, 2 Oct., 1842; married in Brooklyn, Conn., 30 April, 1805, George Brinley, son of Edward and Sarah (Tyler) Brinley, born in Boston, 24 Oct., 1774; died in Hartford, Conn., 21 Jan., 1857. Merchant in Hartford in later years.

Children:

1638   CATHERINE HUTCHINSON, b. 12 Feb., 1806; d., *s. p.*, 21 July, 1832; m. Oct., 1825, Samuel Howard Huntington, who d. 4 Dec., 1880, aged 86; he was a judge; lived in Hartford.

1639   SARAH TYLER, b. 6 Mar., 1808; d. 27 Sept., 1812.

1640   HARRIET PUTNAM, b. 28 Apr., 1810; d. 31 Oct., 1811.

1641   HARRIET PUTNAM, b. 13 May, 1812; d. 4 Sept., 1845.

1642   ELIZABETH, b. 6 Nov., 1814; d. 28 Sept., 1862.

1643   GEORGE, b. 15 May, 1817; d. 17 May, 1875; m. F. E. Terry.

1644   SARAH TYLER, b. 25 Dec., 1818; d. 28 Dec., 1818.

1645   ANNE, b. 19 Mar., 1820; d. 13 Oct., 1860.

1646   SARAH, b. 1 Sept., 1822; d. 21 May, 1836.

1647   EMILY MALBONE, b. 27 Oct., 1824; m. H. K. Morgan.

1648   PUTNAM, b. 18 Feb., 1827.

1649   EDWARD HUNTINGTON, b. 22 Jan., 1829; m. Mrs. R. M. Bradford.

GEORGE BRINLEY was for many years at the head of a drug store in Boston, succeeding Dr. Dix, and there laid the foundation of a large fortune. He was a warden of Trinity church, Boston. In late years he resided at Hartford. His wife was a lady of strong sense and high excellence of christian character. Their house was the home of the clergy of the church.

VI. **690 Elizabeth** (*Daniel, Gen. Israel, Joseph, Thomas, John*), born 24 Sept., 1794; died 1844; married George Sumner, M. D., her cousin, son of George and Mary (Tyler) Sumner, No. 1619.

Mr. Sumner graduated from Yale in 1813; for some years a physician at Hartford, and Professor of Botany in Trinity College; he died 20 Feb., 1855.

Children:

1650 ELIZABETH, m. Myron Wilson.

1651 CATHARINE R. m. 25 Sept., 1856, Hezekiah Huntington, of Hartford, who d. 20 Feb., 1865.

1652 MARY, m. 20 Oct., 1858, Joseph Warren Newcomb, of Hartford, who d. at Burlington, N. J., 17 Oct., 1866; m., 2d, C. M. Bidwell, of E. Hartford.

1653 GEORGE.

1654 HARRIET G., m. William Chipman, who d.; and she m., 2d, Mr. Hazzard.

VI. 691 John Pope (*Peter Schuyler, Gen. Israel, Joseph, Thomas, John*), born in Brooklyn, Conn., 9 May, 1786; died in Cambridge, N. Y., 10 Oct., 1867; married 5 Jan., 1813, Elizabeth, daughter of Doctor Jonathan Dorr, of Cambridge, N. Y.

Children :

1655 A SON, d. in infancy.

1656 MARY, adopted daughter; niece of Mrs. Putnam. Present address, Mary Putnam Thatcher, 339 Lafayette ave., Brooklyn, Ct.

MR. PUTNAM graduated from Williams College in 1809, and studied law at Albany with Abraham Van Vichten. In January, 1813, he removed to Cambridge, where he lived until his death. He was a good lawyer; a faithful student of the bible; an ornament to society and a strong arm to help in church affairs; a most affectionate husband and father; a sympathetic friend.

VI. 695 Nathan (*Peter Schuyler, Gen. Israel, Joseph, Thomas, John*), born in Brooklyn, Ct., 22 Aug., 1787; died in North Adams, 3 Dec., 1841; married at North Adams, 2 July, 1816, Maria, daughter of Richard and Lellis (Chase) Knight. She died 8 Feb., 1845.

Mr. Putnam resided at Adams, Mass., where he practiced law; at one time postmaster. He was a graduate of Williams College.

Children :

1657 LILLIE MARION, b. in Northampton, 7 Feb., 1818; d. 17 Feb., 1891, at No. Adams; m. 28 Nov., 1832, Edward Norman, M.D. Ch.: Emily W., m. —— Hayden; present address, Mrs. Emily N. Hayden, 66 Centre street, No. Adams.

1658 LUCY ALIDA, b. 1 Oct., 1819,; d. 28 June, 1844; m. Mortimer
      Wadhams.
1659 NATHAN KNIGHT, b. 26 Dec., 1821; d. 23 Mar., 1822.
1660 ANN ELIZA, b. 27 Mar., 1827; d. 30 Nov., 1844; m. 2 Sept., 1841,
      Charles Emerson.

VI. 696 Peter Schuyler (*Peter Schuyler, Gen. Israel, Joseph, Thomas, John*), born in Brooklyn Conn.; died in Elyria, Ohio, 1858, aged 69; married Miss Stephens.

Children :

1661 SON.
1662 DAUGHTER.

MR. PUTNAM at one time was a merchant in Cleveland, but at the time of his death was a member of the Lorain Bar. He performed the duties of a magistrate in Elyria for many years in a most faithful manner.   At one time a resident of Marietta, Ohio.

VI. 699. Doctor Samuel, (*John, Samuel, John, Nathaniel, John*) born about 1740; married about 1761, Elizabeth Kimball, who died Oct., 1804, aged 66. Administration on his estate granted 6 Nov., 1789, to widow Elizabeth who gave bonds with James Bancroft and Amos Putnam.

Children :

1663 BETSEY, b. 3 April, 1762.
1664 SAMUEL KIMBALL, b. 27 Feb., 1765; d. 21 Nov., 1847.
1665 MARY, b. 23 Sept., 1766; m. 4 Dec., 1803, Nathaniel Cumming.
1666 SARAH, b. 6 Mar., 1768.
1667 JOHN, b. 2 Sept., 1769; 19 Sept., 1778.
1668 WILLIAM, b. 1 Sept., 1771; d. 3 Feb., 1835.
1669 JAMES, b. 5 Aug. 1773; d. Nov., 1776.
1670 JAMES, b. 23 Nov., 1777; d. 18 Nov., 1807.

DR. SAMUEL PUTNAM accompanied Dr. Amos Putnam, with whom he was studying, in the French and Indian campaign as " waiter."   He settled in Salisbury, and afterward in Reading and Lynnfield.

VI. 702 John (*John, Samuel, John, Nathaniel, John*),
born in Sudbury, 13 June, 1746 ;[119] died in Chester, Vt., 9
Sept., 1838; married in Marlborough, Mass., Dec., 1771,
Mary, daughter of Robert Baker, born there, 20 August,
1747.

Children :

1671 JESSE, b. in Marlborough, 31 July, 1772.
1672 ROBERT, b. 25 June, 1774.
1673 AN INFANT, b. 1776 ; d. 3 Oct., 1778.
1674 POLLY, b. in Ashburnham, 23 July, 1778 ; m. 1802, John Hoar.
1675 BETSEY, b. in Lancaster, 9 Jan., 1781 ; m. 1801, Ezra Sargent, Jr.
1676 JOHN, b. in Lancaster, 31 March, 1783.
1677 RACHEL, b. 19 Apr., 1785 ; unm., in 1835.
1678 SALLY, b. in Chester, Vt., 1 Sept., 1790 ; m. 1812, Ebenezer Hoar.

JOHN PUTNAM was above the common stature and of a robust constitution, being hale and hearty at ninety. At various periods he lived in Ashburnham (1775–9), Lancaster,
and finally in Chester, Vt.

His name occurs on the Lexington Alarm lists as marching
in Capt. Deliverance Davis' company, Col. Asa Whitcomb's
regiment.

VI. 703 Nathan (*John, Samuel, John, Nathaniel,
John*), born in Sudbury, 26 July, 1749 ; died in Lexington,
Ky., 26 June, 1833, of cholera, and was buried in the garden of his estate on Hall street, Lexington ; married 20 Oct.,
1774, Dorothy, daughter of Daniel and Dorothy (Goss)
Whitney, born in Stow, 23 Dec., 1751 ; died in Wendall,
27 Dec., 1825.

Children :

1679 DANIEL, b. 29 April, 1775 ; bapt. in Ashburnham, 16 July, 1775 ;
      d. 22 Sept., 1775.
1680 DOROTHY. b. 2 Dec., 1776 ; bapt. in Ashburnham, 18 May, 1777 ;
      d. in Eddyville, Ky., 19 Dec., 1832 ; " weak as a child but being
      restored to health," m. Nathan Gates, of Stow, and had " four
      daughters and two sons, and eight or ten of the fourth genera-
      tion." The children were : Dorothy. Nathan. Maria. Anne.
      Joseph.

[119] Another account, b. 13 June, 1745.

1681 NATHAN, b. 18 Mar., 1779; d. in Wendall, 4 Nov., 1817.

1682 SAMUEL. b. 19 June, 1781.

1683 SARAH, b. 15 Sept., 1783; m. Daniel Ridge (or Rider) of Leicester. "Sarah has had a chequered fortune; they have been raised from low to high degree and have now sunk to low." Writing of Ridge, the author says: " he has a large share of ingenuity in the mechanical line, and has met with many disappointments and losses, is now picking up again." They lived in Lexington, Ky., and Cincinnati, Ohio. Ch.: Sarah. Daniel. Lucy. Orily. Joseph. William. Emily. Susanna. John. Nathan. " Orily, Sarah, Daniel, Joseph, all dead."

1684 LUCY, b. 19 May, 1786; m. 8 Mar., 1802, Aaron Lawrence, of Hollis, N. H. " Lucy married Mr. Aaron Lawrence; his fortune has been diversified; began well but lost his health; moved from place to place, at last to Vermont, where he is doing well;" " have not lost a child;" "have never seen such an agreeable family, all well looking and most are beautiful. One son and two or three daughters are married." " Lucy has three or four grandchildren." Ch.: Lucy, m. Ambrose Pease. Aaron, m. Lucretia Claggett. Mary R., m. Perkins W. Wiley. Daniel, of Newmarket, d. 1833. Jane D. Alona A. Willimian C. Dorothy M. Nancy B. Sarah S. Eliza A. James P.

1685 JAMES, b. 2 June, 1778; "an unfortunate youth, much inclined to society and sport; chose a sea faring life and has been heard from for many years past;" went to sea in 1819.

1686 JOSEPH WASHINGTON, b. 10 Aug., 1790.

1687 MARY, b. 24 Nov., 1791; m. John Davis, a farmer in Hancock, where they lived. Ch.: V. Harriet. James. George. Maria. Charles. Sarah J.

NATHAN PUTNAM lived in Grafton, Stow, Ashburnham and Wendall, Mass., and Lexington, Ky. He joined his brother John at Ashburnham. While at Stow he kept an inn. In 1778, Nathan Putnam and wife were granted letters of dismissal from the church, on account of difference of opinion in regard to infant baptism.

There is a curious manuscript written by Nathan Putnam and now in the possession of his descendants in Kentucky, from which the above account of his children was taken, touching on every variety of subject. One is a satire on " Calvin'sCreed," very well taken, and showing the author to be a man of shrewd sense and somewhat of an Unitarian or Universalist in his belief.

VI. 705 Capt. Daniel (*John, Samuel, John, Nathaniel, John*), born in Sudbury, 27 Sep.,[120] 1755; died in Windham, Vt., 21 Oct., 1819; married, first, at Ashburnham, 18 Mar., 1777, Elizabeth, daughter of John Oberlock (or Overlock, whose children were all known as Lock), a German emigrant who settled in Ashburnham in 1758. Mary, widow of John Oberlock, died at Winchendon at the home of Capt. Daniel Putnam.

His first wife dying 8 Aug., 1787, he married, second, 29 Nov., 1787, Kezia, daughter of William and Hannah (Whitcomb of Harvard) Pollard, of Ashburnham, born 15 Feb., 1765.

Children by Elizabeth, all born in Ashburnham!

1688　JOHN, b. 1782; shoemaker; lived in Williamstown. He married and left one or two daughters.

1689　DANIEL, b. 1783; left home, unm., and had not been heard from as late as 1835.

1690　JACOB, b. 1785.

1691　LEVI, b.1786; d. 3 June, 1796.

1692　ELIZABETH, b. 1787; d. inf.

1693　AN INFANT, d. at time of mother's death.[121]

Children, by Kezia:

1694　WILLIAM, b. Ashburnham, 18 Jan., 1789.

1695　SILAS, b.　　　"　　10 Mar., 1790.

1696　JONAS, b.　　　"　　7 Sept., 1792.

1697　ABEL, b.　　　"　　8 Jan., 1794; d. 2 July, 1878.

1698　MARY (called Poliexena by Abel), b. Ashburnham, 15 Mar., 1795; m. Shepard Marvin, of Ashburnham.

1699　JOSEPHA, b. Ashburnham, 27 July, 1796; m. Simon Davis.

1700　LAURA, b. Ashburnham, 7 May, 1798; m. Samuel Cox.

1701　MYRA, b. Winchendon, 11 Mar., 1800; m. William Sheldon.

1702　PLINA, b. Winchendon, 21 Nov., 1801.

1703　ELMIRA, b. Winchendon, 5 July, 1803; m. Richard Empy, of Camden, Oneida Co., N. Y. Both her husband and a son served in the late war.

1704　ROSINA, b. Winchendon, 5 Sept., 1805.

1705　AURILLA, b. Royalton, Vt., 14 May, 1807; m. Oliver Porter.

CAPTAIN DANIEL PUTNAM, with his brothers John and Na-

---

[120] Family Rec. in possession of Mr. Abel Putnam of Saratoga has it 25 Oct.
[121] Perhaps same as 1692.

than, settled in Ashburnham about the opening of the Revolution. During Sept., 1776, he enlisted in Captain Manasseh Sawyer's company, Col. Dike's regiment and served, the latter portion of the time as sergeant, until 21 Jan., 1777. In 1779, he was chosen one of the Committee on Correspondence.

In July, 1781, upon the reorganization of the militia he received a commission as second lieutenant of seventh company, 8th Reg., and on May 2, 1787, captain. In this year he was chosen on a committee to draft a petition for pardon for Capt. Job Shattuck, then under sentence of death for participating in Shays' Rebellion. Captain Putnam was conspicuous in the business and military affairs of the town, but in 1798 he removed to Winchendon, and in 1810 to Windham, Vt., stopping for a time at Royalton, Vt.

VI. 706 Asa (*John, Samuel, John, Nathaniel, John*), born in Sudbury, 5 Sept., 1758; died 29 Mar., 1837; married Lucy Haynes of Sudbury; married, second, Catherine Early of Princeton, born 13 Oct., 1762; died 1 Feb., 1821.

Child, by first marriage:

1706   JAMES, b. 11 Nov., 1784.

Children, by second marriage:

1707   LUCY HAYNES, b. 4 Mar., 1792.
1708   ASA, b. 8 Aug., 1793.
1709   DENNIS, b. 4 June, 1795.
1710   CYRUS, b. 6 Apr., 1797.
1711   ADAM, b. 16 July, 1799.
1712   ELBRIDGE, b. 27 July, 1802; d. in the army.
1713   ELIZABETH.
1714   SALLY.
1715   MOSES, b. 21 Nov., 1806.

ASA PUTNAM lived in Stow. He served during the Revolution; enlisting 3 May, 1775; and was in various service in 1775 and 1777. There is an Asa Putnam, private, on roll of Capt. John Gleason's company, of Framingham, stationed for some time at Kingston, Rhode Island, 1777.

VI. 711 Elisha (*Asa, Josiah, John, Nathaniel, John*), born in Danvers, 16 Mar., 1741; died there 16 Feb., 1817; married in Danvers, 18 Oct., 1764, Rebecca Brown.

Children :

1716 ASA, b. 23 Sept., 1765; adm. granted to him on his father's estate 15 Apr., 1817.

1717 REBECCA, bapt. 29 Nov., 1767.

1718 SALLY.

1719 ELIZABETH.

1720 MEHITABLE.

VI. 718[122] Asa (*Josiah, Josiah, John, Nathaniel, John*), born in Danvers, Aug., 1743; died 7 Sept., 1795; married 24 July, 1766, Anna Collins. Removed to Brattleboro, Vt. His widow, Anna, married about 1800, Col. Benjamin Simonds of Berkshire Co., Mass.

Children :

1721 PERLEY, b. 10 Mar., 1767.

1722 LEWIS, b. 22 Aug., 1769.

1723 SERAPHINA, b. 7 Sept., 1772; m. Jonathan Smith of Bath, Me. She was living in her 86th year. Ch.: Gardner C., and Asa, b. 12 Apr., 1792. Lucy S., b. 31 Aug., 1794. Daniel S., b. 25 Oct., 1796. Fanny, b. 7 Feb., 1799; Hannah, b. 4 Mar., 1805. Lydia A., b. 11 July, 1811. Oliver B., b. 12 Nov., 1812. Andrew S., b. 8 Oct., 1815. William, d. young. David, d. young. Jackson, d. young.

1724 EBENEZER, b. 4 Sept., 1779.

1725 JOSIAH, b. 1 Aug., 1781.

1726 ALFRED, b. 10 May, 1784.

1727 SEWALL, b. 23 Sept., 1786.

1728 SYLVIA, b. 25 May, 1789; d. at Cattaraugus, N. Y., 2 Oct., 1883; m. 11 Feb., 1811, Zane A. Hamilton, of Aurora, who d. in E. Aurora, N. Y., 5 Dec., 1863. Ch.: Catherine A., b. 20 Nov., 1811; d. 28 Nov., 1860; m. Wm. A. Steuben. Mary Putnam, b. 22 Aug., 1813; d. in Chicago, 4 Mar., 1879; m. 15 Jan., 1838, Edward Raymond.[123] Collins, b. 17 Aug., 1814; d. 10 Aug., 1834. Abuckus, b.

---

[122] For No. 717, see under No. 407.

RAYMOND.

[123] I. Richard Raymond of Salem, Mass., mariner; and of Norwalk and Saybrook, Conn. He was made a freeman 14 May, 1634, and received grants of land in Salem in 1636. He was an enterprising shipmaster and trader. In 1662, he removed to Norwalk, where the immediate descendants of his son John mostly resided; but two years later he removed to Saybrook, where he died, in 1692, aged about ninety years. By his wife Judith, he had children: *John*. Bathsheba, bapt. 6 Aug., 1637; m. 29 July, 1659, Humphrey Coombs. Joshua, bapt. 3 Mar., 1639; m. Elizabeth Smith, and settled in New London, Conn. Lemuel, bapt. 3 Jan., 1640; prob. d. *s. p.* Hannah, bapt. 12 Feb.,

22 Mar., 1817; d. 13 Apr., 1878; m. Caroline Messich. Charles, b. 15 June, 1819; d. 17 Mar., 1820. Seraph S., b. 20 Mar., 1821; d. 17 June, 1862; m. Charles P. Jackson. Charles S., b. 16 Nov., 1822; d. 17 Apr., 1891; graduated from West Point in 1843, served in the Mexican War and afterwards lived at Fond du Lac and Milwaukee, Wis.; he rose to the rank of Major general in late civil war; m. 9 Feb., 1849, Sophia Shepard. Sylvia, b. 23 Feb., 1824; d. 8 May, 1864; m. Dr. Edw. Bishop. Anna M., b. 25 Oct , 1826; d 17 Mar., 1851; m. Levi S. Crawford. Lucy E., b. 5 Oct., 1828; m. Salmon L. Johnson, lived in Cattaraugus, N. Y. William A., b. 21 Aug., 1832; d. 14 Sept., 1834.

1729 HARVEY, b. 5 Jan., 1793.

VI. 721 Josiah (*Josiah, Josiah, John, Nathaniel, John*), born 8 June, 1749; died 1 May, 1835: married 12 Sept., 1771, Sybil Smith, born 11 July, 1743, died 3 Dec., 1824. Lived in Weston, now Warren, Mass. Marched to Cambridge upon the alarm of 19 April, 1775.

Children:

1730   EUNICE, b. 2 July, 1777; d. 17 Oct., 1857; m. 2 Feb., 1803, Zebadiah Allen, b. 17 Jan., 1766; d. 15 Jan., 1808. Ch : Eliza, b. 31 May, 1804; d. 30 July, 1850; m. 1 May, 1823, Lyman Day, b 18 Mar., 1797: and d. 14 Apr., 1867. Sally, b. 10 Feb.,1806; d. 18 Dec., 1852; m. Joseph King, Mar., 1827, b. 1781; and d. 14 Apr., 1855. Ambrose, b. 9 Sept., 1807; d. 1 Sept., 1881; m. 2 Apr., 1835, Ruby Beebe, b. 27 Sept., 1808, and d. 22 Jan., 1880.

1642; m. Oliver Manwaring of Salem and New London. Samuel, bapt. 13 July, 1644; m. Mary Smith; d. *s. p.* Richard, bapt. 2 Jan., 1647; d. abt. 1680. Eliza, bapt. 23 Apr., 1649. Daniel, bapt. 17 Apr., 1653; m. Elizabeth Harris, and settled at Lyme, Conn.

II. JOHN, eldest son of Richard; m. 10 Dec., 1664, Mary, dau. of Thomas Betts of Norwalk. John was living as late as 1694, but was dead in 1699.

Children: John, b. 9 Sept., 1665. *Samuel*, b. 7 July, 1673. Thomas, b. abt. 1678. Hannah.

III. SAMUEL, son of John, m. 1 Apr., 1696, Judith, dau. of Ephraim Palmer, of Greenwich. He lived in Norwalk and died probably in 1739. Children: Samuel, b. 7 May, 1697. John, b. 12 Feb., 1699; prob. d. early. Ephraim, b. 9 Sept., 1701. Joshua, b. abt. 1702. Mary, b. abt. 1705; m. John Brown. *Simeon*, b. at " Old Well, " Norwalk, Conn., 1711.

Samuel Raymond deeded land in 1733 and in 1738, to his son Simeon; and under date of 20 Mar., 1739-40, Samuel, Joshua, Ephraim, and Simeon Raymond, divide land left them in common by their father Samuel Raymond. (*Norwalk Rec. Vol. 8, p. 253.*)

IV. SIMEON, son of Samuel, m. Hannah. He held a captain's commission at the breaking out of the troubles in 1775, which he resigned, and was active in the Revolution. His property was burned by Tories. He d. at Norwalk, July, 1795.

Children: Hezekiah, b. 22 Jan., 1743. Jedediah. Nathaniel. Uriah. *William*, b. 11 Jan., 1747. Moses. Ruth, b. 1 Nov., 1755. Aaron, b. 9 Aug., 1759. Anna. Hannah.

V. WILLIAM, son of Simeon, m. 21 Jan., 1768, Ruth, dau. of Nathan Hoyt of Norwalk. He removed to Granville, N. Y., and died at Bethany Centre, N. Y., 18 Feb.,

1731 WILLIAM, b. 29 Mar., 1774; d. 13 Oct., 1796.

1732 LYDIA, b. 11 Aug., 1778; d. April, 1847; m. Josiah Howland of Barre, Mass. Ch.: Josiah P. Rufus. William L. Timothy J.

1733 TARRANT, b. 1 Apr., 1780; d. 27 Feb., 1837; m. Nancy Shepard.

1734 RUFUS, b. 25 July, 1782; d. 18 Jan , 1847; m. Augusta Peabody Lived in Rutland.

1735 SALLY, b. 10 May, 1784; d. 24 July, 1864.

1736 JAMES, b. 6 Feb., 1786; d. 6 Aug., 1817; m. Eliza Carpenter. Lived in N. Y.

1737 ASA, b. 30 Apr., 1788; d. in Weston, 7 Sept., 1829.

1738 HENRY, b. 14 Aug., 1793; d. 21 June, 1829; m. Sophia Blair, b. 29 Aug., 1792, d. 18 Oct.,1829.

VI. 725 John (*John, John, John, Nathaniel, John*), born in Salem Village, 10 Dec., 1743; married in Danvers, 31 Oct., 1765, Abigail Small.

His name disappears from the tax list in Danvers after 1767.

Children :

1739 REUBEN.

1740 RUTH, perhaps bapt. Danvers, 9 Aug., 1767.

1741 JOHN, perhaps bapt. Danvers, 26 Feb., 1769

1742 LYDIA.

1743 NABBY.

1744 BETSEY.

1745 SALLY.

1832. His wife d. 26 Apr., 1808, and he m. 2d, Aug., 1808, Sarah Meech, b. 6 May, 1760 Children: Anne, b. 6 Mar., 1769. Elizabeth, b. 5 Aug., 1770. Wm. d. y. Ruth, b. 5 Apr., 1775. Wm., b. 10 Aug., 1777. Nathan, d. y. Charlotte, b. 4 July, 1782. Sarah, b. 10 June, 1785. Frances, b. 21 July, 1787. Polly, b. 16 Aug., 1789. *Nathan Hoyt*, b. 10 Oct., 1791.

VI. NATHAN HOYT, son of Wm., m. at Granville, 7 May, 1812, Marcia Kellogg, b. 7 Feb., 1788. He made several removals westward, finally settling at Cambridge City, Ind., where he d. 6 Aug., 1874. His wife d. 9 Aug., 1849, and he m. 2d, 9 May, 1850, Mrs. Elvira Lawrence, b. 18 Oct., 1810; she d. 27 Nov., 1863.

Children: Marciaetta, d. y. Nathan H., b. 19 May, 1814; d. 13 Apr., 1850. *Edward*, b. 5 Feb., 1816. Nathan, b. 24 Mar., 1817. Chas. H., b. 10 Nov., 1818. Helen E., b. 22 Sept., 1820. Ravand R., b. 26 Feb., 1823. Henry R., b. 4 June, 1825. Marcia, b. 19 Jan., 1827. Wm., d. y. Sarah, b. 25 Aug., 1830. Mary, d. y.

VII. EDWARD, son of Nathan H., of Chicago, Ill.; m. Mary P. Hamilton (No. 1728); m. 2d, 8 Nov., 1883, Mrs. Persis E. Belden.

Children, Amelia, b. 13 Mar., 1840; m. J. C. Richards of Chicago and Marcia b. 29 Apr., 1847; m. 2 Sept., 1869, Robert E. Jenkins of Chicago. Their children are George Raymond, b. 26 July, 1870. Marcia, b. 2 Sept., 1872; d. 21 July, 1878. Helen Mary, b. 5 Aug., 1874. William, b. 23 July, 1876; d. 13 Aug., 1876. Edith D., b. 7 Apr., 1879.

VI. **726 Deacon Daniel** (*John, John, John, Nathaniel, John*), born in Salem Village, 19 Apr., 1748; died in Fitchburg, 26 Apr., 1813; married in Salem, 14 Dec., 1769, Rachel, daughter of William Small of Danvers, born in Salem, 5 Apr., 1743, and died in Fitchburg, 26 Jan., 1819.

Children :

1746   PHEBE, b. 20 Sept., 1770; d. in Fitchburg, 12 Nov., 1827; m. 26 July, 1791, Abiel, son of Daniel and Hannah Holt, b. in Andover, 1766 and d. in Rindge, N. H., 18 June, 1826. Ch.: Abiel, b.1791; d. 10 June, 1864; m. Nov., 1815, Edah Darling. Daniel of N. Y., d. 1871. Nathan, d., unm., 1827. Edah Putnam, b. 29 Sept., 1804; d. *s. p.*, 1861; m. 1859, Wm. B. Phelps. Liberty, m. Lucy Wheeler. See History of Rindge and Ashburnham, N. H.

1747   DANIEL, b. 5 Sept., 1772.

1748   RACHEL, b. 1 Nov., 1775; d. in Fitchburg, 1 Sept., 1862; m. Feb., 1797, Elias Messenger, who d. there 9 Feb., 1820, aged 46 years. Ch.: Geo. Small, b. 31 May, 1798; m. 2 Oct., 1823, Sylvania, dau. of Thos. and Lydia (Davis) Thurston, b. 13 Feb., 1798. Abel, b. 7 Jan., 1801; d. unm. Elias, b. 26 Apr., 1806; d. in Lowell, *s. p.*; m. Susan Boutelle. Daniel. b. 14 Sept., 1808; m. 14 Feb., 1834, Eliza Simonds, who d. 15 Dec., 1860; m., 2d, 7 Aug., 1861, Mary S. Jones.

1749   EDAH, b. 20 Nov., 1777; d. Nov., 1839; m. as his 2d w., 1810, David Baldwin. He d. in Fitchburg 16 June, 1830. Ch.: Calvin, b. 15 Oct., 1810, of Leominster. Edah, b. 2 Apr., 1812; m. —— Kendall of Ashby. Daniel, b. 16 May, 1814, removed to California. Asenath, b. 8 Dec., 1817; m. Charles Boutelle of Leominster; she d. there 21 Apr., 1868. Roxanna, b. 13 Feb., 1822; m. Joseph Perkins; and removed to Minnesota.

1750   GEORGE SMALL, b. 21 July, 1780.

1751   ISAIAH, b. 22 May, 1782.

1752   SAMUEL, b. 4 Sept., 1785.

DANIEL PUTNAM early settled in Fitchburg and became an active and honored citizen. He was magistrate and deacon. Representative 1787–1793 and 1788 and 1797 delegate to the Constitutional Convention.

VI. **727 Deacon James** (*John, John, John, Nathaniel, John*), born in Salem Village, 16 July, 1750; died there, 21 Aug., 1819; married there, 16 Sept., 1773, Eunice, daughter of Nathaniel and Mary (Swinnerton) Pope, born 21 Feb., 1751, and died 6 Mar., 1808.

Children :

1753 EUNICE, b. 9 May, 1775; d. 16 Oct., 1801.
1754 MARY, b. 20 Mar., 1780.
1755 RUTH, b. 16 Oct., 1785; d. 6 May, 1816.

VI. 728 Peter (*John, John, John, Nathaniel, John*), born in Salem Village, 3 Oct., 1751; died 29 Mar., 1802. The account of his administrator, Zerubabel Porter, was rendered 16 Jan., 1810. He married 27 Feb., 1783, Eunice, daughter of Elias and Eunice Endicott, who died 24 Dec., 1854, aged 96 years, 5 months, at the time of her death the oldest person in Danvers as well as of Governor Endecott's descendants.

Children[124], born in Danvers :

1756 PETER, b. 1784; d. *s. p.* about 187–; m. Mar., 1818, Abigail Goss who d. 1858. Lived on the same estate as his father, grandfather and probably great grandfather Putnam. The house has been destroyed by fire. It stood back of the Asylum. He was quite eccentric and published a pamphlet entitled " The Life and Times of Peter Putnam. "
1757 RUTH, b. 25 Mar., 1786; m. 23 Jan., 1814, Asa Hutchinson, son of Jeremy and Sarah (Putnam) Hutchinson of Danvers, b. 4 Mar., 1777; d. 11 May, 1854. Ch.: Eben., b. 15 Oct., 1814. James Putnam, b. 15 Dec., 1816. Hannah, b. 17 April, 1820. Mary, b. 26 June, 1823; m. James A. Bartlett. Sarah, b. 3 Oct., 1828.
1758 SALLY, b. 1792; m. prev. 1010, David Davis, morocco manufacturer.

VI. 729 Amos (*John, John, John, Nathaniel, John*), born in Salem Village, 25 May, 1752; died in Winchester, N. H., after 1835 ; married June, 1781, Lydia Hovey.

Children :

1759 AMOS, b. 17 Feb., 1782.
1760 LYDIA, b. 1 Sept., 1783; m. 2 July, 1820, George Tufts. Ch.: Amos Putnam, b. 12 July, 1823.
1761 MARY, b. 4 Oct., 1785; m. 23 Jan., 1815, Eleazer Reed. Ch.: Mary Lydia, b. 16 Dec., 1816. Amos Putnam, b. 29 Aug., 1818.

[124] Joshua, George and Amos are given by D. B. Putnam as additional children, if so they died very young, as Peter, Ruth and Sally, all minors, are the only ones mentioned in settlement of Peter's estate.

1762 SAMUEL, b. 5 Dec., 1787.
1763 SARAH, b. 24 Nov., 1789.
1764 ELIZABETH, b. 2 Apr., 1791.
1765 SUSAN, b. 4 June, 1793.

VI. 730 Doctor James Phillips (*Amos, John, John, Nathaniel, John*), born in Salem Village, 21 Apr., 1745; died in Danvers, 4 March, 1824; married   1768, Mary,[125] daughter of Rufus and Mary (Conant) Herrick, of Pomfret, born at Cherry Hill, North Beverly, 17 Aug., 1749; and died 13 Dec., 1840, aged 91 years, 3 months.

Children, born in Danvers :

1766 AMOS, b. 4 Jan., 1772; d. 24 Oct., 1848.
1767 RUFUS, b. 19 July, 1774; d. 12 May, 1855.
1768 POLLY, b. 29 Sept., 1778; d. 18 Apr., 1856; m. William Putnam (No. 1668), of Salem.
1769 HANNAH, b. 23 Sept., 1783; d. 22 May, 1855.
1770 BETSEY, b. 11 Nov., 1785; d. 7 Apr., 1847.
1771 LYDIA, b. 7 Aug., 1792; d. previous to April, 1856.

DOCTOR PUTNAM practised in Danvers. At one period he lived in the Clark house which stood where now is the Danvers station on the Eastern Division of the B. & M. R. R. Co.

Elderly people in Danvers well remember the two daughters of Dr. Putnam, Hannah and Betsey. They kept a private school to which the children were generally sent. Many are the anecdotes told of their discipline and management. Among their scholars was the Rev. A. P. Putnam. A memorial shaft over their graves in the Wadsworth cemetery has recently been erected by their former pupils.

VI. 734 Andrew (*Edmund, John, Nathaniel, John*), born at Salem Village, 15 Jan., 1750–1; died in New York City, about 1785; administration granted to Israel Putnam, 3d, 16 Nov., 1785; married, 1 Sept., 1774, Mary, daughter of Col. Jeremiah and Sarah (Andrew) Page of Danvers, born 9 Sept., 1755. She married, second, Benjamin Kent.

---

[125] A descendant of Roger Conant and Henry Herrick.

Children :

1772 HULDAH, m. 28 Jan., 1802, John, son of William and Elizabeth
(Girdler) Hines, b. 1775; d. 26 Oct., 1811. Ch.: Mary, b.
30 Sept., d. 21 Oct., 1802. John, b. 7 Nov., 1803; d. 8 Mar.,
1885; m. Hannah B. Dodge; the father of Ezra Dodge Hines,
Asst. Registrar of Probate for Essex Co. William, b. 8 Aug.,
1805; d. 19 Jan., 1806. William, b. 17 Jan., 1808. [126]

1773 ISRAEL, b. 2 June, 1777; d. 8 Sept., 1860.

1774 ANDREW, d., unm., prev. to 1834.

ANDREW PUTNAM had rather a chequered career. He was
occasionally in office from 1778–1780, but in 1782 got into a
law dispute with Dr. Endicott and finally left Danvers, going
to New York. He seems to have made some pretensions to
practising medicine. Pynchon's diary gives some interesting
facts concerning "Dr. Andrew Putnam." He owned land in
Danvers and Marblehead. He was possibly the Andrew
Putnam who was commissioned captain, 24 Apr., 1778, of
the 7th company, 8th Essex regiment Mass. Militia.

VI. 735 Israel (*Edmund, John, John, Nathaniel,
John*), born in Salem Village, 20 Nov., 1754; died in Dan-
vers, Aug., 1820; married 8 July, 1788, Anna, daughter of
Elias and Eunice (Andrew) Endicott.

Children :

1775 ELIAS, b. 7 June, 1789; d. 8 July, 1847.

1776 JOEL. b. 2 Aug., 1791; d. 30 Apr., 1803.

1777 NANCY, b. 30 Oct., 1795; m. Nathaniel Boardman. Ch.: Israel
Putnam, b. 16 Apr., 1817; d. 1876. Mr. Boardman m., 2d,
Anna, dau. of David Putnam (No. 939).

1778 ALDEN, b. 2 Nov., 1801; d. 14 Apr., 1803.

1779 MARY, b. 2 Sept., 1804; d. s. p., Manchester, N. H.; m. Israel, son
of Israel and Betsey (Rea) Endicott, b. at Danvers, 20 Nov.,
1799; d. in Wolfboro, N. H.

ISRAEL PUTNAM, says the *Essex Register*, Salem, Mass.,
announcing his death, "was a highly respected and worthy
citizen," a pure and upright man, he was withal of a very de-
vout spirit. He embraced the Universalist views which his
father had accepted. He headed, April 22, 1815, a list of

[126] For a very interesting account of the Hines family, see Salem Press Historical
and Genealogical Record for October, 1891.

27

names, twenty-four in all, which were appended to a paper organizing those who signed it into the First Universalist Society of Danvers. In furtherance of the object to establish stated preaching of the doctrine which they professed, the subscribers, with other friends, met six days later, on the 28th, at the Brick School House, District No. 3, in which most of them lived, whereupon Mr. Putnam was chosen Moderator and Treasurer, with Warren Porter as Clerk; and measures were adopted to engage the services of ministers and to raise money to defray the necessary expenses. Rev. Edward Turner and other clergymen of the faith had already, in previous years, preached in the School House from time to time; but now there came to be a more regular supply, Rev. Hosea Ballou and Rev. (afterward Hon.) Charles Hudson and other noted men occupying the desk. Thus early, Universalism was established in Danvers. Mr. Putnam, it is believed, occasionally read to the little knot of believers certain sermons which he himself wrote, out of his deep interest in the new movement and the views which it was designed to propagate. One or more of these he printed in pamphlet form and circulated in the neighborhood. One of them was a discourse, entitled "Universal Death in Adam and Life in Christ, containing a Refutation of the Doctrine of Total Depravity and Endless Misery," (1817), and was a very well written and ably reasoned production. Though the sermon was marked with admirable temper, it called forth a scurrilous printed rejoinder from a Mr. Dole, one or two other publications on either side giving the continued discussion of the subject.

About the time Mr. Putnam died, the little society lost another of its highly esteemed and greatly beloved members, Mr. Joseph Porter. Rev. Barzillai Streeter preached and printed a sermon, occasioned by the death of these two excellent Christian men, in which he paid a fitting tribute to their noble characters and to the brave and decided stand which they had taken for the cause of religious liberty, as against the oppressive creeds and Parish Rate System which had been in vogue. Mr. Putnam was a conscientious and thoughtful man, much venerated by all who knew him, specially devoted to religious matters, and exceptionally familiar with the Scriptures. His wife was a remarkably bright, intelligent and interesting person, strongly marked by the characteristics of the family whence she sprang. Both were interred in the old Burial Ground at the Plains.

VI. 737 Edmund (*Edmund, John, John, Nathaniel, John*), born in Danvers, 15 Jan., 1772; died in Beverly, 26 Mar., 1828; married in Beverly, 19 Oct.,[127] 1795, Martha, daughter of William, junior, and Hannah Trask of Beverly, baptized 23 June, 1776, died 19 Jan., 1811. He married, second, 19 Sept., 1813, Sarah Choate, who died 1843. He was a trader in Beverly.

Children, born in Beverly :

1780 WILLIAM, b. 7 Sept., 1796; d. 4 Mar., 1848; of Beverly.

1781 SARAH, b. 20 Feb., 1798; d. 5 June, 1829; m. 21 Dec., 1819, Robert G. Bennett (whose first wife was Hannah, dau. of Benjamin and Emma Low, b. 1790, d. 10 July, 1818). Ch.: Hannah, b. 13 Oct., 1820.

1782 EDMUND, b. in Beverly, 24 Jan., 1800; d. 9 May, 1872.

1783 JOHN, b. 17 June, 1802.

1784 MARTHA, b. 4 June, 1804; m. Jacob Edwards. Ch.: Jacob. Martha A. Hannah. Edmund. Sarah.

1785 HANNAH, b. 28 May, 1806; m. Ebenr, son of Ebenr and Lydia (Rea) Smith, b. in Beverly, 12 Oct., 1804. Ch.: Ebenezer, b. 27 Sept., d. 11 Nov., 1832. Hannah Putnam, b. 27 July, 1834. Eliza, b. 8 Sept., d. 7 Nov., 1836. Charles F., b. 10, d. 28 July, 1838. Charles F., b. 24 June, 1839. Eliza P., b. 6 Aug., 1841; d. 21 Apr., 1842. Ellen, b. 20 June, 1843. Albert, b. 30 Sept., 1845. Maria.

1786 ELIZABETH, b. 1 Oct , 1808; m. 20 Sept., 1828, William, son of William and Mehitable Elliott, b. in Beverly, 24 Dec , 1804, d. 18 Jan., 1831. Ch.: Emma. Elizabeth.

1787 MARY ANN, b. 15 Sept., 1810; d. 21 Nov., 1873; m. 4 Apr., 1830, William Ellingwood, son of John Porter and Desire (Wellman) Webber, b. 22 Mar., 1807, d. 23 Feb., 1874.' Ch.: William Ellingwood, b. 18 Jan., d. 24 Mar., 1831. Mary C., b. 27 May, 1832. Ellen M., b. 19 Apr., 1834; d. 17 Apr., 1835. Sarah E , b. 20 Mar., 1836. Martha Jane, b. 29 Mar., 1838. William Porter, b. 15 Oct., 1841. Edmund Putnam, b. 26 Aug., 1843. Ellen, living in 1880. Charles Henry, b. 30 Mar., 1845. Georgianna Putnam, living in 1880.

[127] Or July 26th?

VI. 740 Jacob[128] (*Amos, Amos, John, Nathaniel, John*), born in New Salem, 2 Nov., 1758; died there; married Sally, daughter of Daniel Putnam. He married, second, at New Salem, 27 Dec., 1787, Rebecca Patrick of Western now Warren.

Child, by first marriage:

1788 SAMUEL.

Children, by second marriage:

1789 SALLY, m. ——— Boyce of Blanford; two sons.
1790 TRUISSA, m. Jonathan Gregory of New Salem.
1791 MELISSA, d. y.
1792 STILLMAN.
1793 MELVIN.

VI. 745 Aaron (*Amos, Amos, John, Nathaniel, John*), born in New Salem, 19 July, 1773; died at Houlton, Me., 13 Feb., 1849; married at New Salem, 16 Jan., 1794, Isa Patrick of Western, sister of Mrs. Jacob Putnam (No. 740). Mrs. Putnam previous to her marriage was a school teacher, she died at Houlton, June, 1867.

Children:

1794 AMOS, b. in New Salem, Oct., 1794; d. 29 Dec., 1849.
1795 JAY STILLMAN, b. in New Salem, 9 June, 1803; d. 5 Aug., 1880.
1796 LYSANDER, b. in Woodstock, N. B., 27 Dec., 1806; d. 27 Sept., 1886.
1797 AARON RANDOLPH, b. in Houlton, 30 July, 1813; d. about 1874; m. 1840, Maria Burleigh of Houlton. They removed to Illinois in 1854 and both died, the wife one year after the husband, leaving no children.

AARON PUTNAM bought one-eighth of the grant to New Salem Academy in Maine and in 1805 in company with other pioneers settled Houlton. The other purchasers of this grant were, John and Joshua Putnam each one-tenth, Varney Pierce, Joseph Houlton, Rufus Cowles, John Chamberlain, William Bowman, Consider Hastings, Thomas Powers.

The grant was in disputed territory, claimed by both the United States and Great Britain so that the early settlers took great risks in purchasing of the Massachusetts party.

[128] The records of New Salem previous to 1857 were mostly destroyed by fire.

The early settlers lived in log cabins and were satisfied with the simplest of food, dress and utensils, while the farm was being cleared. Then came a frame house, easier communication with the outer world, and soon one was as comfortable in northeastern Maine as in western Massachusetts. Previous to 1813 Aaron Putnam had erected a saw mill and it was in that year that the frame house commenced to supersede the log cabin.

During the early settlement and until after the war of 1812, the families in town were few. Aaron Putnam, his wife and family, his mother, his brother Joshua's family, the Rices, Shaws, Houltons, all connections and all determined to stick. The suffering from cold and scarcity of provisions some years was great. During the year 1813 deserters from the British garrison across the river were frequently in town, and generally the settlers helped their escape, although having no means of defense they were at the mercy of the British and so forced to be neutral.

Mrs. Putnam once dared a provost's guard to enter her house where a deserter was rocking the cradle in plain sight, and where he remained in safety until a suitable opportunity opened for his escape.

The early settlers reached Houlton by sailing from Boston to the mouth of the Saint John River, then up the river to Frederickton. Here they embarked in small craft and proceeded as far as Woodstock; there the families remained while young men went to prepare a bridle path to the settlement. The first visit to Houlton by Mr. Putnam and Mr. Houlton was in 1804, at which time they were nearly lost in the forest.

When, in 1836, the Unitarian movement reached Houlton, Aaron Putnam gave the land for the church, and his sons, the Pearce family and the Houlton "connection" contributed the funds.

In the "Story of Houlton," Mr. Francis Barnes, lately deceased, has told the sufferings and successes of the pioneers in a most interesting manner. To him I am indebted for most of the material concerning the descendants of Amos Putnam who settled in Maine.

VI. 746 John (*Joshua, Amos, John, Nathaniel, John*), born in New Salem, 2 Nov., 1762; died there, 13 Jan., 1827; married there, Sally, daughter of Isaac and Sally Rich of New Salem, who was born in New Salem, 4 Mar., 1765, and died in Houlton, Me., 25 Mar., 1852. John Putnam was captain in the second regiment Massachusetts Militia.

Children, born in New Salem :

1798 JOSHUA, b. 3 Mar., 1794; d. 21 June, 1873.

1799 EUNICE, b. 20 May, 1796; d. in Amity, Me., 20 May, 1845; m. Capt. James Ballard of Amherst, Mass.

1800 JOHN VARNUM, b. 4 Aug., 1802; died 21 April, 1879.

1801 SALLY, m. John Sawin of Wendall and Cambridge, Mass.

1802 ESTHER, d. aged about 15 years.

VI. 748 Joshua (*Joshua, Amos, John, Nathaniel, John*), born in New Salem, 8 Feb., 1772; died in Houlton, Me., 14 June, 1835;[129] married Oct., 1796, Betsey Baker of Bakersfield, Vt.

Children :

1803 ROMANE LYNDES, b. in New Salem, 30 June, 1798 (according to Bowdoin College record, 20 June, 1799); d., unm., in Australia, subsequent to 1863. Entered Bowdoin with class of 1829 but never graduated. Went to California and in 1852 to Australia.

1804 STERNE, b. 6 June, 1800; d. Aug., 1881.

1805 FANNY, b. 27 Sept., 1802; d. 6 Jan., 1829; unm.

1806 MARIA. b. 30 May, 1805; d. 2 Mar., 1806.

1807 JAMES BAKER, b. 9 May, 1807.

1808 JOHN, b. in New Salem, 26 Sept., 1809; d. 11 Aug., 1831, while in school at Limerick.

1809 JOSEPH B., b. in New Salem, 1 Oct., 1811; d. in Houlton, Me., 25 Mar., 1829.

1810 FRANKLIN, b. in Houlton, Me., 16 May, 1814.

1811 HARRIET, b. 12 July. 1817; d., unm., 21 Nov., 1860.

JOSHUA PUTNAM moved with his family from New Salem to Houlton, Me., about 1812. He was a thick set, strongly built man; with large broad features; but his wife was some-

---

[129] Another authority gives his death as occurring in Feb., 1834.

what less than average stature. During the winter of 1817, which was unusually severe, it is recorded that for six weeks there was not a morsel of bread in the house. The people in the settlement lived upon salmon.

VI. 750 Daniel (*Uzziel, Amos, John, Nathaniel, John*), born in New Salem; died there; married there, 20 June, 1789, Mary Putnam of New Salem.

Children, born in New Salem :

1812 VERLINA, m. previous to 1837.
1813 SUMNER, m. previous to 1837. Did he remove to Claremont, N. H.? See No. 1824.
1814 SALLY, b. 16 Nov., 1795; d. of paralysis, at New Salem, 18 Jan , 1865, unm.
1815 TARRANT, b. Feb., 1801.
1816 VARNEY.
1817 DANIEL, d. about 1800.
1818 ISRAEL.

VI. 751 Samuel (*Uzziel, Amos, John, Nathaniel, John*), of New Salem, born there, Oct., 1767; died Jan., 1850; married Hepzibah Pierce of New Salem, who died Sept., 1844.

He bought the mills at Orange of Joseph Putnam, which were destroyed by fire in 1815, but rebuilt by Samuel and his sons.

Children :

1819 WILLIAM, b. in New Salem, 7 July, 1792.
1820 JOHN, b. in New Salem, 2 Sept., 1794.

VI. 752 Major Joseph (*Uzziel, Amos, John, Nathaniel, John*), born in New Salem, 18 Oct., 1773; died in Orange, Jan., 1812; married, 1796, Hannah Kellogg, born 29 May, 1777.

Owned mills in Orange which passed into possession of Daniel and Samuel Putnam. Joseph, William and John Putnam were successively proprietors of the hotel at Orange.

Children :

1881   UZZIEL, b. 5 Sept., 1797.

1822   POLLY, b. 25 Mar., 1800; d. at Athol, 3 June, 1866, unm. Was in the millinery business in Boston and Athol. Buried in North Orange.

1823   JOSEPH WARREN, b. 14 Aug., 1802; lost at sea; unm.

1824   HANNAH, b. 2 May, 1805; d. 1 Apr., 1869; m., 1st, [120] —— Essick; m., 2d, her cousin Sumner Putnam (No. 1813), who died in Claremont, N. H.

1825   EXPERIENCE, b. 7 July, 1807; d. 16 Aug., 1809.

1826   BENJAMIN GANSON, b. 9 Feb., 1810; d. 19 July, 1877.

1827   JOSEPH KELLOGG, b. 10 May, 1812; d. 21 Jan., 1866.

VI. 753 Uzziel (*Uzziel, Amos, John, Nathaniel, John*), born in New Salem. Living at Popagon, Mich., in 1834.

Children:

1828   UZZIEL (Hon.), of Popagon, Mich.

1829   JOHN.

1830   ORLAN.

1831   ANNA, m. Dr. Leeden.

1832   ZILPHA.

There were other children.

VI. 756 Daniel (*Daniel, Amos, John, Nathaniel, John*), born in Danvers, 3 Oct., 1762; died in Newbury, Vt., 19 Dec., 1802; married 27 Jan., 1789, Sarah, daughter of Joseph and Sarah (Porter) Putnam, born 5 Feb., 1765 and died 13 Feb., 1834.

Children :

1833   BETSEY, b. 22 Jan., 1791; d. 29 Aug., 1791.

1834   DANIEL, b. 9 Jan., 1792.

1835   BETSEY, b. 12 May, 1794; m. 10 Oct., 1816, Michael Carlton, b. 4 Nov., 1793. Ch.: Michael, b. 13 Aug., 1817. Sally Putnam, b. 18 Mar., 1819. Mehitable B., b. 10 Dec., 1820. Betsey, b. 17 July, 1824. Martha and Mercy, b. 30 June, 1827. Harriet N., b. 30 June, 1830. Horace D., b. 5 May, 1833.

1836   JOEL, b. 28 July, 1796.

1837   SALLY, b. 17 Mar., 1800; m. 27 Aug., 1823, Dudley C. Kimball, b. 21 Nov., 1800. Ch.: Daniel Putnam, b. 25 July, 1824. Joseph Porter, b. 10 Jan., 1826. Charles, b. 5 Nov., 1827. Mehitable, b. 3 Feb., 1832.

[120] According to Mr. James M. Crafts, to whom I am indebted for many dates, Bial Smith

VI. 760 Amos (*Daniel, Amos, John, Nathaniel, John*), born in Danvers, 11 Oct., 1778; died in New Salem, 19 Jan., 1867 (family record has it 16 Jan); married at New Salem, Jan., 1806, Lydia, daughter of Varney and Hannah (Putnam) Pearce of New Salem, born there, 17 Feb., 1782 and died there, 3 June, 1815. He married, second, Mrs. Rhoda (Childs) Smith, who died in New Salem, 13 Apr., 1873, aet. 84 years, 3 mos., 8 days. She was born in New Salem, and was the daughter of David and Lydia (Hemenway) Childs.

Mr. Putnam was a farmer in New Salem, whence he had removed from Danvers. He and his children had dark hair and black eyes. In middle age weighed about 190 lbs.

Children :

1838   SAMUEL ~~VARNEY~~, b. in Danvers, 9 Nov., 1806. *d. May 30, 1911*

1839   MELISSA, b. in New Salem, 7 Sept., 1808; m. 29 Mar., 1829, Robert Cook of New Salem. Living (1890) in Cambridgeport. *d. 1898*

1840   ELIZABETH, b. in New Salem, 7 Dec., 1810; m. 30 Oct., 1837, Frederick Kellogg of Orange.

1841   DANIEL VARNEY, b. in New Salem, 9 Oct., 1813; d., *s. p* , 18 Dec., 1883; m. Oct., 1836, Cleopatra Bryant. They lived in New Salem where Mr. Putnam carried on a farm. He was selectman nine years. He was 5 ft. 7 in. tall, 190 lbs., and had brown hair and eyes.

VI. 762 Nathaniel (*Jacob, Nathaniel, Benjamin, Nathaniel, John*), born in Danvers, 24 April, 1738; died in Wilton, N. H., 20 May, 1790; married 2 Dec., 1762, Mary Eastman of Hampstead, N. H., who died 28 Dec., 1777. He married, second, 17 Sept., 1778, Phebe[131] Snow, who married, second, 18 Jan., 1795, Jonas Thayer of Heath.

Children, born in Wilton, N. H. :

1842   PETER, b. 29 Nov., 1763.

1843   ELIPHALET, b. 23 Jan., 1766; d. 24 or 25 Feb., 1826.

1844   JONATHAN, b. 1 Dec., 1767; d. 29 Sept., 1770.

1845   JONATHAN, b. 29 July, 1770; d. 27 Oct.. 1839.

1846   ELIZABETH, b. 25 Apr., 1772; d. 9 Dec., 1845; m. 22 Feb., 1798, Joseph, son of Joseph and Molly (Ritter) Dodge, of Shirley and Hancock, N. H. Ch. : Joseph, held many important political

---

[131] According to Kendrick S. Putnam, Mary Snow.

offices. Nathaniel of Boston, m. a sister of the late Gov. Gilmore of N. H. Persis, m. John P. Beckwith. Mary, m. Ebenezer Hutchinson. Eliza, m. Hugh Gilmore, brother of Gov.
Gilmore. Parentha, m. Warner Hutchinson.

1847 PHILIP, b. 15 Mar., 1775.

1848 MARY, b. 18 Sept., 1777; living in 1885 at Andover, Vt., unm.

Children, by second marriage :

1849 PHEBE SNOW, b. 27 June, 1779; d. 14 Dec., 1786.

1850 HANNAH, b. 24 Oct., 1780; d. 29 May, 1854; m. 30 Nov., 1797, Selah
Severance of Heath. Thirteen ch., eight living in 1876, one of
whom was Mr. Lorenzo Severance of E. Sherburne, Mass.

1851 CALVIN, b. in Wilton, N. H., 8 June, 1782; d. 9 May, 1857.

1852 ABIGAIL FOX, b. in Wilton, 9 July, 1785; d. 7 Aug., 1846; m. David
Kinsman of Heath. Twelve children.

VI. 764 Stephen (*Jacob*, *Nathaniel*, *Benjamin*,
Nathaniel, *John*), born in Salem Village, 24 Sept., 1744;
died in Rumford, Me., 29 June, 1812; married Olive Varnum, born in Dracut, 7 Mar., 1742.

Children, mostly born at Temple, N. H. :

1853 STEPHEN, b. 31 Aug., 1765.

1854 OLIVE, b. 2 Oct., 1766; m. 17 July, 1797, Samuel Hinkson. No
children.

1855 SAMUEL, b. 29 May, 1768.

1856 ESTHER, b. 23 Apr., 1770; d. y.

1857 MARY, b. 10 Apr., 1772; m. 20 Sept., 1794, Robert Hinkson of Rumford, Me., who m., 2d, in 1815, Sally, widow of Nathan Silver.
Ch.: Polly, b. 7 Sept., 1795. Patty, b. 1 Mar., 1797. Robert,
b. 17 June, 1798. Sally, b. 1 Oct., 1799. Sullivan, b. 29 Aug.,
1801; d. 24 May, 1809. John, b. 31 Apr., 1803. Esther and
Rachel, b. 9 Jan., 1805. Daniel, b. 7 Nov., 1807. Phebe, b. 19
Nov., 1808. Lewis, b. 18 Apr., 1813. (For further particulars
see History of Rumford, Me., by W. B. Lapham.)

1858 ELIZABETH, b. 11 July, 1774; d. in Upper Canada; m., 1798, John
Puffer of Society. Ch. : John. Betsey. Seth. Pamelia. Prudence. Lavina. Daniel. Jacob. Zilphia.

1859 ISRAEL, b. 31 Mar., 1776.

1860 ABIGAIL, b. 6 Mar., 1778; m. Isaac Newton. Ch.: Israel, b. 5
Dec., 1802. Olive, b. 25 Dec., 1804. Galen, b. 31 Aug., 1805.
Isaac, b. 25 Jan., 1807. Phila, b. 26 Oct., 1808. David, b. 28
May, 1810. Jacob, b. 21 Jan., 1811. Stephen, b. 3 July, 1814.
Lydia, b. 10 Sept., 1815. Abigail, b. 6 July, 1817. Vianna, b.
1 Aug., 1819. Rosanna, b. 9 Mar., 1821. Cyrus, b. 18 Sept.,
1823.

1861 RACHEL, b. 28 Feb., 1780; d. inf.

1862 JACOB HARRIMAN, b. 28 Dec., 1781; d. inf.
1863 RUTH, b. 25 Sept., 1783; m. 14 July, 1810, Matthias Puffer. Ch.:
      Ruth, b. 1 Oct., 1810; m. Joseph Hinkson of No. 10.

STEPHEN PUTNAM bought a farm in Temple, which adjoins Wilton and Lyndeboro, N. H., and there settled. He
built a grist mill there. In 1776 he signed the Association
Test, but in June, 1777, he with others was obliged to show
cause why they should not be considered unfriendly to the
new government. His answer satisfied the meeting. Shortly
after the Revolution he moved to Rumford, Me., where his
son Stephen had already settled. Here also he built a mill
and became quite an influential person. He had great mechanical ability, in fact was a "Jack at all trades."

VI. 765 Col. Philip (*Jacob, Nathaniel, Benjamin,
Nathaniel, John*), born Mar., 1742 (according to the His-
tory of Wilton, born 4 Mar., 1740); died in Wilton, N. H.,
10 Oct., 1810 (Hist. of Wilton, 18 Nov.); married, first,
19 June, 1764, Abigail Jaquith, who died 4 Sept., 1765.
He married, second, 10 Jan., 1767, Hannah Jacques, born 7
July, 1741, and died in Wilton, 22 Sept., 1819 (History of
Wilton, 1829).

Child, born in Wilton:

1864 ABIGAIL, b. 28 July, 1765; d. 29 Aug., 1765.

Children, by second wife:

1865 ABIGAIL, b. 1 Sept., 1767; d. in Wilton, 6 May, 1831; m. 8 July,
      1789, Hon. Abiel Wilson, b. in Andover, 1760, and d. in Wilton,
      N. H., 26 July, 1824. Ch : Abiel, b. 7 Apr., 1790. Putnam, b.
      9 Oct., 1791. James, b. 24 Nov., 1793; d. 21 Aug., 1796. James,
      b. 4 Dec., 1796. Abigail, b. 8 Jan., 1799: d. 4 Jan., 1831. Han-
      nah, b. 10 June, 1801. Inf. dau., b. 29 Apr., d. 30 Apr., 1803.
      Inf. dau., b. 29 Apr., d. 16 May, 1803. Joseph, b. 3 June, 1804.
      John, b. 19 May, 1806; d. 26 Mar., 1852. Philip, b. 8 Feb.,
      1809; d. 31 Jan., 1810. (See Hist. of Wilton, N. H., for further
      particulars.)
1866 HANNAH, b. 16 Apr., 1769; m. Samuel, son of Major Jonathan and
      Huldah (Nichols, from Middleton, Mass.)Burton of Wilton, b.
      8 Apr., 1767. They, in company with their brother Jonathan
      Putnam, settled in Andover, Vt.
1867 RACHEL, b. 9 Feb., 1771; d. in Wilton, unm., 30 Sept., 1793.

1868 SARAH. b. 20 Aug., 1773 (13 Jan., Hist. of Wilton); d. 26 Nov., 1838; m. as his second wife, Rev. Abel Fiske, who was b. in Pepperell, Mass., 28 May, 1752, and d. in Wilton, N. H., 21 Apr. 1802. Ch.: Theophilus, b. 4 Dec., 1801.

1869 PHILIP, b. 13 Jan., 1781; d. in Wilton, N. H., 22 June, 1834.

COL. PHILIP PUTNAM served in the French and Indian War, and in the Revolution commanded a company mustered 26 Sept., 1776, for three months service, at the battle of White Plains; he also served one month at Saratoga in 1777. His title of colonel was obtained in the militia.

He was selectman three years, and represented Wilton in the state legislature for nearly a score of years.

He was an exceedingly prosperous farmer and for many years one of the three largest tax payers in Wilton.

The following Putnams, resident in Wilton in April, 1776, signed the non-intercourse resolutions of New Hampshire: Philip Putnam, Jacob Putnam, Caleb Putnam, Nathaniel Putnam and Jacob Putnam, junior.

VI. 766 Joseph *(Jacob, Nathaniel, Benjamin, Nathaniel, John)*, born in Wilton, N. H., 28 Feb. (28 July, History of Hancock), 1744; died in Marshfield, Vt., 17 Nov., 1826; married, in spring of 1763, Miriam Hamblett, of Wilton, who died in Marshfield, 12 Feb., 1836.

Children :[132]

1870 JOSEPH, b. in Wilton, N. H., 6 Dec., 1763.

1871 MIRIAM, b. in Wilton, N. H., 21 Jan., 1766; d. in Temple, N. H., 20 Mar., 1777.

1872 JOEL, b. in Wilton, 19 June, 1768; d. 21 June, 1769.

1873 GIDEON. b. in Wilton, 26 Mar., 1769; d. 8 June, 1769.

1874 HANNAH, b. in Temple, 18 May, 1770; m. Thomas, son of Thomas and Alice Boynton, of Hancock, N. H. Mr. Boynton was a teacher; he d. in Washington, Vt., 18 Aug., 1847.

1875 SARAH, b. in Temple, 17 Mar., 1773; m. 28 Feb., 1799, John Spaulding, b. in Lyndeborough, 1 Sept., 1772, d. in Marlow, 28 Aug., 1866; lived also in Warner, Hancock and Alstead. Ch.:

[132] In regard to the dates of birth and death of the Wilton branch, I have generally followed the MSS. of Perley Putnam, who had frequent communication with the Wilton families, the early part of this century. The History of Wilton differs occasionally. See also History of Hancock.

(Rev.) John, b. 30 June, 1804. (Doctor) Nehemiah, of Nashua, Iowa. Sally, d. y. Rachel, d. y. Betsey, b. 11 Dec., 1806. Joseph Putnam, b. 13 Oct., 1809; d. in Leominster, 18 April, 1880.

1876 MEHITABLE, b. in Temple, 4 Apr., 1775.

1877 GIDEON, b. in Temple, 26 May, 1777.

1878 SUSANNAH, b. in Temple, 1779.

1879 MARY, b. in Temple, 1781.

1880 JACOB, b. in Society Land, 18 Mar., 1784.

1881 ELIZABETH, b. in Society Land, 2 Oct., 1786; d. in Montpelier. Vt., 2 Dec., 1831; m. 15 Mar., 1810, Joseph Barnes of Litchfield, who d. in Milford, N. H., Mar., 1862. They lived in Goffstown, N. H., Marshfield, Vt. (1816), and Montpelier. Ch.: Louisa, b. 17 Apr., 1811. Charles E., b. 2 June, 1812; of Boston, inventor. Laurinda, b. 27 Apr., 1814. William, b. 13 Sept., 1816. Lenora, b. 19 Aug., 1818. Lucy P., b. 14 Sept., 1820. Lucinda, b. 1822. Joseph K., b. Sept. 1829.

JOSEPH PUTNAM had a fair complexion, brown hair and blue eyes; of medium height (5 ft. 10 in), firmly built, broad shoulders; he had an iron constitution. Of temperate habits, just in his dealings, of a progressive mind, and great firmness and steadfastness of character, he was beloved by his family and admired by his neighbors. Throughout his his life he adhered to the old style of dress.

He built his house, which is still standing, remodeled and moved from the original site, in Society Land, where now stands the Bennington Hotel. He built the first bridge across the river at this point, and it was long known as Putnam's bridge. Between 1782–9 he bought nearly the whole of the site of the present village of Bennington, and owned the water power of the falls on the Contoocook. In 1794, his estate was detached from Society Land and attached to Hancock.

In an account written by E. D. Putnam, of his grandfather Joseph, he tells of the first settlement in Temple on a piece of land deeded to him by his father, situated in what had been formerly Wilton.

There Hannah was born, and the succeeding five children. At that time that country was but sparsely peopled and Mr. E. D. Putnam states that his grandfather often related to him tales of the early times : how the wolves would render night terrible with their howling and how on account of the the bears and wolves it was necessary to shut up the sheep nightly.

The stream now called Whiting's Brook was then known as Putnam's Brook, and there Joseph erected the second grist mill built in Temple. In 1782 he abandoned that situation and located at the great falls on the Contoocook, and erected a saw and grist mill, buying land on both sides of the river, completely controlling the water power. His land was in 1794 annexed to Hancock. Repeated offers were made him to sell but he refused until 1804, when he removed to a farm in Alstead, and, feeling that the time was passed when he should labor, called his son Gideon to carry on the farm, and later Jacob. Upon the latter moving to Marshfield, Vt., in 1820, his parents accompanied him and died there.

He belonged to the church of England, later the American Episcopal church.

VI. 768 Jacob *(Jacob, Nathaniel, Benjamin, Nathaniel, John)*, born in Wilton, N. H., 15 Nov., 1747 ; died in Wilton, N. H., 2 June, 1821 ; married there, 1770, Abigail Burnap, who died there, 10 June, 1812. He married, second, 1813, Mrs. Lucy Spofford, of Temple, N. H.

Children,[133] born in Wilton :

1882 JACOB, b. 4 Oct., 1771.
1883 ABIGAIL, b. 29 Apr., 1773 ; d., unm., at Wilton, 20 Feb., 1827.
1884 JOHN, b. 24 Nov., 1774 ; d. 16 Feb., 1835.
1885 CALEB, b. 7 Oct., 1776 ; d. 17 Nov., 1777.
1886 CALEB, b. 24 Mar , 1779 ; d. Sept., 1862.
1887 RUTH, b. 20 Jan., 1781 ; d. 7 Aug., 1801, unm.
1888 EDITH, b. 21 Feb., 1783 ; m. —— Cooper, of Francestown, N. H.

VI. 769 Archelaus *(Jacob, Nathaniel, Benjamin, Nathaniel, John)*, born in Wilton, N. H., 15 Oct., 1749 ; died in Chester, Vt., 22 Oct., 1816 ; married Mary Nichols, of Danvers, Mass.

[133] The records of Temple give "Jacob, of Jacob and Mehitable Putnam, d. 29 June, 1772. Mehitable, do., d. 29 Aug., 1775."

Children, all but the two youngest, born in Wilton :

1889   ARCHELAUS, b. 11 June, 1776.
1890   ANNA, b. 26 Oct., 1777; m. 8 July, 1798, William Thompson, Jr.
1891   MARY, b. 19 July, 1779; m. Abijah Allen.
1892   SUSANNA, b. 14 Jan., 1781; m. Timothy Thompson.
1893   HULDAH, b. 10 May, 1782; m. 12 Feb., 1809, Joseph Williams.
1894   AMY, b. 2 June, 1784; m. 7 Feb., 1809, Nathan Whitman.
1895   PETER, b. 26 Dec., 1785.
1896   ABIGAIL ELLIOT, b. 8 July, 1787; m. Jonathan Ransom.
1897   SALLY, m. Henry Edwards.
1898   SAMUEL, b. 1 May, 1789.
1899   BETSEY, b. in Andover, Vt., 1793; m. Charles Wolf.
1900   LYDIA, b. 11 Feb., 1796; m. 3 Feb., 1823, John Pierce.

ARCHELAUS PUTNAM lived with his father in Wilton until the latter's death in 1781, and then, selling out to Lt. Oliver Whiting of Temple (1790), he removed to Andover and erected some mills. From Andover he removed, about 1800, to Chester, Vt.

He was one of the two inhabitants of Wilton who refused to sign the non-intercourse resolutions of April, 1776, and in 1780 was fined £10 "for not doing his turn in the war."

VI. 770 Caleb *(Jacob, Nathaniel, Benjamin, Nathaniel, John),* born in Wilton, N. H., 10 March, 1751; died before Fort Ticonderoga, 22 or 27 August, 1776; married Amy ———, who married, second, 30 Nov., 1778, Ebenezer Pearson, of Duxbury School Farm.

Child :

1901   A DAU, who was living in 1776.

CALEB PUTNAM, in a deed from John Cram, is styled "blacksmith." He served in Captain Taylor's company at Winter Hill, and was in Captain Barron's company in the Ticonderoga expedition. His brother Peter also died at Ticonderoga.

VI. 774 Archelaus *(Archelaus, Nathaniel, Benjamin, Nathaniel, John),* born in Danvers, 6 Nov., 1740; died there 14 April, 1800 (gravestone); married at Danvers, 1761, Abigail Goodrich.

Archelaus Putuam was known as "junior." He held many town offices.

Children, born in Danvers :

1902 ABIGAIL, bapt. 15 May, 1763; m. ——— Trask, of Danvers. Ch.: Samuel. Mary, m. Joseph Porter, of Danvers. Sarah.

1903 ARCHELAUS, b. 16 Jan , 1762.

1904 CALEB, b. 24 Nov., 1763: settled in Newburyport, but was, perhaps, a resident of Danvers in 1833. It is possible his descendants are to be found in the South.

1905 LYDIA. b. 25 Oct., 1765; m. James S. Parker and settled in Wilton, N. H. Ch.: Lydia. Abigail. James Swan, d. prev. to 1835. Hepzibah Ruggles. Nancy. William.

1906 MEHITABLE, bapt. 6 Dec., 1767.

1907 MARY, m. Capt. John, son of John and Martha (Putnam) Endicott, of Salem. b. in Danvers, 13 Jan., 1765, and d. there 29 Nov., 1834. He m., 2d, Mrs. Fidelia (Bridges) Kettelle, by whom he had four children. Ch., by Mary: John, b. Nov., 1791; d. Apr., 1808. Samuel, b. 26 Oct., 1793. Maria Cecilia, b. 20 Jan., 1798; m. John Gardner. George Washington. b. 15 Jan., 1800. Martha, b. 17 Jan., 1803; d. Nov., 1816. John, b 19 May, 1805.

VI. 776 Ephraim *(Archelaus, Nathaniel, Benjamin, Nathaniel, John)*, born in Danvers, 14 Sept., 1744; died in Lyndeborough, N. H., 11 May, 1821; married, autumn of 1768, Rachel Cram, born 16 April, 1746 and died 29 April, 1833.

Children, born in Lyndeborough, N. H. :

1908 JONATHAN, b. 14 Sept., 1769; d. 27 Sept., 1843.

1909 MEHITABLE, b. 6 Dec., 1772; m. 20 Feb., 1801, Robert Ritchie, who d. 17 Nov., 1832. Ch.: Mary, b. 7 Sept., 1804.

1910 ARCHELAUS, b. 16 Mar., 1775; d., unm., Feb., 1839.

1911 EPHRAIM, b. 7 Jan., 1778; d. 20 Feb., 1785.

1912 ABIJAH, b. 30 Nov., 1780; d. 16 Feb., 1785.

1913 EPHRAIM, b. 30 Apr., 1785; d. 11 June, 1862.

1914 NATHANIEL, b. 22 Aug., 1788; unm., in 1834.

1915 AMOS, b. 21 July, 1791; d. 1794.

EPHRAIM PUTNAM was always known as "Danvers" Ephraim, thus distinguishing him from two others in Lyndeborough bearing the same names. He represented Lyndeborough in a convention of deputies which met in 1775, and was generally active in town affairs. In 1834, eight male Putnams, descended from him, were living in Lyndeborough.

VI. 777 Nathaniel *(Archelaus, Nathaniel, Benjamin, Nathaniel, John)*, born in Danvers, 17 May, 1746; died 5 Nov., 1800; married in Beverly, 11 Feb., 1773, Mary Ober, who died 3 Jan., 1788. He married, second, 10 Dec., 1788, Ruth Butler, of Essex, born 28 July, 1768.

Children, born in Danvers:

1916   NATHANIEL, b. 22 Mar., 1774.

 1917   MARY, b. 2 Feb., 1776; m. Levi Carr, of Carr's Island, Salisbury, later of Newbury.

 1918   HITTIE, b. 17 Sept., 1777; m. S. Pindar.

 1919   LYDIA, b. 3 Oct., 1779; m. —— Coffin.[133]

 1920   PHEBE, b. 15 Nov., 1781; m. (Maj.?) Moses Black, of Danversport?

 1921   REBECCA, b. 11 Oct., 1783; d. y.

 1922   PRISCILLA, b. 25 June, 1785; m. E(dward?) Stone, of Beverly.

 1923   ARCHELAUS, b. 19 June, 1787; m., 1817, Sarah W. Noyes, of Andover. He was a cabinet maker in Danvers.

Children, by second marriage:

1924   BETSEY, b. 7 Mar., 1789.

1925   SALLY, b. 11 Apr., 1791.

1926   REBECCA, b. 3 May, 1793.

1927   PAMELIA, b. 9 May, 1795; m. Thomas Symonds, of Topsfield. Among their ch. was Jacob, (he m. Harriet Arnold), who became father of Clara Drew Symonds, wife of Geo. E Barstow, son of Hon. Amos C. Barstow, of Providence, R. I.

1928   LOIS, b. 2 Sept., 1797.

NATHANIEL PUTNAM was a member of Capt. Jeremiah Page's company which marched to Lexington April 19, 1775, and he is on the Coat Rolls as serving before Boston during the siege.

During the war he held various town offices, was constable, surveyor of lumber, tything man, etc., etc., and also after the war although less frequently. He was taxed for two " top-chaises."

VI. 785 Ephraim *(Ephraim, Nathaniel, Benjamin, Nathaniel, John)*, born in Salem Village, 14 or 15 June, 1744; died there 1799; married Lucy Spaulding.

---

[133] Bible of Mrs. Clarissa (Carr) Currier, w. of John Currier, Jr., dau. of Levi Carr.

Children :

1929 EPHRAIM.
1930 DANIEL, b. in Lyndeborough, 1770; d. 1841.
1931 SARAH.
1932 ELIZABETH, d. unm.
1933 JOHN, d. unm.

VI. 788 Jesse (*Ephraim, Nathaniel, Benjamin, Nathaniel, John*), born in Lyndeborough, N. H., 21 Sept., 1750; married Rachel, widow of Timothy Carlton, of Wilton, N. H., and daughter of Nathaniel and Abigail Putnam, of Wilton. Soon after marriage they moved to Guilford, Vt., thence to Buffalo, N. Y.

VI. 789 Ensign David (*Ephraim, Nathaniel, Benjamin, Nathaniel, John*), born in Lyndeborough, N. H., 6 March, 1753; died there, 1820; married there, 18 June, 1778, Abigail, widow of John Johnson, and daughter of Jeremiah and —— (Roberts) Carlton, born in Lyndeborough, and died there, 5 Jan., 1835, aged 84.

Toward the end of the French war, Mrs. Putnam's mother, then a young girl, lived with her parents Nathaniel and Hannah Roberts in the block-house. Once, when all the men were absent, the Indians attacked the place but were frightened away by the presence of mind of Mrs. Roberts and her daughter. By her first husband Mrs. Putnam had: David, died 1813, unmarried; Osgood, married Betsey Daker; Hannah, born 6 Feb., 1777, married Daniel Putnam.

Children :[134]

1934 AMY, b. 17 Mar., 1779; d. 17 Dec., 1866; m. Gideon Cram, of So·
        Lyndeborough.
1935 TIMOTHY, b. 19 July, 1781; d. —— 1847; m. Rachel Duscomb of
        Wilton; m., 2d., Patty Cheever, of Lowell.
1936 ABIGAIL, b. in Lyndeborough, 1 June, 1785; d. 30 July, 1836,
        unm.
1937 DAVID, b. in Lyndeborough, 19 June, 1790; d. 10 June. 1870.
1938 SARAH, b. 19 Aug., 1793; living in 1890; m. Jonathan Clark, of
        Lyndeborough.
1939 JEREMIAH, b. in Lyndeborough; d. y.

[134] The Dascomb family record makes Amy, b. 6 Mar.; Timothy, b. 20 May, 1782.

DAVID PUTNAM obtained his commission in 1781, in the 14th company, 9th regiment N. H. militia. In 1786-87-1794 he was constable. He was the pioneer Baptist in Lyndeborough, and was extremely active and instrumental in establishing a church there.

VI. 791 Aaron *(Ephraim, Nathaniel, Benjamin, Nathaniel, John)*, born in Lyndeborough, N. H.; died there (living 1834); married —— Lee. He married, second, at Lyndeborough, 28 April, 1789, Phebe Farnham, or Varnum, of Lyndeborough.

Children :

1940 WARD, b. Nov., 1781.
1941 AARON.
1942 WILLIAM.

Children, by Phebe :

1943 JOSEPH.
1944 CALVIN.
1945 ISRAEL, b. 1797.
1946 ELISHA.
1947 EPHRAIM.
1948 BENJAMIN, of Bradford, N. H.
1949 EPHRAIM TOWNS, b. in So. Lyndeborough, 13 Jan., 1803.

VI. 792 John *(Ephraim, Nathaniel, Benjamin, Nathaniel, John)*, born in Lyndeborough, N. H., 1760; died in Bradford, Vt., 5 Nov., 1837; married at Lyndeborough, 30 Nov., 1783, Olive Barron, sister to Gen. Micah Barron. She died in 1858. Moved to Bradford, Vt., 1787.

Children :

1950 OLIVE, b in Lyndeborough, 28 Jan., 1785; m. Moses Collins, carpenter. They lived in Michigan. Ch.: William. Barron. David. Hartwell. Jonathan. Moses. Lucy. Hannah. Sarah. Alvin. Five others.
1951 SARAH, b. 5 Oct., 1786; m. Ebenezer Chapin of Newbury, Vt., clothier. Ch.: Luther. John, of Chicago. Putnam. Paschal-Paoli. Ebenezer, of Chicago. Sarah, m. —— Cummings; lives in Wisconsin.
1952 JONATHAN, b. in Bradford, Vt., 19 June, 1789; m. Mary Stockwell.

1953 REBECCA, b. 8 July, 1791; m. Isaac Stockwell. Mr. and Mrs. Stockwell d. in Danville, Canada East. Ch.: Christina. Emira Emeline. Sarah. Isaac. John. Olive.

1954 JOHN, b. 22 May, 1793; m. Mary Pukett.

1955 MICAH BARRON, d. æt. 2 yrs.

1956 HANNAH, b. 17 Mar., 1797; m. John Pearsons, of Bradford. Ch.: Alonzo, b. 8 Sept., 1818. Daniel, b. 14 Apr., 1820. William, b. 19 Dec., 1824. George, b. 7 Aug., 1830. Elizabeth, b. 25 Apr., 1836. Four others.

1957 EPHRAIM, b. 30 July, 1799; m. Rachel Stoddard.

1958 ELIZABETH, b. 22 Feb., 1802; m. Israel Prescott, wheelwright. Ch.: Alma. Martha. Jane. Mary. Samuel. Charlotte.

1959 WILLIAM, b. 8 Aug., 1807.

VI. 815 Capt. Israel (*Tarrant, Tarrant, Benjamin, Nathaniel, John*), born in Sutton, 22 May, 1767; died there, 23 Feb., 1853; married there, 29 Jan., 1795, Hannah, daughter of Jonathan and Hannah (Dudley) Woodbury, born 27 March, 1772, and died 20 Sept., 1795; married, second, 21 April, 1796, Hannah, daughter of Lazarus and Hannah (Chase) LeBarron, born 22 Jan., 1776, and died 30 June, 1861.

Children:

1960 HANNAH LEBARRON, b. 18 Mar., 1797; d. at New York, 12 Apr., 1875; m. 21 Oct., 1821, Jabez Hull, of Providence, R. I., and Millbury, where he d. 2 Oct., 1844. Ch.: Hannah C., b. 6 Oct., 1822; d., unm., June, 1845.

1961 LEBARRON, b. 19 Aug., 1799.

1962 TARRANT, b. 18 May, 1801.

1963 MARY LEBARRON, b. 7 Nov., 1803; d. 4 Sept., 1894; m. 15 Nov., 1831, Dr. Leonard, son of Aaron and Hannah (Greenwood) Pierce, b. 8 Dec., 1793; of Sutton and Canton, Illinois, where he d. 30 Aug., 1843. Mrs. Pierce returned to Sutton and lived on the LeBarron estate with her daus. She was a woman of great ability and a successful teacher. Ch.: Mary Frances, b. 18 May, 1834; d. unm., 9 May, 1891. Ellen Douglas, b. 22 Aug., 1836; m. 16 Nov., 1864, Marcius Milner Hovey; ch.: John W., b. 24 Aug., 1865; d., unm., 13 Jan., 1889, at H. C. Marcius Milner, b. 15 June, 1875.

1964 ISRAEL, b. 25 Dec., 1805.

1965 EDWIN, b. 9 Jan., 1808; d., unm., 20 Dec., 1836, in New York City, where he had engaged in business with great success. The business house which he established, continued by his brothers, was well known for half a century.

1966 FREDERICK WILLIAM, b. 3 Aug., 1810; d. 16 Aug., 1813.

1967 FREDERICK AUGUSTUS, b. 29 May, 1813; a physician in New York; unm.

1968 THEODORE ELIJAH, b. 11 Sept., 1815; d. in Sutton, 4 July, 1885.

1969 CAROLINE PRISCILLA, b. 3 Aug., 1818; m. 29 Nov., 1889, Dr. Ne-hemiah Chase Sibley, who d. 4 Oct., 1844. Ch.: Richard H., d. y. She m., 2d, 25 Apr., 1849, Stephen Merrihew, lawyer, of New York. Ch.: Caroline P., b. in N. Y., 22 May, 1850. The-odora, b..31 Aug., 1853; m. 8 Apr., 1886, James G. Rieck. Geo. W., b. 17 Sept., 1856.

ISRAEL PUTNAM kept a "general store" in Sutton for many years. He was known as "Captain," having obtained his title from a militia commission. He was a fine horseman and had a large herd of cattle and sheep of which he was very proud. He was a man of sterling worth. Of Mrs. Putnam, a descendant writes : " she was one of those old-time women who always found their home and family their highest place of usefulness." Although living to a great age she retained all her faculties, light-heartedness, and interest in the young-er generation to the end.

VI. 823 Judge Samuel (*Gideon, Tarrant, Benja-min, Nathaniel, John*), born in Danvers 13 May, 1768; died 3 July, 1853; married 28 Oct., 1795, Sarah, daughter of John and Lois (Pickering) Gooll, born 28 Nov., 1772, and died 22 Nov., 1864.

Children :

1970 SAMUEL RAYMOND, b. 2 Mar., 1797.

1971 HANNAH, b. 21 June, 1799; d. 4 Aug., 1872; m. 9 Dec., 1822, Thomas Poynton Bancroft, b. 20 Dec., 1798, and d. 16 Mar., 1852. Ch.: Elizabeth I., b. 8 Nov., 1823; d. 23 Sept.,1851. Sarah Ellen, b. 17 Jan., 1826; d. 6 May, 1837. Thos. P., b. 5 Jan., 1829; d. 30 May, 1838. Sam'l Putnam, b. 23 Nov., 1834; d. 30 Nov., 1850. Ellen, b. 22 May, 1838. Robert Hale, b. 21 April, 1843.

1972 LOUISA, b. 4 Oct., 1801; d. 7 Oct., 1876; m. 3 Sept., 1821, Joseph Augustus Peabody, b. 7 Aug., 1796, and d. 18 June, 1828. Ch.: Elizabeth Smith, b. 31 July, 1822; d. 13 Dec.,1869; m. 15 Jan., 1845, Caleb Wm. Loring, b. 31 July, 1819. Sarah L., b. 6. Nov., 1823; d. 1832. Catherine, b. 12 Oct., 1826; d. 8 Jan., 1848. Josephine Augusta, b. 12 June, 1828; m. 6 Nov., 1851, William

Gardner Prescott (their dau. Edith, b. 20 Apr., 1853; m. 2 Nov., 1874, Roger Walcott, b. 13 July, 1847, (Lt. Gov. Mass.), and have: Huntington F., b. 1875, d. 1877; Roger, b. 25 July, 1877; Wm. P., b. 1 June, 1880; Sam'l H., b. 9 Nov., 1881; Cornelia F., b. 8 Feb., 1885). Wm. H., b. 22 Feb., 1855; d. 1864. Linzie, b. 27 Nov., 1859. Catherine E., b. 19 Feb., 1863.

1973 MARY ANN, b. 20 Aug., 1803; d., *s. p.*, 10 Apr., 1845; m. Charles Greeley Loring, b. 2 May, 1794; d. 8 Oct., 1867.

1974 CHARLES GIDEON, b. 7 Nov., 1805.

1975 ELIZABETH CABOT, b. 11 Nov., 1807; d. 12 Feb., 1881; m. 2 Apr., 1829, John Amory Lowell, b. 11 Nov., 1798, and d. 31 Oct., 1881. Ch.: Augustus, b. 15 Jan., 1830; m. 1 June, 1854, Katherine B. Lawrence, b. 21 Feb., 1832. (Ch.: Percival, b. 13 Mar., 1855. Abbott L., b. 13 Dec., 1856. Katherine, b. 27 Nov., 1858; m. Alfred Roosevelt. Roger, d. y , and Elizb., b. 2 Feb., 1862. May, d. y. Amy, b. 9 Feb., 1874). Eliz. R., b. 27 Feb., 1831; m. Francis P. Sprague. Ellen B., b. 1 Nov., 1837; m. 8 Apr., 1858, Arthur Theodore Lyman, b. 8 Dec., 1832. (Ch.: Julia. Arthur. Herbert. Ella. Susan L. Mabel. Roger. Ronald T.) Sara Putnam, b. 24 June, 1843; m. 18 May, 1876, Geo. B. Blake, who d. 17 June, 1884, (Ch.: John A. L.).

1976 SARAH GOOL, b. 1 June, 1810; d. 10 Dec., 1880; m. 20 Mar., 1832, Francis B. Crowninshield, b. 23 Apr., 1809, and d. 8 May, 1877. Ch.: Mary, b. 17 Jan., 1833; d. 6 May, 1834. Sarah, b. 22 Dec., 1834; d. 24 Nov., 1840. Benj. W., b. 12 Mar., 1837; m. Katherine M. Bradlee. Alice, b. 22 Nov., 1839; m. 17 Mar., 1864. Josiah Bradlee. Louisa, b. 7 Jan., 1842; m. 8 Oct., 1860, Francis E. Bacon. Francis, b. 8 June, 1845; d. 23 Apr., 1847. Emily, b. 9 Dec., 1847; d. 18 May, 1879.

1977 JOHN PICKERING, b. 21 June, 1813.

SAMUEL PUTNAM was the only one of the ten children of Gideon who lived to attain maturity. His delicate youth gave no promise of the long and useful life to come. As a boy he attended school at Beverly and later at Andover. Thence to Harvard being in the same class as John Quincy Adams, and from which institution he graduated in 1787. In 1794 he was admitted to the Essex Bar, having studied law with Judge Parsons at Newburyport, in preference to adopting the profession of teacher selected by his father. He soon established himself at Salem and obtained a lucrative practise, at the same time giving more or less attention to politics. In this later field he was successful, representing

Salem in the General Court in 1812, and the county as senator in 1808, 1809, 1813, 1814.   During his last term as
senator Chief Justice Sewall died, and Governor Strong appointed Mr. Putnam to the vacant seat on the bench of the
Supreme Court.   In 1825 he received the degree of Doctor
of Laws from the University of Cambridge, England. - For
twenty-eight years he remained on the bench, during which
time no one could justly complain of his decisions which have
been praised by the most learned judges of our own time.

He took great pride in his place at Danvers, and great interest in all that pertained to the history of the family.   In
his youth he saw the soldiers under Arnold march by on their
way to Quebec, and had seen a British regiment parade under the command of General Gage, and the events in the life
Israel Putnam and others of the family were familiar gossip
to his ears.

In July, 1834, he wrote the following letter to Col. Perley
Putnam, of such general interest, that it is inserted here:

"The Register of Deeds shows that the family became proprietors of considerable tracts of land.   The homestead of my
farm I believe has always been owned by some of the descendants from the common ancestor.   They have generally
been plain common-sense, industrious men.   They have not
been very rich, but in comfortable circumstances.

I have known very many of this numerous family (probably as numerous as descended from any of the first settlers
of Salem) and have had traditionary accounts from many
others.   Of a few only I will speak.   For I have not time to
speak of many who are as deserving as those are of whom I
shall make mention.

James Putnam (No. 378) of Worcester, was a distinguished counsellor at law, and the patron of John Adams,
the late president of the United States.   He adhered to the
parent country, and removed to New Brunswick where he
held a judicial office, with great reputation under the Crown.
His descendants have been very respectable, have merited
and received the rewards due to their continued allegiance

and fidelity. One of them returned to England and was particularly favored by Prince Edward now deceased.

We can now look to the period of the Revolution without the bitter feelings which then agitated the country. And it is clear (to my mind at least) that many of those who adhered to the old government were as true men as many of those were who shook off their allegiance.

For example, I think that James Putnam, Daniel Leonard and Jonathan Sewall loved their country as well as John Adams, John Hancock and Samuel Adams.

Ebenezer Putnam (No. 374), of Salem, the grandfather of the postmaster, was very distinguished in the medical department. If I am not mistaken he was the brother of James Putnam of Worcester. I remember his appearance and his civility to me when I was a boy. His person moved alertly. I have heard aunt Clark say that his house was broken open in the night; that he went down alone in the darkness, seized and detained the burglar, who was a much larger man than himself. If he had been a soldier he would have been as fearless as he was skilful as a physician. Ebenezer Putnam (No. 960), the father of the postmaster,[135] was a gentleman of most excellent spirit as well as of great truth and honor. I knew him very well. In any case of morals it would have been safe to follow the dictates of his mind.

I remember your grandfather, Dr. Amos Putnam (No. 271), of Danvers. He was in great practice as a physician and surgeon, and of a most courteous and gentlemanly deportment. He was the physician in my father's family. It used to be said that he acquired his skill in surgery in the war of 1756. Some of the family have distinguished themselves in war; General Israel Putnam (No. 90), is known to the world certainly as a soldier of great bravery. I was once at his house in Brooklyn where he treated me with great hospitality. He showed me the place where he followed a wolf into a cave and shot it; and he gave me a great many anecdotes of the

---

[135] Eben Putnam, of Salem, father of Prof. Fred. W., of Cambridge, and grandfather of the compiler of this genealogy.

war in which he had been engaged, before the Revolution, tracing the remarkable events upon a map. He was once taken by the Indians and tied to a tree to be put to death according to their fashion. They threw their tomahawk into the tree by the side of his head, and after amusing themselves in that way, for some time, they lighted up the fire and danced and yelled around him. When they were thus engaged, one of the tribe, a chief who had been once a prisoner of Putnam and treated kindly by him, arrived at the spot and recognized his friend in their intended *victim*, immediately released him from impending slaughter. General Putnam said that their gestures in the dance were so inexpressively ridiculous that he could not forbear laughing. I expressed some surprise that he could laugh under such circumstances, to which he mildly replied, that his composure had no merit—that it was constitutional, and then said that he had never felt any bodily fear.

I can as easily credit that assertion as the one which Governor Morris made of himself, viz.: "that he never felt embarrassed by the presence of any person whomsoever in his life." And I am inclined to think that both of them spoke the truth, concerning their own sensations. In 1786 he rode on horseback from Brooklyn to Danvers and made his last visit to his friends there. On his way home he stopped at the colleges at Cambridge where the government of the college paid him much attention. It was in my junior year. He came to my room; his speech was then much affected with palsy.

I knew his son Daniel Putnam. He has visited me in Salem. His letter to General Dearborn, repelling the charge or insinuation of cowardice at Bunker Hill, was in matter and manner precisely what became him. I have several letters from him, which show that his mind was much cultivated. His manners were frank and gentlemanly.

I have had an opportunity in the examination of applicants for pensions to obtain affidavits of some who were engaged in the battle of Bunker Hill, proving that General Putnam was there encouraging the men and exposing himself with his accustomed fearlessness, in the fight at the rail fence. *Prescott* was in the redoubt, at some distance higher up the hill, fighting like a lion. If the ammunition had not failed he would have maintained the ground which he so long and so gloriously defended. Col. Sweet has given a very interesting account of that battle.

Gen. Rufus Putnam (No. 212) of Marietta, served with great reputation in the Revolutionary war. He united great discretion to great bravery. I have often heard Governor Strong speak of him with very great respect, and he knew him intimately and was as good a judge of men as I have ever known. He was the father of the State of Ohio. His descendants there are said to be very numerous. I have often heard my father speak of one of the Putnams who was called "Lieutenant David" (No. 85) as one of the lion-hearted men of his time. I believe he belonged to a troop of horse, which was commanded by Captain Gardner, but of that I am not certain. I have seen some Indian trophies in the possession of Samuel P. Gardner of Boston which had been taken by his ancestor, Captain Gardner. Most of the family have been farmers, and among them I think William Putnam (No. 231), of Sterling, was the most distinguished. The late General Bowdoin gave the charge of Elizabeth Islands to him.

Some of the family have been successful in commerce; of those I think the late Oliver Putnam (No. 1455), of Newburyport, was the most eminent for talents. He cultivated letters for the love of them. He was self taught, and, as is often the case with such men, he was well taught, in all that he attempted. He left a considerable sum in trust for a high school in Newburyport, and was there greatly esteemed.

I have often heard my father say that some of the family moved to Charleston, S. C., and were merchants. But of their fate I knew nothing. I think it was Benjamin (No. 414) who went to Carolina.

Some of the family are now distinguished scholars in Divinity. The Rev. Israel W. Putnam (No. 1022) is nearly or quite at the head of the orthodox clergy in New Hampshire; the Rev. George Putnam (No. 1253), of Roxbury, is one of our most eminent Unitarian clergymen in this state. I have lately had occasion officially to be informed that the Rev. Rufus A. Putnam of Fitchburg is one of four clergymen who by a testator were named as trustees to dispose of a large estate for such religious objects as they should think proper. I do not know that gentleman, but the fact to which I allude shows that he is deemed both honest and discreet.

Some of the family have been good shipmasters. I recollect many, but will speak only of one. I recollect that Mr. Vidaurne, the chief justice of the court of Pennsylvania, called to see me, and when about to go away he desired me to direct him to the house of Capt. Hiram Putnam, who brought Mr. V. to this country from Peru. He was put on board of Captain Putnam's ship by the Peruvian government, against the will of Mr. V., and Mr. V. said "I never should forgive myself if I were to go from the country without taking leave of Captain Putnam, and thanking him for his great kindness to me while I was on board his ship."

Those of the family who have been mechanics, have been generally intelligent and laborious men. My father was a carpenter and a farmer. His share of his father's estate was only thirteen acres of land. By his industry and perseverance assisted by my mother, whose untiring assiduity was without bound, he was enabled to acquire and leave to me the farm which his ancestors had possessed from the first settlement of the country. He did that besides educating two sons in college and making a comfortable provision for his family at home, which from sickness and other causes was very chargeable.

A great many examples of such industry will occur to your recollection. But I know there have been some of the family who have not conducted themselves well. The instances however have been rare considering the great number of descendants from John Putnam.

Generally the descendants of John Putnam have been distinguished more for industry, perseverance, honesty and firmness than for genius or brilliancy. I could illustrate this remark by a great many examples, but I have not time to do it.

After all it is of no consequence that we record that Abraham begat Isaac, and Isaac begat Jacob, and so on, unless we imitate as far as we may the virtues of Abraham, Isaac and Jacob.

I hope not to have tired your patience. But you may retaliate, by a copy of your genealogical tree, when you shall have completed it."

VI. 832 Benjamin (*Benjamin, Benjamin, Benjamin, Nathaniel, John*), born in Danvers, 28 April, 1757; died there, 9 July, 1812; married there (12 April, Flint Gen.) 5 March, 1777, Miriam, daughter of Elisha and Miriam (Putnam) Flint, born in Danvers, 4 Nov., 1759, and died in Haverhill, 20 Oct., 1830. She married, second, Moody Spofford, of Georgetown.

Children, born in Danvers:

1978 RUTH, b. 12 Oct., 1777; d. in Plaistow, N. H., 19 Mar., 1827; m. Rev. Reuben Peaslee, of Plaistow. Ch.: Moses Flint, b. 13 Jan., 1801; d. in Haverhill, 18 Aug., 1868; m. 29 Nov., 1821, Sally Bradley, of Plaistow, N. H.

1979 SETH, b. 22 Dec. (2 Flint Gen.), 1779; d. 1 Apr., 1864.

1980 BENJAMIN, b. 20 Mar., 1782; d. 27 Aug , 1850.

1981 MIRIAM, b. 4 Oct., 1784; d. in Haverhill, 23 Dec., 1862; m. 24 Apr., 1808, Moses, son of Rev. Gyles and Lucy (Cushing) Merrill, of Haverhill, b. there, 12 Sept., 1776, and d. there, 6 Dec., 1864. Ch.: Gyles, b. in Haverhill, 13 Mar., 1816; m. 28 Nov., 1849, Elizabeth, dau. of Leonard and Grace Watson, b. in Mickleover, Derbyshire, Eng., 26 Jan., 1816.[146]

[146] Children of Gyles and Eliz. Merrill are: Gyles, b. in Roxbury, 6 Oct., 1850; d. in Haverhill, 3 Aug., 1880; m. 14 Nov., 1878, Helen M. Burnham. Moses Putnam, b. 27 Jan., 1852; d., unm., at Haverhill, 13 Apr., 1878. James Cushing, b. in Charlestown, N. H., 9 Sept., 1853; m. 10 May, 1878, Ella Frances Johnson. Samuel, b. 1 Jan., 1855; m. 1 Oct. 1887, Estelle Minerva, dau. of Gilman E. and Alenda (Kincaird) Hatch. Both Mr. and Mrs. Samuel Merrill are on the editorial staff of the Boston Globe. See New Eng. Hist. Gen. Reg. for October, 1891, for an ancestral chart of Gyles Merrill.

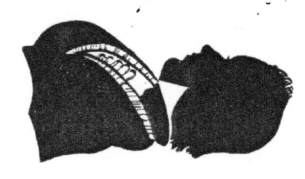

BENJAMIN PUTNAM.

(BENJAMIN, BENJAMIN, BENJAMIN,
NATHANIEL, JOHN.)

MIRIAM (FLINT) PUTNAM.

WIFE OF BENJAMIN.

From the original silhouettes in the possession of Gyles Merrill, Esq., of Haverhill, Mass. Mrs. Putnam was a daughter of Elisha Flint of Danvers, and a lineal descendant of John Putnam through each of his three sons. The devices above the forehead and under the chin in her picture are intended to represent the bows of the cap-strings.

1982 EUNICE, b. 14 May, 1787; d. in Clayton, N. Y., 28 Oct., 1871; m. Daniel Gardner. Ch.: Putnam, b. 8 Apr., 1811. Miriam, b. 25 Nov., 1813. Emma, b. 15 Feb., 1815. Daniel, b. 21 Feb., 1817. Sally, b. 3 Feb., 1819. Ebenezer, b. 29 Apr., 1821. John Nichols, b. 7 Oct., 1823. Willard, b. 16 Apr., 1826.

1983 EMMA, b. 9 Nov., 1789; d. in Danvers, 24 Dec., 1866, *s. p.*; m. John Nichols, of Danvers, who d. the same day as his wife.

1984 SALLY, b. 29 Mar., 1793; d. in Danvers, 30 Dec., 1866; m. 12 May, 1814, Abel, son of Andrew and Eunice Nichols, and lived on the old Nichols farm Ch.: Abel, b. 14 June, 1815; d. 13 May, 1860; an artist. Sarah, b. 13 May, 1818; d. 14 May, 1887; m., 1st, 19 Nov., 1839, Charles Page; m., 2d, 14 May, 1869, Eben G. Berry, both of Danvers.

BENJAMIN PUTNAM and wife Miriam joined the church in Danvers, 1 Nov., 1778. It was not until 1786 that he held any town office; that year he was tythingman, but from that time on he was frequently called upon to serve the town in various positions. He lived on North street in the house pictured opposite page 61. The silhouettes are from originals in Samuel Merrill's possession.

VI. 833 Timothy (*Timothy, Stephen, Benjamin, Nathaniel, John*), born in Danvers, 1756; died in Middle Stewiacke, N. S., 9 Oct., 1840; married in Truro, N. S., 1785, Janet, third daughter of Robert and Esther (Moore) Hunter, born in Truro, 18 Jan., 1763, and died in Middle Stewiacke, 26 Feb., 1841.

Children, born in Middle Stewiacke:

1985 LETITIA, b. 1786; d. 27 Apr., 1822; m., 1808, James Rutherford, Sr., and had one son and six daughters.

1986 ROBERT, b. July, 1788.

1987 TIMOTHY, b. 26 Oct., 1790.

1988 JOHN, b. May, 1793.

1989 ESTHER, b. 31 Dec., 1796; d. 3 May, 1868; m. 17 Mar., 1818, James Barnhill, and had three sons and five daus.

1990 ELIZABETH, b. 1799; d. suddenly, 14 Apr., 1821; m. Feb., 1820, James Dunlap, and had one son.

TIMOTHY PUTNAM was carried to Nova Scotia by his mother when not more than six years of age. He settled in Middle Stewiacke. An erroneous tradition has been current for many years amongst his descendants that he was a loyal-

ist. He became the progenitor of a numerous and worthy
family, who have sustained the Putnam characteristics as well
as their Yankee cousins.

VI. 835 Matthew (*Phineas, Stephen, Benjamin, Nathaniel, John*), born in Danvers, 2 Aug., 1756; died there, 25 Dec., 1828; married 17 March, 1778, Ruth, daughter of Nathan and Mary Smith, born 15 Jan., 1755, and died 20 Feb., 1841.

Children, born in Danvers :

1991 PHINEAS, b. 10 Sept., 1778; d. 10 Jan., 1854.
1992 POLLY, b. 29 Apr., 1783; d. 18 Apr., 1856; m. 1801, Seth Putnam.
1993 MATTHEW, b. 26 May, 1785.
1994 RUTH, }
1995 SALLY, } twins, b. 27 Jan., 1792.
1996 BETSEY, b. 26 May, 1794.
1997 HANNAH, b. May, 1799; d. 25 Nov., 1800.

VI. 836 Joseph (*Phineas, Stephen, Benjamin, Nathaniel, John*), born in Danvers, 12 Apr., 1761; died 8 Nov., 1853; married 19 Nov., 1790, Fanny (No. 974), daughter of Col. Enoch and Hannah (Putnam) Putnam, born 7, Aug., 1764, and died 28 June, 1858, aet. 93 yrs., 10 mos., 20 days.

Mrs. Joseph Putnam's mother was a daughter of Stephen Putnam (No. 315).

Child :

1998 CLARISSA, b. in Danvers 2 Aug., 1792; d. 26 July, 1888; m. 2 Dec., 1819, John, son of Levi and Mehitable (Nichols) Preston of Danvers, b. there, 16 Dec., 1790; d. 28 May , 1876. Ch.: **Charles Putnam**, b. 24 Sept., 1820; d. 27 Oct., 1887; m. 29 Jan., 1845, Sarah Hubbard, dau. of Moses and Ruth (Stuart) Hook, b. in Fremont, N. H., 30 Dec., 1820. (Ch.: Charles H., b. 22 Mar.,

---

HUBBARD.

I. RICHARD HUBBARD of Salisbury, 1665; d. 26 June, 1719. He was a blacksmith. He m. Martha, dau. of Wm. and Ann (Goodale[137]) Allen, b. in Salisbury, 1646 and d. there, 4 Oct., 1718.
He may have been of Dover, N. H., 10, 11, 1658; if so was not

137 Richard Goodale from Yarmouth, Eng., settled in Newbury about 1638, removed to Salisbury where he died 1676. His wife Dorothy d. 27, 11, 1664; and his second wife Mary, d. 31 May, 1683. Ch.: Ann, d. May, 1670; m. Wm. Allen who d. 1686. Richard who settled in Boston.

1863.) John Preston was, as was his son and grandson, a selectman of Danvers, and also representative to General Court.
Chas. P. and Chas. H. were both trustees of the Peabody Institute and Charles P. was also trustee of the Danvers Insane
Hospital and Sec'y of the Essex Agricultural Society.

---

taxed there in 1661. A romantic story with but little to commend
it concerning his birth and coming to this country will be found
in the History of Candia, N. H., In 1694–5 he was deputy to the
General Court from Salisbury and for some time lived in Boston, where his son Joseph had settled. Ch.: Mary, b. 19 Jan.,
1667; m. 17 Nov., 1686, Tobias Langdon, from whom descended
the Govs. Langdon of New Hampshire. *John*, b. 12 Apr., 1669,
settled at Kingston, N. H. A child who died 1672. Dorothy,
b. 7 Apr., 1673; m. John Stevens. Joseph, b. 4 June, 1676; m.
4 Aug., 1698, Thankful Brown. (One of their ch. was the Hon.
Thomas Hubbard, b. 4 Aug., 1702; d. 14 July, 1773. Member
of the Council, and Treasurer of Harvard College.) Judith, b.
9 July, 1679; prob. m. at Boston, 7 Nov., 1699, Obadiah Emons.
Comfort, b. 17 Jan., 1681–2; m. 7 Nov., 1699, Joshua Weeks.
Jemima, b. 11 Nov., 1684, living unm. in 1718. Kezia, b. 11
Nov., 1684; m. 16 Dec., 1701, Joseph True. Richard, b. 9 Mar.,
1686–7; d. 20 Jan., 1687–8. Eleazer, b. 27 Oct., 1689, left descendants in Salisbury.

II. LT. JOHN (Richard), d. in Kingston, N. H., 25 Sept., 1723; m.
    1688, Jane (Collyer) of Salisbury. Ch.: Richard, d. y. John, b.
    17 Jan., 1690–1. Jeremiah, b. 27 Aug., 1692; m. Mercy John-
    son. Mary, b. 29 Nov., 1694. *Richard*, b. 27 Dec., 1696; m.
    Abigail Davis. Martha, b. 8 Oct., 1698. Jane, b. 10 June,
    1700. Anna, b. 22 July, 1702; d. 1775; m. Rev. Wm. Thompson
    of Scarboro. Keziah, b. in Salisbury, 10 July, 1704; m. 1 Jan.,
    1734, John Libby. Dorothy, b. in Kingston, 8 Jan., 1708. John,
    d. y. Jemima, b. 3 Mar., 1711; prob. m. John Messerve of
    Scarboro. John, b. 28 Jan., 1715.

III. CAPT. RICHARD (John, Richard), d. in Kingston; m. Abigail Da-
    vis, who d. 25 Sept., 1733; m., 2d, 16 Oct., 1734, Abigail Taylor,
    who d. 9 Dec., 1768. Ch.: *Dorothy*, b. 25 July, 1722; m. 1741,
    Sam'l Small of Scarboro. Eliz'b, b. 25 Sept., 1724; m. Sam'l
    Libby of Scarboro. Martha, b. 26 Nov., 1726. Abigail, b. 22
    Nov., 1728. Grace, b. 22 Sept., 1730. *John*, b. 12 Apr., 1733.
    Mary, b. 21 May, 1735; m. John Stevens. *Grace*, b. 8 Jan.,
    1736–7; m. 13 July, 1758, Samuel Stuart. Anne, b. 17 Oct.,
    1738. Marg't, b. 30 Aug., 1740. Richard, b. 3 Dec., 1742.
    Benjamin, b. 12 Nov., 1744. Sarah, b. 16 Feb., 1751. Jed_
    diah, b. 16 July, 1755.

IV. DOROTHY (Richard, John, Richard), m., 1741, Samuel, son of
    Sam'l (grandson of Francis of Kittery) and Anna (Hatch)
    Small of Scarboro, b. 26 May, 1718. Their dau. Dorothy, b. 14

VI. **837** Timothy (*Phineas, Stephen, Benjamin, Nathaniel, John*), born in Danvers 17 Feb., 1763 ; died in Danvers 6 July, 1838 ; married 10 Mar., 1794, Hannah (No. 975), daughter of Col. Enoch Putnam, born 21 May, 1771 and died 22 June, 1830. "June 22, 1830, my dear wife departed this life fifteen minutes before eleven of the clock."

Children, born in Danvers :

1999   ELBRIDGE GERRY, b. 4 Sept., 1794.
2000   WILLARD, b. 13 June, 1796.
2001   ADRIAN, b. 14 June, 1803.
2002   GUSTAVUS T., b. 6 Dec., 1810.

TIMOTHY PUTNAM enlisted at the age of sixteen and served throughout the Revolution bearing the hardships of the terrible winter at Valley Forge. He came home bare-footed. Otis Putnam, Esq., of Danvers, has in his possession the gun Timothy carried through the war. Mr. Adrian L. Putnam

---

Jan., 1762 ; bur. 1 Oct., 1846 ; m. 4 Dec., 1781, Dominicus, son of Enoch and Elizabeth (Plummer) Libby, b. in Scarboro, 27 Dec., 1751 and d. 18 Dec., 1822. He was a Revolutionary soldier, and a great great grandson of John Libby, born in England about 1602. Capt. Enoch, son of Dominicus above, b. 23 Feb., 1787 ; d. in Richmond, Me., 11 Mar., 1863 ; m. Eliz'b, dau. of Capt. Wm. Welch, and had Mary Ann, b. in Richmond, 20 Jan., 1822 ; m. Col. Laurens, son of Lawrence and Olive (Small) Joyce, b. in Brunswick, Me., d. in Richmond, Texas. Their dau. Elizabeth m. Frank Tucker of Roxbury and had Florence Maude, who married Eben Putnam (Fred. W., Eben., Eben., Eben., James, James, John, John) of Salem.

IV.   GRACE (Richard, John, Richard), m. at Kingston, 13 July, 1758, Samuel Stuart. Their son Sam'l m. Hannah Brown, and had Ruth, who m. Moses Hook, father of Sarah Hubbard Hook wife of Chas. P. Preston (see No. 1998).

IV.   DR. JOHN (Richard, John, Richard), m. 30 Apr., 1754, Joanna Davis, who d. in 1807, æt. 74. Ch.: Margaret, b. 2 Apr., 1755. Nane, b. 25 Feb., 1757. John, b. 28 Sept., 1759 ; d. in Brentwood, Me., 22 Apr., 1838 ; his son, also a physician, was Hon. John, b. 22 Mar., 1794, Governor of Maine, in 1850-2. Richard, b. 1 May, 1764. Francis, b. 17 Dec., 1761.
Further details about this Hubbard family, the principal part pertaining to the early generations having been supplied by the compiler of this (Putnam) genealogy, will be found in "One thousand years of Hubbard History," p. 85.

of Provincetown, a grandson, has the family bible and several heirlooms, amongst which is a small silver spoon marked "H. P." and a china plate with "T. H. P." in gilt in the center. This plate is one of a set made to order in China.

Timothy Putnam occupied for a time the old Putnam house, since removed which formerly stood in Summer street. A part of this property is now known as Oak Knoll. He had in a marked degree the old-fashioned courteous and dignified manners. The four sons were of medium stature and very industrious men. Elbridge, Willard and Gustavus were much interested in music. Adrian was a farmer and settled on the old homestead on Elm St., Danvers, while Elbridge and Gustavus built on either side.

VI. 838 Ezra (*Phineas, Stephen, Benjamin, Nathaniel, John*), born in Danvers, Mar., 1771; married 28 Nov., 1799, Sally, daughter of Israel and Sally (Eppes) Putnam of Danvers, born there, 6 Mar., 1779 and died 20 Aug., 1811. He married, second, 16 June, 1813, Hannah, daughter of Jacob Granger of Andover, Vt., born Nov., 1775.

Children:

2003 SALLY, b. 5 Jan., 1801.
2004 KENDALL, b. 3 Jan., 1803; d. Mar., 1837; of Wells Co., Ind.
2005 NEWTON, b. Jan., 1805.
2006 FRANKLIN, b. Dec., 1807.
2007 MARY W., b. Oct., 1809; m. Asa Parker. Ch.: Sarah H., b. Sept., 1827.
2008 EZRA G., b. Apr., 1814; d. Mar., 1837, in Wells Co., Ind.
2009 WILLIAM, b. May, 1815; d. Mar., 1837, in Wells Co., Ind.
2010 CHARLES, b. June, 1816; d. Mar., 1837, in Wells Co., Ind.

EZRA PUTNAM settled in Cavendish, Vt. In 1836, he removed with his family, except one son, to Wells Co., Indiana, where several of the children died of a prevailing epidemic. The survivors returned to Cavendish.

VI. 841 Deacon Rufus (*Aaron, Stephen, Benjamin, Nathaniel, o'n*), born in Danvers, 7 May, 1764; died in Beverly 21 (or 14?) Mar., 1836, "sick but a few days;"

31

married 10 Dec., 1793, Mary, daughter of Deacon Asa Putnam, born 11 Aug., 1765; died in Beverly, 28 Jan., 1840.

Children, born in Beverly:

2011 AARON, b. 21 Apr., 1796; d. in Beverly, 30 Mar., 1801.
2012 RUFUS, b. 12 Apr., 1800.
2013 AARON, b. 14 Apr., 1802; d. in Beverly, 17 Jan., 1803.
2014 WILLIAM, b. 10 Nov., 1803.

DEACON RUFUS PUTNAM removed to Beverly in 1800 and bought the Leech homestead at Royal Side.   His son William lived there after his father's death.

VI. 845 Simeon (*Aaron, Stephen, Benjamin, Nathaniel, John*), born in Danvers, 22 Nov., 1776; died there, 24 July, 1834; married 1 Dec., 1801, Deborah Brown, born in Boxford, 22 Oct., 1782.

Children, born in Danvers:

2015 LYDIA, b. 19 Feb., 1803; d. 25 Feb., 1805.
2016 SIMEON, b. 3 June, 1805.
2017 AARON, b. 9 Apr., 1807.
2018 AUGUSTUS, b. 22 Apr., 1810.
2019 EDWARD BROWN, b. 24 May, 1812; d. Apr., 1843.
2020 ELIZABETH GARDNER, b. 14 Feb., 1815; d. 28 Oct., 1834.
2021 ISRAEL HERBERT, b. 19 Jan., 1819.

SIMEON PUTNAM was a farmer in Danvers.

VI. 846 Stephen (*Moses, Stephen, Benjamin, Nathaniel, John*), born in Danvers, 20 May, 1772; died 18 Sept., 1821; married 19 Sept., 1797, Sarah daughter of John and Rebecca Burton of Wilton, born in Wilton, 8 June, 1772 and died in Mason, N. H., 29 July, 1840.   He built and ran a gristmill at Barnes' Falls, Wilton.

Children:

2022 STEPHEN, b. 11 Nov., 1797.
2023 SYLVESTER, b. 8 Feb., 1799; d. *s. p.* in Mason, N. H., 25 July, 1846; m. 1 May, 1842, Elizabeth Hill, who m., 2d, —— Chamberlain of Mason and died about 1888.
2024 HIRAM, b. 13 Nov., 1800.
2025 REBECCA, b. 31 Aug., 1802; m. —— Adams. Ch. : a son and dau. Is supposed to have lived in Andover.

2026 CYRUS, b. 13 Sept., 1804; his dau. Lizzie M., b. 17 June, 1844; m. A. A. Forbush of Washington, D. C.

2027 SARAH, b. 20 Feb. (July), 1808; d. in Salem, 1887; m. ――― Baldwin. Two ch., of which Lucia was the younger.

2028 MOSES, b. (22) 30 July. 1810; m. July, 1844, Mary Ann, dau. of Daniel Barton of Ware who d. there in 1885. Lives at Ware (1892).

2029 IRA V., b. 22 Sept., 1813; d., unm., at Memphis, Miss., 1841.

2030 JOHN FRANKLIN, b. 2 Mar., 1817.[138]

VI. 849 Aaron Kimball (*Moses, Stephen, Benjamin, Nathaniel, John*), born in Wilton, N. H., 11 Jan., 1784; died there, 25 Mar., 1871; married 12 Dec., 1808, Polly Shattuck of Temple, N. H., who died 10 Oct., 1841, aged 54 years; married, second, Nancy Wright of Mason, N. H., who died 28 Aug., 1875, aged 68 years. He was a carpenter and later conducted a small farm on a scientific and profitable basis.

Children :

2031 MARY RUSS, b. 17 Sept., 1809; d 10 Oct., 1838.

2032 EVELINE, b. 31 Mar., 1811; m. 22 Apr., 1832, William Emerson of Wilton, b. 13 Dec., 1805. Mr. Emerson was associated with his father-in-law in business for many years. He also held many town offices. Ch.: Sumner Brooks, b. 25 Feb., 1834. Charles A., b. 6 Feb., 1837. Mary, b. 26 Jan., 1841; d. 8 May, 1845. Martha, b. 8 May, 1843; d. 7 Sept., 1855. Henry L., b. 6 Feb., 1845. Willisk, b. 10 Apr., 1849. Mary E., b. 13 Aug., 1851. Lenora, b. 12 July, 1855.

2033 SARAH, b. 15 Feb., 1813; m. 25 Dec., 1834, John Mills, a large boot and shoe manufacturer in Milford, N. H. Ch.: Sarah N., b. 19 Jan., 1856.

2034 AARON KIMBALL, b. 13 Dec., 1814; d. 1 Aug., 1816.

2035 AARON KIMBALL, b. 23 Jan., 1817; d. 16 Mar., 1818.

2036 LEVI, b. 4 Dec., 1818.

2037 HARVEY, b. 21 Sept., 1820.

2038 DANIEL PRATT, b. 9 July, 1822; m. Miss Peavey. No. ch. Lived in Bethlehem, but lately in Cleveland, O.

2039 MATILDA ROCKWOOD, b. 23 Oct., 1824; d. 16 Sept., 1886; m., 1st, 1 Jan., 1855, Samuel F. Maynard of Wilton, who d. 10 Aug., 1856. Ch.: Samuel F., b. 15 Feb., 1856; d. 23 June, 1886. Mrs. Maynard m., 2d, 9 Nov., 1865, Deacon Charles Wilson, of New Ipswich, N. H., and also of Wilton.

[138] Mrs. Hammond of Swanzey, N. H., gives these dates of children's birth with exception of second and last one year later. Parenthesis enclose the Hammond dates.

2040 RUFUS, b. 3 Mar., 1827.

    2041 ANNA JANE, b. 26 July, 1829; m. Stephen C. Coburn. Lives in Milford, N. H.

    By second wife :

    2042 MARY CORNELIA.

VI. 851 Moses (*Stephen, Stephen, Benjamin, Nathaniel, John*), born in Danvers 4 Nov., 1775; died 10 Sept., 1860; married 28 Apr., 1803, Betsey, daughter of Israel and Sally (Eppes) Putnam, born in Danvers, 9 Oct., 1782, and died 23 Oct., 1864.

    Children, born in Danvers :

2043 ALFRED, b. 13 Feb., 1804; d. 8 Sept., 1835, at Danvers.

    2044 HARRIET, b. 11 May, 1806; d. 13 May, 1891; m. 3 Dec., 1833, Dea. Samuel Page[139] son of Samuel and Clarissa (Page) Fowler, b. 22 Apr., 1800; d. 15 Dec., 1888. Ch.: Clara Putnam, b. 20 Mar., 1836; m. 25 Nov., 1856, Geo. Edson, son of Alex. E. and Ellen R. (Tucker), DuBois, b. in Randolph, 24 Feb., 1829 and d. there, 3 Nov., 1859. (Ch.: Ellen Tucker, b. 16 Dec., 1857.) Mrs. DuBois lives in Danvers. Samuel Page, b. 6 Dec., 1838. Harriet Putnam, b. 25 July, 1842; resides in Danvers.

    2045 SALLY EPPES, b. 21 Apr., 1808; d. 6 July, 1808.

    2046 LOUISA, b. 16 Aug., 1809; d., unm., 24 Aug., 1842.

    2047 SUSANNA HERRICK, b. 20 Apr., 1812; d. 18 Nov., 1891; m. 21 June, 1832, Daniel F. Putnam.

---

[139] Dea. Fowler was born in Danvers and died there, having been very active in all matters pertaining to the welfare and educational interests of the town. A prominent member of the Essex Institute he contributed greatly to the literature of Essex County. His children are descended in nine ways from John Putnam, the emigrant, as follows :

1. Harriet, Betsey, wife of Moses, Israel, David, Joseph, Thomas, John.
2. Moses, Stephen, Stephen, Benj., Nath'l, John.
3. Miriam, wife of Stephen, John, John, John.
4. Sam'l P. Fowler, Clarissa Page, Sam'l Page, Sarah Andrews, Genger Porter, Sarah, James, John, John.
5. Sarah, mother of Sam'l P. Fowler, Archelaus, Nath'l, Benj., Nath'l, John.
6. Mehetable, wife of Archelaus, Caleb, John, John, John.
7. Hannah, wife of John, Benj., Nath'l, John.
8. Rebecca, wife of Capt. Sam'l Page, William, David, Jos., Thos., John.
9. Elizabeth, wife of Wm., Josiah, John, Nath'l, John.

While many of the old Danvers families by intermarriage can claim descent by two or more lines from John Putnam, yet this record is truly remarkable.

A portrait and memoir of Dea. Fowler may be found in volume 26 of the Essex Inst. Historical Collections.

Just as this goes to press the information reaches me that Miss Harriet P. Fowler has presented to the Essex Institute at Salem an old cupboard carved in the fashion of the 16th century, which is known to have been the property of her ancestor Benjamin Putnam, and is thought by some, with reason, to have been brought from England by our first ancestor. E. P.

Jacob Putnam

2048   CLARISSA, b. 8 May, 1814; d., unm., 12 Apr., 1836.

2049   ISRAEL EPPES. b. 20 Oct., 1816; d. 1 Oct., 1838.

2050   MOSES WATTS, b. 9 Oct., 1818; d. in Philadelphia, 16 Jan., 1888;
        m. 8 Dec., 1846, Mary B. Steele.

2051   EMELINE, b. 15 June, 1821; m. 11 June, 1844, Joseph S., son of
        Major Moses Black.   Ch.: Israel Putnam, b. 27 Apr., 1845;
        m. 1869, Mary Alice Currier.   Joseph Willis, b. 13 Apr., 1847;
        d. 13 Dec., 1851.   Joseph Walter, b. 12 Sept., 1851; m. 2 July,
        1879, Susan L. Farnham.   George Franklin, b. 30 Apr., 1854; d.
        Oct., 1893.   Emeline Louisa, b. 19 Nov., 1856; d. 16 June, 1863.
        Mrs. Black m., 2d, Charles A. Putnam (No. 2067).

MOSES PUTNAM was apprenticed to learn the shoe business,
when fourteen years of age, to John Porter of Danvers. By
successive steps he rose in business till he became one of the
largest manufacturers and wealthiest men in Danvers.

VI. 854 Jacob (*Stephen, Stephen, Benjamin, Nathaniel, John,*), born in Danvers, 17 Nov., 1780; died 18 Jan., 1866, at Salem; married 1 June, 1819, Susanna, daughter of Capt. James and Susanna (Howard) Silver of Salem, born there, 17 Apr., 1800 and died in Salem 25 June, 1872.

Children, born in Salem:

2052   SUSAN SILVER, b. 24 Feb., 1820; m. 10 May, 1842, Judge Thos.
        Bancroft son of Asa T. and Judith (Little) Newhall of Lynn, b.
        2 Oct., 1811; died in Lynn 25 Sept., 1893, æt. 82 yrs. Ch.:
        James S., b. 13 Aug., 1843.   Susan A., b. 19 July; d. 29 Aug.,
        1845.   Thos. B., b. 12 Dec., 1846; d. 18 Sept., 1847.   Thos. L.,
        b. 31 Dec., 1857; d. 2 Sept., 1862.   Caroline P., b. 27 Jan., 1860;
        m. J. A. Heath.   Judge Newhall was elected Mayor of Lynn
        but declined.

2053   JAMES SILVER, b. 7 Mar., 1822; d. 26 Sept., 1873; m. 20 Oct., 1870,
        Mary Daland Cheever.

2054   SARAH AUGUSTA, b. 25 May, 1824; d. 4 Dec., 1825.

2055   SARAH AUGUSTA, b. 19 Nov., 1826; m , 19 Aug., 1847, John Andrew
        son of Andrew and ——— (Tebbetts) Heath, b. in Bath, Me., 8
        Aug., 1811.   They live in Boston.   Ch.: Jacob Putnam, b. 29
        June, 1848; d. 14 Mar., 1887.   John A., b. 27 Oct., 1850; m. his
        cousin Caroline P. Newhall 15 June, 1886.   Nath'l, b. 15 Feb.,
        1852.

2056   CAROLINE ELIZA, b. 10 Feb., 1829; d. 24 Dec., 1829.

2057   GEORGE FRANKLIN, b. 28 July, 1831.

2058   CAROLINE ELIZA, b. 15 Dec., 1833; m. 4 Oct., 1860, Thos. Witteridge Osborne.   Ch.: C. E., b. 15 Dec., 1833; d. 18 Apr., 1861.

2059   MARY ELLEN, b. 15 July, 1837; d. (1847?).

JACOB PUTNAM was the pioneer of the leather industry in
Salem. When a lad, although not having the advantages of an
education equal to some yet his native wit and shrewdness of
observation stood him such good service, that he as a man was
one of fine education and talents. In 1805 he made a voyage
to Calcutta and immediately upon his return established himself in the leather business which he successfully followed until
death removed him from an active sphere of usefulness. He
was a man of untiring energy, unfaltering patriotism, and of
sound judgment and great business sagacity. The business
he built up is still carried on by his son, George F. Putnam of
Boston. This business extended into all the various lines,
dealing in hides, tanning, currying, marketing the finished
product. During the commercial activity of Salem, he engaged in the shipping business, importing in his own vessels,
products of South America and Sumatra.

As a private citizen of Salem, he did much good, although in
a manner not calculated to attract attention. His death was
lamented by a circle of friends of all stations in life who will
always remember him as a kindly and benevolent gentleman.

During the war of 1812 he was an active member in the Salem company.

VI. 855 Samuel (*Stephen, Stephen, Benjamin, Na-
thaniel, John*), born in Danvers, 30 Oct., 1782; died 15
Aug., 1856; of Danvers, shoe manufacturer; married 26
March, 1808, Polly Herrick.

Children, born in Danvers:

2060 GEORGE ADAMS, b. 23 July, 1808.

2061 STEPHEN, b. 19 Feb., 1810.

2062 MARY HERRICK, b. 23 Feb., 1812; m. 16 Feb., 1836, Elbridge
Trask of Danvers. Ch.: Samuel Putnam, b. 4 July, 1836; d.
Feb., 1841. Elbridge Payson, b. 2 June, 1840. Mary Elizabeth,
b. 12 Aug., 1842; m. 1 May, 1862, Austin Martin, of Beverly.
Samuel Putnam, b. 1 Feb., 1845; d. 3 Apr., 1881; m. 17 June,
1875, Eliza C. Means of Essex, who d. 24 Oct., 1885. Charles
Willie, b. 8 May, 1846. Almira Putnam, b. 14 Dec., 1850; m.
16 June, 1872, C. Loring Elliott of Danvers. Caroline W., b.
30 Aug., 1854.

2063 SAMUEL, b. 18 Oct., 1813; d. unm., 18 Feb., 1833.

2064 WILLIAM N., b. 10 Aug., 1815; d. unm., 5 Mar., 1843.

2065 THOMAS MEADY, b. 15 Sept., 1817.

2066 ALBERT, b. 18 Feb., 1819.

2067 CHARLES AUGUSTUS, b. 3 May, 1821; d. 13 Feb., 1893.

2068 ALMIRA AUGUSTA, b. 3 Apr., 1823; d. 21 Jan., 1875; m. 13 Jan.,
1853, Haskell Perley of Georgetown. Ch.: Eleanor P., b. 21
Apr., 1854; m. 25 Dec., 1882, Newell H. Tilton of New Salem,
N. H. Mary H., b. 3 July, 1858. Julia A., b. 22 Dec., 1861.

2069 ELIZABETH H., b. 6 Feb., 1825; d. 30 Dec., 1864; m. 23 Apr., 1860,
Aaron Foster of Wenham.

2070 HENRY ALONZO, b. 13 May, 1827.

2071 MARTHA JANE, b. 1 July, 1829; d. unm., 19 Feb., 1833.

2072 ELLEN Maria, b. 28 Mar., 1831; d. unm., 10 June, 1833.

VI. 856 Ebenezer (*Stephen, Stephen, Benjamin, Nathaniel, John*), born in Danvers, 4 Feb., 1785; died there, 1877; married 8 Oct., 1809, Betsey, daughter of Nathaniel and Emma (Porter) Webb, born 11 Dec., 1790 and died 18 April, 1843; married, second, 7 May, 1844, (Mrs.?) Priscilla Dutch, born 9 Sept., 1797 and died 18 April, 1856; perhaps daughter of Daniel and Lucy (Staniford) Dutch, of Salem. Married, third, 25 Nov., 1857, Mrs. Sophia Clement, born in New Hampshire.

Children, born in Danvers:

2073 EDWIN FRANCIS, b. 19 July, 1810.

2074 ADDISON WEBB, b. 4 Mar., 1812; d. 28 Oct., 1835.

2075 ELIZABETH ANN, b. 4 Mar., 1814; m. 16 Feb., 1837, William Cheever, of Long Island.

2076 SALLY HERRICK, b. 11 Feb., 1816; d. at Danversport, 12 Feb.,
1881; m. 17 Apr., 1838, Henry, son of Samuel and Clarissa
(Page) Fowler, b. in Danvers, 15 Sept., 1810. Ch : Henry P.,
b. 24 Feb., 1839. Addison W., b. 26 May, 1841. Adelaide, b.
23 Sept., 1843. Betsey P., b. 4 Nov., 1846. Eliza P., b. 24 Jan.,
1849. Sarah P., b. 11 Aug., 1853. Rebecca, b. 26 Jan., d. 20
July, 1859.

2077 MARGARET DALE, b. 24 Dec., 1817; m. 7 May, 1844 (8 Apr., 1840,
Ropes Gen.), Joseph White, son of William and Rachel Ropes,
of Danvers, b. 14 Mar., 1816. Ch.:

2078 HANNAH JANE, b. 11 Nov., 1819; m. 2 Oct., 1844, Francis A.
Boomer: lived in Iowa, 1889.

2079 MARY ANN, b. 30 July, 1821; d. in Danvers, of consumption.

2080 EUNICE ADALINE, b. 25 Aug., 1823; d. in Danvers.

2081 EMILY AUGUSTA, b. 20 Sept., 1825; d. ———; m. 16 Feb., 1853,
John Black.

2082 Eben Henry, b. 16 Dec., 1827; d. in Boston, 27 May, 1856.
2083 Caroline Amanda, b. 31 Aug., 1829; m. 10 Oct., 1853, Abraham Babbitt.
2084 Franklin Weston, b. 17 Sept., 1831.
085 Georgianna, b. 20 April, 1837.

Ebenezer Putnam was an active business man of Danvers, at first as a shoe manufacturer, from which business he retired in 1844, after forty years' experience, and afterward as a grocer. In 1835 and '36 he represented Danvers in the General Court and from time to time held many important town offices.

The males of this family had light hair and eyes.

VI. 863 Henry (*Daniel, Daniel. Benjamin, Nathaniel, John*), born in Reading, 7 May, 1755; died there in November, 1806; married 9 Nov., 1775, Mary Hawkes, of Lynnfield, who died 21 Jan., 1794. He married, second, 18 Feb., 1796, at Charlestown, Lucy, daughter of Peter and Ann (Adams) Tufts, born 12 Nov., 1767 and died 10 June, 1849. She married, second, June, 1811, Jacob, son of Capt. Isaac and Betsey (Flint) Osgood (see Osgood Genealogy).

Children, born in Reading :

2086 Daniel, b. 1777; d. in Inf.
2087 Henry, b. 28 June, 1778; d. at New York, 1827.
2088 Polly, b. 30 Sept., 1780; d. 27 Feb., 1807; m. 11 Apr., 1799, Dr. Nahum Fay, of Charlestown.
2089 Joshua, b. 4 Sept., 1782; d. 6 Oct., 1834.
2090 Daniel, b. 14 Oct., 1785; d Nov., 1792.
2091 Sally, b. 1 Oct., 1790; d. ———; m. John Gulliver, of Taunton. Mrs. Gulliver was a truly remarkable woman. Ch.: John Putnam, b. May, 1819; d. at Andover, 25 Jan., 1894; m. 8 Sept., 1845, Frances Woodbury, dau. of Elizur and Amanda (Steele) Curtis of Torringford, Conn., who d. 9 Mar., 1892. (Ch.: Wm. C. of N. Y. Francis. Julia of Rockford, Ill. Mary of Northampton.) Prof. Gulliver held the chair of "Relations of Christianity to Science," at Andover Theological Seminary. Sarah, b. in Boston, 18 Dec., 1823; m. 17 Oct., 1855, Rev. Lewellyn, son of Selden Mather and Rebecca (Nott) Pratt, b. in Saybrook, Conn., 8 Aug., 1832. He has filled professorships at Knox and Williams Colleges and at Hartford Seminary. (Ch.: Waldo Selden, b. in Philadelphia, 10 Nov., 1857; m. 5 July,

1887, Mary E. Smyly; they live in Hartford. Thos. Putnam, b. 24 Jan., 1863; d. 12 Jan., 1867.) Daniel Francis, b. in Boston, 29 May, 1826; m. 16 Sept., 1852, Mary Eunice, dau: of Henry and Eunice Edgerton (Huntington) Strong, b. 27 Oct., 1827.. He was a physician in Boston; now a resident of Norwich, Conn.; grad. at Yale and Jefferson Medical Coll. at Phila. (Ch.: Henry Strong, b. 31 Oct., 1853; m. 3 Sept., 1887, Harriet Evans, and had Wm. and Henry S., d. y. Arthur H., b. 13 Dec., 1856; m. 8 Apr., 1885, F. A. Emerson, and had Edith. Gertrude P., b. 27 Nov., 1858; d. 1 Jan., 1862. Charlotte C., b. 11 Sept., 1860. Fred P., b. 30 Aug., 1865. Eunice H., b. 13 Sept., 1867. Benj. W., b. 2 July, 1869. Robert J., b. 7 June, 1872.) John Gulliver was a merchant in Philadelphia and Boston.

2092   DANIEL, b. 8 Feb., 1793; d. 8 Dec., 1817. He was a merchant in Boston.

HENRY PUTNAM responded to the alarm of the 19th April, 1775 and served nine days in Capt. John Flint's company. He lived in North Reading, was chosen a deacon in the church of the second parish in 1778, and was a man of influence in the place. He lived in the house formerly occupied by Rev. Daniel Putnam, his grandfather.

James Otis, the patriot, was harbored and cared for for many years by Mrs. Osgood. Otis was killed by lightning at her home.

VI. 864 Doctor Aaron (*Daniel, Daniel, Benjamin, Nathaniel, John*), born in Reading, 11 April, 1757; died in Boston, May, 1812; married in Medford, 9 May, 1780, Rebecca, daughter of Aaron and Rebecca (Pool) Hall, of Medford, born 9 Nov., 1760 and died Oct., 1803. Dr. Aaron Putnam and wife were admitted to church in Medford 28 May, 1786; dismissed to church at Charlestown 29 April, 1792. He married, second (published 17 Nov., 1805), Sarah Fayerweather, of Cambridge.

Children :

2093   AARON HALL, b. in Medford, 24 Mar., 1782; d., unm., in Charlestown, 30 May, 1809. Delivered an oration 4 July, 1805, before the Federal Republicans of Charlestown, which was printed.

32

2094 FITCH POOL, b. in Medford, 15 Nov.. 1788, d. in Charlestown, 16 July, 1820.

2095 JOHN INGALLS, b. in Medford, 23 April, 1788; d., unm., Aug., 1835.

2096 REBECCA, b. in Medford, 26 Aug., 1791; d. 21 Aug., 1793.

2097 A SON, d. 21 Aug., 1793, æt. 2 yrs.

2098 CHARLES, b. 26 Oct., 1794; d. 27 Oct., 1794, " æt. 8 days."

2099 CHARLES, b. 14 Dec., 1795; d. 12 or 15 Jan., 1796. ·

2100 CHARLES, b. 7 Apr., 1797; d. aged a few days.

2101 SARAH, b 11 July, 1798; m. Dr. Tyler, of Hopkinton, N. H.

DR. AARON PUTNAM was settled in Medford for ten years, but on account of a limited practice removed to Charlestown and engaged with Messrs. Morse & Woodbridge in the manufacture of baking powder, which however proved an unsuccessful venture. In 1801 he had the position of agent to purchase sixty-five acres of flats fort he U. S. navy yard. He dealt quite largely in real estate, and in 1800 sold to the United States four acres of land in Charlestown for the navy yard. During the struggle for independence he was a surgeon's mate in Colonel Frye's regiment in 1775, in the 26th regiment in 1776, and was appointed surgeon in Vose's regiment, 1 July, 1777; discharged 26 Oct., 1777.

VI. 875 Rev. Aaron (*Aaron, Daniel, Benjamin, Nathaniel, John*), born in Pomfret, Conn., 26 Oct., 1786; died 20 Dec., 1831; married, Oct., 1815, Mary Green, of Rhode Island, who died 17 Oct., 1820; married, second, Mary Abel, of Philadelphia.

He was a graduate of Brown University 1806 or '7; and was a Presbyterian minister, settled at Cherry Valley, N. Y.

Child :

2102 ELIZABETH AVERY, b. 23 Aug., 1816; m. 31 Mar., 1836, Benj. F. Cleveland,[14] who d. 25 Jan.. 1851, æ. 48. She m., 2d, 1877, Morton Eddy, of Fall River. Ch., by 1st m. : Lucy G. Sarah L. Aaron P. Catherine. Henry G.

Children, by second wife:

2103 SARAH.

2104 AARON.

2105 LOUISA, d. in inf.

2106 LUCRETIA, m. David Winton (living in 1885).

[14] For descendants see Avery Genealogy.

VI. 878 Daniel (*Israel, Israel, Benjamin, Nathaniel, John*), born in Chelmsford, 4 Feb., 1759; died at Framingham, 6 March, 1819; married, 1789, Hannah Alexander, born in Boston, 28 March, 1769? and died at Carmel, Me., 3 July, 1852. He was engaged in hop growing at Littleton, but in 1814 was engaged by Col. Calvin Sanger at his cotton factory in Framingham.

Children :

2107 LUCINDA, b. in Chelmsford, 1 Nov., 1793; d. in Waltham, 28 Dec., 1872; m. Theodore Wyman.

2108 DANIEL, b. 27 Nov., 1798; d. in Minnesota, 28 May, 1876; m., 1st, Marcia Hatch; m., 2d, Mrs. Pamelia Hilton. Lived in Framingham in 1822.

2109 HANNAH, b. in Littleton, 23 Mar., 1800; d. in Medway, Nov., 1880; m. Elihu Hixon.

2110 SARAH, b. 15 Dec., 1801; d in Carmel, Me., June, 1860; m. Lewis Mayo.

2111 ISRAEL, b. 20 Nov., 1803; m. Adeline White; lived in Dover, Me. Lived in Framingham in 1823.

2112 MARY, b. 18 June, 1805; d. Bangor, Me., 1 July, 1878; m., 1st, Timothy Mayo; m., 2d, Wm. Swett.

2113 ANN, b. 21 Mar., 1807; d. in Monroe, Me., 16 June, 1864; m. Israel Stearns.

2114 MARTHA, b. 12 Mar., 1809; d. 1811.

2115 RACHEL, b. 16 July, 1811; d. in Carmel, Me.; m. Lewis Mayo.

VI. 884 David (*Jonathan, Israel, Benjamin, Nathaniel, John*), born in Chelmsford, 1758; adm. of his estate to his widow, 1 Aug., 1785; married, 1780, Relief Pierce, of Chelmsford, a sister of Gov. Benj. Pierce, and aunt of Franklin Pierce, President of the United States.

Children :

2116 LEAFY, b. 26 October, 1781; d. in Charlestown, N. H., April, 1870; m. 6 Feb., 1803, Joseph Danah, b. in Tyngsboro, 15 Aug., 1779 and d. in Charlestown, N. H., 9 Mar., 1863. Ch., b. in Charlestown, N. H.: Charles, b. 12 Nov., 1803; d. in Carthagena, S. A., 4 June, 1826. Lefe Pierce, b. 4 May, 1805. Elizabeth, b. 12 May, 1807; d. in Concord, 15 Jan., 1823. Amanda, b. 28 April, 1809; d. 4 June, 1857; m. Henry H. Sylvester. Joseph, b. 4 Apr., 1813; d there, 13 April, 1884. Jane Maria, b. 7 July, 1815. Robert Kendall, b. 7 Dec., 1818; d. in Boston. David Putnam, b. in Concord, Mass., 26 Mar., 1823; d. 7 Mar., 1875; m. Mary Morse. Henry Hurd, b. in Chester, Vt., 4 Oct., 1825; lives in Boston.

2117 DAVID, b..1783.
2118 HANNAH, b. 1785.

DAVID PUTNAM served as a private in Capt. Ford's company of Chelmsford in the campaign against Burgoyne in Sept., 1777.

VI. 892 Joseph (*Jonathan, Israel, Benjamin, Nathaniel, John*), born in Chelmsford, 4 March, 1771; died 18 Oct., 1858; married, 1794, Abigail, daughter of Tarrant Putnam, born 13 July, 1768 and died, 1797; married, second, 1798, Nancy, daughter of Joseph Putnam, of Danvers; died 1 Sept., 1865, aged 91 years, 3 months, 22 days. Farmer at Chelmsford.

Children, by first wife :

2119 A CHILD; d. y.
2120 ISRAEL, b. 1797; d. y.

By second wife :

2121 ELIEL, b. at Middleton, 23 Apr., 1800; d. 31 Mar., 1868.
2122 OSGOOD, b. 25 Oct., 1801.
2123 MARTHA T., b. 23 Sept., 1803; d. 13 Feb., 1873; m., 1827, Joseph Chamberlain. Ch. : Joseph Augustus, b. 1828. John Franklin, b. 1830. Martha, b. 1833. Adams, m. Hattie Avery (one ch. Florence M.).
2124 ISRAEL, b. 14 Jan., 1805.
[2125 STEPHEN, b. 17 Nov., 1807; d. 7 Apr., 1884.
2126 FRANKLIN, b. 3 Aug., 1809; d , unm., 27 Jan., 1881; "d in Newton, 24 Jan., 1881, æt. 71 yrs., 5 mos., 24 dys." He was a merchant.
2127 ANN E., b. 14 Mar., 1811; m. 8 Nov., 1838, Hezekiah Bryant son of Nelson Crooker of Boston, b. in Amherst, N. H.; d. in Boston, 28 Oct., 1868. She lives in Newton. Ch. : Ann Juliet, b. 6 Oct., 1839; d. 16 Feb., 1869; m. 27 Sept., 1864, Albert Day, jr., of Boston. (Ch. : Henry H., b. 19 Nov., 1865. Juliet, b. 27 Oct., 1868.) Joseph Putnam, b. 1841; d. 1843. Mary Elizabeth, b. and d. Nov., 1844. Henry W. C., b. 1847; d. 1858.
2128 JULIA AMANDA, b. 1813; living 1886; m. George W., son of Joseph (Joseph) Putnam, and had one dau., Julia Alexandria.
       All of these eight children lived to be between 70 and 80 yrs. of age.

VI. 894 Stephen (*Jonathan, Israel, Benjamin, Nathaniel, John*), born in Chelmsford, 1776; married Eunice Phippen.

Children :

2129 ANN, m. Jonathan Cass.
2130 MARTHA, m. Benjamin Ireson. Ch.: Eunice. Lydia, m. Thomas
Lewis. William. Eveline. Martha Ann, m. Horace Lewis.
Mary Angelina. Franklin, d. during Rebellion.

VI. 895 Eleazer Porter (*Tarrant, Israel, Benjamin, Nathaniel, John*), born in Danvers, 8 Dec., 1758; died in Corinth, Vt., 1813; married 28 April, 1781, Rebecca Smith, of Topsfield, born 29 June, 1760 and died at Corinth, Vt., 15 April, 1816.

Children :

2131 SAMUEL PORTER, b. 6 Dec., 1783.
2132 ISRAEL, b. in Danvers, 25 Mar., 1785.
2133 BENJAMIN, b. 1 Sept., 1788.
2134 HIRAM SMITH, b. 14 Nov., 1793.
2135 HARRIET SMITH, m. —— Ormsby, of Fairlee, Vt. Ch.: four.
2136 SALLY, b. 14 Sept., 1798; d. 1850; m. ——Raymond, of Corinth.
A dau. d. prev. to 1834.
2137 LOUISA, b. 4 June, 1803; m., 1837, E. C. Scott; lives at Atlantic, Mass.

ELEAZER PORTER PUTNAM about 1790, removed from Danvers to Newbury, Vt., thence to Corinth, Vt.

VI. 896 Israel (*Tarrant, Israel, Benjamin, Nathaniel, John*), born in Danvers, 22 Nov., 1760; married in Corinth, Vt., April, 1788, Susanna Heath, born 2 July, 1767. Removed to Topsham, Vt.

Children, born in Newbury, Vt. :

2138 BETSEY, b. 15 July, 1789; d. 5 Dec., 1819; m. John B., son of Dudley and Mehitable (Barker) Carlton, of Newbury, Vt. who d.
Mar., 1873. Ch.: Horatio Nelson, b. 31 May, 1815; m. 19 Mar.,
1843. Sarah Ann Prescott, of Newbury, Vt.; no ch.
2139 JESSE, b. 21 Dec., 1790; m. 18 Apr., 1816, Eliza Groew.
2140 SUSANNA, b. 27 Feb., 1794; d. in Fonda, N. Y., *s. p.*, abt. 1856;
m. Jan. or Feb, 1820, Luke Cross, of Topsham, N. H.

VI. 897 Asa (*Tarrant, Israel, Benjamin, Nathaniel, John*), born in Danvers, 28 Dec., 1763; died ——; married ——.

Children (large family) :

2141

Lived in 1834 at Brookfield, N. Y., and afterwards at Essex, N. Y. He was a deacon, also a successful and wealthy farmer.

VI. 903 Tarrant (*Tarrant, Israel, Benjamin, Nathaniel, John*), born ———; died previous to 1834; married ———. Of Newbury, Vt.

Children:

2142 DANIEL PORTER.
2143 MARY JANE.
2144 A DAU., d. prev. to 1834.

VI. 907 Moses (*Nathaniel, Cornelius, Benjamin, Nathaniel, John*), born in Sutton, 23 Jan., 1758; administered on estate to Stephen Putnam, 2 May, 1826; married 24 June, 1774, Mary Allen, of Sutton.

Children, born in Sutton:

2145 DEBORAH, b. 26 June, 1780.
2146 POLLY, b. 25 Sept., 1781.
2147 STEPHEN, b. 24 Dec., 1782; d. 28 Nov., 1836.
2148 NATHANIEL, b. 13 Feb., 1785.
2149 ELIJAH, b. 9 Oct., 1786; d. 31 Dec., 1788.
2150 MOSES, b. 17 Aug., 1788; m. prev. to 1835, ——— Livermore.
2151 ELIJAH, b. 16 July, 1790; m. prev. to 1835.
2152 SALLY, b. 14 July, 1792; m. 3 Apr., 1811, Abraham Howard.
2153 STILLMAN, b. 15 Jan., 1797; d. 17 Aug., 1798.
2154 SUKEY, b. 13 June, 1799; d. 22 Aug., 1803.

VI. 911 Bartholomew (*Bartholomew, Cornelius, Benjamin, Nathaniel, John*), born in Sutton, 13 July, 1774; died there, 25 July, 1811; married there, 4 Sept., 1801, Hannah, daughter of Tarrant and Hannah (Putnam) Sibley, born 22 May, 1784; and died 9 June, 1827. Her father was of Sutton, a maltster, married 22 April, 1779. Mrs. Putnam married, second, Aaron Putnam (No. 1219) by whom she had a son Sibley, born 1821, who was a merchant in Worcester and died there 1887.

Children, born in Sutton:

2157 RUSSELL, b. 3 Feb., 1802.
2156 POLLY, b. 4 Apr., 1804; m. in Oxford, Aug., 1822, Asa, son of Increase and Mary (Barrett) Stearns, of Holden, b. in Northbridge, 25 Aug., 1800 and d. in Shrewsbury, Aug., 1865. Mrs.

Stearns is still (1890) living. Ch., b. in Sutton: Osborn, b. May, 1824; d. 1888. Henry Putnam, b. 18 Apr., 1828. Andrew Jackson, b. 29 Mar., 1830. Charles Sibley, b. in Shrewsbury, 16 Apr., 1844. Of these the two latter are in business at 285 Congress street, Boston. Henry P. is the physician in charge of the Retreat for the Insane at Hartford, Ct. He is a graduate of Yale and served as surgeon U. S. Vol. In 1857 he m. Annie Elizabeth, dau. of James and Elizabeth (Shaw) Stone, of Glasgow, Scotland, b. there, 1830. Ch.: Henry Stuart, b. in Marl. boro, 12 Aug., 1858; of Salem, Mass.; of the class of '81 Williams, Yale Univ. Law School, 1884; m. 7 May. 1889, at Beverly, Mary, dau. of Henry King and Anna M. (Olmsted) Olmsted, of Hartford, b. there, 20 Jan., 1865. (Ch.: Stuart O., b. 19 April, 1891.) Ellen Brodie, b. in Hartford, 1867; d. 1878. Charles Stainer, b. in Hartford, 1869.

2157   CLARK, b. 18 Feb., 1806; living 1827.
2158   PRUDENCE, b. 19 Feb., 1808; d. æt. 32; m. Clark Dalrymple of Providence, R. I.
2159   LEONARD, b. 25 Apr., 1810; d. y.
2160   ZILPHA, b. 8 Apr., 1812; d. y.

VI. 913 Edward (*Bartholomew, Cornelius. Benjamin, Nathaniel, John*), born in Sutton, 26 Jan., 1782; died there; will dated 1 June, prob. 6 Aug., 1811: wife Lydia, infant son aged four months; only child now living.

Child:

2161   EDWARD, b. Jan. or Feb., 1811; mentioned in grandfather's will, 1822.

VI. 920 Abner (*David, Cornelius, Benjamin, Nathaniel, John*), born in Sutton, 14 May, 1775; died 25 June, 1859; married in Sutton, 13 March, 1799, Amy (No. 1 25) daughter of Captain Archelaus and Sarah (Putnam) Putnam, born in Sutton, 7 Oct., 1779.

Children, born in Sutton:

2162   RUTH, b. 12 June, 1800.
2163   SALLY, b. 29 Apr., 1802; m., 1st, Darius Putnam; m., 2d, Tourtellot Inman.
2164   HARVEY, b. 29 Nov., 1804.
2165   ANNA or AMY, b. 3 Nov., 1806; m. 23 Oct., 1831, Charles H. Newton.
2166   ARCHELAUS, b. 3 Dec., 1808.
2167   WILLARD, b. 7 Feb., 1811.

2168 DEXTER, b. 14 Nov., 1813; m. 16 Mar., 1840, Ruby Titus, dau. of
        of Lewis and Betsey Torrey, of Sutton, b. there, 31 Jan., 1821.
2169 LOUISA, b 14 Oct., 1816.
2170 LAWSON, b. 18 Sept., 1820.

VI. 921 Cyrus (*David, Cornelius, Benjamin, Nathaniel, John*), born in Sutton, 21 Aug., 1777; married there, 17 May, 1800, Lucinda, daughter of Simeon and Betsey (Wellington) Hathaway, of Sutton, born 31 Oct., 1781.

Children, born in Sutton :

2171 SALMON, b. 29 Dec., 1800.
2172 DAVID, b. 6 Feb., 1803.
2173 PRUDENCE, b. 20 Dec., 1804; d. 28 Dec., 1804.
2174 LUCINDA, b. 5 Oct., 1806; d. 14 Jan., 1845; m. Merritt Cook, of
        Sutton.
2175 HORACE, b. 16 Feb., 1809.
2176 MARY REID, b. 2 Oct., 1811; d. 15 Jan., 1812.
2177 PHILANDER, } b. 10 Mar., 1815.
2178 LEANDER,   }

VI. 923 Cornelius (*David, Cornelius. Benjamin, Nathaniel, John*), born in Sutton, 25 Jan., 1782; married Abigail Bigelow.

Children :

2179 POLLY, b. 1 June, 1804.
2180 DARIUS, b. 30 Sept., 1806.
2181 LUCY, b. 3 Sept., 1808.
2182 ULVA ABIGAIL, b. 18 Jan., 1811; m. 2 Dec., 1832, Nathan, son of
        John and Hannah (Putnam) Waters, of Sutton. Ch.: Anna C.,
        b. 26 Jan., 1835; m. A. Aldrich. Ulva M., b. 27 Mar., 1837.
        Marion, b. 26 Mar., 1842; m. Henry Inman. Samuel, b. 25 Mar.,
        1845. Adelaide P., b. 20 Apr., 1848; m. E. E. Burdon. George
        B., b. 23 Feb., 1852.
2183 HARRISON BIGELOW, b. 18 Apr., 1813.

VI. 926 Joseph (*David, Cornelius, Benjamin, Nathaniel, John*), born in Sutton, 23 Feb., 1790; died there (after 1840); married there, 26 Dec., 1813, Polly Putnam; married, second, Fanny Whittemore, of Leicester.

Children :

2184 MARIA LOUISA, b. 4 Jan., 1815.
2185 PALMER, b. 1 May, 1817.

2186 MARY ELIZABETH, b. 3 July, 1819.
2187 SIMEON, b. 17 Nov., 1821; d. in Minnesota; Methodist minister.
2188 ALEXANDER, b. 29 June, 1824; a merchant in Worcester.
2189 GEORGE WHITTEMORE, b. 11 Aug., 1827; of Anoka, Minn., where
        he has held many public offices.
2190 CHARLES VERNON, b. 6 July, 1829; a merchant in Worcester
2191 PORTER FRANKLIN, b. 21 July, 1831.

VI. 927 Capt. Jeremiah (*Jonathan, Jonathan, Jonathan, John, John*), born in Danvers, 31 Oct., 1737; died 16 Sept., 1799; married 3 Feb., 1763, Rachel Fuller.

Children, born in Danvers:

2192 THOMAS, b. 8 Oct., 1763.
2193 EUNICE, b. 3 Jun., 1766; d. 20 Mar., 1817; m. 18 July, 1795, Israel
        son of Lt. Col. Israel and Mehitable (Porter) Hutchinson of
        Danvers. Ch.: Mehitable P., b. 22 July, d. 22 Oct., 1796.
        Eunice, b. 19 Dec., 1797; d. 11 Mar., 1866; m. Capt. John Ken-
        ney; removed to Gloucester. Elisha, b. 27 Sept., 1799; d. 30
        Aug., 1860; of Haverhill. Mehitable P., b. 23 Apr., 1805; d. 22
        Apr., 1837; m. 9 Sept., 1830, Dan'l Davenport of Andover.
2194 JEREMIAH, b. 21 Nov., 1769.
2195 APPHIA, b. 23 May, 1772.
2196 ELIJAH.
2197 LEVI.
2198 RACHEL.

JEREMIAH PUTNAM served from February to December, 1756, in the company of Capt. Andrew Fuller, at Crown Point, and again from Mar., to Nov., 1758 under the same commander. He enlisted 6 Apr., 1759, in Col. Plaisted's regiment. When the alarm of 19 April, 1775, came, he was one of those who responded being a member of Capt. Jeremiah Page's company. After the fight at Lexington he enlisted in the army as sergeant, 11 May, 1775, and rose to the rank of captain. He was taken prisoner at Long Island at which time he was an ensign in Col. Hutchinson's regiment. He was a brave soldier and gallant officer.

Hanson says of him, "He was a useful citizen and discharged faithfully the trusts reposed in him."

Over his grave in the Plains cemetery is a stone bearing the following epitaph:

"In memory of Capt. Jeremiah Putnam who died Sept.

33

16, 1799, Aged 63 years. An Officer under the Immortal Washington."

> This modest stone, what few vain mortals can,
> May truly say; Here lies an Honest Man."

VI. 933 Nathan (*Jonathan, Jonathan, Jonathan, John, John*), born in Danvers, 8 Sept., 1749; died there 10 Apr., 1823; married 23 Oct., 1771, Hannah, daughter of Dr. Amos Putnam, baptized 24 Sept., 1749, and died 26 Nov., 1802.

Children:

2199 NATHAN, b. 18 March, 1773.

2200 PERLEY, b. 16 Sept., 1778.

2201 DAVID, b. 23 Dec., 1780; d., *s. p.*, at Salem 15 May, 1866; m. 25 July, 1805, Sarah Abbott, b. June, 1792, d. 13 Dec., 1856. He was prominent in militia circles and rose to the rank of general. In 1807 he was one of the marshals appointed to receive President Monroe upon the occasion of his visit to Salem. At one time, he was an unsuccessful candidate for mayor of Salem He was a man of considerable prominence and worth. For many years he was a merchant in the dry goods trade. He adopted two nephews of his wife, by the name of Abbott: one known as Abbott Putnam lived for a while in Danvers; the other, David, was born 24 Dec., 1816, and is probably the "young artist of promise," who died at St. Andrews, N. B., 9 Apr., 1840, "Æt. 25 years." These young men are not known to have left any descendants.

2202 AMOS, b. 10 Feb., 1785; d. 20 June, 1850.

2203 HANNAH PHILLIPS, b. 23 Nov., 1786; d., unm., in Salem, subsequent to 1870. She presented to the Essex Institute a cup, porringer and snuff box of silver, marked with the initials J. & S. P., probably James and Sarah Putnam.

2204 JOHN, b. 20 May, 1791.

NATHAN PUTNAM was a member of Capt. Hutchinson's company which responded to the alarm of 19 April, 1775, and which suffered severely in the fight at Arlington, while making a brave stand. His brother Perley was killed. The following advertisement appeared in the "New England Chronicle, or Essex Gazette" for May 25, 1775. "Lost in the Battle of Menotomy,[141] by Nathan Putnam, of Capt. Hutch-

---

[141] The ancient name for Arlington, between Cambridge and Lexington.

inson's Company, who was then badly wounded, A French Firelock, marked D., No. 6, with a marking iron, on the Breech. Said Putnam carried it to a cross Road near a mill. Whoever has said Gun in Possession, is desired to return it to Col. Mansfield of Lynn, or to the Selectmen of Danvers, and they shall be well rewarded for their trouble. Danvers, May 16, 1775." He re-enlisted in Capt. Putnam's company, 19th Reg., 6 Oct., 1775. Constable 1785 and in 1787, he and Benjamin Putnam were of a committee to regulate the schools for the following winter.

VI. 936 Aaron (*Jonathan, Jonathan, Jonathan, John, John*), born in Danvers, 6 Sept., 1756; married Olive Osborne. After Mr. Putnam's death, she joined her sons in New York.

Children :

2205 PARLEY, went to sea and never was heard from; supposed to have been killed in Spain.
2206 NATHAN, } settled in N. Y. State probably Otsego County.
2207 JEREMIAH, } Nathan afterward went to Mich.
2208 SARAH, b. in Greenfield Hill, Conn., m. Moses Jennings who was born in Fairfield, Conn , about 1753. Ch. : Sam'l Henry. John. Eunice. Abbie. Mary. m. abt. 1845, at London, Eng., Chas. M. Mee, who came to America and settled in Brooklyn. (Ch. : Rev. Chas B. of Indepedence, Iowa. Sophia. James Putnam.)
2209 LYDIA, m. Isaac Bertine. She d. in Conn.
2210 EUNICE, m. Wm. Phillips. She d. in Conn.

AARON PUTNAM removed to Connecticut. He served in the Revolution, in 4th Conn. Reg. as private 1780–83. Of Fairfield, Conn., 1790 (Essex Deeds).

VI. 938 Joshua (*David, David, Jonathan, John, John*), born in Danvers, 3 Sept., 1789; married 12 Dec., 1820, Elizabeth Ashby of Marblehead.

Children, born in Danvers :

2211 ELENOR JANE, b. 27 Oct., 1821; d. 13 May, 1826.
2212 MARY ANN, b. 24 June, 1823.
2213 ANN ASHBY, b. 13 Sept., 1825; d. 22 Oct., 1828.
2214 JOSHUA HOLTON, b. 13 Nov.. 1829; m. at Boston 17 June, 1852, Josephine Cross.

VI. 942 Bartholemew (*Bartholomew, Bartholomew, James, John, John*), born in Salem, 2 Feb., 1737–8; died 17 Apr., 1815; married 13 May, 1760, Sarah, daughter of Gamaliel and Priscilla (Webb) Hodges, born 31 July, 1740, died 17 Oct., 1830.

Children :

2215 SARAH, bapt. 12 Sept., 1762; m., 1st, Thomas Palfray, (one son Thomas, d., unm.); m., 2nd, 2 Sept., 1784, Stephen son of Jonathan and Elizabeth (Saunders) Webb, b. 21 Sept., 1756, d. 11 Oct., 1831. Ch.: Hon. Stephen P. Webb.

2216 ELIZABETH, bapt. 9 Dec., 1764; m. Winthrop Gray.

2217 PRISCILLA, bapt. 24 Aug., 1766; d. (adm. 21 Apr.,) 1807; m. 11 Nov., 1787, Henry Clark son of John and Ann (Furneaux) Clark.

2218 RUTH, bapt. 17 July, 1768; d. 24 June, 1790; m. 2 Mar., 1789, Michael, son of Jonathan and Elizabeth (Saunders) Webb of Salem, b. 19 July, 1762; d. 12 Nov., 1839.

2219 BARTHOLOMEW, bapt. 20 Sept., 1772; d. unm.

2220 WILLIAM, bapt. 15 Sept., 1776; d. unm.

BARTHOLOMEW PUTNAM lived in Salem on the site of the present East Church. In 1778 he marched (4 Aug.) with the volunteers from Salem to Rhode Island, also in the campaign of 1779 when a company marched to Providence from Salem. He was the first collector of the port of Salem, under the new constitution.

VI. 959 Sarah (*Ebenezer, James, James, John, John*), born in Salem, 30 Aug., 1765; died there 20 Dec., 1801; married 17 Apr., 1791, Nathaniel, son of Judge Nathaniel and Priscilla (Sparhawk, daughter of Rev. John and Jane (Porter) Ropes, of Salem, born 13 June, 1759 and died 8 Aug., 1806. He married, second, 12 Apr., 1803, Elizabeth Cleveland.

Children, by Sarah :

2221 NATHANIEL, b. 1 Aug., 1791; d. 21 Aug., 1791.

2222 NATHANIEL, b. 24 July, 1792; d. 30 Aug., 1793.

2223 NATHANIEL, b. 14 Oct., 1793; d. in Cincinnati, Ohio, 19 July, 1885; m., at Cincinnati, 10 July, 1826, Sarah Evans, dau. of Wm. and Ruth (Hanford) Brown of Cincinnati, b. in Cincinnati 10 July, 1802, d. 7 Jan., 1873. Ch.: Sarah Putnam, b. 27 Mar., 1827.

Isabella Brown, b. 17 Jan., 1829; d. 11 Nov., 1834. Eliz'b Cleveland Orne, b. 28 Mar., 1831; d. 27 Aug , 1832. Nath'l, of Salem, H. C. 1855; b 17 Jan., 1833; d. *s. p.* in Salem, 6 Feb., 1893. Wm. Augustus, b. 22 Dec., 1834; d. 3 Feb., 1879. Eliza Orne, b. 7 Mar., 1837. John, b. 29 Aug., 1839; d. 16 Jan., 1842. Abigail Pickman, b. 7 Jan., 1842; d. 1 Feb., 1842. Mary Pickman, b. 30 Mar., 1843. Mr. Ropes was a prosperous merchant in Cincinnati. All the children, except three youngest, born in Cincinnati; they at Covington, Ky.

2224 SALLY FISKE, m. 19 May, 1817, Joseph Orne, who d. 1 Sept., 1818. Ch.: Eliz. Ropes, b. 27 Feb., 1818; d. *s. p.* 8 Mar., 1842.

2225 ABIGAIL PICKMAN, b. 20 Oct., 1796; d. *s. p.* 23 Apr., 1889.

NATHANIEL ROPES was a merchant in Salem, and lived there and on his farm in Danvers. His father was one of the noted men of Colonial days. Judge Ropes was graduated at Harvard in 1745 and was a Justice of the Court of Common Pleas, in 1766 Chief Justice, and in 1772 placed on the Bench of the Superior Court of Judicature. He was also representative to the General Court, and a member of the Executive Council. At the time of pre-revolutionary troubles, he, in common with most of the principal people of wealth and education, was averse to the radical movements on foot and this with his official position rendered him obnoxious to the commoner sort of persons. While ill with small pox, his house was assailed by a mob, who broke in the windows, and threatened to assassinate him. The strain was so severe, in his weak state, that he died the next day, 18 Mar., 1774. He and Doctor Eben Putnam were great friends, which was afterward cemented by a marriage between the families. His residence, on Essex street, opposite Cambridge St , was occupied by his granddaughter Mrs. Orne and after her death by her nephew Nathaniel Ropes. Recently it has been moved back and is now the residence of the Misses Ropes who have kept the old house externally nearly as it was but the interior unfortunately was recently damaged by fire.

VI. 960 Ebenezer (*Ebenezer, James, James, John, John*), born in Salem, 1768; died there 25 Feb., 1826; married, first, 22 May, 1791, Sarah, daughter of Gen. John and

Lydia (Phippen) Fiske of Salem, born 30 June, 1772, and died 7 Jan., 1795; married, second, 13 Nov., 1796, her sister, Elizabeth Fiske, born 19 July, 1778 and died Mar., 1808.

Children, born in Salem:

2226 EBENEZER, b. 27 Aug., 1792; d. 5 July, 1796.
2227 HARRIET, b. 5 Feb., 1794; d. 22 Nov., 1794.

By second wife:

2228 EBENEZER, b. Sept. 6, 1797; d. 3 Apr., 1876.
2229 HARRIET, b. and d. 22 May, 1799.
2230 JOHN FISKE, b. 25 May, 1800; d. 14 July, 1881.
2231 CHARLES FISKE, b. 19 Oct., 1802; d. 31 Dec., 1862.
2232 GEORGE, b. 10 Jan., 1804; d. 4 Dec., 1860, unm. He was a well known druggist in Salem, and a great lover of flowers and fruits, which he cultivated with great success.
2233 EDWARD, b. 23 Jan., 1806; d. 21 Nov., 1852.
2234 FRANCIS, b 3 Jan., 1808; d. 26 Mar., 1878.

EBENEZER PUTNAM was one of those men whose every instinct was naturally correct. As a boy, his life is unknown, except that he was a pupil, in 1778, of Rev. Asa Dunbar, the intellectual young colleague of Rev. Thomas Barnard of the First church in Salem. It is probable that he was fitted for college by Mr. Dunbar, that gentleman having, by reason of continued ill health, resigned his pastorate of the church, but this is by no means certain.

Young Putnam entered Harvard in 1781, at the age of thirteen, and was graduated in 1785. Among his classmates were Theodore Lincoln, Henry Ware, Nathan Hayward, Samuel Emerson, Jabez Upham, Paul Fearing and Barzillai Gannett. Samuel Putnam and John Quincy Adams were of the class of 1787, while Nathan Reed whose friendship was lasting had been graduated in 1781.

The stirring times of the Revolution, the hardships and annoyances his family had suffered during the contest, probably helped to give him that liberality of character, which especially distinguished him in after life. Shortly after reaching his majority, in 1791, he married one of the charming daughters of Gen. John Fiske, at that time one of the noted men of Salem. General Fiske claimed as his ancestors a long line of

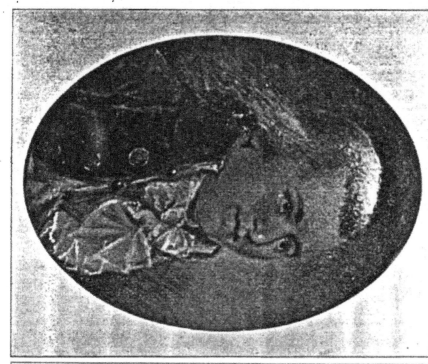

EBENEZER PUTNAM ESQ.

NO. 960.

ELIZABETH (FISKE) PUTNAM.

more or less distinguished ministers, more than one of whom had suffered bitter persecution as well here as in old England. He had shown the same spirit while in command of vessels of war, as his ancestors had shown in maintaining their right to believe as they chose. His title of general was obtained in the militia when, having accumulated a large fortune by his industry and bravery, he left the sea and settled down to the usual life of a retired Salem ship-owner and nabob. That Mr. Putnam was a welcome son-in-law is evident; for, within two years of the sad loss of his wife he took as a bride the General's youngest daughter.

A Salem lady used to say she well remembered the occasion of the entrance of the bride and groom in church the Sunday following the marriage. The bride wore a gown of rich white brocade, white satin bonnet and white veil and walked up the aisle on the arm of her husband, a man as well favored by good looks as herself. The miniatures, from which the illustrations here given were taken, were painted at about this time. Until his marriage he had lived with his mother, his father having died in 1788, in the house on Washington street; but either upon his first or second marriage he removed to the house still standing on the southwest corner of Bridge and Lemon street, to which was attached a fine garden of several acres. In this house were born his children and from there he returned to the house on Washington street, soon after the death of his mother which occurred in 1807. While living in this house he experienced those reverses of fortune which obliged him to part with much of his property. In 1810 he seems to have been drawn into commercial enterprises of what nature is not known, but he is remembered to have in the latter years of his life conducted business as a lumber merchant with a wharf near the present North Bridge. Shortly after the close of the War of 1812, he was forced to part with the greater portion of his property, so much that his sons were each obliged to begin life without capital. His eldest son in particular was forced to abandon the plans he had formed for his life work.

In his times of prosperity, Mr. Putnam was a large owner of real estate both in Essex County, in Maine and New Hampshire. He was one of the proprietors of Union wharf and held other wharf property and was one of the owners of the new mills on Crane river in Danvers as well as of a distillery in Salem. These investments came to him in part from his father and part by his marriage with Miss Fiske.

The War of 1812 and the failure of the Essex bank were sources of loss or ruin to many a Salem merchant and it is presumed these were among the causes which led to his loss of property rather than from any mismanagement of his estate.

It is related of him that his generosity was abundant and that he was constantly looking out for those he could help. Upon one occasion he noticed the household goods of some family upon the roadway and inquiring who was moving was informed that so and so was ejected for non-payment of rent; he promptly ordered the goods back and settled the bill. This is but one of the many similar accounts I have heard of his good deeds.

Judge Samuel Putnam wrote in 1834 concerning him, he " was a gentleman of most excellent spirit as well as of great truth and honor. I knew him very well. In any case of morals it would have been safe to have followed the dictates of his mind." The *Essex Gazette* of date of 28 Feb., 1826, said of him, "He was graduated at Harvard University in 1785 and was highly respected through life for strictest principles of integrity and honor." He died on Saturday the 25th Feb., and was buried the following Monday at half-past three o'clock.

Of Mrs. Putnam who died in March, 1808, the following obituary appeared in a Salem paper:

"Mrs. Elizabeth Putnam, aged thirty, wife of Mr. Ebenezer

Putnam, and youngest daughter of the late Gen. Fiske. This beloved woman was distinguished by her domestic virtues. She inherited all the benevolence which made her Father dear to his fellow citizens, with all those domestic attachments, which form the fond parent, the good wife, and the choicest of friends. She was Mr. Putnam's second wife, and both wives were daughters of the late Gen. Fiske, who has only one daughter living."

VI. 962 Doctor Archelaus (*Archelaus, James, James, John, John*), born in Danvers, baptized 9 Dec., 1744; died in Danvers, 1800; married 12 Nov., (11 Oct.,) 1786, Nabby Bishop of Medford, born 5 Oct., 1753 and died in Medford, 17 Dec., 1807; daughter of John and Abigail (Tufts) Bishop.

Children, born in Danvers:

2235 JOHN BISHOP, b. 1788; d. prev. to 1813.
2236 JAMES Augustus; b. 1 Dec., 1792; d. 14 Apr., 1864.
2237 ABIGAIL BISHOP; d. unm. 1829, æt. 35 years.

VI. 968 James (*James, James, James, John, John*), born in Worcester, 16 Nov., 1756; died in England, 2 Mar., 1838. He never married. A graduate of Harvard in 1774, he retired to Worcester, but early in 1775 was obliged to leave that place in company with his father, on account of his loyalist sentiments. He took an active part during the siege of Boston in organizing companies from the loyalist refugees cooped up in that town; but so far as we know none of these organizations took part in any of the fighting about Boston. He held the commission of lieutenant. Later he was at New York and Halifax and through the influence of the Duke of Kent, with whom he had formed a friendship, he was appointed to the commissary department of the British army. He was one of the trustees for the estate of the Duke of Kent and the only one who retained the position through the entire period of the trusteeship. At his death he left a good estate. During his life he was respected by all who came into contact

34

with him and letters are extant from the Duke of Kent,[142] which bear testimony to the high estimation in which he was held. One of which is as follows; .

Addressed "James Putnam Esqr.
6 Holles St."

Kensington Palace.
June 7th 1801.

DEAR PUTNAM

Having understood from you in conversation yesterday that you hoped to have an audience tomorrow of Sir William Scott on the subject of your situation as Marshall of the Admiralty at Halifax to which I had the good fortune of getting you named, I thought it might be both satisfactory and useful to you to be able to produce to that highly respectable and valuable man, my written sentiments as to the manner in which you have discharged your duties in the military situation you held in North America during the period of seven years that I commanded at Halifax, I therefore herewith enclose the same wishing you all the success in obtaining the object for which you are solicitous, that you so justly merit. I remain with the highest esteem & regard Dear Putnam

Ever Yours Most Sincerely
Edward, General and Commander in Chief
of His Majesty's Forces in North America.

VI. 970 Ebenezer (*James, James, James, John, John*), born in Worcester, 26 Jan., 1763 ; died in Fredericton, N. B., 3 April, 1798 ; married 2 Dec., 1786, Elizabeth, daughter of Hon. John and Dorothy (Paine) Chandler, born 20 Feb., 1770, and died in Lancaster, 18 Jan., 1820. He was graduated at Harvard, 1779. Registrar of deeds and wills at Fredericton, N. B. His wife is buried in Worcester, where the last years of her life were passed.

Children :

2238 ELIZABETH KNOX, b. 28 June, 1789; d. 19 Nov., 1789.
2239 JAMES, b. 27 Nov., 1790; d. in Worcester, 18 Aug., 1810, of rheumatic fever, while studying medicine with Dr. Nathan Smith at Dartmouth College. He was graduated at Harvard, 1808.

142 Father of Victoria, Queen of England, etc.

2240 JOHN CHANDLER, b. 26 Dec., 1793; d., *s. p.*, 1840, at Hartford,
      Conn.; m. 5 Sept., 1831, Abby, dau. of Stephen and Abigail
      Smith, b. Apr., 1805. He was a merchant in Boston. An
      adopted dau. m. William Lincoln, of Boston.

2241 CHARLES S., b. 24 June, 1796; d. 17 Feb., 1837.

2242 FRANCIS EBENEZER, b. 18 June, 1797; d., *s. p.*, 17 Aug., 1836;
      H. U. 1815. Lawyer at St. Andrews, N. B.; m. 27 Mar., 1820,
      Hannah Curry, who d. in Boston, 1839. Studied law with Ward
      Chipman, Jr., at St. John.

VI. 972 Col. Jethro (*Enoch, Jethro, James, John, John*), born in Danvers, 22 Dec., 1755; died there 20 May, 1815; married there 21 Sept., 1784, Mary, daughter of Hon. Samuel and Mary (Warner) Holton, of Danvers, born there, 26 June, 1760, and died there, 29 April, 1840.

Children, born in Danvers:

2243 HIRAM, b. 30 Jan., 1786.

2244 HARRIET, b. 22 May, 1787; m. —— Adams.

2245 PHILEMON, b. 12 Oct., 1789.

JETHRO PUTNAM was colonel of the Danvers regiment.

VI. 977 John (*John, Eleazer, Eleazer, John, John*), born in Preston, Conn., 7 March, 1765; died in Hinsdale, Mass., 21 Jan., 1826; married 13 April, 1791, Philusa Curtis, of Hampton, Conn., who died in Hinsdale, 4 March, 1836, aged 66 years.

Children:

2246 MARTHA, b. 9 Mar., 1792; d. soon after birth of her daughter;
      m. 20 Mar. (18 Feb., T. R.), 1810, G. W. McElwain, who d. at
      Plainfield, Conn. Ch.: Martha Philena, m. Charles Wright, of
      Hinsdale, afterward of Pittsfield.

2247 MARY, b. 11 Aug., 1793; m. 1 Jan., 1815, Dr. John Kittredge, of
      Hinsdale. Ch.: John Putnam, b. 8 Aug., 1815. Mary Sophia,
      b. 6 May, 1817. William C., b. 6 June, 1819. Frederick C., b.
      20 May, 1821; of Dalton, Mass. Samuel C., b. 13 Feb., 1825.
      George W., b. 28 May, 1828. Mary E., b. 6 May, 1829. Philena
      C., b. 28 Aug., 1833. Martha M., b. 16 Dec., 1834.

2248 SOPHIA, b. 22 Oct., 1797; m. 27 Jan., 1820, Daniel Nichols, who d.
      3 June, 1836. Ch.: Henry Putnam, b. 26 Sept., 1821; of Wor-
      cester. Philena Curtis, b. 6 Oct., 1827; A. F., b.——; of
      Worcester. Mrs. Nichols m., 2d, Jacob Booth, and d. about
      June, 1871. No children by the 2d marriage.

2249   JOHN, b. 12 Nov., 1799; d. 7 Mar., 1800.
2250   HENRY, b. 31 July, 1801.
2251   JOHN, b. 21 Apr., 1803.

JOHN PUTNAM moved, in 1790, from Cummington, Conn., to Hinsdale, then the west parish of Partridgefield. At this time Berkshire County was just beginning to attract settlers. He was a man of correct habits, strong mind and few words. At his death he left a good estate. During life he was noted for his great strength and iron constitution.

VI. 979 Jedediah (*John, Eleazer, Eleazer, John, John*), born in Preston, Conn., 6 Feb., 1769; died in Volney, N. Y., 3 Jan., 1826; married Lois Cheesborough, of Stonington, Conn.

Children, born in Brooklyn, Conn. :

2252   SAMUEL.
2253   HANNAH.
2254   JEDEDIAH.
2255   JOHN ; d. prev. to 1838.
2256   HARRIET.
2257   THOMAS.
2258   WILLIAM.
2259   MARY.

JEDEDIAH PUTNAM removed from Brooklyn, Conn., about 1815, to Volney, N. Y., although another authority states that in 1806 he moved to Manlius, N. Y., thence farther west.

VI. 988 Captain David (*Fuller, Jephtha, Eleazer, John, John*), born in Sutton, 26 Jan., 1753; married 15 Jan., 1781, Martha, daughter of Amos and Abigail (Cobb) Waters, of Sutton, born 22 Sept., 1759; she was appointed administratrix on her husband's estate 7 June, 1795.

Children, born in Sutton :

2260   RUFUS, aged 15 years, Sept., 1796; m. 15 Dec., 1805, Sally Sibley.
2261   SIMEON WATERS, aged 13 years in Sept., 1796.
2262   PATTY, m. Capt. Peter Putnam.
2263   POLLY.

2264 FULLER. Adm. on estate of Fuller Putnam, late of Sutton, a soldier in the United States army, to Rufus Putnam, 4 Jan., 1814.
2265 SALLY.

VI. 991 John (*Fuller, Jephtha, Eleazer, John, John*),
born in Sutton, 8 July, 1760; died there; administration
granted to Sylvanus "only son" 1 May, 1827; married, first,
22 Aug., 1781, Huldah, daughter of Amos and Abigail
(Cobb) Waters, of Sutton, and sister to the wives of Capt.
David and Capt. Abner Putnam, born 19 Dec., 1761, died
April, 1796; married, second, 14 June, 1798, Mrs. Ann
(Powers) Cox, from whom he was divorced Sept., 1817, on
account of incompatibility of temper. He gave her a small
farm in Sutton. She died about 1836. Married, third, in
Connecticut, 15 Dec., 1819, widow Dorcas Collar, daughter
of Peter Sibley, who survived him.

Children :

2266 JOHN, b. in Ward.
2267 SYLVANUS, b. in Auburn, 24 Jan., 1791.
2268 SARAH, b.———; m. 26 Dec., 1813, Otis, son of Joshua and Caroline M. (Hathaway) Morse, of Sutton, b. 30 Nov., 1790.
2269 A DAU.; m. Joseph Putnam.
2270 HULDAH, m. 8 Jan., 1809, Peter, son of Solomon and Mary (How-
ell) Stockwell, of Sutton, b. there 29 Nov., 1784.

By second wife :

2271 HARRY, d. in early manhood, unm.
2272 STEPHEN, b. 25 April, 1799.
2273 MARY, b. 27 Nov., 1800.
2274 GARDNER, b. 26 Oct., 1801.

By third wife :

2275 RUTH, b. 26 Mar , 1820.
2276 ESTHER, b. 28 Oct., 1822; m. Freeman F. Sibley.

VI. 998 Jacob (*John, Jephtha, Eleazer, John, John*),
born in Sutton, 21 Nov., 1764; died in Marblehead, 25
Nov., 1820, administration on estate of Jacob Putnam, of
Marblehead, hairdresser, granted to widow Hannah 20
Feb., 1821; married in Marblehead, 9 Oct., 1785, Hannah

Mugford, a sister of Mrs. John Putnam, and died in Marblehead, 18 April, 1826.

Children:

2277　LYDIA, m. —— Proctor.
2278　HANNAH, m. William Russell, of Marblehead, mariner.
2279　BETSY W., m. —— Stacey.
2280　OLIVE, m. Elias Hulen, Jr., of Marblehead, mariner.
2281　MARY ANN, unm., in 1822.

JACOB PUTNAM was a hotel keeper in 1806, when he was adjudged *non compos*. His wife was a daughter of Capt. James and Lydia Mugford, and therefore brother to the gallant young Capt. James Mugford, commander of the Franklin, a small armed vessel of sixty tons, with which he cut out the transport Hope and carried her into Boston harbor. On his return he was unsuccessfully attacked by a boat party of 200 British, but lost his life in the fray. This was the 19 May, 1776, when he was just twenty-seven years old. He left a widow Sarah.

Jacob Putnam was a U. S. pensioner at the time of his death.

John, a younger brother of Jacob, also married a sister Mary of Captain Mugford. She married second a Kimball and was a widow a second time in 1809. She and John were married 3 Jan., 1790. I know nothing further about him.

VI. 1001 Simeon (*John, Jephtha, Eleazer, John, John*), born in Charlton, 10 Aug., 1769; died in Peabody; married 2 Feb., 1794, Martha Batchelder.

Children:

2282　MARTHA, b. 26 Nov., 1794; d., unm.
2283　SALLY, b. 5 Feb., 1796; m. 19 Apr., 1818, John Wheeler, of Salem, b. in Brookfield. Ch.: John Simeon, b. in Salem, 3 Aug., 1827. Sally B., b. 22 Aug., 1833; d. young.
2284　MARY B., b. 18 May, 1802.
2285　JEFFERSON, b. in Charlton, 20 Oct., 1804; d. 12 Apr., 1864.
2286　REBECCA, b. 4 Apr., 1807.
2287　LINCOLN S., b. 5 Oct., 1809.

VI. 1006 Abijah (*Benajah, Jephtha, Eleazer, John, John*), born in Sutton, 30 July, 1777; died there; married 15 May, 1803, Betsey, daughter of Jonathan and Belote (Bartlett) Burdon, of Sutton, born 7 Sept., 1784, living in 1877.

Children, born in Sutton :

2288 SALLY, b. 22 June, 1803.
2289 MELONA, b. 4 June, 1805; m. Nicholas Woodward.
2290 VILOTA, b. 26 June, 1807.
2291 LUTHER, b. 16 Feb., 1809.
2292 JASON, b. 14 Feb., 1811.
2293 LYMAN, b. 28 Jan., 1813.
2294 JAMES. b. 7 Feb., 1816.
2295 EMERY, b. 20 July, 1818.
2296 SYLVANUS, b. 12 Sept., 1821; m. 3 Mar., 1840, Ann M. Lynch, of Sutton.
2297 SALLY, b. 26 Nov., 1823.
2298 RUFUS, b. 19 Nov., 1827.

VI. 1010 Sylvanus (*Benajah, Jephtha, Eleazer, John, John*), born in Sutton, 11 May, 1791; died in Montpelier, Vt., 19 Sept., 1854; married 16 Sept., 1815, Lucinda, daughter of Benjamin and Hannah Bancroft, of Petersham.

Children :

2299 A DAU., b. Dec., 1816; d. æ. 1 week.
2300 SUMNER, b. 21 Feb., 1818
2301 SON, b. Dec., 1820; d. æ. 3 mos.
2302 MARIA, b. 12 June, 1823; m. N. F. Atkins, of Toulon, Ill.; left two sons.
2303 AUGUSTA, b. 17 July, 1828; m., 1852, A. H. Whitcomb. Ch.: Henry. Jenny.

VI. 1017 Sarah (*Tarrant, Samuel, Eleazer, John, John*), born in Danvers, 5 Oct., 1769; died 28 Feb., 1858; married 12 Oct., 1789, Capt. Hezekiah, son of Samuel and Ede (Upton) Flint, born in Danvers, 31 Jan., 1766, and died 22 Sept., 1818.

Hezekiah Flint lived in what is now Peabody. He was a master mariner and ship owner. For interesting particulars concerning his life, see page 50 of Flint Genealogy.

Children :

2304 SARAH PAGE, b. 20 Dec., 1800; d. at North Andover, 22 Jan., 1875; m. in Danvers, 5 Feb. 1824, Hon. Daniel Putnam. son of Daniel and Phebe (Upton) King,[143] b. 8 Jan., 1801, d. 25 July, 1850. Ch.: Ellen Maria, b. 16 Jan., 1825; d. 4 Mar., 1849; m. Isaac Osgood Loring. Caroline Watts, b. 21 Jan., 1826; d. 12 Mar., 1889; m. Isaac O. Loring. Sarah Page, b. 14 April, 1828; d. 28 June, 1863; m. Gayton P. Loring. Benjamin Flint, b. 12 Oct., 1830; d. 24 Jan., 1868; m. Abbie Jane Farwell. Daniel Webster, b. 1 Mar., 1833; m. 27 Apr, 1858, Mary Robinson Harwood; m., 2d, 25 Apr., 1866, Jennie Walker, dau. of Woodbury Bryant and Eliz. J. (Walker) Purington,[144] of Topsham, Me. Edward Everett, b. 1 Aug., 1835; m. Annie M. Couillard; m., 2d, Katie R. Woodman. Rebecca Cleaves, b. 18 Nov., 1837; d. 15 Feb., 1867.

2305 BENJAMIN HEZEKIAH, b. 6 June, 1804; d. 9 Nov., 1820.

VI. 1018 Elizabeth (*Tarrant, Samuel, Eleazer, John, John*), born 19 Aug., 1771; died 17 Nov., 1842; married 24 Aug., 1794, John, son of Samuel and Ann (Williams) Derby, born 28 May, 1770; died 1 March, 1834. Mr. Derby was a tailor and a worthy citizen. For many years he represented Salem in the General Court.

Children :

2306 JOHN, b. 21 Feb, 1795; d. at E. Saginaw, Mich., 7 Aug., 1874; m. 17 July, 1819, Rebecca Punchard; m., 2d, 26 July, 1853, Mrs. A. L. Cobb, dau. of Dr. Nathan Weeks.

2307 TARRANT PUTNAM, b. 14 Aug., 1796; d. 6 Mar., 1850; m. Rachel Ropes; m., 2d, Elizabeth P. Pierce.

2308 CHARLES, b. 20 July, 1798; d. 23 Sept., 1868; m. at Nashville, Tenn., 18 Feb., 1820, Nancy, dau. of Henry and Betsey Ann Pulling, who d. 19 Nov., 1878. Ch.: Perley, b in Murfreesboro, Tenn., 26 Oct., 1823; m., Salem, Dec., 1, 1850, Harriet, dau. of Wm. and Abigail (Punchard) Knight, b. 1 Feb. 1827. Mr. Derby is an accomplished genealogist and has aided materially the compiler of this genealogy. In early life he was a portrait painter and engraver. John Henry, b. in Lynn, 26 May, 1826; d. in Salem, 15 May, 1830. Charles W., b. in Derry, N. H., 8 Nov., 1827. Sarah Putnam, b. in Danvers, 28 Jan., 1832; d. 14 Mar., 1832.

---

[143] Mr. King was state representative and senator; speaker of the House, president of the Senate, and representative to Congress. He resided in that part of Danvers, now Peabody.

[144] She was born 5 July, 1843. Ch.: Elizb. W., b. 11 Feb., 1867. Tarrant Putnam, b. 18 Mar., 1869. Caroline W., b. 19 Jan., 1871. Annie Purington, b. 9 July, 1873. Grace W., b. 24 Apr., 1878. Mr. King is a merchant in Boston.

2309 PERLEY, b. 9 May, 1800; d. at sea 2 Dec., 1821, while attempting the rescue of others.

2310 SARAH PAGE, b. 2 July, 1802; d. at Boston, 16 July, 1861, unm.

2311 ELIZABETH, b. 16 July, 1804; d. 16 Dec., 1870; m. 7 Apr., 1825, Ferdinand Andrews.

2312 MARY ANN, b. 1 May, 1806; d. at Boston, 24 Mar., 1887.

2313 HANNAH, b. 25 Jan., 1808; d. 1 June, 1840; m. 1 Nov., 1837, Jonathan Fox, son of Rev. Sam'l Worcester.

VI. 1020 Perley (*Tarrant, Samuel, Eleazer, John, John*), born in Danvers, 16 Dec., 1776.

Child :

2314 PERLEY, b. 13 Jan., 1798; lived in Franconia, N. H.

VI. 1022 Israel Warburton (*Eleazer, Samuel, Eleazer, John, John*), born in Danvers, 24 Nov., 1786; died in Middleborough, 3 May, 1868; married in Andover, 2 Dec., 1815, Harriot, daughter of Peter and Hannah (Porter) Osgood, of Andover, born there, 28 March, 1791, and died in Portsmouth, N. H., 10 June, 1832; married, second, 29 April, 1833, Mrs. Julia A. Osgood, of New York, widow of Samuel Osgood, junior, and daughter of Samuel Osgood, Esq., being cousin of his first wife. See Osgood Genealogy.

Children :

2315 CHARLES ISRAEL, b. in Portsmouth, 28 Dec., 1816.

2316 SAMUEL OSGOOD, b. in Portsmouth, 17 Aug., 1818; m., 1st, 13 June, 1848, Elizabeth Noble, dau. of J. D. Whitney, of Northampton, who d. June, 1863; m , 2d, Mrs. Olivia Shipman; lives in San Francisco, Cal.

2317 EDWARD WARREN, b. in Portsmouth, 1 May, 1820; d. in North Whitefield. Me., 2 Sept., 1863. Entered Brown University from Phillips Andover Academy, 1836. Graduated from Dartmouth College 1840. Taught school at Beaufort, S. C., and in 1843 entered the Episcopal Seminary in New York, but in December of that year joined the Roman Catholic Church and entered the college at Worcester. He preached at Albany, Providence, Milwaukee, and North Whitefield, Me., where he was settled thirteen years. He was of medium height, blue eyes and very dark hair.

2318 FRANCIS BROWN. b. in Portsmouth, 16 Jan.. 1822; d. at sea, 12 Mar., 1851. In 1840, entered the commission business at New York, and in Milwaukee, 1846. In Oct., 1850, went to Isthmus of Panama as secretary for the Panama Railroad, and d. on his

35

way home the next year. He was buried at Kingston, Jamaica.
He likewise joined the Roman Catholic church. His eyes were
blue and hair dark.

2319 HARRIOT OSGOOD, b in Portsmouth, 12 Sept., 1823; m. in Middleborough, 7 Sept., 1852, Charles Frederic, son of Peter Hoar
and Nabby (Sproat) Pierce, b. there, 7 Sept., 1817. Ch.:
Charles Frederic, b. 11 Feb., 1863; resides 1223 Pine St., San
Francisco, Cal. Mary Porter, b. 10 Sept.. 1865; d. 6 Apr., 1867.

2320 HORACE MOSSE, b. in Portsmouth, 29 June, 1825; d. 21 Dec.,
1832.

2321 WILLIAM FULLER, b. in Portsmouth, 5 Sept., 1827; d. in Middleborough, 11 Feb., 1853.

2322 JULIA MARIA, b. in Portsmouth, 13 Feb., 1830; d. in Middleborough, 6 Aug., 1859; m. Alfred S. Thayer, of Boston.

2323 LUCY MACKINTOSH, b. in Portsmouth, 24 Apr., 1832; m. Franklin
S. Thompson, of Middleborough.

REV. ISRAEL WARBURTON PUTNAM was the very foremost
of Congregationalist divines of his times, although he entered
the ministry somewhat late in life, his father and others not
believing that he was destined for the church.

His early education was obtained at Franklin Academy,
North Andover, where he was prepared for college. He was
graduated from Dartmouth College in 1810, and commenced
to study law with Judge Samuel Putnam at Salem, but after
two and a half years he became convinced that his duty was
to labor in the ministry, and entered Andover Theological Seminary in 1812. He was ordained at Portsmouth, 15
March, 1815, and continued in the ministry there for twenty
years until dismissed at his own request. During this period
he was very active in theological matters. His well known
" Thanksgiving Sermon " was preached at Portsmouth in
1826. One of his earliest articles was published in the Pan-
oplist in 1813, entitled, "Does the Bible contain any doctrines
contrary to reason?" He became a trustee of Dartmouth
College in 1820, and was trustee of Berwick Academy from
1820 to 1835. Installed at Middleborough, Oct., 1835,
where he remained until his death. The degree of Doctor of
Divinity was conferred by Dartmouth in 1853.

During his long and useful life, he showed great interest in educational and historical matters. His researches in regard to the genealogy of the Putnam family were quite extensive, he having entertained the idea of publishing the results, but afterward generously placed his manuscript in the hands of Col. Perley Putnam.

His grandfather, Archelaus Fuller, was a member of the Provincial Congress at Cambridge and Watertown in 1775, and died a colonel in the Revolutionary army.

VI. 1024 Doctor Archelaus Fuller (*Eleazer, Samuel, Eleazer, John, John*), born in Danvers, 3 Oct., 1792; died in Beverly, 11 Aug., 1859.

Graduated at Dartmouth College 1819, and became preceptor of Moore's Charity School at Hanover (1821–4). He then commenced the study of divinity at Andover, but in 1826, on account of ill health, abandoned his studies. Resolving upon the study of medicine, he graduated from the medical school at Dartmouth in 1829, and after a preliminary course of study with Dr. Nathan Crosby of Lowell, commenced practice the same year at Portsmouth, N. H.

In July, 1836, he settled in Windham, N. H., but ill health against which he had always struggled forced him to abandon professional work. He therefore retired in 1840 to Danvers. He died in Beverly, whither he had removed in 1844. He was an excellent man and physician.

VI. 1025 Samuel (*Eleazer, Samuel, Eleazer, John, John*), born in Danvers, 14 June, 1794; died in Brooklyn, N. Y., 20 March, 1859; married 5 Aug., 1819, Betsey, daughter of Elijah and Hannah (Putnam) Pope, of Danvers, and neice of General Israel Putnam. She died subsequent to 1877.

Children :

2324 SARAH ELIZABETH.
2325 SAMUEL WARBURTON, b. 1823; of Trenton, N. J., 1877.
2326 MARY POPE.
2327 EMILY S.
2328 HARRIET.

SAMUEL PUTNAM was educated at Phillips Andover Academy, and commenced teaching at Marblehead, thence to Portsmouth, where he taught eight years. In 1831, in company with Theodore Ames of Salem, he opened a school for boys in Brooklyn, N. Y., occupying a building erected for their use by citizens of Brooklyn and called " Classical Hall." Upon Mr. Ames' retirement in 1837, Mr. Putnam continued the school at his residence. As a teacher he was widely known and highly respected.

Several of his daughters possess his ability and occupy posts as teachers.

VI. 1033 Allen (*Henry, Henry, Eleazer, John, John*), born in Danvers, 25 Oct., 1762; killed by a fall, at Marietta, Ohio, in 1807; married in Danvers, 20 April, 1785, Nancy Porter, daughter of Amos Porter, Jr., of Danvers, and Marietta, Ohio.

Children :

2329   ANNA, m. David B. Nash.
2330   ROSELLA, m. Daniel Griswold Stanley.
2331   CLARISSA, unm.
2332   SARAH, m. David DeLong.
2333   HARRIET, m. Hugh Jackson.
2334   HENRY, lived near Quincy, Ill.
2335   THOMAS, d. 1823, æ. 19.
2336   GEORGE W., lived in Illinois.
2337   MARTHA, m., 1st, Robert Gard; m., 2d, —— West.

ALLEN PUTNAM was the first of Gen. Rufus Putnam's party to leap ashore at Marietta, from the Mayflower. Two years later, he and his brother-in-law Amos Porter returned to Danvers, walking all the way, got their families and started back. On account of the Indian war, they remained in western Pennsylvania two years, reaching Marietta again in 1795. They settled in Fearing, an adjoining township to Marietta.

VI. 1036 Jonathan (*Henry, Henry, Eleazer, John, John*), born 13 Sept., 1766; married —— Skidmore.

Child :

2338 HENRY, b. 26 Sept., 1794; d. 31 Aug., 1820.

VI. 1038 Frederick (*Henry, Henry, Eleazer, John, John*), died in Salem ; married 25 May, 1790, Sally, daughter of Ezekiel and Abia Marsh, of Danvers, born there, 3 July, 1773, and died in Salem, 28 Nov., 1816.

Child :

2339 LEVI, b. 14 Nov., 1791; d. in Lynn, 1824; buried with military honors; cordwainer. In his will mentions aunt Desire Batchelder, uncle Henry Batchelder, uncle Thomas H. Marsh, grandfather Ezekiel Marsh. Will dated 6 Feb., prov. 5 Oct., 1824.

VI. 1048 Henry (*Eleazer, Henry, Eleazer, John, John*), born in Medford ; died, 1810, at Savannah, Georgia ; married at Nassau, 1780, Frances, daughter of Dr. James Fraser, formerly of Charleston, S. C., but later of Nassau, New Providence, whither he had repaired upon the evacuation of Charleston by the British. He is said to have been a loyalist and an officer in the British army. He died in 1790 aged 60 years. Mrs. Putnam died very suddenly on the plantation near Savannah, prior to 1800.

Mr. Putnam married, second, Priscilla Croom, of Putnam Co., Ga., who was born about 1780, and died in April, 1873.

Children :

2340 GEORGE, who d. about 1845 at Savannah, Ga., where he is buried.
2341 HARRIET FRANCES, b. 1789; d. 18 Oct., 1856; m. John Carnochan.

By second wife :

2342 ADELINE.
2343 JAMES MADISON, b. 12 Mar., 1811.

HENRY PUTNAM[145] is said to have settled in Georgia about 1786, in company with his "brother" Benjamin (No. 414). This is evidently an error, but while it is not a certainty that Henry was the son of Eleazer, yet it is known he was a near relative of Benjamin and all the facts seem to point to the position here given him as being correct. Henry (No. 1054), son of Roger, brother of Benjamin (No. 414), was according to family tradition killed in the war of 1812.

[145] I am indebted to Mrs. Annie L. Winters for aid in establishing the line of this branch of the family.—E. P.

VI. 1049 Doctor Elijah (*Eleazer, Henry, Eleazer, John, John*), born in Medford, 1769; died in Madison, N. Y., Jan., 1851; married Phoebe, daughter of Capt. Abner Wood, born in Madison, and died about 1854.

Children, born in Madison:

2344 FRANCES, b. 1 Mar., 1799; d. 3 May, 1877; m. Dr. Jonathan Guernsey.

2345 JOHN, b. 1800.

2346 PHOEBE, b. 1803; d., *s. p.*, 1843; married Lyman Root, a merchant of Madison.

2347 SAMUEL, } b. July, 1805.
2348 SYDNEY,   }

2349 HAMILTON, b. 5 Sept., 1807.

2350 HARRIET, b. 1809; d., 1847; m. Isaac Chamberlain.

2351 MARY, b. 15 Mar, 1811, d., *s. p.*, 9 July, 1864; m. Adin Howard.

2352 CAROLINE, b. 1812; d. 4 Feb., 1838.

2353 HENRY LOCKE, b. 1816

DOCTOR ELIJAH PUTNAM moved form West Cambridge to Peterboro in 1801, thence to Madison, N. Y. (March, 1802), where he located and practised medicine for forty years. He was a true christian gentleman and a good physician.

VI. 1052 John (*Roger, Henry, Eleazer, John, John*), born in Charlestown or Medford, April, 1777; died suddenly at Topsfield, 16 June, 1826; married 21 April, 1814, Polly, daughter of Isaac and Dolly (Dickenson) Wilson, 3d, born in Danvers, 10 May, 1781.

Children:

2354 JOHN WILSON.

2355 MARIA W., b. in Danvers, 17 July, 1814.

2356 DANIEL W., b. in Reading, 21 July, 1816.

2357 DOLLY W., b. in Topsfield, 8 Oct., 1819; d. in Danvers, 26 May, 1850.

VI. 1055 Gilbert (*Roger, Henry, Eleazer, John, John*), born 1785; died in Malden, 5 Oct., 1820; married 30 Nov., 1811, Betsey Thayer, daughter of Amos and Joanna (French) Sampson, born in Charlestown, 15 Oct., 1789; of Danvers and Malden.

Children :

2358   BETSEY, b. in Danvers, 13 June, 1813; d., unm., 25 Apr., 1874.
2359   JOANNA SAMPSON, b. in Everett, 28 May, 1817; lives with her brother in Charlestown, unm.
2360   RACHEL SAMPSON, b. in Everett, 24 Oct., 1815; d. 25 Sept., 1817.
2361   GEORGE SAMPSON, b. in Everett, 20 Apr., 1819.

VI. 1056 David (*Roger, Henry, Eleazer, John, John*), born in Medford, 20 April, 1791; died ———; married 14 Jan., 1814, Mary, daughter of Nathaniel and Polly (Newman) Davis, of Lynn, born 24 June, 1796.

Children, born in Danvers :

2362   DAVID, b. 21 Oct , 1814; d. 4 Aug., 1833.
2363   HENRY, b. 24 Nov., 1816.
2364   MARY ANN, b. 17 Jan., 1819.
2365   BETHIAH, b. 5 Apr., 1821.
2366   JOSEPH WARREN, b. 5 Sept., 1823.
2367   SARAH, b. 9 Mar., 1826.
2368   NATHANIEL DAVIS, b. 28 Feb., 1829.
2369   JOHN, b. 7 Dec., 1831.
2370   CHARLES HENRY, b. 16 Feb., 1834.
2371   CLARISSA FIDELIA, b. 17 Mar., 1836.
2372   ELIZA GERTRUDE, b. 26 May, 1838; d. 18 Dec., 1840.
2373   ANGELINE, b. 7 Jan., 1840.
2374   LAURA JANE. b. 5 Feb., 1842.

VI. 1058 Benjamin (*Roger, Henry, Eleazer, John, John*), born in Medford; living in Waltham, 1836.

Children :

2375   HARRIET.
2376   CLARISSA.
2377   THOMAS.
2378   BENJAMIN.
2379   MARY ANN.
2380   SARAH.
2381   ? GEORGE.

VI. 1059 Ebenezer (*Roger, Henry, Eleazer, John, John*), born in Medford, about 1786; died in West Cambridge, 1848, of consumption; married, first, 1 Jan., 1806, Sally Patterson, who died 1826; married, second, Ann Lawrence of Groton, who died within six months; married, third, Mrs. Corning.

Children :

2382 EBENEZER, b. in Charlestown, 9 Oct., 1806.
2383 ABBY CARTER, b. in Danvers, 25 Oct., 1808; d. 20 Feb., 1827; m.
        Calvin Harris. Ch.: Calvin P., b. 12 Feb., 1807; with Breed
        & Burton, 1886 Broadway, N. Y., (1880).
2384 CHARLES, b. in Danvers, 5 Aug., 1810; d. in Medford, 10 Feb.,
        1856.
2385 JOSEPH P., b. in Danvers, 5 Nov., 1812; never m.
2386 SALLY A., b. in Medford, 8 Jan., 1815; d. in W. Cambridge, 30
        June, 1845; m., July, 1835, Thomas F. Frost.
2387 WILLIAM A., b. in Medford, 15 Oct., 1817.
2388 CLARISSA, b. in Medford, 18 Sept., 1819; d. abt. 1864; m., 1st, 3
        Jan., 1847, William W. Frost, who d. 19 Apr., 1855; m., 2d,
        David Hunt, of Woburn.
2389 SUSAN, b. in Medford, 11 Aug., 1821.
2390 HENRY, b. in Medford, 15 Mar., 1823; d. 16 Mar., 1823.

By third wife :

2391 HOWARD.
2392 ABBY C.
2393 MARY A.

VI. 1060 John Allen (*Billings, Henry, Eleazer, John,
John*), born in Newburyport, 27 Nov., 1775; died there;
married there, 3 May, 1801, Sarah Davis.

Children :

2394 JOHN C., b. 12 Sept., 1803; d. in Newburyport abt. 1833.
2395 HENRY, b. 24 Sept., 1805; d. young.
2396 SALLY, b. 28 Oct., 1807; d. young.
2397 MAY, b. 10 June, 1809; d. young.
2398 GEORGE, b. 5 Apr., 1811; d. young.
2399 JANE, b. 22 June, 1812; m. —— Glidden, of Biddeford, Me.
2400 AARON, b. 25 Dec., 1818; d. young.

Vl. 1069 Joseph (*Billings, Henry, Eleazer, John,
John*), born in Newburyport, 15 April, 1794; died there, 16
June, 1873; married, first, 25 Aug., 1816, Elizabeth Danforth, b. 11 April, 1797; d. 20 Sept., 1833; married, second, 19 Jan., 1834, Patience Jacobs, daughter of Robert and
Patience Wiley, born in Gilmanton, N. H., 10 Feb., 1799;
died 2 June, 1870.

Children, born in Newburyport :

2401 JOSEPH BILLINGS, b. 26 Apr., 1817; m. 5 June, 1841, Sarah H.,
        dau. of William Bickum, of Bradford; lived in Danvers.

2402 ANN CARR, b. 21 Mar., 1819; d. in Newburyport; m. 15 Jan , 1843, John Laskey, of Newburyport and Charlestown. Ch.: Ann Elizabeth. Jennie. Both dead.

2403 ELIZABETH, b. 18 May 1821; m. John Paul, of Lynn. Ch.: Ella

2404 LUCY JANE, b. 10 Sept., 1823; d. in Lynn, 2 Apr , 1855; m. 28 Nov., 1844, William Paul, brother of John Paul. Ch.: Charles W., b. 25 Aug., 1845; d. 6 Mar., 1878. Lucy Jane, b. 20 Apr., 1849.

2405 HENRY LOCK. b. 15 Aug., 1825; m. Mary J. Cockrane

2406 HANNAH, b. 2 Sept., 1827; d. Oct., 1828.

2407 HANNAH, b. 22 Mar., 1831; m., Dec.. 1850. Freeman Chapman, who d.———. Ch.: Edgar, of Saugus. Others.

2408 HARRIET, b. 15 June, 1833; d. 8 Oct , 1833.

By second wife :

2409 FRANCIS WILEY, b. 3 Nov., 1834; m. 16 Dec., 1859, Ann Maria Newman, who was b. 31 Oct., 1837. No ch Lives in Newburyport.

2410 LYDIA GOODHUE, b. 3 Nov., 1836; m. 20 Nov., 1858, her brother-in-law, William Paul. Ch.: two; d. young.

VI. 1072 Augustus (*Benjamin, Henry, Eleazer John, John*), born ———; died 1818; married, 1815, Mary Tiben, who married, second, in 1820, Mr. Shaw.

Child :

2411 MARY, d. æt. one year.

VI. 1073 John Gustavus (*Benjamin, Henry, Eleazer, John, John*), born in Savannah, Ga., 1796; died at Madison, Fla., 1 May, 1864; married in Virginia, 3 Oct., 1838, Sarah Attaway. third daughter of Samuel Lewis, of Fredericksburg, Va., a nephew in the second degree to Gen. Washington. Mr. Lewis' grandfather, George Lewis, married Betty, only sister of Washington. Mrs. Putnam was also a first cousin of the princess Murat, who was Catherine Willis, daughter of Col. Bird Willis and Mary Lewis, the sister of Samuel Lewis. Mrs. Putnam died 28 Oct., 1871.

Children :

2412 CAROLINE LEWIS, b. in Tallahassee, Fla., 4 Aug., 1839; unm.

2413 CATHERINE MURAT, b. in Madison, Fla., 5 July, 1842; m. 15 Jan., 1867, Philip S. Duval. Ch.: Henry S., b. in Tallahassee, 14 Mar., 1868. Philip P., b. in Madison, 2 Feb., 1871. Sarah A., b. in Savannah, 24 Nov., 1873.

2414 MARY MALCOLM, b. in Wakulla Co, Fla., 11 July. 1844; m. 15 Jan., 1868, Fred. P. Shaffer. Ch.: John P., b. in Madison, 25 Sept., 1870; d. 18 Nov., 1874. Robert F., b. in Orange Co., Fla., 22 May, 1873: d. 2 Oct., 1890. Lucy M., b. in Madison, 24 Dec., 1884.

2415 JOHN LEWIS, b. at Madison 28 Jan., 1848.

2416 ANNIE ATTAWAY, b. at Madison, 28 Jan., 1848; lives at Washington, Ga., unm.

2417 LUCY DARNGEFIELD, b. in Madison, 18 July, 1852; m., Jan., 1881, Edwin Wiley, who d., *s. p.*, at Sparta, Ga, 14 May, 1882.

VI. 1076 Judge Benjamin Alexander (*Benjamin, Henry, Eleazer, John, John*), born in Savanna, Ga., about 1800; died in Palatka, Fla., 25 Jan., 1869; married, March, 1830, Helen, youngest daughter of Hon. Ephraim Kirby, of Litchfield, Conn., and an aunt of Gen. Kirby Smith.

Child :

2418 CATHARINE, b. 1 Jan., 1831; educated in school at Washington; m. Dr John C., son of John C. Calhoun, of Charleston, S. C. Ch.: John C., d.———. Benj. P., of Palatka, Fla., a judge. She m., 2d, Wm. Lowndes Calhoun, a brother of her first husband. Ch.. Wm. Lowndes, d. ———.

BENJAMIN PUTNAM entered Phillips Andover Academy in 1817, and graduated at Harvard in 1823. In 1847 he was described by Hon. Daniel P. King, as a man of high character and an eminent lawyer. He then lived at St. Augustine.

VI. 1077 William (*Caleb, Caleb, John, John, John*), born in Danvers; baptized there, 10 Aug., 1746; died 1832; of Middle Stewiacke, N. S.

Children :

2419 WILLIAM, b. (1777)?

2420–28 NINE DAUGHTERS.

WILLIAM AND CALEB PUTNAM were in Salem, 1 Aug., 1772, and acknowledged a deed, dated 30 July, 1772, whereby they sold for £111 to William Putnam of Danvers 22 acres bounding on William and Peter Putnam's land running along the Topsfield road till it reached Aaron Putnam's land. They

were of Shubenacadie, N. S., and a year later Caleb, who held
his brother's power of attorney, and his mother Elizabeth
Upham, sold all their rights in 19½ acres, beginning at the side
of a lane which runs to Peter Putnam's house, and bounded
by said Peter's and Mary Andrew's land, etc. Acknowledged
in Salem. Elizabeth, wife of Richard Upham, was of Onslow, N. S.

VI. 1078 Caleb (*Caleb, Caleb, John, John, John*),
born in Danvers; baptized there, 15 June, 1750; died Sept.,
1838; married, 1775, Letitia, daughter of Robert and Esther
(Moore) Hunter,[146] of Truro, N. S., born in New England,
1755; died, 1785; married, second, 1787, Jane Fulton.

Children, born in Maitland, N. S. :

2429　ELIZABETH, b. 7 Sept., 1776: d., Sept., 1832; m., 1799, Robert
Brydon, who d. at Tatmagouche, in 1856, leaving two sons
and three daughters.

2430　WILLIAM, b. 1 Feb., 1779.

2431　ESTHER, b. 14 Mar., 1781, m., 1808, Robert, eldest son of Gavin
and Elizabeth (Hunter) Johnson, and removed to Ohio in 1805;
one son, three daughters.

2432　MARY, b. 7 Aug., 1783; d., Jan., 1870; m, Dec., 1807, James
Douglas, who d. Apr., 1842; 4 sons, 1 dau.

2433　CALEB, b. 12 July, 1785.

By second wife :

2434　JAMES.
2435　ROBERT.
2436–41 SIX DAUGHTERS

VI. 1085 Caleb (*Peter, Caleb, John, John, John*),
born in Danvers, 3 July, 1776; died in Rome, N. Y., 24
May, 1819; m. Elizabeth, who had administration of her
husband's estate.

Children :

2442　PETER, of full age, 1823; of E. Bloomfield, Ontario Co., N. Y.
2443　ANDREW, of full age, 1823; of Canandaigua, Ontario Co., N Y.
2444　CALEB, of full age, 1823; of Canandaigua, Ontario Co., N. Y.

[146] Mr. Hunter was one of the grantees of Truro township and one of the pioneers,
having settled there about 1760. He died 7 Feb., 1810, æ. 77; his wife died 14 Oct., 1807,
æ. 74.

ELIZABETH, of full age, 1823; m. prior to 1823, Horace Eggleston, of Pembroke, N. Y.

2446 HARRIET, æ. above 16 in 1823; m. prior to 1823, Horatio N. Carr, of Stephentown, Co. Rensselaer, N Y.

2447 VOLANTINE, b. 1802.

2448 SARAH, æ. 18 in 1823.

2449 GEORGE, æ. 11 in 1823.

2450 WILLIAM HENRY, æ. 14 in 1823.

2451 ANNA, æ. 9 in 1823.

CALEB PUTNAM removed to Bolton and engaged in the business of tanner. He was a resident of Bolton in 1792; but that same year seems to have bought land in Schenectady, N. Y. (deeds at Albany). He finally settled in Rome and acquired considerable property, owning many thousand acres in Rome, Paris, Lee, Canandaigua, and neighboring places. From the settlement of his estate in 1823, it appears that the homestead and tannery came into the possession of his eldest son Peter during the father's lifetime.

End of Volume One.

CPSIA information can be obtained
at www.ICGtesting.com
Printed in the USA
BVOW09s0601140717

489194BV00006B/34/P